Transnationalism
and Society

Transnationalism and Society

AN INTRODUCTION

Michael C. Howard

McFarland & Company, Inc., Publishers
Jefferson, North Carolina, and London

LIBRARY OF CONGRESS CATALOGUING-IN-PUBLICATION DATA

Howard, Michael C.
Transnationalism and society : an introduction /
Michael C. Howard.
p.   cm.
Includes bibliographical references and index.

ISBN 978-0-7864-6454-8
softcover : 50# alkaline paper ∞

1. Transnationalism — Social aspects.   2. Emigration and
immigration — Social aspects.   3. Cultural pluralism.   I. Title.
JV6225.H69   2011   320.54 — dc22   2010054420

BRITISH LIBRARY CATALOGUING DATA ARE AVAILABLE

Cover photograph © 2011 by Duncan Walker
Front cover by Bernadette Skok (bskok@ptd.net)

Manufactured in the United States of America

*McFarland & Company, Inc., Publishers
Box 611, Jefferson, North Carolina 28640
www.mcfarlandpub.com*

CONTENTS

PREFACE

I began work on *Transnationalism and Society* while developing an undergraduate international studies course on transnationalism. There were no suitable introductions to the topic and the readings available tended to be oriented towards specific disciplines rather than being cross-disciplinary. The present work is intended to provide a multidisciplinary introduction to transnationalism and society. I have sought to provide sufficient examples to enable the reader to gain an appreciation of the nature and complexity of the topic — to put flesh on the bare bones.

My own interest in transnationalism began in the 1980s with an emphasis on transnational corporations and transnational labor relations. While teaching at the University of the South Pacific in Suva, Fiji, I became associated with the Transnational Corporations Research Project at the University of Sydney and with a regional project on workers' education in the South Pacific undertaken by the International Labour Organization. At the time the study of transnational corporations dominated scholarly studies of transnationalism, whereas attention to its broader social aspects was limited. The University of the South Pacific itself is a transnational setting in that it is a regional institution that serves more than a dozen countries in the South Pacific and recruits faculty from around the world. After the military coups of 1987 in Fiji I became involved with another aspect of transnationalism, the refugees that resulted, especially those coming to Vancouver to join the established Fijian community there.

Living and teaching in Vancouver since leaving Fiji has helped to reinforce my sense of the importance of transnationalism. As I discuss in the chapter on cities, some cities are more transnational than others, and Vancouver is definitely one of the world's more transnational cities. This is reflected in its demography, cultural life, and economy. Moreover, like other such cities around the turn of the century it has not simply become more transnational in its character, but the character of its transnationalism has become much more complex, especially as it is integrated into the Asia-Pacific region. Writing the present book can, thus, be seen as a response to my immediate environment — to the society in which I live — but it is also a response to an increasingly important aspect of life for millions of people, one that will become far more important in the years to come.

1

AN OVERVIEW

The study of transnationalism has received increasing attention in recent years in response to a number of developments ranging from the use of the internet to the activities of terrorist organizations such as al-Qaeda. This reflects the extent to which transnational relations have become more important to a larger number of people around the world, in part because of improvements in communication and transportation. That said, transnationalism is not new and has been around since ancient times. In the past as well as at present, transnational relations have played an important role in the generation of wealth and economic development, innovation in technical fields, the enrichment of the arts, in fact in almost all aspects of human life, far beyond the number of individuals or groups directly involved in transnational activities. The main difference between transnationalism now and in the past is that today the number of people involved in transnational social relations is not only far greater than it was in the past in both absolute and relative terms, but it involves a much wider range of people from different social backgrounds to the point that rather than being somewhat exceptional it is becoming increasingly commonplace. Scholarly attention on transnational social relations, however, has been relatively slow to develop. That is starting to change, but it still lags far behind the rapidly growing importance of such relations.

Transnationalism refers to relations across state boundaries. The present work focuses on social aspects of transnationalism and on the kinds of societies created through transnational relations. We are interested in individuals, groups, and other social entities that maintain a meaningful presence in or are part of a social system within one state while also maintaining significant relations with others in different states to the extent that they can be viewed as forming cross-border societies. There are many types of transnational social relations, ranging from family networks to those of criminal organizations and religious orders. In addition, as with all societies, those based on transnational relations have a cultural dimension. Thus, we will look at cultural aspects such as language and the arts of transnational societies as well in order to gain a more comprehensive picture of the nature of these societies.

The focus of the chapters that follow is on transnationalism in the modern world since the 1500s, with an emphasis on developments from the 1800s to the present. While important transnational relations existed in the past, the scale and scope of such relations has increased significantly in modern times beginning with the appearance of global trade and empires in the 1500s. This process intensified in the 1800s, due in part to innovations in transportation and communication, and the growth of transnationalism has accelerated even further since the 1940s. Thus, while a few hardy souls braved the voyage between New Spain and southern China to trade for limited quantities of luxury items in the 1600s, in the 1800s hundreds of ships were sailing across the Pacific between China and the Americas on a regular basis transporting not only greater quantities of trade goods, but also thousands of people as permanent or temporary migrants. The development of mass air travel during the latter half of the 1900s made it possible for even larger numbers of people to move back and forth across the Pacific in a matter of hours, while improvements in communication and literacy have meant that rather than a few letters taking months or years to travel across the sea, large numbers of people on both sides of the Pacific can now maintain regular almost instantaneous communication.

Terminology

Use of the term nation within transnationalism can cause some confusion because of the way in which it has come to be used interchangeably with the term state even though the two words refer to different entities. The English word nation comes from Latin — in this case the word *nationem*— and refers to "A distinct race or people, characterized by common descent, language, or history, usu. organized as a separate political state and occupying a definite territory."[1] It is related to the Latin verb *nascor*— I am born, I grow, spring forth. In this sense, transnationalism could refer to what is commonly termed ethnic relations and, while ethnic relations can be relevant to transnationalism, the meaning of nation in regard to transnationalism needs to be understood primarily in relation to the state. Thus, rather than ethnic relations, transnationalism refers to what, perhaps, more accurately could be called trans-state relations, although, as will be discussed below, it also pertains to relations of ethnic or national groups across state boundaries. State has a variety of meanings, but in this context it refers to "the body politic as organized for supreme civil rule and government; the political organization which is the basis of civil government; hence, the supreme civil power and government vested in a country or nation" or "A body of people occupying a defined territory and organized under a sovereign government."[2]

While nations and states may coincide, often they do not. The creation of most modern states entailed encompassing more than one existing national or ethnic group. Thus, before there was a United Kingdom or China there were a variety of tribal or national groups already living in the territories that came to be included within their boundaries. People from a variety of nations or ethnicities inhabit most states in the modern world. A particular national group may well comprise the dominant group within a state, but nationally homogeneous states are a rarity and inclusion of national groups within a state may well be contested. These national or ethnic groups are not of concern in the context of transnationalism except in cases where relations are maintained between members across state borders.

Relations between members of the same ethnic or national group living adjacent to one another on opposite sides of a border between two states are one form of transnationalism. Another form of transnationalism involves relations that are maintained between members of a national/ethnic group who have migrated to another state with members of the same group who still live in the original homeland. This form of transnationalism involving migrants can also involve those who have migrated to a number of different states who form networks that may or may not involve relations with people living in the ancestral homeland.

The ambiguity surrounding use of the term nation is reflected in the ways in which people create social identities and organize themselves into groups. Individuals have multiple identities and belong to a variety of groups. Some of these are distinct from one another, while others are more layered or situational in their nature. People's identities in relation to state citizenship and ethnicity may coincide, may be layered (as in viewing oneself as an American and also as an Asian-American and ethnic Vietnamese, Chinese, etc. living in America), or may be contested or denied (as with supporters of separatists movements).

People also often have other important identities beyond being members of an ethnic group or citizens of a state that are also of relevance to transnationalism. These can include, for example, racial identities, religious identities, occupational identities, and even generational identities. Such identities may be linked or at least subject to efforts to link them (as in instances where people seek to identify a particular religion with a state) and are almost always layered (as in a person not simply being a Christian, but also a Catholic or Methodist). In our study of transnationalism we are interested in how people organize themselves socially according to such identities across state borders.

The State, Ethnicity, Nation Building, and Transnationalism

Transnationalism is essentially about humans creating boundaries and then crossing them. The creation of these boundaries entails processes of exclusion and inclusion by which membership within what is being bounded is defined, including some and excluding others. We are concerned especially with two types of boundaries here: boundaries of ethno-national groups and state boundaries. The state is the basic unit within which ethno-national groups reside in the modern world and states and inter-state relations provide the context within which transnationalism occurs. Conditions within states influence how people set about to create and then develop transnational relations. Such conditions influence people's decisions about migration, how migrants settle into their new home, and what sort of relations people maintain with co-ethnics in other states.

The existence of diverse ethnic groups within even the most ethnically homogeneous states raises an important issue in relation to transnationalism in that even migrants from such states have not only an identity related to the state, but they may also have an ethnic identity within their state of origin that differs from the majority. It is, of course, the immigrant groups that are of primary concern here since this is where the greatest potential for transnational relations lies. While the ethnic identities of the immigrant groups mentioned above refer to the states of origin of the immigrant groups, as was mentioned in the previous section, immigrants may also identify themselves on the basis of ethnic or ethno-national identity. Sometimes people use both identities, employing one or the other depending on the context, while others may prefer to use only one of their potential identities. This is true both in terms of identification in relation to a person's status within a state and in regard to transnational relations.

We will use the Black Tai to highlight some of the ambiguities that exist in regard to ethno-national identity and the relevance of this to transnationalism.[3] The Black Tai are a group of people who share a perceived common ancestry and language belonging to the Tai language family who settled in the highlands of what is today northwestern Vietnam over a thousand years ago with more recent migrant groups being found in Laos, Thailand, France, and the United States. Prior to the establishment of French colonial rule in Indochina in the 1880s the Black Tai maintained their own political entities that were largely autonomous from neighboring lowland states to which they paid symbolic tribute. Although formally incorporated into the French colonial state of Tonkin (contemporary northern Vietnam) in the late nineteenth century, the Black Tai were able to retain considerable autonomy. As a result, during the French colonial period most Black Tai did not speak Vietnamese, which was the language of the lowland Kinh who were the ethnic majority in the colonial state, or identify with a Vietnamese state.[4]

Some of the Black Tai in Tonkin who had sided with the French against the communists following World War II migrated to neighboring Laos, where small groups of Black Tai had already settled over the centuries, after the Vietnamese communists defeated the French in Tonkin in 1954. Later, when war broke out in Laos between the communists and Royal Lao government, many of these Black Tai sided with the government. A number of these Black Tai then fled across the Mekong River to Thailand after the communists defeated the Lao government in 1975, where they were placed in a refugee camp by Thai authorities. From there they were allowed to migrate to Iowa in the United States.

Although the older members of this group were born in what is today considered Vietnam, many were born in Laos and in the United States they are usually categorized as coming from Laos. In regard to language, Black Tai is their first language, while a few of them speak Vietnamese and an even larger number of them speak Lao as a second, third or fourth language — some also speak French. The Black Tai refugees in the United States form a distinct community and generally identify themselves primarily as Black Tai rather than as Lao or Vietnamese. They recognize their ethnic homeland as being in a territory that is now part of the Vietnamese state, while also recognizing links to Laos because of the time spent there and because some of them were born there, but for the older members of this group in particular these identities are of far less importance than that of Black Tai. In the United States they have relations with other refugees from Laos (including people from other Tai-speaking groups, ethnic Lao, and Hmong) and there has been some intermarriage, resulting in some blurring of ethnic and transnational identities among younger people.

Initially the communist governments in Vietnam and Laos made it impossible for these refugees to maintain contact with relatives who remained behind in Vietnam and Laos, helping to ensure the primacy of the Black Tai identity over identification with the states of Laos or Vietnam. Reforms in these two countries in the 1990s allowed the Black Tai refugees to re-establish contact with relatives in Vietnam and Laos. Some of the Black Tai in the United States have made visits to relatives in Vietnam and Laos and a few Black Tai from these countries have migrated to the United States in recent years.

On the basis of kinship and their ethno-national identity as Black Tai, the Black Tai in the United States today are part of a transnational network that incorporates Black Tai living in the United States, Laos, Vietnam, and France. All of these Black Tai continue to view their ancestral homeland as located in what is now Vietnam (which they commonly refer to by its Tai name of Muang Thanh rather than its Vietnamese name of Dien Bien Phu) and place primacy on their ethnic identity as Black Tai. While they recognize that their relatives in Vietnam and Laos are citizens of those states, there is ambiguity in such an identity on their part. Thus, while they recognize some association with the Vietnamese state because of its control over their homeland, they generally equate the ethnic category of Vietnamese in the United States with lowland Kinh as distinct from themselves.

Forces that promote, allow, or hinder assimilation influence ethno-national identity within a state and can influence transnational relations. Assimilation is the process by which social and cultural distinctions between ethnic groups are minimized or eliminated. The specifically cultural dimension of this is referred to as acculturation, a process whereby the members of an ethnic group adopt aspects of the culture of another group as a result of contact or incorporation into a polity. Complete assimilation into the dominant national group and adoption of its culture tends to end or at least to greatly reduce transnational associations and especially those that are based on ethno-national origins.

Assimilation can result from coercion or from less overt forces and often is a process that takes place as a result of a mixture of the two. The Black Tai assimilated a variety of Mon-Khmer speaking peoples as they settled in Vietnam, Laos, and Thailand and established small feudal states. These Mon-Khmer speaking peoples were not forced to adopt Tai culture beyond recognition of its feudal order, but there were material and cultural incentives to do so. Most of these non–Tai peoples adopted Tai names and Tai styles of dress and spoke one of the Tai languages initially as a second language but gradually as their sole language. Over time virtually most or all vestiges of their Mon-Khmer heritage disappeared. In the case of the Black Tai who settled in what is now Thailand, over time most of them too were assimilated to become part of the larger Thai national majority and ceased to see themselves as Black Tai.

Another potential identity that can be formed on the basis of being a Black Tai is to identify with Tai-speaking peoples in other countries on the basis of a shared heritage. While historically the tendency has been for Tai-speaking groups to segment rather than to amalgamate, in recent years there have been efforts to highlight commonalities in cultural terms. This includes, for example, academic gatherings where Tai peoples from throughout Asia have come together. Considerable interest was generated, for example, at a Thai studies conference held in Chang Mai, Thailand, in 1996 by the attendance of a group of Tai people from northeastern India. This was the first time that Tai from India had been invited to an international gathering of this type. The event took place in the context of a cultural revival among Tai in India[5] and in growing interaction among Tai peoples as a result of the greater openness of the communist regimes in Vietnam, Laos, and the PRC. This openness, for example, resulted in many people in Thailand going as tourists to northwestern Vietnam to explore their Black Tai cultural roots and in ethnic Thai scholars from Vietnam visiting Thailand.

Nation Building

Despite frequent claims to the contrary by nationalist leaders, most modern states as presently constituted did not exist prior to the nineteenth century and in many cases prior to the twentieth century and efforts to forge a unified national identity within states therefore are also usually recent developments. In modern times pressure to assimilate and forge a single national identity within a state often is associated with the process of nation building — the process of constructing or shaping a unified national identity within a state using the power of the state. Nation building is often seen as a crucial component of state building — strengthening the state. Commonly the process involves efforts by the dominant ethno-national group in the state to identify their culture with the state, which is perceived of essentially as a nation-state, and then seeking to promote conformity on the part of those belonging to other national groups.

Taking Indonesia as an example of modern nation building,[6] the thousands of islands that constitute the state of Indonesia have no history of political unity prior to the early twentieth century, when the Dutch brought the entire area under its control. The Dutch had been in the region since the 1600s, but had sought to include certain portions of the region within their colonial realm only in the late nineteenth and early twentieth centuries, when they established control over the area corresponding to the modern Indonesian state. Java was the most populous island in the colony and also served as the center of Dutch administration.

When Indonesia became independent in the late 1940s the new government was dominated by Javanese, but recognition of the new state's hundreds of other ethno-nationalist groups was articulated under the banner of "Unity in Diversity." Indonesia was able to avoid one of the problems confronting many modern states when seeking to establish a national language. The language chosen, Indonesian, was a modern creation based on an existing trade creole language that had been used around the islands. Thus, it was almost everyone's second language. Despite such slogans and a relatively neutral national language, the history of modern Indonesia has been marked by efforts to promote Javanese culture as the national (i.e., state) culture and local resistance to these. This can be seen in policies aimed at promoting Javanese batik patterned clothing as national dress and as the symbol of the Indonesian state — an effort that in some parts of the country met with considerable resistance. In the case of one of Indonesia's more troublesome provinces, Papua (formerly known as Irian Jaya), where there is no tradition of making or wearing batik-patterned clothing, a compromise was achieved in the 1990s through the creation of batik clothing featuring local motifs rather than ones from Java.[7]

There are many instances where nation building has created a backlash and generated ethno-nationalist movements by those resisting such efforts at assimilation and acculturation. The goals of such movements range from having their right to exist within the state as a distinct group with its own particular cultural traditions recognized to seeking separation from the state. It is common for people living in an area where such issues arise to support a variety of approaches. In the case of the Indonesian province of Papua, for example, which was only brought under Indonesian control in 1963 in the face of considerable local opposition, a separatist movement known as the *Organisasi Papua Merdeka* (Free Papua Movement) emerged and remains active today. While opposition to Indonesian authority within Papua remains strong, many Papuans favor greater autonomy rather than full independence. As with many ethno-national independence movements, there are a number of OPM supporters who have gone into exile — in this case to neighboring Papua New Guinea as well as to Australia and the Netherlands—from where they have sought to lobby for independence and to provide support for the independence movement, and thus giving the movement a transnational character. Moreover, such exiles tend to identify themselves as Papuans rather than as Indonesians.

While many states in the modern world are composed primarily of ethno-national groups with relatively long histories of living in the regions included within the state's boundaries, there are also states that are composed mainly or even completely of migrants. Of course, if the time frame is long enough it can be said that migrants settled most states. Going back even a mere 1,000 years in most instances leaves few indigenes. Nevertheless, there are some states that are primarily inhabited today by the descendants of those who settled only during the past 500 years (i.e., roughly in modern times). These include states like the United States, Argentina, Canada, and Australia as well as all of the states in the Caribbean. There are even states that were uninhabited in the not too distant past. Mauritius, in the Indian Ocean, which today (2008) has about 1.3 million inhabitants, was completely uninhabited when Portuguese sailors landed on the island and established a small temporary settlement In the 1500s, and it was not until the French took it over it 1715 that the first sustained settlement of the island began. Mauritius was under British rule from 1810 to 1968, and most inhabitants trace their migratory origins to the period of British colonial rule. Most migrants came from India (Indo-Mauritian 68 percent), but others arrived from continental Africa (Creole 27 percent), Madagascar, France (Franco–Mauritian 2 percent), the United Kingdom, and China (Sino-Mauritian 3 percent).

The issue of nation building also arises in the case of such migrant states, but in these instances it is the culture of the dominant colonial power that was most important in shaping the cultural configuration that comes to be identified as national. Usually the colonial power was also the main source of migrants, but as with Mauritius, this is not always the case. The colonial heritage of these and other states that were formerly under European colonial rule serves in various ways as the foundation of transnational links in the post-colonial world. Having at one time shared a common language, having histories that overlap, and possessing some legal and other institutional frameworks in common creates enduring bonds, especially among elites.

These bonds have been given international recognition through the creation of such entities as the Commonwealth of Nations (also known as the British Commonwealth), the *Organisation Internationale de la Francophonie* (International Organization of the Francophonie, and also known as *La Francophonie*), and the Organization of Ibero-American States (*Organización de Estados Iberoamericanos* in Spanish and *Organização dos Estados Ibero-Americanos* in Portuguese). These bodies serve to promote transnational relations among their members in a variety of ways. The Commonwealth was established in 1921 as the British Commonwealth, with the term British dropped in 1949. Its members include countries that at one time were associated with Britain through some kind of colonial relationship. At present there are 53 members. It sees as its main goals the promotion of democracy, good government, human rights, and development. *La Francophonie* was established in 1970 and includes members with some former attachment to France. At present there are 56 member states, 3 associate members, and 14 observers. In addition to promoting peace, democracy, and human rights, it seeks to promote use of the French language. The Organization of Ibero-American States was founded in 1949 and the office of its secretariat is in Madrid. Its members include states that were formerly colonies of Spain and Portugal. There are 24 members. Its aims are the promotion of democracy, regional integration, and cooperation in the fields of education, science, technology, and culture.

The process of nation building is rarely so heavy-handed as to openly proclaim as its goal the eradication of all but the dominant national culture. There are, of course, examples of state policies of ethnic cleansing, but most states at least pay lip service to multiculturalism and ethnic pluralism. Even an authoritarian state like Burma (Myanmar), where the military regime is carrying out ethnic cleansing campaigns against members of ethnic groups such as the Shan and Karen who are opposed to their role, on the surface presents itself as a multicultural state that encourages ethnic diversity.

Multiculturalism as a policy aims at recognizing, promoting, and creating a tolerant environment for ethnic and cultural diversity in state and private sector institutions and within the society at large. For migrant ethnic groups such a policy often creates a favorable environment for the maintenance of transnational relations. As an official policy with some basis in reality, multiculturalism was first adopted by the government of Canada in 1971 in response to efforts to promote biculturalism, which focused on relations between Anglo-Canadians and French-Canadians. A similar policy was adopted by Australia in 1973. Both Canada and Australia are predominantly migrant societies that initially received most of their migrants from Europe, but by the 1970s were receiving an increasing number of migrants from other parts of the world, especially Asia. Their policies of multiculturalism served not only to improve the status of non–European migrants but also to support the arrival of a larger percentage of migrants from such regions, to add greater complexity to the notion of what constitutes the national identity, and to create more diverse transnational networks on the part of their citizens.

Citizenship

In recent years, greater recognition of multiculturalism by states has also resulted in a more tolerant attitude towards transnationalism in many instances. One important area where this can be seen is in the recognition of dual citizenship. All states have different categories of people living within them. These include citizens, permanent non-citizen residents, temporary residents with work or study permits, illegal aliens, and officially recognized refugees. The category of citizen may be further divided into those who were born in the state as citizens, those who became naturalized citizens, and those of either of these two sub-categories who also hold citizenship in another country (dual nationals).

Permanent residents include a variety of migrants who have established permanent residency in the country, but who have not sought or been granted citizenship. This category may include people who have married citizens, but who themselves do not have citizenship. Another group of people belonging to this category are retirees who have settled in another country for various reasons, such as warm weather or a lower cost of living. The number of people living away from their homeland on temporary work or study permits in the world is quite large. For some of these people this is a temporary situation and they plan on returning home once their contract or studies are finished. For others, moving from contract to contract around the world is essentially a permanent feature of their life. Such people include employees of multinational agencies like the United Nations as well as certain professionals like petroleum or mining engineers and geologists. Illegal aliens include a wide range of people who move to other countries in search of improved economic conditions or to flee hardships at home. In some countries (such as the United States and Thailand) they form a significant part of the workforce. While some refugees lack legal status in the countries to which they have fled, others are granted official status (often in conjunction with the United Nations High Commissioner for Refugees). These people often find themselves confined to refugee camps and, while there may be a goal of permanently resettling them back in their home countries, in the host country, or in a third country, often they remain in the camps for long periods of time, forming semi-permanent communities.

Policies on how one becomes a citizen of a country vary considerably. While most people today simply become citizens of the country that they are born in because their parents were citizens of that country, there are also a relatively large number of people who acquire citizenship through other means or who change citizenship in the course of their lives. This process is known as naturalization: the acquisition of citizenship by somebody who was not a citizen of that country when he or she was born. In some countries naturalization is a relatively simple matter. In Canada and Belgium citizenship can be obtained without much difficulty after three years of continuous residence as a permanent resident. Most other countries have more difficult requirements. An additional complicating factor in some cases is the requirement for documentation, such as a birth certificate. Refugees, illegal migrants, people living in areas subject to warfare, and often those simply living in remote areas of a country commonly do not possess such documents.

An especially important issue in relation to transnationalism that has arisen in recent years is that of dual citizenship. The policies of states vary considerably in this regard and there is considerable debate about its merits and demerits. Critics of dual citizenship raise questions in relation to rights and responsibilities and expectations. Those favoring it tend to highlight the potential benefits in strengthening international relations. Countries such as the Peoples Republic of China revoke a person's citizenship if that person is granted citizenship elsewhere. In the case of Saudi Arabia, taking out citizenship in another country carries criminal penalties. But an increasing number of countries have come to recognize the legality of dual citizenship or at least made some effort to accommodate it.

Vietnam offers a useful case study of a country that has become increasingly lenient towards those living abroad who have ancestral or direct links to Vietnam. The official term for overseas Vietnamese is *Nguoi Viet Hai Ngoai*, but they are more commonly called *Viet Kieu*, a Sino-Vietnamese term meaning Vietnamese sojourner. Before 1975 there were about 300,000 Vietnamese living in France, the United States, Laos, Thailand, Cambodia, and a few French colonies (such as New Caledonia). The Vietnamese War, which ended in 1975, Vietnam's brief war with China in 1979, and a program of sending laborers to the Soviet Union and other Eastern bloc countries (on contracts, but some did not return) resulted in a huge movement of people out of the country. At present there are over three million Overseas Vietnamese. The largest number, over 1.6 million, live in the United States. Other large numbers of them are to be found living in such countries as Cambodia (600,000), France (250,000), Australia (160,000), Canada (160,000), and Taiwan (over 120,000). Officially there are only around 26,000 Vietnamese living in Russia, but unofficial estimates place the number in excess of 100,000. In addition to these countries Vietnamese are to be found living throughout Europe. There are also some in Latin America: about 10,000 in Mexico live mainly in Tijuana and an estimated 1,000 live in Brazil. There are even about 200 living in Israel, where they came as refugees between 1976 and 1979, and two on the island of Guam, where they landed by boat as refugees.

Prior to the 1990s the Vietnamese government placed considerable restrictions on the ability of its citizens to travel abroad, limited issuing passports to those who traveled in an official capacity, and viewed overseas Vietnamese with considerable hostility, branding them "cowardly traitors." Those who immigrated had to do so illegally and it was extremely difficult for Overseas Vietnamese to remain in contact with relatives in Vietnam. At the same time, it was hard for non–Vietnamese to visit Vietnam. Those doing so came mainly in official capacities and their movements and interactions with Vietnamese in the country were severely restricted. As a result, few Vietnamese living in Vietnam married non–Vietnamese, making the issues of naturalization and dual citizenship of little significance at the time. During the 1990s, Vietnam began to open itself to foreign visitors, eased restrictions of interaction between citizens and foreigners, and made it easier for Overseas Vietnamese to make return visits.

The easing of restrictions on travel and interaction resulted in a growing number of marriages between Vietnamese and non–Vietnamese. A large number of Vietnamese women married men from South Korea and Taiwan in particular, often through marriage brokers. By 2001, Vietnamese women comprised 49 percent of the foreign brides in Taiwan and 118,300 Vietnamese women had married Taiwanese men (mainly through the services of marriage brokers) by 2005.

The growing number of marriages between Vietnamese and non–Vietnamese led the Vietnamese government to establish a number of regulations on international marriage in the early 2000s. These included prohibitions on marriages where the partners did not have a common language of communication and in cases where the age gap was considered to be too great. A number of citizenship issues arose from these marriages. One had to do with the emergence of people being left stateless as a result of divorce. Thus, in the case of Vietnamese women who had married Taiwanese men, the UNHCR found that about 3,000 women had become stateless after divorces. These were women who had given up their Vietnamese citizenship at the time of their marriages and become naturalized Taiwanese citizens, but had then given up their Taiwanese citizenship after their divorces when they returned to Vietnam, where they sought to have their Vietnamese citizenship restored. While such women eventually could restore their Vietnamese citizenship, their children who had been born in Taiwan faced more serious obstacles since they had not previously been Vietnamese citizens. Among the problems faced by these women and their children was that their children were not allowed to attend public schools.

A revised Citizenship Law passed in 1998 that came into effect on 1 January 1999 still did not recognize dual citizenship and continued to require those who took out non–Vietnamese citizenship to renounce their Vietnamese citizenship. Government views of Overseas Vietnamese, however, were changing. They were no longer characterized as traitors, but as valuable assets who could provide Vietnam capital and needed skills. New laws allowed Overseas Vietnamese to invest and own property in Vietnam and made it easier for them to visit and reside there. This change in attitude was symbolized by a visit by the president of Vietnam, Nguyen Minh Triet, to Little Saigon (the largest Overseas Vietnamese community) in Orange County, California, during a trip to the United States in June 2007. As government views of Overseas Vietnamese began to change, so did its attitude towards Vietnamese married to non–Vietnamese and its position on dual citizenship. Visa restrictions on non–Vietnamese married to Vietnamese citizens were progressively eased and in 2008 the government moved to allow dual citizenship.

The director of the Department of Justice Administration in the Ministry of Justice, Mr. Tran That, commented in a 2008 interview,[8] while the 1999 Citizenship Law did not recognize dual citizenship, "the reality is that most Vietnamese who live abroad actually have dual nationality because the countries where they live do not require them to relinquish their Vietnamese citizenship." He added, "The Law on Citizenship must be amended in a way that benefits all Vietnamese people and protects the rights of Vietnamese expatriates. Most Vietnamese people who move abroad permanently want to become citizens of their adopted countries without shedding their Vietnamese citizenship. If we don't have proper policies, these people lose some of their rights and benefits in both countries. We must safeguard their interests and anticipate the consequences of changing the law at the same time…. We must change our way of thinking and not be so old-fashioned. We must realize that it's perfectly normal for someone to want to change their citizenship if they move to another land to live."

In November 2008 Vietnam's National Assembly passed a revised Citizenship Law that came into effect in July 2009, allowing overseas ethnic Vietnamese with foreign passports to acquire Vietnamese nationality, provided that they had not renounced their Vietnamese citizenship. Under the new law, Overseas Vietnamese would be able to apply for citizenship at embassies and consulates around the world and those who claimed dual citizenship would be treated the same as ordinary Vietnamese.

Another category of citizenship that has come into being in recent years is supranational citizenship. A number of regional bodies and treaties have made it easier in recent years for citizens of the states relating to them to travel from one of the states to another as well as to reside, study, and work in these states. Under the Maastricht Treaty in 1993 the European Union went further and created the category of European Union citizenship. Under the treaty EU citizenship was granted to "Every person holding the nationality of a Member State," while noting, "Citizenship of the Union shall complement and not replace national citizenship."

Globalization, Transnationalism, and Culture

Modern transnationalism takes place within the context of what is commonly referred to as globalization. Globalization is the process of transforming local phenomena into global ones. It can refer to phenomena of an economic, technological, political, social, or cultural nature. In relation to economics, it is used to refer to the integration of state economies into the international or global economy. In regard to technology, it refers to the global spread of types of technology. In terms of politics, it refers to political relations that transcend state boundaries and assume a global dimension. In social and cultural terms, it refers to forms of social organization and cultural expression that transcend state or local boundaries and assume global dimensions.

Obviously, transnationalism and globalization are related, but they are not the same. As Hannerz has remarked, "I am ... somewhat uncomfortable with the rather prodigious use of the term globalization to describe just about any process or relationship that somehow crosses state boundaries. The term transnational is in a way more humble, and often a more adequate label for phenomena which can be of quite variable scale and distribution."[9] Moreover, as Dicken reminds us, "We must never forget that all 'global' processes originate in specific places."[10]

Whereas globalization emphasizes deterritorialization, transnationalism is grounded in the existence of ethno-national groups and states. In his discussion of social spaces, Faist remarks: "There is a marked difference between the concepts of globalization and transnational social spaces: transnationalization overlaps globalization but typically has a more limited purview.... Whereas global processes are largely decentered from specific nation-state territories and take place in a world context above and below states, transnational processes are anchored in and span two or more nation-states."[11]

Both the concepts of transnationalism and globalization have figured in a debate concerning the future of both the state and the nation. As Willis, Yeoh, and Fakhri have noted, "much early work on the process of 'transnationalism,' particularly in the field of cultural studies, dwelt on the death of the nation."[12] By way of example, they cite Appadura, who asserts, "States throughout the world are under siege."[13] According to this line of thought, the threat from above comes from international organizations such as the International Monetary Fund and World Trade Organization as well as transnational corporations. The threat from below, so the argument runs, is from migrant networks and transnational activists.

These authors have greatly exaggerated the impact of such threats to both states and nations. Rather than their withering away, it is more accurate to view recent developments as a "reconfiguration,"[14] and even this may be too strong a term, since states have never been all-powerful and have always existed within a broader context in which their borders are permeable to varying degrees. As in the past, modern states serve as gatekeepers that seek to influence the flow of people, goods, and ideas across their borders. Some states try harder than others to restrict or influence such flows, but none are able to completely halt this flow or to influence it absolutely.

Writings on globalization include discussions about the emergence of global culture, which is often viewed as a threat to local cultures. There is undoubtedly some truth to this, but it is also important to keep in mind that cultures constantly change and have always been subject to outside influences, just not to the extent that they are at present. The process of globalization has led to the widespread belief that humankind is moving towards a homogenous global culture. Anthony Smith has offered to critique of this notion: "the idea of a 'global culture' is a practical impossibility, except in interplanetary terms. Even if the concept is predicated on *Homo sapiens,* as opposed to other species, the differences between segments of humanity in terms of lifestyle and belief-repertoire are too great, and the common elements too generalized, to permit us even to conceive of a globalized culture."[15] He views such globalized culture as it exists as being too artificial and lacking in emotional content to be able to supersede more deeply held beliefs that have evolved within local contexts. In his view, the state in its effort to create a national culture is a far more powerful force in the modern world than the supposed global community. The state, he argues, can offer people a sense of a shared past, present, and future that is far more powerful than the whole of humankind.

Although the forces of globalization do exert some influence on how modern cultures are evolving, we are certainly not on the verge of witnessing the creation of a globalized culture and many aspects of what is perceived to be globalized culture may be best viewed from a transnational perspective. Even the dreaded hamburgerization of the world, which is often held up as symptomatic of global cultural homogenization, has failed to live up to this promise of homogeneity. The hamburger is, in fact, an interesting food item from a transnational perspective. With its origins linked to minced beef made in Germany, what was commonly referred to as Hamburg Steak was brought to the United States by German migrants in the early nineteenth century and by the latter part of the century the bun had been added to produce the American hamburger.[16] Thus, an item of German cuisine was integrated into the American menu and then transformed into a distinctively American food item.

The rise of American power and influence after World War II saw the gradual spread of the popularity of the hamburger to other countries, sometimes through American-owned restaurants and sometimes through local ones—e.g., the first Wimpy Bar opened in London in 1954 serving hamburgers with British-style chips. The spread of hamburgers by American-based transnational corporations is identified in particular with McDonald's, which was established in California in 1940. McDonald's began its international expansion with a restaurant in British Columbia, Canada, in 1967, followed by one in Costa Rica in 1970, and additional restaurants in Japan, the Netherlands, Germany (the first McDonald's to serve beer), and Australia in 1971. Over the next two decades McDonald's opened restaurants in an additional 53 countries. Hamburgers have proven to be popular in Japan and, while McDonald's has been very successful, it has faced considerable competition, especially from local hamburger chains such as MOS Burger, which was founded in 1972. In addition, Japanese versions of the hamburger have also been developed like the MOS Rice Burger that features buns made of rice mixed with barley and millet. Likewise, in the Philippines, McDonald's competes with Filipino-owned Jollibee, which serves its own versions of hamburgers alongside more traditional Filipino dishes and in 1998 controlled 69 percent of the local burger business (Liddle 1998). From the transnational perspective it is also of interest to note that these non–American hamburger chains have begun to operate outside of their country of origin, catering to markets that identify with their particular country of origin rather than some broader globalized one. MOS Burger has restaurants in Taiwan, Singapore, Hong Kong, Thailand, and Indonesia that cater in particular to Japanese expatriates and tourists. Jollibee has restaurants in 12 countries outside of the Philippines including the United States (in California, where there are large numbers of Overseas Filipinos), Saudi Arabia, Dubai, the PRC, Hong Kong, Vietnam, Malaysia, Indonesia, and Brunei. These restaurants cater especially to Filipino expatriates and migrant workers. In the case of American-based transnational purveyors of hamburgers such as McDonald's, while Americans may visit them while overseas for a taste of America, for local people the cultural context of eating hamburgers in such restaurants may entail a desire for a little exposure to American culture, but it may also be related to other factors ranging from price to perceived cleanliness or modernity.[17] Moreover, as with their local competitors, McDonald's often has varied its offerings to cater to local tastes.

Any discussion of globalization and culture must also take into account the impact of modernization on cultures. To expect that a group of jungle foragers will retain the same cultural beliefs and practices once they have settled down and become farmers, miners, or factory workers is impossible. This is especially true once you add the influence of putting their children in schools and providing them with access to radios, televisions, and now the internet. Aspects of their former culture may survive through language retention, story telling, songs and dances, or marriage customs, but a great deal will disappear as their lives change.

Culture change today, as it was in the past, is the result of the interplay and to some extent the tension between the local-level, state-level, and international-level as they relate to and are influenced by modernization. In this regard, the local-level may not be as important as it was in the past, but its significance has far from disappeared. Nor has the state ceased to play an important role in its efforts to influence the content and flow of goods and ideas across its borders and among its citizens. Technological innovation plays an important role in the entire process. Thus, the inventions of automobiles, airplanes, electricity, and so forth are manifestations of modernization as are ways of thought associated with scientific rationality and the spread of literacy and formal education. While the general thrust of such innovation is to promote greater interaction and interconnectedness, the cultural impact is far from uniform. Literacy can be used as a means of spreading propaganda or critical thought, to undermine cultures or to help preserve them. The internet has proven as much a boon to scientific research as it has to the fanatical ravings of Islamic jihadists wishing to restore a medieval caliphate.

An interesting question arises concerning the extent to which such innovations in communication have served to undermine local culture. To begin with it is important to recognize that global culture arrives locally in a disjointed fashion that creates opportunities for it being integrated into the local culture rather than being something that necessarily overwhelms local cultures. Local cultures may be viewed as differing from more generalized ones in part because they are more a reflection of face-to-face interactions and lived experiences. Seeing something on television is not the same as experiencing it first-hand. And yet, in the modern world a great deal of what shapes even our local cultures is not solely based on first-hand experience. Given the number of hours that many people spend in front of computer and television screens every day versus how much time they spend in face-to-face interactions, it is obvious that cultures are increasingly shaped by what we view and hear through such media — media that has greatly reduced the importance of distance along with physical contact. The more interactive forms of media in particular can assume a greater feeling of reality that usurps some of the significance of the local. At the same time, modern technology has made it possible to record, preserve, and share many aspects of local cultures far more than in the past. In the past a local dance could only be witnessed first-hand and its preservation required that it be taught by one generation to the next. Now, once its movements have been recorded not only can it be shared globally, future generations can recreate it even if it does cease to be performed for a time.

Language is one part of culture where the impact of modernization and globalization has been keenly felt in recent years. Estimates on the number of distinct languages spoken around the world at present and in the recent past vary a great deal. This is in part a reflection in ambiguity over what constitutes a distinct language. Mutual intelligibility is the general criterion, but even with this as a criterion it is not always easy to determine linguistic boundaries. In any event, estimates range from 5,000 to 6,000, with many of these languages being spoken by only a few hundred people or even less.

New languages tend to evolve as a result of the relative physical, social, or political isolation of a group of people in relation to their neighbors. Thus, over 1,000 different languages are spoken on the island of New Guinea, where a small number of people have lived for tens of thousands of years without the existence of unifying political structures much beyond the village level for most of that time. Increasing interaction and the creation of larger political units tends to reduce linguistic diversity and this process has accelerated in the modern world.

It is also important to keep in mind that many people speak more than one language. Often people speak a so-called mother tongue as well as at least one other language with varying degrees of proficiency. This second language may be one spoken by a neighboring people or the official language of the state where this is different than one's mother tongue. It may also be a language used in commerce or one's field of employment.

A number of linguistic developments characterize the modern world. One of these is the extinction of many languages. There are many efforts to preserve or revive languages on the verge of extinction, but the general trend is overwhelming. State-sponsored education, improved communication, and greater mobility of people all play a role in this process. Another development is the spread of languages across the globe to a greater extent than in the past. Especially in large cities in countries with large migrant populations such as the United States, Canada, and Australia, it has become common for teachers to be confronted with students speaking dozens of different languages from around the globe. A classroom in Vancouver may include not only students speaking English, Cantonese, Mandarin, Spanish, and Punjabi as their first (and sometimes only) language, but there may also be students whose first languages are Mnong, Jarai, Lao, and Karen. Whether or not some of these languages continue to be spoken by second-generation migrants depends on a variety of factors relating to the size of the migrant community and how it is integrated into the wider society.

The emergence of global languages is a third development. In the past languages such as Latin, Mandarin, Spanish, Portuguese, French, and English spread as a result of imperial or colonial conquest, religious conversion, and migration. This resulted in such languages being spoken not only in their country of origin, but also in other parts of the world. The most widely spoken languages in the world today in terms of native speakers are Mandarin (885 million), Hindi (500 million to 680 million), English (375 million), Spanish (350 million) and Arabic (280 million). The picture become more complicated when we include people who speak these languages as a second language. This includes 100 million to 250 million additional speakers in the case of Mandarin, Hindi, Spanish, and Arabic, but an additional 1.4 billion people in regards to English. Except for English, those who speak these languages as a second language generally live within the main countries where these languages are spoken as official languages but whose mother tongue is another language.

English is distinct from the other top five in terms of its global breadth and especially in terms of its use in global contexts. In addition to being either "the" or "an" official language in 53 countries (Arabic ranks no. 2, being an official language in 25 countries), English has emerged as the global *lingua franca*. It is the dominant language in communication, international travel, science, entertainment, and diplomacy. The Science Citation Index, for example, covers 6,400 of the world's leading journals in science and technology and 95 percent of the articles in these journals are written in English.

English is also the most widely used language on the internet, but this dominance is being challenged as internet use grows around the world. In 2008 the top ten languages used on the internet were English (29.4 percent), Mandarin (18.9 percent), Spanish (8.5 percent), Japanese (6.4 percent), French (4.7 percent), German (4.2 percent), Arabic (4.1 percent), Portuguese (4 percent), Korean (2.4 percent), and Italian (2.4 percent).[18] The top ten languages are used by 83.6 percent of internet users. Hindi is notably absent from this list and reflects the fact that many internet users in India use English.

The process of culture change within and between the local-level, state-level, and international-level is influenced by political and status-related considerations. In the case of nation building those who are politically dominant in a state generally seek to promote their cultural values to their fellow citizens, sometimes by force but usually through slightly more subtle means. Even when coercion is not used local people may be influenced by what they perceive as the superiority of the cosmopolitan culture of elites within the state. While pride in local cultures is widespread, so to is the desire to adopt at least some aspects of cosmopolitan culture. Here again, the role of modern means of communication is important in regard to serving as a means of promoting fashions and ideas emanating from non-local sources. But it is important not to oversimplify. Thus, while modern forms of communication have promoted the spread of popular youth culture globally, beneath its surface uniformity there is considerable local variation, and modern technology has also allowed for the dissemination of these local variants transnationally. As hip-hop culture spread to Vietnam, for example, it assumed decidedly Vietnamese characteristics not just in terms of language, but also in regard to the treatment of topics—focusing more on topics of concern to Vietnamese youth than to Black Americans.

Annalists have used two terms when discussing what has taken place as global and local cultures meet and mix: creolization and hybridization. To some extent these terms can be used interchangeably. A hybrid is a combination of two or more different things that is intended to produce a particular objective. In cultural terms it is the outcome of the blending of distinct cultures to produce something that is new. Creolization traditionally referred to the outcome of contact between African slaves and French or Spanish settlers in and around the plantations of the Caribbean. In linguistic terms creole refers to a simplified hybrid language called a pidgin that developed to fulfill the communication needs in the absence of a common language being adopted as the mother tongue of a people. The term pidgin was first coined to refer to the speech form that had evolved in Canton, China, in the nineteenth century as a result of interaction between Chinese and British and American traders. Similar linguistic developments had previously taken place in European-run plantations around the world where laborers speaking a variety of languages were brought together from distant lands and they and the plantation managers developed a simplified means of communication. Pidgins evolved into creole languages in a number of instances not only among descendants of plantation workers as in Haiti but also in cases such as Papua New Guinea and Vanuatu where people speaking a great variety of languages were brought into contact with one another as a result of the creation of a colonial state.[19]

The term creolization as it is used today refers to a broader process of cultural mixing than just language that results in the creation of a creole culture. Hannerz has remarked, "It used to be that there were only some handful of historically recognized creole cultures, mostly in the plantation areas of the New World, but now we sense that 'creole' cultures may be turning into more of a generic term, or wider applicability."[20] He adds, "What is at the core of the concept of creole culture is a combination of diversity, interconnectedness, and innovation, in the context of global center-periphery relationships."[21] The diversity concerns the confluence of separate and quite different traditions with historical roots in different continents. While it is marked by the inequality between the center and periphery, "The cultural processes of creolization are not merely a matter of a constant pressure from the center toward the periphery, but a more creative interplay." Using the example of Nigeria, Hannerz says "creolist concepts may be useful in putting together a coherent understanding of a national culture; probably not the kind of homogenizing, boundary-making, past-enhancing understanding that nationalists tend to prefer, but a more dispassionate mapping of the ordering of the cultural inventory."[22]

As Hannerz points out, creolization is also of relevance to the debate surrounding cultural homogenization in the face of globalization: "The rhetoric of global homogenization by way of the market, I would suggest draws many of its overly generalized examples from the highly visible consumption pattern of this market segment. These are the people frequenting major department stores, reading *Time* and *Newsweek* perhaps, preferring transplanted fast-food chains to the local street stalls, and — in good years — even flying into London or Paris for shopping safaris."[23] One should not ignore the role of such people as cultural models, but they are only a part of a complex picture: "The market frame ... does not only present us with the spectre of global homogenization, but also striking instances of cultural innovation through creolization." In regards to popular culture, one finds "striking instances of cultural innovation through creolization.... Creolized music, art, literature, fashion, cuisine, often religion as well, come about through such processes. The cultural entrepreneurs of the periphery carve out their own niche, find their own market segment, by developing a product more specifically attuned to the characteristics of their local consumers.... They draw from organizational forms, technology, and culture drawn from transnational sources, but use these in new and original combinations."[24]

Transnational Social Spaces and Their Context

The notion of transnational social space has been central to the analysis of transnational relations and communities. Faist defines transnational social spaces as "combinations of ties, positions in networks and organizations, and networks of organizations that reach across the borders of multiple states" and emphasizes that they are dynamic: "Cultural, political and economic processes in transnational social spaces involve the accumulation, use and effects of various sorts of capital, such as educational credentials, skills and know-how, and social capital, mainly resources inherent in or transmitted through social and symbolic ties."[25]

Faist identifies three forms of transnational social space: (1) transnational kinship groups that engage in reciprocal relationships based on social norms and expectations, (2) transnational circuits that are created through the exploitation of insider advantages such as through ethnically based trading networks, and (3) transnational communities that are created on the basis of solidarity and collective identity.[26] He cautions that transnationalism and these related concepts should not be seen as replacing other concepts such as assimilation of immigrants or ethnic pluralism, but as adding to the repertoire of conceptual tools at our disposal for understanding migration and cross-border relations.[27] He also points to the need to recognize that considerable differences exist not only between the characteristics of the relationships found in each of these categories but there are also significant differences within the categories. Taking transnational communities for example, there is a considerable difference between a community formed mainly on the basis of the flow of remittances in transnational families between first-generation migrants within reciprocally organized households and centuries old diasporic communities that span part of the globe such as the Jewish diaspora.

As with other forms of social exchange, those of a transnational character entail a sense of mutual obligations and expectations of the actors that are associated with specific social ties and are based on exchanges and services in the past that often involve reciprocity and expectations that such exchanges and services will occur in the future. Those involved in transnational relations share a sense of solidarity with others on the basis of such things as kinship or local community membership and this includes various collective representations in the form of shared beliefs and symbols. Individuals benefit from such relations by gaining access to information and to more economic, human, and social capital. As Faist reminds us, however, transactions based on such norms not only provide benefits, but they can also restrict freedom and there are sanctions in the form of revenge and retaliation.[28]

Transnational communities characterize situations in which strong and dense ties connect those who have migrated and those who have remained behind over time and across space. Such communities can be based on a shared village, town, city, region or state of origin or a shared ethno-national identity.

Transnational diasporas constitute a specific type of transnational community (although it has become increasingly common practice to employ the term more broadly). Diasporas are created when a group suffers some kind of traumatic event that leads to the dispersal of its members. Jews provide a prototype. Armenians and Palestinians are other examples. Diasporic communities share a vision and memory of a lost homeland or an imagined homeland still to be established. Diasporas can only be called transnational communities if the members develop some significant social and symbolic ties to the receiving country, while also maintaining or creating links with fellow exiles in other countries. The difference between diasporas and other forms of transnational communities becomes clear when we compare the Jewish diaspora before the establishment of the state of Israel with other global communities such as Chinese entrepreneurs and traders for whom an actual homeland still existed.

The individual is the basic unit for creating a transnational social space and people create transnational social spaces for a variety of reasons. These can be viewed as motivational factors. Portes, Guarnizo, and Landolt highlight three types of reasons: (1) economic initiatives of transnational entrepreneurs who mobilize their contact across borders in search of suppliers, capital, and markets; (2) political activities of party officials, government functionaries, or community leaders whose main goals are the achievement of political power and influence in the sending or receiving countries; and (3) socio-cultural enterprises of a family nature as well as those oriented towards the reinforcement of a national identity abroad or the collective enjoyment of cultural events or goods (musical folk groups, sports teams, beauty contests, celebrations of holidays, etc.).[29] Whatever the reasons for forging transnational relations, they are based on expectations of benefits and a mix of norms that include notions of reciprocity and senses of obligation.

Historically the search for profit has been the most important motivating factor promoting the creation and maintenance of transnational relations. This has manifested itself especially in long-distance trade. Thus, the desire of Neolithic peoples to obtain obsidian, which was used to make sharp blades, led to the emergence of trade in the Middle East as early as 14,000 B.C. since many of the consumers lived at some distance from sources of obsidian. Discussing the dangers of travel and market difficulties faced by early long-distance traders in his history of trade, Bernstein asked the question, "Why would anyone risk life, limb, and property on journeys that might carry him from hearth and home for years on end, yielding only meager profits?"[30] The answer to this, he says, is simple: "the grim trading life was preferable to the even grimmer existence of the more than 90 percent of the population who engaged in subsistence-level farming." Even small profits from trade were sufficient "to support an upper-middle-class existence" and made the trader "a rich man" when compared to most other people. Moreover, it is important to understand that trading in ancient and medieval times was rarely an individual undertaking and often was a family or ethno-national group specialty.

International trade is an important context to transnational social relations. This was especially true until recent decades, when long-distance commercial activities were the focus of even more of the transnational activities in the world than at present since the difficulties and costs associated with transnational activities constrained those of a non-commercial nature to a greater extent than today. Missionaries, pilgrims, mercenaries, diplomats, and others who traveled over long distances tended to follow established trade routes and usually to travel in the company of long-distance traders and the sailors or caravan personnel who assisted them. Because of this, the volume of international trade provides a general idea of the changing amount of transnational activity. Rostow seeks to quantify the volume of world trade for the period 1720 to 1971.[31] Using 1913 as equal to 100, the volume of world trade in 1720 is 1.13. This provides an indication of relatively how little trade took place at this time. The volume of world trade grew slowly over the next century, reaching only 3.1 in 1820. From then until 1913 (just before the start of World War I), the volume of world trade more than doubled about every twenty years. This boom period in world trade paralleled a dramatic increase in worldwide migration and in transnational activities in general. After this period of pre–World War I growth, the volume of world trade declined after the war and then stagnated at around the 1913 level into the 1940s (it was 103 in 1948).

The post–World War II period witnessed a return to growth in world trade at an even faster pace than during the latter half of the nineteenth century, with the volume doubling about every decade from 1948 to 1968 (when it reached 407). By 1970 the volume of world trade was 490, almost 500 times what it had been 250 years earlier. The volume of world trade has continued to grow rapidly since then. As a report by the World Trade Organization remarked in 2006, "world trade has grown twenty-seven fold in volume terms since 1950, three times faster than world output growth."[32] There has also been a change in the nature of world commerce in association with this growth in trade volume. Dicken refers to the integration of the world economy prior to 1914 as "shallow integration, manifest largely through trade in goods and services between independent firms and through international movements of portfolio capital."[33] In contrast, he says, "Today, we live in a world in which deep integration, organized primarily within the production networks of transnational corporations (TNCs), is becoming increasingly pervasive."[34]

International trade has political aspects in that such economic activities take place within a political and legal framework. This includes state-to-state diplomatic and trade agreements as well as regional and global multilateral agreements. Thus, the growth of world trade following World War II has taken place within the context of the General Agreement on Tariffs and Trade (GATT), a multilateral agreement regulating trade among about 150 countries that was signed in 1947.

Merchants and other business people pursuing foreign markets and trade goods also do so within a social context. Those engaged in international trade may seek to utilize existing networks of co-nationals living in the country where they are conducting business or may work through a network of intermediaries who are adept at negotiations between locals and foreigners. Such activities may take place within what Faist has referred to as transnational circuits, but circuits can also exist in relation to transnational merchant or business communities. In the past foreign merchants often lived in distinct merchant enclaves. Today such expatriate merchants rarely live in such enclaves, but they often form part of a distinct expat community.

The creation of expat or other transnational communities requires the existence of strong social and symbolic ties of the migrants to their country of origin. The extent of their association with the country of immigration varies. Expat business communities often have only limited associations with their country of residence, whereas other communities of long-term immigrants may be highly assimilated and have strong ties to their country of residence. Links between these communities and their country of origin may be perpetuated by a continued flow of immigrants, but also require continued communication and exchange of goods, services, and ideas back and forth. Return visits of migrants may also play an important role in creating and maintaining such communities. In regard to this last point, while there has always been a back-and-forth movement of immigrants, only recently has it reached a critical mass where a large number of people are able to live dual lives—to have homes in two countries and to make a living through continuous regular contact across state borders. In the past such transnational lives were lived only by a relatively small number of people because in large part to the difficulties in international travel. It is significant today that not only has the number of people living transnational lives increased dramatically, but that those doing so has come to include many non-elite—i.e., there has been a democratization of transnationalism.

Those who lived transnational lives in the past included a relatively limited range of people: long-distance merchants, long-distance sailors, diplomats, civil and military employees of large empires, and an assortment of itinerant specialists (including mercenaries and religious practitioners). Such categories of people still account for a significant proportion of transnationals today, with imperial employees being replaced by employees of international organizations. We can add to these more traditional categories of transnationals a category of unskilled and semi-skilled workers who are to be found in huge numbers the world over working in construction as domestics and so forth living transnational lives and forming transnational communities. This is a modern phenomenon made possible by the advent of rapid, inexpensive transportation.

Enabling Factors

We have already discussed how factors such as trade agreements can be conducive to the formation of transnational social relations. In this section we will look at technological factors that enable people to create transnational relations, focusing on the role of transportation and communication — what Dicken refers to as "space-shrinking technologies"[35] — and at how innovations in these areas have contributed to the development of transnationalism. Thus, while transportation may not be a cause of international trade and of the transnational relations that come into being as a result of such trade, international trade cannot take place without the means to transport the goods and traders. For example, as Bernstein points out, "Not until ... around 1500 B.C. would humans begin to exploit the camel's ability to carry hundreds of pounds of cargo across otherwise impenetrable territory" and "Without the domestication of the camel, the trans–Asian silk and trans–Arabian incense routes would have been impossible."[36]

Hannerz remarks, "Distances and boundaries are not what they used to be."[37] In regard to distances, this certainly is an understatement. Progressively more dramatic changes in communication and travel over the past couple of centuries have changed the nature of transnationalism by making communication and travel over great distances faster and easier and accessible to more people than ever before. These changes serve as preconditions for the development of modern transnationalism.

Transnationalism existed in the past, but it was more restricted. Migrants in earlier times often did not maintain transnational relations or did so to only a very limited extent in large part because of the constraints placed on them by existing communication and transportation capabilities. The barriers that distance posed in the past have not disappeared, but they certainly have diminished thanks to air travel and various forms of electronic communication.

Transportation

Until recently humans traveled on foot, on animal (or in something pulled by animals), or in a boat or ship. Sea travel was an especially important means of moving over long distances in the past and improvements in sailing technology and knowledge of the seas in modern times played an important role in the development of transnationalism in the modern world. Casson makes the point that "Until the coming of the railroad, the water was the only feasible medium for heavy transport and the most convenient for long distance travel."[38]

Although ships have been carrying peoples and cargo over extensive parts of the world since ancient times, most of these ships traveled only within particular regions, and the number of people and quantity of goods sailing over long distances was relatively limited. Moreover, it was not until after 1492 and the voyage of Christopher Columbus that major sea links came to be created across the Atlantic and then the Pacific filling in the final gap in establishing a truly global system of transportation.

Modern Europe's global maritime expansion can be said to have begun with the patronage of Dom Henrique (1394–1460), better known as Prince Henry the Navigator for his patronage of maritime sciences. Under his patronage Portuguese ship-builders created a new style of round-hulled, lateen-rigged ship known as the caravel. This ship allowed the Portuguese to carry relatively large cargoes and to sail closer to the wind than previous European vessels. Its improved cargo-carrying capacity and speed proved to be a tremendous boost for Portugal's maritime trade and exploration. While Columbus's voyages have received the most attention in regard to voyages of exploration during this remarkable period of maritime history, almost as important for the newly emerging world system was the voyage of Vasco da Gama from Lisbon around the southern tip of Africa to Calicut and back between 1497 and 1499, which served to open the trade routes and lands of Asia to Europe and to the establishment of Portuguese trading posts scattered across Asia from Goa to Macau. It was not long before the Spanish, Dutch, and English were also sending their ships to the far-flung corners of the globe in search of trade and to establish colonies.

Columbus's voyages set in motion the Spanish conquest and colonization of a great deal of North and South America. The Spanish did not stop there, but pushed on in search of a route to the riches of the Orient: the spices of eastern Indonesia and the silks of China. Ferdinand Magellan set sail from Spain with a fleet of five ships in 1519 in search of the Spice Islands of the East Indies. Although he died in the Philippines, which he claimed for Spain, one of his ships with only 18 of the original 230 crew still alive made it back to Spain (accompanied by some Malay sailors) in 1522, accomplishing the first circumnavigation of the world. One of the legacies of this voyage was that the Philippines became a colony of Spain and the base of trade between Spain and China. This trade was carried out by a fleet referred to as the Manila Galleon and entailed Spanish ships with New World silver sailing from Acapulco to Manila via Guam to trade the silver for Chinese silk, porcelain, and lacquer ware as well as spices and then returning via California to Acapulco.[39] The fleet began sailing in 1565 and continued sailing once or twice a year until the early 1800s. The voyage from Manila to Acapulco took about four months. The galleons that were built for this trade were the largest ships of their time, weighing between 1,700 and 2,000 tons and able to carry goods and up to 1,000 passengers. The *Concepcion*, which was wrecked in 1638, was about 49 meters long and weighed around 2,000 tons.

Such ships served to issue in the Modern Age in which trade and the flow of people for the first time became truly global in scope.

During the nineteenth century sailing was revolutionized by the construction of new "extreme clippers" such as the *Cutty Sark*.[40] The *Cutty Sark* was launched in 1869 and was designed for the tea trade between England and China. It was capable of sailing at sustained speeds of 28 km/h to 32 km/h and, while its initial voyage from Shanghai to London took 122 days, later the ship was to gain the reputation of being the fastest ship of its kind and was able to sail between Australia and England in as little as 67 days.

Rather than such extreme sailing ships, it was steam engine powered ships that gained the ascendancy during the latter half of the nineteenth century, especially after the opening of the Suez Canal in 1869.[41] The canal cut the distance traveled by ships from Bombay to London from over 18,000 to less than 10,000 kilometers. The transcontinental railroad had been opened across the United States a few months earlier in the same year and the Indian subcontinent was crossed by rail the following year. Such speedy travel made possible by these developments was highlighted in Jules Verne's 1873 novel, *Around the World in Eighty Days,* in which Phileas Fogg and his valet Passepartout circumnavigated the globe in 80 days traveling largely by railroad and steamship. Travel around the world by sea was made even shorter — by about 13,000 kilometers — with the opening of the Panama Canal in 1914.

In the early nineteenth century ocean-going ships were designed primarily to carry cargo and not passengers. Catering to passengers became more important during the nineteenth century as an increasingly large number of people were carried to distant destinations around the world as migrants, contract laborers, colonial civil servants, and in other capacities. The Black Ball Line of New York City, founded in 1817, became the first shipping company to be concerned with the comfort of its passengers. It had four packet ships that sailed between New York City and Liverpool. Packet ships were primarily used to carry mail, but they could also carry passengers. The number of ships catering to passengers increased in the 1830s, with the British and North American Royal Mail Steam Packet (later called the Cunard Line) dominating the business. The first Cunard ship was the *Britannia,* launched in 1840. Its transatlantic crossing took 14 days. There were an increasing number of ships that focused on carrying passengers across the Atlantic in the 1850s and 1860s. Mark Twain chronicled such a voyage in his 1867 book *The Innocents Abroad, or The New Pilgrims' Progress,* in which he describes a voyage to Europe and the Holy Land with a group of religious pilgrims on board the *Quaker City.* The *Quaker City* was a side-wheel steamship built in 1854 that could sail at a speed of 24 km/h.

Huge numbers of European immigrants sailed across the Atlantic during the latter half of the nineteenth century (see Chapter 2). These immigrants sailed on ships that were built mainly to carry cargo as what was referred to as "steerage" or between-deck class. They were placed between the upper deck and the storage hold in a level created by the construction of what was called the between deck, where temporary partitions were erected and used for steerage accommodation. The steamship *Adriatic* (launched in 1872) of the White Star Line is an example of such a ship. It could accommodate about 800 steerage passengers, 50 first class passengers, and 50 second class passengers. In 1843 an emigrant could expect to pay 20 *speciedaler,* for the voyage from Norway to New York, plus $1.75 for the landing fee in New York.[42] The average crossing time from Norway to New York was 53 days, but could take as long as 100 days. By 1899 ships were being built with what were called third class, which was similar to second class but more crowded, and fourth class. The Cunard Lines steamships *Saxonia* and *Ivernia* (built in 1899) could carry 1,600 such passengers each.

The Germans and British in particular built very fancy steamships catering to passengers in the early twentieth century, such as the *Mauritania* and *Lusitania* of the Cunard Line.[43] The *Mauritania* was designed to carry 560 first class passengers, 500 second class passengers, 1,400 third class passengers, and had a crew of 800. Its top speed was 46 km/h. J.P. Morgan's White Star Line built the *Olympic* and *Titanic* (which sank on its maiden voyage in 1912). These were the first cruise ships to emphasize comfort over speed. The interwar years (1920–39) were the heyday of such fancy cruise liners. The passengers on these ships were mainly wealthy tourists and they were not fitted to carry immigrants in steerage. During World War II these large ships were used to carry troops. After the war the ships transported refugees to the United States and Canada and North American businessmen and tourists to Europe. Air travel undermined the use of cruise ships after World War II and passenger ships went into a sharp decline. It is important to note, however, even if they no longer carry very many people, ships still carry over 90 percent by weight of the goods that are traded internationally.

The history of commercial aviation and its role in changing how we travel can be viewed from the perspective of the airplanes that have been flown and its evolution from a relatively dangerous means of travel for a few to a form of safe travel for the masses. Air services initially focused on carrying mailbags and dirigibles and airplanes were able to carry relatively few passengers. Commercial air travel was initiated by Frankfurt-based DELAG (*Deutsche Luftschiffahrts-Aktiengesellschaft*), which was founded in 1909. The first international scheduled air service was by Aircraft Transport and Travel (1916–1921) of the United Kingdom in 1919 between London and Paris

Early commercial airline travel in the 1920s is associated especially with two airplanes: the Ford Tri-Motor and the Fokker F.VII. The Ford Tri-Motor, popularized in recent years in the Indiana Jones movies and books such as *Indiana Jones and the Sky Pirates,*[44] first flew in 1926.[45] Ford claimed that it was the safest airliner in the world. The Ford Tri-Motor carried eight to nine passengers (12 maximum) and introduced what was advertised as coast-to-coast service in the United States. In fact, passengers traveled by rail from New York City to Port Columbus, Ohio, before boarding the plane for a flight to Waynoka, Oklahoma, where they boarded another train to Clovis, New Mexico, where they then flew on to Los Angeles. The Dutch Fokker F.VII was built between 1925 and 1932.[46] It could carry eight (and a maximum of 12) passengers and had a cruise speed of 170 km/h. The F.VII's popularity suffered after a variant, the F.10, crashed in 1931, killing famed football coach Knute Rockne. While the Ford Tri-Motor was built entirely of metal, the Fokker F.VII was built of plywood and it was subsequently banned from use on commercial flights.

Among the airlines using the F.VII was KLM (*Koninklijke Luchtvaart Maatschappij,*

Royal Aviation Company), founded in 1919 and now the oldest airline company in the world that is still operating under its original name. KLM's first flight was between Amsterdam and London in 1920. Scheduled services began later the same year and it carried a total of 440 passengers in 1920. KLM began flying to the Netherlands East Indies (Indonesia) in 1929 using the F.VII. For a time, this 14,400-kilometer flight was the longest scheduled airline route in the world. Comparing the number of passengers carried by KLM in 1920 and 1930 provides an indication of the growing importance of air travel. In 1930 the airline carried 15,143 passengers, compared with only 440 a decade earlier.

A 1932 article in *Flight* magazine discusses this route and new air routes in the Dutch East Indies. Citing an increase in the number of airline passengers flying within the Dutch East Indies (14,457 in 1929 and 18,248 in 1930) largely as a result of new routes within Java and from Java to Palembang and Medan in Sumatra and to Singapore that commenced in 1930, the article boasts, "There is no doubt that the public now regard the air service as an integral part of the lines of communication in daily use in this country."[47] The flight from Amsterdam to Batavia initially was every two weeks until in October 1930 it began weekly service. The route from Amsterdam to Batavia included stops in Budapest, Athens, Cairo, Baghdad, Bushire (Bushehr, Iran), Jask (Iran), Karachi, Jodhpur, Allahabad, Calcutta, Akyab (Sittwe, Burma), Rangoon, Bangkok, Medan, and Palembang. The journey took 11 to 12 days each way. The fare was fl. 2,200 "inclusive of full board and lodging at hotels en route" with a baggage free allowance of 15 kg.

Airline travel began to emerge as an alternative to travel by railroad and steamship in the 1930s. The Douglas Aircraft Company of Long Beach, California, founded in 1921, was at the forefront of introducing new commercial aircraft during this time.[48] The Douglas DC-2 was introduced in 1934. It only had 14 seats, but it is widely credited with demonstrating that air travel could be safe and reliable, as well as comfortable. It was the DC-2's successor, however, the DC-3 —featured in a number of Hollywood movies including a half-scale model that appears at the end of the 1942 movie *Casablanca* and more recently the 2008 James Bond movie *Quantum of Solace*— that revolutionized air transport in the 1930s. It was much easier to fly than previous airplanes and American airline companies quickly ordered 400 of them. A total of 16,079 were eventually built in the United States, Russia, and Japan. The DC-3 could carry 21 to 32 passengers. Its amenities included sleeping births and an in-flight kitchen. It had a cruise speed of 240 km/h. Stopping to refuel three times, it could cross the United States eastbound in 15 hours and 17.5 hours westbound.

While today it is known mainly as a manufacturer of helicopters, Sikorsky Aircraft Corporation (founded in 1925) was primarily associated with seaplanes in the late 1920s and 1930s.[49] The four-engine S-42 was introduced in 1934. It could carry up to 37 passengers and had 14 sleeping births. It was capable of flying 3,088 km non-stop at a maximum speed of 300 km/h. Designed for Pan American World Airways, they were known as Flying Clippers or Pan Am Clippers. A total or ten were built.

Pan American began in 1927 as a seaplane service in Key West, Florida, that had the rights to carry mail to Havana.[50] The airline acquired a virtual monopoly on carrying international mail for the United States in Latin America and established extensive routes for mail and passengers in Latin America. The airline initiated a program of rigorous long-distance training for its pilots and flight crew and built a network of seaplane anchorages for its planes. Pan American began service across the Pacific in 1935. This route ran from San Francisco to Honolulu, then on to Canton with stops at Midway, Wake, and Guam on the way. Once in Canton, passengers were able to fly to various cities in China on China National Aviation Corporation (today known as China Airways), which had been acquired by Pan American in 1933. Pan American began semimonthly flights to Singapore in 1941. This allowed people to fly between San Francisco to Singapore in only six days—previously it has taken 25 days. Pan Am also flew Boeing 314 flying boats, the first of which were delivered in 1939 and began regular service across the Atlantic between New York and Southampton in the United Kingdom. The fare for passengers was U.S. $375 (equivalent to over $5,000 today).

Looking at the number of passengers carried by KLM again, we can see that there was a dramatic increase after World War II. In 1950 the airline carried 356,069 passengers. International air travel changed and continued to grow in importance in the 1950s with the introduction of new airplanes such as the Douglas DC-6 and Lockheed L049 Constellation that were much faster and larger than previous passenger aircraft. The DC-6 commenced regular flights in 1947 and about 700 of them were built between 1946 and 1959. It had been designed initially as a military transport plane, but was re-designed for long-range commercial use after World War II. It was designed to carry between 54 and 102 passengers. Some versions featured Pullman-type sleepers. It has a range of 4,840 km and has a cruise speed of 507 km/h. It came to be used by a large number of airlines around the world for domestic and international flights. For example, Pan American first used it for transatlantic tourist flights in 1952 and British Commonwealth Pacific Airlines (1946–54) used it for its flights between Sydney and Vancouver, which had stops in Auckland, Nadi (Fiji), Canton Island, Honolulu and San Francisco. Its durability is attested to by the fact that about 100 of these planes are still in use today in Alaska and South America.

The Lockheed L049 Constellation was developed in cooperation with Trans-World Airlines in 1945. Its initial flight was from Washington to Paris with stops in Gander and Shannon. It was designed to carry 62 to 95 passengers (maximum 109), has a range of 8,700 km, and a cruise speed of 547 km/h. Eight hundred fifty-six of them were built between 1943 and 1958. It was the first passenger airline to have a pressurized cabin. Pan American used this plane for its Flights 001 and 002, which were initiated in 1950. These were the first scheduled around-the-world flights. The route was San Francisco, Honolulu, Tokyo, Hong Kong, Bangkok, Calcutta, Delhi, Beirut, Istanbul, Frankfurt, London, and New York. The flight westbound took 46 hours. Pan American also introduced economy class at this time.

Jet airliners were introduced in the late 1950s. De Havilland operated the first jet-powered airliner in 1949—the Comet. The Comet began commercial flights in 1952, but a series of crashes in 1953 and 1954 resulted in the planes being grounded and interest in jet-power waning. It appeared for a time as if the future lay with turboprops such as the British-built Vickers Viscount and Lockheed Electra. Meanwhile Boeing had been producing jet-powered planes for the military (such as the B-52, which was introduced in 1952) and began work on a commercial jet. Douglas also began work on a commercial jet. In 1955 Pan American placed orders for 20 Boeing 707s and 25 DC-8s. Other airlines quickly followed suit and the age of jet travel began.

The jet-powered four-engine DC-8 began flying in 1958. DC-8s carry between 124 and 259 passengers. Variants of the DC-8 have a range of 3,445 km to 7,410 km and have maximum cruise speeds of around 950 km/h. The first 707s were delivered in 1958, with the last one being built in 1979. Variants of the 707 carry between 110 and 202 passengers, have a range of about 6,800 km, and a maximum cruise speed of about 1,000 km/h. The 707 began flying scheduled service between Paris and New York in 1958 — the first non-stop flight to Europe by a commercial carrier.

Air travel took another leap with the introduction of the Boeing 747-100. Known as the Jumbo Jet, the airplane was designed to carry a maximum of 366 passengers with a three-class configuration or 452 passengers with a two-class configuration. Its cruising speed is 893 km/h and its maximum range is 9,800 km. Commercial Boeing 747 flights began in 1970, with the first commercial flight being between New York and London. Subsequent versions of the plane carry more passengers, fly faster, and farther. The 747-400 model that was introduced 1989 can carry up to 524 passengers, has a cruising speed of 913 km/h, and a range of 13,500 km.

Such huge long-range aircraft helped to generate a massive jump in the number of people flying worldwide. With a total fleet as of 2008 of 173 airplanes (including 26 747s), over 30,000 employees, and more than 90 destinations, KLM carried 9,715,069 passengers in 1980 and over 16 million in 1990. For someone living in the Netherlands wishing to visit in Indonesia rather than months at sea on a potentially dangerous and relatively expensive voyage around the Cape of Good Hope and across the Indian Ocean as was the case in the early nineteenth century, or the 11 to 12 day flight of the 1930s, it is now possible to travel safely at a relatively modest cost and to make the journey in a matter of hours. You can leave Amsterdam and arrive in Jakarta 16 hours and 30 minutes later.

Communication

People have not only been traveling faster than ever before over the past two centuries, they have also been able to communicate much better with one another even if they do not leave home. Literacy and the ability to write were quite low worldwide at the beginning of the nineteenth century. Even in England, where government-funded public education only became available in 1870, in 1841, for example, 33 percent of men and 44 percent of women signed their marriage certificate with a mark since they could not write. In many parts of the world in the nineteenth century reading and writing was the preserve of small numbers of priests, administrators, and other elites. In India, for example, the literacy rate was estimated to be only 3.2 percent in 1881 and 1882 and it had only increased to 12.2 percent by 1947. There has been a steady increase in India's literacy rate since then of about 10 percent per decade until by 2008 it was 61 percent. At present over 80 percent of the world's population is literate.

The spread of literacy made it potentially easier for people spread out across the globe to communicate with one another, but turning this into reality also required the development of a dependable and affordable postal system. Postal systems existed within empires in the ancient world and merchants living in different commercial centers devised means of writing to one another in the medieval world, but these means of sending letters were not widely employed and sending letters across borders was especially difficult.

The modern postal system began in England in the early nineteenth century. Rowland Hill, an educator and tax reformer, advocated establishing an inexpensive postal system in a series of pamphlets written between 1835 and 1837. Postage in England at the time was extremely expensive. For example, it cost one shilling to send a letter from London to Edinburgh — the equivalent of a day's wage for a factory worker — even though, as Hill pointed out, the actual cost for delivering this letter was only one thirty-sixth of a penny thanks to the railroad. Hill joined forces with Richard Cobden, a prominent advocate of free trade, to promote what was referred to as the penny post. As Cobden noted, "Cheaper postage ... would allow the fifty thousand Irish working in Manchester to regularly write to their loved ones back home."[51] The penny post came into being in 1840, laying the basis for the modern inexpensive postal system.

The railroad allowed for the delivery of mail at greater speed and at a reduced cost between points linked by rail service initially within countries (e.g., England in 1830 and the United States in 1864) and only gradually across borders. International mail was often delivered by ship until the twentieth century. Packet ships designed to carry mail entered into service between Wales and Ireland and between Dover and Calais in the early 1600s. Regular packet service between England and the West Indies began in 1702 and was later extended to North America. The British began airmail service on a limited basis in 1911, regular service in Europe started after World War I, and airmail service between England and India commenced in 1929. Transpacific airmail service between San Francisco and Manila (on the Pan American route) started in 1935 and across the Atlantic in 1939 (New York–Bermuda-Portugal-Marseilles).

The Treaty of Bern created the General Postal Union in 1874, which became the Universal Postal Union in 1878. It established a system whereby: (1) there should be a more or less uniform flat rate to mail a letter anywhere in the world, (2) foreign and domestic mail should be treated equally by postal authorities, (3) monies collected for international postage was to be retained by each country, and (4) stamps issued by the member states were recognized internationally. The UPU is now a United Nations agency with its headquarters in Bern and there are at present 191 members of the UPU.

Additional means of transnational communication were provided by the electrical telegraph and telephone. Optical telegraphs are ancient and employ signals made with smoke and beacons. Semaphore lines employing a series of towers to send visual messages were employed in Europe in the late eighteenth and nineteenth centuries. These were soon superseded by electrical telegraphs, which were first used on a regular basis in 1833 in Göttingen. Efforts to lay a telegraph cable across the Atlantic commenced in 1857, but it was not until 1866 that regular telegraphic communication was possible across the Atlantic. England and India were connected by telegraphic cable in 1870 and Australia was connected by cable in 1872. Telegraphic communication across the Pacific began in 1902, making it finally possible to send a telegraph around the world. Wireless or radiotelegraphy began to be developed in the 1890s, with the first signal being successfully sent by Guglielmo Marconi in 1896. Wireless telegraphy became more widely used in the early twentieth century as efforts were made to improve the technology and lower the cost of sending messages. The system was fully automated in 1935 with the introduction of telex machines. Germany was the first country to establish a worldwide telex system in the 1930s, for official communications.

Efforts to improve on the electronic telegraph also led to invention of the telephone — a means of communication that does not require literacy. Although there were earlier versions of such a communications device, Alexander Graham Bell was awarded a patent to the telephone in 1876 and the first long-distance telephone line was strung over 58 miles in California in 1877. Commercial development of the telephone was rapid and by 1904 there were over 3 million telephones in use in the United States. Breaking free of wire connections via radiotelephones began as early as 1926, but their use remained quite limited until the 1970s, when the first commercial cellular networks were launched. These early cellular phones were used mainly in vehicles.

It was with the launching of the so-called second generation of cellular phones in the early 1990s that cellular telephone use became widespread and their use increased sharply following the introduction of third generation systems in 2001. Cellular phone technology has allowed a large number of people worldwide to gain access to telephones than would otherwise have been possible. By 2005 there were an estimated 2.4 billion cell phone users. It is significant that there are large numbers of users not only in developed countries, but also in many developing countries as well — there are over 400 million cell phone users in the People's Republic of China and over 50 million in Indonesia. These are countries where only a few years ago relatively few people had access to telephones. In general, improvements in telephone technology and the reduced cost of making telephone calls have allowed people around the world to talk to one another more frequently over great distances, across borders, and even when in remote areas.

No form of communications has had as much of an impact on the promotion of transnational linkages as the internet. Early networks were created in the 1960s, with the term internet being coined in 1974, but use of this technology remained quite limited until after it was opened to commercial interests in 1988. The World Wide Web was invented in 1989, but even then it was used mainly within academic circles until the mid–1990s. The subsequent increase in use of the internet has been phenomenal. Around 360 million people used the internet in 2000. By the end of 2008 there were about 1.6 billion people using the internet, representing 23.5 percent of the world's population.[52] Also interesting is the distribution of users by percentage of total population: from a high of 73.1 percent in North America to a low of 5.6 percent in Africa.

The improvements in transport and communication discussed above have made it easier for people to move about the globe and to remain in contact with one another. Such technological changes have made it much easier to create and maintain transnational relations.

2

MIGRATION IN THE MODERN WORLD

Migration refers to movement from one place to another. Such movement can be temporary or permanent. Usually it also entails movement across an administrative boundary of some kind. In the present context we are concerned with migration across state boundaries. Migration is often an essential prerequisite for transnationalism. The act of migration itself, however, is not sufficient to create transnationalism. In fact, most past migrants and most descendants of migrants historically have not and many migrants at present do not maintain transnational lives or, at best, maintain only minimal transnational relations. For migrants or their descendants to become transnationals requires something extra in that not only have they adapted to their current home country to a significant degree but they have also maintained or created meaningful connections with countries where they have previously lived or that they consider to be their ancestral homeland or with others from their ancestral home living in yet other countries.

There are a handful of basic concepts that are fundamental to understanding the characteristics of international migration.[1] To begin with there is the difference between pioneer migration and chain migration. Pioneer migration refers to migrants moving to a new destination for the first time whereas chain migration refers to the migrants who follow the path of pioneer migrants forming a chain of migration to a particular destination. A second group of characteristics relates to frequency. Primary migrants are those migrating for the first time. Return migrants are those who return to their original country of emigration with the intention of taking up residence there again. Transilient migrants are migrants who move on to a second destination from their first destination. Circular or recurrent migrants are those who frequently move between two or more places as with seasonal laborers. The term transmigrant is sometimes used to refer to migrants who live in either the country of emigration or of destination, and commute back and forth between the two locations for life periods.

It is also common to make a distinction between voluntary and involuntary migration. Voluntary migrants are those who choose to migrate while involuntary migrants are those who are forced to migrate. Voluntary versus involuntary migration is not always easy to distinguish and there are clearly degrees to which migration is a voluntary act. Slaves are clearly involuntary migrants, while refugees may not have to leave their homes, but not doing so can have dire consequences and, therefore, their decision is largely involuntary. The situation can be more ambiguous in the case of labor migrants who are moving from severely impoverished situations to ones with greater opportunities.

In trying to understand reasons for migration consideration should be given to how individuals make decisions concerning migration. Individuals do not make decisions about migration in a vacuum. In a general sense there are push factors and pull factors. These terms refer to the factors that push people to leave home and pull factors that pull people towards a particular destination. These include encompassing structural factors that encourage or discourage migration such as levels of economic inequality between states, labor markets, and state institutions that relate to migration.

Perceptions of relative differences between a person's homeland and possible place of immigration are important motivational factors for voluntary migrants. The destination is viewed as being relatively better in one or more ways. Historically economic factors have undoubtedly been the dominant motivating factors for most migrants, but it is important to recognize that there may be others. A person with a well-paying job in northern Canada may willingly accept a reduction in economic benefits to move to Hawaii because of weather differences and a general perception that Hawaii is some kind of paradise. A sense of adventure or a desire to do good works may also be considerations. A person may leave home to join the circus, work on a freighter, or teach English in a foreign land motivated by a sense of adventure or may become a religious missionary or aid worker in another country based on a desire to help others.

A person may dream of migrating, but how to actually achieve this desire? Negotiating the intricacies of migrating from one country to another is not an easy matter and often requires the help of others. Faist points to the importance of social networks to immigration.[2] Network analysis does not help to understand initial decisions of pioneer migrants, but it does help to explain the direction of international migration and the dynamics of migration flows and, in particular, why more migration flows once it has taken off. Migrant networks become self-sustaining because of the social support that they provide prospective migrants. The glue that holds migrant networks together includes the shared cultural values of members such as their feelings of obligation, reciprocity, and solidarity towards those they perceive as sharing some kind of identity or group membership. Thus, networks are often formed on the basis of family membership, kinship, sharing a common place of origin (neighborhood, village, town, city, region, or country), ethnicity, or occupation. Such migrants feel that they should help one another. Those who are members of migrant networks often provide resource to those seeking to migrate. These may include material help as well as the sharing of information about how to migrate and how to adapt to new environments.

As mentioned above, migration merely creates an opportunity for establishing transnational relations. The actual creation of these relations depends on a variety of factors. At the level of the individual this relates to personal decisions and what Faist refers to as transnational life projects.[3] A person's stage of life influences decisions about migration and mobility and the nature of transnational ties. Such decisions take place within a broader social context that are influenced by notions of reciprocity and solidarity such as among family members or members of the same ethnic group. They also tend to take place within transnational communities that have arisen out of the creation of dense and strong social and symbolic ties forming a durable transnational network that is based in part on such notions of reciprocity and solidarity. The creation of these transnational networks and communities is also influenced by the existence of structural opportunities that allow and encourage them to develop.

Faist combines network analysis and the concept of social capital to help understand patterns and decisions about migration as well as the development and maintenance of transnational networks and communities.[4] Social capital is primarily a local asset and can be transferred cross-nationally only under specific conditions. Especially for pioneer migrants the expected costs and risks of international movement are high. However, once official policies and other groups support migration, pioneer migrants and other facilitators take heart. As mechanisms such as migrant networks evolve that make obligations, reciprocity, solidarity, and other social resources more easily transferable across state borders, the choice to migrate increases among the pool of potential migrants.

A particularly important question concerns how the descendants of migrants maintain transnational connections—i.e., how does a strong and dense circular flow of people, goods, ideas, and symbols extend beyond the first generation of migrants. Related to this is a question about how migrants adapt to their new environment while at the same time maintaining transnational social spaces. Such developments also can be analyzed in terms of structural conditions that allow and encourage transnational relations to persist over time as well as the persistence of transnational community and social group ties over generations based on social capital and a host of norms related to reciprocity, obligation, and a sense of a shared identity the crosses state borders.

In addition to the migrants themselves, in examining how migration relates to the creation of transnational social relations, it is important not to forget those employed in the migration process. This includes a range of people involved in the migration enterprise such as government officials, operators of migration-related businesses, and a host of recruiters, brokers, and crews of ships and planes. These people are not only crucial to making migration possible, but they themselves may lead transnational lives in their activities that encourage and facilitate the movement of people across borders.

Patterns of Migration

The flow of migrants across borders from 1500 to the present has not been even in terms of absolute numbers and as a percentage of the total world population. It is common to speak of waves of migrants and such waves are not continual. Thus, while it may seem like there are a large number of migrants around the world at present, recent migration figures are not all that high when compared to the period from the mid–1800s to the outbreak of World War I.

There have been three waves of international migration since 1500. The first of these waves occurred during the so-called Age of Discovery from 1500 to the early 1800s and included voluntary migration and contract labor migration from Western Europe and the movement of slaves from Africa to newly colonized lands primarily in the Americas. The second wave took place between the mid- to late 1800s and early 1900s.[5] It coincided with the industrialization of Western Europe and the boom in international trade mentioned in the last chapter and included large-scale migration from Europe to former colonies in the Americas and Southwest Pacific as well as large-scale recruitment of contract labor migrants from certain Asian countries such as India and China to European colonies and the United States. Again, coinciding with patterns in international trade, the third wave begins with the aftermath of World War II and runs to the present. This wave starts with the movement of people across borders as a result of the rise of communism in Eastern Europe and China and the decolonization process elsewhere. From the 1960s labor migrants and refugees moving from one developing country to another as well as from developing to developed countries have been the dominant patterns.

Within any particular period of migration a limited number of countries are the main sources and destinations of migrants. The concept of chain migration is important here since once the process of migration starts, more people tend to follow. In contrast, where the process of migration does not begin to any appreciable extent most people tend to stay put.

An especially important dimension of the pattern of international migration is the relative economic status of the countries from which migrants are moving from and to. We can characterize this broadly as South-South, South-North, and North-North migration. South-South migration refers to migration between two relatively poor or developing countries. South-North migration refers to migration from a relatively poor or developing country to a relatively wealthy or developed country. North-North migration refers to migration from one relatively wealthy or developed country to another. These are obviously very broad categories. Thus, Laos and Thailand are both developing countries, but while Thailand is a middle-income country and relatively well off compared to many developing countries, Laos is one of the poorest countries in the world. While migration from Laos to Thailand can be categorized as South-South migration it takes place between countries that are very unequal economically, but the degree of economic difference is less than in the case of a person from Laos migrating to the United States.

Most South-North migration is from former colonies or the result of selective recruitment. During the latter part of the twentieth century about 65 million migrants settled in states with a high degree of industrialization and in oil rich states. One-third of these migrants went to France, Germany, Italy, Japan, the United Kingdom, and the United States.

Colonial ties not only shaped initial transnational social relations to a large extent in the major modern recipients of migrants such as the United States, Canada, Australia, and Argentina, but following independence the colonial heritage continued to influence the patterns of migration not only in terms of relations with the former colonial master itself, but also in terms of orienting their migration policies so as to favor migrants coming from the same part of the world as the former ruler. Thus, in the case of the countries cited above under colonialism they received migrants mainly from the United Kingdom and Ireland or Spain. After independence the United Kingdom and Ireland or Spain remained important sources of migrants, but these former colonies also received migrants from a wide range of other European countries as well. Thus, their transnational orientation remained towards Europe or to other countries outside of the world that shared such a European orientation.

Asian migration to such European-oriented countries is noteworthy in regard to transnationalism since such migrants serve to challenge this orientation. As we will see, Asian migrants in relatively small numbers were accepted in these Euro-centric countries in the nineteenth century largely to fill specific labor requirements and generally with the understanding that it was temporary. Despite this, small Asian migrant communities did settle in these countries, but in countries such as the United States and Australia they faced considerable discrimination and further migration from Asia during the late nineteenth century and throughout the first half of the twentieth century was severely curtailed by migration policies. This meant that while there were translational social links between these countries and Asia these did not form a large part of the transnational networks of these countries. This situation changed dramatically in the late twentieth century as Asian migration to many of these European-oriented countries has grown substantially. These countries now are home to relatively large Asian ethnic communities with transnational ties to Asia. This situation has increasingly challenged the Euro-centric nature of such countries, pushing them towards a transnational, cultural, and political orientation that is more global in its orientation.

Involuntary International Migration

The recruitment and shipment of slaves is the most extreme form of involuntary migration, but there are other forms as well. There is a long history of forcing those convicted of crimes to leave a community or country. In modern times this has occasionally taken the form of sending convicts to distant sites away from the home country known as penal colonies. Refugees constitute another category of involuntary migrants. Refugees are persons who have left their home country because of a fear of being persecuted for reasons of race, religion, nationality, membership of a particular social group, or political opinion. Each of these forms of involuntary migration relates to transnationalism in somewhat different ways and how they have done so has changed over time.

Slavery has a long history and was widespread throughout the world well into the nineteenth century. The number of slaves has declined since then, but despite it being illegal worldwide there are still slaves in some countries. Historically most slaves were either obtained within the society possessing them or from nearby areas. Even in Africa, the majority of people taken into slavery in the modern era have remained in close proximity to their homeland. In the context of transnationalism, however, we are primarily interested in those slaves who are transported over long distances from their point of origin.

In the case of Africa, before the development of the European slave trade to the Americas in the 1500s the vast majority of African slaves who were exported from the continent were shipped from East Africa to the Arabian Peninsula. Zanzibar became the major slave-trading center for the Islamic world with an estimated 50,000 slaves a year passing through Zanzibar. The ruling Arab elite of Zanzibar maintained it as a base for exporting slaves and ivory from the interior of Africa and Arab slave traders often led their own expeditions into the interior of Africa to obtain slaves.

Modern European involvement in the African slave trade began with the Spanish and Portuguese. African slaves were present in both countries prior to their voyages of exploration and establishing colonies beyond Europe, but both countries became increasingly involved in trading and using slaves as their colonial empires expanded. The Portuguese established control over several of the important centers of slave trading on the east coast of Africa in the 1500s. The economies of the Portuguese settlements in Africa relied heavily on the export of slaves, largely to the Americas. African slavery in the British and French colonies in the Caribbean became increasingly important in the late 1600s when they switched from using European labor to African slave labor as their plantation economies changed focus from tobacco to sugar. European slave traders shipped between 12 million and 13 million salves from Africa, mainly to the Americas. The trans–Atlantic slave trade peaked in the late 1700s before going into decline and eventual abolition in the 1800s.

There were a total of 61 African ports involved in the trans–Atlantic slave trade and while slaves from Africa were scattered around the Americas, there were some patterns to where slaves from particular locales ended up.[6] Thus, in the case of Brazil, an estimated 42 percent of the slaves came from Angola, 13 percent from the Congo, 9 percent from the DR Congo, 10 percent from Gabon, 6 percent from Madagascar, and 9 percent from Mozambique. The pattern in the Caribbean was somewhat different: 15 percent from Angola, 6 percent from Benin, 8 percent from Cameroon, 8 percent from Gabon, 15 percent from Ghana, and 17 percent from Nigeria.

Slaves taken from their homelands usually go on a one-way trip and, although they become an integral part of the slave-owning society, they are in no position to create transnational social relations. Slavery creates transnational relations largely in regard to those who are engaged in the slave trade, such as the Arab traders of Zanzibar and the English traders who dominated the trans–Atlantic slave trade. These people often spent long periods away from home operating out of established trading and procuring centers near to the source of the slaves, then transporting them by land or sea to locales where they were sold. Slavery might also contribute indirectly to transnationalism as in the case of Africa slavery in the European colonies of the Caribbean, where for a time slavery provided an economic basis for the plantation economies that developed in the Americas and that supported European colonists and colonial administrators, who sometimes maintained a transnational existence. In the contemporary context, African slavery in the Americas is of relevance in the sense that many descendants of these slaves have become interested in exploring their roots in Africa.

Political and religious conflicts have produced refugees throughout the modern period[7] and refugees have played an important role in the creation of transnational social relations. In the past, however, the majority of refugees, in part because of difficulties in communication and travel, either lost contact with their homelands or maintained only limited contact. For example, between 1471 and 1835 the Kinh of Dai Viet (modern northern Vietnam) gradually conquered the kingdom of Champa, which occupied much of modern central and southern Vietnam. This conquest resulted in a number of Cham fleeing to neighboring Kambuja (modern Cambodia), Siam (modern Thailand), and Melaka (in modern Malaysia). These Cham refugees largely lost contact with their homeland. This led to the formation of what essentially was two distinct Cham groups: those who remained behind in what became Vietnamese territory and those forming the Cham diaspora. Differences between the two communities emerged, including distinct dialects and religious traditions (the Cham in Vietnam either being Hindus or what are called Old Muslims and many of those constituting the diaspora being what are called New Muslims as a result of Malay influence). The legacy of this can be seen in the fact that at present in addition to about 60,000 Cham living in the old Champa homeland in southern Vietnam, an additional 20,000 Cham live in Vietnam near the border with Cambodia, approximately 300,000 live in Cambodia, 4,000 in Thailand, and 2,000–10,000 in Malaysia.[8]

Despite difficulties in travel and communication, some refugees in the past were able to form transnational networks. Often in such cases few links remained to the original homeland and the networks were formed between groups of refugees from the same homeland who scattered to numerous other countries. The Jews of the Iberian Peninsula provide a good example of one such group. Ferdinand of Aragón (1479–1516) and Isabella of Castile (1474–1504) not only conquered the final Muslim territory on the Iberian Peninsula (the emirate of Grenada), unified Spain and oversaw the beginning of Spanish exploration and colonization of the Americas, but they also organized the Inquisition, which led to Jews and Muslims being forbidden to live in Spain. Jews were required to become Christians within four months or leave Spain. Some converted, while about "150,000 sold out hurriedly and left for Portugal, where they were fleeced further and then sent away to the Ottoman Empire, Italy, the Netherlands, and elsewhere"[9]— places that afforded greater tolerance. As for the domestic impact of this policy, Fagg adds, "in the long run the loss of about a tenth of her [Spain's] population, the most skilled and hard-working at that, was ruinous."[10] The Inquisition was also set up in the Spanish American colonies in the 1570s (for example, tribunals in Mexico City, Lima, and Cartagena).[11] In the case of Portugal, Manoel I (reigned 1495–1521) of Portugal married one of Ferdinand and Isabel's daughters and in 1492 he too instituted measures to force the Jews in Portugal to convert or leave. As in Spain, some Jews converted, while some of them left.

Amsterdam was an especially important destination and from here a number of Jews with commercial interests developed transnational networks across Europe and stretching around the world. Poliakov writes about Jewish refugees with international banking interests.[12] A member of one such family was based in Amsterdam in the 1700s, two of his brothers were in London, two more in Italy, and there were also various cousins and nephews in France and Turkey. Jewish merchants were especially active in areas under control of the Dutch West India Company (*Geoctroyeerde Westindische Compagnie*). Formed in the early 1600s, the Dutch West India Company engaged in trade in the Caribbean, the east coast of North America, the northeast coast of South America, and the west coast of Africa. It was especially active in the trans–Pacific slave trade. The company established a number of colonies, including New Netherlands (including modern New York and New Jersey), Suriname, and in 1630 it established the colony of New Holland (modern Recife) in Brazil. Jews, including merchants and moneylenders, were a major presence in New Holland, until Catholic Portuguese settlers revolted and drove them out in 1654.[13] Some of the Jewish refugees from New Holland returned to Amsterdam, while others went to other territories of the Dutch West India Company. This included a group of 23 who sailed to New Amsterdam (modern New York).[14]

World War I (1914–17) and its aftermath created a large number of refugees around the world and many of these refugees, who were cut off to varying degrees from their homeland, formed transnational networks between the various countries where they settled. The best known of these are the Armenians. The Armenian Kingdom of Cilicia lost its independence in 1375 and over the next few centuries a number of Armenians migrated away from their homeland. A sharp increase in involuntary migration by the Armenians took place as a result of the Armenian Genocide, which took place between 1915 and 1917 as the Ottoman Empire's military slaughtered and forcibly relocated large numbers of Armenians.[15] Toynbee estimated that about 600,000 Armenians died during deportation or were massacred.[16] Those who escaped from the Ottoman Empire migrated all over the world. A large number settled nearby in Russia, the Ukraine, Georgia, Bulgaria, and Greece. Many also immigrated to territories under British control, including India, Pakistan, Singapore, Burma, Hong Kong, Sudan, South Africa, and New Zealand. Others settled in Ethiopia, the Philippines, China, and Japan. Armenian culture survived in many of these diasporic communities and Armenian merchants in particular often formed transnational networks.

The Communist Revolution of 1917 and the Russian Civil War (1917–23) between the White Army and the Bolshevik Red Army that followed the Communist Revolution in Russia also generated a large number of refugees. These refugees included anti-communist White Russians (often called White émigrés), Mensheviks, and Socialist-Revolutionaries as well as Russian Orthodox Christians and others who were less politically inclined. Most of the refugees initially fled to the Baltic countries of Estonia, Latvia, Lithuania, Poland, and Finland, or south to Turkey. Many then moved on to Yugoslavia, Bulgaria, Czechoslovakia, Germany, France, the United Kingdom and the United States. Large Russian émigré communities were formed in cities such as Istanbul, Belgrade, Berlin, and Paris. Those who lived in Siberia and the Russian Far East and fled tended to go to China (especially to Shanghai), Japan, or Central Asia. A total of one to two million refugees left Russia between 1917 and 1920, and smaller numbers continued to flee during the 1920s and 1930s.

These Russian refugees also formed transnational networks linking their various communities, although doing so often was difficult since many of them lacked official citizenship or immigration status. Thus, between 100,000 and 200,000 White émigrés from Siberia and the Russian Far East fled to Harbin in northeastern China in the early 1920s.[17] In 1920 the Chinese government broke relations with Imperial Russia, effectively leaving the Russians living in Harbin stateless. The situation became even more difficult for the local Russian community in 1924 when the Chinese government signed an agreement with the Soviet government requiring that all employees of the Chinese Eastern Railway be either Soviet or Chinese citizens. Many of the Russians in Harbin took out Soviet citizenship, but others chose to remain stateless and eventually lost their jobs with the railway. The Japanese occupied Manchuria in 1931 and established the Manchukuo puppet state. When the Soviet Union sold its interest in the China Eastern Railway to the Japanese in 1935 many of the Russians in Harbin left for the Soviet Union. Most of these returnees were subsequently arrested during Stalin's Great Purge (1936–8) on charges of espionage and counter-revolutionary activity. Others moved to Chinese cities such as Shanghai, Beijing, Tianjin, and Qingdao.

The Russian community in Shanghai, which grew to around 25,000 in the mid–1930s, was for a time one of the most important communities of Russian refugees. Mikhail Maximovitch (1896–1966), who later became Saint John of Shanghai and San Francisco, was one of the most important members of this community and a crucial force in maintaining its transnational relations.[18] He was born in Russia, his family moved to Belgrade in 1921 and in 1925 he graduated from Belgrade University in theology. He was ordained as a monk in Kiev and became bishop of the Russian Orthodox Church Abroad congregation in Shanghai in 1934. He continued his work during the Japanese occupation and was elevated to archbishop after the war in 1946. When the communists took power in China the Bishop Maximovich and the Russian community in Shanghai fled to a refugee camp that was run by the International Refugee Organization on the island of Tubabao in the Philippines. There were about 5,000 Russian refugees in the camp and subsequently they were resettled in the United States and Australia.[19]

Solomon Bard was another prominent Russian refugee from Harbin.[20] He was born to a Russian Jewish family in Siberia and lived with his family in Harbin, where they fled because of the revolution. They then moved to Shanghai, where he attended a British school. He graduated from Hong Kong University's medical school in 1939 and then worked as an army medic while interned in a prisoner or war camp during the Japanese occupation. Following the war he served as Director of the Student Health Service at Hong Kong University. He served as Executive Director of Hong Kong's Antiquities and Monuments Office from 1976 to 1983 and Assistant Music Director of the Hong Kong Chinese Orchestra from 1983 to 1987. He retired in 1993 and moved to Australia, though retaining close contact with Hong Kong after his retirement.

Multinational organizations have come to play an increasingly important role in dealing with refugees since the early twentieth century. Their activities led to the creation of institutionalized refugee camps under their supervision and have influenced the status and placement of refugees. Their presence has also led to the creation of employment for persons involved in the treatment of refugees, adding to the growing number of people working worldwide for such multinational organizations. Coordinated international involvement with refugees began in response to the problems faced by refugees fleeing the Russian Revolution and Russian Civil War with the founding of the High Commission for Refugees (HCR) by the League of Nations in 1921. Norwegian explorer and scientist Fridjof Nansen (1861–1930) was appointed the High Commissioner for Refugees and in 1922. During the 1920s the mandate of the HCR was expanded to include Armenian, Assyrian, and Greek refugees from Ottoman policies of genocide. The Nansen International Office for Refugees replaced the High Commission for Refugees in 1930. Its main achievement was creation of the Nansen passport for refugees. The rise of Nazism in Germany and the subsequent flood of refugees from Germany led the League of Nations to create a special body to deal with them in 1933, the High Commission for Refugees Coming from Germany. The High Commission's mandate was increased to include refugees fleeing the Nazis in Austria and Sudetenland as well.

The upheavals of World War II and its aftermath resulted in millions of refugees. A proposal by President Franklin Roosevelt of the United States led to the creation of the United Nations Relief and Rehabilitation Administration (UNRRA) in late 1943. Initially the activities of the UNRRA focused on displaced persons who were citizens of signatory countries, but in response to requests by Jewish organizations concerned with the fate of Jews who were German citizens in 1944, the mandate was expanded to include those who had been forced to leave their home countries because of their race, religion or activities. Immediately after the war the UNRRA provided assistance to around eight million refugees in Europe and Asia. This included operating Displaced Persons camps in Europe until 1947 and in East Asia (in China and Taiwan) until 1949.

The newly formed United Nations established the Office of the United Nations High Commissioner for Refugees (UNHCR) in 1950, with its headquarters in Geneva, Switzerland. It took over from the UNRRA with a mandate to protect and support refugees at the request of the United Nations or particular countries. Its activities include the voluntary repatriation, local integration, and third country resettlement of refugees. The UNHCR operates under the auspices of the United Nations Convention Relating to the Status of Refugees that was signed in 1951.

The flow of post–World War II refugees was related primarily to the spread of communist control over countries in Eastern Europe, China, North Korea, North Vietnam, and Cuba and to disruptions linked to the process of decolonization (e.g., the partition of India). The communist defeat of the Nationalist forces of the Republic of China in 1949, for example, resulted in several million Chinese fleeing as refugees and, again, many of these refugees came to form transnational networks outside of the newly established People's Republic of China. About two million of these Chinese fled to Taiwan with Kuomintang (KMT, Chinese Nationalist Party) leader Chiang Kai-shek. Economic conditions and political repression associated with the so-called White Terror during the period of martial law (1949–87) under the KMT government resulted in a number of Chinese who had initially fled from the mainland to Taiwan migrating once again. Many of these people migrated to the United States, which recognized the Republic of China and had relatively liberal immigration policies towards migrants from that country. Significantly, unlike many earlier migrants to the United States from southern China who tended to live in distinct Chinatowns, these migrants from Taiwan, who were often relatively well educated and who spoke Mandarin rather than Cantonese or one of the other southern Chinese languages, commonly settled in ethnically diverse neighborhoods or formed their own communities. Improvements in economic and political conditions in Taiwan in the 1980s resulted in a decline in the number of people leaving and even to some returning.

In addition to those going to Taiwan, a number of Kuomintang soldiers and their families in Yunnan were driven across the border into Kokang in Burma's Shan State in 1949. There the United States supported them in preparing for an invasion of southern China and they also became deeply involved in the opium trade.[21] In late 1960 and early 1961 an offensive by the Burmese army drove most of the Kuomintang across the border to Thailand and Laos. In Thailand they mainly settled in and around Mae Salong. The Thai government granted them asylum in part for their support in fighting against local communist insurgents. At present there are about 20,000 descendants of the Kuomintang in Thailand. In recent years they have established links with relatives and other Chinese living in Taiwan.

The seizure of power by communists in Vietnam, Laos, and Cambodia also created a wave of refugees. The French defeat by the Viet Minh in 1954 led to the partitioning of Vietnam into the communist-dominated Democratic Republic of Vietnam in the north and the anti-communist Republic of Vietnam in the south. Even before 1954 some Vietnamese had left to avoid the conflict, but the number of refugees increased dramatically in 1954. A number of anti-communist Vietnamese went to France as refugees, where their presence precipitated a split in the local Vietnamese community between anti-communists and communist supporters. The largest number of refugees, however, left the Democratic Republic of Vietnam for the Republic of Vietnam under the provisions of the Geneva Accord, whereby people were given 90 days to leave one of the Vietnams for the other. About 800,000 left the north for the south and about 150,000 people left the south for the north.

Communist victories in these three countries in 1975 led to a large number of people fleeing beyond their borders as refugees—the UNHCR recorded 665,955 refugees from the three countries during the decade following the war, but Pongsapic and Chonwattana estimate the number to be closer to one million.[22] The categorization of these refugees raises interesting points concerning their identity in relation to state and ethnicity as discussed in Chapter 1. Thus, the refugees from Laos included not only ethnic Lao but also a number of other ethnic groups whose members did not always readily identify with the Lao state. This is especially true of the Hmong, who constituted the largest ethnic group among those coming from Laos. Even in the case of Vietnam there were significant numbers of refugees from the Central Highlands (e.g., Jarai, Ede, and Bru) who only marginally at best identified with the Vietnamese state.

Most of these refugees initially found themselves in about a dozen refugee camps in Thailand, while some also crossed the border into China and others went by boat to Malaysia, Hong Kong, the Philippines, and elsewhere. Looking at the camps in Thailand, the UNHCR recorded that there had been 702,772 refugees in the camps by 1986. Of these refugees, 75.6 percent (531,347) of them were resettled in third countries, 4.9 percent were relocated, 1.7 percent voluntarily repatriated, and 17.8 percent (125,047) remained in the camps (most of these have since been closed and the inhabitants either repatriated or resettled). The distribution of those who were resettled provides a good idea of how extensive the spread of such refugees often is under the supervision of multinational organizations such as the UNHCR. Of the 548,771 who had been resettled from the camps in Thailand by the end of 1986, most went to the United States (378,487, 69 percent), followed by France (73,357), Canada (34,912), and Australia (31,217). The following additional countries accepted more than 500 refugees from the camps: Germany, New Zealand, China, Switzerland, Belgium, Japan, Argentina, the United Kingdom, Italy, the Netherlands, Austria, Norway, and Spain.

Changes in the communist world since the late 1980s have had important implications for refugee populations from former or reformed communist states in that it became increasingly possible for refugees and descendants of refugees to re-establish contact with the countries from which they or their parents fled. This has taken the form of communication, visits, and even migration in some cases. Since the 1990s, for example, political reform in Vietnam, Laos, and Cambodia has allowed refugees and their descendants to re-establish contact with family members who remained behind and to build important transnational networks. In the case of the Cham, the communist seizure of power in Vietnam and Cambodia in 1975 had traumatic results for the Cham in both countries. The Cham in Vietnam had actively fought against the communists and they were targeted after the communist victory. A number of these Cham fled to the United States as refugees. The situation was even worse for the Western Cham in Cambodia where the Pol Pot regime slaughtered large numbers of them. Some of these Cham were able to escape as refugees. The total number of Cham refugees living in the United States is over 3,000 and there are another 1,000 in France and a small number in Australia. The Cham who had fled were largely cut off from those who remained behind, who found themselves largely cut off from the outside world. Political reforms in both countries in the 1990s allowed Cham living in the United States and elsewhere to re-establish contact with family members in Vietnam and Cambodia, including visits. Today, for instance, an increasing number of Cham in Vietnam are able to visit relatives living in the United States and elsewhere. This has meant that the transnational network of Cham refugees has been expanded to include Cham in Vietnam and Cambodia and modern forms of communication and travel, which are now available to Cham in these two countries, have made it easier for Cham to stay in touch with one another around the world. Family ties are not the only component of this Cham transnational network. Religion has also been a factor. In recent years Islamic fundamentalism has gained influence in the Cham communities in Malaysia and Cambodia, largely as a result of activities by Saudi Arabian Muslims, and these fundamentalist Cham Muslims have sought to spread their beliefs among the Cham Muslims in Vietnam. Small numbers of Cham Muslims have also migrated to other Muslim countries and there are small numbers living in Saudi Arabia, Yemen, Libya, and Indonesia.

Political reforms have not put an end to the flow of refugees from these countries.

Vietnam and Laos in particular remain single-party, authoritarian communist states in which political and religious freedoms are restricted. Harsh government treatment of Central Highlanders in Vietnam in relation to the religious practices of those who are Protestants and disagreements between members of local ethnic groups and Kinh migrants from the lowlands attracted to the region by the coffee boom led about 1,000 Central Highlanders to flee across the border to Cambodia in 2001. About 900 of these refugees were placed in two UNHCR–run refugee camps in Mondolkiri Province. The UNHCR brokered an agreement for their voluntary repatriation, but this broke down when Vietnamese government officials refused to allow UNHCR monitors into the Central Highlands to oversee the repatriation. The camps were then closed and the refugees moved to Phnom Penh, where about 700 were processed for resettlement in the United States. Further repression by government authorities and conflict in the Central Highlands over the next couple of years led more refugees to flee to Cambodia. Between 2002 and 2005 the UNHCR oversaw the repatriation of several hundred of these refugees and the Cambodian government forcibly repatriated another 94. Arrest and interrogation of some of the returnees by Vietnamese authorities prompted more Central Highlanders to flee to Cambodia, including those that Human Rights Watch dubbed "double back returnees" (i.e., they returned to Cambodia as refugees a second time).[23] In light of the ongoing problems faced by these Central Highlanders, in 2005 the United States, Canada, and Finland agreed to begin resettling them. In the case of Canada, by 2009 about 200 had been resettled in Vancouver. An important difference from the situation in the past, however, is that these refugees have been able to remain in fairly regular contact with relatives back in Vietnam and have even begun to sponsor some relatives through normal immigration channels.

Conflicts and repressive governments around the world have ensured a continual flow of refugees in recent decades, ensuring that refugees continue to be significant to transnationalism. In 2007 the UNHCR reported a total of 21,018,589 refugees falling under its mandate. These included 7,979,251 in Asia (2,974,315 in Southeast Asia, 2,580,638 in the Middle East, 1,304,189 in South Asia, 901,525 in East Asia and the Pacific, and 218,584 in Central Asia), 5,069,123 in Africa, 4,740,392 in Europe, and 3,229,822 in the Americas.

Politics often plays an important role in creating refugees and it is not surprising that refugee groups often continue to take an active interest in the political affairs of the country from which they initially fled. In this regard transnational political relations are often especially important in refugee communities— more so than is often the case with other types of migrant communities. This is especially true when members of the refugee community continue to support and even to engage in oppositional politics to those in power in the home country. Contemporary examples include anti-communist Cuban and Vietnamese refugees in the United States and elsewhere as well as a host of refugees from ethnic and regional conflicts scattered around the globe. A degree of caution is required, however, when assessing the significance of such political activities for the refugee community as a whole since they are often the work of a small group of activists who may receive considerable external attention while having relatively little support within their own community. This is especially true when looking at the evolution of such communities over time as they become more integrated into their new homelands, particularly as a new generation is born there that did not experience the events that led to people becoming refugees firsthand.

The ethnic Vietnamese communities in North America provide a good example of the changing significance of transnational politics in such communities. Many of the initial refugees in 1975 and immediately thereafter had been members of the government or military in the Republic of Vietnam (aka South Vietnam) when it was defeated by the communists in 1975. Their flight from Vietnam was traumatic and once they had settled in North America many harbored a hatred for the communist regime back in Vietnam and many dreaming of its eventual defeat. The nature of the regime in Vietnam meant that there was little scope for these refugees to engage in political activities there, but they were able to form a lobbying group against the communists outside of Vietnam and they sought to keep loyalty to the Saigon government and opposition to the communists alive within ethnic Vietnamese communities in North America as well. Symbolically this took the form of flying the flag and playing the anthem of the Republic of Vietnam at public events, including those of a cultural or religious nature. After reforms in Vietnam in the 1990s made establishing relations between Vietnam and overseas Vietnamese easier, some anti-communist activists sought to thwart this, at times violently. There were also a few who saw the new opening as creating opportunities to try to change Vietnam by quietly making contact with and offering assistance to those within Vietnam who sought to promote democratic reforms. By the mid–2000s, thirty years after the fall of Saigon, however, support for either style of political activities had become minimal within the ethnic Vietnamese communities in North America. While initially those who had gone back to Vietnam to visit relatives often were forced to do so secretly for fear of being branded communists and being subjected to violence, by the mid–2000s even family members of those who had been prominent in the Saigon government were openly visiting Vietnam on a regular basis, opposition to visits by prominent individuals from Vietnam to North America was less common than before, and anti-communist speeches and symbolic support of the Republic of Vietnam had become far from universal in public gatherings within North American ethnic Vietnamese communities.

Voluntary Labor Migration: Contract Laborers

Voluntary labor migrants are people who move to another country either permanently or temporarily to take up employment. Many of those who migrate for this reason temporarily do so under some kind of contract. Castles defines contract labor as temporary international movements of workers, which are organized and regulated by governments, employers or both.[24] A form of contract labor was employed during the early period of English colonization in North America when indentured workers were recruited from England for the American colonies.

The decline and eventual abolition of slavery in the face of labor demands of plantations, mines, and infrastructure projects in European colonies and the newly independent settler states of the Americas in the nineteenth century created a huge demand for contract labor.[25] People from China, India, and Japan were the main targets of recruiters of contract laborers destined for Southeast Asia, the South Pacific, the eastern Pacific Rim, the Indian Ocean region, and the Caribbean. Colonial relations often were important factors in recruiting contract laborers. Thus, the British recruited laborers from India for their other colonies, the French recruited laborers from Tonkin (northern Vietnam) for their other colonies, and the Dutch recruited laborers from Java for their other colonies. In addition, everyone in need of contract laborers also looked to China and Japan.

Contract labor recruitment remains important at present. The pattern of recruitment tends to reflect demographic and economic differences, in that the countries doing the recruiting not only are more wealthy than those from where laborers are recruited, but they also tend to have either relatively small populations in relation to their labor needs such as in the oil-rich Gulf States of the Middle East or low levels of population growth such as in Western Europe. Contract laborers today generally are recruited from nearby sources, such as Turkish workers in Western Europe and South Asian workers in the Gulf States. However, in part because of the relatively low cost of international travel, distance is not always a factor, as exemplified by the presence of large numbers of Filipino nurses in Western Europe and Thai agricultural workers in Israel.

Contract labor is important in relation to transnationalism because it creates conditions that allow for the emergence of transnational social relations involving those engaged in the labor trade and on the part of the workers themselves. Unlike slaves, whose journey is a one-way affair, contract laborers usually intend to return home at the termination of their contract or once they have saved what they consider enough money to return home. Historically, many of these workers, especially those migrating to more distant locales from their homes, in fact did not return home, but settled in the countries where they had gone on contract. Others, however, especially those going to places closer to home, did return home at the end of their contract (provided they survived). In some instances, after staying home for a time these people signed on to go back to work as contract laborers, becoming what contractors sometimes refer to as old hands.

In the case of Indian contract laborers during the colonial era, indentured laborers from India were recruited to work on plantations following the abolition of slavery in the British Empire in 1833.[26] Over the following century the largest numbers went to work in the British colonies of Burma, Ceylon, and Malaya, and others went to work in and around the Indian Ocean, South Pacific, and Caribbean. It is important to point out that most of these colonies had no ethnic Indian residents prior to the arrival of contract laborers and other Indian migrants who were able to move about within the British Empire. Davis estimates that around 30 million Indians emigrated (mainly as contract laborers) between 1834 and 1937 and that 24 million of these eventually returned to India — thus, about six million settled outside of India.[27] Today there are significant ethnic Indian populations in a number of countries around the world as a legacy of British colonialism and the indentured labor system such as in Mauritius (where they comprise roughly 70 percent of the country's population), Trinidad and Tobago, Guyana, South Africa, and Fiji.

We will use Fiji as a case study. The British annexed the Fiji Islands in 1874 and promoted the development of sugar plantations. By the early 1900s sugar accounted for about
80 percent of the exports of the colony. Since the indigenous Fijian population was largely
off limits as a source of labor for the plantations and recruitment from other Pacific
Islands was inadequate to meet the needs of the industry, the larger sugar plantations
turned to India. Between 1879 and 1916, 60,553 indentured laborers were brought to Fiji
from India. The recruitment of indentured workers in Fiji ended in 1916 and all of the
remaining contracts ended in 1920. They came under a *girmit* to work 5 days a week for
five years at 1 shilling per day. They were provided with free transportation back to India
if they worked in Fiji for ten years. If they worked only five years then they had to pay
their own way home. Over two-thirds of the workers were between the ages of 20 and 30
and 30 percent were women.

Initially the colonial government, the plantation owners, and the indentured laborers
themselves viewed their status in Fiji as temporary. They lived in barracks near the fields
where they worked, commonly sent any money saved back to relatives in India, and
regarded India as their home. They were an enclave population in Fiji rather than a
transnational one. This situation changed as an increasing number of these indentured
workers decided to remain in Fiji after their contracts were completed. By 1911 roughly
75 percent of the indentured laborers rather than returning to India or renewing their
contracts had settled on agricultural land as smallholder owners or tenants. Coulter
reported, "In 1938 about sixteen thousand Indians were engaged in agriculture, and some
eighty-five hundred in various trades and commerce."[28] In its early days the emerging
Indo-Fijian society faced limitations because of the composition of its population, especially the lack of women, religious specialists, and others needed to form a complete functioning society. By the 1920s the situation had changed considerably, in part because of
the arrival of independent Indian migrants from India and elsewhere in the British
Empire, including women, Hindu and Muslim religious practitioners, professionals, and
merchants. Not only had Indo-Fijians integrated themselves into the colonial economy
and society of Fiji, but they also developed cultural institutions. Today, Indo-Fijians look
upon the 1920s and 1930s as a period of cultural revival: "There were orthodox Hindu
schools and Arya Samaj schools; those attached to mosques with children reciting the
Quran in Arabic; schools attached to Sikh gurudwaras or temples."[29] Writing about the
"Indian festivals and bazaars" that had been "transplanted to Fiji" during this period,
Coulter noted that there were differences—e.g., "The length and number of Hindu and
Mohammedan religious festivals in Fiji, particularly the former, have been reduced" and
"Similarly, less time is spent on wedding celebrations in Fiji."[30] This revival had transna-
tional dimensions in that many of the religious specialists involved came from India and
Indo-Fijians continued to see India as an important cultural reference point.

While developing their own political consciousness in Fiji, Indo-Fijians did so in
reference to developments in India and political activists from India and elsewhere in the
British Empire play a role in the process. The Indian political leader Mohandas Gandhi
(1869–1948), who had worked as a lawyer in South Africa from 1893 until 1915, wrote
critically of the indenture system in Fiji and his disciple C.F. Andrews visited Fiji and

wrote reports on the condition of Indo-Fijians on three occasions. Coulter commented in regard to the situation around 1940, "Close touch between the Indians in Fiji and events in India has kept the immigrants and their children informed of the activities of the National Congress party."[31] This influence continued to be felt as Fiji itself moved towards independence in the 1960s. For example, Norton cites a 1966 speech by an Indo-Fijian politician associated with the local predominantly Indo-Fijian Federation Party that makes reference to politics in India: "Federation Party is your party.... It is a party of poor people, like the Congress Party [in India].... The Congress was the party of the poor, and India didn't gain its independence until Mahatma Gandhi went from village to village to unite the people."[32]

Fiji gained independence in 1970 and at the time Indo-Fijians comprised about half of the population. Political uncertainty around the transition led a small number of Indo-Fijians to migrate to English-speaking countries such as Australia, New Zealand, and Canada. The fact that such migrants did not consider going to India was a reflection of these people's perceptions that such countries offered better opportunities than India, but also reflected the declining importance of India to Indo-Fijians over time. To younger Indo-Fijians India had become little more than a distant part of their culture heritage. The military coups of 1987[33] led to a substantial migration of Indo-Fijians primarily to these same countries where they already had family connections.[34] At present there are about 340,000 Indo-Fijians still in Fiji, with an additional 48,000 living in Australia (2006), 37,000 in New Zealand (2006), 31,000 in the United States (2000), and 25,000 in Canada (2004). These migrant Indo-Fijian communities maintain substantial and close transnational relations with Indo-Fijians still in Fiji and the other Pacific Rim countries. They have little or no contact with India but in their new homes sometimes find themselves in the ambiguous position of often being treated as ethnic Indians alongside migrants from India.

Similar developments can be seen in the other countries where Indian indentured laborers settled. In these countries too over the years relations with India declined. In the case of South Africa, for example, where at present there are about 1.2 million ethnic Indians, very few speak any Indian language and contact with India is minimal, although movies and music from India are popular. A total of over 500,000 Indians went to the British West Indies as contract laborers between 1838 and 1917. At present there are especially large populations of Indo-Caribbeans in Trinidad and Tobago, Guyana, and Suriname as well as smaller numbers scattered around the rest of the region. Some descendants of Indian migrants to the Caribbean subsequently migrated to other countries. This group is comprised mainly of Indo-Trinidadians and Indo-Guyanese, with the former being the majority. There are around 700,000 Indo-Trinidadians living in the United States, Canada (mainly in Toronto), and the United Kingdom. The British Indo-Caribbean community numbers over 30,000 and is made up mainly of Indo-Trinidadians. While these groups rarely have links with India, they often maintain important transnational links with the Caribbean. Even though in recent years India has sought to establish closer relations with ethnic Indians living outside of the country, for the Indo-Fijian and Indo-Caribbean descendants of Indian indentured laborers their most important transnational relations are to be found within networks of fellow Indo-Fijians and Indo-Caribbeans rather than among those who could be categorized as Overseas Indians.

Whereas Indian labor recruitment during the colonial era took place within the British Empire, Chinese contract laborers were recruited to work in a wider range of locales. Destinations included the Philippines, the Dutch East Indies, northern Borneo, Siam, Vietnam, Cambodia, the Malay Peninsula, Burma, various European colonies in the South Pacific, Australia, Hawaii, the United States, Canada, a variety of European colonial territories in the Caribbean, Mexico, and several different independent countries in Central America and South America. As with their Indian counterparts, many of the destinations (i.e., those in North and South America and Africa and the Indian Ocean) for Chinese contract laborers had no existing ethnic Chinese communities. Southeast Asia was different in this regard in that there were long-established ethnic Chinese communities scattered throughout the region, largely as a result of a history of long-distance trade.

Since it has been of considerable relevance to the creation of ethnic Chinese communities and their transnational relations it is also important to note that these laborers generally came from particular areas within China and from particular non–Mandarin speaking ethno-linguistic groups. Unsettled conditions in China during the mid–nineteenth century, and the Taiping Rebellion in particular, led to a widespread increase in poverty and encouraged many people living in the southern coastal areas of Guangdong and Guangxi provinces (and to a lesser extent Fujian and Hainan Island) to emigrate. These were mainly speakers of the three dominant southern coastal languages of China: Hakka, Min Nan (which includes Teochow and Hainanese), and Yue (Cantonese).

The recruitment of Chinese workers was a multinational affair in which ethnic Chinese played an important role. Chinese businessmen engaged in recruiting workers (commonly referred to by Europeans as coolies) and shipping them on junks to the Malay Peninsula, the Dutch East Indies, and the Philippines as early as 1823.[35] In 1842, when the British gained control over Hong Kong under the terms of the Treaty of Nanking, the Chinese labor contractors began using European ships and henceforth British[36] and American[37] companies dominated the shipment of Chinese contract laborers. Meagher makes the point that the involvement of British and American shipping in transporting Chinese laborers to Southeast Asia made it a relatively simple step to expand the business to North America, South America, and Australia.[38] The recruitment business itself came to be dominated by European companies and by two British firms in particular, Tait and Company and Syme, Muir and Company. Europeans and Americans relied on Chinese brokers (*khe-tau*) to deliver the recruits to the firms.

In addition to Hong Kong, contract laborers were shipped out of the treaty port of Amoy (modern Xiamen), Canton, and Macau. Macau emerged as the main point of departure for contract laborers, in part because the Portuguese authorities were more lax in regulating the trade than the British. Macau's economy had been seriously undermined with the establishment of the British presence in Hong Kong in 1842 and the contract labor trade was widely viewed as a means of improving the situation. The export of Chinese laborers from Macau started in 1851 after the British increased restrictions on the trade in Hong Kong.[39] The labor trade in Macau was conducted largely by British and Chinese capital. Critics of the system pressed the Portuguese government to forbid the trade because of the poor treatment of workers in Cuba and new regulations for transporting contract laborers were put in place in 1873.

Most contract laborers were young men. They often married before going abroad to work and left their wives and children behind. Northrup notes that convincing Chinese to leave home was not easy, but resistance weakened in the face of stories about the Gold Mountain from those who were returning from the goldfields of California (and later British Columbia and Australia).[40] Having decided to go abroad to work, as Lee points out, "Most Chinese probably wished either to visit temporarily or to sojourn only long enough to accumulate sufficient savings to enable them to return home in triumph rather than settle permanently."[41]

In fact, many of these laborers did not return to China. In the case of workers going to the United States, for example, Lee comments, "Despite their intentions, many stayed in the United States much longer than they had originally planned, and some never made it back to China at all."[42] Government policies on the receiving end in regard to the status of Chinese workers varied. British colonial administrations, for example, tended to look favorably on Chinese deciding to settle. In the case of the Malay Peninsula, Francis Light of the British East India Company, who established a trading post for the company on the island of Penang in 1786, favored promoting Chinese immigration, as can be seen from a 1794 statement that he made: "The Chinese ... are the only people of the east from whom a revenue may be raised without expense and extraordinary efforts of government."[43] The Chinese population on the peninsula began to increase significantly after Stamford Raffles of the British East India Company established Singapore as a trading post for the company in 1819.[44] The city's Resident William Farquhar (reigned 1819–23) introduced a policy of unrestricted immigration to help spur the colony's economic growth and this served to attract a large number of Chinese. They were the largest ethnic community in Singapore by 1827 and by 1845 represented over half of its population. Andaya and Andaya remark of British colonial policy in Malaya, "As a rule of thumb, the British believed, the rate of Chinese migration and the numbers of Chinese settlers were a reliable index of economic progress."[45] In recognition of the importance of the Chinese to the peninsula's economy the British commonly appointed officials who could speak at least one Chinese language in the states and in 1877 the colonial administration established the office of Chinese Protectorate in Singapore to look after issues relating to the Chinese population. For its part, in 1893 the Chinese government ended restrictions on emigration, making it easier for Chinese to migrate to Malaya and elsewhere. Britain reaffirmed liberal immigration policies in 1911, allowing unrestricted immigration from China and other countries such as India. Such openness changed, however, with the onset of the Great Depression in 1929 and restrictions on immigration were introduced in 1931.

Attitudes of the British settler colonies and former colonies—the United States, Canada, Australia, and South Africa—to Chinese contract workers and immigrants also changed according to economic conditions. Large numbers of Chinese were recruited to work on railroads and plantations in the case of the American South after the abolition of slavery[46] and others came to find their fortunes in the goldfields. Initially these countries encouraged or at least officially tolerated Chinese immigration. Thus, among other things, the Burlingame Treaty of 1868 between China and the United States effectively eliminated restrictions on Chinese immigration. This favorable legal framework coincided with improvements in transportation to facilitate the movement of Chinese workers. Most of them (along with Japanese workers) sailed on the Pacific Mail Steamship Company, which was founded in 1848 and established a route from San Francisco to Hong Kong, or the Occidental and Oriental Steamships Company (founded in 1874). Under such favorable conditions, from the outset of the gold rush until 1882 about 300,000 Chinese came to the United States. Most of these immigrants were single men who intended on returning to China, but many of them remained. This is reflected in population figures. There were only 4,108 Chinese in the United States in 1850. This number had increased to 34,933 in 1860 and by 1880 had grown to 105,465.

Tolerance of Chinese immigrants in the United States eroded with the onset of the Long Depression of the 1870s that began with the Panic of 1873 and lasted until 1879. Prior to the depression there had been considerable demand for Chinese labor in many areas, but with the depression not only did demand decline, but European-Americans and European migrants began competing for many of these jobs. There was a marked increase in anti–Chinese sentiments on the part of these groups that sometimes manifest themselves in anti–Chinese riots. They also led to growing opposition to Chinese immigration within the American Congress. Pressure from Congress resulted in the Burlingame Treaty being renegotiated in 1880 and Chinese immigration being suspended. Then the Chinese Exclusion Act was passed in 1882, which halted Chinese immigration for ten years and prohibited Chinese from becoming American citizens.[47] The Exclusion Act was extended for another ten years by the Geary Act of 1892 and became permanent in 1902. The Chinese Exclusion Act did not completely stop the flow of Chinese migrants to the United States,[48] but it slowed it to a trickle. This can be seen from the fact that the number of Chinese living in the United States in 1880 was about the same as the number of Chinese-Americans in the United States in 1940, a little over 100,000. Shortly after gaining independence Australia also passed an act to curtail further Chinese immigration, the Immigration Restriction Act, in 1901. Hostility towards Chinese immigrants was present in independent Canada during the latter part of the nineteenth century and was given formal expression with passage of the Chinese Immigration Act in 1923 that banned additional Chinese from entering Canada. Anti-Chinese sentiments on the part of the white community in South Africa resulted in many Chinese being repatriated after the colony became independent in 1910.

The existence of well-established maritime transportation between China and the United States allowed for Chinese workers still to be recruited for the sugar plantations of Hawaii, which was an independent kingdom until 1893 and remained an independent republic until it was annexed by the United States in 1900, after the passage of the Chinese Exclusion Act. In fact, the Pacific Mail Steamship Company and Occidental and Oriental Steamships Company were granted a monopoly on supplying the islands with Chinese migrants in 1883.[49] Between 1852 and 1887 56,720 Chinese (mostly from Zhongshan Prefecture in Guangdong) came to Hawaii as laborers.[50] About 60 percent of these workers remained in Hawaii at the end of their contracts rather than returning to China.

As with Indian contract workers, Chinese contract workers played an important role in the establishment of permanent ethnic communities in many countries as a result of significant numbers of the workers remaining after the end of their contracts rather than returning to China. Thus, in the case of Malaya by 1911 there were 917,000 Chinese, representing 34 percent of the total population and the number continued to increase until by 1941 there were 2,378,000 Chinese, accounting for 43 percent of the population.[51] While some of these Chinese migrant settlers continued to live in the rural areas where most had initially been employed, many of them gravitated to urban areas. Chinese were especially prominent in the growing urban areas of Southeast Asia. Thus, the 1891 census of Malaya indicated that Chinese accounted for 79 percent of Kuala Lumpur's 43,786 residents. Siam had a relatively long history of Chinese migration largely in relation to long-distance trade and already in 1828 Chinese comprised about half of the new city of Bangkok's 77,300 inhabitants. While Siam recruited Chinese workers for employment in rural areas, during the latter part of the nineteenth century it also recruited large numbers to build its urban infrastructure. Metropolitan Bangkok had a population of 867,457 in 1909 and about half of its residents were Chinese. In the former settler British and Spanish colonies (such as Peru, which boasts the largest ethnic Chinese population in Latin America) the Chinese also gravitated towards urban areas, often settling in distinct so-called Chinatowns, but they tended to comprise smaller portions of the total urban population than in Southeast Asia.

Chinese contract workers remained in contact with their homeland primarily through letters and by money back to family members. In regard to remittances, Purcell, for example, remarks, "There are whole districts in Canton and Hokkien provinces that are supported by remittances from Malaya."[52] Temporary visits back to China during long sojourns or on the part of those who settled outside of China were rare. After studying files on hundreds of Chinese immigrants to the United States between 1882 and 1941, Lee found "that only 4 percent were able to make two visits home to China, while another 9 percent made only one visit during their years in America."[53] Those who engaged in commercial activities rather than working as laborers tended to be the ones who maintained the most active transnational links back to China,[54] especially those involved in businesses that required importing goods from China, such as sellers of herbal medicines.[55]

Politics in China also had an impact on overseas Chinese populations. In the first decade of the 1900s overseas Chinese found themselves drawn into political conflicts in China between the Manchu Dynasty and the Republicans led by Sun Yat-sen. In an effort to gain support from overseas Chinese, in 1909 the Manchu government in China claimed that all those who could claim Chinese descent through the male line no matter where they were born or presently lived were Chinese citizens. It urged these Nan Yang Chinese to send money back to China to help the royal cause against the Republicans and to return home. The Republicans also were active trying to gain support among overseas Chinese and the Republican leader Sun Yat-sen made numerous visits to overseas Chinese communities. The establishment of the Republic of China in 1911 served to promote a sense of pride in being Chinese among Chinese living outside of China at the same time that many were adapting to a permanent life in their new homes.

Domestic Chinese politics continued to be significant to overseas Chinese contract laborers and settlers in the 1940s as they took sides in the struggle between the Nationalists and Communists for supremacy in China. The Chinese contract workers of the tin mines of Banka Island in Indonesia provide an example. Chinese had been recruited to work in the mines for a long time prior to World War II and those who were stranded there when the war broke out worked as virtual slaves for the Japanese during the war. The mines were damaged during the war, but were soon resuscitated and in 1947 there were 9,435 Chinese and 3,952 Indonesian workers employed in the mines.[56] Poor working conditions in the post-war environment led to labor strikes and general unrest among the workers and a number of them joined the communist union *Serekat Kaum Buruh*. Many of the Chinese laborers expressed a desire to return to China and others left to work in Singapore where ages were higher and the work easier, but by 1949 as conditions in China deteriorated most of those still in Indonesia appear to have decided that it was better to remain. The Chinese community on Bangka initially was divided between those who supported the communists and those who supported the Nationalist Kuomintang, but support for the Nationalists largely disappeared after the communist victory in China in 1949.[57]

Turning to contemporary contract labor recruitment, currently the Philippines is one of the largest sources of migrant workers in the world and provides a good case study illustrating the diversity of occupations involved in such recruitment and the range of countries where they are recruited at present. There are around 11 million Overseas Filipinos or persons of Philippine origin living outside of the Philippines. This number includes permanent migrants and their descendants as well as temporary migrants (many of these being contract migrant laborers). About one million Filipinos migrate each year to work through contract employment schemes. The history of Filipino labor migration begins with the recruitment of Filipino workers for the plantations of Hawaii starting in 1909 and later for the farms of California. A new wave of migration began in the mid–1970s in response to economic problems within the Philippines and opportunities presented by the Middle Eastern oil economies.

The Marcos government initiated its Labor Export Policy in 1974 aimed primarily at sending skilled manual laborers to Saudi Arabia and the neighboring oil-rich countries. As the number of Overseas Foreign Workers (OFWs) grew the government created more agencies to promote labor migration and to look after the affairs of those who were recruited. The Overseas Workers' Welfare Administration was established in 1977 and in 1982 the Department of Labor and Employment (DOLE) established the Philippines Overseas Employment Administration (POEA) to license private recruitment agencies, to process the applications of OFWs, and to facilitate the provision of contract labor to foreign employers (including maritime agencies that recruit workers as crews for ships). The DOLE also established 34 Overseas Labor Offices attached to Philippine consulates in the main labor importing countries. In addition to skilled manual laborers, a wide range of other types of workers also began to be recruited, including nurses, teachers, doctors, engineers, domestic servants, and unskilled factory workers.

Rather than reducing the flow of OFWs the fall of the Marcos government in 1986 saw a sharp increase in the number during the Aquino administration (1986–92). However, the government instructed the POEA to take a more active role in looking after the welfare of OFWs than it had during the Marcos period. By 1993 there were about 500,000 OFWs and they were sending around U.S. $2.5 billion back to the Philippines annually. After the hanging of a Filipina maid by the authorities in Singapore and in response to over 10,000 complaints received from OFWs by the Philippine Overseas Workers Welfare Administration in 1994 (including a number of cases of physical abuse and rape in the Middle East in particular), President Ramos (1992–8) appointed an advisory commission initially to look into the specific problems faced by maids and then expanding its mandate to include other problems of OFWs. The commission recommended that the Philippines stop sending maids to some Middle Eastern and Asian countries and a short time later, the negative publicity surrounding the problems of OFWs led the government to pass the Migrant Workers and Overseas Act of 1995,[58] which sought to play down the role of migrant workers and their foreign exchange remittances as a means of promoting national development and to emphasize the need to look after the welfare of such workers. In keeping with such sentiments, the Act tightened regulations pertaining to the recruitment of overseas workers, required workers to register with Philippine embassies overseas, and took other steps to legally protect migrant workers. The government also indicated that it wished to reduce the number of workers going overseas and to create conditions within the Philippines that would keep these people home. At the time that the Act was passed there were about 4 million Filipinos working overseas, including around 800,000 women (600,000 of these in the Gulf States of the Middle East). In response to concerns that a reduction in the number of OFWs would hurt the economy because of a drop in remittances from the overseas workers, the government expressed the hope that this could be offset with foreign investment in the Philippines.

The policies of 1995 had little lasting impact on the recruitment of overseas workers other than to create a few more means of looking after their welfare, and subsequent administrations have returned to actively promoting the recruitment of migrant labor. By 2007 there were around 9 million Filipinos working abroad with about 1 million new workers going overseas each year — representing about 11 percent of the country's population. There were also a sizeable number of undocumented overseas workers. About half of the 9 million workers were on contract as official OFWs. Significantly, while two-thirds of these workers were re-hires and maritime workers, one-third of them were new hires. Moreover, the percentage of women being hired has been increasing and constituted about half of the new hires in 2007. The combined remittances sent to the Philippines by OFWs as well as by other temporary migrant workers and Filipinos living abroad in 2007 officially was over U.S. $14 billion — a figure representing 10 percent of the GNP of the Philippines. As much as another U.S. $7 billion was sent back to the country through informal channels. In comparative terms this level of remittance places the Philippines in the big league of remittance recipients, ranking number four behind India, the PRC, and Mexico.

The Middle East remains the destination for the largest number of OFWs (around 2.5 million) with the majority going to Saudi Arabia, followed by the United Arab Emirates, Qatar, and Kuwait. Smaller numbers also go to Bahrain. The second major destination includes neighboring countries in East Asia and Southeast Asia. While the official number of Filipino migrants in Japan is only around 60,000, estimates of the actual number of Filipinos living in the country are commonly several times that number, reflecting the presence of many Filipinos who are undocumented or living in the country illegally. Likewise, although official Taiwanese figures place the number of contract workers at around 85,000, Filipino figures indicate that there are 155,000 contract workers in Taiwan. There are also around 150,000 Filipinos working in Singapore (mainly as domestic helpers), 130,000 working in Hong Kong (also mostly as domestic helpers), and 50,000 working in South Korea. Quite a large number of Filipinos have migrated to Malaysia, especially to Sabah, and while some are in the country on legal contracts, most are in the country illegally.

In recent decades large number of Filipinos have migrated to Western Europe temporarily as contract workers or, in some instances, as permanent migrants. The largest number of these migrants (about 300,000) has gone to Spain — it has had a small Filipino community since the colonial period — primarily to work as domestic helpers, in healthcare (mainly as nurses), and as industrial workers. The United Kingdom has recruited large numbers of Filipino nurses and caregivers and there are also sizeable Filipino migrant communities in Italy, Germany, France, and Greece.

Reflecting a past colonial association, the largest number of Filipinos living overseas is in the United States (over 4 million). Most of these are permanent migrants and many of the recent migrant workers come as nurses. There is also a large Filipino population in Canada (over 400,000). Again, many of these are permanent migrants, but many enter the country as temporary contract workers, especially as domestic helpers. The Philippines and Mexico also share a common history as colonial subjects of Spain. During the Spanish colonial period a number of Filipinos migrated to Mexico on the Manila Galleon. These included sailors, soldiers, and artisans. Economic development of the coastal and border regions of northwestern Mexico in the early 1900s attracted some Filipino migrants from California who came to work as fishermen and farm laborers. A third group arrived in Mexico from Spain in the 1930s as refugees from the Franco regime. One aspect of the common colonial legacy is that Mexican immigration law grants special status to citizens of the Philippines and starting in the 1970s a large number of Filipinos began migrating to Mexico with the intent of subsequently moving on to the United States. The most recent group of Filipino migrants to Mexico is migrant contract workers and in 2009 there were 309 OFWs in Mexico.

As with Indian and Chinese contract workers before them, Filipinos coming to new territories to work as contract laborers initially formed an enclave and, although they contributed to local economies they were barely integrated into the local society. Likewise, as increasing numbers of these workers, often joined by other Filipino migrants, settled in these countries local ethnic Filipino societies evolved with transnational relations. Subsequently contract workers who come to these countries, even temporarily, tend to take part in these local ethnic societies, using the same facilities to send money back to the Philippines, attending ethnic gatherings, and shopping in stores that cater to Filipinos. They and local ethnic Filipinos are also able to keep abreast of life in the Philippines on a regular basis through the internet and broadcasts of Filipino television programs. Moreover, in addition to communication with the Philippines being much easier than in the past, relatively inexpensive air travel means that trips back to the Philippines are easier and more affordable than in the days of trans-oceanic travel.

Voluntary Labor Migration: European Colonial Administration and Settlers

To some extent colonialism always involves migration. At the very least a handful of administrators and soldiers are needed to look after a country's colonial possessions. However, there are almost always other migrants lured by perceived economic opportunities or driven by a desire to spread religious beliefs associated with the colonial power. Thus, all colonies have at least a small expatriate population either there on a temporary basis or intending to settle more permanently (though still possibly dreaming of retirement back home).

The 1921 census of Fiji, for example, at the time a British colony, listed 3,878 Europeans out of a total population of 157,266 — a little over 2 percent of the population. The governor of the colony at the time was Sir Cecil Hunter Rodwell. He had been appointed in 1918 to replace Sir Ernest Bickham Sweet Escott who had served as Governor for six years. Sir Rodwell graduated from Cambridge with a BA in 1897, then was appointed to the staff of the High Commissioner for South Africa in 1900, became Imperial Secretary for Mauritius in 1904, where he remained until being appointed Governor of Fiji and High Commissioner for the Western Pacific in 1918.[59] Underneath the Governor were dozens of European colonial civil servants, ranging from the Chief Justice and Judicial Commissioner for the Western Pacific, Attorney-General, Colonial Secretary, Colonial Treasurer, Chief Medical Officer, Commissioner for Works, and Commandant of the Fiji Defense Force at the top of the hierarchy to the Clerk, interpreter and Canteen-keeper of the Leper Asylum and Clerk and Typist of the Printing Office at the bottom. While some of these government employees were permanent residents in Fiji, others were there for a limited time before moving on to another post in another colony. The Commandant of the Fiji Defence Force (and Inspector-General of the Constabulary) in 1924 was Colonel G.J.L. Golding. He had been a lieutenant in the Cork Artillery from 1889 to 1893 and then served with the Bechuanaland Border Police in the Matabele War of 1893 and the Natal Mounted Rifles and Johannesburg Mounted Rifles during the war in South Africa from 1899 to 1901. He then served in various positions in northern Nigeria from 1903 to 1910. Next he served in the police in Trinidad, becoming chief of police in 1912. During World War I he helped raise and commanded the Windward Islands contingent of the 1st British West Indies Regiment and was promoted to the rank of major. After the war, in 1919 he was appointed Inspector-General of the Fiji Constabulary and then in 1922 he also became Commander of the Fiji Defence Force.

The religious side of European colonial Fiji in 1924 included the Right Rev. L.S. Kempthorne, Bishop of Polynesia of the Church of England; Monseigneur Bishop C.J. Nicolas, S.M., Vicar Apostolic of the Roman Catholic Church; the Rev. G.L. Johnson of the Presbyterian Church; and the Rev. A.J. Small, Chairman of the Wesleyan Methodist Church. The 1907 *Cyclopedia of Fiji* provides biographical information on several of the religious figures in Fiji in the early 1900s.[60] Bishop Nicolas was born in Metz, Lorraine, in 1860 and studied in Metz and Dublin. He received his priesthood in Lyons in 1888 from Bishop Lamaze of Tonga and was then sent to New Caledonia before moving to Fiji in 1889. As for the Rev. Small, he was born in London in 1854 and in 1863 came to Sydney with his parents. He established a business in Australia and was active in the Methodist Church and was ordained as a minister in 1879 and promptly sailed to Fiji. He worked on the island of Bau for 8 years and then moved to Suva, where he was appointed Chairman of the church in 1900. All of the prominent religious figures at the time were born outside of Fiji, but once migrating to Fiji generally spent the rest of their lives working there.

The elected members of the Legislative Council of Fiji included Sir Maynard Hedstrom, Hon. Major Henry Marks, and five other prominent members of the local European community. Sir Hedstrom had been born in Levuka, Fiji, in 1872 — Levuka being center of the European settler community in pre-colonial Fiji — and sent to Melbourne for his higher education (graduating with a BA from Melbourne University in 1888). He was the primary partner in the Levuka firm of Brown and Joske and Hedstrom that grew into one of the largest local businesses. Henry Marks was born in Melbourne in 1861 and migrated to Fiji in 1881 where he settled in Suva and established himself as an export and import trader. He then worker as a labor agent traveling to the New Hebrides, New Caledonia, and the Solomon Islands, before returning to Suva and setting up as a general merchant and commercial agent. His company, Messrs. Henry Marks and Company Limited, became one of the leading commercial firms in the colony and he took an active role in a number of other businesses as well such as Suva Soap and Oil Company and Fiji Shipping Company. In addition to such local businessmen there were also European employees of foreign firms operating in the colony, such as the Bank of New Zealand, Bank of New South Wales, the Union Stream Ship Company of New Zealand, the Colonial Sugar Refining Company of Australia, and Burns Philp of Australia. While many of the Europeans in the business sector were either born in Fiji or migrated to the colony on a permanent basis, some came on a more temporary basis to work for foreign companies with operations in Fiji.

To varying degrees these people formed part of a transnational colonial society that was linked to Great Britain and to other nearby current and former British colonies, Australia in particular. Even those colonial officials who remained in Fiji for only a short time found that they were integrated into local colonial society not only through their work, but also in their social lives. While this segment of Fiji's society was in many ways distinct from that of the indigenous Fijians and the Indian and Chinese migrants, forming part of what is commonly referred to as a plural society, there were points of contact through work and, especially in the case of elites, socially. Moreover, while the local social roots of some of the colonial civil servants were not well developed, others spent a major portion of their lives in Fiji — some even retiring there after completing their period of service. Even for those colonial civil servants and European migrants who settled in Fiji, however, relations with Great Britain, Australia, or other such countries tended to remain important to them through family connections, work, and culturally.

It can be seen from the example of Fiji that even such a small colony hosts a significant expatriate population of temporary and permanent migrants. The majority of European colonies in Africa and Asia followed a similar pattern to Fiji. Quite different were the so-called settler colonies, where there was a major flow of migrants from Europe with settler migrants in several instances becoming the majority of the colony's inhabitants. Spain and Portugal encouraged their citizens to migrate to their colonies in the New World starting in the early 1500s, the British and French encouraged their citizens to migrate to their New World colonies a little later, while the United Provinces (the Netherlands) favored recruiting employees for its overseas economic ventures more than promoting permanent settlement of migrants.

In addition to the number of migrants going to the settler colonies an important question in regard to potential transnational relations concerns the ethnicity or nationality of the migrants. In general the European colonial powers favored their own citizens as migrants, but they also allowed certain people from other European countries to migrate to their colonies. Thus, while the majority of settlers going to Jamestown in the early 1600s were from Great Britain, the initial groups of settlers also included Polish and German artisans.[61] Religion and other cultural links often played an important role in this regard. The Spanish were open to Irish Catholics migrating to their colonies and Protestants from Germany could migrate to Dutch and English colonies with relative ease. Even in the early days of colonial migration, however, the situation was often even more complex. From our discussions earlier in the chapter, it should also be remembered that most of these colonies often received sizeable numbers of slaves and contract laborers from non–European regions — adding to the ethnic mix of these colonies.

Using Australia as an example, European settlement of Australia began with the founding of a penal colony in the vicinity of present-day Sydney in 1788. British settlement of the rest of the colony spread slowly over the next few decades, until it was given a substantial boost with the onset of the Victoria Gold Rush (1851 to late 1860s).[62] While most of colonial Australia's migrants came from the United Kingdom and Ireland, there were also migrants from elsewhere in Europe and a few Chinese began to arrive in 1854.[63] The gold rush was only the beginning of the flood of immigrants coming to Australia during the latter half of the nineteenth century. The flow was sustained by policies of providing assistance for migrants from Europe. Agriculturalists, rural workers, and domestic servants were the main categories given assistance. Australia's population growth rate during this period was "considerably above all other countries in the western world, and a substantial portion of the increase came from immigration. Between 1861 and 1890 about two-fifths of the addition to population was due to migration, almost all from Great Britain and Ireland. Australian colonial governments took the leading part in encouraging migration by directly offering help with cheap passages and land grants (about 40 per cent of total immigration was assisted)."[64] The rate of migration slowed considerably during the 1890s as a result of an economic depression and drought and did not pick up again until the post–World War I period.

In addition to migrants from the United Kingdom and Ireland, other groups of European immigrants coming to Australia during the colonial period included relatively small numbers of Germans, Italians, and Greeks. The limited numbers of migrants coming from these countries in part reflected relative costs and distance of travel to some extent, especially before the opening of the Suez Canal. It was simply much cheaper and easier for migrants from the European continent to go to the Americas than to Australia. Nevertheless, some did make the extra effort.

Colonial policies and racist attitudes favored European migrants and generally discouraged migrants from closer regions of the world. In addition to the Chinese who were attracted primarily by Australia's gold rushes, small numbers of people from the Pacific Islands and Asia also migrated, but usually as contract laborers to meet specific labor requirements. For example, Japanese, Malays, Filipinos, and Pacific Islanders were recruited to work as pearl divers in Western Australia, the Northern Territory, and Thursday Island in Queensland starting in the 1870s and peaking between 1889 and 1891, when Broome was the largest pearling center in the world.[65] While Europeans controlled the pearl industry at the outset, Japanese assumed a dominant position and people from a variety of national backgrounds were recruited to work. Thus, prior to 1890 most of the pearl divers were of European descent, but recruitment of an increasing number of divers from the Asia-Pacific region who worked for less resulted in few Europeans continuing to dive. An agreement with Dutch colonial authorities allowed the industry to recruit Indonesian pearl divers. Most of the Malay divers returned home when their contract expired and the Immigration Restriction Act passed by the government of newly independent Australia in 1901 seriously hindered further recruitment. The Japanese had begun to migrate to Australia to work in the pearl industry in the 1880s. Most of them initially came to work as divers. Some were also involved in boat-building and other aspects of the industry especially after the British and Japanese governments signed an agreement in 1894 allowing Japanese to settle in Australia. In fact, the Japanese became so important to the pearl industry that they were exempt from the immigration restriction placed on Asians in 1901. The industry also attracted Chinese migrants who had already settled in Australia and mainly ran shops or worked as cooks.

While a few Pacific Islanders worked as pearl divers, most of the Pacific Islanders who migrated to Australia in the nineteenth century came as contract laborers recruited to work on sugar plantations in Queensland. Around 62,000 Pacific Islanders—called Kanakas—were recruited between 1863 and 1904. They came mainly from the Solomon Islands and the New Hebrides (modern Vanuatu). The restrictive legislation passed in 1901 restricted entry of additional Pacific Islanders on work contracts and led to the deportation of most of them who were living or working in Australia.

Migrants to Australia from the Middle East included mainly Christian Lebanese from Ottoman controlled Lebanon who started arriving in the 1870s in the face of deteriorating conditions for them under Ottoman rule. The largest number of Lebanese migrated to the United States, but Lebanese migrants went to a number of other countries as well, including a few to Australia. Since they were classified as Asians, further Lebanese migration to Australia was restricted in 1901 and those already in Australia were barred from citizenship.

There were several thousand Afghans and other Muslims brought to Australia as contract laborers during the 1800s, primarily to serve as camel drivers.[66] In addition to Afghanistan those recruited included men from Baluchistan, Kashmir, Sind, Rajasthan, Egypt, Persia, Turkey, and Punjab. A total of about 3,000 were recruited to work in South Australia, starting with a group of 18 Afghans in 1838. Most of the cameleers went to work on outback stations using camels to transport goods, while some also assisted in the exploration of parts of Western Australia in the 1870s and later worked for the Overland Telegraph Line. Haji Mulla Merban (died 1897), from Kandahar, emerged as one of the most important community leaders. He originally worked for the Overland Telegraph Line out of Port Darwin. He went back to Afghanistan for three years and then returned to Australia and settled in Adelaide where he married a European woman and became the religious leader of the local Afghan community upon completion of the Adelaide Mosque in 1888. Most of the camel drivers eventually returned to the Middle East, but some settled in Australia. Of those who settled in Australia, many remained single, some married Aboriginal women, and a few married European women. A number of them established their own businesses providing camel transport as well as in other areas.

We can see from the above discussion that a variety of factors including the colonial government's immigration policies, the cost of transportation, and cultural preferences meant that colonial Australia's migrant population came mainly from the United Kingdom, with much smaller numbers coming from other European countries, and even fewer coming from Asia and the Middle East. Moreover, since most of the Asian and Middle Eastern migrants came as contract laborers only a small portion of these remained as settlers. The implication for transnationalism was that transnational relations between settlers in Australia and the rest of the world focused primarily on relations with the United Kingdom.

Post-Colonial Voluntary Migrants

The end of colonial rule in theory can lead to significant changes in migration policies as newly independent countries close their borders to sources of migrants that existed during the colonial period or seek new sources of migrants. In addition, political and economic turmoil surrounding the transition from the status as a colonial to that of an independent state may be a major disincentive for would-be migrants as well as producing emigration of those who have suffered from changing circumstances or who perceive that they will suffer under the new postcolonial order.

The United States was the first of the modern post-colonial states and has been the modern world's most important destination for voluntary migrants. The population of the newly independent country according to the 1798 census was 3,929,214. This included

2.5 million people of British ancestry (English, Irish, Welsh, and Scottish), about 750,000 people of African ancestry, and around 50,000 Native Americans. Almost half of the remaining 600,000 were of German ancestry (about 280,000) with the rest including about 80,000 people of French ancestry, 20,000 of Spanish ancestry, and 20,000 from Sweden and other Scandinavian countries.

The flow of immigrants to the United States increased considerably during the decades prior to the Civil War. From only 143,400 in the 1820s, the number of legal immigrants increased to 2.6 million in the 1860s. Immigration to the United States during this period was related in large part to labor demands in the United States and to adverse conditions in parts of Europe. With the end of the Civil War in 1865 and the growth of northern industry and the country's westward expansion, the United States experienced a massive influx of migrants that continued well into the early 1900s. At the outset of this period the 1870 census placed the country's population at 38,555,983. The population of the United States by 1900 was around 76 million—doubling the 1870 figure in just 30 years. Taylor refers to the United States as a "distant magnet" for migrants from Europe.[67] In fact, improvements in sea transportation, as discussed in Chapter 1, served to make it a not so distant magnet.

While many of the migrants coming to the United States from 1870 to 1910 were from the traditional sources in northwestern Europe, an increasing number also came from new sources. As for the traditional countries of emigration, "By 1914 Ireland, Sweden, Switzerland and West Germany had virtually exhausted their stock of potential emigrants."[68] In addition, industrialization in parts of Europe such as western Germany turned these regions into importers of labor rather than exporters.[69] Only the United Kingdom, with a rather poorly performing economy in the decades before World War I, continued to produce large numbers of emigrants. Italy and Eastern Europe (especially the Balkans and Jews from the Russian Empire) became major sources of new migrants to the United States during the 1890s. This trend accelerated between 1900 and 1910, when about three-quarters of immigrants from Europe came from eastern and southern Europe. In regard to Italian migrants at this time, most were men and many were "Birds of Passage"[70] who intended to work for a time and then return to Italy. While about 25 percent did go back to Italy (the highest rate among migrants to the United States) until World War I stopped further return migration, the majority remained in the United States.

During the early 1920s anti-immigration sentiments, especially on the part of union leaders, came to focus on the increasing number of migrants who had been arriving from Italy and Eastern Europe. These feelings led the American Congress to pass a series of increasingly restrictive immigration bills,[71] starting with the Emergency Quota Act in 1921. The 1921 Act created a quota system that limited immigrants from any particular country to 3 percent of the persons from that country who were living in the United States in 1910 (professionals were exempt from the restrictions). The total allowed under this quota system was 357,802 per year with over half of the quota being set aside for immigrants from northwestern Europe, and it severely curtailed the number of immigrants coming from eastern and southern Europe. Even greater restrictions were put in place on the immigration of those deemed undesirable with the Immigration Act of 1924 (aka the Johnson-Reed Act). This Act established a quota system based on country of origin that was to remain in place until 1965.

Outside of Europe the 1924 Act placed no restriction on immigration from Latin America, while it barred immigrants from almost all of Asia. As for Europe, the 1924 Act placed two restrictions. First, the quotas for immigrants were reduced to 2 percent of the population by country who were resident in the United States as of 1890 — that is, prior to the onset of massive immigration from eastern and southern Europe. Second, the annual quota for any country could not exceed a number related to the inhabitants who originated from that country residing in the United States in 1920. The total number of immigrants allowed under the 1924 Act was 164,667 per year. In regard to regions, 86 percent of the quota was for northwestern European countries and Germany, Great Britain, and Ireland received the largest quota. The quota for Germany, for example, was about 57,000. As for those countries now facing reductions, in the case of Italy, whereas before World War I about 200,000 Italians a year had been immigrating to the United States, the quota for Italy was 4,000 per year. The 1924 Act also established preferences for the type of migrant to be admitted, favoring family members of those who had already migrated and persons with agricultural skills.

The effects of the quotas (and the onset of the depression in 1929) can be seen in the numbers of immigrants coming to the United States in the first part of the 1900s. From 1911 to 1920 5.7 million migrants had arrived and in the 1920s 4.1 million. During the 1930s only 528,400 migrants came to the United States.

World War II and the Soviet Union's subsequent occupation of East Europe displaced millions of people in Europe. Many of these people found themselves in Displaced Persons camps from where most were allowed to migrate to a variety of non-communist countries. Reflecting the existing bias against Jews and other Eastern Europeans, there was considerable opposition in the United States to accepting such Displaced Persons (DPs). Despite opposition in public and within the American Congress, lobbying efforts by Earl Grant Harrison (who had served the United States Commissioner of Immigration and Naturalization from 1942 to 1944 and then as the American representative on the Intergovernmental Commission on Refugees from 1945 to 1946) and others on behalf of displaced Jews and others in Europe led to passage of the Displaced Persons Act of 1948.[72] The 1948 Act and subsequent legislation allowed about 600,000 DPs to migrate to the United States. In addition to Jews the DPs coming to the United States included about 55,000 *Volksdeutschen* (ethnic Germans living outside of Germany). Movement of these people was handled both by the American government and by a number of ethnic and religious organizations.

The Immigration and Nationality Act of 1952 (aka the McCarran-Walter Act) offered only minor changes to the 1924 Act. Overtly racial aspects of the quota system were eliminated, but the quotas themselves maintained the biases against Asians and certain other groups. Under the 1952 Act the number of immigrants (not counting those who were exempt from the quota on the basis of professional skills and refugees) was increased to 270,000 per year. Asians continued to be excluded for the most part and most European migrants still came from northwestern Europe until 1965. This began to change when

Congress repealed the system of quotas based on country of origin and restrictions on Asians with the Immigration and Nationality Act of 1965 (aka the Hart-Celler Act) and introduced a system of preferences based on family unification and skills.[73] The 1965 Act allocated 170,000 visas per year to the "Eastern Hemisphere" (i.e., the Asia-Pacific region) with a maximum of 20,000 going to any one country and in 1968 the "Western Hemisphere" (i.e., Latin America) was allocated 120,000 visas. These visas were to be granted on a first-come, first-served basis. In addition, the number of family reunification visas was unlimited. These legislative reforms resulted in the number of immigrants coming to the United States growing once again, especially after 1965. Thus, during the 1950s about 2.5 million migrants had come to the United States, with the number in the 1960s increasing a little to 3.3 million. In the 1970s the number rose to 4.5 million, and then in the 1980s to 7.3 million, and to over 9 million in the 1990s. From 1961 to 2000 a total of 24 million migrants came to the United States—an average of about 600,000 per year. As a result of such immigration there were 19.8 million foreign-born people in the United States, representing 7.9 percent of the population.

Growth in the number of immigrants entering and residing legally in the United States was given a boost by two additional acts. First by passage of the Immigration Reform and Control Act in 1986 that allowed for the granting of amnesty to about 3 million migrants who were living illegally in the country. Second, by the Immigration Act of 1990 that added an extra 175,000 immigrant visas per year (half being reserved for skilled applicants).

Not only did the 1965 Act and subsequent acts serve to increase the number of immigrants, but the composition of the migrant population also changed radically. Thus, "In the 1950s, 53 percent of all immigrants were Europeans and just 6 percent were Asians; by the 1990s, just 16 percent were Europeans and 31 percent were Asians. The percentages of Latino and African immigrants also jumped significantly."[74]

Changes in naturalization and immigration policies mentioned above had an important influence on the Asian population in the United States. The Asian population in the United States in the past was largely indicated in the census through the category of Asian foreign born. In 1850 the census reported that there were only 1,135 such people, representing only 0.1 percent of the total foreign born in the country. This number had increased to 107,630 by 1880, thanks in part to an influx of Chinese migrants as a result of the gold rushes and railroad construction discussed earlier in the chapter. As a result of anti–Asian immigration policies in the United States the number of Asian in America in 1920 was only 237,950 (representing only a little over 1 percent of the total foreign born). In the aftermath of the Korean War the number of Asian Americans grew as immigration policies became more liberal and in 1960 their population had reached 490,996 (5.1 percent of the total). By 1970, only ten years later and five years after passage of the Immigration Act of 1965, the number had grown to 824,887 (8.9 percent of the total).

A much more dramatic change took place in the United States in the wake of the Vietnam War and this has had important implications for the changing nature of transnational relations between the United States and the rest of the world. In 1980 the number of Asian foreign born was 2,539,777, representing 19.3 percent of the total foreign born.

In terms of ethnicity, the number of people identifying themselves as Asian by ethnicity in 1980 was around 3.8 million. By 1988 this number had increased to 6.5 million, an increase of 70 percent, with Asians by then representing over 25 percent of the foreign born. During these years between 268,000 and 281,000 immigrants arrived from Asia each year. Most of these new immigrants were admitted under a family reunification policy. The countries providing the largest numbers of immigrants included China, South Korea, Philippines, and India. The number of migrants coming from Asia continued on a large scale during the 1990s, and in 2000 there were 11.9 million people in the United States who identified themselves as Asian: including 3.5 million Chinese, 3 million Filipinos, 2.8 million Indian, 1.6 million Vietnamese, 1.6 million Koreans, 1.2 million Japanese, 200,000 Cambodians (Khmers), 200,000 Pakistanis, 200,000 Lao (from Laos), and 150,000 Thais (from Thailand). The number was 13.1 million in 2006, representing 4.4 percent of the population. Roughly 50 percent of these people live along the west coast, where they are heavily concentrated in urban areas. The 2000 census recorded 4.2 million Asians in California (12.3 percent of the population) and 700,000 in Hawaii (58 percent of the population). In other states the Asian population ranged from 6.7 percent (Washington) to 0.7 percent (West Virginia) of the population.[75]

In addition to their growing overall number, Asians living in the United States since the 1960s have come from a more varied range of countries than previously. The most significant change can be seen in the growth in the number of Asian Indians and non–Filipino Southeast Asians. Most of the growth in the non–Filipino Southeast Asian population can be traced to America's involvement in the Vietnam War between the 1960s and 1975 and the subsequent flood of refugees from Vietnam, Cambodia, and Laos. Thailand was a close ally of the United States during this period and a large number of Thais came to the United States during and immediately after the war period. Thus, the number of Thais migrating to the United States grew from 5,000 in the 1960s to 44,000 in the 1970s. An additional 64,400 Thais migrated to the United States in the 1980s. Many of the Thai migrants come from the impoverished northeastern part of Thailand. Many have settled in Los Angeles (over 80,000 as of 2002). The presence of this large Thai community, which maintains close relations with Thailand, has resulted in Thais often referring to Los Angeles as the 77th province of Thailand. Political reforms in the communist states of Vietnam, Laos, and Cambodia have also meant that these ethnic groups in the United States also now maintain important transnational relations with their countries of origin.

Contemporary Migration Patterns

On 28 October 2002 the United Nations issued a press release "Number of World's Migrants Reaches 175 Million Mark: Migrant Population Has Doubled in Twenty-five Years."[76] Its *International Migration Report* for 2002 indicated that migrants or people living outside of their country of birth accounted for about 3 percent of the world's population, with 56 million migrants in Europe, 50 million in Asia, and 41 million in North

America. Moreover, the report noted that 60 percent of the migrants lived in developed countries where they account for about 10 percent of the population and 40 percent in less developed regions where only about 1 in 70 persons is a migrant. The report also highlighted the importance of remittances from migrant workers: "in 2000, remittances from abroad augmented GDP by more than 10 per cent for countries such as El Salvador, Eritrea, Jamaica, Jordan, Nicaragua and Yemen."[77] The United Nations *World Population Policies 2005* reported in 2005 that the number of migrants had increased to 186,579,300.

According to the UN's 2005 report the United States accounted for 20.56 percent of the total number of migrants in the world: 38,355,000. Among the other countries, Germany had 10,144,000 migrants (5.4 percent of its population), Saudi Arabia 6,361,000 (25.25 percent), Canada 6,106,000 (18.76 percent), India 5,700,000 (0.5 percent), the United Kingdom 5,408,000 (9 percent), Spain 4,790,000 (20.79 percent), Australia 4,097,000 (20 percent), the People's Republic of China 3,852,000 (0.3 percent), Pakistan 3,254,000 (2 percent), the United Arab Emirate 3,212,000 (71.4 percent), Hong Kong 2,999,000 (42.6 percent), Israel 2,661,000 (37.9 percent), Japan 2,048,000 (1.6 percent), Singapore 1,843,000 (42.6 percent), Kuwait 1,669,000 (62.1 percent), Malaysia 1,639,000 (6. percent), and Argentina 1,500,000 (3.9 percent).

In addition to looking at the total number of migrants around the world it is important to look at the sources of new migrants.[78] In the case of the United States, the main destination for migrants in the world, in 2006 there were 1,266,264 legal immigrants. Of these, 552,093 were from the Americas (including 146,609 from the Caribbean, 173,753 from Mexico, 18,207 from Canada 18,207, and 138,001 from South America), 440,391 were from Asia (including 87,345 from the PRC, 24,386 from South Korea, 61,369 from India, 74,607 from the Philippines 74,607, and 30,695 from Vietnam), and 146,211 were from Europe (11.5 percent of the total, including 17,207 from the United Kingdom, 17,142 from the Ukraine, and 17,052 from Poland). These figures point to the relatively small number of migrants coming from the United Kingdom and other English-speaking countries in contrast to the very large number of migrants who come from Latin America and Asia. The relatively large number of Asian migrants (about 35 percent of the total) is especially noteworthy and highlights the growing contribution of this part of the world to the ethnic mix of the United States and the growing importance of transnational relations between Asia and the United States.

What of the other two main English-speaking countries that receive migrants: Canada and Australia. Canada's migrant intake in 2004 was 235,824, with Asia representing an especially important source of migrants, representing about 59 percent of the migrants legally entering the country. Canada received 139,706 migrants from Asia in 2004 (including 37,280 from the PRC, 28,183 from India, 13,900 from Pakistan, and 13,900 from the Philippines), while receiving only 28,873 from the Americas (including 12,306 from South America and 6,470 from the United States) and 37,359 from Europe (26.7 percent of the total, including 5,816 from Romania, 5,353 from the United Kingdom, 4,382 from Russia, and 4,046 from France). Australia received 131,593 legal migrants in 2006. There were 58,587 from Asia (44 percent of the total, including 10,272 from the PRC and 11,286 from India), 31,062 from Europe (23.6 percent of the total, including

23,290 from the United Kingdom), and 22,777 from Oceania (including 19,643 from New Zealand). From these figures we can see that the vast majority of Canada's migrants are from Asia, while English and French speaking countries, the source of most earlier migrants, now provide relatively few migrants. Australia receives the highest percentage of migrants from English-speaking countries, but a larger portion of the migrants now come from Asia.

The pattern of immigration in Europe is different from the above cases because of the free flow of people allowed within the European Union that has contributed to considerable migration within the region. Muenz provides a brief survey of migration within the European Union as of 2005 and notes, "Of the 474 million citizens and legal foreign residents of the EU/EEA and Switzerland, some 42 million were born outside their European country of residence. In absolute terms, Germany had by far the largest foreign-born population (10.1 million), followed by France (6.4 million), the UK (5.8 million), Spain (4.8 million), Italy (2.5 million), Switzerland (1.7 million), and the Netherlands (1.6 million)."[79] If we look at German patterns of migration we see that it received 558,467 legal immigrants in 2006. Of these, 383,658 came from within Europe (68.7 percent, including 151,743 from Poland, 23,353 from Romania, 17,650 from Italy, and 13,633 from France) and although Asia migrants accounted for most of the remainder (102,445 or 18.3 percent), 29,589 of these came from Turkey (5 percent of the total and 28.9 percent of the Asian immigrants) with other sources including the PRC (12,941), India (8,911), Vietnam (4,491), and Thailand (4,174). Thus, while Asian and other non–European migrants are increasingly in evidence in Europe, the overwhelming majority of migrants still come from within Europe itself.

It is apparent that Asians have come to represent an increasing percentage of international migrants in recent decades. However, international Asian migration is most noticeable within the Asia-Pacific region (i.e., within Asia and across the Pacific to the United States and Canada) and to the oil producing countries of the Middle East. In writing about the growing importance of trans–Pacific migration, Skeldon (1995) noted that as of 4 May 1984 more commercial aircraft crossed the Pacific than the Atlantic for the first time.[80] He points out that while Asia accounted for about 8 percent of migrants to the United States and 5 percent or less of annual migrants to Canada and Australia in the mid–1960s, by the early 1990s Asians accounted for 43 percent of annual migrants to the United states and Canada and 49 percent for Australia. As we saw in the immigration data cited above, this trend has continued into the 2000s. Skeldon adds, "It is the movement of Chinese peoples that is ultimately likely to make the greatest impact on the destination societies over the long term. As China develops we can expect to see an even greater involvement of its people in international flows. Chinese migrants with their high levels of education, entrepreneurial skills, and financial resources are likely to have the biggest impact on host countries."[81]

3

CITIES

In the present chapter we will focus on cities and their transnational character. Individuals with transnational lifestyles can live almost anywhere, but they tend to concentrate in particular communities. Historically transnational communities have been found especially in ports and other trading entrepôts and in the capital cities of empires. In this regard, the size of the community is not so important as its function. Thus, many of the trading entrepôts in the past were relatively small towns whereas just because a community becomes large enough to be designated a city does not mean that it is particularly transnational in its orientation. In this regard, it is important to think in terms of degrees of transnationalism. Although most cities will have at least a few transnational residents, the number and overall importance of such individuals to the city as a whole can vary a great deal ranging from relative insignificance to serving a major role in the life of the city.

Transnationalism and Cities

Cities not only attract people from immediately surrounding areas, but also from greater distances as well who come to settle permanently or temporarily to carry out administrative tasks, conduct business or simply to visit. Likewise, while the day-to-day existence of most urban-dwellers is devoted to tasks of a local nature, many may also maintain important links and engage in transnationally oriented activities.

The bulk of people in most cities tend to share similar cultures and form part of a relatively coherent social structure. Cities may also attract migrants with very different cultural traditions. Some of these migrants gradually are assimilated into the dominant culture, while others form relatively stable ethnic enclaves. Urban residents who are part of the cultural majority as well as those forming distinct cultural minorities may or may not maintain significant transnational ties. Those people living in cities who are part of transnational networks and communities and those cities in which such transnationals form a significant part of the population are of primary interest here. Looking at transnationalism from another perspective, while cities are not the only settings where transnational communities are found, they are the primary locales where people with transnational links live in the modern world. This is largely because cities often serve as important hubs of international commerce, transportation, and communication. For this reason, cities are a special importance to the study of transnationalism.

Not all cities, of course, are home to significant transnational communities. In general, the most transnational cities are capital cities, major transportation hubs, and border towns. Such cities include those that can be characterized as global cities in which transnational links play a major role in their existence as well as cities with important transnational links but where transnationalism plays only a relatively minor part of the overall life and economy of the city. Thus, any modern capital city will have at least a small transnational population associated with foreign embassies and multinational agencies such as those of the various United Nations bodies. Even Pyongyang, capital of North Korea and perhaps the least transnational city in the world, hosts embassies from about two dozen countries (those of Russia and the PRC being the largest), a few foreign technicians, and representatives from a small number of foreign multinational agencies and non-governmental organizations (although many of these have ceased operating in the country in recent years). Sorenson estimates that the "total number of foreign residents is no more than a few thousand" out of a total population of between 1.2 and 2.4 million.[1] Most capital cities, however, have much larger transnational populations, including not only those who are resident in official capacities (often along with at least some family members), but also numerous representatives of private companies and locals and other foreign residents with transnational ties.

Expats and Extraterritoriality

Foreign migrants living in cities include settler migrants and temporary migrants. The adaptation of these two categories of migrants tends to be different since most settler migrants intend on remaining in the city and putting down roots while temporary migrants tend to adopt a lifestyle reflecting the transient nature of their stay. Expatriates (*expatria,* out of country/fatherland) constitute a category of migrant that transcends both categories. In contemporary usage an expatriate ("expat" being the shortened version) is a person who resides temporarily or permanently in a country other than the one where the person was brought up and retains legal residence in another country. In the late 1700s and early 1800s the term referred to someone who had been driven away or banished from or who had renounced allegiance to that person's native country. Over time it assumed more of a voluntary and less drastic meaning such as referring to British retirees living in a Spanish beach community.

The status of such foreigners varies a great deal as does the extent to which they retain a separate existence from the local population. Extraterritoriality is an example of the recognition of the separate status of foreigners. This refers to the exemption of certain categories or people (or places such as embassies and military bases) from local jurisdiction. Those granted extraterritoriality interact with the local population in some circumstances, but lead lives that are in many ways removed from local society. Extraterritoriality tends to create a distance between foreigners and local people that diminishes the prospects of an expatriate developing transnational links involving the city or country of residence. Nevertheless, even expatriates who have been granted extraterritoriality can form their own distinct societies that differ to some extent from those in their home countries and, thereby, creating a type of transnational society.

Extraterritoriality has a fairly long history. The Byzantine government granted extraterritoriality to the residential quarters of Pera and Galata in Constantinople of expatriates from the republics of Genoa and Venice in the 1200s. European colonial powers commonly sought extraterritorial rights for their citizens in the 1800s. The Bowring Treaty between Britain and Siam that was signed in 1855 provides an example of an agreement granting extraterritorial status to foreigners. King Mongkut of Siam and the Governor of Hong Kong, Sir John Bowring, acting as Britain's envoy, signed it as a treaty of friendship and commerce. Among it provisions was the right of British subjects to trade freely in all of Siam's seaports, to buy and sell freely to any Siamese individual, to reside permanently in Bangkok (where they were also allowed to buy or rent property freely), to travel freely within the country with passes provided by the British consul, and they were placed under the jurisdiction of the British consul rather than being subject to the laws of Siam. This was the first time that Siam granted extraterritoriality to foreigners. The Bowring Treaty had a major impact on Siam's economy and promoted commercial relations with Britain and British territories in Asia. It also helped to provide a framework that kept European powers from colonizing Siam. In terms of transnationalism it helped to promote the emergence of a significant European expatriate community in Bangkok that played a major role in the country's development. Siam subsequently signed similar treaties with 13 other European countries and with Japan. These treaties remained in effect until the 1930s, when the absolute monarchy was overthrown and the nationalistic government that came to power signed new treaties in 1937 and 1938 that did not include extraterritoriality provisions.

As in the case of the Genoese and Venetians in medieval Constantinople, extraterritoriality can also be used to establish distinct communities of foreigners within a city that are outside of the laws of the city, sometimes referred to as international zones. During the 1800s, for example, European states were able to establish international zones in Shanghai for their citizens that were exempt from the laws of China. One of these was known as the International Settlement and the other the French Concession. In addition to granting Hong Kong Island to Britain ("in perpetuity"), the Treaty of Nanking that was signed by Britain and China in 1842 at the end of the First Opium War (1839–42) opened five ports for foreign trade (Canton's Shameen Island, Amoy [Xiamen], Fuzhou, Ningbo, and Shanghai) and laid the basis for the creation of the extraterritorial zones in Shanghai. The British and American foreign concessions were combined to form the Shanghai International Settlement in 1863,[2] while the French retained a separate concession. Although these concessions were granted extraterritoriality, unlike Hong Kong, they were still part of China. The population of the concession grew from 15 foreigners in 1844 to 38,940 foreigners and 1,120,860 Chinese in 1935.

The Shanghai Municipal Council, which was established in 1854, governed the concession. Hann makes the point that "The foreigners—mainly British and Americans—who came to Shanghai in the very early years were self conscious of the fact that they ought to govern themselves, without in any way being subjected to a higher authority like their compatriots in Hong Kong."[3] Thus, the Shanghai Municipal Council functioned as a relatively autonomous body with elected members drawn from the mixed expatriate community of the concession (resident Chinese from the Chinese Ratepayers Association were given seats on the council in 1927). Members of the council and its staff included citizens of Britain, the United States, Australia, New Zealand, Denmark, and Japan.

The buildings of the concession reflected European tastes and a distinct expatriate society developed with residents of the concession commonly being known as Shanghai-landers. The number of Chinese living in the concession grew by about 400,000 after war broke out between China and Japan in 1937 and people sought refuge in the concession. The concession also offered refuge to a large number of Jews fleeing persecution by the Nazis in Germany until the Japanese closed this avenue in 1941. After occupying Shanghai the Japanese put an end to the concession in 1943.

Most expatriates do not live in such exclusive zones or enjoy the rights of extraterritoriality. American expatriate artists, musicians, and writers who went to live in Europe during the latter part of the 1800s, the inter-war years of the early 1900s, and the 1950s and 1960s often lived in distinct neighborhoods in cities like Paris, but local people also lived in these neighborhoods. Thus, so many American black artists, writers, and musicians came to live and work in the Montmartre area of Paris that it came to be known as the Harlem of Paris, but it was certainly not a predominantly black neighborhood like Harlem. Montmartre, which was located outside of the city limits, became a popular Parisian drinking area in the 1800s and the home to several well-known nightclubs, including the Moulin Rouge and Le Chat Noir. By the latter part of the 1800s it had also become a popular area for artists from France and elsewhere in Europe. Pablo Picasso and Amedeo Modigliani, for example, lived there in the early 1900s.[4]

Today, as in the latter part of the nineteenth century, the term expatriate is often used to refer to businessmen and professionals working abroad for multinational or transnational companies or who simply have moved abroad in search of employment opportunities. While transportation today is faster, easier, and less expensive than in the past the basic characteristic of this type of expatriate has changed little from the colonial era except that today recruitment for positions is on more of a global scale than being limited primarily to within the confines of colonial empires. That said, transnational companies from non–English speaking countries such as the PRC still tend to recruit expatriate workers from their own cultural backgrounds, and although those from English-speaking countries recruit more globally than in the past, they still require fluency in English and tend to recruit from within the confines of the former British Empire.

There is a stereotype that expatriates during the high tide of European colonialism maintained cultural barriers from the locals and that considerable stigma was attached to "going native." While this certainly was the case to some extent, especially in British colonial territories, it was never absolute. Modern business and professional expatriates face few formal barriers to interacting with locals, but cultural views and practices tend to limit such interaction and expatriates often gravitate to other expatriates, thus forming expatriate communities that are distinct from the local society. The formation of such communities is often reinforced beyond the work place through social and religious organizations, international schools, expat hangouts (bars, restaurants, and hotels), and media catering to the expatriate community.

Social clubs have played an important role in expatriate communities since the 1800s. Singapore's Tanglin Club, for example, was founded in 1865 to cater to the social and recreational needs of the British expatriate community. Construction commenced the following year on a clubhouse in the Claymore Estate area that included bowling alleys, billiard rooms, stables, and a dance floor. German expatriates in Singapore built their own club, the Teutonia Club, that had around 200 members and a large clubhouse, which was seized as enemy property in 1914 and today is the Goodwood Park Hotel. Whereas, some colonial era clubs vanished with the end of European colonialism, many of them simply transformed to become social clubs catering to nationals and post-colonial expatriates. Shortly after independence, in 1962 the Singapore government asked clubs such as the Tanglin Club to have at least 50 percent Singaporean membership. The Tanglin Club responded by changing its constitution to allow a maximum of 51 percent Singaporean membership. Demand among Singaporeans to join quickly grew along with Singapore's economy. This led to waits of up to nine years for Singaporeans to be admitted to membership and to debates over allowing a larger percentage of Singaporeans members that ended up in a case before the country's High Court. At present the club has about 5,500 members from some 70 different countries.

In addition to reading newspapers and magazines from their home countries, during the latter part of the nineteenth century specialized local media catering to expatriates also emerged in many parts of the world. Allen, for instance, reprints several cartoons from 1920s issues of the *Straits Produce,* "a satirical fortnightly which had been keeping Europeans in Singapore and Malaya amused since the 1880s."[5] In addition to reading dated copies of newspapers from home, beginning in 1887 Americans living in Europe could also read the *Paris Herald,* a European edition of the *New York Herald* that was published in Paris, and the forerunner of the *International Herald Tribune.* The *IHT* began publishing simultaneously in Europe and Hong Kong in 1980 and is one of the leading newspapers read by English-speaking expatriates around the world today. For contemporary expatriates the internet has made it possible to read a much wider range of media from home that is current. Satellite and cable TV programs from expatriates' home countries are also widely available. In addition today there are also numerous websites catering to expatriates such as ExpatForum.com, hkexpats.com, expatfinder.com, expatriates.com, alloexpat.com/Vietnam (or another country), and expatfocus.com. The website expat communities.com/vietnam-expatriates, for example, is comprised mostly of advertisements and includes sections on Expat Vietnam, Hanoi International Women's Club, Living in Vietnam, Meetups, Real Post Reports, and Viet Nam News.

International Schools play an important role in catering to the needs of expatriate families and in creating a distinct expat culture. Such schools also have come to play a part in socializing local children who attend them to international expat culture. The

United Nations International School of Hanoi, for example, is a private, coeducational, English-language school that enrolls students from pre-kindergarten through grade 12. It is located near the international compound where foreigners formerly were required to live in Hanoi prior to the opening of the country in recent years. The school was established in 1988 to cater to the children of United Nations personnel and other expatriates living in Hanoi. It has about 100 full-time faculty members from the United States, Canada, the United Kingdom, Australia, New Zealand, France, Belgium, Sweden, Denmark, South Korea, and Vietnam. There are about 900 students from over 50 countries—including Vietnam, South Korea, the United States, Japan, Sweden, the United Kingdom, Denmark, Germany, Australia, Canada, Switzerland, Belgium, France, Malaysia, and Indonesia. Increased demand for such education in Hanoi led to the founding of the Hanoi International School in 1996 as a joint-venture between Vietnam's Centre for Education Technology (30 percent) and International School Development Inc. of the United States (70 percent). In its first year of operation there were 54 students from 15 countries. The school became a member of the European Council of International Schools in 1998 and by the early 2000s had over 250 students from 35 countries.

Foreigners who migrate to cities include not only expatriates who have come to do a particular job for a relatively short time, of course, but also many migrants who come to settle more or less permanently. Some of these migrants eventually become citizens while some remain on the basis of other statuses such as that of permanent resident. Permanent residency is a status whereby a person who is not a citizen is nevertheless allowed to reside in a country indefinitely. There are a large number of countries that grant permanent residency. Member states of the European Union allow citizens to move to other member states than their own and attain permanent residence status after 5 years. Many of these countries also allow non–EU citizens to acquire permanent residence status. The major former settler colonies Argentina, Australia, Brazil, Canada, Chile, New Zealand, South Africa, and the United States also grant such a status. Elsewhere in the world the availability of this status is relatively rare and these tend to be states with major transnational economic interests. Other states that grant permanent resident status include Brunei Darussalam, the PRC (as of 2004 for the PRC as a whole with the status already available for Hong Kong and Macau), the Republic of China, Japan, Malaysia, and Singapore in Asia. It is also available in Mexico and Guatemala in Latin America, Israel and Iran in the Middle East, as well as in Russia and the Ukraine.

Chinatowns

Foreign settler migrants in cities often, initially at least, reside in distinct neighborhoods that form ethnic enclaves. The best known and most universal of these are so-called Chinatowns. Chinatowns are distinct parts of an urban area usually outside of China (the Chinese area in the Shanghai International Concession was also called a Chinatown) where there is a concentration of ethnic Chinese in residence and Chinese-owned businesses. In recent decades many Chinatowns have evolved from being simply ethnic neighborhoods to also serving as tourist destinations.

Many of the oldest Chinatowns are located in Southeast Asia and East Asia, where Chinese merchants established trading outposts that evolved into permanent communities. Examples of such early Chinatowns are to be found in the Binondo district of Manila, Cho Lon in Saigon (Ho Chi Minh City), the Yaowarat Road area in Bangkok, and Nagasaki's Shinchiachi district. Taking Cho Lon as an example, ethnic Chinese have a very long history of living in what is now Vietnam, especially in the north, which was part of the Chinese empire for almost a thousand years. Chinese migrants settled in the central and southern parts of Vietnam as the area came under Dai Viet's control, especially in commercial trading centers on the coast such as Hoi An. The Chinese in this region became embroiled in the Tay Son rebellion in the 1770s[6] and after Tay Son rebels carried out an attack on the ethnic Chinese (referred to in Vietnam as Hoa) living in Bien Hoa in 1778, these Chinese fled and settled in the Cho Lon area. After they were attacked again by the Tay Son rebels in 1782 the Chinese built a more substantial settlement that included embankments to prevent flooding and named the settlement Tai Ngon ("embankment" in Cantonese). Later the town came to be known as Cho Lon ("big market" in Vietnamese) and developed into a sizeable town. A 1943 handbook describes Cho Lon in the late 1930s as the largest city in Cochinchina (southern Vietnam) with a population of 145,000 and notes, "The town is not only an important river port and commercial center, but is also the greatest industrial centre in Indo-China. There are over twenty rice mills, three distilleries, several soap works and a match factory."[7] Adding, the "Chinese to-day form the larger part of the population" and that it is "the market and entrepôt not only for all the rice of Cochin-China and Cambodia, but also for many other products such as hides and skins, dried fish, pepper, tea, sugar, coffee, and vegetable oils."[8] Cho Lon and Saigon (Saigon had a population of 111,000 at the time) were joined in 1932 to form a single urban area known as the Région Saigon–Cho Lon. The urban area came to be known only as Saigon in 1956 and Cho Lon became in effect the city's Chinatown. In addition to its commercial enterprises, Cho Lon also had a number of distinct Chinese cultural institutions, including a school and several Buddhist temples that cater mainly to ethnic Chinese. Migrants from Fujian built the Quan Am Pagoda in 1816 and later in the century built the Tam Son Hoi Quan Pagoda. The goddess Thien Hau (who is believed to be able to ride through the sky on a mat and save people in trouble at sea) is worshipped by most of the coastal ethnic Chinese and the Cantonese built the Thien Hau Pagoda in Cho Lon in the early 1800s. Chaozhou migrants built the Nghia An Hoi Quan Pagoda in Cho Lon. Cha Tam Catholic Church was built in Cho Lon in the 1890s catering primarily to local Chinese Catholics. There are also pagodas in Cho Lon that cater mainly to ethnic Kinh (Vietnamese) such as the Phung Son Pagoda, which was the first pagoda built in the area (between 1802 and 1820 on the site of an older Funanese structure) and a mosque that Tamil Muslims built in 1932.

A second generation of Chinatowns appeared in the mid to late nineteenth century as Chinese migrants settled around the globe. Many of these Chinatowns were established in port cities in English speaking countries such as the United States and Canada, especially as Chinese migrants flocked to gold rush areas around the English-speaking world. The recruitment of Chinese laborers in the English-speaking world and Latin America during the latter part of the 1800s also played a role in the development of these China-towns. These were essentially urban enclaves that served the needs of a migrant community that made few efforts and was not encouraged to assimilate into the surrounding society. The residents in these Chinatowns generally did not take an active part in the larger economy beyond providing labor and services such as laundries. As with the earlier Chinatowns, the populations of these newer ones came primarily from the coastal area of southeastern China (especially Fujian and Guangdong) and included speakers of Cantonese, Hakka, and Teochow (aka Chaozhou). Such ethno-linguistic differences were significant within the Chinatowns and sometimes resulted in conflicts within the local Chinese community.

San Francisco's Chinatown was the first to be established outside of Asia.[9] Large numbers of Chinese migrants, primarily from Guangdong, arrived in the port of San Francisco to seek their fortunes in the California gold rush and later to work in railway construction. This Chinatown was established in the 1850s in an area where the city government and private property owners allowed Chinese migrants to live and purchase property. As was mentioned in the last chapter, external relations turned especially hostile after the economic panic of 1873 and the flow of migrants was largely cut off following passage of the Chinese Exclusion Act of 1882. Members of the community formed the Chinese Consolidated Benevolent Association to assist the ethnic Chinese living in Chinatown and to represent their interests to the outside world. The community also experienced a growth in criminal activities often involving organized gangs (commonly referred to as tongs). The 1906 San Francisco earthquake completely destroyed the Chinatown area. After plans emerged to move the Chinese community outside of the inner city area, the Benevolent Association enlisted support from representatives of the Chinese government and local business interests to ensure that Chinatown was re-built in and around its original area. The new Chinatown was reconstructed in a manner that was more accessible to non–Chinese and that could serve as a tourist attraction.

San Francisco's post-earthquake Chinatown exemplifies the newer generation of Chinatowns that emerged around the world in the 1900s. While such Chinatowns sometimes serve at least to some extent as residential areas for ethnic Chinese (especially newly arrived migrants), they are primarily ethnic Chinese commercial areas that cater not only to the ethnic Chinese community, but also to the city's wider population and to visiting tourists. Moreover, such Chinatowns often also include ethnic Chinese who migrated to the city from other parts of the world rather than China itself (such as Sino-Vietnamese "boat-people" who fled Vietnam as refugees in the early 1980s) and even non–Chinese Asians attracted by the commercial prospects associated with doing business in such a neighborhood. Thus, many modern Chinatowns feature not only Chinese restaurants but also a variety of restaurants featuring foods from other East Asian and Southeast Asian countries such as Japan, Korea, Vietnam, and Thailand. These newer Chinatowns are located in a variety of cities around the world, including many cities other than the more traditional gateway ports (such as the new Chinatown in Las Vegas, Nevada).

While it is apparent that Chinatowns serve various functions related to ethnic Chinese living in cities around the world, what roles do they play in relation to transnationalism? The older Chinatowns had clear transnational roles in relation to long-distance trade and serving the needs of contract workers. They also provided cultural links between migrant Chinese communities and China through activities such as the staging of Chinese opera performances. Chinatowns today are fairly marginal to long-distance commerce, even that involving local ethnic Chinese, but they do continue to serve as venues for the sale of goods imported from China on a small scale, and some ethnic Chinese import-export businesses are located in Chinatowns. Recent Chinese migrants to cities rarely live within the confines of Chinatowns any longer, but they may work for ethnic Chinese businesses located there (often because of their lack of knowledge of the local national language) and shop for familiar goods and eat familiar foods that are found in Chinatowns. Herbal medicine, tea, and grocery shops are among the commercial enterprises commonly still found in Chinatowns that mainly sell goods imported from China (or elsewhere in East Asia and Southeast Asia), although many of these goods are now often also available outside of Chinatowns as well. In recent years, the Peoples Republic of China has used Chinatowns around the world as part of its initiative to build ties with overseas Chinese. One symbolic act in this regard is the donation of arched entryways (*paifing*) by the PRC to local Chinatowns (such as the one in Havana, Cuba). Following the communist takeover of China, many of the ethnic associations in Chinatowns had political links with the Republic of China, but in recent years relations with the PRC have become increasingly important.

The development of ethnic Chinese commercial centers catering more to middle class tastes in suburban areas is another recent development. These new areas more closely resemble modern commercial areas in East Asia than the older Chinatowns and often play a more important role in the lives of ethnic Chinese and other East Asians and Southeast Asians living in cities than the older Chinatowns. Little Hong Kong in Richmond, British Columbia, Little Taipei in Monterrey Park, California, and Little Shanghai in Ashfield, New South Wales, provide examples of such communities.

Transnationalism and Modern Cities from 1350 to 1800

Prior to the ascent of Europe, in the early modern world (1350–1500) nine out of ten of the largest cities of the world were located outside of Europe with most being in Asia: Beijing, Hangzhou, Guangzhou (Canton), Vijayanagara, Gaur, Cairo, Tabriz, and Constantinople (Istanbul). Most of these cities were politically important and served at various times as capitals of empires. The significance of transnationalism to these cities varied, however. Transnational relations were most important in the case of cities where long-distance trade was a major activity, such as Hangzhou, Guangzhou, and Tabriz. In contrast Beijing and Vijayanagara ruled over large empires where international commerce was concentrated elsewhere and they benefited from the wealth generated by such trade indirectly. It is also worth noting that a number of these cities either were already in decline or were soon to begin to decline in 1500 as a result of adverse political considerations.

Beijing was the largest city of the world from around 1425 until the mid–1600s, with a population of around 672,000 by 1500 (it regained this status from the early 1700s to the early 1800s). The city (named Jingshi at the time) became the primary capital of the Ming rulers in 1421. Transnational relations under the Ming, however, were limited mainly to a few ports while their capital city remained fairly isolated from the world beyond China's borders. Hangzhou and Guangzhou, also located in China, had grown and prospered from maritime trade during the time of the Southern Song Dynasty (1127–1279) and although the Mongols moved the center of political power back to the north both cities continued to flourish as centers of international maritime trade. While Guangzhou suffered following the outbreak of the Red Turban Rebellion in 1351 both cities again grew and prospered under Ming rule in the 1400s as China's foreign maritime commerce flourished and they were home to large numbers of foreign merchants engaged in long-distance trade. The population of Hangzhou had grown to around 250,000 under the Southern Song and after a period of decline by 1500 the population of Guangzhou had recovered to around 150,000. The transnational character of these two cities was about to change, however, as China progressively closed itself off to the outside world during the 1500s.

South Asia possessed two of the world's largest cities in 1500, Vijayanagara and Gaur, but both cities went into decline during the century as a result of conquest by Muslim forces associated with the Sultanate of Delhi. Vijayanagara (City of Victory, located in modern Karnataka, India, and also known as Hampi) was the second largest city in the world in 1500 with a population of around 500,000. Durant remarks that it was "probably the richest city that India had yet known."[10] Harihara Raya I (reigned 1336–56) founded the city as his capital on the site of a religious center in 1336.[11] Nocolo Conti visited the city in 1420 and estimated its circumference to be about 60 miles. Domingo Paes visited the city around 1520 to 1522 as a member of a Portuguese delegation from Goa to the court of King Krishnadevaraja and described it as being "as large as Rome" and "the best-provided city in the world ... for in this one everything abounds."[12] He said that it had over 100,000 houses, implying a population of around 500,000 people. Most of the city's inhabitants were poor serfs and laborers, but in addition to the nobility there were also merchants. Paes described the city's marketplace: "Going forward, you have a broad and beautiful street, full of rows of fine houses and streets of the sort I have described, and it is to be understood that the houses belong to men rich enough to afford such. In this street live many merchants, and there you will find all sorts of rubies, and diamonds, and emeralds, and pearls, and seed-pearls, and cloths, and every other sort of thing there is on earth and that you may wish to buy."

Vijayanagara served as the capital of the empire that bears its name. The empire ruled over much of southern India and although the city itself was inland it controlled important coastal trading ports that generated considerable wealth for the capital. As noted by Paes, "The said kingdom has many places on the coast of India; they are seaports with which we are at peace, and in some of them we have factories, namely, Amcola, Mirgeo, Honor, Batecalla, Mamgalor, Bracalor, and Bacanor."[13] Cotton was among the important agricultural products in the drier regions of the empire and its production supported a large weaving industry with a number of major weaving centers. The rainy hill region of Malad (in modern Karnataka) produced spices such as pepper, cardamom, turmeric, and ginger. Textiles, spices, as well as other goods such as gemstones and gold were transported to Vijayanagara for sale in its markets. Foreign merchants sometimes visited Vijayanagara to purchase such goods, but for the most part they operated out of the coastal trading entrepôts and it was from these ports that the empire's goods were exported to the Middle East, Europe, Southeast Asia, and China.

Although international commerce was limited mainly to a few coastal towns, this trade had an important impact of the lives of people throughout the empire. In addition to producing goods destined for the international market, the inhabitants of the empire also received benefits from the wealth it generated. Thus, the wealth produced from this trade helped to support patronage of the arts and literature in the capital and throughout southern India. The rulers promoted the Hindu religion and the capital boasted a large number of religious buildings and numerous lavish religious festivals. The empire encompassed peoples from a variety of different cultures throughout southern India and its capital included people from the various groups under its control.

In 1500 Gaur had a population of around 200,000 and was the second largest city in India and the seventh largest in the world. It was located inland on a channel of the Ganges and served as a regional political center off and on from 1204 until 1574. Smith notes, "As at Vijayanagara, numerous European travelers described the riches of the city, and recent archaeological surveys have documented abundant evidence of long-distance exchange including Chinese celadon and blue-and-white wares, as well as imported stone and marine shells."[14] Like Vijayanagara, however, the centers of long-distance trade were located closer to the sea, while Gaur exerted political control that allowed it to profit from this trade.

Three of the world's other largest cities in 1500 — Cairo, Tabriz, and Istanbul (Constantinople) — were located within Muslim ruled territories in the Middle East. For 1,000 years Constantinople as capital of the Eastern Roman or Byzantine Empire had been one of the most important and cosmopolitan cities in the world, when it fell to Muslim forces commanded by Mehmet II in 1453. The majority of the 30,000 inhabitants of the Byzantine city who had survived the siege were deported and Mehmed II then set about to repopulate the city by forcing Muslims, Christians, and Jews from around his empire to move to the city.[15] The census of 1477 gave the population of the city as consisting of 9,486 Muslim households, 3,743 Greek households, 1,647 Jewish households, 267 Christian households, and 31 Gypsy households. There was also a spate of construction including the Grand Bazaar in 1455, Topkapi Palace in 1459, and the Faith Mosque in 1463. There was a great deal more construction during the reign of Suleiman the Magnificent (reigned 1520–1566). At the time of Mehmet II's death in 1481 the population of the city had reached 80,000 and by 1500 it was around 200,000 (its population in 1800 was about 400,000). As capital of the Ottoman Empire the city regained some of its transnational character as it attracted a wide range of diverse peoples from around the empire as well as diplomats, merchants, and others from beyond its borders.

Cairo had a population of around 400,000 in 1500, which represented a decline from previous levels.[16] Previously the port city of Alexandria had been the center of transnational activity in Egypt and it remained an important international commercial center under Muslem rule, although its position was gradually eclipsed with the rise of Cairo further inland. A military encampment named al-Fustat had been established in the area where Cairo was to emerge in AD 641. In 969 the Fatimid leader Jawhar founded a new city nearby called al-Mansuriyah. The city's name was changed later to al-Qahirah (The Victorious)—the name Cairo being a European version of the name. It grew as the Fatimid capital and as the capital of Saladin of the Ayyubid dynasty. Cairo grew even larger under the Mamluks who established their capital there in 1260. The first century of Mamluk rule was especially prosperous for the city and there was a great deal of construction of public and religious buildings at this time. The trade in Asian spices that passed through Cairo from the Red Sea ports to Alexandria contributed a great deal to the city's prosperity. Cairo suffered from the Black Death in 1348 and this and other epidemics saw the city decline in size and wealth during the latter part of the 1300s. The city's marginalization to the spice trade in the late 1400s added to the decline of the city. The Ottomans defeated the Mamluks in 1517 and the status of the city was reduced from an imperial capital to that of a provincial capital. By the time Napoleon captured the city in 1798 the population of Cairo was less then 300,000.

Tabriz was the third largest city in the Middle East in 1500 with a population of around 250,000.[17] Its growth and prosperity was linked to its political importance as well as to its role in international trade. Although the city was established earlier,[18] it was destroyed by an earthquake and rebuilt under the direction of a wife of the Abbasid caliph Harun al-Rashid named Zubaidah in AD 791 and she is commonly credited as the founder of the city. Tabriz became capital of the Ilkhanate during the reign of Arghun Khan (reigned 1284–91) and Ghazan Khan (reigned 1295–1304) undertook a program of construction that included new city walls, numerous public buildings, and caravansaries to serve traders coming overland along the Silk Road. The city also served as capital of the Kara Koyunlu Black Sheep Turkomen confederation (encompassing adjacent parts of Armenia, Azerbaijan, Turkey, Iran, and Iraq) from 1375 to 1468 and the Ak Koyunlu White Sheep Turkomen confederation from 1469 to 1501. Tamerlane sacked the city in 1392, but this did no lasting damage. Shah Ismail I (reigned 1502–24) made it the capital of the Safavid (Persian) Empire. It remained capital of the empire until 1548, when the capital was moved to Qazin. The Ottomans occupied the city briefly in 1514, again between 1585 and 1603 and once more in 1724. In addition to its political importance, throughout this long history the city served as a major commercial hub for long-distance traders with goods flowing through the city from Central Asia, the Middle East, and South Asia. The local population is predominantly Azeri, but as the capital of various empires and as such an important commercial center the city's population has included a range of different ethnic groups from the surrounding area (e.g., Persians, Kurds, Armenians, and Assyrians).

While urban populations in Europe were growing, European cities in 1500 were still relatively small on a world scale.[19] The population of medieval Europe had peaked in the 1200s and then declined considerably in the 1300s and early 1400s as a result of wars, famines, and diseases. Europe's population remained relatively stagnant until the mid–1700s—thanks to ongoing plagues, famines, and wars—and only then did Europe's population began to grow once again. Paris was the largest city in Europe in 1500 with a population of around 185,000 and was not an especially transnational city at the time. Most of Europe's other major cities were located in Italy and were actively engaged in international trade: Venice, Milan, and Naples each had populations of around 100,000 and Florence and Genoa around 50,000 each. In England the population of London was only about 60,000 (its population grew to about 300,000 by 1700). Seville was the largest city in Spain.[20] When Ferdinand III of Castile (1199–1252) captured Seville from the Moors in 1248 most of its 300,000 Moors left the city. By 1500 it had a population of between 40,000 and 60,000 and was Spain's largest city. In contrast, Cadiz had a population of only 3,015 in 1534 (22 percent of its inhabitants in 1484 were Genoese),[21] and Madrid's population in the mid–1500s was around 20,000. Seville became the administrative center for Spain's empire and grew in size and wealth during the 1500s. By 1588 it had a population of around 150,000. Meanwhile, Madrid, which became Spain's capital in 1560, had a population of only 35,000 by 1570. Given the relatively small size of Spanish cities in the early 1500s it is little wonder that Hernán Cortés and his band of 600 conquerors was amazed by the sight of the Aztec capital of Tenochitlan when they first laid eyes on it in 1519. Tenochitlan at the time had a population of over 200,000.[22]

The period from 1500 to 1800 witnessed significant changes in the urban configuration of the world in response to the growing imperial and economic power of Europe. The global dimensions of the new European empires also meant that for the first time in world history the power of colonial administrations based in Europeans cities and the financial reach of commercial networks extending from these cities assumed global proportions. While most of the world's largest cities were still in Asia, a number of European cities entered the top 10. The big three in China (Beijng, Guangzhou, and Hangzhou) remained in the top 10, while in Europe Paris had been joined by London and Naples, with London moving to the no. 2 spot globally. Within Asia, the large South Asian cities had declined while three of the top 10 cities were now in Japan.

The growth of Japan's cities, especially Tokyo, during this period is an interesting one from the perspective of transnationalism. Edo (modern Tokyo) grew from a small fishing village in the 1400s to a city of 1 million in 1721, the largest city in the world at the time. The rise of modern Japan is closely linked to two men: Imperial Regent Toyotomi Hideyoshi (1536–1598) and Shogun Tokugawa Ieyasu (1543–1616). Toyotomi Hideyoshi, who played a major role in the unification of Japan, promoted trade with Europeans while at the same time seeking to curtail the activities of Christian missionaries. Tokugawa Ieyasu founded the Tokugawa shogunate that established rule over all of Japan in 1600. He also was a proponent of foreign trade, while at the same time being suspicious of foreigners. Initially he sought to open Edo to foreign trade, but Europeans preferred to trade in the ports of the southern island of Kyushu, especially Nagasaki, and China rejected his proposal for trade with that country. What developed instead was restricted trade through certain ports during what was referred to as the *Nanban boeki jidai* (Southern Barbarian trade period). Historians commonly date this period from

1543 when the Portuguese first arrived in Japan to 1543 when foreign traders were almost completely banned from Japan. In addition to foreign ships coming to southern Japanese ports during this period, Japanese sailors and merchants also operated to the south of Japan with small Japanese enclaves appearing in trade entrepôts such as Hoi An in central Dai Viet.

The end of the *Nanban* trade period and the onset of the closed-door period (*sakoku*) began with government efforts to restrict the activities of Japanese Christian converts in 1612. Foreign trade was restricted to Nagasaki and Hirado on the island of Kyushu in 1616 and thousands of Christians were executed in the 1620s. The edict closing the country came into effect in 1635. Japanese were forbidden to leave the country and if they did they were not allowed to return. A number of Japanese living abroad at this time decided to remain outside of Japan. Some trade continued and in 1636 the Dutch were allowed to operate out of a small artificial island named Dejima in Nagasaki harbor (as an artificial island it was not considered to be on Japanese soil) and the Chinese out of a quarter in Nagasaki town. Some Portuguese also were allowed to remain for a few more years before they were expelled and the English were permitted to conduct trade for a time. By the mid–1600s foreign activities in Japan were allowed only to a limited extent in Nagasaki.

The growth of cities in Japan was a reflection of the country's political unity and of its increasing population under more peaceful conditions. Japan's population in the 1500s was around 26 million as compared to under 5 million for England and 16 million for France. Japanese cities, however, even more than their Chinese counterparts were largely cut off from the world beyond.

In contrast to the cities of East Asia, most of the cities of Southeast Asia were closely linked to international commerce even after the early decades of the 1500s. Melaka (Malacca) was the most important trade entrepôt in Southeast Asia during the 1400s with a population of around 100,000, comprised of people from all of the major maritime trading regions of Asia. It was perhaps the most transnational city in the world at the time. The Portuguese occupation of Melaka in the 1500s reduced its commercial importance and saw its population decline to around 25,000.

The other large cities in Southeast Asia in the early 1500s with populations in the 100,000 range included Thang Long (Hanoi), Ayutthaya, Pegu, Aceh, Banten, Makassar, and Mataram, and there were also a few cities with populations of around 50,000 such as Pattani and Surabaya.[23] International commerce was important to most of these cities and many of them were relatively large in relation to the population in the surrounding hinterland, sometimes requiring them to import food over considerable distances. Reid makes the point that "Southeast Asia in the period 1500–1660 should ... be seen as highly urban, in relation both to other parts of the world and to its own subsequent experience."[24] Long-distance trade played an important role in the region's urbanization and resulted in these cities manifesting a transnational character.

Ayutthaya (also spelled Ayudhya) provides a good example of such Southeast Asian cities. It is located about 60 km from the sea up the Chao Phraya River and is surrounded by a large flat fertile area. U Thong, who appears to have come from a "powerful Chinese merchant family" and to have married the daughters of important local rulers,[25] founded the city in 1351. U Thong assumed the name Ramathibodi and established a state "based upon an uneasy alliance between Tai manpower from the western portion of the state, Khmer prestige and statecraft from Lopburi and the eastern provinces, and Chinese (and other Asian) commercial power concentrated at the center in the port-capital" of Ayutthaya.[26] In cultural terms, a Siamese culture evolved in Ayutthaya that was a mixture of the cultures of the local Tai, Khmer, and Mon as well as the Chinese. Added to this was Buddhist religious elements from Sri Lanka that were blended with aspects of Indian Hinduism and local religious beliefs and practices.

After a period of instability and decline in the late 1500s, under King Naresuan's (reigned 1590–1605) leadership the population of the city and kingdom grew once again and foreign trade resumed "thanks to continuing good relations with the Portuguese, the Spanish Philippines (with whom Neresuan had concluded a treaty in 1598), China, Japan, and the Ryukyu kingdom."[27] During his reign Ayutthaya grew into an even larger and more cosmopolitan city than before 1569. By 1600 its population reached around 300,000 (the total population of the kingdom at the time was only about 1.7 million). The Tai rulers of Ayutthaya actively promoted foreign trade and attracted merchants from Persia, Japan, India, other parts of Southeast Asia, China, and Europe. The rulers also employed Cham, Portuguese, and Japanese as their bodyguards and elsewhere in the military.

Some of the foreigners living in Ayutthaya obtained high positions in the royal court. A Persian named Sheik Ahmad who along with his brother had arrived in the country in 1602 was appointed head of the section of the ministry of finance and foreign affairs that dealt with Muslim traders, then head of the ministry itself, and finally prime minister.[28] His son succeeded him as prime minister around 1670. This family's influence was curtailed with the rise of a Greek named Constantine Phaulkon, who had arrived in the kingdom in 1675 as a merchant (he was married to a woman of Japanese-Portuguese-Bengali ancestry) and who became the king's close counselor and was appointed to the offices of chief of foreign trade. According to Wyatt, "Outsiders thus were enabled not only to rise rapidly to high official positions but also to found veritable dynasties of royal officers who, generation after generation, monopolized certain state offices and played prominent political roles. Their descendants ... continued in such position into the twentieth century."[29]

King Ekathotsarot (reigned 1605–10) received the first Dutch ships to arrive in Ayutthaya and sent diplomatic missions to Portuguese Goa in 1606 and to the Netherlands in 1608. English ships visited Ayutthaya in 1612 and both the English and Dutch established factories in Pattani in the southern part of the kingdom and in Ayutthaya itself. The English and Dutch had difficulty competing with Asian traders in Ayutthaya and for a long period during the 1600s the English ceased trading there. European interest in trade with Ayutthaya focused especially on obtaining deer hides for export to Japan. In general the kingdom's main exports included rice, spices, agar wood, sappan wood, lac, and benzoin. Its main imports included cloth from India, firearms (especially those of European manufacture), and silver, along with a variety of luxury goods for the capital's elite. In addition to foreign traders coming to Ayutthaya, the kingdom sent its own ships (usually with Chinese or Sino-Siamese crews) to China and Japan.[30]

Foreigners generally were not allowed to live within the core area of Ayutthaya (a common practice in Asian cities at the time) and many of Ayutthaya's resident foreigners lived in distinct areas on the outskirts of the city. These were also the areas where commercial activities involving foreigners took place. The Japanese, for example, had a large community living in what is sometimes referred to as the city's Japanese village. The Japanese community in Ayutthaya was in existence by 1540. Many of them dispersed to other parts of the kingdom in 1569 as a result of the Burmese sacking of the city, but the Japanese community in Ayutthaya grew again and was sufficiently large that 500 Japanese fought with Naresuan in 1593 at the battle of Nong Sarai. The community seems to have ranged in size during this period from between 800 and 3,000. Official diplomatic relations were established between Japan and Ayutthaya in 1604 during the reign of Japan's Shogun Tokugawa Ieyasu and Ayutthaya's King Ekathotsarot. After this the number of Japanese arriving in Ayutthaya to conduct trade and sometimes to settle increased from several hundred a year to as many as 7,000. Japanese communities also existed in other towns in the kingdom. Yamada Jisayimon Nagamasa was official leader of the local Japanese community and of the Japanese who had volunteered for military service in the early 1600s and played an active role in the kingdom's politics, which eventually resulted in his being poisoned by agents of the king. Nagamasa's son assumed his father's position as leader of the Japanese community and orchestrated a revolt in 1633. After the revolt failed local Japanese were massacred and the Japanese quarter in Ayutthaya was burned.

Narai (reigned 1656–88) became king "with the aid of his supporters and of the Japanese-Thais, Pattani Malays and perhaps Persian Muslims."[31] Narai's Persian prime minister imposed a royal monopoly on foreign trade in 1662 to help finance expensive wars with neighboring kingdoms. This adversely effected the Dutch in particular who withdrew from Ayutthaya. To lure them back King Narai sent a mission to Batavia and a treaty was negotiated in 1664 that not only returned their monopoly on the export of hides but also granted them extraterritoriality. During King Narai's reign French involvement in Ayutthaya increased at the expense of other foreign interests. French Jesuit missionaries had arrived in Ayutthaya in 1662 and opened a seminary. A French mission arrived bearing letters from King Louis XIV of France and Pope Clement IX in 1673. King Narai reciprocated with a letter sent to France in 1680. It was lost at sea but a second mission in 1684 made it to Paris. The two countries established diplomatic relations and negotiated a trade agreement in 1685–6. A treaty was signed in 1687 after France sent 6 warships and a force of 650 troops to Ayutthaya that allowed the French to establish a fortress at Bangkok. Under the terms of the treaty King Narai also promised to convert to Catholicism. This part of the treaty was never carried out, but the French did set themselves up in Bangkok. Foreign Muslims sought to counter the increasing influence of European Christians in the city and kingdom. The Safavid ruler of Persia Shah Sulaiman sent a mission to Ayutthaya in the 1680s to try to convert Narai to Islam. Then in 1686 a group of Bugis-Makassarese (originally from the island of Sulawesi) living in Ayutthaya, apparently along with some Muslim Cham, plotted to overthrow Narai and place one of his younger brothers on the throne if he converted to Islam. The plot failed and many members of the Bugis-Makassarese community were killed.

After the king became terminally ill in 1688 a revolt took place in reaction to what many Siamese view as the excesses of the French and Phaulkon that led to Phaulkon being executed and a number of other foreigners being killed, the French in Bangkok being besieged and forced to leave the kingdom, and several French Catholic missionaries being temporarily imprisoned and their converts being persecuted. Significantly, unlike China and Japan, Ayutthaya did not seek to close itself off from all foreigners. Having checked what those leading the revolt saw as the excesses of the French and Phaulkon, other foreigners were allowed to continue their activities, although the level of foreign involvement in the kingdom remained considerably reduced from what it had been before. Even the French priests were released and allowed to resume trying to make converts—with a notable lack of success. Ayutthaya fell to Burmese invaders in 1767. The Burmese wrecked the city and carried off most of its wealth and many of the people still living in the city at the end of the siege. After the Burmese were repulsed the Siamese capital was moved to Bangkok. Ayutthaya itself slowly revived as a small provincial town in the heart of Siam's rice growing region to the north of Bangkok. The 2006 census gives Ayutthaya's population as 54,888.

Modern Imperial and Colonial Cities

European colonialism witnessed the rise of two types of transnational cities: imperial cities at the heart of the empires and colonial cities scattered around the colonies. These cities served administrative, economic, and cultural functions linked to colonial rule. While all of the major European states possessed colonial territories the British and French empires were the most extensive during the 1800s and first half of the 1900s. London and Paris were at the center of empires that extended around the globe and both cities developed transnational characteristics.

London became Europe's first city to have a population in excess of 1 million in 1800. One hundred years later it had a population of around 5 million. The growth of London during the first half of the 1800s was in large part a result of domestic factors such as government policies associated with the Enclosure Movement that pushed people from throughout the British Isles to move from rural areas to urban ones. During the latter part of the 1800s and first few decades of the 1900s London also began to attract migrants from elsewhere in Europe such as Italians, French, and Russian Jews. A few South Asian and Chinese migrants also came to London first mainly as sailors on British ships and as domestic servants of families that had lived in Asia and brought their servants with them on their return to England. The Navigation Act of 1660 restricted the number of Asian sailors (known as *lascars*) serving on English ships to one-quarter of the crew. Most of these sailors returned home, but some remained in England. While small numbers of Asians from parts of the British Empire settled in London prior to the mid–1900s the numbers were relatively small and London remained overwhelmingly a British city with its main non–British residents being other Europeans.

In the case of the South Asians, many of the earliest migrants were Bengali and other Muslims brought to England by the British East India Company.[32] Sake Dean Mahomet was one of the Bengali migrants and he opened the Hindoostane Coffee House in 1810, London's first Indian restaurant.[33] Fisher estimated that there were over 40,000 South Asians living in Britain by the mid–nineteenth century, many of them in London.[34] They included sailors, soldiers, businessmen, as well as diplomats and students. The number had grown to around 70,000 by 1900, about 50,000 of these being sailors. The South Asian community in and around London was relatively scattered. The South Asians who settled in London spoke English and many of the early male settler migrants, as distinct from those living in London on a more temporary basis, married local English women. England's first mosque (Masjid-e-Abu Hurairah) was built in the port city of Cardiff in 1860, followed by mosques in Woking and Liverpool in 1889. Construction of London's Fazl Mosque began in 1924 and it was inaugurated in 1926. Followers of the Ahmadiyya movement in India provided the money to build the mosque.

Coming mainly as sailors as well, the Chinese in England initially settled mainly in the ports of London and Liverpool.[35] The 1891 census indicated that there were only 582 people living in England who were born in China and in 1896 the number was only 387 (80 percent of them being males and most of these were seamen). China itself opened an embassy in London in 1877. Many of the early male Chinese settler migrants married local English women.

The Chinese migrants tended to live in distinct neighborhoods in and around London's port area (where South Asian and Japanese sailors also lived while in England). Europe's first Chinatown was established in Liverpool in the early 1800s and London's Chinatown was established in the Limehouse area in the 1880s. Most of the Chinese settlers living in the Limehouse area were from Canton and other coastal areas of southern China. In the 1890s Chinese also settled in the nearby Poplar area. Those settling in Poplar were mainly from Shanghai. These small Chinatowns contained lodging houses for seamen and shops providing Chinese goods as well as opium dens and brothels. The first Chinese restaurant in London was opened in 1907. The 1911 census enumerated 1,319 Chinese-born residents in England along with 4,595 Chinese seamen serving in the British Merchant Navy.

With the outbreak of World War I the British government considered bringing a large number of Chinese laborers to England to overcome wartime labor shortages, but this initiative was blocked by trade unionists and the Aliens Restriction Act, which was extended in 1919, served to keep further Chinese immigration in check. As a result of such restrictions, the 1921 census enumerated only 2,419 Chinese-born residents. This number included 547 laundrymen, 455 seamen and 26 restaurant workers. The killing of Chinese protestors in the Shanghai International Settlement in May and June 1925, followed by the resultant Canton-Hong Kong strike from June 1925 to October 1926 resulted in a decline in Chinese immigration to England.[36] Thus, the 1931 census recorded only 1,934 Chinese-born residents in England.

Rather than as a magnet for immigrants from the British Empire, London's role as an imperial capital prior to World War II was primarily that of an administrative center with institutions in the capital related to the management of the empire. Formal British administration of its colonial territories began in 1660 with the establishment of a Council for Foreign Plantations, which was later expanded to become the Council for Trade and Plantations. Eventually a Colonial Office was created, which from 1854 was under the direction of the Secretary of State for the Colonies. Under the Secretary was a bureaucratic establishment that included hundreds of individuals based in London. Among the Colonial Office's departments located in London was the Oversea Settlements Department, which provided assistance to "British subjects wishing to settle overseas within the Empire, or to emigrate to foreign countries." The Crown Agents for the Colonies served as the commercial and financial agents for the colonies and protectorates and employed a large staff in London.

In addition to such government bodies that were directly responsible for the administration of the empire, there were a host of institutions based in and around London with functions closely related to Britain's imperial activities. These included educational institutions such as the Royal School of Mines (founded 1851) and the subsequent Royal College of Science (founded 1881) that provided personnel with technical expertise to the empire, University College that produced a large number of graduates who became important figures in Britain's imperial history as well as individuals who played important roles in their home countries after independence including Mohandas Gandhi of India and Jomo Kenyatta of Kenya, and the London School of Tropical Medicine (along with the Tropical Diseases Bureau).

There were also the financial institutions centered within the City of London that conducted financial activities around the world, making London the largest financial center in the world in the 1800s. During the latter part of the 1800s the City of London was transformed from a community mainly of business people to a center of business offices housing such financial entities as the London Stock Exchange, the Bank of England, and Lloyd's of London. As a consequence, as the financial importance of the City of London increased its population decreased (from 112,000 in 1861 to 31,000 in 1900) as people moved into the surrounding suburbs. The Port of London was the other important part of London catering to the country's imperial domains. In 1800 about 800,000 tons of goods passed through the port. By 1900 the amount had increased to 8 million tons.

The Great Exhibition of the Works of Industry of All Nations (or simply The Great Exhibition and also known as the Crystal Palace Exhibition) that was held in 1851 served an important role as a symbol of Britain's global power in the mid–1800s.[37] There were over 13,000 exhibits in total from Britain, a number of other European countries, the United States, and many of the colonies, protectorates, and dominions within the British Empire, ranging from a Jacquard loom to the Koh-i-noor diamond. Over 6 million people attended the exhibition. Funds generated from the Great Exhibition were used to establish the Victoria and Albert, Natural History, and Science museums. The first America's Cup yacht race was also held in conjunction with the exhibition. The area was also used in 1893 for the site of the Imperial Institute of the United Kingdom, the Colonies, and India, which was opened to celebrate the Jubilee of Queen Victoria. The Imperial Institute served "to promote the utilization of the commercial and industrial resources of the Empire by arranging comprehensive exhibitions of natural products, especially of the Dominions, India and the Colonies, and providing for their investigation and for the collection and dissemination of scientific, technical, and commercial information relating to raw materials." Several committees that included prominent members of the colonial administration, academics, and representatives of important British companies that had activities within the Empire oversaw the activities of the Colonial Institute.

The dismantling of the British Empire after World War II gave rise to the transformation of London from a city primarily of English people who administered a large empire to a city that no longer ruled much of the world (although a great deal of world finance still flowed through London) but was more of a global city in terms of its population. Thus, as early as 1951 the British census enumerated a Chinese population of 12,523 (about 4,000 of these being ethnic Chinese who had migrated from Malaya). By 1961 the number of Chinese had grown to 38,750. Many of these were young male laborers who came from Hong Kong's New Territories. The reaction to the flow of migrants from the former colonies (the majority of them settling in London) began with the Commonwealth Immigrants Act in 1962 that sought to restrict the number of migrants. Despite this and subsequent restrictions such as the 1981 British Nationality Act the number of non–European migrants to Britain continued to increase (e.g., the 1971 census enumerated 96,030 Chinese in Britain).

Colonial cities included cities such as Sydney and Toronto that were inhabited almost entirely by new foreign migrants to settler colonies and colonial cities in colonies with large indigenous populations where the foreign migrant population comprised a relatively small percentage of the total population of the city. In terms of transnationalism these colonial cities, the latter type in particular, are significant since they were created primarily to play a transnational role linking the colony to the colonial power. Batavia (modern Jakarta), the capital of the Dutch East Indies (Indonesia), provides an early example of such a city. A census in 1673 indicated that it had a total population of 27,068. This number included only 2,024 Dutch, along with 13,278 slaves, 611 Javanese, 981 Balinese, 2,747 Chinese, 1,339 South Asian Muslims, and 5,362 Portuguese-speaking Indonesian soldiers called *Mardijkers*.[38] This kind of profile remained much the same in the nineteenth and early twentieth centuries, with such cities having small European communities, a few Eurasians, various migrants from other colonies, usually some Chinese, and a majority of inhabitants from around the colony. The Europeans commonly included people born in the colony and other long-term residents as well as those who were there for shorter periods such as those in the upper ranks of the colonial civil service.

The city of Rangoon (recently re-named Yangon) was re-built after the Second Anglo-Burmese War in 1852 along plans designed by a member of the British engineering corps. Writing shortly after independence, Lewis described the city as "imperial and rectilinear. It was built by a people who refused compromise with the East, and has wide, straight, shadeless streets, with much solid bank-architecture of vaguely Grecian inspiration. In the town one is constantly taken back to Leadenhall Street; while down on the Rangoon river-front the style is that of the London Customs House."[39] As for the people living in the city during the colonial era, R. Talbot Kelly remarked, "on landing, the first impression received is the Indian character of the place, for among all its varied nationalities the Indian native seems to predominate. The dock coolies, in simple loincloth and turban, are mostly Madrassees or Chittagonians, the 'gharry' or cart, and 'tikka gharry,' or hired vehicle, walahs half-bred Indians, while in the street, ablaze with coloured costumes, the dominant types are Hindus, Tamils, Madressees, Cingalese, and Chinese. The Burman seems crowded out here.... Even the police in the streets are drawn from that fine body of men the Sikhs.... The Chinese are largely in evidence. Most of the river carrying trade is in their hands; quite the best shops and houses in the native quarters are theirs.... There is, of course, a large Burmese population in Rangoon, but it is mainly to be found in their own quarters."[40]

Kelly's observations are born out by census figures from the British colonial period. The 1931 census reported that more than half of the population of Rangoon (which was about 400,000 in the 1930s) was Indian. The Indians living there, however, were a mixed group including people from all over India. Indians (along with Chinese) comprised a significant portion of the city's middle class of merchants, traders, and landowners. The Chettiars were at the top of local Indian society. Indians owned a great deal of the land in Rangoon and they paid more than half of its municipal taxes. There were also many Indians in the city's lower classes. Large numbers of migrant workers arrived by sea in Rangoon. Some moved on elsewhere in the country, but a significant number remained to work in Rangoon.

The number of Europeans (mainly English) living in the city was quite small, but they included most of the colony's administrative and managerial elite. There was also a small Eurasian population that held posts in the colonial administration and in British-owned firms. As noted by Kelly, the Chinese were especially important around the waterfront, where the city's Chinatown and a number of Chinese temples (such as the Hokkien Association's Kheng Hock Keong Temple) are located. There was also a population of white-collar middle class Burmese. This group consisted of Burmese who had taken advantage of British colonial rule to leave their villages and attend school and take many of the newly created salaried and professional positions available in Rangoon and other large towns. For the most part each of these ethnic groups lived in residentially distinct areas. Under British rule the city also attracted a small but significant number of Tai-speaking Shan from the Shan states (1,277 in the 1872 census). In the surrounding area they became market gardeners that provided produce to the urban market.

Since we will be discussing Singapore later in the chapter, mention should be made here of that city as well. Founded in 1819 by Stamford Raffles of the British East India Company, the city remained under British rule until 1963. Like Rangoon, under British rule the city attracted large numbers of Indian and Chinese migrants and considerably fewer Malays from the neighboring Malay Peninsula. Singapore's population in 1921 was 425,912 — 414,230 of these were classified as Asiatics, 6,231 were Europeans (about 1.5 percent of the population), and 5,451 were Eurasians. The Asian population included a large number of migrants from China, followed by South Asians, and the Malays. Both the Chinese and South Asian populations were mixed groups. The Chinese were predominantly from various ethno-linguistics groups in southern China. The Europeans were overwhelmingly from Britain, but also included significant numbers of people from other English-speaking countries such as the United States and Australia as well as others from Western Europe.

Singapore was an important colonial administrative and economic center in Asia. Singapore along with the Straits Settlements was made a separate administrative entity from India in 1867. Singapore served as the seat of government for the Straits Settlements that included Penang and Malacca as well as several other territories such as the Cocos Islands and Christmas Island and later responsibility for Labuan and Brunei was added. Singapore's transnational character was enhanced as it emerged as an important regional financial and commercial center. Its importance was evident from the number of ships that passed through the city. *The Colonial Office List* for 1924 notes, "Over 50 lines of seagoing steamers touch at Singapore."[41] There was regular service to England via Sri Lanka and India and to the Netherlands. Within the region there was regular service to the Dutch East Indies, Hong Kong, China, Japan, Vietnam, Siam, and Australia. The value of Singapore's trade peaked in 1926 at U.S. $1.9 billion before declining to U.S. $500 million by 1933.[42] Over half of the trade was with Europe and North America with 60 percent of this amount going to the United States.

The companies based in Singapore included a number of agencies for British and other firms as well as local firms that traded within the region and several large firms owned by local Chinese. Paterson, Simons & Co. provides an example of an important Singapore-based trading company. Rawson, Holdsworth and Co. established the original company named Holdsworth, Smithson and Co. in Singapore in 1821. The company became Paterson, Simons & Co. in 1859. The company was one of the earliest trading houses in Singapore and dealt in a wide range of goods. It exported tropical products including copra and pineapples (and later rubber) from the Malay Peninsula, Borneo, and the Dutch East Indies to Europe and elsewhere and imported cloth and other manufactured goods from Europe. The company also became an agent or representative for numerous shipping lines (e.g., the Ben Line, Gibb Line, Union Line, Mogul Line, Nippon Yusen Kaisha, and the Tata Line), insurance companies, and a variety of other firms. Within the region it served as an agent mining companies such as the Pahang Kabang, numerous companies involved in plantation agriculture, and for the Jahore Government. Prior to World War I the company itself had opened branches in Penang, Kuala Lumpur, Klang, and Port Swettenham.

Singapore was also home to a number of important retail companies that served domestic and regional markets. Among the best known of these is Robinson & Co., which was established by Australian Phillip Robinson and James G. Spicer (who had been keeper of the Singapore jail) in 1858 under the name Spicer and Robinson. It became Robinson & Co. in 1859 after Spicer left the partnership and was replaced by George Rappa, Jr. Robinson sent sales representatives throughout the surrounding region and King Mongkut of Siam was among the company's customers. Phillip Robinson died in 1886 and his son Stamford Raffles Robinson took over the business with A.W. Bean as his partner. Under his direction in the 1890s the company expanded the number of its representative traveling in Malaya and later opened stores in Kuala Lumpur.

United Engineers Ltd. provides an example of a local engineering firm that also came to play an important regional role. Richard Riley and William Hargraves formed the company Riles, Hargraves & Co. in 1865. The company built bridges, the Fort Canning Lighthouse, and steamships. Samuel Erskine and J. Howarth founded Howarth, Erskine & Co. in 1875. Their company specialized in the design and construction of iron and steel structures and waterworks. The two companies were joined in 1912 to become United Engineers Ltd. As the company's history notes, "From the very beginning, the Group was a well established Asian company with presence in Malaysia, Thailand, Hong Kong, China and Singapore." Its activities in Malaya expanded with its acquisition of Federated Engineering Company of Kuala Lumpur. During the 1920s the company was manufacturing or importing a great deal of the heavy equipment used by Singapore's industries. The company played a major role in Singapore's construction boom in the 1930s. In 1932 it also became the local distributor for Carrier air conditioners (the American Dr. Willis Carrier had invented the air conditioner in 1902). The company installed Singapore's first air conditioner in the Chinese Club (European clubs such as the Tanglin Club were air conditioned only later).

World War II and its immediate aftermath brought an end to the European colonial world that led to the transformation of the European imperial and colonial cities. London and Paris remained important global cities in economic terms and became magnets for migrants from around the world (especially from former colonies), but were no longer at the center of vast empires. The fates of colonial cities varied. Those that had been the capital of colonies commonly became the capitals of newly independent countries and those that had been ports remained ports, but the relations of these capitals and ports to the world were often altered in relation to the foreign relations of the newly independent countries. Singapore emerged from the destruction of World War II once again to become a major regional commercial center and to expand its global importance. In contrast, Rangoon began to retreat from the world, especially after 1962 when the country's military rulers largely cut the country off from the outside world.

The rise of communism in the post–World War II also played a role in the direction taken by those former colonial cities that found themselves under communist rule. The French left Hanoi after their defeat in 1954 and many of the Vietnamese who had sided with them or who were opposed to the communists left as well, either migrating to France or to South Vietnam, which remained free from communist rule until 1975. To the extent that Hanoi maintained a transnational existence in the years immediately after 1954 these were primarily with its communist allies, especially the Soviet Union and its Eastern European satellites. Foreigners, however, had to live in closed compounds and relations between foreigners and Vietnamese were tightly regulated.

Megacities and Global Cities

Two categories of city are of special concern to the study of modern transnationalism: the megacity and the global city. Megacities are cities with populations in excess of 10 million people. Such cities are a feature of the modern world and did not exist in the past. They reflect not only the growing population of the world but also the increasing concentration of that population in urban areas. In 1800, cities were smaller and they were few in number. Only about 3 percent of the world's population lived in cities and a city of a few hundred thousand people was considered huge. Beijing, with an estimated population of 1.1 million, was the largest city in the world in 1800, followed by London (861,000), Guangzhou (about 800,000), and Edo (Tokyo) (685,000). The six other largest cities in the world, with populations ranging from 570,000 to 377,000 included two in Japan (Osaka and Kyoto), one other in China (Hangzhou), Constantinople, and Paris and Naples in Europe. The urban configuration of the world changed dramatically during the 1800s, mainly because of the Industrial Revolution and the rise of the West's political and economic influence. The average population of the world's ten largest cities was about 630,000 in 1800 and six out of ten of these cities were located in East Asia. In 1900 the average population of the ten largest cities was around 2.6 million and only one of these cities was in East Asia (Tokyo)—the other nine were in Europe or North America. The growth of British industry and imperial power saw London grow into the world's most populous and wealthiest city with a population of 6.5 million in 1900. Manchester was the ninth most populous city with a population of 1.4 million. New York City had grown from global insignificance to become the second most populous city in the world (4.2 million). Other cities on the top ten list with populations ranging from 3.3 million to 1.4 million included Paris, Berlin, Chicago (which was founded in 1833), Vienna, St. Petersburg, and Philadelphia.

The number of cities in the world with populations of over one million reached 83 in 1950. New York City had become the world's largest city (12.5 million), eclipsing London, which fell to the number two spot (8.9 million), and becoming the world's first megacity. The average population of the top ten cities had grown to over 6.5 million and, again, there was an interesting change in the configuration. Six of the top ten cities were still in Europe and North America (New York City, London, Paris, Moscow, Chicago, and the Rhine-Ruhr metropolitan region), but the list also included Tokyo (7 million), Shanghai, Buenos Aires, and Calcutta (Kolkata). The latter half of the 1900s witnessed a dramatic increase in global urbanization. By the end of the century an estimated 47 percent of the world's population lived in cities and there were almost 500 urban areas with populations of over 1 million. Moreover, as of 2007 there were 27 megacities in the world and the average population of the top ten had grown to 22 million people. The configuration of these large cities across the globe has continued to diversify with Asian cities assuming an increasing prominence in the list. Tokyo, having been on the top ten list since 1800, had risen to number one with a population of almost 34 million people. A group of six cities from several different parts of the globe with populations ranging from 25 to 20 million follows Tokyo: New York City, Seoul, Mexico City, Mumbai (Bombay), Delhi, and São Paulo. The remaining megacities are also widely scattered across the globe, but 10 of the 20 are from East Asia, Southeast Asia, and South Asia: Osaka, Shanghai, Kolkata, Manila, Jakarta, Karachi, Beijing, Dhaka, Lahore, and Bangkok. The other megacities include Los Angeles, Cairo, Tehran, London, Paris, Buenos Aires, Istanbul, Rio de Janeiro, Lagos, and Moscow.

Size is not everything and while all megacities have significant transnational aspects, the significance of transnationalism varies among these cities and there are also smaller (but not necessarily small) cities with even more important transnational characteristics.

The transnationalism of a city is linked to the second urban category mentioned above: the global city. Saskia Sassen coined the term global city (replacing an earlier term, world city).[43] While the term megacity focuses on the size of a city, the term global city emphasizes influence and connectedness. Global cities have an exceptional concentration of wealth, power, skills, and other resources. The concept focuses on economic factors and especially international commerce. Sassen also makes the important point that their global orientation results in a tendency for them to have more in common with one another than with other cities in their home countries.

There have been various ranking of global cities using a variety of criteria. A ranking conducted by A.T. Kearny and the Chicago Council on Global Affairs "focused on the 60 cities that shape our lives the most" using the criteria of business activity, human capital, information exchange, cultural experience, and political engagement.[44] The authors note, "The world's biggest, most interconnected cities help set global agendas, weather transnational dangers, and serve as hubs of global integration. They are the engines of growth for their countries and the gateways to the resources of their regions."[45] The top ten cities on their list are: New York, London, Paris, Tokyo, Hong Kong, Los Angeles, Singapore, Chicago, Seoul, and Toronto. It is interesting to note that only five of these cities appear on the list of 27 megacities. Looking at the list of megacities it is also informative to see where the 7 largest megacities are placed on the global cities list: Tokyo is no. 4, New York is no. 1, Mexico City is no. 25, Mumbai is no. 49, Delhi is no. 41, and São Paulo is no. 31. Such a difference reflects the extent to which Latin America and South Asia are a good deal less important globally than Europe, North America, and East Asia. The global importance of East Asia and Southeast Asia can be seen not only from the presence of 4 cities from the region in the top 10 (compared with 4 from North America and 2 from Europe) but more broadly from there being 10 East Asian cities on the list and 6 Southeast Asian cities. Sub-Saharan Africa in contrast provides only two cities on the list: Johannesburg no. 50 and Lagos no. 53.

The focus on economic criteria and international commerce should not blind us to other factors that make cities important globally. One in particular that comes to mind is religion. This criterion would place Rome, Mecca-Karbala, and Jerusalem at the top of the list, yet Rome is no. 30 on the *Foreign Affairs* global cities list and the other three are not on the list at all.

Contemporary Transnational Cities in Asia

If we look at contemporary cities of the world by size,[46] 13 of the top 25 cities are located in Asia as of 2009: two in Southeast Asia, six in East Asia, and five in South Asia:

    1 — Tokyo (Japan) — 33,800,000
    2 — Seoul (South Korea) — 23,900,000
    4 — Delhi (India) — 22,400,000
    5 — Mumbai (India) — 22,300,000

  8 — Manila (Philippines) — 19,200,000
10 — Shanghai (PRC) — 17,900,000
11 — Osaka (Japan) — 16,700,000
12 — Kolkata (India) — 16,000,000
13 — Karachi (Pakistan) — 15,700,000
14 — Guangzhou (PRC) — 15,300,000
15 — Jakarta (Indonesia) — 15,100,000
19 — Beijing (PRC) — 13,200,000
20 — Dhaka (Bangladesh) — 13,100,000

Size and a city's extent of transnationality, of course, do not necessarily correlate. It is also important to be aware that while all of the cities listed above do have many residents and institutions with transnational connections for some of these cities (e.g., Osaka, Kolkata, and Dhaka) such linkages are a relatively minor part of their overall urban landscape. Moreover, Hong Kong and Singapore, two of the region's most important transnational cities, while large, are quite a way down on the world ranking of cities by population: Hong Kong is no. 43 with 7.2 million people and Singapore is no. 71 with 4.7 million. Just how different cities of comparable size can be in terms of transnationality is perhaps most apparent in the cases of Yangon and Singapore, Southeast Asia's least and most transnational cities. Yangon has a population of 4,850,000 (no. 67), while Singapore has a population of 4,700,000 (no. 71). These two examples serve to point to the importance of post-colonial government policies in regard to transnationalism. Whereas Singapore's government has sought to promote ties to the outside world more than most other governments in the world and views itself essentially as a transnational trading state, the military rulers of Myanmar (Burma) have sought to limit ties between their country and the rest of the world as much as possible and created an atmosphere that is relatively hostile to transnationalism.

Even if national and city governments are relatively open to transnationalism, this does not mean that it will develop in a particular city to a significant extent — at least over a relatively short period. For example, whereas some of the PRC's coastal cities have become much more transnational since the 1990s, the country's interior cities remain far more isolated from the world outside of the PRC. This is in part a reflection of the lack of infrastructure connecting them to the outside world — a situation that is starting to change. The Chinese city of Chengdu (no. 61 worldwide in size and about the same size as Saigon), with a population of around 5.6 million (11 million counting the surrounding region), is the capital of the province of Sichuan and its leadership has aspirations of seeing it become a global city. There are relatively few overseas Chinese from Chengdu (or Sichuan) and historically ever since the Han conquered the city it has not been particularly international in its orientation. World War II was something of an exception in that the city became the capital of Chiang Kai-shek's Kuomintang government and a base of Allied operations against the Japanese. It was the last city to fall to communist forces in late 1949. Although most flights from Chengdu's Shuangliu International Airport are to domestic destinations there have been an increasing number of

international connections in recent years with direct flights now available to a number
of neighboring Asian countries and KLM flying to Amsterdam. The Chengdu Hi-Tech
Industrial Development Zone was approved in 1991 but only open to enterprises from
APEC countries in 2000. Chengdu is home to about 12,000 domestic companies. In contrast, so far only around 30 foreign enterprises have established branch plants (e.g., Intel,
IBM, NOKIA, Motorola, Siemens, Canon, Xerox, and Microsoft) and only a handful of
international financial institutions (HSBC, Standard Charter, AMRO, BNP Paribas) have
opened branches. Moreover, the number of resident expatriates remains relatively small,
although there are 10 international schools and about half a dozen foreign consulates.
Thus, Chengdu is becoming more transnational, but by world and even Chinese standards
it is still mainly simply a very large provincial city.

The major cities of Southeast Asia present an interesting array of transnational cities
(with the exception of Rangoon/Yangon):

  8 — Manila (Philippines) — 19,200,000
15 — Jakarta (Indonesia) — 15,100,000
31 — Bangkok (Thailand) — 8,750,000
57 — Saigon/Ho Chi Minh City (Vietnam) — 5,650,000
67 — Yangon/Rangoon (Burma) — 4,850,000
71 — Kuala Lumpur (Malaysia) — 4,700,000
71 — Singapore — 4,700,000

A ranking from the most to the least transnational would place Singapore as the
most, Manila a close second, Bangkok, Saigon, Kuala Lumpur, and Jakarta in the middle
range, and Yangon as the least. Let us look briefly at Singapore as a case study.

Singapore was a major international commercial and communications hub under
British rule and it remained so after independence in 1965. The government of independent Singapore has successfully pursued a policy of promoting industrialization, development of modern international financial and service sectors, and direct foreign
investment and at present the city-state has the fifth highest per capita income in the
world and massive foreign exchange reserves (over U.S. $170 billion). Although a mixed
group of ethnic Chinese form the majority (about three-quarters), the country also has
large Malay and South Asian ethnic communities as well as one of the largest percentages
of resident expatriates of any country in the world. The city-state's economy relies heavily
on imports and exports. This is reflected in its port being one of the busiest in the world
(e.g., until overtaken by Shanghai in 2005 it was the world's busiest port in terms of cargo
tonnage and most years ranks number one in terms of number of containers and trans-
shipment) and the fourth largest foreign exchange trading center in the world (after London, New York City, and Tokyo).

From a social perspective Singapore's transnationalism has several dimensions,
including the transnational orientation of its resident citizens, the transnationalism of
Singaporeans living abroad, and the transnationalism of its resident expatriates. State
policies immediately after independence tended to place restrictions on transnationalism.

Even before independence the government of Singapore in 1960 had prohibited dual citizenship. The number of non-citizens working in Singapore declined to 30,900 (2.9 percent of the population) in 1970. As Yeoh points out, "Although strict controls initially were imposed on unskilled foreign workers, these were relaxed as the country became more industrialized."[47] Singapore began attracting large numbers of unskilled workers for the manufacturing, construction, and domestic service sectors from other Asian countries such as India, Bangladesh, Sri Lanka, the Philippines, Indonesia, and Thailand. The number of non-citizens working in Singapore doubled in the 1980s and grew even more rapidly in the 1990s and early 2000s until by 2005 there were 797,700 non-citizens living in Singapore on resident permits, representing 18.3 percent of the population. As of 2006 there were also an additional 290,188 people (7.2 percent of the population) living in Singapore as Permanent Residents (they are entitled to most rights and duties of citizens, but cannot vote). While many of Singapore's resident citizens are descended from migrants who came to the country in the 1800s or early 1900s and have few if any functioning family connections to their country of origin, 2005 census data indicate that 596,108 residents (including citizens and Permanent Residents), representing 18.3 percent of the population, were born outside of Singapore: 306,998 in Malaysia, 163,503 in the PRC–Hong Kong–Taiwan, 61,308 in South Asia, 32,785 in Indonesia, and 15,137 elsewhere in Asia.

In an interview former prime minister Lee Kuan Yew remarked on the importance of these new migrants to maintain Singapore's economic position: "Over time the MM [minister mentor, Lee Kuan Yew] says, Singaporeans have become 'less hard-driving and hard-striving.' That is why it is a good thing, the MM says, that the nation has welcomed so many Chinese immigrants" and "describes the country's new subjects as 'hungry,' with parents who 'pushed the children very hard.'"[48]

There are in effect two categories of foreign workers in Singapore: (1) unskilled and low skilled and (2) skilled (including professional and managerial workers, who are referred to as "foreign talent"). About 580,000 of the 670,000 foreign workers in the country in 2006 were in the first category with the remaining 90,000 in the second. Government policies toward these two categories of workers are quite different. Government policy discourages unskilled and low-skilled migrant workers in particular from trying to settle permanently in Singapore. Once in the country they are only allowed to work for the employer and in the type of job designated in their work permit and once their employment is over they are required to leave the country within seven days. Such migrants are not allowed to bring their families with them and may not marry Singaporeans.

In contrast to unskilled migrant workers, government policy is to encourage highly skilled workers to come to Singapore. This is related to the government's desire to see Singapore as a global center not only in finance but also in technical areas such as information technology. Not only has the government made it increasingly easier for skilled workers to become Permanent Residents, but it has also made an effort to make living in Singapore appear more attractive to such professionals. This has included, in particular, a push to develop the arts in the city-state — such as an initiative to promote Singapore as a "Global City for the Arts." These policies are predicated not only on the government's desire to sustain a high level of economic development but also from concern over the relatively low birth rate on the part of Singaporean citizens (1.24 children per woman in 2005).

The number of people who make the transition from Permanent Resident to citizen in Singapore is fairly small. During the early 2000s only about 6,000 to 7,000 people per year became citizens. Government efforts to make becoming a citizen easier resulted in the number increasing to about 13,000 people in 2005. To apply for citizenship a Permanent Resident must be at least 21 years old and have resided in Singapore for at least six years immediately prior to the application for citizenship. There are also checks on their suitability in terms of being of good character and being in a financial position to support themselves and any dependents. Despite recent increases in the number of people becoming citizens, whereas Singapore allows a large number of foreigners to reside and work in the city-state, the vast majority of these people remain expatriates and only a very small percentage of those who migrate to Singapore settle and become citizens.

In the past most of the skilled professionals migrating to Singapore came from English-speaking countries (primarily the United Kingdom, the United States, and Australia) or from Japan and South Korea. Since the 1990s a large number have also come from India and the China.

Transnationalism among Singaporean citizens assumes a number of forms. Given the large number of enterprises in Singapore that are either foreign owned or do a significant amount of their business internationally, many Singaporeans are either employed directly by firms with significant international interests themselves or that do business with such firms. As members of an affluent society many Singaporeans are able not only to travel abroad for holidays but many of them also spend extended periods outside of Singapore as students or in relation to work. While Singapore itself boasts highly respected tertiary institutions, many young Singaporeans still choose to study abroad — primarily in English speaking countries. In 2008, for example, there were 8,848 Singaporeans studying in tertiary institutions in Australia[49] as well as another 15,000 Singaporeans studying in Singapore at Australian affiliated institutions. Another 5,000 and 6,000 Singaporeans study in the United Kingdom with the United States also being a major destination for Singaporean students.

In addition to students and other Singaporeans temporarily living abroad, there are a large number of people of Singaporean ancestry or who themselves were born in Singapore living outside of Singapore — especially in Australia, the United Kingdom, the United States, and Canada. In recent years there has been an increasing amount of fictional writing dealing with the lives of these overseas Singaporeans[50] along with numerous websites devoted to Singaporean expats.[51] In the case of the United Kingdom, there are a little over 40,000 Singaporean-born people living there — over 9,000 of them in London and most living in the surrounding area (about 3,000 in Scotland and 300 in Northern Ireland). Singaporean migration to Australia dates back to the gold rush days, when there were a few dozen Chinese Singaporean migrants, and then picking up again recently (966 in 200 and 1,464 in 2002). The Museum of Victoria in its *Origins* website on immigrant communities in Victoria writes: "Between 1986 and 1996 the size of the community in Victoria doubled to 6,557 people. In 2001, 7,661 Victorians were Singapore-born in 2001. Today most live in urban Melbourne, and 43% are aged between 15 and 29, reflecting the high proportion of students. Many are employed as professionals, and work in property and business services. The Singapore-born population in Victoria is predominantly of Chinese ethnicity, followed by Malay and Indian. Almost half are Christians; a further 20% are Buddhists or Muslims. The most common language spoken at home is English, followed by Mandarin and Cantonese. Organisations supporting the Singaporean community in Victoria include the Merlion Club, which fosters business networks and community fellowship."[52]

Around 800 Singaporeans give up their citizenship each year. A survey by Singapore Polytechnic in 2009 reported that more than half of the Singaporean youths aged 15 to 20 said that they would migrate if given the opportunity.[53] This loss of people and the threat of even greater losses in the future have helped to prompt debate within Singapore about the granting of dual citizenship and to lead the government in 2006 to establish the Overseas Singaporean Unit to coordinate and initiate programs to engage overseas Singaporeans and make them feel more an integral part of Singapore society.

4

Marriage and Families

Marriage and the creation of family networks across state boundaries are an extremely important component of transnationalism. There are a variety of forms of transnational marriage. These include alliances between elites across borders, transnational marriages within ethnic or national groups, and inter-ethnic transnational marriages. Once these marriages take place there are issues concerning the type of family that is created. Within the immediate family the important question here concerns the extent to which it becomes a transnational family — i.e., to what extent are linguistic and cultural traditions of the migrating spouse maintained and to what extent are relationships with relatives of the migrating spouse maintained. The degree of assimilation of the family may have some impact on this. Relative wealth is also a factor, although in general it is easier now for even the poor to maintain transnational relations through communication (e.g., mail, telephone, and internet) and visits than in the past. Governments on both ends play a role as well: especially the extent to which governments in the home country of the migrating spouse allow communication and travel and the policies of the country of residence concerning encouragement of marriage to non-nationals.

Marriage Alliances Between Elites Across Borders

Transnational marriages of elites probably date back to the earliest chieftanships as powerful figures sought to enhance their position and forge alliances through marriages with surrounding groups. This pattern of international political marriage persisted with the formation of early states and the histories of most states and empires includes numerous references to such marriages. Cleopatra VII Philopator (69–30 BC) of Egypt's marriage to the Roman Marcus Antonius (Mark Antony) provides one of the most famous examples of such transnational elite marriages in the ancient world. Transnational marriages were relatively common among the feudal elites of medieval and early modern Europe and remained widespread in the modern period. Among the more famous of such transnational marriages towards the end of the period of absolute monarchs in Europe was the marriage between Marie Antoinette of Austria and Louis XVI of France. Marie Antoinette

Josèphe Jeanne de Habsbourg-Lorraine (1755–93) was born in Vienna to the Holy Roman Emperor Francis I and the Empress of Austria, Maria Theresa. She married Louis-Auguste, the Dauphin of France, when she was 14. After the death of Louis XV, Louis-August became King Louis XVI of France and Marie Antoinette became Queen of France and Navarre. Louis XVI was deposed during the French Revolution and during the Reign of Terror in 1793 she was beheaded.

As the political power of Europe's feudal aristocracy declined, transnational marriages to European aristocrats assumed a new role in the late 1800s and early 1900s in providing respectability to newly rich capitalists from the United States. Writing about the French Riviera at this time, Galbraith remarks, "the Riviera was pre-eminently the resort of the European aristocracy, and from this came its major service. Daughters of the American rich could here be traded for the esteem that went with older landed wealth or title, or sometimes merely the title. By this single simple step the new wealth achieved the respectability of age."[1] He cites the example of the Churchill family with its palace at Blenheim and title of Marlborough: "It was natural, therefore, that a Duke of Marlborough should marry Consuelo Vanderbilt for a initial payment of $2,500,000. More was later invested in repairing Blenheim, which was run down, and a great new London house. In all, the Marlborough connection cost around $10 million. The results, however, were excellent. The robber-baron connotation was almost completely excised from the Vanderbilt family tradition."[2] This business saw the appearance of marriage brokers ("often impoverished women of imagined social rank") and Galbraith highlights the scale of the business: "By 1909, by one estimate, 500 American heiresses had been exported for the improvement of the family name, along with $220 million."[3]

Although modern nationalist politics may have made transnational marriages among political elites less popular than in the past they continue to take place. Queen Elizabeth II and Prince Philip provide a contemporary example of a transnational marriage among political elites. Prince Philip was born on the island of Corfu in Greece as Prince Philippos of Greece and Denmark in 1921. His father was Prince Andrew of Greece and Denmark (1882–1944), who was a son of King George I of Greece (1845–1913) and a member of the German House of Schleswig-Holstein-Sonderburg-Glücksburg, which includes the royal houses of Greece and Denmark as well as Norway. George I's wife was Grand Duchess Olga Konstantinova of Russia (1851–1926). His mother was Queen Olga of Greece. Formerly she had been Princess Alice of Battenberg. She was a daughter of the First Marquis of Milford Haven (formerly Prince Louis of Battenberg) and Lady Milford Haven (formerly Princess Victoria of Hesse and by Rhine). Lady Milford Haven's mother was the Grand Duchess of Hesse and by Rhine. Princess Alice was also a granddaughter of Queen Victoria of Britain and sister of Queen Louise of Sweden. He gave up his Greek and Danish titles shortly before he married Princess Elizabeth, the daughter of King George VI of Britain in 1947.

There are contemporary examples of transnational marriages among political elites from other parts of the world as well. Jordan's King Abdullah II's wife Queen Rania (Rania Al-Yassin), for example, was born in Kuwait to Palestinian parents who were from Tulkarm, Palestine. Queen Rania studied Business Administration at the American University in Cairo, Egypt, and then went to work for Citibank and Apple Computer in Amman,

Jordan, after graduation. The case of Sonia Gandhi is an especially interesting one that highlights to political problems that may accompany a transnational marriage in the modern world of nationalist politics. Former Indian Prime Minister Rajiv Gandhi (son of Indira Gandhi and grandson of Jawaharlal Nehru) married Edvige Antonia Albina Maiono (Sonia Gandhi) from Italy (born 1946). Rajiv attended university at Cambridge University in the United Kingdom where Sonia was attending the Bell Educational Trust's language school. They met in a Greek restaurant in 1965 and after marrying moved to India where they lived with his mother for several years and he worked as an airline pilot. Rajiv initially remained out of politics, but became involved after the death of his younger brother Sanjay in 1980. Rajiv was elected prime minister after the assassination of his mother in 1984 and Sonia was forced into public life. Her foreign birth sparked criticism from extreme nationalist elements. After Rajiv's assassination in 1991, Sonia became more directly involved in politics and criticism of her foreign birth by nationalists such as those associated with the Bharatiya Janata Party, but within the Congress Party as well, increased. Despite such criticism she became President of the Congress Party, an elected member of the Lok Sabha, and chairperson of the ruling United Progressive Alliance within the Lok Sabha.

Transnational marriages by contemporary feudal elites can have adverse consequences in the face of nationalist sentiments or elitist traditions. Thun Kramom Ying Ubolratana Rajakanya Sirivadhana Barnavadi (aka Ubolratana, born 1951), the eldest daughter of Thailand's King Bhumibol and Queen Sirikit, for example, was forced to relinquish her royal titles when she married American Peter Ladd Jensen. Ubolratana was born in Lausanne, Switzerland, prior to her father's return to Thailand and assumption of the throne following the death of his older brother. Ubolratana studied mathematics at MIT and public health at UCLA in the United States. She had met Peter Ladd while at MIT and in 1972 they married and settled in the United States. By marrying a commoner (and it did not help that he was a foreigner) she was forced to give up her royal titles and was given the title Thanpuying (i.e., Dame) Ubol Ratana Jensen in their place. The couple had three children and initially relations between Ubolratana and her family in Thailand were limited. Relations eventually improved and she paid a visit to her family in Thailand in 1980 and made several trips to Thailand over the next several years in relation to important family events (e.g., the wedding of her younger sister Princess Chulabhorn in 1982, the celebration of her father's sixtieth birthday in 1987, the celebration of her mother's sixtieth birthday in 1992, and the funeral of her grandmother in 1996). Members of her family also paid Ubolratana occasional visits in the United States during this period as well. Ubolratana and her husband divorced in 1998 and she and her family moved to Thailand in 2001. No longer married to a foreigner and commoner, Ubolratana was given a new quasi-royal title of *Tunkramom Ying* without restoring the royal *Chao Fa* title to her.

Transnational Marriages Within Ethno-National Groups

Many of the pioneer migrants who settled away from their country of origin in the past were single males who settled within ethnic enclaves where there were relatively few women. Marriage to women of other ethnic groups already living in the country was sometimes a possibility and this tended to hasten assimilation of the male migrants and lessen the prospects of maintaining not only a distinct ethnic identity but also transnational connection to the country of origin. A second option was to seek a spouse from one's country or place of origin and to bring her to the new country as a migrant. This strategy tended not only to reinforce a distinct ethnic identity in the country of settlement, but also to perpetuate at least a degree of transnationalism, especially where the assistance of co-ethnics was used in obtaining a bride.

Mail-Order and Picture Brides

Settler immigrants seeking a spouse from their country of origin or ancestry or from the same ethnic group within that country may visit the country themselves in search of a spouse, but often they remain where they have settled and turn to an intermediary to assist in arranging a marriage. This was especially true in the past when travel was more difficult and costly. Such forms of matchmaking may be done by members of the immigrant's own family, by friends, or by professional matchmakers or matchmaking firms. Providing so-called mail-order brides to single male settlers dates to the early days of European settlement in the New World. Thus, in 1619 the Virginia Company of London sent 90 single English women to the Jamestown settlement with their passage being paid for in tobacco: "one hundredth and fiftie [pounds] of the best leafe Tobacco" per woman. Mail-order brides from Europe continued to go to the United States during the 1700s and 1800s, sometimes coming from the same country as the man seeking the marriage but sometimes from other European countries as well.

As was discussed in the chapter on migration, most of the East Asian migrants (e.g., from Japan, China, and Korea) coming to English-speaking settler colonies in the 1800s and early 1900s were either single unmarried males or married males who left their wives behind. Those who remained to settle in the new country either brought their wives over to join them or often sought to arrange for their marriage to a woman from their country of birth and then to bring her to the new country. Many of these women came as so-called picture brides, referring to the use of photographs of the men and women in seeking to arrange a marriage.

Makabe provides accounts of the experiences of Japanese picture brides coming to Canada in the early 1900s.[4] She notes that Japan at the time was undergoing rapid social and economic change in the form of industrialization and urbanization and, while it was not impossible for young women to go to the big cities and find work ... it was almost impossible for a country-bred, uneducated, ordinary woman to become independent, either economically or socially. Going to Canada or the United States was practically the only means of improving one's status."[5] The author notes of the women she interviewed, they had "a strong drive to work and make money.... They also declared that if passage from Japan had been unrestricted they might have crossed the ocean alone, not as brides.... From the brides' viewpoint, a typical attitude was 'I would have married anybody, as long as I could get to America.'"[6] She also reminds us that arranging marriages for "practical reasons" was fairly common in Japan at that time.[7] Here is one of the women's accounts of her desire to migrate and how her marriage was arranged: "From our village, two of us came to Canada.... In some parts of Oshima-gun, a lot of people emigrated to Hawaii or Canada, depending on the village. I'd heard tell of people from my village who'd gone to Hawaii. My cousin had gone too. But if you looked at the whole village, there weren't many emigrants ... I wanted like anything to go to America, even though if couldn't have known anything about the country. My cousin was in Seattle, and he was running a big business with his wife. We wrote to each other, and it seemed America was such a good place to live that I started wanting to go.... My cousin had gone from Hawaii to the U.S. and was working in tailoring and sundries, and in his photos he looked as if he was really living in style.... My husband's village was about three miles from mine, and people there heard that I wanted to go to America. My husband's parents came around, saying that it was just about time for their son to get married, so our parents decided on it. I was still only 18 years old, I didn't know what kind of man he was, but I was happy as long as I could get to America. It was easy to make money in America. My family was poor."[8] Her husband was 30 at the time and, as was common practice, there was a wedding ceremony without the groom being present in his parent's house. The woman sailed to Canada with two other brides.

Most Japanese-Canadians at the time lived in British Columbia and many of the men worked in the forest or fishing industry. The society that they lived in was a very closed one in which people worked very hard and rarely interacted with people outside of their own ethnic group. Thus, Japanese-Canadian society prior to World War II developed largely in isolation from the wider Canadian society: "Canada was to the very end a foreign society that had little relation to them."[9] Some male migrants returned to Japan or moved on to the United States, while for those who remained in Canada ties back to Japan were maintained primarily through letters. For the picture brides, their trip to North America was almost always a one-way trip and the mail also formed their primary link with Japan.

After Japan annexed Korea in 1910, Koreans also became involved in arranging picture bride marriages. In her description of Korean picture brides in Hawaii, Kim makes the point, "Single Korean men [in Hawaii] sent for picture brides not necessarily because they could not find other women to marry — although that was true in many cases — but mainly because they specifically wanted to marry a Korean woman."[10] In the relatively open multi-ethnic environment of Hawaii at the time there were more opportunities for migrants to marry across ethnic boundaries than was the case for Japanese in British Columbia. One of Kim's informants said, "Neighborhood people with eligible daughters just wanted to marry their daughters off to my pap. There was this Portuguese man who wanted my papa to marry his nice-looking daughter. There was another Hawaiian family who had to have my papa as a son-in-law." In response to one generous offer, "Papa said he wanted the house and the lot, but he couldn't think of marrying anyone except a Korean girl."[11] For the Korean picture brides coming to Hawaii, in addition to ties back home through the mail, many of them also became actively involved in the Korean independence movement, which had an active and important base in the Korean migrant community in Hawaii. Thus, Korean women in Honolulu formed the Korean Women's Relief Society in 1919 as part of their effort to promote the cause of Korean independence.

The picture bride system was also widely used among some European and Middle Eastern migrant groups. Papanikolas writes of Greek immigrant picture brides coming to the United States in the early 1900s: "Young Greek women arrived, each sent by her family with a picture in hand to recognize the man she was to marry. A few women were fortunate to have a mother or father accompany them until the wedding took place, after which they returned to Greece. Several brides often traveled together, but most came alone and afraid."[12] One of the problems of course (and this was true with Japanese and Korean migrants as well) is that the photos did not always look much like the brides or grooms when they met: "Chicanery ruled: a younger, prettier sister's picture; a photograph of a better-looking friend with a full head of hair, or of the handsome American movie actor Rudolf Valentino."[13]

Members of the widely dispersed Armenian diaspora who had survived the Turkish genocide also often resorted to the picture system of arranged marriages. Kaprielian–Churchill writes, "Armenian and non–Armenian newspapers and tracing agencies and a far-flung informal network of family, friends and compatriots served to reunite families and to bring together eligible men and women. Through the auspices of intermediaries men and women in places as distant as Brantford, Ontario and Beirut, Lebanon, were linked up. In the pre–Genocide society, certain individuals had engaged in matchmaking, but in the post–Genocide period, everyone became a potential matchmaker: a woman chose a mate for her son and brought the girl to Canada with her; another woman picked a girlfriend from her orphanage for her brother in the United States; a man selected a bride for his nephew in Argentina. Another man travelled to Marseilles where he found his prospective wife, the cousin of a friend, in a shipload of refugees who had landed the previous day. They married and returned to Canada on the return voyage of the same ship that had brought him to France." In regard to the use of photos, she writes, "Sometimes, after being linked up by a matchmaker, a man and woman exchanged photos and corresponded. If they liked each other, the man proposed" and provides an example in one of the narratives: "A person came from Canada to our village. A friend in Canada had asked him to find him a suitable girl. He said he would pay all the necessary costs of bringing the girl to Canada. The visitor thought I was suitable. He showed me a man's picture. We didn't write, just a picture. I came here. We saw each other here. I arrived here on December 1 and was married on December 21."[14]

Communication and travel are easier today and while there are modern versions of male order and picture brides it is more common today for people looking for spouses from their country of origin or ancestry to travel there themselves and meet the prospective spouse face-to-face. Even where face-to-face meetings take place this often occurs after an initial connection is made by intermediaries or by one of those involved in response to advertisements.

Transnational Indian Arranged Marriages

While many overseas Indians find spouses within the country where they reside these days, quite a few also seek spouses either in India or from among Overseas Indians living in other countries. Thus, Indo-Fijian parents of Gujarat origin will sometimes send a daughter on a chaperoned world tour to explore marriage possibilities—the preference being a spouse from a comparable background. Nearby Overseas Indian communities in Australia and New Zealand are the most common hunting grounds and this works both ways with ethnic Indian families in these countries also sometimes looking to Fiji for spouses for their children. Thus if an ethnic Indian family in Australia hears of an Indo-Fijian family with a marriageable daughter they may contact her parents who, if interested, will supply her photo. If things go well, the girl's father may then travel to Australia to start making arrangements.

Divakaruni has surveyed thirty years of matrimonial columns in *The Times of India* and discovered a number of trends relating to transnational marriages. He comments, "The first ad I cited from 1969, when the original swell of Indian immigrants came to the United States, declared that the bride-to-be should be willing to go abroad. This would demonstrate her adaptability: she agreed to endure the hardships of a strange land. But resettlement was certainly not something that either she or her parents would wish for: the popular feeling was that only boys who couldn't make it in the home country went abroad. As late as 1979 expatriate men looking for hometown wives needed to prove their worth and not be finicky.... Over the course of the next twenty years the tide turned. By 1989 being a prospective groom or (rarer) bride who lived abroad was a distinct advantage. Someone thus situated could unabashedly demand more.... And although England, Canada, or Australia was acceptable, by last year [1999] the United States had become the destination of choice, for which many bargaining points were willingly surrendered.... By last year *The Times of India* had a long column titled 'NRI [nonresident Indian]/Green Card.' And the Internet had arrived in the marriage supermarket.... As more immigrants settle abroad, NRIs are beginning to prefer other NRIs, or at least 'Green card holder H-1 visa'—a status that allows the recipient to live and work in the United States for long periods. This is in part to ensure cultural compatibility and in part a response to a prevalent urban legend about unscrupulous Indians who marry NRIs in order to get a green card and then shrug off their spouses with a quick divorce."[15]

The improved status of Overseas Indians in the overall Indian marriage market is highlighted in a recent quote by an Overseas Indian living in Australia who told a reporter from *The Australian,* "There is a lot of interest in leaving India and an Indian-born person with Australian permanent residence who is looking for a spouse is in a favourable situation in selecting an attractive partner."[16] The quotation is cited in an article on what is referred to as "a surging number of Indian brides heading the migration growth in Australia."[17] The article notes that in the year 2007-8 Indian-born migrants in Australia sponsored 2,782 brides and 496 grooms, an increase from 434 brides and 149 grooms in the year 1996-7, while the total number of visas issued under Australia's spouse and fiancée program to Indians increased from 25,500 in 1996-7 to 38,931 in 2007-8. A large number of the migrants who are sponsoring brides and grooms from India entered the country under the category of skilled migrant: 15,865 migrants from India applied for permanent residence in Australia under the skilled migration program in 2006-7. Bhandari cites the example of "Mamta, 29, [who] came to Australia two years ago on a spouse visa, which she got six months after getting married. Her husband, an electrical engineer, had come to Sydney four years ago under the skilled migrant programme."[18]

Transnational Chinese Arranged Marriages

Oxfeld provides a case study of transnational marriages between members of ethnic Hakka Chinese communities in Calcutta and Toronto and residents of Mei Xian County in Guangdong Province, China.[19] She refers to these as "marriages in a de-territorialized community," noting the "de-territorialized community in this case is created at least in part by the very marriage alliances across national borders" that she describes.[20] The county has a history of people migrating to Southeast Asia and India as far back as the 1800s. During the 1800s and early 1900s young men who were about to migrate would sometimes marry before leaving. The fate of these marriages varied with the men occasionally sending for their wives once they had successfully established themselves economically abroad, others merely sent money back to their wives but never themselves returned, while others were never heard from again and either died or established new lives abroad. She describes one fairly typical marriage in which the woman went to live in the home of her future husband while an infant, where she was referred to as a "little daughter-in-law."[21] When the two came of age they were married and her husband migrated to India with his brother. He returned after a few years for a brief visit, she became pregnant with a son, and he went back to India. He returned once more, this time she became pregnant with a daughter, and he then went back to India and she never heard from him again. On a happier note, Oxfeld mentions the case of a man who migrated to Calcutta in 1936, where he established a tannery and once it became successful he sent for his fiancée, who had been living with his family, and his younger brother.[22] The economic success of such migrants appears to have played a major role in determining the fate of the marriage or engagement.

After the communists seized power in China, maintaining links between Hakka in China and overseas became difficult: "The policies of the Communist government did not favor families with overseas relatives. Not only were there practical difficulties in traveling in and out of China, but a woman's natal family could actually suffer as a result of having an overseas Chinese relation." While initially remittances could still be sent, actual visits by relatives living overseas were rarely possible, and during the period of the Cultural Revolution in the late 1960s and its aftermath in the 1970s almost all contact between Chinese Hakka families and their relatives overseas were cut: "'If you had an overseas Chinese relative,' one villager told me, 'they might even accuse you of being a spy. So people, if they had any connections, just kept it a secret.'"[23] The communists began to reverse this isolationist policy after 1978 and not only did they make it easier for family members to renew their connections with relatives overseas, but gradually they came to encourage such links.

Oxfeld's study highlights the multi-state nature of such transnational ethnic marriage networks. As with Overseas Indians, Overseas Hakka not only marry Hakka from China, but also Overseas Hakka living in countries other than their own. Many Hakka and other

Chinese in India were deported or interned during the Sino-Indian conflict of 1962. This treatment by the Indian government left many of the Hakka living in Calcutta, where Oxfeld conducted her study, feeling insecure and "By the early 1980s, emigration of some family members had become an important strategy for the Calcutta Chinese, economically and politically, and there are now few Calcutta Chinese families who do not have at least some family members who live abroad."[24] Toronto is a particularly popular locale to search for a spouse and migrate. As Oxfeld notes, this trend made it more difficult for those who remain in Calcutta to find a spouse and resulted in young men increasingly looking to China for brides. Looking for a bride is somewhat different today than it was in the past, however, since Hakka women in China are more independent than they were in the past: "While 'love marriages,' or marriages where the partners choose each other based on an emotional and romantic bond, are still in the minority, almost all marriages in Mei Xian are at least undertaken by mutual consent. A matchmaker may introduce a couple, or try to set up a channel of communication between them, but ultimately the decision is theirs."[25] The relative independence of young Hakka women from Mei Xian has made it more difficult for Overseas Hakka to find a bride there than in the past. Even when a young woman's parents may favor such a proposed union the young woman has veto power and may well already have a local boy friend.

Relative Status and Vietnamese Transnational Marriages

Constable draws attention to issues related to the relative statuses of transnational marriage partners.[26] While sometimes women marry men of higher socio-economic status than themselves in transnational marriages, as she notes, "Contrary to popular assumptions, the brides [in transnational marriages] are not necessarily poor, nor do they categorically marry men who are above them on the socioeconomic ladder."[27] Even though the bride's home country may be poorer than that of the groom, the bride herself is not necessarily poor. Modern transnational marriages often involve brides from the middle class in their home countries, where, as Constable remarks, "a middle-class income can afford them meals out, maids, entertainment, and other luxuries that are far more expensive and difficult to come by in the United States, Western Europe, or Japan."[28] In her study of Filipina-Japanese marriages, Suzuki examines "the tensions between the lived realities of Filipinas married to Japanese and their Filipino families' fantasies about the women's presumed upward mobility through transnational marriage" and the "clash between lived realities and imaginations" of the brides themselves once they settle into such a transnational marriage and find that in some ways they have married down and face unexpected hardships.[29]

Thai examines such status difference in Vietnamese transnational marriages between those who are to some extent unmarriageable in their respective countries, highly educated women in Vietnam and low-wage ethnic Vietnamese males in the United States.[30] The difficulties faced by such people are in part related to the demographics of their respective societies. As a result of warfare during the 1960s and 1970s Vietnam, as is often the case with countries that have been at war, subsequently found itself with more women than men, an imbalance that persisted even two decades after the war. The imbalance is even more marked in the overseas Vietnamese (*Viet Kieu*) population, but in reverse. Within Vietnam, this demographic situation has made it difficult for some women to find husbands, including those with higher education who are somewhat older than the norm when they start to look for a husband because of the years that they have spent in school. *Viet Kieu* people with lower incomes are disadvantaged in their search for a spouse by their relative lack of wealth. One option is to marry outside of the ethnic Vietnamese community, but low-income (and generally lowly educated) *Viet Kieu* are less likely to be in a position to do this since they generally are more cut off from the surrounding society than their co-ethnics who are wealthier and better educated. The result on the one hand is a number of highly educated women in Vietnam looking for husbands from abroad (*Viet Kieu* or others) and on the other hand, poor and poorly educated *Viet Kieu* men looking for brides in Vietnam. As Thai illustrates, where such marriages occur there are often problems because of a clash of expectations since the men want traditional wives while the women are hoping for a husband who is more liberal in outlook.

As in the case of the Hakka Chinese, the contemporary rise in the number of Vietnamese transnational marriages has been made possible by changing policies on the part of the communist government in Vietnam from one of isolationism to more openness. In Vietnam this greater openness only began to take shape in the late 1980s and was slow to develop, but in recent years official attitudes towards *Viet Kieu* have changed considerably from suspicion and underlying hostility to viewing the *Viet Kieu* population in a relatively positive light, especially as potential sources of capital. A similar transformation has taken place within the *Viet Kieu* population, which for years was dominated by anti-communists who made it difficult for their fellow *Viet Kieu* to visit or have any relations with communist Vietnam. Their hold on the *Viet Kieu* community has weakened considerably in recent years, especially as the number of second-generation *Viet Kieu* increases—people with no first-hand experience of the war or the harsh realities of life under the pre-reform communist regime. Thus, the number of *Viet Kieu* visiting Vietnam increased from 160,000 in 1993 to 360,000 in 2002. This trend has continued to increase with the number of *Viet Kieu* returning home for New Year (*Tet*) increasing from 200,000 in 2002 to 500,000 in 2007.

A look at transnational marriages within the *Viet Kieu* community of Vancouver, where about 30,000 of Canada's ethnic Vietnamese live, presents a somewhat different picture than that presented by Thai's study of *Viet Kieu* in the United States and points to the importance of changes that have occurred over time. Most ethnic Vietnamese in Vancouver either migrated as a family unit or married ethnic Vietnamese or non–Vietnamese from Vancouver or elsewhere in North America rather than seeking spouses in Vietnam. The demographic imbalance is largely taken care of among younger ethnic Vietnamese in Vancouver by marrying outside of the Vietnamese community. To the extent that there have been transnational marriages between ethnic Vietnamese in Vancouver and Vietnamese from Vietnam these appear to be most common among those who were born in Vietnam or in refugee camps in the 1970s and early 1980s and then raised in Canada rather than those who were subsequently born in Canada. There also seems to be a marked decrease in interest of finding a wife with traditional values over time to the point that such a consideration is relatively rare among those born in Canada.

That said, there does seem to be a correlation between educational and income levels and the extent to which young men are likely to prefer a wife who is more traditionally Vietnamese in her cultural orientation.

As for the spouses' relative levels of education, until recently only a few ethnic Vietnamese in Vancouver remained in school after high school. This situation has changed as more of those who were born in Canada go to college or university. For the few highly educated ethnic *Viet Kieu* living in Vancouver finding a spouse within the overseas Vietnamese community has been a challenge. In one instance, a young woman with a Ph.D. who had been born in Vietnam went back to Vietnam where she took up with her boyfriend from high school. Another young man who had been a teacher in Vietnam before migrating to Canada married a medical doctor from Vietnam and she migrated to Canada to join him. In both of these cases the relationships are between people of roughly similar socio-economic statuses and with similar cultural orientations. Most transnational marriages between Vancouver ethnic Vietnamese and Vietnamese from Vietnam are between ethnic Vietnamese men in Vancouver with relatively low levels of education and non-professional jobs ranging from factory workers to fishermen to women in Vietnam who also have relatively low levels of education and who are either from rural areas (the Mekong Delta region in particular) or from the lower socio-economic strata of Saigon or other cities. Thus, they come from comparable backgrounds, although the families of the brides are generally materially poorer than the Canadian groom. As for the grooms, usually they will only look for a wife in Vietnam once they feel that they have the material means to support her. Nevertheless, there is often a degree of initial disappointment on the part of the young woman as she is confronted with the realities of life in Canada and finds that it is not like in the movies—that she often has to work harder and that money is more difficult to come by than expected. This is especially true of those from urban backgrounds.

Inter-Ethnic Transnational Marriages

The marriage of Mark Antony to Cleopatra attests to the existence of inter-ethnic marriages since antiquity. Such marriages, however, have always been relatively rare, which may account for the attention that they often receive. There are a variety of ways that such marriages come about and a couple of these are the most common. This includes temporary migrants, travelers, or tourists who meet someone during their sojourn abroad. Another pattern is for marriages to be arranged as with foreign mail-order brides. This is a modern development on a large scale, but arranged transnational marriages among political are certainly an ancient form of such marriages.

Inter-Ethnic War Brides

So-called war brides are one version of transnational inter-ethnic marriage involving temporary sojourners. Such marriages have probably been taking place for as long as young men have been going off to war, but the term is usually used to apply to marriages that took place in relation to wars of the 1900s, World War I, World War II, the Korean War, and the Vietnam War in particular.[31] They commonly involve soldiers who are stationed in a foreign country for a time marrying local women and then arranging for them to migrate when the soldiers return to their home country. Most of the war brides of World War II who migrated between 1942 and 1952 were European — about 100,000 from the United Kingdom, 150,000 to 200,000 from elsewhere in Western Europe (especially France, Italy, and Germany) — or from Australia (15,500) and New Zealand (1,500). While the majority of these brides went to the United States, there were also about 44,000 who migrated to Canada, mainly in 1946 on so-called war bride ships that took them to Halifax.

In the above instances, the bride and groom were from different countries but they often shared a generally similar cultural orientation and often the same language. More problematic from a cultural and immigration perspective, especially in light of the racist immigration policies and attitudes of many people of the day, were marriages between Western Allied soldiers and Asian women. As Reimers notes, "Wherever American troops have been stationed, GIs have married foreign women and brought them to the United States. Thus the Philippines, Thailand (during the Vietnam War), Vietnam, Japan and the NATO nations have produced a sizeable number of such immigrant women, and they help account for how nations such as the Philippines and Korea can exceed the 20,000 annual limit."[32]

During World War II and during the occupations immediately after the war American and Australian soldiers married women from a number of Asian countries, including Japan, China, the Philippines, India, and Burma. The American Congress repealed the Chinese exclusion acts during the war since China was an ally and not only allowed Chinese living in the United States to bring family members from China but also to become citizens. The War Brides Act of 1945 and Soldier Brides Acts of 1946 and 1947 temporarily gave soldiers the rights to bring wives back to the United States, with the 1947 act in particular allowing this "irrespective of race." These acts were temporary and it was not until passage of the McCarran-Walter Act in 1952 that racial restrictions were permanently lifted and American soldiers were allowed to bring back brides without concern for their race.[33] The result was the largest influx of Asian migrant women in American history as 72,700 Asian women migrated to the United States between 1947 and 1964. The largest number of these came from Japan (45,853), but there were also 14,430 from the Philippines, 6,423 from Korea, and about 6,000 from China. The impact of this legislation in the case of Japanese brides meant that while less than 900 had come prior to 1952, 4,220 arrived in 1952 alone.[34]

Most of the Korean war brides came as a result of the Korean War, when over 500,000 Allied troops served in Korea, and the continued presence of American soldiers in South Korea has meant that there has been a continuous stream of Korean wives married to American soldiers migrating to the United States. Initially there were very few Korean migrants coming to the United States: only 10 in 1950, 32 in 1951, and 127 in 1952. The numbers increased sharply after passage of the McCarran-Walter Act. As

Reimers points out, "When [American soldiers] married Korean women, they began a new immigration channel. Korean "war brides" constituted the largest single share of the newcomers during the first years of renewed immigration, and since that time Korean women have continued to marry GIs and follow them when the soldiers were reassigned to the United States or elsewhere. Between the outbreak of the war and 1965, when a new immigration law was passed, over 15,000 Koreans entered the United States, 40 percent of whom were married to United States citizens, mostly soldiers."[35] He estimates that the total number of Korean women married to American soldiers migrating to the United States from the 1950s to the mid–1990s to have been between 90,000 and 100,000.

In the case of Australia, as was mentioned in the chapter on immigration there were a few war brides from Japan as a result of the participation of Australian troops in the postwar occupation of Japan. As O'Malley writes, "By 1952, Japanese war brides were permitted to enter after Gordon Parker married a local girl early in the occupation of Japan and asked to bring her to Australia. Other Australians with the occupation force in Japan also applied to be married, quickly creating a policy headache for the government. But there were strict rules, overseen by the Australian embassy in Japan and the local police, which screened all prospective brides to ensure they were not communists, criminals or prostitutes and had passed an exhaustive medical check. The examination and investigation was considered more stringent than that required for any other migrant. Even tougher was coping with attitudes to Japanese in the 1950s. The first war bride to arrive in Queensland, Shigeko Brown, who travelled to Cairns in 1953 to live with her husband Bill, remembered the painful taunts when she ventured out."[36]

Contemporary Transnational Cross-Cultural Marriages

While most contemporary transnational marriages are between people with similar national or cultural backgrounds, there are also a large number that take place between people with different backgrounds. To some extent such marriages reflect the nature of international travel, higher education, and work in the modern world as more people, especially young people, travel abroad as tourists, to study, and for employment. Those who travel or live away from their home countries often mingle with people of like backgrounds, but many also come into contact with people from different countries and cultures and end up forming relationships that end in marriage. Choice of residence in such cases following marriage varies. Often the couple comes to reside in the husband's country, but especially in instances where one person is from a relatively poor country and the other from a wealthier one the relative economic status of the countries may be a determining factor. There are, however, many examples of young men from developed countries marrying young women from developing countries and the couple then residing in the wife's country. The number of Italian restaurants scattered throughout Thailand is testimony to the number of Italian men who have married Thai women and decided to seek their fortunes in Thailand rather than returning to Italy. Such marriages take place within the context of the laws of the respective countries regarding travel, marriage, residency, and citizenship and the bureaucratic difficulties associated with such marriages

often serves to test the strength of the bonds between newly married or engaged couples—to say nothing of the problems associated with cross-cultural relationships.

The marriages discussed in the paragraph above are the result of chance encounters. Another form of transnational marriage, although less common, has received the most attention in scholarly and popular literature as well as from the mass media. These are arranged transnational marriages involving some type of brokering agent or agency. As Constable notes, most of these marriages are between men in developed countries and women from poorer countries.[37] She cites the example of the Philippines as "a popular place of origin of marriage migrants."[38] Of the 175,000 Filipinas who engaged or married foreigners between 1989 and 1999, 40 percent (over 70,000) married someone from the United States, 30 percent (over 53,000) someone from Japan, 8.8 percent from Australia, 4.2 percent from Germany, 3.8 percent from Canada, 1.9 percent from the United Kingdom, and 11 percent from other parts of the world (mainly other Western European countries and Asian countries such as Taiwan). While some of these marriages were to overseas Filipinos, many were to non–Filipinos such as the Japanese men discussed by Suzuki.[39] Constable adds, however, "Whereas many contemporary marriage-scapes fit the pattern of brides from poorer countries and grooms from richer ones, it is important to stress that such migrations are shaped not only or simply by economic geographies but also by 'cartographies of desire' [or] 'sites of desire'.... Recent marriage-scapes both reflect and are propelled by fantasies and imaginings about gender, sexuality, tradition, and modernity."[40] Thus, "Men's openly stated assumptions about the 'traditional' moral values and character of Asian women as well as their less openly expressed ideas about their erotic sexuality, and women's assumptions about 'modern' outlooks, power, or attractiveness of Western and other foreign men are factors in their motivations to meet and marry."[41] Such images do not always reflect reality, and the failure of the marriage to a foreigner to meet expectations can lead to loneliness, depression, and even to brides running away or divorcing their husbands. Of course, such marriage may also simply be part of a strategy to obtain foreign residency or citizenship in which the wife plans from the outset to leave her husband as soon as these are obtained.

Demographics and a range of other socio-economic factors have contributed to the growth of transnational marriage markets in Taiwan and South Korea involving men from these countries seeking brides from poorer Asian countries such as Vietnam and Thailand. South Korea is an especially interesting case since it is ethnically one of the world's most homogeneous countries. The number of marriages between South Koreans and foreigners has increased dramatically in the 2000s. They represented 4 percent of marriages in 2000 and by 2005 had grown to 13.6 percent of marriages,[42] but declining to a still high 11.1 percent in 2007.[43] Demographically the pattern reflects an imbalance of males over females, which is in large part a result of South Korean's favoring sons over daughters (a similar pattern has emerged in many other Asian countries). Technology that allows parents to determine the gender of a fetus, which has been widely available since the 1980s, has played a major role in this development because of the resultant common practice of aborting female fetuses. The situation has been exacerbated by South Korea's low birth rate. Thus, an article in *The Korea Times* entitled "South Korea's

Birthrate World's Lowest" (22.05.09) highlighted that fact that "South Korea's birth rate was the world's lowest for the second consecutive year.... A South Korean woman gives birth to 1.2 babies on average, based on statistics of 2007. The figure was the same as a year before, and has fallen from the 1990's rate of 1.6 and 2000's 1.4. The country ranked at the bottom among 193 nations, along with Belarus, Bosnia-Herzegovina, the Czech Republic, Poland, Slovakia, and Ukraine."[44] Other countries with very low birth rates include Russia and Japan at 1.3, Germany, Spain, and Macedonia at 1.4, and Canada and Cuba at 1.5, while Nigeria at 7.2 and Afghanistan at 7.1 have the highest rates.

Rural areas in South Korea have been especially hard hit by the demographic imbalance that has resulted not only from abortions of female fetuses—with 110 boys being born for every 100 girls—but also by a large number of young women leaving for cities to study or work. Thus, whereas nationally in 2006 one in every eight marriages was to a foreigner, in rural areas four out of every ten marriages was to a non–Korean. The other group that is prominent in actively searching for foreign wives is urban divorced men, which is a relatively large group as a result of South Korea's relatively high divorce rate.[45]

Who are these foreign brides? Kim found that in 2007 53.4 percent were Korean-Chinese, 19.8 percent Vietnamese, 4.9 percent Japanese, 4.5 Filipino, and 1.9 percent Mongolian.[46] Other countries that are popular for recruiting brides include Thailand, Cambodia, Uzbekistan, and Indonesia. Thus, although the number of foreign brides coming to South Korea has increased sharply in the 2000s, over half of them are Koreans from the PRC who share roughly similar cultures and languages. There were about 2 million ethnic Koreans in the PRC in 2000. Most of them live in the northeast of the country near the border with North Korea and many have relatives in North Korea. There are also about 60,000 to 70,000 ethnic Koreans living in Beijing.

Among those who are culturally and linguistically different, Vietnamese brides are especially popular. Lee, Seol, and Cho found that Korean-Chinese tended to marry South Korean men from cities who were divorced and that many of these Korean-Chinese women themselves were divorced.[47] They also found that these women were the most likely to subsequently divorce or separate from their South Koreans husbands. In contrast, women from Vietnam and elsewhere in Southeast Asia tended to marry South Korean men from rural areas who had not been married before. Moreover, these marriages had a low rate of divorce and these women were the most adaptive to South Korean society as indicated by relatively high rates of South Korean citizenship and employment.

A survey of 1,235 Korean-Chinese, 677 Vietnamese, 516 Filipino, and 389 Japanese wives in North Cholla province found that 56 percent said that they were generally happy with their marriage and only 8 percent said that their married life was unsatisfactory. A large number of the women said that economic difficulties had made their marriages harder than expected — 75 percent said that they wanted to get a job to improve their financial security. As for their reasons for marrying to begin with, 36 percent said that they had married because they loved their grooms and 38 percent because they wanted to move to a more affluent country and be able to help their families back home. In response to the results, Lee Yong-Hwan of the Hansun Foundation for Freedom and Prosperity commented, "If love is the reason for a cross-cultural marriage, there would be little room for disillusionment, but if money is the reason, the marriage is more likely to end up being a disappointment."

Most of these marriages are arranged by matchmaking agencies and typically involve the men going on marriage tours where they are introduced to possible brides. Such tours typically cost around U.S. $10,000 and rural government often subsidize this cost in an effort to overcome problems of depopulation. Such firms emerged in the late 1990s specializing in finding foreign brides (mainly Korean-Chinese) for rural farmers and the physically disabled. By 2003 there were between 2,000 and 3,000 such firms and the range of people they were serving and of countries where they were recruiting brides had expanded considerably. The national government has provided encouragement for the search for foreign spouses as seen through its 2006 "Transition to a Multicultural, Multiethnic Society" policy, and views such marriages as an answer to a number of problems such as the low birth rate, high divorce rate, and imbalance of the sex ratio.[48]

Onishi provides an account of the experience of a young man from South Korea on a marriage tour to Vietnam: "It was midnight here in Hanoi, or already 2 a.m. back in Seoul. But after a five-hour flight on a recent Sunday, Kim Wan Su was driven straight from the airport to the Lucky Star karaoke bar, where 23 young Vietnamese women seeking Korean husbands sat waiting in two dimly lit rooms. 'Do I have to look at them and decide now?' Kim asked, as the marriage brokers gave a brief description of each of the women sitting around a U-shaped sofa. Thus, Kim, a 39-year-old auto parts worker from a suburb of Seoul, began the mildly chaotic, two-hour process of choosing a spouse. In a day or two, if his five-day marriage tour went according to plan, he would be wed and enjoying his honeymoon at the famed Perfume Pagoda in the Huong Tich Mountain southwest of here. After an initial setback — his first three choices found various reasons to decline his offer — Kim narrowed his field to a 22-year-old economics major in college and an 18-year-old high school graduate. 'What's your personality like?' Kim asked the college student. 'I'm an extrovert,' she said. The 18-year-old asked why he wanted to marry a Vietnamese woman. 'I have two colleagues who married Vietnamese women,' he said, adding, 'The women seem devoted and family-oriented.' One Korean broker said the 22-year-old, who seemed bright and assertive, would adapt well to South Korea. Another suggested flipping a coin. 'Well, since I'm quiet, I'll choose the extrovert,' Kim said finally, adding quickly, 'Is it O.K. if I hold her hand now?' She came over to sit next to him, though neither dared to hold hands. She spelled out in her name in her left palm: 'Vien.' Her name was To Thi Vien."[49]

Onishi also interviewed the owners of international marriage agencies. One of the interviewees pointed to the difficulties faced by young men in finding brides: "Nowadays, Korean women have higher standards.... If a man has only a high school degree, or lives with his mother, or works only at a small- or medium-sized company, or is short or older, or lives in the countryside — he'll find it very difficult to marry in Korea." In addition to Vietnam's relative poverty when compared to South Korea, returning to our discussion of intra-ethnic transnational marriages it will be remembered that Vietnam has a gender imbalance of females over males, which is a factor that encourages the export of brides. One of the marriage agency owners, however, pointed to the prospects for the market becoming more difficult in the future: "But this business will get more difficult as those countries get richer.... Now, even a disabled Korean man can find a Vietnamese bride. But eventually Vietnamese women will ask why they have to go marry a Korean man when life in Vietnam is good."[50] Given Vietnam's rapid economic growth in recent years it is increasingly likely that the market there will become more difficult for Koreans and other foreigners very soon.

While Taiwan is more multi-ethnic than South Korea, ethnic Chinese constitute the vast majority of its population. Taiwan's Ministry of Interior indicates that 240,837 foreign spouses migrated to Taiwan between 1987 and 2003 with 57.8 percent of these coming from the PRC and 42.2 percent from Southeast Asia. By 2006 the number had increased to 384,000 with 65.1 percent coming from the PRC and 34.9 percent from Southeast Asia and elsewhere.[51] As for where the women came from, in Southeast Asia: 57.5 percent were from Vietnam, 23.2 percent from Indonesia, 5.3 percent from Thailand, and 5.3 percent from the Philippines. Marriage is the only legal means of immigration to Taiwan from the PRC. Vietnamese brides are especially popular in part because of the perception that they share Confucian family values with ethnic Chinese men from Taiwan. The demographic impact of this large number of foreign brides is that they and their children now number more than the country's aboriginal population. Beyond demographics the presence of Vietnamese women in Taiwan can also be seen in the increasing number of Vietnamese restaurants and stores run by them throughout the country.

The reasons why Taiwanese men seek foreign brides are similar to those in South Korea. In addition to demographic factors, men must also contend with changing attitudes towards marriage on the part of women. As an article on BBC News notes, "Many Taiwanese men travel to China and South East Asian countries, especially Vietnam and Indonesia, to find brides. They say they have to do so because Taiwanese women are putting careers ahead of marriage, delaying getting married or not marrying at all."[52] The Taiwanese grooms tend to be in there 30s, not to be very well educated (9 years of school on average), and relatively poor. These factors combined make it very difficult for them to find brides in Taiwan. As for the Vietnamese brides, they tend to be several years younger than the grooms, many of them being 15 to 18 years old. On average they have about 6 years of schooling and most come from relatively poor rural families.

Friends or family members who are already married to a Vietnamese or who have worked in Vietnam arrange many of these marriages. As in South Korea there are also matchmaking agencies in Taiwan that operate in Vietnam, sometimes with a branch office located there. The same BBC News article reported, "matchmaking agencies have developed a booming business, charging men as much as $9,000 to help them find a wife.... The men are shown photo albums or videos of the women, they pick the one they want and after only one trip to see the woman, they marry her, sometimes on the spot. Our correspondent says that many of the women agree because they are motivated by the chance to live and work in Taiwan and send money home."[53]

The growing number of foreign brides in Taiwan and difficulties that they face there as well as problems associated with matchmaking agencies have given rise to concern both in Taiwan and Vietnam and to legal reforms. Hsia complains that foreign wives in Taiwan suffer from economic difficulties, social isolation, and discrimination.[54] The term *dalu mei* (mainland wench) that Taiwanese commonly used to describe wives from the PRC is indicative of discriminatory attitudes. The widespread perception is that many of these marriages are not real and that the women have come to work as prostitutes. The children produced by such marriages also often face discrimination. Hsia also point to problems that foreign wives have in obtaining citizenship because of various legal constraints (including financial requirements).[55]

In the face of abuses of the system, such as fake marriages to allow women to come to Taiwan to work as prostitutes, in early 2009 the Taiwanese government announced plans to reform the commercial international marriage business: "To preserve Taiwan's image and ensure that marriages are treated as a serious matter not as a business, the government says that from now on companies can only charge the customers for the airfare, hotel expenses and administrative costs. Violators will be fined up to $30,000. The agencies will also be strongly advised to encourage both parties to get to know each other better."[56] Around the same time the Vietnamese government announced its own plans to reform the business by setting up a government-run matchmaking agency to arrange marriages between Vietnamese women and foreign men based in Saigon: "The authorities say they want to regulate the sector, which they say is currently run by illegal groups. Police have targeted events in recent years where dozens of women from poor backgrounds, seeking a better life, are paraded before potential suitors. The men are often on short "marriage holidays" from South Korea and Taiwan. Correspondents say that some women in Vietnam see overseas marriage as a route out of poverty and the practice is widespread in some rural areas. But many women fall foul of unscrupulous brokers and are sold into prostitution; while others are forced into marriages they do not want.... The government says it hopes the plan will help prevent the abuse of Vietnamese women by criminal organisations, or by their new husbands."[57]

The use of matchmaking agencies to arrange marriages of local men to foreign brides has also proliferated in recent years in the United States, Canada, Australia, and Western Europe. The brides come from a variety of sources with the Philippines, Russia, Ukraine, Colombia, and Mexico being especially popular sources. Constable compares contemporary inter-cultural transnational arranged marriages from an American perspective with those in the past: "Today's correspondence relationships are notably different from the older historical cases of frontier brides, proxy brides, and picture brides in terms of the technology they utilize. But they are perhaps not so different in the extent to which they are regulated by laws and policies that are in turn influenced by public opinion and racial prejudice.... A key difference in [such] marriages today is how they cross ethnic/racial and national lines, whereas the older forms of marriages involved couples whose experiences differed greatly but who were of the same ethnic or national background."[58] The main technological difference, of course, is the introduction of the internet, which is widely used today in searches for foreign spouses. The racist issues are especially evident in cases involving marriages between men of European ancestry and Asian women.

Constable reports that in 1998 there were over 350 websites with the stated aim of introducing American western men to prospective foreign brides and 70 percent of the women listed on the sites were from the Philippines.[59] The number of sites has increased since then and the nationality of the women has become more diverse, there being a larger number of women on these sites from Russia and other Eastern European countries in particular.[60] As for matchmaking firms in the United States that specialize in arranging transnational marriages, Harris writes, "Over the past decade, the number of such brokers nationwide has grown from a handful to roughly 600.... Each year, up to 12,000 American men find wives through for-profit international marriage brokers, say sponsors of the congressional legislation."[61] Harris provides an example of one such marriage: "Divorced, single and in his mid–30s, Sam Baar wasn't comfortable with the bar scene or nightclubs. Yet the Phoenix computer technician still longed to meet someone and settle down. So Baar went online and did what hundreds of other spouse-seeking men have done: He pursued a relationship in another country, and he found a wife. In November, Baar went to Cartagena, Colombia, with Phoenix-based A Foreign Affair, one of the largest international marriage brokers in the United States. On the first day, Baar said, he found the love of his life, and four days later he proposed."[62] Harris interviewed Lynn Visson[63] about such men: "Visson said the men are typically between 35 and 45, divorced or never married, and many are in the computer business. Most earn between $50,000 to $80,000 a year, she said. 'They [the men] have been very busy, completely zonked out or devoted to work, and they are too old for the bar scene,' Visson said. 'So, where do you find someone?' She said the American men appeal to foreign women, especially those in Russia, because the men are willing to adopt their children and American men live longer than Russian men on average. They also are perceived to drink less."[64]

As in Taiwan, there has been criticism of the role of commercial firms in arranging transnational marriages in the United States. In the case of America such criticism has focused largely on spousal abuse of foreign women and critics have sought to link the business with exploitative forms of human trafficking. Constable offers a critique of the critics who she views as often being overly simplistic and misleading by focusing on the more sensational cases of abuse in such marriages.[65] Harris interviewed the operators of one such firm, A Foreign Affair, who characterized "their international dating service is as harmless as a 'high school dance'" and took offense by characterizing them as running a mail order bride firm: "You can't pay us any amount of money to arrange a marriage for you.... We simply introduce people who think they would like to meet and hopefully build a relationship and marry someday."[66] Harris also cites a report by the United States Citizenship and Immigration Services stating "marriages arranged through these services would appear to have a lower divorce rate than the nation as a whole, fully 80 percent of these marriages having lasted over the years for which reports are available."[67]

Transnational Family Networks

The Philippines provides a good example of a country where transnational family ties are of considerable importance. About 10 percent of the population of the Philippines lives overseas and a very large percentage of families in the Philippines have family members living in other countries. Tyner estimates that transnational Filipino families have members living in 160 countries.[68] Similar figures exist for many other countries such as those in South Asia. Many other countries in the Caribbean, Latin America, and the South Pacific also have large numbers of transnational families, but they tend not to be spread quite so widely around the world. Transnational families are also a common feature of the main countries that receive migrants such as the United States, Canada, Australia, and Argentina.

There are two means by which transnational family networks are formed. Migration across borders and transnational marriages may lead to the creation of transnational family networks where members of the family make an effort to maintain relationships across borders. Transnational family networks may also be formed where the creation of state boundaries has divided families but family members continue to maintain relations despite this political obstacle. No matter how they are formed analysis of such networks entails examination of the context within which they develop and the content of the networks.

The context or social space within which transnational family networks exist, which we discussed initially in the first chapter, includes such factors as government policies that favor or dissuade communication and travel across borders, the cultural environment within which family members live, their economic statuses, and technical factors related to cross-border communication and travel. Cultural values that promote family solidarity are important motivating factors as are related calculations based on the perceived advantages to be gained through reciprocity among family members.

Hindrances on the parts of governments in modern times include especially the isolationist policies of communist governments that seized power in various countries around the world in the 1900s, which cut off family members from their relatives living in non-communist countries for a time. Liu provides an interesting case study of a transnational ethnic Chinese family.[69] Family members migrated to the United States in the late 1800s where they worked as asparagus farmers and ran an herbal medicine business. Family members subsequently moved back and forth across the Pacific for business and education. Liu argues that instability and other problems in China and racial hostility in the United States combined to make transnational family life a focal point of the social existence of family members. Vietnamese refugees who left Vietnam following the communist seizure of power in northern Vietnam in 1954 and their conquest of the central and southern part of the country in 1975 found maintaining contact with family members remaining in Vietnam difficult until reforms began to open the country more to the outside in the late 1980s. Once communication with and travel back to Vietnam became easier in the 1990s overseas Vietnamese still had to contend with the hostility of anti-communist extremists in the overseas Vietnamese community that made open contact with family members difficult and especially actual visits to Vietnam. It was not uncommon for overseas Vietnamese to try to keep such visits secret for fear of reprisals at home that sometimes took the form of physical attacks and having their homes set afire. There were also lingering problems on the Vietnamese side, especially from low-ranking government officials. Such problems have receded in recent years as Vietnam has become increasingly open, as government officials have become more tolerant of overseas Vietnamese, and as the hold of anti-communist extremists on the overseas communists has waned. Economic growth in Vietnam has also provided an attraction for overseas Vietnamese, who have invested in businesses and real estate back in Vietnam to a considerable extent in recent years. A growing number of older overseas Vietnamese who were born in Vietnam have also considered returning to Vietnam to retire. All of these factors have combined to create a large number of transnational ethnic Vietnamese families with bases in two or more countries.

Family reunification policies on the part of governments have played an important role in maintaining relations between migrants and family members in their countries of origin. In the case of the United States, for example, the 1965 Immigration and Naturalization Act eliminated the old quota system based on national origin and established a new system based on family reunification and occupation. Especially important is the distinction between quota (i.e., those categories of migrants that continued to be subject to various quotas) and non-quota categories of immigrants. Immediate relatives of American citizens (whether naturalized or not)—including spouses, minor children, and parents—constitute a non-quota category. As Constable points out, the "unintended consequence of the reforms was a sharp increase in Asian and Latin American immigration."[70] Another consequence was an increase in the percentage of women. Thus, she notes, "during the 1997 fiscal year, out of 796,000 immigrants over 25 percent were spouses of U.S. citizens (170,226) or legal permanent residents (31,576). Of these spouses, 66 percent (over 132,000) were women." Looking at Filipino migrants to the United States, Constable found not only that the absolute number of immigrants increased (665,000 Filipinos coming to the United States between 1965 and 1984), but that while during the first ten years following the Act the number entering under the employment and reunification categories was about equal, in the mid–1970s the occupational category dropped to about 20 percent of all immigrants, due to stricter entry requirements for professionals," and the vast majority of immigrants came under the reunification category.[72]

Technological changes and access to means of travel and communication, which were discussed in the first chapter, have had an important impact on the maintenance of transnational family networks. Changes in communication include such things as the introduction of the penny post and other improved and less expensive mail delivery, the spread of access to telephones, and the internet. The internet has revolutionized communication within transnational families by allowing low cost almost constant communication to an increasing number of people worldwide. Air travel has also played an important role in making face-to-face contact among family members easier.

The content of transnational family networks may include exchange of news, information, and resources as well as other forms of assistance (such as help in obtaining visas). The sending of remittances by temporary labor migrants to their relatives back home was mentioned in the chapter on migration. What is of particular interest in the present context is the continuing flow of remittances by settler migrants back to relatives in their country of origin or ancestry. Hugo uses the term remittance to refer not only to money, but also to other goods, services, and guarantees that migrants deliver to their place of origin.[73] Hugo's study of Javanese migrants is of relevance in the present context also because of its finding that circular migrants sent the most money home while permanent migrants sent back far less. Looking at households receiving money from migrant family members, he found that circular migrants provided 60.2 percent of the incomes to the households to which they were associated, whereas permanent migrants provided only 8 percent.[74] This difference reflected not simply the type of migration, but also the fact that the households of circular migrants tended to be poorer than those related to permanent migrants.

Hugo's study points to the importance of the economic status of migrants in determining the level and role of remittances. Remittances from those who have migrated to wealthier countries from poorer ones are of most importance to families from poorer backgrounds that see migration primarily as a means of improving the family's pool or access to wealth. In her study of transnational Filipino families, Suzuki refers to how "families originally located in economically weak countries have begun to maintain themselves transnationally,"[75] and the flow of remittances is the primary form that this maintenance takes. Their significance (and often frequency) declines among wealthier families. For middle class transnational families the flow of money often resembles that of many non-transnational families where money is sent on special occasions as a gift (such as for birthdays and weddings) or in cases of emergencies.

Suzuki has noted in the case of Filipino transnational families that the "form and content of family ties" among members are different from those of families that are more localized within the Philippines.[76] This is especially true in the case of gender roles and gender-based expectations whereby Filipino women living outside of the Philippines are confronted with both increased expectations of their ability to play the traditional male role of provider to family members back in the Philippines while also being subjected to traditional expectations of as female as a care giver: "As women's earning power increases, their new role of family provider ironically incorporates material care into their maternal care,"[76]

Skeldon points to how the two-way flow of migrants in the contemporary Asia-Pacific region has led to the creation of "a curious new form of spatially extended family" that is a product of Asian migration and modern communication and includes "astronaut" fathers who leave their wife and kids in a home purchased in the destination country and returns to his initial homeland to work and "parachute" children who are placed in a home in the destination country (sometimes with relatives) while the parents stay in their homeland to work.[77] By 1993 there were already an estimated 40,000 parachute Asian children living in the United States.

An additional issue concerns differences between role and behavioral expectations of family members in the country of origin or ancestry and those associated with dominant cultural traditions within the countries of settlement. This is an especially important issue in regard to gender and the socialization and behavior of children. Where cultural differences between countries are not so different, as with transnational marriages between Taiwanese men and Vietnamese women, problems may be minimal. However, when cultural differences are greater, as in the case of Muslim migrants from Middle Eastern and

North African countries living in North America and Western Europe, there can be considerable tension. One of the more dramatic and highly publicized manifestations of such tensions is so-called honor-killings by Muslems. Honor killings involving the murder of a family member who is believed to have brought dishonor on the family.[78] The United Nations Population Fund (UNFPA) estimated that around 5,000 take place annually. Most of these occur in Asian, Middle Eastern, and North African Muslim countries, but they also take place among Muslim migrant families in Western Europe and North America. Such murders in North America and Europe reflect problems of adapting to a very different cultural environment on the part of migrant families rather than something specific to transnational families, but they relate to transnationality insofar as they represent efforts by families to maintain the cultural traditions of their home or ancestral country.

5

TRANSNATIONAL CORPORATIONS

Transnational corporations (TNCs) are also known as international corporations, multinational corporations (MNCs), or multinational enterprises (MNEs). A TNC is a corporation that manages production or delivers services in more than one country. While it is common to think of TNCs as massive corporations that span the globe like Royal Dutch Shell and Wal-Mart, they can also be small enterprises (sometimes referred to as micro-multinationals) employing relatively few people but still operating in more than one country. In the present chapter we are more concerned with the social and cultural aspects of TNCs than their economic dimension. This relates both to their role as transnational employers and as a transnational link between people living in different countries.

Modern Transnational Corporations

The Dutch East India Company (*Vereenigde Oost-Indische Compagnie,* United East Indian Company, VOC), which was established in 1602, is generally considered to be the first modern transnational company since it was the first transnational enterprise to issue stock.[1] Unlike its modern counterparts, beyond simply trading, the VOC established colonies, waged war, negotiated treaties with states, and issued its own coins. Although it was a Dutch company its employees included not only people from the Netherlands, but also many from Germany and from other countries as well. Also, while most of its shareholders were Dutch, about a quarter of the initial shareholders were Zuid-Nederlanders (people from an area that includes modern Belgium and Luxemburg) and there were also a few dozen Germans.

While the VOC mainly operated in what later became the Dutch East Indies (modern Indonesia), the company also had important operations elsewhere. During the 1640s and 1650s the VOC pushed the Portuguese out of Sri Lanka and took over their control of the cinnamon trade with Europe. The VOC then conquered the Malabar Coast of southern India, leaving the Portuguese with only Goa. The VOC established a base at the Cape of Good Hope in southern Africa in 1652 in order to re-supply its ships sailing between the East Indies and Europe. The company established additional trading posts along India's

Malabar Coast, at Tjutjura (Chunchura, Hougly) in Bengal, at Malacca (Melaka) on the Malay Peninsula, in the Kingdom of Ayutthaya (Thailand), at Canton, on the island of Formosa, and in Japan. The VOC established its trading post in Japan on the island of Hirado in 1609, but as a result of the closed-door (*sakaku*) policy of the Tokugawa shogunate, in 1638 it was forced to close this post and in 1639 transfer its operations to the island of Dejima in Nagasaki harbor. The Dutch maintained a post on Dejima from 1641 until 1860 (after the VOC had been dissolved). Janus Henticus Donker Curtis (born Arnhem, 1813–79) was the last Dutch commissioner for Dejima. The VOC also maintained a number of bases in the Middle East such as those at Mocha (Mokka, Al Mukkha; 1621–1739) in Yemen and at Gamron (Bandar-e Abbas; 1638–1758), Kirman (Kerman; 1659–1744), Khark (known as Fort Mosselstein; 1753–66), and Isfahan (1623–1747) in Persia.

Huybert Visnich established the VOC trading station at the Persian capital of Isfahan in 1623 at the same time that the company concluded a commercial treaty with Shah Esfahan. Their office there allowed them to conduct negotiations directly with the shah while also engaging in trade, which largely involved exchanging spices for Persian silk. The VOC trading post at Gamron bought silk, wool, and attar of roses (rose oil) and sold spices, cotton textiles, porcelain, opium, and Japanese lacquerware. The post had a staff of around 20 Europeans (mostly Dutch) and 20 Persians. Baron Tido von Kniphausen, who had been the VOC agent at Basra, built Fort Mosselstein on the island of Khark (near Basra) in 1753. This post mainly sold Javanese sugar and Indian cotton textiles. The VOC also maintained a post at Shiraz to purchase attar of roses. Armenians represented the company in Shiraz, although European employees from its other posts would often stay there during the summer.

At its peak in 1669 the VOC had over 50,000 employees along with an army of around 10,000. Its fleet was comprised of over 150 merchant vessels and 40 warships. It was the largest and richest company in world history up to that point, but it was about to stagnate and drift towards terminal decline, culminating in its bankruptcy and dissolution in 1800, when the Batavian Republic assumed its debts and took over control of its possessions.

Trouble for the company began in 1662, when it lost its base on Formosa to the Chinese. The VOC had built Fort Zeelandia at Anping (Taiman) between 1624 and 1634. A Swedish nobleman named Frederick Coyett (born Stockholm, c. 1615–87) was appointed the twelfth governor of Formosa in 1656. Previously he had served twice as the VOC's commissioner (Opperhoofden) at Dejima (1647–8, 1652–3) and he was the first Swede to travel to Japan and China. The Ming general Zheng Cheng-gong (aka Koxinga) laid siege to the Dutch fort in 1661. Koxinga had an army for 25,000 men and 400 warships to lay siege to the 2,000 Dutch troops at Fort Zeelandia. The siege lasted nine months. Coyett surrendered after fresh water had begun to run out, the loss of 1,600 of his men, and when it became apparent that the VOC was not sending reinforcements from Batavia. Coyette managed to reach Batavia, where VOC officials imprisoned him for 3 years for the loss of Fort Zeelandia and then exiled him to the island of Rosengain in the Banda Islands until he was pardoned in 1674. His son Balthaser Coyett (1650–1725) later became a VOC employee and served as governor of Ambon from 1701 to 1706 — and Balthaser's son Frederik Julius Coyett (1680–1736) also worked for the VOC.

In addition to the loss of Formosa political instability in China and trade restrictions in Japan meant trouble for the VOC's operations in East Asia. Thus, the company was no longer able to obtain Chinese silk by 1666 (it substituted Bengali silk). Back in Europe the Third Anglo-Dutch War (1672–4) disrupted the company's trade with Europe and the resultant sharp increase in the price of pepper in Europe brought the British East India Company into competition with the VOC in this market. The VOC also found itself in competition with the French East India Company and the Danish East India Company until in 1721 it was forced to give up trying to dominate the shipment of spices to Europe and the British East India Company was able to assume a dominant position on the Malabar Coast.

Having lost control of the spice trade, the VOC diversified into trading in tea, coffee, textiles, and sugar. Such commodities were increasingly in demand in Europe by the late 1600s and early 1700s and the VOC had ready access to capital to finance this new direction (in part because of the flow of silver from the New World to Europe). Thus, using New World silver to buy Asian commodities for export to Europe, the VOC was able to substantially increase its size.[2] The increased scale of operations meant more costs to the company as it employed more people in more places and operated more and more ships. At the same time, profits from these new commodities were substantially less than had been the case in the past with spices and while the company grew during the mid–1700s it did not generate much in the way of profits. Along with poor profits, the company was poorly managed and suffered more than most companies at the time from corruption and poor performance by its employees (the high mortality and morbidity rates of its employees did not help). Such external factors as political setbacks and increased competition along with its internal failings eventually led to the company's demise.

Early Western transnational companies like the VOC tended to focus on trade. They were closely identified with a particular country and their activities were often closely linked with the political fortunes and interests of their home countries abroad. While shareholders might come from a variety of countries, those from the home country tended to dominate. The language and culture of the home country usually was dominant as well. In the foreign countries where they operated locals closely identified these companies with their home countries. Overseas employees included people from the home country who came out on contracts generally intending to return home at some point, but a number settled overseas. There were also local employees ranging from clerks to laborers. The two groups were kept separate and paid at radically different rates. The locals in many instances included a group of people of mixed European and local background such as Anglo-Indians. Moreover, European companies sometimes hired local people from particular ethnic groups. Thus, the corporate society was patterned along ethno-national lines in a hierarchical manner.

The social organization and cultures of many contemporary transnational corporations retain aspects of the older companies. Thus, most modern transnational corporations are still identified with a particular state that is also where their headquarters is located. However, in recent decades there has been a shift away from such a pronounced identification with a particular country and its language and culture and many corporations have become more multicultural within the context of a deterritorialized international corporate culture.

Transnational Oil Companies

The VOC's main legacy was a major Dutch colonial presence in Southeast Asia where future Dutch transnational companies would come to operate. Royal Dutch Petroleum Company (aka *Koninklijke Nederlandsche Maatschappig Tot Exploitatie van Petroleumbronnen in Nederlandsch-Indië* and *N.V. Koninklijke Nederlandsche Petroleum Maatschappij*), founded in 1890, provides an example of a newer generation of Dutch TNC that came into being in the late 1800s. The oil industry in the Dutch East Indies effectively began when the first concession was granted in Langket, northern Sumatra, in 1883. The Royal Dutch Petroleum Company soon came to dominate the industry in the Dutch East Indies.

The 1924 *Handbook of the Netherlands East-Indies* notes, "This company gradually established connections with various other companies for the buying of the crude product, its shipping and distribution, with the aim of securing for itself a place in the world market. Beyond the Dutch East Indies also, it is steadily extending its sphere of activity for that purpose. The Royal Dutch Petroleum Company presents an example of a world wide organization, which has made it possible to bring the petroleum industry in the Dutch East Indies to a high degree of perfection."[3] As for the actual shipping of the oil beyond the Dutch East Indies, a small amount was carried by the Netherlands Indian Tank Steamship Company, some was shipped by the Asiatic Petroleum Company Ltd. (mainly to British territories such as India, the Straits Settlements, the Malay States, Egypt, as well as to Australia and the Philippines), but most was carried by the Anglo Saxon Petroleum Company.

The Anglo Saxon Petroleum Company was a branch of the "Shell" Transport and Trading Company. Shell was a British company founded by Marcus Samuel and Samuel Samuel in 1897. The initial company had eight oil tankers. The brothers' father Marcus Samuel has established an import-export business named M. Samuel & Co. that traded with the Far East in 1833. The brothers carried on with the import-export business with Marcus establishing "Shell" Transport and Trading Company to import sea shells for sale to collectors in London and Samuel, in partnership with his brother, later founding Samuel Samuel & Co. in Yokohama, Japan (a trading company that played a major role in the industrialization of Japan). While on a trip to the Black Sea to collect shells in 1890, Marcus realized the business potential for shipping oil and founded the shipping company after his return to England — the first of his oil tankers was named the *Murex*. His new oil tankers were the first to be allowed to transport oil through the Suez Canal and the company began shipping oil between Europe and Singapore and Bangkok.

Motivated to a large degree by competition with the American oil company Standard Oil that was owned by John D. Rockefeller, Royal Dutch Petroleum Company and "Shell" Transport and Trading Company joined in 1907 under the name Royal Dutch Shell.[4] The Dutch had a 60 percent share of the new company and the English 40 percent and Henri Wilhelm August Deterding (1866–1939), who was head of Royal Dutch Petroleum Company, became the chairman of the new company, giving it a predominantly Dutch identity. The company had 38 tankers and in 1910 it launched the *Vulcanus,* which was propelled by two 400 hp diesel engines, making it the first ocean going motor driven tanker. The company also expanded its exploration and production activities beyond the Dutch East Indies to areas of British influence in Sarawak and Brunei on the island of Borneo, where its subsidiary the British Malayan Petroleum Company discovered commercial reserves at Seria in Brunei in 1929, and in Venezuela and Mexico. As the world wide demand for oil increased dramatically after World War I, in large part because of growing use of motor vehicles, the company undertook exploration and began production in California, Venezuela, Iraq, and Saudi Arabia. The Middle East had emerged as an especially important source of oil. By the late 1920s it was the largest oil company in the world, supplying 11 percent of the world's oil. While still a Dutch-English company its ties to the colonial possessions of these countries had weakened and it had become much more global in its operation.

In addition to the Great Depression, changing political conditions in the world in the 1930s had an important impact on Royal Dutch Shell. It had bought Mexican Eagle Petroleum Company in Mexico in 1919 (changing its name to Shell-Mex Ltd. Mexican Eagle in 1921), which made it the leading oil firm in the country. The government of Lázaro Cárdenas nationalized Mexican Eagle in 1938 (it then became Petróleos Mexicanos, PEMEX). There were also problems for the company in Venezuela. Then in 1939 the Germans invaded the Netherlands and the company had to move its Dutch offices to Curacao with the London office focusing on support of the Allied war effort.

The post–World War II period witnessed a severing of the company's link to Indonesia, when its assets there were nationalized in 1957 (becoming the state-owned oil monopoly Permina, which in turn became Pertmina in 1968). In addition, its assets in Iran were sequestered between 1951 and 1953 and the Suez Crisis of 1956–7 disrupted shipping. Such losses and problems were offset by new discoveries and production elsewhere, especially in Nigeria's Niger delta, in Sarawak and Brunei, in the Middle East, and in the Gulf of Mexico. Shell had drilled its first offshore oil well in the Gulf of Mexico in 1947 and by 1955 had 300 offshore wells. Discovery of the Yibal oil field in Oman led to greatly increased production there in the 1960s. The company also began producing natural gas in the Netherlands and North Sea. Political problems and the global expansion in oil production led to the introduction of the supertanker. Sumitomo Heavy Industries in Japan built the first of these in 1979 (it was 458 meters long with a capacity of 564,763 DWT).

In regard to transnational social relations, an additional important change in the 1960s related to personnel policies on the part of Shell. These changes reflected political, economic (especially in terms of markets), educational, and social trends in the post-colonial world favoring greater diversification in terms of the nationality of employees by large transnational corporations such as Shell. As the company's official history notes, "During the 1960s, Shell took the decision to internationalise the company. A policy of placing local people in top positions in a given country was adopted and the recruitment of Asians, Africans and South Americans was pursued, giving them as much independence as possible. This diversification of staff reflected the wider political changes of the end of

Empire and its attitudes, and this far-sighted decision took Shell into the modern world."[5] Shell not only had operations in a wide range of countries, but also came to employ people at all levels from these countries, producing a large multi-ethnic transnational workforce. The company itself underwent a structural reorganization in 2005, when the partnership between the two original companies was dissolved to create a single company named Royal Dutch Shell. Thus, it was no longer a transnational partnership but a single transnational company (with its headquarters in the Hague). The company's website describes Royal Dutch Shell as "a global group of energy and petrochemical companies. With around 102,000 employees in more than 100 countries and territories." As the Fortune Global 500 index of companies notes, in 2009 it was also the largest corporation in the world with revenues of U.S. $458,361,000,000 (pushing it just ahead of no. 2 ranked Exxon Mobil).

Other oil companies appearing on the list after the top two include BP no. 4, Chevron no. 5, Total no. 6, ConocoPhilips no. 7, and China Petroleum & Chemical Corp. (Sinopec) no. 9. The inclusion of Sinopec, which is 71.84 percent state owned, points to an important aspect of the oil industry — the extent of state involvement. Thus, while to some extent private oil companies are becoming more transnational in terms of both their operations and employees, a great deal of the industry remains linked to particular states.

The Fortune Global 500 list is only one criterion for judging the relative size of companies. Energy Intelligence publishes the *Top 100 Ranking: The World's Oil Companies* annually using a wider range of criteria to assess their relative size and looks at both private and state-owned enterprises.[6] According to its 2009 list the relative ranking is: no. 1 Saudi Aramco (100 percent), no. 2 NIOC (Iran) (100 percent), no. 3 Exxon Mobile, no. 4 PDV (Venezuela) (100 percent), no. 5 CHPC (China) (100 percent), no. 6 BP, no. 7 Shell, no. 8 ConocoPhillips, and no. 9 Chevron. Its report notes, "Majority state-owned national oil companies now make up 27 of 50" of the largest oil companies. Using the narrowest criteria, oil reserves, only state-owned enterprises appear in the list of top ten oil companies in terms of reserves: Saudi Aramco, National Iranian Oil Co., Qatar General Petroleum Corp., Iraq National Oil Co., Petróleos de Venezuela, Abu Dhabi National Oil Co., Kuwait Petroleum Corp., Nigerian National Petroleum Corp., Libya National Oil Corp., and Sonatrach (Algeria). Exxon-Mobil is no. 17 and Royal Dutch Shell is no. 22 on this list.

While some of the state-owned oil enterprises operate entirely within state borders (or almost entirely) and employ mostly citizens of the same state, some of them also have transnational aspects, although they remain much more tied to and to identify more with a particular state than private transnational corporations. The largest of these state-owned oil companies, Saudi Aramco, provides a good case study. As Saudi Arabia expanded the extent of its control over the company until it became entirely state owned in 1980 the company also sought to reduce its reliance on foreign employees in managerial and technical areas through the training of Saudi nationals. By 1980 Saudis constituted about 22,000 out of the company's 38,000 employees, although at managerial and supervisory levels non–Saudis still constituted 55 percent of those employed. Ali Naimi became the company's first Saudi executive vice president in 1982 and company president in 1984.

Aramco contractors employed an additional 20,000 workers, many of these being foreign contract workers. Aramco also diversified the sources of its foreign employees, most of who initially were from the United States. There were 3,400 American employees of the company in 1980, with other foreign employees coming from 44 countries. By 1989 there were 31,712 Saudis (73.3 percent) out of a total workforce of 43,248 and the number of American employees had declined to 2,482. Although the number of foreigners employed by Saudi Aramco and its contractors has declined, there still are a number of foreigners employed by the company and its contractors in Saudi Arabia.

Saudi Aramco's major contractors include both domestic and transnational companies. Transnational contractors used by Saudi Aramco include many of the major transnational companies that provide services worldwide to the oil industry: Baker Hughes (the world's third largest oilfield services company), Samsung Engineering (based in Seoul, South Korea), Technip (based in Paris, with 23,000 employees worldwide), Schlumberger (the world's largest oilfield services company, which operates in about 80 countries and employees over 87,000 people from 140 countries), Halliburton (based in Houston with operations in over 70 countries), BJ Services Company (an oil and gas equipment services company based in Houston), Rosen Inspection Technologies (based in Switzerland with operations in over 80 countries), Foster Wheeler Energy (an engineering design and construction services company based in New Jersey) and Fluor Corporation (and engineering, procurement, construction, and maintenance services company based in Irving, Texas, that began working in Saudi Arabia in 1947 and currently has about 36,000 employees and, according to its 2009 annual report, has employees in 66 countries[7]).The transnational nature of Aramco entails not only employing foreigners within Saudi Arabia and working with numerous non–Saudi companies, but also conducting business outside of the country through a number of subsidiaries that are primarily involved in marketing and shipping. These include Aramco Services Company, Aramco Associated Company, and Aramco Training Services Company with their headquarters in Houston; Saudi Petroleum International with its headquarters in New York City; Aramco Overseas Company B.V with its headquarters in the Hague; Saudi Petroleum Overseas Ltd. with its headquarters in London; and Vela International Marine Ltd. with its headquarters in Dubai. Saudi Petroleum International, for example, arranges scheduling, loading, storage, transportation, and delivery of Saudi Aramco's crude oil to refineries in Canada and the United States (it handles about 15 percent of the crude oil coming to the United States). Aramco Training Services Company operates an international exchange program to train employees of Saudi Aramco and its affiliates and promotes programs to facilitate mutual understanding between Saudi Arabia and the United States. These subsidiaries have both local employees as well as Saudi Arabian employees who reside in these foreign countries.

The Fortune Global 500

The Fortune Global 500[8] was launched in 1989 to replace a list of only American companies and the list has changed over the years not only in which companies it lists and their order, but also in the relative importance of particular sectors and the geographical distribution of the companies in terms where they are headquartered. While oil companies have dominated the upper portion of the list since 1990, other sectors have become increasing important since then and, although the United States remains the headquarters of most companies, the list of headquarters has broadened.

In regard to corporate headquarters, North America and Western Europe dominate the list, but a significant number of companies are also based in East Asia. The list of countries with more than 10 headquarters is: United States—140, Japan—68, France—40, Germany—39, PRC—37, United Kingdom—26, Switzerland—15, Canada—14, South Korea—14, Netherlands—12, and Spain—12. By region this breaks down to North America—154, Western Europe—129, East Asia—129. In addition to countries it is also important to see where the headquarters are located in terms of cities: Tokyo—51, Paris—27, Beijing—26, New York—18, London—15, Seoul—11, Madrid—9, Toronto—7, Zurich—7, Osaka—7, Moscow—7, and Munich—7. While some of these companies (especially the Chinese ones) are largely national companies, many of them are transnational and it is not surprising to see that the cities listed here also tend to figure prominently among the world's major transnational cities.

Transnational Corporations of the People's Republic of China

The companies on the Fortune 500 list from the PRC generally are based in Beijing, with a few in other cities such as Shanghai and Hong Kong. Whereas the state is the largest (and sometimes the exclusive) owner of the companies on the list based in Beijing and elsewhere in the PRC except for Hong Kong, Hong Kong–based Jardine Matheson (no. 411) is privately owned. Also, while Jardine Matheson is transnational, almost all of the other companies operate predominantly within the PRC. Among the large PRC state enterprises operating outside of the country, the most prominent are China National Petroleum Corporation (CNPC, no. 13 on the 500 list) and China Ocean Shipping (COSCO, no. 327 on the list, but no. 2 among shipping companies). Although both CNPC and COSCO are predominantly state-owned enterprises, the social nature of the transnationalism of these two companies is quite different with COSCO evolving to look increasingly like Western transnational corporations (at least as they were during the colonial era) while CNPC remains more guarded in its integration into the transnational world.

The history of the PRC's commercial shipping industry, and COSCO in particular, provides a useful picture of the country's integration into the world economy and the emerging transnational nature of such companies. COSCO's operations have generated considerable controversy over the years because of its close association with the People's Liberation Army and the periodic use of its ships and containers to transport illegal weapons, narcotics, and humans and concern over its use as a means of expanding the PRC's political power around the world. Mair, for example, refers to COSCO as "the merchant marine for the People's Liberation Army.[9] Despite this, COSCO is increasingly viewed simply as just another transnational corporation.

The creation of the Chinese-Polish Joint Stock Shipping Company (CHIPOLBROK), which began operation in Tianjin in 1950, appears to be the PRC's first joint venture. The

China Ocean Shipping Company (COSCO) was founded in 1961, with operations conducted out of Guangzhou. Its first passenger liner, the *Guanghua,* was used to transport ethnic Chinese wishing to leave Indonesia and migrate to the PRC because of instability in Indonesia at the time. The first voyage by a COSCO ship to Western Europe took place in 1967. COSCO entered the container business in 1978 and sent its first international container ship to Sydney, Australia.

In regard to transnationalism, COSCO's signing an agreement for overseas contract employment with Iino Kaiun Kaisha Ltd. (IINO Lines of Japan, which operates oil tankers and other tankers and bulk carriers) in 1979 was an important development. This was the first time that a company from the PRC became involved in the international manning of ships. Another milestone was in 1988 when COSCO transformed its joint venture in the United Kingdom into a wholly owned subsidiary, COSCO (UK) Ltd. COSCO's container operations are operated by COSCO Container Lines Co. Ltd., which is part of what was renamed the China Ocean Shipping (Group) Company (COSCO Group) in 1992. Accordingly COSCO (UK) Ltd. became COSCON (UK) Ltd. As COSCO's operations in Western Europe expanded COSCO Container Lines Europe GmbH was established in Hamburg, Germany, in 2005 to serve as the regional headquarters for the various COSCO operations around Europe. COSCO presently has 40 offices and subsidiaries scattered around Europe. The senior management of COSCO Container Lines Europe GmbH and the subsidiaries such as COSCON (UK) Ltd. is Chinese. However, most of the lower-level managers and other employees are citizens of the country where the subsidiary operates.

Back home in the PRC, COSCO remains closely tied to the state. However, since 2002 it has traded shares on various stock exchanges. This began in 2002 when shares were offered on the Shanghai Stock Exchange. Shares were offered on the Hong Kong Stock exchange in 2005. In addition, its subsidiary COSCO Corporation (Singapore) Ltd. offered shares on the Singapore Exchange in 2004, the first sate-owned enterprise from the PRC to be sold on this exchange.

Turning to the oil company CNPC and its emergence as a transnational corporation, investment by the PRC's government in oil outside of the country began in 1993 — coinciding with the PRC becoming a net importer of oil and the government's desire to secure supplies of oil internationally: "China's imports have grown from about 6 percent of its oil needs a decade ago to roughly one-third today and are forecast to rise to rise to 60 percent by 2020."[10] The PRC reorganized its oil and natural gas industry in 1998 to create three companies: CNPC, Sinopec, and CNOOC. CNPC was to focus on land-based upstream activities (e.g., exploration and production), Sinopec on downstream activities (e.g., refining and distribution), and CNOOC on offshore production.

While Sinopec and CNOOC have some operations outside of China, CNPC is the PRC's main international investor in oil. Sinopec focuses on handling the downstream aspects of foreign investments such as refining and distribution to retail outlets in the PRC, but has also made some foreign investments itself (e.g., in Iran and Oman). Most of CNOOC's production is within the PRC, but it has recent projects in Indonesia and Nigeria. CNPC's website characterizes the company as follows: "CNPC is China's largest oil and gas producer and supplier, as well as one of the world's major oilfield service providers and a globally reputed contractor in engineering construction. With a presence in almost 70 countries, we are seeking an even greater international role.... China National Petroleum Corporation (CNPC) is an integrated international energy company. Based in China, we have oil and gas assets and interests in 29 countries in Africa, Central Asia–Russia, South America, the Middle East and the Asia-Pacific.... Providing oilfield services and engineering construction in 44 countries around the world."[11]

CNPC's first transnational investments were relatively modest ones in existing areas of exploitation in Canada (in Alberta) and Thailand (the Banya development block). The next year it purchased rights to the Talara Oilfield in northwestern Peru, its first foreign oilfield development project. Oil was discovered in the Talara Basin in 1869 and at present there are 48 fields being worked there.[12] The CNPC field had been worked for over a century and the company hoped to increase production. In 1996 CNPC invested in Sudan (more on this shortly) and in 1997 in Kazakhstan and Venezuela. The pace and range of CNPC's foreign investments increased in the 2000s: Burma in 2001; Indonesia, Oman, Syria, and Turkmenistan in 2002; Chad, Ecuador, Niger, and Russia in 2003; Iran, Mauritania, and Tunisia in 2004; Libya and Mongolia in 2005; and Equatorial Guinea, Nigeria, and Uzbekistan in 2006. Most of these projects were relatively modest by industry standards, but they served to spread CNPC's operations around the world.

The largest of the PRC's foreign oil projects have been in Kazakhstan and Sudan, where the only projects that produce more than 100,000 bpd are located. Since Kazakhstan is located immediately to the west of the PRC and Kazakhstan is the world's third largest oil producer, the motivation for investment here is quite obvious. In addition to investing in oil production in Kazakhstan, CNPC in conjunction with Kazakhstan's KazMunyaGas also built a pipeline linking the two countries. Investments in countries like Kazakhstan and Mongolia are essentially in the PRC's backyard and take place in countries where the PRC has long-standing political and cultural relations. Investments in Southeast Asia (e.g., the PRC has become a major investor in Indonesia's oil and gas industries) and the Middle East (e.g., Oman has been one of the PRC's main suppliers of oil for some time) also take place in relatively familiar territory. Of particular interest transnationally is the PRC's increasing investment further afield in Africa and Latin America since this is an important part of the PRC's emergence as a global economic actor.

While a substantial amount of the PRC's oil imports still come from the Middle East (mainly Saudi Arabia, Iran, and Oman), Sudan and Angola have emerged as its other top suppliers and the PRC is now the second main importer of African oil in the world with Angola serving as its number one source (ahead of Saudi Arabia). The PRC's investments and overall involvement in Sudan has attracted considerable attention largely because of the political context. The PRC's involvement in Sudan's oil industry has developed in tandem with its becoming the main supplier of weapons to Sudan (including construction of three arms factories in the country), forging close diplomatic relations between the two governments, and the PRC's involvement in infrastructure projects in the Sudan (many of these tied to bilateral aid from the PRC). Between the 1990s and late 2000s CNPC invested around U.S. $10 billion in Sudan, while Sinopec has built a pipeline to

Port Sudan where the Petroleum Engineering Construction Group of the PRC has built a U.S. $215 million tanker terminal.[13]

Unlike COSCO, which employs a large number of locals in its foreign operations, oil companies from the PRC rely almost entirely on employees imported from home. This has resulted in 5,000 to 10,000 people from the PRC working in Sudan over the past ten to fifteen years. This includes a number of decommissioned soldiers from the People's Liberation Army who are employed to provide security, especially to operations in southern Sudan and the Darfur region. The Chinese workers in the Sudan live in relative isolation from the Sudanese. Goodman describes "Chinese laborers based in a camp of prefabricated sheds [who] work the wells and lay highways across the flats to make way for heavy machinery," while "Only seven miles south, the rebel army that controls much of southern Sudan marches troops through this sun-baked town of mud huts." He adds, "But the Chinese laborers are protected: They work under the vigilant gaze of Sudanese government troops armed largely with Chinese-made weapons."[14] In many instances, Sudanese soldiers drive local people out of areas where oil production is planned or under way. Goodman interviewed local Nuer in southern Sudan: "'The Chinese want to drill for oil, that is why we were pushed out,' said Rusthal Yackok, who was blinded, his wife and six children killed. 'Now, I have no family, no cows,' he said. 'I have nothing. My life is totally destroyed.' Today, people in Leal try to coax crops from unproductive soil. They line up at wells drilled by an aid organization and await the next shipment of food aid. 'Oil has brought devastation to our lives,' said Stephen Mayang, a father of three whose legs were badly hurt during the attack.... A recent report in the state-controlled China Business News quotes a Chinese foreign affairs official as saying that Beijing has asked Khartoum to 'send troops' to areas in which Chinese companies operate."[15] The Sudanese government's perspective concerning the Chinese is different: "In an interview in Sudan's capital, Khartoum, Energy and Mining Minister Awad Ahmed Jaz praised his Chinese partners for sticking to trade issues. 'The Chinese are very nice,' he said. 'They don't have anything to do with any politics or problems. Things move smoothly, successfully. They are very hard workers looking for business, not politics.'"[16]

The Global Middle Class

The nature of transnational corporations in the modern world is closely linked to the emergence of what is widely called the new global middle class. Members of this class constitute many of the employees of TNCs (especially in managerial, professional, and technical positions), the main consumers of their goods and services, and it is their values that tend to shape the way that such corporations are evolving. In the case of the PRC, for example, the growing energy needs of its middle class is one of the main factors sending the country's oil companies around the globe and, at the same time, these companies are major employers of middle class Chinese at home and abroad.

The growing middle class of the developing countries of the world has received considerable attention from academics and marketing specialists in recent years. A 2009 article in the *Economist* highlighted the fact that over half of the world's population belongs to the middle class largely as a result of economic growth in countries such as the PRC and India.[17] In the case of the PRC the percentage of the population categorized as middle class increased from 15 percent in 1990 to 62 percent in 2005. Around 2007 or 2008 the number of middle class people in such countries became greater than the number of the developed countries. As Das points out, this expansion of the middle class has changed consumption patterns and shifted "the balance of spending power to middle-income economies."[18] Particularly important in this regard is not merely the spending power of this group, but specifically the fact that it has sufficient income to devote a significant portion of it to discretionary spending rather than on basic necessities. This means that a large number of people in middle-income countries are able to spend money on consumer goods, health care, and on improving the education of their children.

Brazilian economist Eduardo Giannetti da Fonseca describes members of the middle class as "people who are not resigned to a life of poverty, who are prepared to make sacrifices to create a better life for themselves but who have not started with life's material problems solved because they have material assets to make their lives easy."[19] By way of an example of middle class dynamism and changing life-styles the article describes a Chinese civil servant who left government employment to go into commodities trading and then developed the country's first sky resort near Harbin. Fifteen years ago the PRC had no ski resorts and few skiers. By 2009 there were 300 ski runs in the country catering to around 3 million skiers. As for the resort near Harbin, "Every weekend the resort is packed with IT executives, bankers and media glitterati. This is the emerging markets' new middle class at play."[20] Similar developments have taken place in regard to golf, such as the U.S. $1 billion 12-course Mission Hills golf complex near Shenzen that was first opened in 1992 and has grown steadily, although the sport caters more to elites than to the emerging middle class.[21] There are over 200 golf courses in the PRC and the Mission Hills Golf Club "is accredited as the world's largest by Guinness World Records, and recently ranked 17 out of 100 in a poll of 'Top 100 Courses You Must Play' according to Golf World."[22]

One common indication of achieving middle class status is to have about one-third of one's income available for discretionary spending—i.e., what is left after paying for food and shelter. This is being middle class in relative terms, but the *Economist* article also points out that "In practice, emerging markets may be said to have two middle classes. One consists of those who are middle class by any standard—i.e., with an income between the average Brazilian and Italian. This group has the makings of a global class whose members have as much in common with each other as with the poor in their own countries. It is growing fast, but still makes up only a tenth of the developing world. You could call it the global middle class. The other, more numerous, group consists of those who are middle-class by the standards of the developing world but not the rich one. Some time in the past year or two, for the first time in history, they became a majority of the developing world's population: their share of the total rose from one-third in 1990 to 49% in 2005. Call it the developing middle class."[23]

Both of these middle classes are important, but their spending habits and how they relate to the world beyond the border of their own country differ in some ways. In a country like Vietnam, for example, members of the developing middle class tend to travel by motorcycle, while members of the global middle class increasingly travel by car, although a joint-venture company in Vietnam probably made both vehicles. To take another example, large numbers of the PRC's emerging middle class now take foreign holidays, usually in the form of cost-conscious package tours to some destination not too far from home. In contrast, an increasing number of the PRC's global middle class take foreign holidays much like their counterparts in Japan or South Korea.

Surjit Bhalla's forthcoming book *Second Among Equals: The Middle Class Kingdoms of India and China* is cited extensively in the article in the *Economist*. Bhalla describes there being three middle class "surges" since 1800. The first surge was the creation of the mass middle class in Western Europe in the 1800s, the second with the post–World War II baby boom, and the third being the current surge in the emerging countries. Bhalla produces a table that shows the middle class in 1820 as constituting only a few percent of the world's population. By 1890 it was nearing 10 percent and by 1938 (thanks in part to the boom in the 1920s) it was well over 20 percent. It passed 30 percent between 1960 and 1980, and then grew slowly until the current surge got underway in the 1990s. Bhalla adds that the current surge has resulted in the number of middle class people in Asia overtaking the number in the West for the first time since 1700. Moreover, the surge is far from over. Again, quoting the *Economist,* "The surge across the poverty line is a period of accelerating growth both for the new middle class and for the country it inhabits. That should continue for a couple of decades. By most estimates, the global middle class will more than double in number between now and 2030. This will have profound social consequences, as happened in previous middle-class surges."[24]

In comparing India and the PRC, whereas over half of the population of the PRC has already achieved middle class status, the process has been much slower in India. In 2005, when the middle class constituted 62 percent of the PRC's population, it was only about 5 percent of India's. However, India's National Council for Applied Economic Research estimates that the percentage will grow to 20 percent by 2015 and 40 percent by 2025. In regard to India's emerging middle class, Dibroy makes the interesting point that "When India opened up in the early 1990s, the middle class was often cited to sell the attractiveness of India's domestic market. Figures of 300 million were bandied about, but producers realized to their chagrin that this market was elusive and did not, in fact, exist. Depending on the product, the market might very well be 30 million. In part, the problem arises from using income as the criterion in defining middle class, ignoring heterogeneity beyond income categories."[25] To some extent this was a matter of confusing the emerging middle class of India with its global middle class. Nevertheless, Dibroy adds that despite the initial exaggeration or confusion, the "30 million is now approaching 300 million."[26] Thus, the predicted middle class market in India is now becoming a reality.

Vietnam's Middle Class

While a great deal of attention has focused on the middle classes of the PRC and India, it is important to recognize that a similar process is taking place in many other countries around the world, especially in Asia[27] and Latin America. Vietnam provides another useful case study. With a population of 86,116,560 (July 2008 estimate) Vietnam may not be as populous as India or the PRC yet it has more people than many developed countries and is rapidly emerging from being one of the poorest countries in the world to achieving middle-income status.

While placing considerable emphasis on an inward looking nationalism, Vietnam's communist party had important transnational aspects from its very beginning through the close links of Ho Chi Minh and some of its other leaders with fellow communists in other countries, especially the Soviet Union. Once they came to power in the north in 1954 such ties were maintained and reinforced, for example, by sending people to study in communist countries. As a result, many communist elites and non-elite professionals had spent years in such countries and commonly spoke Russian or other eastern European languages. This represented a small portion of the total population, but it was a group that played a very important role in the life of the country. Moreover, such foreign links were commonly seen as important, especially as a source of scarce resources. Following the collapse of communism in the Soviet Union and Eastern Europe and the subsequent reforms in Vietnam that began in the late 1980s the country witnessed the emergence of new elites and of a new middle class, both of which owed their existence to the country's growing private sector. Moreover, both groups found themselves more able to and more interested in interacting with an increasingly wider range of non-communist countries in many different ways—visiting as tourists, studying abroad, reestablishing contacts with family members living outside of Vietnam, forging business links with non–Vietnamese, and so forth. Significantly, the government itself changed from hostility towards such ties to suspicion, then to acceptance, and finally to a very positive attitude.

A 2007 article in the Communist Party of Vietnam's magazine provides the party's view of the country's new middle class: "Our national renewal process sets the objective of building a rich people and strong country. Obviously, democracy and civilisation will be further manifested as more people join the middle class, so that 'the poor will have sufficient food and the sufficient will become richer' as Ho Chi Minh said. Now that Vietnam has become a WTO member and is integrating into the global economy, the role of middle class households, who are increasing in the population, should be promoted to further stabilise and develop the country. If this population is growing bigger, the social gap between the rich and the poor will be narrowed and negative social polarisation will be limited. It can be said that the middle class group consists of eminent people from all social strata. They include skilled workers, farmers and artisans, scientists with highly valued work, and dynamic small and medium business people. These people, therefore, play a rather important role in the formation of the socio-economic position of social classes as well as relations in many aspects of the social and population structure. Recently, with the increasing number of skilled employees in the private economic sector, particularly in the foreign invested sector, changes have taken place in the social structure among the middle class. Well-to-do households working in the foreign invested sector, with a rather high standard of living, have followed a dynamic and modern lifestyle. Further changes will take place, and not only in the standard of living and lifestyle of the middle class in Vietnam during the industrialisation, modernisation and international integration process as a WTO member."[28]

Vietnam's per capita GDP went from U.S. $114 in 1990 to U.S. $620 in 2006 (GDP per capita in terms of PPP in 2006 is estimated at $3,100). During this same period the poverty rate declined from almost 60 percent of the population to between 30 percent and 20 percent. As elsewhere in the developing world, Vietnam's middle class is largely found in its cities. McCool cites a study by TNS market researchers indicating that annual per capita gross domestic product in households in Saigon was about $2,400, which is three times the official nationwide figure of $720 for the year.[29]

Even more so than the PRC, Vietnam's growth and the emergence of its new elite and middle class has been linked to market reforms as the emergence of private enterprise. Enterprise reforms began in Vietnam in 1989. The previous year (1988) there were 3,092 state industrial enterprises, 32,034 industrial cooperatives, 318 private domestic enterprises, and 1 enterprise with foreign capital. A decade later, in 1998, there were 1,821 state industrial enterprises and 949 industrial cooperatives, 5,714 private domestic enterprises, and 830 enterprises with foreign capital. While Vietnam, like the PRC, continues to suffer from the drag on its economy created by many of its remaining state enterprises, their number has continued to decline and their overall economic importance shrinks each year.

Foreign investment and overseas development assistance have also contributed to Vietnam's economic growth since the 1980s. Both of these grew significantly as Vietnam was opened to the non-communist world. FDI commitments reached $8.6 billion in 1996 and then dropped sharply to $600 million in 1999. This drop was in part due to the Asian economic crisis, but many foreign investors were finding it too difficult to make money in Vietnam. This was in part a reflection of the still relatively small domestic market reflecting the still fairly small number of middle class people in the country and the relatively small amounts of discretionary income available to the country's emerging middle class in absolute terms. During the boom years of the early 1990s foreign investors were willing to sign deals even if initial prospects were not encouraging. Faced with a relatively small domestic market and widespread corruption losses accumulated faster than expected and many companies pulled out or decided not to move ahead with investment plans. More recently, however, the government has taken a more accommodating approach to foreign investment and once again foreign investment in Vietnam is booming. At the same time the domestic market has grown as the country has witnessed its own middle class surge not just in terms of numbers but also in regard to the amount of discretionary income available. This surge has been helped, especially in the south of the country, by investments and remittances from overseas Vietnamese.

Public displays of wealth in Vietnam began to emerge in the mid–1990s in the form of increasingly larger private family homes such as those that appeared in Hanoi's West Lake District. Much of this initial personal wealth was in the hands of corrupt government officials. Such ill-gained wealth was sometimes used to start private sector businesses and before long these individuals were joined by a rapidly growing number of individuals whose wealth was based on non-government sources, ranging from overseas financial support to local entrepreneurial success.

Golf has become an increasingly popular game among members of this newly rich elite and it is a sport that provides transnational links between Vietnamese and nationals from other countries. The game was popular during the colonial era among French expats and local elites. With the coming of the communists the courses were closed. Today there are about a dozen golf clubs in the country and 30 or more under construction. The King's Island Golf Club near Hanoi, which opened in 1993, was one of the first of the new generation of golf clubs. The following year the old royal golf course in Dalat was reopened as the Dalat Palace Golf Club with financial backing from Larry Hillblom, one of the founders of DHL, and managed by Jeff Puchalski, who had been a golf pro at the Wilshire Country Club in Los Angeles. Like these two, most courses in Vietnam are joint ventures with significant foreign investment and with foreigners serving in the top management positions, but most of the other employees being Vietnamese. Most players are also foreigners, but gradually that is changing: "Several years ago, Dalat Palace and Ocean Dunes began giving free lessons and rounds to dozens of Communist Party officials at the provincial level. In 1997, Mr. Puchalski even put on a golf clinic at Da Lat, paying to bring senior leaders from Hanoi. As a result, the government seems to have developed a greater appreciation for the game. Mr. Puchalski said that many leaders now play regularly.... Interest in the game has also spread to the nouveau riche of Vietnam."[30] The game has yet, however, to gain popularity among middle class Vietnamese, even those who could be classified as global. Given that membership in the King's Island Golf Club, for example, is over U.S. $60,000 and the lack of relatively inexpensive courses near urban areas this is perhaps understandable.

In addition to a wealthy elite, in recent years Vietnam has also witnessed the growth of an increasingly affluent middle class based on incomes from small businesses, employment by larger foreign and domestic firms, and in some cases an ability to combine government employment with side incomes from the private sector. As in other developing countries, Vietnam has seen the rise of both an emerging and a global middle class. A growing number of skilled professionals employed by large domestic and foreign corporations in Vietnam earn salaries of U.S. $5,000 a month and more. They pay little tax on this salary, have few basic expenses beyond housing, and, thus, have considerable discretionary income. Many members of this new middle class have access to the internet, international media, and, increasingly, travel outside of Vietnam in relation to their work and for leisure.

The emergence of this class can be seen in the growing number of apartment complexes and other residential units that are being built to cater to this class in Saigon, Hanoi, and a few other booming cities such as Danang. The changing status of this group can also be seen in transportation. Ten years ago such individuals aspired to own a Honda Dream that could easily be wheeled into their small apartments at night. More and more members of the middle class are now buying or at least aspiring to purchase their own automobile. To put this in dollar terms, whereas a basic 100 cc Honda Super Dream sells for $1,800, the base price for a Ford Focus (Ford's least expensive model in Vietnam) is $28,500, with many popular car models in Vietnam selling in the $50,000 range. The move to the new residential units is spurred not only by a desire for a newer and fancier place to live, but also by the need for a place to park a car. Like the middle classes in other emerging economies the one in Vietnam is also purchasing a wide array of consumer goods that were not even dreamed of ten years ago: "The middle classes of the Socialist Republic of Vietnam have taken quite well to capitalism. Whether it is families dining at fancy restaurants, businessmen buying luxury cars or people shopping for vanity items, conspicuous consumption is popular, especially in Ho Chi Minh City [Saigon] and Hanoi.... The children of the middle class increasingly eat Western food, use mobile phones and the Internet and enroll at international schools that until a few years ago catered almost exclusively to expatriates. They are sometimes called cadre kids, the sons and daughters of couples connected to the elite ruling group or of businessmen whose entrepreneurial skills in the new economy have completely transformed the lifestyle of their extended families."[31]

The country's automotive industry is a useful indicator of people's changing economic status. It is also an industry with a significant transnational character. In the mid–1990s it was still quite rare to see private automobiles on the road. Most automobiles were government-owned, assigned to government employees for use, and the bulk of them were made in the Soviet Union or Eastern Europe. Domestic automobile production started in 1951 with the opening of Auto Hoa Binh, a state-run manufacturer of military vehicles. The situation began to change in 1991 when Auto Hoa Binh formed a joint-venture partnership named Vietnam Motors Corp. (VMC) with Colombian Motors of the Philippines and Nichmen Corporation of Japan. VMC began assembling passenger vehicle kits supplied by Kia of South Korea, Mazda of Japan, BMW of Germany, and Subaru of Japan. While a number of other foreign automobile companies began producing cars in Vietnam in the 1990s (e.g., Mitsubishi, Isuzu, Hino, Daihatsu, and Toyota of Japan; Fiat of Italy; Daewoo of South Korea; Daimler Benz of Germany; and Ford from the United States) the domestic market remained weak. In late 1997 the vehicle assembly plants in Vietnam had a combined production capacity of 83,260 vehicles, but only 21,000 vehicles were sold in Vietnam in that year and three-quarters of these were imports. This meant that these plants were fighting over a market of about 5,000 vehicles.

Despite brief setbacks in 1998 and 2008, in general Vietnam's automobile industry has grown since the dark days of the late 1990s in step with the fortunes of the country's elites and middle class. The Vietnam Automobile Manufacturers Association reported that the country's 11 joint ventures sold 43,000 units in 2004, although plants were running at only an average of about 30 percent of designed capacity. As one report at the time commented, "Though Vietnam was more of a motorcycle-oriented country in past years, its passenger car segment witnessed a good growth after Vietnam joined WTO. Rising income and flexible bank loan structure has incited the growth in passenger car segment."[32] By the mid–2000s, the market was growing substantially. In 2007, another report noted, "Both domestically produced and imported vehicle sales doubled during the three-month period, compared with 2006, while the passenger car segment grew by over 200%."[33] There were 16 manufacturers operating in Vietnam by 2010 and sales for the first half of the year (through July) were 59,717 vehicles.[34]

Writing in 2006, McCool noted that the increase in car sales was despite the fact that

"Vietnam is one of the most expensive places in the world to buy a vehicle, with import tariffs as high as 90 percent." He quotes a man in Hanoi who is buying a Honda car for his son who is about to enter university: "In the past, having a bicycle was a dream already, let alone a motorbike — now even farmers go to the field on motorbikes." A manager of a small import-export company who has just spent U.S. $29,000 on a used Mercedes C200 told McCool, "You are first-class citizens if you go to work in a car."[35] Such people have moved from being members of the emerging middle class to being part of the global middle class.

The companies producing automobiles in Vietnam are joint-ventures that employ a mixture of Vietnamese and foreign nationals at top levels and in some technical capacities with the general workforce being entirely Vietnamese. Taking Vidamco as an example, the company is the local subsidiary of GM Daewoo. Daewoo of South Korea was a relatively early entry into Vietnam during the reform period with the Daewoo Hotel in Hanoi serving as an important center for expats. The company already had a close relation with General Motors of the United States when it went bankrupt following the financial crisis that started in 1997 and General Motors increased its stake, with the company becoming GM Daewoo in 2002. Daewoo began operating in Vietnam in 1993.[36] Its assembly plant is located on the outskirts of Hanoi where it produces around 10,000 passenger cars and 500 buses a year. The company proclaims its vision to be: "With the market leader position in passenger car market, every urban Vietnamese family will own one GM Daewoo in their garage by 2020. My first GM Daewoo in my life."[37]

Vidamco's board of directors is comprised of 7 members. Five of these are Korean and 2 Vietnamese.[38] A South Korean, Kim Jung In, is the General Director. He received his undergraduate degree at Sung Kyun Kwan University in South Korea and then received an MBA from the University of Hawaii, Manoa. He began working for Daewoo in South Korea in 1976. He went to the company's New York office in 1986 and then returned to South Korea to serve as Director of Daewoo Automobile Export Division and Foreign Investment. In this capacity he was in charge of sales and marketing in the Pacific Rim, including overseeing automobile sales companies in Hong Kong and Myanmar. He was promoted to the position of Executive Director of the company's Overseas Export, Investment and Development Division in 1997. His work in this capacity included overseeing the development of joint-ventures in the PRC, Vietnam, and Pakistan. Then he became the General Director of Vidamco in Vietnam.

While Dibroy pointed to initial overestimates of the size and wealth of India's middle class, McCool highlights how official statistics in Vietnam tend to underestimate. He cites an interview with a market researcher from London-based TNS Global[39] who told him, "Vietnam is wealthier than what we believe, but we honestly don't know how wealthy." He cites research by TNS showing that in an average household in Saigon, "people spent 2.5 to 7 times more than they said they earned," commenting that "Measuring the new wealth of the middle classes is difficult because Vietnam is largely a cash economy and the personal income tax-collecting system is still in its infancy."[40] As symbolic of this new middle class as its cars, "Singapore-style apartment towers, designer stores, trendy bars and restaurants" is the presence of "Large supermarkets operated by the German retailer Metro and the French-owned retailer Big C [that] are filled at weekends with shoppers buying goods in bulk."[41]

Feeding the World's Middle Class

While transnational corporations have been involved in food production and the import and export of food items since the founding days of the VOC, the retail side was largely left to domestic enterprises until recently. Attention on the involvement of transnational corporations in domestic food consumption over the past couple of decades has tended to focus on restaurant chains such as McDonald's, with its golden arches appearing across the globe from Chisinau in Moldavia to Nadi in Fiji, but that was ranked only 388th in the 2009 Fortune Global 500 list of corporations. Far less attention has been paid to the emergence of transnational grocery store chains and especially their conjoined supermarket and department stores known as hypermarkets. The development of this form of transnational enterprise is closely linked to the rapid growth of in the middle classes of countries around the world and their consumer preferences and they play a far more important role in feeding the global and emerging middle classes than do transnational restaurant chains.

The big three in hypermarkets globally are Carrefour of France (no. 25 in the Global 500 list), Metro of Germany (no. 50), and Tesco of the United Kingdom (no. 56). Groupe Casino of France also operates a large number of hypermarkets around the world. These are huge companies. The Carrefour group currently has over 15,500 stores and 490,042 employees, Metro Group had over 2,200 outlets and employed about 300,000 people in 2009, and Tesco is Britain's largest retailer both domestically and internationally and has 273,024 employees, while Groupe Casino has around 175,000 employees. In regard to their global operations, Carrefour operates in 35 countries and over 56 percent of group turnover derives from outside France. In terms of net sales, in 2008 44 percent of its sales were within France, 37 percent in the rest of Europe, 12 percent in Latin America, and 7 percent in Asia. Metro operates in 32 countries in Europe, Africa, and Asia. It employs peoples from 150 different countries and about half of them worked outside of Germany. Tesco operates in 15 countries outside of the United Kingdom. By late 2004, while 75 percent of group revenue came from within the United Kingdom, the amount of floorspace in its stores was greater outside of the United Kingdom than within for the first time. Groupe Casino focuses on running hypermarkets and supermarkets and outside of France has operations in the Middle East, Indian Ocean, India, and South America.

An important point about these enterprises in relation to transnationalism is that while their headquarters and origins are in particular Western European countries these companies are well integrated into the other countries where they operate in terms of staffing and the sourcing of the products that they sell. Thus, depending on the particular country, these companies source between 90 percent and 97 percent of the products on their shelves locally. Brief histories of these companies provide a sense of how they have spread around the globe beyond Europe in response to perceived emerging markets.

Turning first to Carrefour (meaning crossroads in French), the company began as a single store near a crossroads in the small French town of Annacy, which is located near the Swiss border, in 1957. Carrefour's founders attended seminars in the United States by Colombian-American Bernardo Trujillo, whose theories of sales and distribution included the famous slogan, "No parking, no business." Carrefour opened the world's first hypermarket in France in 1963. Six years later, in 1969, the company expanded beyond France and opened a hypermarket in Belgium. Slowly the company added stores in other Western European countries (Spain in 1973 and Portugal in 1975) as well as in South America (Brazil in 1975 and Argentina in 1982). It opened the first hypermarket in Asia, in Taiwan, in 1989. The company moved into Eastern Europe, opening its first store in Poland in 1997. During the 1990s the company opened stores in a number of other countries in Europe, South America, and Asia, and also expanded its operations outside of France by purchasing existing grocery store chains in some countries (e.g., in Brazil in 1999 and Argentina in 2001). It opened a store in Turkey in 1993. In regard to Asia, it opened hypermarkets in Malaysia in 1994, the PRC in 1995, and in Thailand, South Korea, and Hong Kong in 1996.

Carrefour describes itself as follows: "Over the past 40 years, the Carrefour group has grown to become one of the world's leading distribution groups. The world's second-largest retailer and the largest in Europe, the group currently operates four main grocery store formats: hypermarkets, supermarkets, hard discount and convenience stores.... A pioneering entrant in countries such as Brazil (1975) and China (1995), the group currently operates in three major markets: Europe, Latin America and Asia.... The group sees strong potential for further international growth in the future, particularly in such large national markets as China, Brazil, Indonesia, Poland and Turkey. Wherever it has a presence, Carrefour is actively committed to promoting local economic development. Since retail activities are all about contact with people, the group consistently emphasizes local recruitment plus management and staff training on the job wherever they work. Typically, the Carrefour group will be one of the leading private employers in any country where it operates. Naturally, this is the case for France, where the group was originally founded, but it is also true of such countries as Brazil, Argentina, Colombia, Italy and Greece."[42]

Carrefour's expansion in Asia is especially interesting from a transnational perspective in regard to the problems that it has had and its relations with Asian regional transnational companies. Carrefour expanded rapidly in Asia in the mid–2000s. It opened 36 new hypermarkets in Asia alone in 2007 — 22 of these were in the PRC, a company record for the number of new stores opened in a single year. In 2010 it had 626 stores (including hypermarkets) in Asia, with about two-thirds of these located in the PRC and others in Indonesia, Taiwan, Thailand, Malaysia, and Singapore. Asia accounted for 7.9 percent of Carrefour's total sales in 2009. Exceptions to this pattern of expansion were in Japan, where it sold its 8 hypermarkets to the Aeon Group in 2005, and in South Korea, where it sold its 32 hypermarkets to E-Land in 2006. More recently, partially in response to poor sales in Europe, in 2010 Carrefour announced plans to sell its stores in Thailand, Malaysia, and Singapore.[43] The majority of these stores (40) are in Thailand, where it ranks fourth and well behind market-leader there Tesco Lotus (see below).

Aeon and E-Land are important transnational corporations, especially in the Asian region where they are often in competition with European-based transnational companies like Carrefour. Carrefour's problems in South Korea are interesting and highlight how such companies are not always successful in operating in particular markets. An article about E-Land in www.absoluteastronomy.com notes, "Carrefour Korea, despite its global presence and experiences overseas, struggled to understand the local Korean culture" and, thus, decided to sell its stores to E-Land in 2006."[44] Two years later, in 2008, E-Land re-sold these stores to British-based Tesco. E-Land Group is involved in clothing, retail malls, restaurants, hotels, and construction and operates outside of South Korea through its subsidiary E-Land World in the PRC, Hong Kong, Vietnam, the United States, and Europe.

Aeon makes an interesting study in transnationalism in its own right. Its 2010 annual report is entitled *Aeon 2010: Fully Global, Truly Local.*[45] Aeon is comprised of a group of 155 companies and is Japan's largest retail group in terms of sales. The company was founded in 1758 as a trader in kimono fabrics and accessories. It began to expand outside of Japan in the 1980s, opening Jusco stores in Malaysia and Thailand in 1984 and acquiring the American women's clothing chain Talbots in 1988. The company operates various supermarkets, mostly under the Maxvalu name. Faced with poor market prospects in Japan, its 2010 annual report highlighted a shift in investment emphasis "from domestic to overseas businesses" and especially to Southeast Asia and the PRC.[46] In this regard the report emphasized, "The key to growth in China and the ASEAN region is localizing management for an advantageous synergy between local ideas and Aeon's strengths. We aim for harmonious coexistence with local communities through GMS and supermarket operations closely aligned with local lifestyles and financial services that are appropriate to local business customs."[47] Thus, at a time when European-based Carrefour was withdrawing from some Asian markets because of financial problems in it home territory, Aeon's response to similar conditions was to expand outwards in response to the growing middle class market of neighboring parts of Asia.

Two of the Metro Group's (aka Metro Aktiengesellschaft) subsidiaries are of primary interest in the present context: Real and Metro Cash & Carry. In 2009 Real operated 343 hypermarkets in Germany and another 96 in Poland, Romania, Russia, and Turkey and announced plans to expand into Ukraine. Metro Cash & Carry operates self-service wholesale stores catering to hotel and restaurant operators, caterers, hospitals, and small and middle-sized grocers. As of 2009, it operated 655 stores in 29 countries. Thus, while Metro Group has focused the development of its hypermarkets outside of Germany in nearby emerging markets in Eastern Europe and Turkey through Metro Cash & Carry it has expanded much further around the world occupying a particular niche as a wholesaler to middle class markets.

Metro's top level of management is drawn from around Western Europe rather than solely from Germany. In 2009 its CEO was Swiss, the head of Merchandising German, head of Administration German, head of Human Resources Dutch, head of its Asia Pacific division German, head of its Southern Europe division French, and head of its Eastern Europe division Dutch. In the case of the head of its Asia Pacific division, he is a German who had been with the company since 1963 and had 15 years experience working at the executive level outside of Germany.

Metro Cash & Carry began operating outside of Germany in 1968, when it opened a Makro store in the Netherlands through its subsidiary Makro Zelfbedieningsgroothandel in partnership with Steenkolen Handels-Vereeniging SHV of the Netherlands. It then began expansion into Southern and Western Europe and subsequently into Turkey and Morocco. By the early 1990s it was operating in 200 locations in 12 countries outside of Germany, but still fairly close to home. Since the mid–1990s the company has focused its expansion on what it considers to be "growth markets" in Asia and Eastern Europe. Non-German sales accounted for 44 percent of the company's growth between 2001 and 2004.

In Asia Metro Cash & Carry operates in Vietnam, the PRC, India, Pakistan, Japan, and formerly in Indonesia. Its regional headquarters is in Hong Kong, while its regional operating officer is based in Singapore. It began operating in the PRC in 1996 and in 2009 had 37 stores. It began operating in Vietnam in 2002 and in 2009 had eight stores; in Japan in 2002 and in 2009 had four stores; in India in 2003 and in 2009 had four stores; in Pakistan in 2007 and in 2009 had four stores.

India's *Business Standard* published an interview with the company's regional operating officer for Asia in 2008: "James Scott, Metro Cash & Carry's regional operating officer (Asia) based in Singapore, virtually lives out of a suitcase. With the regional headquarters in Hong Kong and operations across China, India, Pakistan, and Vietnam, Scott travels through the week and gets back home only on weekends. The Englishman was in Mumbai recently to launch Metro's fourth store in India. In a brief interview with *Business Standard*, Scott gives insights on Metro's cash-and-carry model and consumer behaviour in India…. What are your views on consumer behaviour in India? Our business has been consistently growing ahead of the market (faster than the GDP). Consumer behaviour is different in every market, and we stock our assortments according to specific needs. Restaurants in France have different purchasing habits than those in kiosks in Germany. In India, more people buy vegetables than fish and meat. In Mumbai, we can cater to international restaurants with our large assortment of fish and meat."[48]

Metro India's website begins, "Welcome to Metro! The world leader in the self-service wholesale. Offering over 18,000 articles at the best wholesale prices for Hotels, Restaurants, Caterers, Food and Non-food Traders, Institutional buyers and professionals." It has stores in Bangalore, Hyderabad, Kolkata, and Mumbai. The new managing director for India who was appointed in 2007 previously had been expansion director in Russia and was seen as bringing "with him valuable experience gained in emerging markets like Russia and Eastern Europe as well as in-depth knowledge of the wholesale and trading business."[49]

Success in India led the company to move into neighboring Pakistan in 2007, when it opened its first store in Lahore. There are presently four stores in Pakistan: two in Lahore, one in Islamabad, and one in Karachi. Announcing the opening of its Karachi store, the company published an interview with its managing director for Pakistan: "With a population of over 170 million people and more than a million residents in eight cities, Pakistan is a very attractive and important market for our company," said Giovanni

Soranzo, Managing Director of Metro Cash & Carry Pakistan. "We see a vast prospect for our business-to-business wholesale concept and will continue to invest in this country to grow in the coming years. Along with expansion, we aspire to contribute to the economic growth of Pakistan. On average, the capital investment for a new Metro Cash & Carry outlet is 20 million Euros.... Each Metro Cash & Carry wholesale center employs 300 people from the local community. Moreover, 200 people are working at the company's country headquarters in Lahore."[50]

Previously, in 2002, the company had moved into Vietnam and Japan. The company opened its first store in Japan in Tokyo. The newly appointed director for Japan in 2002 was Dutch and he had 17 years prior experience working with other companies in Japan, Hong Kong, and Taiwan, and had worked before that in Italy and Germany. The local operations director was also Dutch, the purchasing director was French, while the deputy purchasing director was Japanese as was much of the remaining staff. As in many of its other operations, the bulk of its products are sourced locally — 90 percent in the case of Japan. The company opened its first store in Vietnam in Saigon and within 8 months of opening its first store there it opened a second one. It managing director in 2002 was Greek. An article by Cadilhon and Fearne on Metro's operation in Vietnam emphasizes the importance of close collaboration with local suppliers and customers built on relatively simple means of sharing information and highlights the extent to which the company needs to become integrated into the local society in order to function effectively.[51]

Not all of Metro Cash & Carry's operations have been successful. It began operating in Indonesia in 2004 under the name PT Metro Supermarket Realty Tbk (MTSM). Based in Jakarta, as late as 2007 it announced plans for expansion in Java, Bali, and Sumatra. The company also engaged in real estate and property management. Then in early 2008 it announced that it was closing its supermarket division. An article in *The Jakarta Post* reported "PT Metro Supermarket Realty Tbk (MTSM) has closed down its trading business due to a steady decline in customers over the last five years, a company official said Saturday. 'The supermarket business has been really slow in the last five years due to a decrease in the number of consumers,' MTSM director Arief Amin said in a report to the Indonesia Stock Exchange on Friday. Arief said the situation had hurt the company's net income, making it impossible for the company to cover its operational costs. 'This is why we closed down our supermarkets.' ... In a public disclosure on Dec. 10, 2007, MTSM's management said last year's profit had fallen short of expectations due to sky-rocketing oil and fuel prices and an increase in natural disasters, all of which had influenced consumer purchasing power. Former chairman of the Indonesian Retail Traders Association, Handaka Santosa, ... said purchasing power was not the only determining factor in the retail industry. 'Numerous other smaller supermarkets, including Tip Top and Hari Hari, are still surviving. It may be that (MTSM's) supermarket division is lacking innovation,' he told *The Jakarta Post*. 'It needs to take into account consumer comfort, promotion and availability of products.' 'Modern consumers are now more concerned about health,' he said, adding that the industry needed to adapt to the changing needs of families, many of which are adopting healthier lifestyles."[52] In this case, even though the managing director was Indonesian, the company had problems adapting to local circumstances.

British-based Tesco PLC has its origins in a stall selling surplus groceries in London's East End established in 1919. Tesco operates Tesco Extra hypermarkets, Tesco Superstores (large grocery stores), Tesco Metro stores (mid-sized grocery stores), Tesco Express stores (neighborhood convenience stores), and One Stop stores. In relation to the comment cited above about Metro's problems in Indonesia is Tesco's promotion of organic and what it calls healthy living products not only in its stores in the United Kingdom, but in its stores in other countries as well.

The history of Tesco's expansion outside of the United Kingdom is similar to the other two companies, but not precisely the same in that its first venture outside of the United Kingdom was a store in Jakarta's Menteng Prada building in 1977 (the store closed in 1999 during Indonesia's economic crisis). This, however, was an isolated development. Its second venture was not until 1992 when the company opened a Vin Plus outlet in Calais selling wine, beer, and spirits. Tesco next moved into the emerging Eastern European market, opening stores in Hungary in 1994, Poland in 1995, and the Czech Republic and Slovakia in 1996. Currently it has a store under construction in Croatia. In 1997 it also began operating in Ireland and in 2003 it began operating in Turkey.

Tesco's expansion in Eastern Europe took place within the context another transnational corporation's decision to sell its Eastern European assets. Kmart — the world's third largest discount store chain after Wal-Mart and Target and operator of hypermarkets known as Kmart Super Centers — was a pioneer in the Eastern European market: "Kmart became the first full-line discount store chain to take advantage of the new free markets of Eastern Europe by purchasing as many as 13 Czechoslovakian retail stores."[53] These were former government-run stores and Kmart's operations in Eastern Europe proved to be quite profitable, but Kmart's financial problems back in the United States forced it to sell its Eastern European stores to Tesco in 1996.[54]

Despite its problems in Indonesia, starting with Thailand in 1998 Tesco began active expansion in the Asian markets. After opening in Thailand in 1998 (where it currently has 607 stores), in 1999, the same year that it closed its store in Indonesia, Tesco expanded its operations in Asia to South Korea. In partnership with one of Malaysia's largest transnational companies, Sime Darby Berhad, Tesco began operating in Malaysia in 2002. Its expansion in Malaysia included the purchase of the Dutch-German-owned Makro wholesale stores in the country and turning them into Tesco Extra stores. Tesco entered the Japanese market in 2003, first buying out local C Two Network discount stores and the next year the Fre'c grocery store chain. Both of these local firms were in financial trouble. Writing about Tesco's move into the Japanese market, Measure and McNeil noted, "Tesco, which trades in 10 countries, has shunned the Japanese expansion route favoured by rival international retailers such as Wal-Mart and Carrefour. While they have opted to buy hypermarkets, Tesco has limited its search to convenience stores and small supermarkets in an attempt to prosper from the Japanese shopping habits—little and often.... A Tesco spokesman said there were 'no plans' to either rebrand the Japanese stores under its red, blue and white banner, or to stock any Tesco own-label products in them. He said the group would continue its cautious approach to expanding in Japan until it better understood the market."[55]

Tesco began operating in the PRC in 2004 (currently 79 stores) and began operating in Indonesia again in 2007. Its move back into Indonesia reflects the economic recovery of that country. In the case of the PRC it purchased a 50 percent share of the Taiwanese Hymall chain, which had stores mainly in the Shanghai area. The success of this investment led the company to increase its share to 90 percent in 2006. In 2007 Tesco launched its Fresh & Easy stores in the western United States. Tesco announced plans to open stores in Pakistan in mid–2009 (the Tesco Pakistan website is currently under construction), starting with locales in affluent suburbs in Islamabad and Karachi. The company also has plans to begin wholesale operations in India (the only type such a foreign company is allowed under current Indian laws) in part to supply the large Indian conglomerate Tata's Star Bazaar stores.

Thailand, where the company operates under the name Tesco Lotus, currently has the most Tesco stores with the largest area outside of the United Kingdom, and the Thai operations account for the largest turnover outside of the United Kingdom after Ireland. Tesco entered the Thai market in 1998 in partnership with the Charoen Pokphand Group, Thailand's largest business conglomerate. Founded by Sino-Thais in 1921, the CP Group's core business is in agribusiness, but it also operates 7-Eleven stores and telecommunications businesses through its True Corporation. The CP Group has around 350,000 employees and has over 250 subsidiaries in 20 countries (it is particularly active in the PRC). In part in response to populist criticism within the country about the growth of hypermarkets, the CP Group sold its share of Tesco Lotus in Thailand to Tesco in 2003, while retaining an interest in the company's operations in the PRC (under the Lotus name). Despite such criticism, Tesco Lotus has thrived in Thailand with the growth of that country's middle class. Tesco Lotus stores have around 20 million customers a month. At the latest count, the company has 24 Supercenters in Bangkok and 31 more in other cities along with hundreds of Lotus Markets, Value stores, and Express stores. Also, the company sources 97 percent of its products in Thailand.

In 2005 Tesco and Carrefour announced the sale of stores to one another in order for each one to concentrate on those countries where they were doing particularly well. Tesco sold its stores in Taiwan to Carrefour and Carrefour sold its stores in the Czech Republic and Slovakia to Tesco. This did not mean an end to competition since both companies continued to operate in countries such as the PRC and Thailand, until 2010, when Carrefour announced plans to sell its stores in Thailand — and Tesco emerged as one of the leading contenders to buy the stores (along with Aeon and others).[56]

In the case of Thailand, Tesco and Carrefour have had to compete with a third chain of hypermarkets, Big C with its Big C Supercenters. The Big C stores were started by another large Thai conglomerate — the Central Group of Companies — that has interests in department stores, hotels, restaurants, and real estate and founded by a Sino-Thai in 1947. The first Central Superstore opened in Bangkok in 1994 — i.e., before Carrefour and Tesco entered the Thai market. In the face of competition from these two companies, in 1999 the Central Group sold a 63 percent interest in Central Superstore to Groupe Casino of France.

Under Groupe Casino's management Big C improved its performance in Thailand

and expanded its operations in Vietnam. Groupe Casino opened the Casino Supermarché in the Saigon suburbs of Dong Nai in 1998 (the first supermarket in the city). After its takeover of Big C in Thailand it renamed its Dong Nai store Big C and opened a series of new Big C supermarkets and hypermarkets in Vietnam. Currently there are three in Saigon, one in Hanoi (the largest of its stores), one in Haiphong, and one in Danang. Big C is the only one of the European hypermarket chains that operates retail stores in Vietnam at present and the company considers these stores to be highly successful. Thus, the company's French manager for the central and northern region of Vietnam shortly after the opening of the Da Nang store reported in an article entitled "Big C Da Nang Overloaded by Customers: Executive Director Laurent Bugeau says People Please Be Patient" that the store had to face a wave of 50,000 customers during its first two days of operation.[57]

Transnational Corporate Culture

Most people working for transnational corporations do not lead what can be characterized as a transnational lifestyle, although their lives may still be influenced by transnationalism. The transnational lifestyle is largely reserved for managers and other skilled workers who move globally through the corporation's operations. There are two aspects of the transnational culture within which such people operate that can be singled out for attention. One is their own lifestyles and the other is how they relate to those they must work with who are from different cultural backgrounds than their own. While we will focus on these two issues, it is important to remember that to some extent even relatively low-level employees of transnational corporations that are operating outside of their country of origin are influenced by transnationalism through the corporate culture within which they work.

As Chan and Douw note, "Many international joint ventures and multinational corporations have discovered that the cultural identities of their employees and many sociopolitical and cultural factors are crucial for corporate success or failure," adding that "cultural conflict is a major problem for the management of transnational enterprises."[58] Hofstede was an early study examining the cultural dimensions of work in such corporate settings highlighting issues related to power distance, individualism versus collectivism, masculinity versus femininity, and risk avoidance.[59] In the case of Western companies operating in the PRC, for example, often cited cultural differences include Chinese particularism versus Western universalism and the Chinese emphasis on maintenance of the collective, interpersonal harmony, conformity to the existing social structure and power hierarchy, face saving, reciprocity, the importance of personal connections (*guanxi*), preference of indirect, informal, non-assertive, non-aggressive, accommodating, compromising ways that avoid direct conflict or confrontation.

In their study of 31 Japanese-owned companies in the Düsseldorf region Germany Lincoln, Kerbo, and Wittenhagen examine differences in cultural patterns and organizational styles between the German and Japanese employees and the problems these pose for communication, cooperation, and morale.[60] Looking at cultural contrasts they highlight issues related to language, interpersonal styles such as personability and politeness, as well as norms regarding the taking of responsibility. They also point to differences in organizational practices such as German specialism versus Japanese generalism and direct and vertical versus indirect and incremental decision-making. Significantly, the authors found that the Japanese-owned companies often sought to find compromises to such differences and in terms of labor relations they fared "no better or worse than comparable German firms."

While such differences no doubt exist, it is important to recognize that at least in some instances such perceived cultural differences between employees of such corporations are strategic ploys or political devices and they may be exaggerated. Chan and Douw remark, "While some cultural differences are real, others are perceived, constructed in the eyes of the beholder, imagined, created artificially and exaggerated — as a result of encounters between two groups, consequently magnifying and hardening whatever initial difference they might have."[61] It is also important to recognize the opposite, whereby perceived cultural similarities may mask differences. Thus, ethnic Chinese from Singapore, Mauritius, and elsewhere around the world point to cultural affinities, which allow them to work with their counterparts in the PRC. While, to some extent such similarities do exist, they too are often exaggerated and belie difference between those who have lived and worked under the PRC's communist regime versus those living in very different social and cultural environments. Such differences are especially noticeable when ethnic Chinese from outside of the PRC interact with people from the PRC working with state-owned enterprises.

While to some extent all transnational corporations share certain basic cultural values as capitalist enterprises they also tend to exhibit the cultural imprint of their country or countries of origin. The most obvious example of this is language. While English serves as a *lingua franca* among transnational corporations, those companies from non–English-speaking countries also rely heavily on the language of the country of origin Such cultural factors are also often apparent in corporate etiquette (bowing, hand-shaking, etc.), forms of recreation (sports, drinking, etc.), as well as in more subtle ways such the cultural patterns associated with the Chinese already mentioned.

As was noted above, such differences sometimes have a political dimension. This can assume many forms. One of these forms is the manner in which intermediaries—often referred to as middlemen, brokers or compradors—do not simply serve as bridges between a company operating in a foreign setting and the local population but sometimes seek to emphasize or maintain cultural differences in order to strengthen their own positions. [62] This aspect of their activities cast them in a negative light in the post-colonial world as nationalist leaders of newly independent states viewed such persons as hindering the transfer of knowledge, skills, and technology. The political dimension of such cultural differences is also apparent in the extent to which the management of the company perceives the ways of doing business emanating from the country of origin as being superior to local ways. Whether it is Western companies operating in the PRC, Japanese companies operating in Hong Kong,[63] or South Korean companies operating in Indonesia, it is common for their managers and other employees from the home country to view their way of doing things as superior to local ways. In this regard, local employees are often judged according to the extent to which they acculturate to this corporate culture and such feelings of superiority are often a source of tension within the overseas operations of transnational corporations.

Writing about the experiences of Western companies operating in the PRC, Chan and Douw note that while Westerners are often "eager to implement in China the corporate culture of their parent companies in terms of liberalism, procedural transparency, encouraging self-motivation and commitment to company rather than self, emphasis on creativity, role flexibility and interchangeability, problem solving, continuous self-development, meritocracy, anti-discrimination, and so on" this has met with varying degrees of resistance in China, especially by those more comfortable with "the traditional Chinese state enterprise style informed by communism, control and authoritarianism."[64] They comment, "Chinese managers are ambivalent about Western ways, attracted to parts of them (for example, transparency, reward based on merit and performance) but also not liking other parts (for example, the preoccupation with techniques, science, rationality or rationalism)." Often, "Chinese managers feel that their local knowledge and expertise are not being fully respected and used, thinking that they have something valuable and useful to teach their non–Chinese colleagues: for example, the importance of patience, face saving, human relationships and local connections (*guanxi*), and proper ways of dealing with Chinese officials."[65]

As for those who work transnational corporations in their overseas operations in recent years, Chan and Douw point out that in the case of foreign companies in the PRC, "some foreign managers, especially those who have worked in China for years and have wisely learned to adapt to the local context, may think and behave differently from their bosses back home in the parent company ... which sets up another dialectic between expatriate managers and the senior management of their parent companies."[66] They add in the case of Chinese managers trained in Western management that such individuals "are hybrids, marginal or translated men and women who live on the margins of two cultures, two social worlds, the Chinese and the non–Chinese, that don't mix or perhaps only mix in the longer term. While they may well be agents of culture change in the joint ventures, they also have their share of anxiety and nervousness because they may well be distrusted by both sides because they belong to neither."[67] Thus, divisions still exist, but the barriers are not absolute and there is a growing tendency even in the PRC on the part of both expatriate and local managers to operate in a mixed cultural manner.

While the corporate culture of some transnational corporations continues to be marked by cultural chauvinism and differences, as the study by Lincoln, Kerbo, and Wittenhagen of Japanese-owned companies in Germany found, it is increasingly common in recent years for differences to be blurred, for compromises to be sought, and for hybrid transnational corporate cultures to emerge.[68] In their study of Sino-German joint-ventures in the PRC, Munder and Krieg found that despite perceived cultural differences on the part of German and Chinese managers, professionals from both countries had a great deal in common and shared a wide range of what they both perceived as modern versus traditional cultural values.[69] The authors argue that the perceived differences are in fact stereotypes that reflect the social separation of the two groups than actual cultural differences. Moreover, both the Germans and the Chinese viewed an awareness of local knowledge as important in order for their companies to operate successfully in the PRC and saw increased localization of corporate culture as a long-term goal more than the imposition of outside cultural values.

This recognition of the importance of local cultural values (and markets) by transnational corporations relates to what Ghemawat refers to as semi-globalization.[70] In his critique of globalized business strategies, Ghemawat examines how one-size-fits-all strategies by corporations have failed because they do not adequately take into account of cross-border differences. Using case studies of Cemex, Toyota, Procter & Gamble, Tata Consultancy Services, IBM, and GE Healthcare, he examines companies that have successfully managed transnational differences through the process of adjusting to such differences (adaptation), overcoming them (aggregation), and finally being able to exploit them (arbitrage).

The example cited above focuses mainly on the growing recognition of the relevance of local cultures to the overall corporate culture of these transnational corporations, thus producing a local transnational hybrid corporate culture. Another important trend is the mixture of personnel, especially at higher levels of management, in such a way that the culture of such management is becoming hybridized to the point that it no longer clearly belongs to any particular cultural tradition, but is best characterized as a global corporate culture. We have already seen how companies such as Metro Cash & Carry can move a Western European manager from one emerging market in Eastern Europe to another in India on the basis of his knowledge of such emerging markets in a general sense rather than his specific knowledge of any one of these markets (although knowledge of particular markets is also valued in the case of this company).

Western Managers in Japanese Corporations

The appearance of Western managers in Japanese-owned corporations is especially interesting in regard to the development of this global corporate culture. Writing in the midst of America's near hysteria about the perceived invasion of Japanese corporations in the late 1980s, when direct Japanese investment in the United States reached 10 times the level that it had been at the beginning of the 1980s, Barlett and Ghohal argued that "The massive shift of assets and resources offshore is likely to become the Japanese companies' Achilles heel rather than their Trojan horse" because of differences in management style between corporate headquarters back in Japan and that of their local operations in the United States. They noted that Japanese investment in the United States was accompanied by a desire to have their operations "closer and more responsive to local market needs and that "while European and U.S. managers have been treating their Japanese competitors' centralized operations as the ideal model for global competitive strategy, Japanese companies have been looking enviously at the politically connected, market-sensitive and locally staffed national units built by their Western counterparts over many decades. From Tokyo to Osaka, the new watchword is *rokaru* (localization)."[71]

The problem, as Barlett and Ghohal saw it, was how "to develop the means to integrate output from new offshore plants and research and development labs into an effective global network, and to give their non–Japanese managers access to and legitimacy in their management system" since "Historically, most Japanese companies have treated their overseas operations as delivery pipelines for products and strategies developed at the center." Japanese companies operating abroad simply had extended their styles of management based on consensus building and shared decision making to their overseas operations. To maintain such a system meant that Japanese companies relied heavily on expatriate Japanese managers— at the time "typically 10 to 20 times the number in comparable U.S. or European companies— whose managers constantly traveled back and forth between the subsidiaries and company headquarters in Japan. They cite the example of Tokyo-based electronics transnational NEC where its corporate managers made more than 10,000 trips abroad in 1983. As Japanese corporations became increasing active overseas in the 1980s the structure began to take a toll on managers who were "finding that they can no longer keep the grueling travel demands required to build consensus and gain commitment from their colleagues scattered around the globe." Moreover, such a centralized management structure by the late 1980s was proving to be a constraint on "their ability to get close to the American customer, create innovative products or take the risks necessary to be profitable in the highly competitive U.S. market."[72]

An added problem was how to integrate the increasing number of foreign managers in the subsidiaries into "their culture-bound decision-making process." While many Japanese companies had come to employ a greater percentage of local managers in their subsidiaries than in the past, top positions remained in Japanese hands and foreigners remained marginal to the core of corporate decision-making: "Through nightly calls to Japan and after-hours meetings together, this expatriate group [of Japanese managers] develops such enormous power and influence that the local management often feels cut out of the communications loop and manipulated in the decision-making process. As a result, many Japanese companies have found difficulty in attracting and retaining top-quality local nationals in key management roles."[73] They cite the example of Motorola after it was acquired by Matsushita where such centralized Japanese management resulted in the loss of most of the company's talented engineers.

Many Japanese transnational corporations had already begun to abandon their centralized management style in favor of a more decentralized one when the Japanese bubble burst and the country entered a prolonged period of economic stagnation. By the end of the 1990s Japanese management was beginning to resemble that of Western transnational corporations to the point that Western managers were being hired at the highest levels by Japanese corporations. Moreover, while the Japanese language continued to be widely used by Japanese-based corporations, use of English had become more widespread at upper levels of management. Yoshida cites an example from Mitsubishi: "Takashi Sato of Mitsubishi Motors Corp. fears he may be transferred because of his poor command of English — a potentiality that was unthinkable until last year. The fear emerged when his new, non–Japanese boss arrived in July from DaimlerChrysler AG. The German manufacturing giant announced in March 2000 that it would rescue Japan's No. 4 automaker by acquiring a controlling stake, currently at 37.3 percent. 'I have to write about half of my documents in both English and Japanese so higher-ups can read them,' said Sato (not his real name), who works in MMC's finance and public relations department in Tokyo. Because he often needs to ask coworkers to help translate documents, he said he is thinking of going to an English-language school." As Yoshida notes, this was not an isolated example: "Like MMC, many top-brand Japanese companies—including Nissan Motor Co. and Japan Telecom Co.—are now under the control of former foreign rivals. The changing climate is having an effect on corporate culture, with the use of English becoming almost a must, and top-down management styles replacing consensus-based management."[74]

Carlos Ghosn is undoubtedly the most prominent foreigner to have assumed a top management position of a Japanese corporation—Nissan in this case. Noting that he is fluent in French, Arabic, English, and Portuguese—and "quickly catching up in Japanese"—CNN refers to him as "the quintessential international businessman."[75] He was born in Brazil, his parents having migrated there from Lebanon. His father worked for an airline and at the age of 6 Carlos returned to Lebanon with his mother, where he completed secondary school at a Jesuit college.[76] He then went to Paris to study, graduating with an engineering degree in 1978. He is a Brazilian, Lebanese, and French citizen. He worked for the French-based transnational corporation Michelin for 18 years, holding positions as a plant manager and head of a research and development branch in France, then serving as its COO for South American operations based in Brazil, and finally as chairman and CEO of Michelin North America based in the United States. He then moved to work for the Renault Group, where he became its executive vice president in 1996 and supervised its operations in South America.

Japanese automaker Nissan was in serious financial trouble in the late 1990s and was forced to seek foreign help. This came in the form of Renault acquiring a 36.8 percent share of the company and Carlos Ghosn becoming Nissan's chief operating officer in mid–1999. He became Nissan's president the following year, and its chief executive officer in mid–2001. Many of Nissan's troubles were blamed on its poor management and Ghosn radically changed its style of management and broke with Japanese business norms at the time by cutting 21,000 jobs (16,500 of these within Japan), closing five of its domestic plants, auctioning 11 of its non-core assets (including its aerospace unit), and announcing that it would buy parts wherever they were cheapest rather than from its traditional suppliers. These moves initially created a great deal of adverse publicity, but when a year later instead of reporting a U.S. $6.1 billion loss as the company had the previous year (the greatest loss that year of any Japanese company) it posted a U.S. $2.7 billion profit (the highest yearly profit ever recorded for the company) he became a national hero.[68] In addition to his positions with Nissan, Ghosn became CEO of Renault in 2005 and also was appointed to the boards of three other transnational corporations: Alcoa, Sony, and IBM. In terms of management within Nissan, not only were all board meetings held in English once Ghosn took over management of the company, but Yoshida quotes a 45-year-old worker from a Nissan-affiliated company, "A decision that would have taken 10 days before can now be made in two hours," and, as a result, "Everybody in my section is in better spirits now. The atmosphere has certainly changed."[78]

Sony Corporation and its current chairman, president, and CEO Howard Stringer provides another example of the transformation of the top management of a major Japanese transnational corporation. Howard Stringer is Welsh by birth. He received a B.A. and M.A. from Oxford University in Modern History and immigrated to the United States, serving in the United States armed forces during the Vietnam War from 1965 to 1967 and becoming a naturalized American citizen in 1985. After leaving the military he worked for CBS as a journalist, producer, and served as president of the company from 1988 to 1995. He went to work for Sony in 1997 and in 2005 he became chairman and CEO of the company. As Brooke points out, "Sony, of course, has always followed an international path that was far more open to foreigners than most Japanese companies. Akio Morita, who founded Sony in 1946, lived for extended periods in New York. Facing entrenched competition at home, he built Sony on overseas sales and overseas investment."[79] Thus, in many ways even before Stringer's rise to become head of the company, Sony was already the most transnational of Japan's major transnational corporations. Nevertheless, its management was still largely Japanese in character.

The transformation of Sony's management culture from being predominantly Japanese to transnational has been gradual and is reflected in the rise of Stringer within the managerial hierarchy. Stringer initially served as head of Sony's North American operations. Faced with serious economic problems, in June 2005 Sony made Stringer chairman and CEO of its entire international operations. He was the first non–Japanese to hold these posts. In May of that year, however, Rioji Chubachi, who is Japanese and a long-time employee of the company who is best known for his role in developing the 8-millimeter video camera, had been appointed president. Brooke reported on the extent to which, by 2005, Stringer's appointment was viewed as normal in Japan: "Japan looked globalization in the eye on Monday. On television, the new chairman of the Sony Corporation, a ruddy-faced Welsh-American wearing a red tartan tie, was giving a news conference in English. Japan didn't blink.[80]

That Stringer's appointment to two of Sony's top positions should be viewed as much more normal than Ghosn's earlier appointment to run Nissan represented considerable change in the overall structure of both equity ownership and management in Japanese-based transnational corporations that has spurred on not just by Japan's financial and managerial problems that had emerged as its bubble economy had burst, but also by increased competition internationally from companies based in the People's Republic of China. The combination of these two factors served to stimulate "a quiet sea change in attitudes toward foreign investment and foreign management."[81] To place Renault's investment in Nissan in perspective, in 1990 foreign ownership of shares on the Tokyo Stock Exchange stood at only 4.7 percent. By 2003 the figure was 21.8 percent. In regard to changes towards greater transnationality, this was reflected in the fact that by 2005 around 100 of the 3,000 companies on the Tokyo Stock Exchange had adopted "American-style corporate governance and transparency rules."[82] Brooke quotes Hiroyuki Hosada, the Chief Cabinet Secretary, who noted at a press-conference held after Stringer's appointment that there was "nothing strange about the appointment," adding that Japanese companies were being internationalized."[83]

The response within Sony itself to Stringer's appointment is indicated by responses made by the chairman of Sony's board of directors Iwao Nakatani, in an interview: "This is the beginning of the new discussion of how corporate governance should be."[84] In fact, Stringer's appointment proved to be just the beginning of Sony's gradual transformation. Faced with record losses in 2008 of around U.S. $2.7 billion, in February 2009 Sony's board of directors voted to make Stringer president as well, ousting Chubachi, who was made vice chairman in charge of product safety, quality, and environmental issues. This coincided with changes in the structure and management of several of the company's divisions along with an announcement that the company was going to shut some of its plants and lay off 16,000 workers. Suzuki and Kondo quote a response to this news by one Japanese analyst: "These moves are bolder than we had anticipated and are positive.... "We believe the new management and organization will be effective in bringing out Sony's potential in this new networked age."[85]

Commenting on Ghosn's radical reforms at Nissan, Toyota Motors chairman Hiroshi Okuda's response at a news conference is especially interesting in relation to transnationalism: "Something so drastic is too difficult for a Japanese manager. It's probably easier for Mr. Ghosn to do that because he has no bonds" with people in the group companies.[86] Yuuki Sakurai, general manager of Tokyo-based Fukoku Mutual Life Insurance Co., made a similar response after Stringer's appointment as president of Sony: "The Japanese can't take decisive actions toward their comrades during hardship.... As a non–Japanese without such loyalties, Stringer is better positioned to conduct the large-scale restructuring that Sony has to do."[87]

We have already discussed Aeon in relation to Carrefour's activities in Asia and Aeon's own expansion outside of Japan. While at the local level management of subsidiary companies and stores is commonly comprised of a mixture of Japanese nationals and locals with people of other nationalities also often playing a role in management as well, until recently the board of directors of the Aeon Group remained exclusively Japanese. In 2009 Aeon made news by appointing its first non–Japanese, Jerry Black, to the board.[88] Black's appointment was directly related to Aeon's decision to place more emphasis on its transnational operations and it was announced that he would be taking charge of Aeon's "business in China [the PRC], Southeast Asia and other places, as well as group strategy."[89] It also highlights the important role of transnational consulting firms to the global operation of transnational corporations such as Aeon. Black graduated from West Virginia University and worked with various retail companies and transnational consulting firms, specializing in assisting with mergers, acquisitions, and transformations of large corporations.[90] He joined the consulting firm Kurt Salmon Associates—"We have the privilege of working with 30 of the world's top 50 — and all of the top 5 — retailers, global and specialty brands"[91]— in 1995, working in their Tokyo office to help build their operations in the Asia-Pacific region. He then moved to the firm's North American headquarters, where his work included "coordinating teams across KSA's North American, European, and Asia-Pacific regions," and he was appointed its CEO in 2008.[92] Aeon was among Kurt Salmon's clients in Japan. The current "team" of KSA's Japan office includes two Japanese nationals and David Hamaty, who is Director of its Asia-Pacific Retail and

Consumer Products Group and, as noted in the company website, "has over 14 years of experience in Japan and Asia" and "is fluent in Japanese."[93]

Not all Japanese companies under foreign management have undergone such radical changes. Yoshida cites the example of International Digital Communications that was renamed Cable & Wireless IDC after it was taken over by British-based Cable & Wireless PLC in 1999 (becoming a 97.69 percent owned subsidiary).[94] Yoshida quotes the Japanese general manager of the company's human resources department, "'The Japanese way is to carefully form a consensus before making a decision. But now we make a decision even if some people are against it.' Quick, transparent decision-making has brought better results to the company, Fujioka continued. And besides, he added, reaching absolute consensus is almost impossible in the first place."[95] Moreover, the company "also revised salary and promotion systems more in line with British standards, applying performance-based evaluations rather than seniority." What the new British management did not do, however, was to drastically reduce the workforce: "IDC is a Japanese company," said Roger Downes, vice president of C&W IDC. "And we cannot change that."[96] Significantly, unlike Nissan, which was a transnational corporation even before Renault acquired a stake in the company, Cable & Wireless IDC was a domestic company and even though now it is a subsidiary of a British-based transnational corporation its operations remain essentially domestic. Moreover, in most instances where foreign firms acquired interest in Japanese domestic companies the language of management remained overwhelmingly Japanese.

It is interesting to speculate about the fate of the corporate culture of the growing number of transnational corporations based in the PRC. Economic activity beyond the PRC's borders can be seen in terms of capital flows relating to overseas investment that rose from less than U.S. $1 billion in 2000 to U.S. $53 billion in 2008 — an amount that Lund, Roxburgh, and Roy point out is "equal to the aggregate of the previous six years."[97] Moreover, sitting on huge foreign reserves, in May 2009 the PRC's State Administration of Foreign Exchange made it easier for companies to raise dollars to invest overseas. So the level of foreign activity will undoubtedly increase substantially in the future.

Since these PRC-based companies are predominantly state-owned enterprises, it is not surprising that their employees are from the PRC and that corporate cultures are overwhelmingly one that has developed within the PRC. Their overseas operations also tend to be more insulated from local societies than those of other transnational corporations. That said, there is evidence of change. Thus, as Lund, Roxburgh, and Roy note, "Asian sovereign-wealth funds are also making some changes. They have increased transparency to allay concerns about their investments. They have also accelerated their hiring of outside financial professionals, tapping the talent being shed by Western banks and other financial institutions."[98] Added to the large number of managers and other professionals form the PRC working in such companies who have received training overseas it is possible that more of a hybrid corporate culture will develop in the future.

6

CRIMINAL ORGANIZATIONS AND NETWORKS

A couple of years ago I found myself chasing away a Nigerian drug smuggler who was harassing one of my field school students in Vientiane, Laos. I was surprised by the appearance of the Nigerian and his associates in Vientiane. Even though such people had been a common sight in Bangkok, especially around the back-packer area of Kao San Road, where they would sell illegal drugs and look for female tourists to convince them to smuggle drugs, this was the first time that I had seen these guys in Laos. The narcotics being smuggled include heroin and methamphetamines that are produced in northern Burma (Mayanmar) from where they are smuggled to neighboring countries and throughout the world. In retrospect, I should not have been so surprised since Nigerian drug smugglers seem to appear wherever there are large numbers of back-packers and by the mid–2000s Laos was a major part of the Southeast Asian back-packer circuit. The Nigerian narcotics smuggling connection with Laos appeared in the international news in 2009 in relation to a case involving 20-year-old Samatha Orobator, a Nigerian-born British citizen, who claimed to have gone on holiday to the Netherlands, Thailand, and then Laos, where she was caught attempting to smuggle heroin through Vientiane's international airport. Sentenced to death, she was allowed to leave Laos after she became pregnant and her case caught the attention of the Western media and she was permitted to serve a life-sentence in a British prison.

Of particular interest here are not so much the foreign tourists who are talked into carrying drugs across borders, but more the network of people who are involved in trafficking on a regular basis and who can be viewed as forming transnational networks and in some instances transnational organizations. This chapter focuses on the social organization of those engaged in illegal activities across borders on a regular basis. As Bunt and Siegel write in regard to transnational crime, "'Transnational' implies that organized crime is in essence cross-border crime."[1] They use the example of human trafficking, which "is almost by definition a transnational crime; the profit for the trafficker lies in the difference in opportunities between different countries." They also point to three common general patterns in transnational organized crime whereby (1)

"Global organized crime follows the usual trade routes and patterns of migration," (2) "major events with global consequences also influence the nature and form of organized crime," and (3) "there is good reason to describe the modus operandi of organized crime as a distinctly local problem" in that "criminals who run international operations often rely on a local power base, propped up by friendships of many years' standing or close-knit families."[2] In regard to the second point they note how such events can have far reaching consequences. They cite as an example how the end of the Cold War and collapse of communism in Eastern Europe can be linked to the involvement of the left-wing movement FARC in the Colombian cocaine trade since the fall of communist regimes in Eastern Europe meant an end of financial support for FARC by these regimes.

Beyond simply committing crimes across borders, transnational criminal organizations and networks have bases in more than one country from which to conduct criminal activity. Thus, in looking at the transnational aspect of such groups and networks we are concerned specifically with the nature of the bases these organizations and networks establish in more than one state and how they link their criminal activities across state borders. While criminals have been carrying out illegal activities across borders essentially since the creation of such borders in the form of smuggling and cross border forays to carry out criminal acts, actual transnational criminal organizations and networks are a relatively recent development that is linked to modern innovations in transportation and communication. Prior to the advent of such innovations as transoceanic steamship travel, transcontinental air travel, and the internet, criminals rarely operated too far from their home base and certainly not on a regular basis. Even the most wide ranging criminal groups, such as maritime pirates who would sometimes conduct raids far from their home strongholds or ports, rarely had a regular presence in more than one locale — they simply raided a distant place and then went home. Thus, the relative ease of modern travel and communication has served to lay the basis for the formation of criminal groups and networks that operate across borders on a regular basis. It should be kept in mind, however, that most criminals and criminal organizations remain highly localized and criminal organizations that operate transnationally are a relatively small, albeit very important, part of criminal activity worldwide.

Nigerian Transnational Criminal Networks

Laos has a long association with narcotics smuggling, having gained considerable notoriety in this regard during the Vietnam War, but the Nigerian connection is relatively new. As noted by Shaw and Wannenburg, "By 1990, Nigerian criminal groups were widely regarded as one of the most significant threats confronting law enforcement agencies in many countries. Nigerian groups were active across the globe, from Latin America to Asia, with particularly sophisticated operations in Europe and North America."[3] They add, "Unlike, say Colombian organized crime, the commodities that Nigerian groups smuggle, most notably heroin and cocaine, are not produced in West Africa. Nigerian criminal groups then act in the majority of criminal exchanges as transporters or middlemen; they have added value not by producing but by buying, moving, and selling."[4] A report by the United Nations Office on Drugs and Crime (2005: 1) begins, "In recent years, transnational organized crime in West Africa, or perpetrated by West Africans elsewhere in the world, has become a major international concern. This has been perhaps most noticeable in regard to drug-trafficking, people-trafficking and fraud. West African criminals operate in a global illicit market, sometimes making working arrangements with other international criminals."[5] Liddick writes of Nigerian criminal activities in the 1990s: "The U.S. State Department estimates that Nigerian criminal gangs working as subcontractors for the Russian Mafiya, Chinese Triads, Colombian cartels, or the various Italian criminal groups import as much as 40 percent of the heroin smuggled into the United States. Since the mid–1980s, over one thousand Nigerian nationals have been convicted of smuggling heroin into the United States. In 1994, Interpol found that Nigerians were the third largest ethnic drug smuggling group in the world."[6]

In testimony before the Subcommittee of Africa of the House International Relations Committee on 11 September 1996, Jonathan Winter, Deputy Assistant Secretary for International Narcotics and Law Enforcement Affairs, reported: "Our law enforcement agencies attest that Nigerian criminal enterprises are organized and active in at least 60 countries around the world. They are adaptable, polycrime organizations. They launder money in Hong Kong, buy cocaine in the Andes, run prostitution and gambling rings in Spain and Italy, and corrupt legitimate business in Great Britain with their financial crimes. Nigerian drug trafficking rings are notorious. The presence today of hundreds of convicted Nigerian traffickers in Indian, Pakistani, Thai, Turkish, and other international prisons is indicative of the international reach of the Nigerian crime rings."[7] More recently, Wannenburg cites the FBI's Organized Crime Section stating that these networks have a presence in 80 countries.[8]

An article in *The Economist* refers to West Africa as "the newest centre for trafficking drugs into Europe," and describes, "A fairly typical recent morning at Murtala Mohammed, Lagos's main airport, [that] saw four traffickers carrying cocaine, heroin or marijuana caught, arrested and X-rayed before noon. All but one of them lived abroad, in Belgium, India and Spain. Stuck without money or just looking for more, they had agreed to swallow the stuff or slip it into their luggage. Since the beginning of the year, Nigeria's Drug Law Enforcement Agency has made 234 similar arrests at this Lagos airport. But this, according to the agency's director-general, Lanre Ipinsisho, is just grazing the surface of the country's booming drug trade."[9] The United Nations Office on Drugs and Crime cites an "experiment at Amsterdam's Schiphol airport [that] involved screening passengers arriving from Aruba and the Dutch Antilles—a favorite drug-smuggling route used by some of the 1,200 couriers arrested at Schiphol in 2001. When Dutch customs officers noticed the increasing numbers of Nigerians using the route, they experimented by checking every single Nigerian arriving at Schiphol from Aruba or the Dutch Antilles for a period of ten days, rather than operating the usual spot-checks only. They found that of the 83 Nigerian passengers using the route over those 10 days, no fewer than 63 were carrying drugs."[10]

The press in most countries around the world carries occasional articles referring to problems with Nigerians involved in narcotics smuggling. For example, a 2006 article in *The Times of India* contained an interview with an officer of the Narcotics Control Bureau: "'Don't even mention Nigerian drug dealers to me. They are a headache,' said a Narcotics Control Bureau officer when asked about nationals from this oil-rich west African republic who have been in the news lately for their involvement in the international drug trade.... We have to understand that Nigerians involved in the drug trade are thorough professionals. Some of them have been at it for decades and have been held by police across the world. They have spent time in jail in every continent.... They speak their own native language to communicate.... Even dreaded members of the underworld prefer to maintain a safe distance from Nigerians...."[11] More recently, a 2009 article in *The Times of India* reported, "Every third foreign national arrested for drug-related offences in the country last year was from Africa and every fourth from Nigeria alone.... African drug syndicates pose a major challenge to drug enforcement agencies in India, primarily because of their trans-national links. Located within reach of the South American cocaine belt, West African nationals, especially Nigerians, play a decisive role in the drug's trafficking. Often, cartels prey on the African diaspora."[12]

Nigerians have been coming to Thailand in large numbers since the 1980s. Many of them come to buy wholesale clothing for export to Nigeria or they bring rough gems from Nigeria to the gem cutters of Bangkok and Konchanaburi. Quite a few come to engage in illegal activities, especially narcotics trafficking. Nigerians were well represented among the 12,528 foreigners in Thai prisons in 2007 and the 395 Nigerians that were transferred back to Nigeria to serve out their prison terms in that year were by far the largest foreign nationality to be repatriated. An article on heroin trafficking to the United States reported in regard to Nigerian traffickers, "Before 1997 Nigerian drug traffickers paid couriers between $2,000 and $5,000 (what an average Nigerian would earn in sixteen years) to transport a pound or two of heroin into the United States. In the late 1990s traffickers began using Express Mail Services (EMS) to ship heroin, concealing it in such items as pots and pans, children's books, and decorative figurines. The use of EMS is far cheaper than couriers, and packages can be mailed anonymously, with less chance of tracing them back to the trafficker if the heroin is discovered. Nigerian traffickers often use Thailand as a base of operation for their heroin trafficking. Most parcels seized originate in Thailand."[13]

Most of the narcotics originate in Burma, but the Nigerians obtain them mainly in Thailand after they have been smuggled from Burma to Thailand. In the case of heroin, the same report cited above stated: "Burma supplied an estimated 14% of the opium produced in the world in 2003, according to the INCSR. Its share of world production has decreased annually since the mid–1990s, when it out produced Afghanistan. The opium produced in Burma, Thailand, and Laos (the Golden Triangle) has traditionally gone by sea from Thailand to Hong Kong or Taiwan, where it was processed into heroin for local use or shipped on to the United States. Trafficking through China is on the increase, and much Golden Triangle opium is being processed into heroin in that country. A growing amount of heroin has been moving through Singapore and Malaysia, despite their strict drug laws."[14] As for methamphetamines, a 2005 report by the National Drug Intelligence

Center of the United States stated, "Burmese criminal groups are the principal producers of methamphetamine tablets in Southeast Asia. Intelligence reports indicate that Burmese criminal groups produce several hundred million methamphetamine tablets annually for distribution in drug markets in Thailand, China, and India."[15]

Nigerian drug traffickers have been turning up in neighboring Southeast Asian countries to the south of Thailand for a number of years. Despite Singapore having strict laws concerning narcotics in the world, a number of Nigerians have been caught smuggling narcotics, primarily at Changi Airport, which is a major international hub for airlines. The death penalty is mandatory in Singapore for anyone caught with more than 15 grams of illegal narcotics and 420 people were executed between 1991 and the end of 2006, mostly on charges of narcotics possession. A recent case involving a Nigerian is that of 21-year-old Iwuchukwu Amara Tochi. He was hanged on 26 January 2007 along with a stateless African, 35-year-old Okeke Nelson Malachy. The two were arrested in November 2004 at Changi Airport after arriving from Dubai with 727 grams of heroin.

In addition to their recent appearance in Laos, Nigerian narcotics smugglers and dealers have also arrived in the PRC. A story in Danwei tells of a Nigerian man charged with drug trafficking and sentenced to death in the Guangdong Province city of Dongguan, located in the Pearl River Delta near Hong Kong: "Both Osonwa Okey Noberts and his girlfriend, Zhang Dongxiang, received the death penalty for selling heroin to Chinese drug dealers, who were also on trial yesterday.... According to the report, this is the first case in Dongguan in which a foreigner was sentenced to death."[16] Anyone caught trafficking with more than 50 grams of heroin in the PRC can receive the death penalty and Noberts and Zhang had sold over 10,000 grams. Zhang testified that Noberts had brought the drugs into China to supply lower-tier drug dealers.

Turning to the case of Samatha Orobator and other Nigerian-born women in the United Kingdom who are involved in Nigerian drug trafficking, an article in the Nigerian newspaper *Daily Sun* refers to a "report that about 238 Nigerian women are currently serving various prison terms for drug trafficking in London.... Seventy of the women are said to be in a single prison, where they constitute a significant percentage of inmates of the prison.... Sadder still is the fact that the case of these women is a tip of the iceberg of the imprisonment of our compatriots for drug trafficking in foreign lands. So many of our citizens are in jail for drug trafficking in many parts of the world." As for reasons behind there being so many Nigerian women in prison on drug charges, while poverty is a factor, the article notes, "Nigeria is not the only country that is ravaged by poverty neither are the imprisoned persons the only poor persons in the country. The problem, we think, can also be traced to the collapse of values and the desperation of many Nigerians to become rich by all means, fair or foul," adding that the "permissive attitude to drug trafficking [in Nigeria] runs contrary to the serious view of the offence in many countries."[17]

Nigerian criminal organizations are commonly described as "criminal networks."[18] The United Nations Office on Drugs and Crime notes, "In the case of West Africa, it is particularly misleading to think of organized crime groups as being solid structures resembling major corporations of crime.... West African criminal networks are generally characterized by their great fluidity and flexibility, qualities that actually can be turned to great advantage in modern, globalized markets, including illegal ones."[19]

The historical and cultural context of the rise of Nigerian transnational criminal networks is to be found in long-standing Nigerian activities as traders, the impact of the 1970s oil boom and its collapse, and the growth of the overseas Nigerian population. As Robinson remarks, "opportunistic to the extreme, Nigerians as a group are historically recognized as the best traders in Africa, and were already doing business with the Arabs before the days of the slave trade," adding in the modern context in reference to so-called 419 scams "if they are nothing else, Nigerians as a group, are without any doubt, Africa's most talented, freewheeling con men."[20]

As for the number of Nigerian-born and people of Nigerian ancestry living outside of Nigeria (which itself has a population of around 140 million), they number around 20 million. Nigerians are scattered across the globe with the largest number of them living in the United Kingdom and the United States. The United Kingdom's 2001 census indicated that there were 90,000 Nigerian-born people living in the country, while the United Kingdom's Foreign and Commonwealth Office estimates in its country profile of Nigeria that there are a total of 800,000 to 2 million people of Nigerian ancestry or birth living in the United Kingdom (a figure that includes people born in the United Kingdom and living in the country illegally). In the case of the United States, the 2000 census enumerated 165,481 people of Nigerian ancestry and birth living in the country. Nigerians are highly concentrated in London in the United Kingdom, while they are quite scattered around the United States.

Significant levels of Nigerian immigration to the United Kingdom and United States began in the 1970s. Most of those migrating at this time came as university students. There was also movement of Nigerians to other parts of West Africa and migration of a large number of West Africans (especially Ghanaians) to Nigeria in search of work following formation of the Economic Community of West Africa in 1975. The United Nations Office on Drugs and Crime views this movement of people in West Africa at this time as contributing to the spread of criminal activities from Nigeria throughout West Africa.[21]

A number of the Nigerians in the United States and the United Kingdom remained overseas to settle in the 1980s as political and economic conditions in Nigeria deteriorated in the wake of the collapse of the oil boom. These migrants were joined by an increasing number of well-educated Nigerians forming part of what is sometimes characterized as a brain drain. The United Nations Office on Drugs and Crime notes, "After the end of the oil boom ... in the early 1980s, Nigerians were also impelled to spread throughout the region and further afield in search of economic opportunity, and to seek out a livelihood, if necessary by any means."[22] The collapse of the oil boom not only sent Nigerians outside of the country, but many West Africans (especially Ghanaians) who had migrated to Nigeria to work during the boom years were expelled when the boom collapsed: "This too was a major stimulus to the development of networks of people with experience of international migration, some of whom were induced to undertake criminal activities."[23] Thus, it was during this period of migration that Nigerian criminal activities quickly spread around the world. Nigerian migration overseas increased sharply in the 1990s, as social and economic conditions in Nigeria remained problematic. This increase can be seen by comparing the 165,481 Nigerians living in the United States in 2000 with the 35,300 reported in the 1990 census. The number of Nigerians enumerated in the United Kingdom from the 1991 to the 2001 censuses increasing by about 90 percent.

What is the nature of these Nigerian criminal networks? The United Nations Office on Drugs and Crime refers to them as being "project-based" along lines similar to businesses operated by legitimate traders.[24] The report cites a description in a 2004 seminar paper on organized crime in Nigeria by Etannibi E.O. Alemika: "The organizational structure [of criminal groups in West Africa] may be similar to [that] employed by legitimate small scale enterprises found [among] ethno-cultural groups disproportionately arrested for drug trafficking. First the enterprises usually involve masters [entrepreneurs] and apprentices [those training to traders or suppliers in particular goods and services]. Second, there is cooperation among the enterprise/entrepreneurs, such that if goods are not available in a given shop it is collected and supplied from another entrepreneur. Third, many of the entrepreneurs have relations or acquaintances abroad that facilitate payment for the imported goods, usually for a commission."[25] In addition, as we have seen from the examples cited earlier, they often recruit people on a one-time basis to carry out a task and such persons know little or nothing about those who are employing them and the overall network involved. As for the networks themselves, the UN report notes, "the practice of recruiting through networks of kinship, typically based on a village or other region of origin, means that the organization of a smuggling or criminal network may be facilitated by cultural codes known to the perpetrators, but more or less impenetrable to outsiders, including law enforcement officers. Relevant examples of this include the practice of administering oaths sworn by reference to religious oracles, and the e of local languages or dialects that make infiltration by outsiders extremely difficult."[26]

There is a degree of specialization among these networks. The UN report mentions that networks involved in prostitution tend to come from Edo State and Benin City "because those individuals who pioneered the trade have kept it in the hands of networks of kin and associates, thus excluding outsiders."[27] Carling states, "Of the approximately 800 Nigerian women who were returned from Italy to Nigeria during 1999–2001, a full 86 per cent came from Edo State. A further 7 per cent came from the neighboring Delta State." Narcotic trafficking is mainly in the hands of "Igbo-speaking people from southeast Nigeria and Yoruba from the south-west, and by southern minority groups."[28]

While Nigerian prostitutes are found in many countries in Europe and elsewhere, Italy is the main destination. Carling discusses the development of this link: "Early Nigerian emigration to Italy in the 1980s was not dominated by prostitution, and those who did arrive to work in the sex industry were often independent and not victims of traffickers. In the first half of the 1990s, however, to enter Italy became more difficult, and an increasing number needed to take loans to cover the costs. Initially the lenders were friends, but gradually it became more common to become indebted to a sponsor. This laid the basis for the establishment of a trafficking system based on a strong pact."[29]

How does the prostitution trafficking network operate? According to Carling, a "Young women's first contact with the trafficking network almost always happens through informal networks. It varies whether it is the woman herself or the other party who first takes the initiative. In many cases, friends or relatives of the woman are the first link. The conversations about traveling to Europe often take place in her home or in other familiar surroundings. The first person with whom the woman is in contact usually has no other role in the trafficking process than to establish contact. The victim may later come to regard this person as somebody who took advantage of her trust to trick her, or as a well-meaning person who was tricked, too. In this phase, the women are lured with promises of work as maids, sales personnel, or hairdressers, or with work in factories or restaurants, or with educational possibilities."[30] The contact person puts the woman in touch with a "madam" who Carling refers to as "the most important person in the network in Nigeria."[31] The madam or another person acts as the sponsor who finances the trip. There is another madam on the European side to receive the woman: "The *madam* in Italy is closely connected to the *madam* in Nigeria; often, they will belong to an extended family."[32] The other important figures in the network include "a religious leader (*ohen*) in Nigeria, the human smugglers who are responsible for the journey (*trolleys*), and a male assistant to the madam in Italy (*madam's black boy*)."[33] The role of the religious leader is to seal the pact between those involved in the operation, which commonly involves overseeing animal sacrifices and other rituals and sanctifying a package containing a variety of symbolic elements such as body materials from the women involved, koala nuts, bent pieces of metal, and soap.[34]

The UN report refers to these Nigerian criminal networks as being "vertically integrated."[35] This involves "having associates at every stage of the trading chain from buying at source (for example, heroin purchased in bulk in Pakistan) to the point of retail sale (typically, at street-level in North America and Europe), with every stage in between being handled by members of the same network." As the report points out, "This both ensures maximum profitability and also enables Nigerian drug-networks to co-exist with the more hierarchical, mafia-style operations that may dominate particular aspects of the trade, such as the more powerful Colombian criminal groups."[36] We will discuss the hierarchical criminal organizations later in the chapter. Within Nigeria itself Robinson mentions that Nigerian criminal enterprises have come to rely on members of the local Lebanese community (which numbers around 31,000) in the north of the country the launder some of their money.[37]

The Golden Triangle

Laos and Thailand, of course, conjure up images of the Golden Triangle and the international narcotics trade centering on the joint border area of Burma, Thailand, and Laos. Formerly the Shan State warlord Khun Sa and at present the members of the Wa ethnic group have been especially prominent among local players operating along the Burma-Thailand border with their operations being linked to international criminal networks that involve them with Italian, American, and Nigerian gangsters.

The Golden Triangle developed in the 1940s in the wake of the communist take-over in China, the end of British colonial order in Burma, and in relation to French policies promoting opium production by highland peoples in Laos and Tonkin (especially the ethnic Hmong producers led by Touby Ly Foung in Laos and ethnic Thai opium brokers led by Deo Van Long in Tonkin). Highland peoples in Mainland Southeast Asia have long-established traditions of opium production for local use and for trade. Urbanization and the rise of large Chinese immigrant populations in the lowlands of French Indochina and Siam increased demand for opium. The trade was largely within state boundaries, with ethnic minorities in the highlands (such as the Hmong) trading opium to intermediaries who were commonly ethnic Tai, who then in turn traded it to lowland traders who were usually ethnic Chinese. During the reign of King Mongkut in Siam in the mid–1800s ethnic Chinese merchants sold opium under a royal franchise. The trade became a royal monopoly administered by civil servants in 1907. The French took a similar approach in Indochina, franchising the sale of opium to ethnic Chinese merchants in Cochinchina in 1862 and establishing similar franchises in other parts of Indochina (including Laos) as they were brought under colonial rule. These franchises were consolidated in 1899 to form a single opium monopoly and refining of opium was centralized in Saigon.

One of the problems facing these lowland opium trading enterprises is the demand soon outstripped the ability of the highlanders productive capabilities. To overcome this shortfall the traders turned to Yunnan in China and later to the Middle East. By the late 1930s there were 2,500 opium dens and retail shops in Indochina that catered to over 100,000 addicts (the figure in Siam/Thailand at the time was around 110,000) and provided 15 percent of the colonial territory's budget — about 60 percent of the opium for this business was imported from Iran and Turkey.[38] This dependence on the Middle East for such a large percentage of the supply led to a crisis with the onset of World War II since shipping between Indochina and the Middle East was disrupted.[39] The French sought a solution by encouraging greater production by the highland Hmong in Laos and Tonkin and did so indirectly through local leaders. It was in this context that the Hmong leader Touby Ly Foung in Laos and the White Tai leader Deo Van Long rose in power and later served as important allies of the French in their fight against communist-led insurgents.

After World War II shipments of opium from the Middle East quickly resumed, with most of it coming from Iran until production there was curtailed in 1955, when Turkey became the major supplier. The seizure of power by the communists in China cut off this source. McCoy argues that it was decisions by the government of Thailand and the French colonial administration in Indochina in the early 1950s to supply the region's addicts from locally grown sources that transformed the Golden Triangle "into the largest single opium-producing area in the world" at the time.[40] In the case of Burma, increased opium production was linked to activities of members of the defeated Kuomintang who had fled to Burma's Shan State from China. From a transnational perspective what is significant here is that production grew beyond simply meeting local needs and the region was transformed from an importer to an exporter of opium. Moreover, whereas in the past, especially prior to a number of countries signing a United Nations Protocol in 1953 agreeing not to sell opium, the international trade had been conducted largely with the blessing of the various governments involved. After 1953 it was increasingly driven underground and came to involve international criminal organizations.

Production of opium and heroin for export in Mainland Southeast Asia in the early post–World War II era was largely in the hands of a few ethnically-based groups that were also involved in political struggles and was concentrated in the areas surrounding the Golden Triangle — Burma's Shan State, northern Laos (with small amounts being supplied by highland peoples in adjacent areas of northern Vietnam), and northern Thailand. Thailand was not as big a producer as its neighbors, but served as the main point of collection for worldwide distribution. Thus, in the 1950s the Kuomintang in Shan State would obtain opium from local highland peoples and then take it across the Thai border, where it was sold to police officers under the direction of the national head of the police force.[41] They carried it to Bangkok from where it was smuggled primarily to Malaysia, Indonesia, and Hong Kong, with only a small amount going to Western Europe and North America.

Within Indochina, the French intelligence service (SDECE) became involved in the trade to help fund its counterinsurgency activities between 1946 and 1954 and in so doing brought Corsican gangsters into the trade as well. McCoy describes the initial Corsican involvement in the trade: "From the nineteenth century onward, Corsicans had dominated the Indochina civil service. At the end of World War II, Corsican resistance fighters, some of them gangsters, had joined the regular army to come to Indochina with the Expeditionary Corps. Many remained in Saigon after their enlistment to go into legitimate business or to reap profits from the black market and smuggling that flourished under wartime conditions. Those with strong underworld connections in Marseille were able to engage in currency smuggling between the two ports.... Moreover, Corsican gangsters close to Corsican officers in Saigon's 2eme Bureau [the SDECE] purchased surplus opium and shipped it to Marseille, where it made a small contribution to the city's growing heroin industry."[42] This Corsican connection went into abeyance in the mid–1950s as the United States replaced France as the main supporter of the government in South Vietnam. It was revived in 1958 by Ngo Dinh Nhu (brother of President Ngo Dinh Diem) who sought to use revenue from the drug trade to fund his counterinsurgency activities, initially using chartered airplanes operated by Corsicans to fly the opium from Laos to Saigon,[43] where most of it was sold to Sino-Vietnamese operating opium dens in Cho Lon. By 1961 planes from Civil Air Transport, which later became Air America, were also involved.

Paul Louis Levet was among the more prominent of Corsican gangsters involved in the regional drug trade.[44] Levet came to Saigon around 1953–54 and began smuggling gold and piasters between Saigon and Marseille. He became involved in opium smuggling and moved to Bangkok in 1955, where he established a front named Pacific Industrial Company. McCoy lists 6 members of Levet's syndicate: Jacques Texier; Jean Giansil, who arrived in Saigon from France in 1954–5; Barthélemy Rutilly, Levet's man in Saigon; Charles Orsini, Levet's contact man in Phnom Penh; and "Tran Hug Dao" (an alias) a Vietnamese in Saigon who worked for the syndicate.[45] He also mentions Roger Zoile, who operated a charter airline based in Laos that transported drugs from the Golden Triangle to Levet in Thailand.[46] In addition to smuggling opium within the region, Levet's syndicate was involved in shipping morphine base that they obtained in northern Thailand to Marseille via Saigon on French freighters. Thai police caught Levet smuggling Burmese opium to Saigon at Bangkok's airport in 1963 and he was deported.

The French port city of Marseille was the heart of Corsican gangster activity in Europe.[47] Corsican gangsters are organized into networks more similar to those of the Nigerians than more formal hierarchical organizations. The Corsicans formed small syndicates to engage in such activities as heroin manufacturing and smuggling, smuggling currency and counterfeiting, and art thefts. The networks spread beyond the island of Corsica and the port of Marseille not only to Southeast Asia but also to various countries in the South Pacific, the United States and Canada, Latin America, North Africa, and the Middle East.

When General Khanh Ky became premier of South Vietnam in 1965 his associate General Nguyen Ngoc Loan, who became head of South Vietnam's Central Intelligence Organization, took over running the opium trade between Laos and Saigon (sometimes via an airdrop in the Central Highlands and then overland to Saigon). Smuggling morphine base (which was made into heroin) increased during the Ky administration. McCoy interviewed an American military officer about this in 1971 who told him, "Loan organized the opium exports once more as a part of the system of corruption. He contacted the Corsicans and Chinese, telling them they could begin to export Laos's opium from Saigon if they paid a fixed price to Ky's political organization."[48] The Ky narcotics organization was partially destroyed in 1968 in relation to the factional political struggle between Ky and General Nguyen Van Thieu after Thieu won the 1967 presidential election, but quickly reinvented itself as the regional narcotics market underwent a dramatic transformation.

Two important developments for Southeast Asia's narcotics market took place in the late 1960s and early 1970s that promoted a surge in production and trafficking: a massive increase in the number of American troops in South Vietnam and improvements in the quality of the heroin being produced locally. Prior to late 1969 and 1970 the Golden Triangle region produced mainly raw opium along with morphine base for shipment to Europe to be made into heroin and fairly crude heroin (referred to as "no. 3") for local consumption and export to Hong Kong, where some was consumed locally and some exported to the United States. A change came "in late 1969 and early 1970, [when] Golden Triangle laboratories added the final, dangerous ether precipitation process and converted to production of no. 4 heroin."[49] This was accomplished by bringing skilled ethnic Chinese chemists from Hong Kong with experience in the process. This improvement was made largely in response to increased demand for heroin in South Vietnam and "Once large quantities of heroin became available to American GIs in Vietnam, heroin addiction spread like the plague."[50] South Vietnamese traffickers provided the heroin to the American soldiers, and after the ousting of Sihanouk in Cambodia in March 1970 they were increasingly bringing the drugs into the country from Pakse in southern Laos via Cambodia rather than through the Central Highlands of Vietnam. The withdrawal of American troops that began just as heroin production was increasing to meet market demands led to a change in the destination of the drugs. Instead of going mainly to South Vietnam in 1971 large quantities began to be shipped to the United States and Western Europe.

Heroin trafficking between Laos and South Vietnam and then between the Golden Triangle and the United States in the early 1970s involved a number of distinct groups working in coordination. Opium poppy cultivation remained centered among Jingpho (Kachin), Shan, and other minority groups living in Shan State and among Hmong, Mien, and other minority groups living in Laos's Xieng Khoang and neighboring provinces in northeastern Laos. Members of these minority groups were also often used for transporting the opium within the mountainous region. McCoy cites CIA sources indicating that the Kuomintang accounted for 90 percent of the opium being shipped out of Shan State at the time, Shan groups 7 percent, and Kachin groups 3 percent.[51]

Collection, transportation, and processing of the opium into heroin was carried out under the direction, control, or protection of the Kuomintang and various local ethnic rebel groups such as the Shan State Army in Shan State and adjacent border area in northern Thailand. In Laos General Vang Pao and his Hmong army and senior Royal Lao Army officers such as General Ouane Rattikone assumed these roles. These elements sometimes worked in concert. McCoy writes of how General Rattikone worked through an officer in General Vang Pao's army to contact a Shan rebel leader in order to arrange shipment of opium from Shan State to Laos.[52] By 1971 there were 21 laboratories producing no. 3 and no 4 heroin in the Golden Triangle region.[53] The largest of these were located near Ban Houei Sai (Houayxay), Laos, which lies across the Mekong River from Chiang Khong, Thailand, and were under the control of General Rattikone.[54] Major Chao La, head of a group of Mien mercenaries, operated another at nearby Nam Keung. The other center of laboratories in Laos at Long Tieng was under General Vang Pao's control. The laboratories in the border area of Burma and Thailand were located near Tachilek on the Burmese side and near Mae Salong and Doi Ang Khang just inside Thai territory.

In the case of opium and heroin smuggled into Thailand, the towns of Chiang Rai, Chaing Mai, and Lampang served as important centers for the drug trade in northern Thailand where smugglers and traders from Shan State came into contact with members of a Chinese syndicate and Thais who were involved in the trade. The drugs then went to Bangkok where they were either taken overland to Malaysia or shipped to Europe (heroin); Malaysia, Singapore, and Indonesia (opium); Saigon (heroin and opium); or Hong Kong (morphine base and opium). As for the opium and heroin smuggled from Laos or from Burma through Laos to South Vietnam, air transport played an important role. The Corsicans, such as Gérard Labenski who operated out of his Snow Leopard Inn at Phong Savan in Xieng Khouang and Bonaventure Francisci who operated Air Laos Commerciale, were pushed out of the business and their role assumed by Air America.

Relative amateurs sometimes smuggled heroin from Southeast Asia to Europe and the United States. For example, Prince Sopsaisana of Laos was caught attempting to smuggle 60 kg of heroin through the Paris airport in April 1971 when he arrived as ambassador-designate. He was carrying heroin for Hmong General Vang Pao that had been refined at Long Tien, Laos. For the most part, however, heroin was smuggled to Hong Kong, the United States, and Western Europe, and elsewhere by members of Chinese, Corsican, and American crime syndicates.

When the communists seized power in Indochina in 1975 much of the transnational drug trafficking involving these countries came to a halt, especially in Vietnam and Cambodia. In the case of Thailand, while efforts to reduce local production of opium in Thailand over the next couple of decades were relatively successful, the country remained a major transit point for smuggling drugs from Burma's Shan State to destinations around the world. As in the past, such smuggling sometimes was the work of amateurs, but more often more organized syndicates were responsible for overseeing the trafficking. Robinson describes a fairly typical syndicate run by a Russian migrant living in the United States in his account of an émigré called Grisha Roizis who had been born in Russia and lived in Israel for a time before migrating to Brooklyn, where in 1991 he decided to become involved in drug trafficking. "He'd seen for years how heroin had lifted other people — namely Boris Nayfeld and Monya Elson — out of the boardwalk tenements and into palatial houses in exclusive, fancy non–Russian neighborhoods. He asked Balagula to please set up a connection for him. Balagula duly introduced him to Nayfeld's consortium of ten Russians and six Italians— their Golden Triangle heroin connection that moved drugs out of Thailand, through Poland and into the States."[55]

Within Shan State, the role of the Kuomintang was gradually reduced in favor of other groups.[56] Khun Sa was a dominant figure for a time. His father was Chinese and his mother Shan and as a young man he was associated with the Kuomintang. He formed his own militia in the 1960s. The Burmese captured him following his defeat by Kuomintang forces in 1967, but he gained his freedom in 1973. He then established a new headquarters at Ban Hin Taek (now part of what is called Thoed Thai) in a frontier area just inside Thailand and established the Shan United Army. By 1985 Khun Sa and his allies controlled drug production and smuggling along most of the border area between Mae Sai and Mae Hong Son. He moved to Rangoon after a largely symbolic surrender to the Burmese in 1996, and died there in 2007.[57]

During the 1990s, prior to his surrender, Khun Sa had already lost his dominant position in the Shan State narcotics business. Dominance had passed to the United Wa State Army (UWSA), which had risen in power after the Wa revolted against the Communist Party of Burma in 1989, and heroin had been joined by methamphetamines as the major drugs being produced and exported from the area.[58] While essentially a local organization, the UWSA's narcotics activities have given it a transnational character. This was highlighted when the New York Field Division of the Drug Enforcement Administration of the United States indicted eight of the leaders of the UWSA on charges of heroin and methamphetamine trafficking. Those indicted included Wei Xuegang (aka Wei Hsueh Kang), special adviser to UWSA's Central Committee, who "became one of the first individuals designated by the United States as a "drug kingpin" under what is termed the Foreign Narcotics Designation Kingpin Act in June 2000.[59]

A United States government press release in 2005 following the indictments stated, "the UWSA, which controls a large section of eastern Burma in the infamous 'Golden Triangle' opium-producing region, is one of the largest heroin-trafficking organizations in Southeast Asia, producing over 180 metric tons of opium in 2004.... The indictments will allow law enforcement agencies in the United States and other countries 'to seek to restrain over $100 million in assets directly traceable to the Wa Army and these defendants as well as ... seize front companies managed and controlled by these defendants which operate in Burma, Thailand, Hong Kong, China and elsewhere and are used to launder the vast illegal profits from the Wa State Army's trafficking operations.' ... The indictment alleges that UWSA and the defendants have engaged in the collection, transport and taxing of opium in the territories under their control; provide security for caravans smuggling drugs from Burma to Thailand, China, and Laos; have manufactured and distributed heroin and methamphetamine to the United States and throughout the world; and have laundered narcotics proceeds through seemingly legitimate businesses."[60]

Despite their investments in Hong Kong and involvement in international narcotics trafficking, the transnational lives of the UWSA indictees are restricted to the southern Yunnan–Shan State–northern Thailand–northern Laos border area. Wei Xuegang is perhaps the most transnational one of the group.[61] He and his two brothers are ethnic Chinese from Yunnan, who fled across the border to Burma's Wa Hills following the communist takeover of China. Wei Xuegang was involved for a time with the Kuomintang-CIA spy network that operated in the border area and then he joined Khun Sa's organization on the Burma-Thai border, serving as its treasurer. In this capacity he traveled extensively in Asia and Western Europe. A falling out with Khun Sa resulted in Wei Xuegang fleeing Taiwan in the early 1980s. He then returned to Shan State to become involved with the UWSA and its narcotics trafficking. He obtained Thai citizenship under the name Prasit Charnchai Chiwinitipanya and frequently visited northern Thailand until he was arrested on narcotics charges in late 1988. He was sentenced but managed to get out of prison and flee across the border. Thai authorities then passed a death sentence on him in absentia and revoked his Thai citizenship. Lintner and Black characterize him as "heroin kingpin and overlord of most of the methamphetamine production in the Golden Triangle."[62] Currently his home is in Panghsang, a hub of Wa activity in northern Shan State near the border with China, where he lives behind tight security.

In the context of the present discussion it is worth noting that the indictments of the UWSA narcotics traffickers mention Laos. While the communist seizure of power in 1975 temporarily disrupted the flow of drugs through and from Laos as the initial revolutionary fervor receded and corruption within the government and military became widespread Laos once again became an important source of drugs smuggled into neighboring Thailand, Cambodia, China (which has emerged as an important market and transit point), and to a lesser extent Vietnam. Laos serves as a transit point for heroin and methamphetamines from Shan State as well as a source of opium. When the United States government began cooperating with the government of Laos in 1987 to try to reduce opium production and narcotics smuggling it reported that Laos was the world's third largest producer of opium. Government figures indicated that estimated opium production declined from 380 tons in 1989 to 180 tons in 1993. Despite this apparent success in reducing production, in 1994 the American government still listed Laos as the world's third largest producer of opium.

At the same time that the United States is trying to counter narcotics trafficking in Laos, the Shan State based traffickers have become increasingly active in Laos, primarily in the border town of Boten.[63] Boten is located in northwestern Laos on the border with the PRC. Their presence grew following establishment of the Boten Border Trade Area by the Lao government in late 2002.[64] The area was established primarily to attract Chinese investors, and its Boten Golden City casino soon became an important center for laundering narcotics income from Shan State. Among those attracted to this area is Bang Ron (aka Surachai Ngernthongfoo), a Sino-Thai who had been a major narcotics trafficker in Thailand, until Thai authorities busted his operation in 1998. He fled across the border to Burma, where he joined forces with Wei Xuegang and the UWSA. Lintner and Black report that he has built a large house in Luang Nam Tha (south of Boten) and "travels frequently between UWSA and NDAA (ESS) controlled areas in Burma and northern Laos."[65]

International Gangster Organizations

The Sicilian Mafia and its offshoots, Japanese Yakuza, Colombian cocaine cartels, Russian Mafiya, and Hong Kong Chinese Triads are the most famous international gangster organizations. Across borders their activities include smuggling narcotics, people, and arms, as well as providing a variety of other illicit goods and services. Within states they are involved in a host of activities ranging from overseeing illegal prostitution and gambling, to illegal waste disposal, running protection rackets, and even many legal activities (often as a means of laundering funds acquired illegally). While these organizations form distinct entities, it is important to keep in mind that while they sometimes come into conflict with other criminal organizations, they also sometimes act in concert. In the present section we will look at the organization and activities of the Yakuza and Triads.

Yakuza

The Yakuza (also known as *boryokudan* and *gokudo*) is the main criminal organization in Japan and one of the largest in the world.[66] Liddick remarks that the Yakuza rank "only behind the Chinese Triads in size"[67] and Linter refers to the Yakuza as "the world's most successful — and powerful — criminal entrepreneurs."[68] There are between 80,000 and 110,000 members that are organized into about 2,500 so-called families.[69] Beyond the usual gangster activities (prostitution, narcotics, protection, child pornography, etc.), "In Tokyo alone, the police have identified more than 800 yakuza front companies, construction companies and pastry shops. The mobsters even set up their own bank in California" and "Japan's Securities and Exchange Surveillance Commission has an index of more than 50 listed companies with ties to organized crime."[70] The origins of the Yakuza can be traced to "the *bakuto*, or traditional gamblers, and the *tekiya*, or street peddlers" who were recruited from among "the poor, the landless, and the delinquents and misfits found in any large society" in the mid–1700s.[71]

As for their organization, "Like the Italian Mafia the yakuza began organizing into families, with a godfather at the top and new members adopted into the clan as older brothers, younger brothers, and children [while severing connections with their actual family]. The yakuza, however, added to that structure the unique Japanese relationship known as *oyabun-kobun,* or, literally 'father role-child-role.' The *oyaban* provides advice, protection, and help, and in return receives unswerving loyalty and service of his *kobun* whenever needed."[72] This structure "was a mirror of the traditional Japanese family in which the father held great and final authority, including the power to choose marriage partners and occupations for his children…. Today, despite encroaching modernization, [this structure] continues to foster a level of loyalty, obedience, and trust among the yakuza unknown within American crime groups except between the closest of blood relatives."[73] While the oyabun-kobun system within Japanese society at large "is generally treated less seriously than in the past" with the oyabun become more of a mentor, "It is almost exclusively within the yakuza that the oyabun-kobun system remains unchanged from its past, existing in a world where kobun will kill others of even kill themselves for the sake of the oyabun."[74]

Oyabun and *kobun* are positions within local Yakuza families. There is also a structure above the family-level that unites the Yakuza organization. The *kumicho* is the boss of the entire Yakuza syndicate. His immediate subordinates include a *saiko komon* (senior advisor) and *so-honbucho* (headquarters chief). Next in the command structure are the various *wakagashira,* who govern gangs within a region. The *wakagasira* is assisted by a *fuku-honbucho,* who oversees several of the gangs within a region. The *shateigashira* is the boss of a gang within the region. The family head may be referred to as an *oyabun* or *kumicho.* There is a ranked structure underneath the family head as well. Directly beneath the family head is a number of *saiko-komon* (senior advisers) who control particular areas within a city. They in turn have a variety of assistants that include accountants, advisers, and enforcers. As with many gangster organizations, Yakuza are mostly males. There are, however, some female Yakuza and they too are given family designations (*o-nee-san,* older sister).

The life of the Yakuza includes important rituals associated with entry into the organization, promotions, peace pacts, and mergers. These also serve to indicate respective positions within the hierarchy. Some of these rituals are performed before a Shinto shrine and most involve a formal exchange of cups of sake (*sakazuki,* sake sharing). Other symbolic and ritual activities include having extensive tattoos (*irezumi*) to indicate Yakuza affiliation and cutting off portions of a finger as penance (*yubitsume*).

The Yakuza began as localized gangsters and their organization eventually spread out across Japan. As Japan became more active in the affairs of neighboring Asian states in the early 1900s so too did the Yakuza. Yakuza joined with rightist, ultranationalist groups and operated across the Asian mainland in the 1920s and 1930s and during World War II they were actively involved in opium trafficking on the Asian mainland.[75] The defeat of Japan in 1945 put a temporary stop to Yakuza operations outside of Japan and their activities took place almost entirely within Japan until the late 1960s (they were extensively involved in black market activities during the American occupation), when they along with Japanese capital and trade spread rapidly across the globe. As Kaplan and Dubro note, "Since the late 1960s, Japanese mobsters had popped up from Paris to

Paraguay, New York to Hong Kong. They were engaged in a growing number of rackets ranging from money laundering to extortion and gunrunning…. By the mid–1970s it was already apparent that the yakuza had made some very powerful friends outside of Japan, both economically and politically. By the 1980s, it was clear that Japanese gangs were becoming a major force in a new era of global organized crime."[76]

Within Japan ethnic Koreans have played a prominent role among Yakuza and South Korea has been an important center of Japanese Yakuza activities. The Japanese had a significant presence in Korea during the latter part of the 1800s and Japanese citizens living in Korea (who numbered 170,000 by 1910) were granted extraterritorial rights in 1876. Japan occupied Korea in 1905 and made it a protectorate in 1910 — a status that lasted until 1945. Koreans also began to migrate to Japan during the colonial period. During World War II large numbers of Koreans were forcibly conscripted to work in Japan (about 670,000) and at the end of the war there were more than 2 million Koreans living in Japan. Korea regained its independence after the war and 1,340,000 Koreans living in Japan were repatriated to Korea, while 640,000 chose to remain in Japan,[77] where they became known as Zainichi Koreans. Although they are only about 0.5 percent of the total population of Japan today, ethnic Koreans are the largest minority group in the country, and one that often suffers discrimination and occupies positions of low socio-economic status. These factors appear to have contributed to the relatively large number of ethnic Koreans among the Yakuza, including a number in high positions.

Hisayuki Machii (1923–2002) was undoubtedly the most prominent of the ethnic Korean Yakuza.[78] He was born in Korea when it was under Japanese rule and moved to Tokyo immediately after World War II, where he became involved in black market activities and formed his own gang in 1948 — the Voice of the East Gang (*Tosei-kai*) — which also became involved in anti-communist strike-breaking. He and his gang came to control pachinko game rooms, then restaurants and bars in the Ginza entertainment district, resulting in Machii coming to be known as the Ginza Tiger, and then moved into selling methamphetamines as well. Machii disbanded the Voice of the East Gang in 1965 and established two front companies for his activities, the East Asia Friendship Enterprise Association (*Toa Yuai Jigyo Kumiai*) and the East Asia Enterprises Company (*Toa Sogo Kigyo*), which was run by his gangster associate Yoshio Kodama. Machii became a major figure in the ethnic Korean community and in Japanese–South Korean relations. Using his political connections in 1970 he came to control a ferry line between Pusan, South Korea, and Shimanoseki, Japan. He also opened a group of clubs and cabarets in Seoul and refurbished some of his old ones in Tokyo. Machii's political ties in South Korea led his involvement in 1973 in a plot by the Korean Central Intelligence Agency (apparently under orders from Park Chung Hee) to kidnap and kill opposition leader Kim Dae Jung while on a visit to Japan. They managed the kidnapping, but Kim was rescued as he was about to be killed. Machii's legitimate economic empire went bankrupt in 1976, but he remained a rich and powerful man with investments and involvement in illegitimate activities not only in Japan but also in South Korea and the United States, where his associates by then were trafficking in drugs.

The ethnic Korean presence within the Yakuza has contributed to the growth not only of activities by Japanese Yakuza in South Korea, but also to the existence of close links between gangsters in the two countries. In regard to this last point, Kaplan and Dubro remark, "The Japanese influence on Korean gangs was so large that yakuza were even training them to be gangsters. When police in Pusan raided Korea's White Tiger gang in 1990, they found evidence that its leaders had attended a ten-day seminar on being mobsters at Yamaguchi-gumi headquarters in Kobe."[79]

Beyond Japan and South Korea the Yakuza tend to operate in conjunction with local criminal organizations or within overseas Japanese communities. Nicaso and Lamothe comment, "In the 1970s the Yakuza went worldwide, operating across Asia, often in conjunction with other Asian crime organizations. Investigators found links between the Yakuza in Japan and Japanese throughout Europe and Hawaii. In America, the Yakuza have formed links, primarily in New York City, with La Cosa Nostra members, buying firearms—relatively cheap in America, but banned, and very expensive in Japan—and coordinating and financing drug operations. Japanese businessmen, brought to mob-run casinos in Atlantic City and Las Vegas by Yakuza-run junkets, often find themselves behind the eight ball after losing at the tables.... In Canada, Yakuza members or associates are involved in organized prostitution through swank businessmen's clubs, widespread money laundering, gambling operations, and loan-sharking."[80]

In addition to laundering money and operating businesses and rackets catering to overseas Japanese and Japanese tourists, Yakuza operate outside of Japan often to obtain people or goods to bring to Japan, such as American guns, women for prostitution, and, of course, narcotics. Ward and Mabrey cite a 1998 figure of there being about 150,000 foreign prostitutes working in Japan.[81] Most are brought into the country legally as entertainers from neighboring Asian countries (especially Thailand, the Philippines, Taiwan, and the PRC), but they also sometimes are brought from farther away such as from Mexico and Peru. Obtaining any of these goods or people often requires Yakuza working with local non–Yakuza criminal organizations since they rarely have their own overseas local organization in place. Thus, the Yakuza liaise with American Mafia (La Cosa Nostra) members in exchanging drugs for guns in the United States and in luring Japanese tourists to Mafia-run gambling operations. Linter mentions that they also have "established links across the Sea of Japan—with Russian gangs in Vladivostok, and other cities in Siberia."[82] Yakuza ship used Japanese cars to Siberia where they trade them for guns and Russian girls.

In California, mainly in Los Angeles, they sometimes work with local ethnic Vietnamese and Korean gangs and at times in partnership with Chinese Triads. In addition to drug trafficking in California, the Yakuza recruit women (including Western women) for prostitution catering to Japanese clients and making pornographic films. In California the Yakuza can operate in a culturally familiar environment among fellow Asian gangsters. Once they leave Los Angeles or San Francisco, however, and head east to Las Vegas and New York they enter Mafia territory where they must deal with culturally different gangsters. While shared interests allow them to work together, it does not appear that the alliances are as strong as is the case with those formed with fellow Asian gangsters.

Hawaii has been a particularly popular locale for the Yakuza operating outside of

Japan. Its multiethnic culture with a large ethnic Japanese population as well as the presence of huge numbers of Japanese tourists and considerable legitimate Japanese investment creates an environment in which Yakuza can comfortably do business. As Kaplan and Dubro comment, "Despite the apparent glut of gangs, the yakuza have had little difficulty joining the ranks of Hawaiian mobsters…. By the early 1970s, yakuza could be seen sunning themselves in full-body tattoos on the beaches of Waikiki."[83] Their businesses include massage parlors, porno movie theaters, bottomless clubs, and adult bookstores, as well as sushi restaurants, gun shops, and real estate investments. They also engage in gunrunning, gambling, and narcotics trafficking.

Yakuza activities in Hawaii started in the early 1970s, coinciding with a boom in Japanese investment and tourism in the islands: "By 1973, the police were keeping a handful of yakuza under surveillance and were beginning to conclude that their presence was no fleeting phenomenon."[84] Kaplan and Dubro cite the case of Wataru "Jackson" Inada, who arrived in Hawaii in 1972: "Shortly after his arrival, he teamed up with a local gangster of Korean descent named John Chang Ho Lee, a man who knew just about everyone in the Honolulu underworld. Together the two hoods formed Mitsui Tours, which catered exclusively to Japanese visitors, and which probably originated the now-common junket of hauling tourists to gun ranges."[85] The following year the pair began trafficking in heroin: "With his cash reserves, his Asian connections, and Lee's distribution network" Inada believed that he could make a fortune. Inada also set up "a prostitution racket, a gambling casino, and a shakedown of local porno shops."[86] He then sought the help of Los Angeles Mafia boss Peter John Milano to smuggle heroin through Los Angeles and on to the Midwest. The operation ended badly with Lee and Milano and a number of associates being arrested. Inada continued trafficking until he and his Korean girlfriend were murdered (possibly by Lee) in 1975 prior to Inada being tried for trafficking.

The drugs smuggled into Hawaii initially consisted mainly of heroin and later mainly methamphetamines. The Yakuza use mainly Japanese couriers who usually pick up the drugs in Bangkok or elsewhere in Asia. They then pass through Guam, Vancouver, San Francisco, or Los Angeles before arriving in Honolulu. About one-third of the Yakuza's estimated gross revenue of around U.S. $10 billion in 1988 came from trafficking in methamphetamines ("ice") and they controlled 90 percent of the flow of illegal methamphetamines to Hawaii.[87] Honolulu-based DEA agent Briane Grey provided a brief overview of the history and changing nature of methamphetamine trafficking in Hawaii in 2004: "The 'Ice' situation in Hawaii is a twofold challenge: Combating the proliferation of Mexican and Asian organizations that are expanding their wholesale and retail distribution in Hawaii and disrupting or dismantling the growing 'Ice' retail networks in our areas of operation…. In the last two years, Hawaii has seen a significant increase in the amount of crystal methamphetamine being distributed and seized. The majority of recent 'Ice' seizures have been linked to Mexican organizations, a significant departure from 'Ice' traditionally supplied by Asian criminal organizations. The profitability of dealing 'Ice' in Hawaii has attracted Mexican organizations that now control the majority of the wholesale methamphetamine distribution to Hawaii. Mexican organizations transport multi-pound quantities from clandestine methamphetamine 'superlabs' located on the

Southwest border and Mexico to Hawaii for distribution.... This drug first appeared in Hawaii around 1985 and was considered to be the 'poor man's cocaine.' During mid 1980s 'Ice' was distributed by Asian youth gangs. At that time, the pure 'Ice' crystals came primarily from the Philippines, South Korea, Hong Kong, Taiwan and Japan. Asian organizations routinely transported drugs from source countries such as Korea, Thailand, and the Philippines through Canada to Hawaii via California to avoid Hawaii's strict U.S. Customs and Border Protection inspections. In the 1990's, the trend shifted and Mexican organizations became the principal 'Ice' suppliers for traffickers in Hawaii."[88] Thus, while the Yakuza continue to operate in areas catering primarily to Japanese tourists in Hawaii, they found themselves unable to compete in the broader area of methamphetamine trafficking in what is essentially a North American market once North American gangsters themselves became involved.

In terms of the amount of money involved, real estate investment has been the other major area of Yakuza activity in Hawaii. This serves mainly as a means of laundering the gangsters' profits. Yakuza real estate investments in Hawaii have followed general real estate trends in the state and were tied especially to the real estate bubble in Japan and Hawaii in the 1980s that collapsed in the early 1990s. Kaplan and Dubro cite the example Asahi Juken that was Japan's second largest condominium builder in the 1980s.[89] Kizo Matsumoto, a former member of the Yamaguchi-gumi Yakuza gang, and three of his brothers established the company. Outside of Japan they first invested in Thailand. They sought to invest in Guam in 1988 but were not allowed to because of their Yakuza connections. After being rebuffed by Guam's authorities they turned to Hawaii. Among their investments in Hawaiian real estate was the Turtle Bay Hilton & Country Club and neighboring Kuilima Resort on Oahu's north shore. Their investment activities in Hawaii ran into trouble when law enforcement officials revoked and indicted two of the brothers on fraud charges and forced Kizo to return to Japan. When the real estate bubble in Japan and Hawaii collapsed the company was $4.5 billion in debt and Yakuza investments in Hawaiian real estate were curtailed for a time.

Triads

The term Triad is used generally to refer to a variety of gangster organizations based in China or associated with Overseas Chinese.[90] Their origins can be traced to a society called the *Tiandihui* (Society of Heaven and Earth) that Buddhist monks in Fujian formed in 1674 with the goal of overthrowing the Qing Dynasty and restoring Han rule over China.[91] This opposition movement spread throughout China and branched into a number of different groups. The name *Sanhehui* (Three Harmonies Society), in reference to the unity between heaven, earth, and humankind, came to be used for some of these groups. Accordingly, triangles featured in the symbolism employed by these groups and for this reason, the British in Hong Kong—which became a center of Triad activity—referred to them as triads—they are also known as *Hung Mun,* Heaven and Earth, *Sam Hop Wui,* or Black Societies. The original purpose of these rebel groups ended with the collapse and overthrow of the Qing Dynasty in 1911, events that they played virtually no role in. After spending most of their lives as rebels and outlaws, many members of these groups were unable to adapt to lives as law-abiding citizens. No longer receiving donations from supporters as rebels, they also found themselves without a means of earning a living. They reformed as secret cults that resorted increasingly to extortion and other criminal activities to support themselves. Thus, like many rebel or revolutionary groups, which often resort to banditry to support themselves from the outset, eventually the band of anti–Qing rebels degenerated into a bunch of gangsters devoid of any political goals.

Whereas the Triads are often associated with Hong Kong, prior to 1949 there were numerous Triad gangs within China itself. There were, for example, the Green Gang (*Hong Bang*) and Red Gang (*Qing Bang*) in Shanghai. Shanghai emerged as an important center of opium trading during the latter half of the 1800s. Adams provides a brief account of the Green Gang.[92] Both of these gangs were formed in the 1800s, recruiting most of their members from men who transported grain and smuggled salt along the Grand Canal. They became active in Shanghai after 1911. As a result of the Opium Wars and Shanghai's European presence and its importance as an international port, there was a brisk opium trade and also considerable local demand for vices. Lintner mentions Jews who had migrated from Baghdad to Bombay to avoid persecution, where they became naturalized British citizens and then expanded their business interests to Shanghai.[93] David Sassoon and Sons and E.D. Sassoon subsequently became Shanghai's largest opium traders. In the early 1900s about one-third of Shanghai's International Settlement's revenue came from the Opium Monopoly. When the trade was curtailed in 1917, it moved to the French Concession.

Tu Yueh-sheng (aka Du Yuesheng and Big-eared Du) was one of the most important leaders of the Green Gang in Shanghai and came to be known as the Opium King of the city.[94] His activities were based in the French Settlement, which Adams refers to as "a noted center of illicit activities where criminals were permitted to operate freely."[95] The French received a share of the profits from gang activities and in return gave the gangs a free hand to the point that they virtually ran the settlement. When Tu arrived in Shanghai the leader of the Green Gang was a man named Huang Jinrong (aka Pockmarked Huang), who also happened to be the chief of detectives—he joined the police in 1892 and rose to prominence with the onset of World War I when many French officers went back to France and he became chief superintendent. Huang operated several opium houses and served as an intermediary when disputes arose within or between gangs. Tu became Huang's protégé.

Until 1918 the opium trade had been largely in the hands of Chinese gangsters from the Treaty Port of Shantou (Swatow) in Guangdong (many of the port's inhabitants are ethnic Teochew and it was a major source of migrants going overseas) who operated out of the British concession. After the British suppressed the trade in 1918 the Shantou gangsters lost their control to the Green Gang in the French Settlement. Tu assumed a leadership position in the Green Gang and unified the gangster organizations involved in opium trafficking in the 1920s. Tu and his associates also pioneered in introducing heroin pills to the Chinese market. European and Japanese pharmaceutical companies produced these pills and "by 1923 the [Shanghai] cartel had to import an estimated 10.25 tons of heroin annually to keep up with consumer demand."[96] After a Geneva Convention ban on marketing heroin came into force in Europe in 1928, Tu and has fellow Green Gang gangsters began manufacturing it in Shanghai with opium shipped from Sichuan. By the 1930s they were producing heroin not only for the huge Chinese market but also shipping it to the United States for sale within the Chinese community and to the Mafia.

By the mid–1920s three gangsters—Tu Yueh-sheng, Pockmarked Huang, and Chang Hsiao-lin—controlled Shanghai's underworld. Their power increased in 1927, when they assisted Chiang Kai-shek's Kuomintang in its suppression of communists and their allies in the labor movement in the city. Chiang Kai-shek subsequently made them honorary advisers to his Nationalist government and Tu became a major general. Following the Japanese invasion, Tu remained of service to the Kuomintang by overseeing the shipment of opium that had been seized as part of the KMT's opium suppression campaign prior to the war from Sichuan to coastal cities under Japanese control such as Shanghai, Hong Kong, and Macau where it was sold.

In a sense the Triad gangs that emerged in the early 1900s were transnational from the outset in that, although particular gangs were quite localized in their primary spheres of operation and in some instances were also associated with particular Chinese ethnic groups, whether in China, Hong Kong or Macau, they had connections with other Triad gangs operating across borders of the other two territories. In the case of Hong Kong, during the inter-war years of the 1920s and 1930s there were a number of Triad gangs operating, each with its own territory. The Triads thrived during World War II under the Japanese occupation of China and Hong Kong. The Japanese military employed Triad members as informers and enforcers, allowed them to operate gambling and opium houses and the Triads provided prostitutes for Japanese soldiers. In return for these services the Japanese destroyed the gangsters' criminal records.[97]

Most of the Triad members in China moved to Hong Kong as the communists came to power there in 1949. McCoy refers to the Hong Kong affiliates of the Green Gang and Teochew gangs in China serving as "welcoming committees" as the gangsters migrated.[98] In addition to opening dance halls, becoming involved in prostitution, and carrying out robberies, the Green Gang members also brought their heroin chemists with them from Shanghai in 1949 and set up laboratories. Tu was among those who moved from Shanghai to Hong Kong in 1949, but he died in 1951 and the influence of the Green Gang with its northern Chinese members waned in the face of competition from the southern Teochew gangs. As for Big-eared Du, Hong Kong authorities would not allow him to be buried in the colony and his ashes were taken to Taiwan, where a statue was erected to honor his service to Chiang Kai-shek.

These Teochew gangs in Hong Kong established control over importing morphine and opium from Thailand to Hong Kong as well as the manufacturing and wholesale distribution of heroin within Hong Kong. As McCoy notes, however, it is the retail distribution end of drug trafficking that is "the most lucrative phase" and this was controlled "by a collection of Cantonese family associations, secret societies, and criminal gangs."[99] These Cantonese groups ran into trouble after violent riots by members of Cantonese secret societies (i.e., Triads) in October 1956 resulted in membership in such societies being outlawed and the police forming a special Triad Society Bureau to suppress them. Police efforts were fairly successful and by the mid–1960s the Teochew gangs had come to dominate this part of the business as well. In addition to controlling the flow of morphine and opium from Bangkok to Hong Kong, these gangs also provided the chemists to the heroin laboratories in the Golden Triangle and were involved in the flow of heroin from Thailand. As evidence of their involvement in the Southeast Asian heroin trade at the time, McCoy cites the example of the arrest of over 60 traffickers by police in Saigon in 1971.[100] All of them were Teochew. He adds that the arrests were only possible because the Teochew syndicate boss in Bangkok believed that he was being cheated by this group in Saigon and decided to use the police as enforcers.

A 1992 report by the Permanent Subcommittee on Investigations of the Committee on Governmental Affairs of the United States Senate provided the following description of Triads in Hong Kong in the early 1990s: "The RHKP [Royal Hong Kong Police] estimate that there are currently about 50 triad societies in Hong Kong, with about 15 of those being very active. While it is very difficult to determine the exact number of triad members in Hong Kong, most authorities agree that there are at least 80,000. Some triads are thought to have as little as 100 members while Hong Kong's largest triad, the Sun Yee On, is believed to have at least 25,000 members. After the Sun Yee On, the next largest triads are the Wo Group, including the Wo Hop To and at least nine other subgroups, which have over 20,000 Hong Kong members. The 14K Triad, including over 30 subgroups, is also believed to have over 20,000 Hong Kong members. The fourth largest group is the Luen Group with approximately 8,000 Hong Kong members. The Tung Group is thought to have approximately 3,000 Hong Kong members. All of these groups also have substantial overseas membership."[101]

After World War II the 14K gang emerged as one of the most powerful gangs operating in Hong Kong. The Kuomintang general Kot Siu Wong founded the 14K gang in 1947. It was named after the street address of its first headquarters in Guangzhou. The letter K added in reference to 14K gold, which is harder and stronger than purer gold. The 14K gang was especially involved in transnational crime beyond the Pearl River Delta area primarily in drug trafficking and later in humans as well. Its activities outside of Hong Kong were boosted in 1956, when British authorities arrested many local gangsters and deported them to Taiwan. Many of the deported gangsters from Hong Kong later became part of Taiwan's *Chulian Bang* (Green Bamboo Gang).

The 14K gang controlled much of the heroin trafficking and became the largest of the Triad gangs. Gang wars involving the 14K gang and its rivals (such as the *Shui Fong* or Water Room gang) had become quote serious in Macau in the late 1990s prior to the Portuguese handing it over to the PRC in 1999. There were over 100 gang-related deaths at the time. The 14K gang was under the leadership of Wan Kuok-koi (Broken Tooth Koi, ethnic Cantonese, born Macau 1956)—a movie named *Casino* was made about him. In addition to violence in Hong Kong and Macau, the 14K gang and its rivals also clashed in other countries. Koi's rivals shot four other 14K gangsters in Bangkok in 1999 on their way back from a visit to Phnom Penh, where the 14K was involved with casinos and from where guns were smuggled to Macau.[102] Koi's main rival in the 1990s was Lai Tung-sang (aka Shui Fong Lai). He escaped to Vancouver, buying a house of Fraserview Drive, in October 1997 on a visa obtained in Los Angeles.[103] Koi's ally in Vancouver was Simon Kwok Chow, owner of Embassy Billiards in Coquitlam and Boss Investment Ltd., and a member of the 14K Triad. He was also known as 426 or Red Pole Fighter and controlled many Chinese gang activities in Canada. After some of Chow's men tried to kill him Lai moved to the Vancouver suburb of Richmond.

After Broken Tooth Koi and his associates killed the head of Macau's Judicial Police, Antonio Marques Baptista, and wounded another officer at a sidewalk café in Macau in 1998 as part of a series of drive-by shootings and car bombings, Broken Tooth Koi was arrested, convicted, and sentenced to 15 years imprisonment, and seven of his fellow gang members received lesser sentences.[104] After these events the 14K gang became far less active in the Pearl River Delta area and refocused its activities elsewhere, especially in North American cities like Los Angeles, San Francisco, and Vancouver, where they have been involved especially in money laundering and loan sharking.

The *Dai Huen Jai* (*Tai Hwin Jai*) or Big Circle Boys (aka *Da Quan Bang*, Big Circle Gang) is one of the newer gangs. It is not technically a Triad gang, but many of its members belong to Triad societies. Former Red Guards who had left the PRC for Hong Kong after the Cultural Revolution formed this gang. It gained a reputation for being especially violent and specialized initially in robbing jewelry stores. The Big Circle Boys returned to the PRC. During the 1980s and 1990s prior to the 1997 handover of Hong Kong the communists of the PRC expressed favorable views of the Triads so long as they did not seek to destabilize the colony and welcomed them to set up business in the PRC. Evidence of this benign view was exemplified in the opening of the Top Ten nightclub in Beijing in 1993. Its owners included Charles Heung of the *Sun Yee On* Triad and Tao Siju chief of the PRC's Public Security Bureau.[105] As for the Big Circle Boys, Lintner characterizes them as "the most powerful crime syndicate in China today" and lists computer hacking among their activities in the PRC.[106]

The Permanent Subcommittee on Investigations of the Committee on Governmental Affairs report also provides a description of the organization of the Triad societies: "Triad societies all display some degree of hierarchy, and a typical triad has members organized by rank. Each rank carries a title and a numerical value, based on triad ritual. The leader of a triad is known as the 'Dragon Head,' and carries the rank '489.' Other 'office bearer' positions also exist, including '438,' which is the second highest rank in a triad, and may be held by several different officials.... Other triad members are known as ordinary members or soldiers, and hold the rank of '49.' The relationships among individual triad members are based on ties between 'Dai-Lo's' (big brothers) and 'Sai-Lo's' (little brothers), where the Sai-Lo's give loyalty, support and sometimes money to their Dai-Lo, in exchange for protection and advice. Although hierarchical in nature, triads tend not to be strictly controlled from the top, in contrast to more familiar crime groups such as La Cosa Nostra. Instead, triad members frequently branch out into their own criminal enterprises. While the triad leadership does not always initiate and direct the activities of all the triad members, triads clearly serve as international networking associations that facilitate such activity. Moreover, monetary profits from criminal activity of triad members often flow to the top in indirect ways, such as through gifts. As one member of the Hong Kong–based 14K triad testified: 'I was not required to pay any percentage of profits to the 14K leadership. Triads do not work that way. Triad members do favors for each other, provide introductions and assistance to each other, engage in criminal schemes with one another, but triads generally do not have the kind of strictly disciplined organizational structure that other criminal groups like the Italian mafia have. For example, a triad member would not necessarily be required to get permission from the dragonhead of his particular triad in order to engage in a particular criminal undertaking — even if the particular deal involved an outsider or even a member of another triad. On the other hand, on the occasion of traditional Chinese holidays such as Chinese New Year, triad members traditionally give gifts to their "big brother" or "uncles" who often are office bearers in the triads.' Further testimony regarding relationships among Chinese crime groups came from Johnny Kon, a convicted heroin smuggler and triad member. He noted the importance of the Chinese concept of "Guan Shi" in facilitating criminal relationships: 'Members of the Big Circle get power from 'Guan Shi' which is a relationship among people. Through such relationships, Big Circle members can call on triad members or other Big Circle members for help.'"[107]

Nicaso describes traditional and contemporary Triad initiation rituals in Hong Kong: "Near the end of the long ceremony, in the real initiation rite, a piece of yellow paper bearing the names of those seeking admission and the words of the 36 oaths is set on fire. Its ashes are mixed with wine, cinnabar and sugar. Then a cockerel is killed and its blood is poured into the cup. Lastly, the master incenser pricks the middle finger of the left hand of the new recruit so a drop of blood appears. When drinking this odd mixture — where his blood gets mixed with that of the other novices— the newcomer must swear never to betray the society and always to be loyal to all its members. In recent times this ritual has changed a little, as the *Sunday Morning Post* wrote quoting an investigator. In one of the most powerful Hong Kong organizations, the Sun Yee On, because of the risk of AIDS the novices will not drink the blood of their peers from a shared cup, but they will simply suck their own blood from their pricked finger."[108]

The Permanent Subcommittee on Investigations of the Committee on Governmental Affairs report also discusses the international dimension of Triad activities: "Although the criminal activities of triad members can be thought of as constituting both domestic and international activities, even domestic activities such as illegal gambling, extortion, and prostitution often have an international element. For example, prostitutes are imported or smuggled, sometimes against their will, over national borders, while proceeds from illegal domestic activities such as gambling are often laundered internationally. International activities include narcotics trafficking, money laundering, counterfeiting currency and credit cards, and alien smuggling."[109]

As for heroin trafficking, a discussion paper on Asian organized crime by the Australian Parliamentary Joint Committee on the National Crime Authority cited a witness who reported: "The main point is that Southeast Asian heroin trade is highly segmented with many independent organizations conspiring to supply the United States and other consuming countries. As heroin moves through the trafficking chain, control of the shipment is transferred several times. In the initial phase, producers and refiners in Burma, Thailand and Laos obtain raw opium from farmers and refine it into heroin. Some three-quarters of the region's heroin refining capacity are concentrated just inside Burma. In the second stage, international brokers in the region arrange the sale, consolidation and movement of large heroin shipments from refineries in Burma through Thailand to trans-shipment points elsewhere in Asia. Next, wholesale buyers, in places like Hong Kong and Singapore, purchase heroin from the brokers and move shipments to the United States for resale. The buyers are frequently connected with Chinese or other international organized crime groups. Finally, retail distribution networks in the United States and Western Europe sell the product on the streets. They often have business connections with the Asian organized crime groups who dominate the wholesale business."[110]

The *Wo On Lok* (*Shui Fong*), *Wo Shing Yee*, and Big Circle gangs are among the Hong Kong–based gangs that are currently most active in Macau. Under Portuguese colonial rule, the Triads came to play an important role for the colony's Chinese inhabitants: "There is a traditional practice in seeking triad assistance in the settlement of disputes and for private protection rather than the assistance of police as Macau citizens have little confidence in the law enforcement agencies under Portuguese administration. Most people have difficulties in understanding the law because most legislation is written in Portuguese, and legal channels for dispute settlement are often time-consuming, expensive, ineffective and involve a complex chain of procedures. Furthermore, legal channels are unavailable to illegitimate businesses such as loan sharking and bookmaking. Thus, triads provide real services and settle disputes among different gambling rooms and different chip roller teams in a more effective and efficient manner than the state."[111]

Gambling casinos are a major institution in Macau, resulting in the former colony being known as the Monte Carlo of the Orient — Loeng refers to it as a Casino State[112] — and the Triads have been involved in them. As was discussed in Chapter 2, Macau was a center of the coolie trade in the mid–1800s. Gambling and opium trading were also important activities and these grew in significance after the end of the coolie trade. The colonial administration awarded the first casino monopoly franchise to the Tai Xing Company in 1937 and prior to World War II levies on gambling and the opium trade accounted for 60 percent of government revenue.[113] The colonial government awarded the franchise to Stanley Ho Hung Sun's Sociedade de Turismo e Diversões de Macau (STDM) in 1962, which currently operate 10 casinos. Loeng points out that over 30 percent of the government of Macau's revenue has been derived from gambling taxes in 1988 and over half in 1998.[114] Moreover, STDM employs 5 percent of Macau's workforce and by 1996 there were over 8 million visitors to Macau, almost all of them coming to gamble.

The Triads gained entry to Macau's casinos in 1984, with the advent of a system of contracting out gambling rooms. Under the contract the room operator is required to purchase a certain number of "dead" chips (*bate-ficha* in Portuguese) each month. As Leong notes, "Before the arrangement of gambling rooms ... the power of the triad societies was limited because they did not have direct administrative access in the casinos and only limited profit was earned from loan sharking and other illegal 'ancillary' activities like prostitution, drug trafficking and smuggling.... With the arrangement of gambling rooms and the establishment of the 'bate-ficha' business in the 1980s, a 'lawless' space was created for triads in the casinos. With the increase in access and wealth, different triad societies began to establish their territories in the casinos and the strongest ones monopolized the 'bate-ficha' business by the late 1990s. The three largest triad societies in Macau in the 1980s and 1990s were the 14K, *Wo On Lok* (also known as *Shui Fong*) and *Wo Shing Yee*, and the Big Circle Boys (*Dai Huen Chai*) was another active gang of criminals in Macau."[115] In addition to gambling, gangs are also involved in prostitution in Macau and bring prostitutes to the city from a variety of countries, including Russia, the PRC, South Korea, the Philippines, Thailand, and Brazil.

Triad gangs also set up operation in Taiwan after the Kuomintang government left the mainland and moved to Taiwan. According to the National Police Administration in Taiwan there are two major Triads in Taiwan, the United Bamboo Gang (*Chu Lien Pang*) and the Four Seas Gang (*Sei Hoi*). The NPA estimated in the mid–1990s that the United Bamboo Gang had over 20,000 members and the Four Seas Gang over 5,000 members.[116]

During the late 1800s and early 1900s the Triads followed the paths of Chinese migration and became established most places where there were significant overseas ethnic Chinese populations. Thus, Triads appeared among the Chinese migrant communities in Singapore and elsewhere in the Malay Peninsula and in North America's Chinatowns.[117]

Secret societies that were offshoots from Chinese Triads existed within Chinese migrant communities in the Malay Peninsula from a relatively early date.[118] For example, the *Ghee Hin, Ho Seng,* and *Hai San* societies (*hui*) existed in the Straits Settlements by 1825.[119] While some of these societies catered exclusively to members of a particular Chinese group, sometimes they catered to more than one. The *Ghee Hin* society in Singapore included five subdivisions representing the five major Chinese ethno-linguistic groups living in the city and the Hakka branch was further divided along clan lines. As Andaya and Andaya note, "When the Chinese migrants came to the Malay world, societies based on clan or dialect associations appeared to be an indispensable organization affording protection and assistance in an alien and often hostile environment. They were also of fundamental importance in maintaining links with China and in preserving Chinese values and culture."[120] They were also closely connected to local ethnic Chinese businesses with prominent businessmen serving as leading members of many of these societies. In addition to such worthy roles, these societies often became involved in intra-ethnic conflicts, such as those among Chinese miners in Larut in the mid–1800s, and sometimes with "the more sinister aspect of extortion, blackmail and control of gambling and prostitution ... and provided an umbrella for the criminal element among them."[121] Trafficking in opium should be added to this list of activities. Moreover, membership often was not voluntary and new migrants commonly were forced to join a society and once a person was a member they could be ordered to carry out a variety of legal and illegal activities.

Combe makes the point that over time many of these societies largely ceased to function as community welfare associations and turned increasingly to crime until they became "synonymous with criminal organizations serving their leaders and gang members purposes rather than the wider community."[122] The trouble that they caused led the British to prohibit them in 1890, although this move only seems to have driven them further underground and into criminal activities. Singapore-based Triads played an important role in post–World War II heroin trafficking. Prior to the arrest of five prominent Triad traffickers by Singaporean police in 1962, "the city was the major distribution center for the Malayan peninsula to the north and the Indonesian archipelago to the south. It was the regional headquarters of four or five international syndicates. Unlimited drug supplies frustrated government efforts at reducing the addict population; frequent seizures of one thousand to two thousand kilograms by customs and police had little impact on the availability of drugs."[123] The role of Singapore in heroin trafficking was greatly reduced in 1962 after the five syndicate bosses were arrested and deported. One of those arrested was a Teochew and he then moved to Bangkok, where he resumed his activities. The Triads of the Malay Peninsula and Singapore also played a role in ethnic conflicts between Chinese and Malays.[124] The 1969 race riots in Singapore provide an example of this. Prior to the outbreak of violence members of a Triad society from Malaya came to Singapore and met with members of two local Triad societies (the *Ang Soon Tog* and *Ji It* societies) to plan attacks on Malays living in Kampong Kedah and the Jalan Tauge-Jalan Ubi areas.

While Triads are no longer very active in Singapore, they continue to have a significant presence in other major cities in the Asia-Pacific region and even farther away in cities such as Cape Town, Buenos Aires, and São Paulo with forays into European cities as well. In addition to narcotics trafficking Triads are also heavily involved in smuggling illegal migrants from Asia to North America and Western Europe (especially the United Kingdom). Nicaso points to Hong Kong's turnover to the PRC as having "forced the Triads to establish bridgeheads in calmer cities where large Asian colonies were present. This was the case in the four Dragon cities (Manchester, Perth, Vancouver and San Francisco) or even in some European capitals such as Budapest and Vienna where the Triads deal in the restaurant extortion racket and low-cost labour."[125] This does not mean that the Triads have left Hong Kong for they are still active there, but the change in government did force them to emphasize their transnationalism to a greater degree. It is also important to note that Triads have become active within the PRC itself. Liddick remarks that "In China, as the mainland opens up to the world, Triad members from Hong Kong, Taiwan, and overseas Chinatowns are swelling the ranks of the several thousand individual Triad societies in the country."[126] The southern Chinese provinces have become major transit points for smuggling heroin from Southeast Asia to destinations elsewhere in China and elsewhere, despite there being death sentences for traffickers.[127] Ward and Mabrey also note that there is other criminal activity in the PRC "by gangs such as Triads, frequently in cooperative ventures involving black market activities, large burglaries, thefts, and hijackings" and that "these gangs are also involved in extortion of small businesses."[128] Moreover, criminal syndicates "are involved in more sophisticated crimes such as prostitution, illegal emigration, slavery, and other forms of vice."[129]

Taking Australia as an example of a country in the Asia-Pacific region where Triads expanded during the latter part of the 1900s, the discussion paper on Asian organized crime by the Australian Parliamentary Joint Committee on the National Crime Authority mentioned above provides a review of Triad and Triad-related activities in that country. In addition to playing a major role in heroin trafficking in Australia, the report notes,

"The attention of Australian law enforcement agencies has focused on Chinese organised criminal activity in relation to a wide range of matters, including drug importation and distribution, illegal gambling, illegal prostitution, extortion, immigration malpractice and money laundering. A relatively new area in which organised ethnic–Chinese are believed to be prominent is sophisticated credit card fraud." In regard to heroin trafficking, the report cites a 1988 statement by the National Crime Authority's Chinese liaison "saying that the Chinese had been linked to every major seizure of heroin in the previous two financial years, totalling 63 kg, and that an estimated 96 per cent of those cargoes seized had been triad-related." Subsequent accounts cited in the report provide similar assessments of ethnic Chinese involvement in the heroin trade with the heroin arriving in Australia being "routed through Bangkok, the Malay Peninsula, Hong Kong and the People's Republic of China."[130]

The chairperson of the National Crime Authority, Justice Stewart, outlined the nature of Chinese gangs in Australia in a 1988 public statement: "Broadly speaking, the Authority's investigations confirm earlier assessments that Chinese criminal elements in Australia have formed criminal associations, modelled to some extent on the traditional Chinese Triad secret societies such as exist in Hong Kong, Taiwan and elsewhere in Asia. These groups involve themselves in a wide range of criminal activities such as drug importation and distribution, extortion, fraud and money laundering. There is no real evidence that these associations follow Triad initiation ceremonies or other rituals, or adopt a strict internal hierarchy. There is evidence however that members of well known Triad societies are resident in Australia and overseas members visit here from time to time for illegal purposes. The power of individuals in these Australian Triad groups seems to be based on accumulated wealth, connections or demonstrated capacity for criminal enterprise rather than on traditional Triad power bases. Many of these people move with comparative ease between Australia, Hong Kong and elsewhere in South East Asia." Justice Stewart also told the Parliamentary Joint Committee on the National Crime Authority in 1988 that "Chinese organised crime was just as entrenched in Melbourne as it was in Sydney, and that there was a strong Western Australian connection too."[131]

In a section on cooperation with other criminal groups, the report of the Australian Parliamentary Joint Committee on the National Crime Authority says: "much of the heroin importation by Chinese criminal groups is directed towards supplying other, non–Chinese, groups for their own distribution networks." As an illustration, in February 1994 the report mentions a former Queensland Criminal Justice Commission officer stating that Chinese heroin importers were the source for an ethnic Romanian drug distribution network on Australia's eastern seaboard. The report also cited Western Australia Police Deputy Commissioner, Les Ayton, as saying: "'An emerging threat is the cooperation that is developing between Chinese and Italian organised groups [that are] complementing each other with their knowledge of importation practices and distribution networks.'"[132]

In his 1988 statement to the parliamentary committee Justice Stewart also mentioned evidence that Chinese criminal organizations were using ethnic Vietnamese as "foot-soldiers."[133] The 1995 Australian Parliamentary report says, "There is more recent evidence that suggests that the Vietnamese are no longer so ready to adopt subordinate roles" and cites a statement by Deputy Commissioner Ayton that "Vietnamese criminals, initially, were used by Chinese organised crime for use as couriers and as part of the distribution network. There is good intelligence and anecdotal evidence that the Vietnamese [criminals] are now emerging as major importers of heroin" and "that Vietnamese criminals were acting in concert with Chinese criminals in serious and widespread credit card fraud."[134] He said that the counterfeit credit cards were being manufactured in Hong Kong and supplied to Australian organized criminal groups.

There is an interesting comment on trends among ethnic Chinese criminals in Australia in the Parliamentary Committee report pointing to changes in the nature of the way their activities are organized and highlighting the flexibility of Ethnic Chinese criminal activity in Australia: "As far as the Committee can discern, there is an increasing tendency to play down the relevance of triad links. It is not clear from the material available to the Committee to what extent this tendency is due to a better understanding of Chinese organised criminal activity, and to what extent it might reflect a shift in the way that activity is being conducted. There are suggestions that the more traditional, triad-oriented, way in which those criminal activities were once organised is increasingly being replaced by a more entrepreneurial, ad hoc, and multi-ethnic approach."[135]

Nicaso also mentions this flexibility of Chinese gangsters in reference to Asian criminal activity in North America, where he characterizes the Triads as "More flexible than the Italian Mafia and much wiser than the Colombian cartels, the Asian gangs represent the new frontier of organized crime."[136] Within North America, Triads are active in numerous cities both in the United States and Canada. Vancouver is an especially important center of Triad activity in North America. As Nicaso and Lamothe point out, "Vancouver's gangland has been dominated by Asian crime organizations since the beginning of the [twentieth] century. The port city has long been in the grip of the Triads."[137] Hong Kong–based gangs active in Vancouver in recent years include Triad gangs like 14K, *Kung Lok*, and *Sun Yee On*, as well as the Big Circle Boys. Members of these gangs both reside in Vancouver and travel back and forth between Vancouver and Hong Kong as well as to the United States and other destinations in Asia. Within Vancouver Triads commonly work in conjunction with local ethnic Vietnamese, Korean, and other ethnic Asian gangs.

One of the significant aspects of contemporary Triad activities in Vancouver and elsewhere in North America is that they have moved beyond local ethnic Chinese communities. The triads also sometimes work in conjunction with La Cosa Nostra, ethnic Russian gangs, and biker gangs, especially in relation to drug trafficking. Nicaso cites a report by Eurispes saying that most of the heroin that is produced and handled by the Triads is now marketed in Canada. As the report remarks, "This is a portent of changing times. For years, in fact, the Chinese Mafia had kept a low profile here. Its visibility was wholly internal to the Chinese community in Canada. Then it passed to the management of larger-scale criminal activities and collaboration with other criminal organizations. Nowadays the *chohai* are not domineering just their kingdoms, the Chinatowns. They've expanded their action range, they squeeze shop owners, they threaten and kidnap men and women unwilling to work for them, and identifying and arresting them is difficult because nobody talks out of fear of their retribution. And silence is the Triads' greatest ally."[138] Within Vancouver Triad members are involved in activities that include drug dealing, gambling, prostitution, and extortion. Their main transnational activities involve drug trafficking and smuggling illegal migrants. The two sometimes overlap with the illegal migrants being used as drug couriers.

Gould provides an in-depth account of Vancouver-based Chinese gangster Steven Wong.[139] When Gould first met Wong (a.k.a. Paper Fan) he was 26 years old, head of the *Gum Wah* Gang, a member of the 14K Triad, and suspected of involvement in heroin trafficking and murder. After Wong faked his death — a reported accident in the Philippines — and left Vancouver Gould sought to track him down following leads about his whereabouts in relation to organized criminal groups in Hong Kong, Macau, Japan, the Philippines, and Cambodia. In the Philippines Gould thought that he was being assisted by the chief of the National Police, Senator Panfilo "Ping" Lacson, who turned out to be closely associated with the 14K Triad. Gould's search for Wong draws attention to the transnational relations of Triad-linked gangsters and to their ties to local criminals and influential persons throughout the Asia-Pacific region.

7

RELIGION

The transnational aspects of religion are so much taken for granted that they are often ignored when thinking about transnationalism. In this regard it is important to think about the origins as well as the processes of diffusion and differentiation that religious traditions undergo and of how they function on a global scale. All religions start out as very localized responses to questions about the nature of the universe and humanity's place in it. However, their followers spread those religions that develop into major ones—like the relatively new global religions Christianity and Islam—beyond the places of origin. In the process and over time local variants evolve, but they remain united by the perceived universalism of their beliefs and often by a transnational organizational structure.

In the present context we are interested primarily in the social aspect of religious transnationalism; i.e., the people who interact and form social groups of followers of a particular religion across national borders. Such social groups exist within an ideological framework that makes the followers of a particular religion believe that they are all part of a community that transcends state boundaries. This is a feature of all of the major religions of the modern world.

Those involved in the work of transnational religion include priests, monks, and missionaries (as well as groups of armed transnational zealots such as medieval Christian crusaders and modern Islamic terrorists). In an ecclesiastical sense, missionaries are persons who are sent with the authority to preach a particular faith, administer the rites of that faith, and to make converts to it. Missionaries may remain within their own state or move to another one and it is these that are of interest here. A pilgrim is simply a person who journeys to some sacred place or places as an act of religious devotion. Most pilgrims do not remain for long in the place of pilgrimage, but some do. Also, while some pilgrims do not roam very far from home or cross borders, other do and, again, it is these that we are interested in. More specifically, in the case of transnational pilgrims there is often a support network or organization to facilitate the movement of pilgrims and it is these that are of most interest in terms of transnational social relations.

Religion and Universality

While many religions claim to be universal, they all are identified with particular places and cultures, or at least they start out that way. The major religions of the world today — Hinduism, Buddhism, Christianity, and Islam — all began in particular parts of the world and developed within certain cultural contexts before becoming worldwide religions. Even when they were spread beyond their homelands, until quite recently they remained associated with certain regions of the globe: Hinduism primarily with South Asia; Buddhism with South, Southeast, and East Asia; Christianity with the Levant and Europe; and Islam with southwestern Asia and northern Africa. The ties of these religions to their place of origin are manifest in the importance of places of pilgrimage in these locales for followers throughout the world. Their spread across these particular regions was intertwined with political developments and the rise of empires within which they flourished. Commerce, colonial expansion, and migration subsequently played important roles in spreading these religions beyond their home regions until today adherents of all of these religions are found scattered across the world and come from many different cultural backgrounds.

The relation between religions and states or empires is a complex and often contested one. Followers of particular religions have often sought to have their religion established as the official religion of the state of which they are citizens, with varying degrees of tolerance for followers of other religions living within the states. Of particular concern in the present context is how religious beliefs influence relations across state boundaries. At the personal level an individual's identities may include both being citizens of a state and membership in a religious community. The manner and extent to which these influence one another is an open question. At the institutional level similar questions arise about the extent to which a religious institution functions as an institution within a state and the extent to which and how it functions as an institution within a global or transnational context. From the perspective of the state questions arise concerning state policies that relate to the international activities of followers of religions and religious institutions.

Two religious issues of concern here relate to the ideologies of religions in regard to perceptions of a global community of believers and the urge to proselytize. Such beliefs are of relevance in the present context to the extent that they lead to the creation of transnational links between individuals and institutions associated with a religion.

Pilgrimages

The activities and religious-based social relations of most followers of a particular religion tend to be highly localized. For most people religious activities consist mainly in taking part in events at their local temples, churches, or mosques where they meet their neighbors on a regular basis. Transnational aspects of these activities rarely go beyond providing financial support for some foreign activity associated with the religion at the urging of religious leaders. Pilgrimages to religious sites in countries other than one's own is a way that many followers of religion do, at least for a short time, engage in a transnational religious undertaking. In addition to the pilgrims, as was mentioned above, there is often a more permanent support structure in place that is involved in getting the pilgrims from their homes to the place of pilgrimage and back home again. This structure may include bodies that are associated with a formal religious institution, government bodies, as well as private enterprises catering to the needs of pilgrims. Such pilgrimages also take place within a context of religious beliefs, norms, and rules relating to transnational pilgrimages as well as secular regulations of the governments of the states through which the pilgrims pass.

Visiting sacred places is probably about as old as religion itself and as belief in certain religions spread the distance that adherents traveled to visit these sites grew. In the case of Asia, for example, pilgrimage to holy places has a long tradition, pre-dating the founding of modern Christianity and Islam, but these early pilgrimages were fairly local in nature. Will Durant notes, "the Jew lived in hopes of one day seeing Zion; and pious pagan Arabs, long before Mohammed, had trekked to the Kaaba."[1] Mohammed adopted the latter in modified form and made a pilgrimage to Mecca a duty of all Muslims and as Islam spread so too did the distance traveled by pilgrims. Such a pilgrimage to a central place of worship also served an important unifying role among followers. As Durant remarks in the case of Islam, "This famous pilgrimage served many purposes. Like that of the Jews to Jerusalem, of the Christians to Jerusalem or Rome, it intensified the worshiper's faith, and bound him by a collective emotional experience to his creed and to his fellow believers. In the pilgrimage a fusing piety brought together poor Bedouins from the desert, rich merchants from the towns, Berbers, African Negroes, Syrians, Persians, Turks, Tartars, Muslim Indians, Chinese — all wearing the same simple garb, reciting the same prayers in the same Arabic tongue."[2]

The Muslem Hajj

The most important transnational pilgrimage for Muslims is the *hajj,* a pilgrimage to Mecca. Islamic religious teachings call on believers to make this pilgrimage at least once in their lifetime. The visit to Mecca is supposed to occur on the twelfth day of the twelfth month of the Islamic lunar calendar. Bianchi characterizes it as "the greatest gathering of humanity on earth."[3] According to Royal Embassy of Saudi Arabia official figures, the number of foreign hajj pilgrims in 1996 was 1,080,465, in 2001 in was 1,363,992, and in 2008 it was 1,729,841.[4] There are also large numbers of pilgrims from within Saudi Arabia itself. Thus, in 2008 the total number of people participating in the pilgrimage was about three million. While the largest number of pilgrims come from Saudi Arabia and its immediate neighbors, hajjis now come from all over the world: "The contemporary hajj is a planetary network that encompasses most lands from London to Cape Town and from Trinidad to Mindanao."[5] This is a relatively recent development. Pilgrims have been coming to Mecca from as far away as Champa for almost 1,000 years, but the number of hajjis from countries beyond the Middle East until recently was quite small.

Bianchi outlines the growth of the hajj network: "During the 1950s, centers of hajj participation were compressed in the western portion of the Arab world between Syria and Yemen. A few outlying centers existed in Senegal, South Africa, and Malaysia, but they seemed remote and disconnected from the Middle Eastern core." The situation began to change in the late 1960s, when "a host of newly independent countries filled in the western and eastern quarters of the network, and a northern quarter emerged in Western Europe. In the 1970s and 1980s, countries with rising hajj activity formed distinct clusters in several regions. Nearly the entire African continent became dotted with local clusters that converged from North Africa, West Africa, and the Indian Ocean. One of the largest groupings arose in Southeast Asia, including Malay-speaking countries, Indonesia, and Australia. The United Kingdom developed into a pole of hajj activity that sits astride a chain of European centers that stretch from Stockholm to Lisbon. By the end of the 1980s, North America and the Caribbean Basin defined the outer limits of a steadily expanding network."[6]

The importance of this pilgrimage to Islam and the specificity of its timing has meant that large numbers of pilgrims from many different countries converge on Mecca at the same time. This creates not only logistical problems, but also conditions that threaten the health of pilgrims. In the past those going on the hajj not only had to contend with the dangers and difficulties of long-distance travel, but also with disease resulting from the gathering of so many different peoples. The return trip from Mecca also often provided a means for the transmission of diseases back to those who had not made the trip. In modern times, while travel has become easier, crowded conditions on ships and airplanes have added to health problems. In addition to contagious diseases, added health problems are posed by the fact that many of those making the pilgrimage are elderly. In recent decades usually a few hundred people die each year while taking part in the pilgrimage, many of them elderly people who die from heart problems or exhaustion. The health of pilgrims is an important issue confronting authorities overseeing the pilgrimage. There was an international outbreak of meningitis following the hajj in 1987 that prompted Saudi Arabian officials to make immunization with the ACW135Y vaccine a requirement for being granted a pilgrim visa. In August 2009 in response to fear about the spread of swine flu among pilgrims Saudi Arabian health officials announced that pilgrims would be required to wear face masks while taking part in the circumambulation, to be vaccinated against the flu two weeks prior to departure, and that visas would not be granted to pregnant women and those who were chronically ill. In response to these health issues many of the home countries of the pilgrims have also taken steps to look after the health of their pilgrims.

For reasons of safety and logistics, Saudi Arabia issues a limited number of visas to pilgrims with specific quotas for individual countries based on population. Out of the 1,575,214 pilgrim visas issued by Saudi Arabia to people from around 100 countries the largest number (214,886) went to people from Indonesia. With 152,000 visas India took the number 2 spot and Argentina with 15 received the smallest number. The number of visas issued to pilgrims from other countries included 10,700 to pilgrims from the PRC, 15,000 from the United States, 25,000 from the United Kingdom, 26,000 from Russia, and 4,800 from the Philippines.

The visa system imposed by the government of Saudi Arabia is only a small part of the transnational structure regulating the flow of pilgrims from so many countries to Saudi Arabia every year. Bianchi remarks, "In one country after another, state pilgrimage agencies have taken over the lion's share of the booming market in religious tourism from private business. Politicians attempt to lure voters by outbidding one another with costly proposals for pilgrimage subsidies and services. Bankers and entrepreneurs scramble to attract investment capital from aspiring hajjis who prepay their expenses with installments savings plans."[6] Moreover, Bianchi points out that beyond the actual trip itself, "Today's hajj is a yearlong cycle of planning, financing, teaching, outfitting, transporting, lodging, doctoring, celebrating, mourning, blaming, and correcting."[7] As will be discussed below, the Dutch and British colonial administrations established bureaucratic structures the deal with hajjis. In the post-colonial world, Malaysia and Pakistan were the first countries to establish significant bureaucratic structures to oversee pilgrims, followed by Turkey and Nigeria. The latter two countries set up systems that whereby the government's role remained limited so as to allow private enterprise to continue to take an active part. The Indonesian government created a hajj bureaucracy next.

Beyond sending the most hajjis to Saudi Arabia these days, Indonesia and its former colonial masters have played an important role in the history of the pilgrimage. Ever since Islam spread to the Indonesian archipelago in the late 1200s and 1300s Indonesian pilgrims have been going to Mecca. Until recently the numbers were relatively small and returning pilgrims were afforded a high status back home on their completion of the trip. Federspeil, writing about the Muslim community in Yogyakarta in the early 1900s, describes a group departing from Penang on a Turkish ship that sailed to Jeddah, "where they were quartered with people who had migrated earlier from Southeast Asia."[8] After completing the rounds they sailed back by way of Johore.

Dutch authorities at the time were concerned that pilgrims would return with radical ideas that might threaten political stability. Christiaan Snouck Hurgronje (1857–1936), the Dutch colonial administration's chief adviser on Islamic affairs from 1889 to 1906, argued that Indonesian hajjis were not in Mecca long enough to be politicized.[9] He saw these pilgrims as simply following the dictates of their religion and not necessarily engaging in political acts or falling under the sway of political indoctrination. In this regard, he drew a fundamental distinction between Islam as a religion and political Islam such as advocated by proponents of a pan–Islamic revival at the time. His primary concern was not the hajjis but those who remained to study in Saudi Arabia for longer times and Malay Muslims who had settled in Mecca and who tried to use their influence through commercial and religious channels to undermine European colonial rule among Malays living in British Malaya and Dutch Indonesia. To counter the influence of this group and to deal with health and other problems encountered by the pilgrims, the Dutch established a bureau to serve hajjis from Indonesia in Mecca.

During the latter part of Hurgronje's tenure as adviser the number of hajjis began to increase thanks largely to the colonial administration's tolerant attitude. In the 1880s, when he began his work, the annual number of hajjis was around 4,000. The average number of pilgrims by the early 1900s was about 7,300 per year. Between then and the onset of World War I the number increased to about 30,000 per year. After the war the number continued to grow, reaching a peak of 52,412 in 1927. Faced with the growth of an independence movement within Indonesia and no longer under Hurgronje's moderating influence in 1927 the Dutch authorities set limits on the number of people allowed to make the pilgrimage each year. This plus the impact of the Great Depression of 1929 resulted in a sharp drop in the number of pilgrims, with only 6,500 going to Mecca in 1940.

In addition to differences of opinion among Dutch officials about the hajj, there were debates among Indonesians concerning the pilgrimage: "Muslim associations held that there was an intrinsic value in the rite, which was worth the expense because of the heightening of religious awareness and civic responsibility that it entailed, even extending to the nationalist movement. Nonreligious nationalists ... argued that the loss of foreign-exchange earnings the pilgrimage entailed harmed both the economy of the Indies and the particular household economies of the people undertaking the pilgrimage."[10]

While Indonesian pilgrims often traveled on Dutch-owned ships, quite a few went first to Singapore and then on to Saudi Arabia. Singapore was the primary departure point for Muslims in Southeast Asia going on the pilgrimage in the 1800s and early 1900s. About 14,000 Muslem pilgrims departed from Singapore in 1900, sailing mainly on British ships. The number varied during this period, with 11,374 going in 1939. "Private pilgrim agents were established in Singapore to facilitate the traffic, making considerable profit by arranging passages and providing accommodations in Singapore and Saudi Arabia."[11] Poorer pilgrims from Indonesia commonly paid for the trip by agreeing to work on plantations in Malaya upon their return under contracts that were arranged by these pilgrim agents. Like the Dutch, the British were concerned with health problems among the pilgrims, leading to enactment of the Indian Pilgrims Regulations and Passenger Ships Ordinance of 1897. In an effort to curtail abuses of pilgrims by pilgrim agents the British began licensing pilgrim agents following enactment of the Pilgrim Passenger Brokers Ordinance in 1905. Under British regulations Muslem pilgrims departing from Singapore had to have a valid British pilgrim's pass and register at the British consulate in Jeddah upon arrival in Saudi Arabia. There was an official pilgrim officer based in Saudi Arabia, who was usually a Muslim Malay from Singapore.

The instability and economic disruption caused by World War II, the war for independence, and the chaos of the Sukarno administration meant that there were relatively few Indonesian hajjis in the 1940s, 1950s, and 1960s. Political stability, economic growth, and an active Ministry of Religious Affairs under the Suharto administration led to increases in the number of Indonesian hajjis starting in the early 1970s. By the mid–1970s the numbers were back to the levels of the 1920s. As the Suharto regime became increasingly pro–Muslim in the 1990s in part to shore up political support — he went on his first pilgrimage in 1991— direct state support for the hajj increased as did its tolerance and support of moderate Muslim organizations that promoted pilgrimages. The result was a dramatic rise in the number of pilgrims by the mid–1990s to over 200,000 per year. Bianchi mentions, "government employees and their families regularly take up about 20 percent of the hajj quota, and another 10 percent is reserved for the armed forces."[12] State support is especially noticeable in Jakarta, the country's capital, where "more than half of all pilgrims are on the public payroll. Bianchi adds, "The Jakarta hajj is a key investment in the political elite's image as God-fearing nationalists who spread Islam through state and society." Moreover, "Since Suharto's pilgrimage, nearly every provincial governor has become a hajj" and "to allay fears that the army was obsessed with rooting out Islamic extremism even where it never existed, Suharto made a special effort to involve military officers in the hajj."[13]

Since the fall of the Suharto regime, the number of Indonesian hajjis has remained high and state support has been maintained. Today in Indonesia the Ministry of Religious Affairs handles arrangements for pilgrims through its director general for hajj organization. Most pilgrims fly with Garuda Airlines and Saudi Arabian Airlines serving as official carriers under contract with the ministry. In August 2009 Garuda agreed to fly 114,434 pilgrims, using three of its own airplanes and leasing an additional 12. A 2009 article in the *Jakarta Globe* reported that 835 crewmembers would be involved, including a number of new crewmembers that would be recruited from different regions of Indonesia to cater to elderly pilgrims who spoke only their local language.[14] Pilgrims would be flown in groups of 300 from 10 departure points: Banda Aceh, Medan, Padang, Palembang, Jakarta, Solo, Surabaya, Banjamasin, Balikpapan, and Makassar.

The pilgrims need to have pilgrim passes and to pass a health check before leaving Indonesia. On 22 August 2009 Vice President Jusuf Kalla announced that a new Indonesian Haj Health Centre (BPHI) would be set up in Mecca to serve and give medical treatment to Indonesian pilgrims who fall ill during their stay in Saudi Arabia. The lease had expired on the building that had been used and the Vice President and Minister of Health visited Saudi Arabia to announce the signing of a five-year lease to house the center in a 9-story building at a cost of U.S. $120,000 per year. The government has credited the existence of the existing center with a decline in the number of Indonesian pilgrims who died in Saudi Arabia each year from 664 in 2006, to 462 in 2007, and 446 in 2008.

The increased global threat posed by Islamic terrorists in recent years and its links to the Wahhabi sect that is prevalent in Saudi Arabia once again has raised concerns over the political impact of the hajj on pilgrims. A study by Clingingsmith, Khwaja, and Kremer provides an analysis of the long-term effects of participation in the hajj based on a survey of over 1,600 Pakistani Sunni Muslims who applied for pilgrim visas in 2006.[15] They compare those who were successful in their application with those who were not (Pakistan allocates visas through a lottery). In general their findings "tend to support the idea that the Hajj helps to integrate the Muslim world, leading to a strengthening of global Islamic beliefs, a weakened attachment to localized religious customs, and a sense of unity ad equality with others who are ordinarily separated in everyday life by sect, ethnicity, nationality, or gender, but who are brought together during the Hajj." In addition, their findings indicated that "While the Hajj may help forge a common Islamic identity, there is no evidence that this is defined in opposition to non–Muslims. On the contrary, the notions of equality and harmony tend to extend to adherents of other religions as well ... Hajjis return with more positive views towards people from other countries."[16]

Christian Pilgrimages to the Holy Land

Pilgrimages by European Christians to the Holy Land began in the AD 300s following the Roman Emperor Constantine I's (reigned 272–337) conversion to Christianity. These tended to involve individuals or small groups, and Christian pilgrimages on more of a mass scale did not develop until the Medieval Period. While groups of European Christians numbering in the thousands sometimes traveled to Palestine during this period (with many dying in the course of the trip), Rome was a major destination of pilgrims within Europe.

Both Rome and Jerusalem and neighboring sacred sites remain important destinations for Christian pilgrims today, even though political conflicts in the Levant have at times served to deter would-be pilgrims from that destination. In fact, the number of Christians visiting the Holy Land is comparable to the number of foreign hajjis visiting Saudi Arabia on an annual basis and this despite the security problems especially since the onset of the Intifada Al-Aqsa by Palestinian extremists in September 2000. A 2009 article in the *Jerusalem Post* reported, "Christian tourism to Israel has increased by 17 percent since Pope John Paul II visited nine years ago, the Tourism Ministry said on Thursday. Nearly 1.8 million of the 3 million tourists who came to Israel last year were Christians, the ministry said. In 2000, 1.5 million Christians came." Moreover, as the article notes, "the number of Christian visitors who defined themselves as pilgrims shot up a whopping 43% over the last eight years, with more than one million in 2008 — more than half of the Christian visitors—calling themselves pilgrims."[17]

Like Muslem hajjis, Christian pilgrims today come to the Holy Land from all over the world. The *Jerusalem Post* article cites Israeli Tourism Ministry information about the origins and religious affiliations of the Christians coming to Israel: "The number of Christian visitors from Eastern Europe and Africa was up dramatically in 2008 compared to 2000, while the figures for Western Europe and Asia fell. Meanwhile, there was a 40% increase in Christians from the United States visiting Israel last year compared to the year 2000, while there were fewer visitors from Latin America, including a 64% drop from Argentina and 37% decrease from Mexico. Last year, more than a million incoming tourists defined themselves as Catholic, 300,000 as Protestant, 360,000 as 'other Christian,' and 75,000 as Evangelicals."[18]

States tend to play a much smaller role in Christian pilgrimages to the Holy Land and such pilgrimages are generally of far less importance to domestic politics than is the case with the Muslim hajj. Rather than states ministries of religious affairs such as are commonly involved with Muslim pilgrims, tourism ministries in the destination countries (especially Israel) are the main government entities involved with Christian pilgrims. A 2008 article in the *Christian Telegraph* noted, for example, "At present both the Israeli and the Palestinian Tourism Ministries and the Israeli police are making efforts to make travel for pilgrims from Jerusalem to Bethlehem and Nazareth as smooth as possible.... The Israeli Tourism Ministry is also working with the Israel Airports Authority to make entry into Israel easier due to the large number of expected tourists arriving at Ben Gurion Airport and at the Taba and Allenby crossings. Earlier this year, Raji Khoury of the Jerusalem-based Shepherds Tours, who organizes Christian pilgrimages, told *Christian Today*, '[Business] was so good until the Lebanese war. It went down as if we started [at zero] in 2000 again. Now it's picked up; now it's really good in 2007.'"[19]

In anticipation of Pope Benedict XVI's visit to the Holy Land in May 2009 Israel's Tourism Ministry established a website for Christian pilgrims in seven languages (English, Spanish, French, Italian, German, Polish, and Portuguese).[20] Highlighting the limited role of the state in this regard, the website includes a list of travel agents that can help arrange pilgrimages in ten countries (in Western Europe as well as the United States, Canada, and Brazil). In British Columbia, the Israeli site links you with Indus Travels, a travel agency that specializes in tours to the Middle East, North Africa, and South Asia and that has its own website that includes a number of individual and small group tours to Israel and the Holy Land such as the Israel Bible Land Tour and Israel Christian Tour. Such private travel agencies play an important role in Christian pilgrimages. In the case of Catholics in the United States wishing to make a pilgrimage to the Holy Land there are numerous specialty travel agencies such as Catholic Pilgrimages that is a division of Glory-Tours, a company with offices in the United States that specializes in "overseas pilgrimages that have a distinct Catholic and Christian interest."[21] In addition to arranging tours itself the company encourages private group leaders to contact them for assistance, noting among the benefits for such leaders the possibility of income generation for oneself or for one's church. For those going on such pilgrimages either as part of a group tour or on their own there are also a number of guidebooks to help pilgrims plan their itinerary.[22] Beyond assisting with the arrangement of tours by pilgrims, as Bajc notes, one of the roles of both government tourism ministries and private and church-based tour operators is to overcome the uncertainty over the safety of visiting the Holy Land with the message that "Jerusalem is a safe place to visit."[23]

While most Christian denominations maintain a presence in Jerusalem and elsewhere in the Holy Land, only some of these play a role in promoting pilgrimages and assisting pilgrims. In many instances their role is an indirect one of providing information to pilgrims about sites. The Franciscan order's *Custodia Terrae Sanctae,* for example, dates its presence in the Holy Land to the creation of the Province of the Holy Land by the Franciscan order in 1217. After the last Crusader stronghold fell to the Muslims in 1291, the order sent two friars each year to the Holy Land to maintain a Christian presence there and to serve as custodians of holy places (a status they were officially granted by Pope Clement VI in 1342). They established themselves at the Sanctuary of the Nativity in Bethlehem in 1347 and over the centuries became custodians of other locales as well (in some of which they have established museums and archives). There are 300 friars from 30 countries serving the *Custodia Terrae Sanctae* at present and its website lists 22 sites in the Holy Land. In addition to such sites, in 1973 it established the Christian Information Center in Jerusalem near the Tower of David and Jaffa Gate. Outside of the holy Land itself, the Custodia's website mentions "It is also represented in many countries of the world, whether by a convent under its direct jurisdiction — as in Rome, Naples, Palermo (Italy), Buenos Aires (Argentina) or Washington, D.C. (USA) — or by a "commisariat" or a center for the dissemination of the message of the Holy Places, as in Madrid

(Spain) or Milan (Italy). Furthermore, the Custodia is represented by a Non-Governmental Organization (an NGO), The Holy Land Association (L'associazione di Terra Santa, ATS), whose main office is in Rome (Italy) and by a foundation, the Franciscan Foundation for the Holy Land, whose offices are in Washington, D.C. (USA)."[24]

Sometimes, though not often, state authorities do take a more direct role in assisting Christian pilgrims. A 2008 Sifynews article from Hyderabad reported, "The first batch of 51 Christian pilgrims from Andhra Pradesh left for Jerusalem on Tuesday under the state government's scheme to help Christians visit places connected with the life of Jesus. The pilgrims left for Bahrain by Gulf Air flight early on Tuesday for their onward journey to Jordan. The state government is providing a subsidy of Rs. [rupees] 20,000 to each pilgrim for the seven-day tour, which covers Jordan and Israel. The pilgrimage including food, accommodation, and transportation costs Rs. 56,000 but with the government providing the subsidy, each pilgrim will have to pay Rs. 36,000 for the tour package.... The state government, which announced the scheme last year, plans to send 900 to 1,000 pilgrims this year and has allocated Rs. 20,000 for the purpose in 2008-09 budget."[25] The article quotes the state's Chief Minister R.S. Rajasekhara Reddy that the "government introduced the scheme because it recognized the right of people to freedom of religion." The Archbishop of Hyderabad Marampudi Joji is quoted as saying that the Christian community had been lobbying for such support for 10 years. The state's minorities finance corporation organized the tour and restricted it to physically fit pilgrims over 50 years of age and couples who were able to support one another during the tour. According to the 2001 census there were 1.2 million Christians in the state, representing only 1.55 percent of the population. Subsidizing Christian pilgrims is part of a broader state initiative to assist the Christian minority that includes creating a separate welfare ministry and finance corporation for them.

Missionaries

As the term is commonly used, a missionary is a follower of a religion who endeavors to convert those who do not share the same faith or works among and provides assistance to less fortunate followers of the religion. Although missionaries may remain close to home or work in different regions of their own country, our concern is with those who go to work in countries other than their own. While to some extent all such missionaries are engaged in a transnational undertaking, the extent of their transnationalism and the content of their transnational activities can vary a great deal. Especially prior to the late 1800s, for example, when travel and communication were more difficult, missionaries to foreign lands sometimes went on a one-way trip and often maintained only sporadic contact with their original homes or with the institutions that sent them.

In addition to promoting religious beliefs, learning and teaching languages is often an important aspect of transnational missionary activity. On the one hand, in many instances proselytizing by missionaries spreads the dominant language of the religion (e.g., Pali, Sanskrit, Latin, English, and Arabic). On the other hand, to function effectively among the people with whom a missionary is working requires that the missionary learn the language of these people. SIL International (formerly the Summer Institute of Linguistics) and its associated institution Wycliffe International (formerly the Wycliffe Bible Translators) provide good examples of the promotion of language learning on behalf of Christian missionaries. While Wycliffe International focuses specifically on translating the Bible into different languages and direct support of Christian missionary activity, SIL International engages in linguistic work of a broader nature.

William Cameron Townsend (1896–1982), who had worked as a Disciples of Christ missionary in Guatemala, founded SIL, which began training missionaries in linguistic principles in 1934. SIL's headquarters is located in Dallas, Texas, and from the 1950s until 1987 language training took place at the Normal campus of the University of Oklahoma. After its contract with the University of Oklahoma was terminated SIL decentralized its language instruction to a number of locales around the world. It has regional offices in Africa (Yaoundé, Cameroon), Latin America (Cuiabá, Brazil; Tlalpan, DF, Mexico; Lima, Peru), Asia (Manila, Philippines), and Oceania (Ukarumpa, Papua New Guinea). In its efforts to assist the work of Christian missionaries around the world, SIL has supported the collection and analysis of data on over 2,550 languages (SIL researchers being the only ones to have studies many of these), published over 20,000 technical publications (mostly of a linguistics nature), and been active in promoting literacy in indigenous languages world-wide. In addition to promoting the Bible into different languages, SIL also provides publications on subjects such as nutrition, farming, and health in minority languages. It also provides linguistics instructors and materials to a number of educational institutions engaged in missionary and theological training in the United States as well as Trinity Western University in British Columbia, Canada.

Buddhist Missionaries

The history of transnational religious missionaries essentially begins with the Emperor Asoka who sent Buddhist missionaries (*dharma bhanaks*) throughout his empire and beyond its borders to surrounding countries as well as west to Europe and North Africa following his conversion to Buddhism in reaction to the brutality of the Kalinga War (265–263 BC). During the Medieval Period Buddhism lost ground to Confucians, Hindus, Christians, and Muslims in many parts of Asia and Europe. It held its ground and continued to gain adherents mainly in the highlands of the Himalayas (e.g., Tibet, Nepal, Bhutan, and some highland areas of northern India) and on Mainland Southeast Asia (e.g., Burma, Thailand, Laos, Cambodia, and Vietnam). Its expansion in these regions continued to be the result of a mixture of the efforts of traveling monks (usually traveling along established trade routes) and the conversion of local rulers and the subsequent consolidation and expansion of their power. The main difference with earlier times was that the monks were not traveling so far. Rather than moving along the Silk Road and the maritime trade route between India and China, these monks mainly traveled along the inland rivers and jungle and mountain trails. While more distant connections with fellow Buddhists in Sri Lanka continued to a limited extent, Buddhism within Southeast Asia during the Medieval Period was relatively localized and often evolved into a syncretic religion that combined aspects of Buddhism, Hinduism, and local animistic and other beliefs.

Buddhist revivals and instances of the spread of its influence occurred in various parts of the world during the 1800s. In the case of Siam (Thailand), for example, Prince (later King) Mongkut formed the Thammayuttika (Ordering Adhering to the Dhamma) in the 1830s in an effort to reform Buddhism in his country. This, however, was an internal affair and not a transnational one except indirectly through its emphasis on paying greater attention to Buddhist texts. The publication of translations of Buddhist writings in the West led to some intellectual interest in Buddhism among philosophers such as Arthur Schopenhauer (1788–1860). However, as Abelson and Keiji have pointed out in regard to Schopenhauer, the link was fairly superficial.[26] The activities of Westerners of a less scholarly inclination, however, played a very important role in the revival and spread of transnational Buddhism. Edwin Arnold (1832–1904), Helena Blavatsky (aka Madame Blavatsky, Helena von Hahn, and Elena Petrovna Gan; 1831–91), and Colonel Henry Steele Olcott (1832–1907) were three of the most important Westerners in this regard.

Edwin Arnold is known primarily as an English journalist and for his writings about Asia.[27] He went to India to serve as principal of the Sanskrit College at Poona from 1856 to 1861. He then returned to England to work for *The Daily Telegraph* newspaper. He published *The Light of Asia* in 1879, an epic dealing with the life of Buddha.[28] While scholars and some Christians were critical of the work it became a best seller and was reprinted numerous times and played an important role in popularizing Buddhism in the West. Arnold was also one of the founders, along with Anagarika Dharmapala, of the Mahabodhi Society in India, which will be discussed below. Arnold's third wife was Japanese and he moved to Japan in later life where he continued to write about Asia.

Helena Blavatsky was born in Russia and left home to wander around the world between 1848 and 1858.[29] Madame Blavatsky claimed that she traveled to Tibet and Sri Lanka in the 1850s, where she says she became a Buddhist.[30] She returned to Russia for a time and then left Russia and immigrated to New York City in 1873, where she developed a reputation as a psychic medium. She and a number of others interested in spiritualism founded the Theosophical Society in 1875. She moved to India in 1879 along with Colonel Olcott to move the headquarters of the Theosophical Society to India, eventually settling on Adyar (near Madras, Chennai) as the site for its international headquarters. She and Colonel Olcott visited Sri Lanka in 1880. While there they both converted to Buddhism (this time the event in her case is known to have happened), although she remained essentially a spiritualist for the rest of her life. More important than her supposed conversion to Buddhism at this time was her close association with the young Sri Lankan Anagarika Dharmapala, whom she encouraged to study Pali and work for the good of humanity. She left India in 1886 and eventually settled in England, where she spent the rest of her life.

While Madame Blavatsky's role in promoting modern Buddhism was somewhat tangential, her colleague Colonel Olcott played a direct and major part.[31] He was born in New Jersey, the son of a Presbyterian businessman. He worked as a journalist and lawyer and served in the army during the Civil War. He became interested in séances and the Spiritualist movement and wrote a series of newspaper articles and a book called *People from the Other World* on them in 1874. He met Helena Blavatsky while visiting one of the séances for his articles and the following year the two of them and others founded the Theosophical Society. Olcott provided the initial funding for the society and served as its president. It was at this time that Olcott officially converted to Buddhism and he is generally considered to be the first American to do so. After arriving in Colombo with Madame Blavatsky in 1880, Olcott became involved in writing about Buddhism for Western readers, promoting Buddhist education in Sri Lanka, and helping to revive the religion within the region. His most famous publication on Buddhism is his *Buddhist Catechism*, which was originally published in Madras in 1881 and is still in print and widely used today. Largely through his efforts as president, the Theosophical Society built numerous Buddhist schools in Sri Lanka. Anagarika Dharmapala worked for Olcott as a translator. Olcott eventually moved back to India to continue his work on behalf of the Theosophical Society. In honor of his contribution to Buddhism in Sri Lanka there are statues of him in front of the Colombo Fort Railway Station and in many of the schools that he helped to found as well as a street named after him in Colombo.

Anagarika Dharmpala (meaning homeless one and protector of the dharma; 1864–1933) was a major figure in the modern revival of Buddhism in Sri Lanka, India, and the West.[32] He was born Don David Hawavitarne to one of the wealthiest merchant families in Sri Lanka. He met Madame Blavatsky and Colonel Olcott at the age of 16 and against the wishes of his father she took him to live at the Theosopical Society's headquarters in Adyar in 1884. When Colonel Olcott came to Sri Lanka in 1886 to campaign for Buddhist schools through the Buddhist Education Fund, Dharmapala joined the Colonel. It was at this time that he renounced the comforts of his life and changed his name. After working with Colonel Olcott and Madame Blavatsky in 1891 he made a pilgrimage to Bodh Gaya and the Mahabodhi Temple, the place of Buddha's enlightenment. Edwin Arnold had visited the site in 1885 and this seems to have provided inspiration to Dharmapala. Upon arrival he found that a Hindu Saivite priest had taken over the temple and turned it into a Hindu temple from which Buddhists were barred from worshipping. In response Arnold and Dharmapala founded the Mahabodi Society. It was first established in Colombo, but in 1892 its headquarters was moved to Calcutta. The society launched a lawsuit against the Hindu priests who controlled the temple and finally in 1949, after Dharmapala's death, the society was successful in being granted partial management of the site.

In the meantime, the Mahabodhi Society served as a catalyst for the revival of Buddhism in India. Mahabodhi Society centers were established around India and a number of Indians converted to Buddhism. Dharmapala spoke to a gathering of Tibetan Buddhists at Darjeeling in 1892 and presented them with a Buddha relic to give to the Dalai Lama. The next year (1893) he was invited to attend the World's Parliament of Religions in Chicago. The success of this trip marked the beginning of his subsequent travels to other countries around the world to lecture and establish viharas. The World Columbian Exposition in Chicago hosted the World's Parliament of Religions, which was the first effort to create a worldwide interfaith dialogue. The gathering served to increase his interest in Eastern religions and especially Buddhism and he came to play an important role in sponsoring activities related to Buddhism in the West.

Dharmapala was invited as a representative of "Southern Buddhism" (i.e., Theravada Buddhism). Among the other invitees were Swami Vivikananda as a representative of Hinduism, Virchand Gandhi as a representative of Jainism, and Soyen Shaku as a representative of Zen Buddhism. These religious figures played a major role in introducing Eastern religions to a wide audience in the United States.[33] (The 2009 Parliament of the World's Religions was held in Melbourne, Australia. It was billed as "the largest interfaith gathering on Earth."[34])

Paul Carus (1852–1919) was among those attending the 1893 World's Parliament of Religions. A German immigrant to the United States, Carus was an influential author and promoter of interfaith dialogue. He invited Dharmapala to give a lecture tour in the United States in 1896 and again in 1902–04. Carus also befriended the Japanese Zen master Soyen Shaku (1859–1919), whom he met at the Parliament. After attending the Parliament Soyen traveled to Sri Lanka to study Pali and Theravada Buddhism for three years. At Carus's request Shaku also sent one of his students, D.T. Suzuki, to the United States to translate Buddhist works for Carus's Open Court Publishing Company.

Dharmapala also traveled to England. His first visit was on his way to the United States and he spent time with Edwin Arnold while there. He announced a desire to establish a monastery there with resident monks from Sri Lanka to promote Buddhism in England. Later he met Mary Foster in Honolulu. She financed the establishment of Foster House in Ealing, which was the first Buddhist monastery (*vihara*) to be located outside of Asia in modern times. It was named the London Buddhist Vihara. She also became Dharmapala's main financial supporter. The London Buddhist Vihara was opened in 1926. It has since been moved to various locations (presently it is located in Chiswick) and ceased operation during World War II when the monks returned to Sri Lanka. In England at this time, in addition to the London Buddhist Vihara, Christmas Humphreys, an English lawyer and judge, founded the Buddhist Society in 1924 — making it the first Buddhist organization to be established in modern Europe. Humphreys initially became a theosophist and then converted to Buddhism. He served as president of the society until his death in 1983. The Society is still in existence and the Dalai Lama became its patron in 1961.

Dharmapala's globetrotting did not detract from his work back in Sri Lanka and India. In Sri Lanka he focused on supporting the construction of schools and hospitals and in India he promoted the construction of a number of new Buddhist temples and monasteries (*viharas*). A new temple at Sarnath was among those built in India, another of the sites associated with Buddha. Dharmapala died there in 1933.

Transnational Buddhist missionary activities were curtailed by World War II, but re-emerged in the 1960s along two paths that intersected at times. One of these paths followed renewed interest internationally — but especially in traditionally non–Buddhist countries in the West — in Buddhism that crossed ethnic lines. The other path catered to the growing Asian immigrant communities by monks from the homelands of the immigrants.

The communist Chinese invasion of Tibet in 1950–1, exile of the Dalai Lama after

the failure of the 1959 Tibetan uprising against Chinese occupation, and ongoing persecution of Tibetan Buddhists by the communist regime are perhaps the most important
developments shaping post–World War II transnational Buddhism. These developments
served not only to create a worldwide Tibetan diaspora, but also to help promote Tibetan
Buddhism as an especially important version of Buddhism attracting worldwide attention
among Buddhists and non–Buddhists alike. Following the defeat of the 1959 uprising the
14th Dalai Lama, Tenzin Gyatso (born 1935), fled into exile in Dharamsala, India, where
Indian Prime Jawaharlal Nehru had given the Dalai Lama and his followers permission
to establish a government-in-exile (known in English as the Central Tibetan Administration or CTA). Today this settlement has become one of the most important centers of
Buddhism in the world and in 2005 and 2008 *Time* magazine named the Dalai Lama as
one of the 100 most influential persons in the world.

About 80,000 Tibetans went with the Dalai Lama into exile in India in 1959. As
MacPherson, Benz, and Ghoso point out, this was "the largest movement out of Tibet to
date."[35] As for the characteristics of these refugees, "Although there were a dispropor-
tionate number of men because the monks and soldiers were at higher risk of persecution
at that time, many women came with families or as nuns."[36] The high proportion
of monks and nuns among Tibetan refugees gives it a distinctive character when compared
with most other refugee and immigrant groups. In 2008 the Central Tibetan Administration's website stated that there were 111,170 Tibetans living outside of Tibet.[37]
Over 80,000 of these people live in India, Nepal, and Bhutan, where the CTA has established refugee settlements (35 in India, 10 in Nepal, and seven in Bhutan), and around
19,000 live elsewhere: 9,000 in the United States (2008), 4,275 in Canada (2006), 1,540
in Switzerland (1998), 1,000 in Taiwan (1998), 650 in the United Kingdom (2008), 533
in Australia (2006), 640 in the rest of Western Europe excluding Switzerland and Scandinavia (1998), 110 in Scandinavia (1998), 66 in New Zealand (2006), and 60 in Japan
(1998).[38] Tibetan migrations have tended to occur in waves, with a second wave coming
in the late 1980s and early 1990s, when around 25,000 Tibetan migrants entered India,
during a period of more liberal treatment of Tibetans by Chinese authorities. A number
of monks and nuns in particular (who constituted about 44 percent of the migrants)
were able to migrate at this time. More recent migrants consist overwhelmingly of monks
and nuns.

The Doeguling Tibetan settlement in Mundgod near Bangalore in southern India
with around 16,000 inhabitants living in nine camps is one of the largest Tibetan refugee
communities outside of Dharamsala. The camps are administered by the CTA and a considerable amount of its financial support comes from the American non-governmental
organization Friends of Tibetan Settlements in India (FOTSI). Mungod is also the site
of the Drepung Gomang Monastic College, named after a monastery in Tibet that
was destroyed by the Chinese. The college website provides the following account of its
founding: "Only about 100 monks [from the original Gomang monastery] managed to
escape with His Holiness the Dalai Lama when he fled Tibet in 1959. They lived first in
Boxa, North India, and then, in 1969, 62 of the surviving Gomang monks were given 42
acres of land in Mungod, south India. There they started to rebuild Drepung Gomang

Monastic Dratsang (college) in its present location."[39] At present the college is home to more than 1.500 monks.

The movement of Tibetan exiles and the emergence of the Dalai Lama as an international figure began in the 1960s. The first group of Tibetans to be resettled outside of the Himalayan region went to Switzerland in the early 1960s under sponsorship by the Swiss Red Cross. An article reprinted in the *Tibet Sun* provides an overview of this early group: "There are now six Tibetan communities in eastern Switzerland at villages in those valleys off the beaten track of tourism. Under arrangements made by the Swiss Red Cross, about 100 more Tibetan refugees, from the 35,000 now living in India, will be arriving here during the next few months. This will bring the total to more than 300, plus some 150 orphans with Swiss families. Typical of those expatriate communities is 'Tibeterhelm Ennethur,' a big chalet on the hillside above Unterwasser, which, since last May, has sheltered 40 men, women and children including two lamas who give the children religious instruction in the evenings but during the day work at a textile mill further down the valley. A dozen other men have been found jobs as carpenters, market gardeners, and labourers—one as an electrician. The two oldest ones, well into their sixties, cope with some of the heavier domestic chores in the chalet. Being skilled tailors, they also make and repair clothes for members of the community."[40]

The Dalai Lama launched the first of his international tours to raise consciousness about the situation facing Tibetans in 1967. Since then he has visited a total of 46 countries. The relative success of the Swiss experience also led the Dalai Lama to approach representatives of the Canadian and United States governments. The Canadian High Commissioner in India was supportive and in 1971 100 Tibetans migrated to Canada, settling in Ontario. The Tibetan Canadian Cultural Centre provides a brief history of the experience of Tibetan migrants in Ontario: "On March 30, 1971 100 Tibetans immigrated to Ontario, Canada. These Tibetans had fled Tibet in 1959 and were living in refugee camps in India. The Canadian government sponsored approximately 200 Tibetans to Canada in the early '70s.... Tibetans were dispersed throughout three Ontario cities: Belleville, Lindsay and Cobourg. Six families settled in Lindsay; 9 families were set up in Belleville and four families called Cobourg home.... As pioneers in this country of the Tibetan identity, the men and women in the Ontario Tibetan community were keenly aware of the need to preserve and share their culture. To ensure that future generations of Tibetans were given a chance to learn their own heritage and traditions, the Canadian Tibetan Association of Ontario was created in 1980."[41] At present the Toronto area hosts the largest Tibetan community in the west (about 3,500 people), followed by New York City (about 3,000 people), with smaller North American communities in Minneapolis, San Francisco, Portland, Boston, Calgary, and Vancouver.

One noticeable difference between the group that first arrived in Toronto and the one that arrived in Switzerland a few years earlier is the absence of monks in the group coming to Canada. Despite the large number of Tibetan monks in exile, not all Tibetan communities in the West have their own monks. For such communities visits by traveling Tibetan monks who today can be seen moving about the globe in significant numbers play an important role in meeting their spiritual needs.

The Dalai Lama has two roles in his international travels: as a Buddhist spiritual leader and as the political leader. Both roles not only link him closely to the Tibetan diaspora, but also to other Buddhists, those from other religions interested in interfaith dialogues, and supporters of the Tibetan cause. The division between the two roles is sometimes blurred and his actions in both roles sometimes elicit protests from the communist government in China The Dalai Lama received his first foreign honors during a visit to California in September 1979, when the mayors of Los Angeles and San Francisco awarded him the keys to their cities. Ten years later in 1989 he was awarded the Nobel Peace Prize. The Canadian Parliament voted unanimously to make the Dalai Lama an honorary citizen of Canada in mid–2006 and a few months later the United States Congress awarded the Dalai Lama the Congressional Gold Medal, the highest award that can be granted by the Congress. The PRC routinely protests such awards and as its economic influence around the world has grown is sometimes able to block them. The Dalai Lama visited the University of Tasmania in mid–2007 and it was announced that he would be awarded an honorary degree by the university in December. The university later withdrew the offer and an Australian senator raised questions about the PRC's influence in the withdrawal since the university received $30 million (Australian) a year from students from the PRC.[42] When Taiwan's Democratic Progressive Party invited the Dalai Lama to visit Taiwan in order to hold religious services in memory of those killed by Typhoon Morakot, the PRC protested the event by canceling attendance by its delegates at several events in Taiwan.[43]

Members of the Tibetan diaspora of course are not the only Buddhists to migrate and then maintain religious ties to their homeland (or homeland in exile in the case of Tibetans) through traveling monks and other means, and Buddhist monks from many countries travel throughout the world today to address quite varied audiences of Buddhists and non–Buddhists. Ties between contemporary immigrant Buddhist communities and Buddhist institutions in their country of origin are often quite important. Immigrant ethnic communities that are predominantly Buddhist commonly seek to establish a Buddhist temple with resident monks, often from their country of origin, as well as to sponsor visits of monks from their home country. Immigrant Buddhists also often send funds back to assist religious institutions in their home country.

As with other religions, Buddhism often plays an important role in the lives of immigrant communities from countries that are predominantly Buddhist. The population of Thailand is mainly Buddhist and Buddhist temples catering to overseas Thai communities are found in many locales where there are large numbers of Thai immigrants. Taking the United Kingdom as an example, the 2001 British census enumerated 16,257 ethnic Thais born in the United Kingdom (i.e., people who's ancestors were from Thailand).[44] The country is also home to a number of other people of Thai descent as well as a large Thai expatriate community (the largest in Europe), bringing the total ethnic Thai population in the country to around 40,000. Women constituted 72 percent of the Thais in the census. More recent figures of Thai immigrants indicate that about two-thirds of the migrants are women marrying British citizens. The largest numbers of ethnic Thais are located in London, Sheffield, Birmingham, and Glasgow. King Rama VI established the *Samaggi*

Samagom (aka The Thai Association in the UK) in 1901 to cater to the Thai community in the United Kingdom. It remains the most important of the roughly 15 Thai secular organizations in the country.

Most Thais in Britain are Buddhists and the community has sponsored the construction of several temples and monasteries in the country. The temples include Wat Buddhapadipa in Wembledon (London, opened 1982) and Wat Charoenbhavana (opened 2004) in Manchester. Viharas include the Amaravati Buddhist Monastery in Hemel Hempstead, Chithurst Buddhist Monastery (aka *Cittaviveka*) in Chithurst, and *Aruna Ratanagiri* in Northumberland. The temples are especially important religious centers for the Thai community while the monasteries are oriented more towards non–Thai Buddhists.

Wat Buddhapadipa was the first Thai temple to be built in the United Kingdom. It serves as a residence for monks and nuns as well as a religious and cultural center for the Thai community in the United Kingdom. The building includes murals painted by two well-known artists from Thailand, Chalermchai Kositpipat and Panya Vijinthanasarn.[45] In addition to celebrating the important Buddhist holidays the temple also hosts a number of other religious activities, such as meditation classes and a blessing ceremony for adopted children, which the temples website describes as "a good thing to do so that children can learn their own culture and religion. Even if they were adopted by an English family, they have an opportunity to learn their own culture and religion and where they came from."[46]

The Venerable Ajahn Chah Subhaddo (aka Acharn Cha, Phra Ajaan Chaa Suphattho and Chao Khun Bodhinyana There; 1918–92), a famous Thai monk, was influential in the founding of the Amaravati Buddhist Monastery and the Chithurst Buddhist Monastery. Ajahn Chah was born in Ubon Ratchathani in northeastern Thailand and was based at Wat Pa Pong in Ubon Ratchathani (founded 1959)[47] and at one time had over 80 monasteries associated with him in the northeast.[48] Ajanh Sumedho (aka Robert Jackman, born 1934 in Seattle) came to Southeast Asia as a Peace Corps volunteer in the early 1960s and from 1967 to 1977 studied under Ajahn Chah at Wat Nong Pa Pong. Ajahn Chah founded Wat Pah Nanachat (aka International Forest Monastery) in 1975, which was the first monastery in Thailand specifically devoted to training English-speaking Westerners, and Ajanh Sumedho served as its abbot.

The English Sangha Trust invited the two monks to visit England in 1977 (Ajanh Chah's dhamma talks had by this time become widely available in English and other languages) with the aim of their helping to establish a Buddhist monastery. Their visit led to the founding of *Cittaviveka* (the Chithurst Forest Monastery) in 1979 with Ajahn Sumedho serving as its abbot. The English Sangha Trust bought land to establish the Amaravati Monastery in 1984 and it was opened the following year. Princess Galyani Vadhana, the sister of Thailand's king, officially opened a new temple building at Amaravati in 1999. Students of Ajahn Chah have opened other monasteries in the United Kingdom as well as in Australia, New Zealand, Italy, Switzerland, and in North America.

While Buddhism, like other major world religions, proclaims its universality, in practice divisions exist between Buddhists in different countries and between Buddhists from different ethnic immigrant communities. In the case of immigrant ethnic communities such as the British Thais and overseas Tibetans discussed above, this reflects the extent to which local Buddhist institutions serve the needs of particular communities and are seen as a part of these communities rather than the larger community of Buddhists as a whole. At an abstract level local Buddhist institutions serve to link their congregations with all other Buddhists around the world, but the most important linkages in practice are with fellow Buddhists of their own ethno-national background around the world, especially to Buddhists in their country of origin or ancestry. Support for local temples and attendance at these temples tends to be overwhelmingly from within a single ethnic community and visiting monks from outside of the country generally are from the same ethnic background. There are important exceptions, such as the Dalai Lama, who attracts multiethnic crowds in his public appearances, but these are not the norm. Other exceptions are found in the case of ethnic immigrant communities of Buddhists that are too small to have their own institutions and have to rely on the institutions of other ethnic groups. Thus, local Lao, Thai, and Burmese immigrant communities may find themselves having to share facilities and even monks, but usually the larger group dominates and the smaller ones often have a goal of eventually establishing their own institutions.

Christian Missionaries

Christian missionary activity is based on what Christians refer to as the Great Commission. One version of the Great Commission appears in Matthew 28:16–20, which has the resurrected Jesus telling the 11 disciples, "Go therefore and make disciples of all nations, baptizing them in the name of the Father and the Son and the of the Holy Spirit, teaching them to observe all that I have commanded you." There are, however, some scholars of early Christianity who doubt that Jesus ever uttered these words and believe that the Great Commission was a later product of the Christian community.[49] Whether or not these were the words of Jesus, Christian missionaries soon set about to spread their religion within the Roman Empire.

Although today Christianity is often portrayed as a European religion, its origins in the Middle East and association with the Roman Empire provided the early Christian church with a base in the Middle East as well. Christianity spread eastward from the Mediterranean as far as China during the medieval and early modern periods. Christian missionaries operating in the East tended to follow the main trade routes along the Silk Road and the maritime trade route to South Asia and on to China and often to mix commerce with religion. The Christian communities that were established farther to the east were relatively small and were often centered on groups of people engaged in long-distance trade. Moreover, the rise of Islam curtailed the growth of Christianity in the East until the age of European colonialism, and the number of missionaries working in the region remained fairly small until modern times.

European discovery, conquest, and colonization of the Americas and Pacific along with the increased European presence in Asia from the late 1400s provided a new impetus for Christian missionary activity as Catholic and Protestant missionaries sought to covert the peoples in these regions to Christianity.[50] Catholic missionaries arrived in the Americas shortly after Columbus's voyage of discovery in 1492. After Columbus returned to Europe Pope Alexander VI issued the bull *Inter Caetera* in 1493 that demarcated spheres of colonization between Spain and Portugal and also called on Spain to promote the conversion of the people in the Americas to Catholicism: "Among other works well pleasing to the Divine Majesty and cherished of our heart, this assuredly ranks highest, that in our times especially the Catholic faith and the Christian religion be exalted and be everywhere increased and spread, that the health of souls be cared for and that barbarous nations be overthrown and brought to the faith itself ... we [the Papacy] command you [Spain] ... to instruct the aforesaid inhabitants and residents and dwellers therein in the Catholic faith, and train them in good morals."[51] Accordingly, Columbus took Catholic priests with him on his second voyage and the first Catholic missionaries to the Americas arrived on the island of Hispanola in what is now the Dominican Republic in 1494 and they had their first baptism in 1496 with the conversion of a man named Guaticaba and the members of his family.

The Catholic Church's encouragement of Spain to convert the people of the Americas was reiterated by Pope Alexander the VI in 1501, when he granted Spain title to its newly discovered lands in the Americas with the condition that the Spanish were to provide religious instruction to the native peoples. This provision helped to ensure that Catholic missionaries accompanied the Spanish conquerors such as Hernán Cortés and Francisco Pizzaro.

Members of four religious orders—the Augustinians, Dominicans, Franciscans, and Jesuits—were primarily responsible for Catholic missionary activities outside of Europe that began in the 1400s. The first three of these orders were all formed in the 1200s: the Franciscans were established by St. Francis of Assisi in 1209, the Dominicans by St. Dominic in 1216, and the Augustinians in 1244 under the influence of Pope Innocent IV who saw it as a counterbalance to the powers of the first two orders (we will discuss the Jesuits, which were formed in the 1500s, below). The orders were already well established in Spain and Portugal when these two countries expanded their international activities in the 1400s and early 1500s. They are of particular interest in the present context since they served to link Catholics around the world back to Spain and Portugal as well as to Rome. The individual monk working outside of Europe became to varying degrees part of the local expatriate or colonial society while also serving as an agent of the Catholic Church based in Rome and operating within the context of Spanish or Portuguese religious and secular policies and interests. Many of the monks who came to live and work outside of Europe became highly immersed in the local society and rarely had direct contact with the wider church organization, while others served essentially as international roving agents of the church, moving around the world to promote and oversee its activities. In the discussion that follows we will focus on three individuals who developed important local roots in their respective areas of missionary work while also playing important roles in Europe promoting missionary activities abroad—Bartolomé de Las Casas, Francisco Xavier, and Alexander de Rhodes.

From the outset there was a duality to Spanish attitudes towards the native people of the Americas. On the one hand there was the view of Columbus, Queen Isabel, and Pope Alexander VI that "the so-called Indians were a gentle, unspoiled people who were eager to accept Christianity and to serve the monarch" and that "the Indians were subjects of the monarchy morally equal to those in the peninsula and that they should become Europeanized Christians as soon as possible."[52] In contrast you had the less benign views of King Ferdinand "who wanted the colonial venture to pay off, regardless of human considerations" and of most of the Spaniards who went to the Americas who "developed extremely unfavorable attitudes towards them. They saw these natives naked, worshipping idols, unmindful of private property, cannibalistic, idle, and engaging in grossly obscene mating and homosexual practices," a view that often led to the conclusion that "the Indians were not even human."[53]

Bartolomé de Las Casas (1484–1566) was the most famous of Spanish Catholic missionaries to work in the New World and is known today for his championing of the native peoples of the Americas.[54] We will discuss Las Casas in some detail in order to provide a glimpse at the transnational activities of this important Catholic priest in the 1500s as he moved back and forth between Spain and its colonies in the Americas.

Las Casas' father and several of his uncles sailed with Columbus on his second voyage to the Americas. His father then took Bartolomé with him when he moved to the island of Hispaniola in 1502. The young man became a priest in 1513 and was also awarded property in Cuba and control over the natives living on it. Reacting against the mistreatment of the native Taino on the island he gave up his property, freed the people living on it, and urged other Spaniards to do the same.

After meeting with a hostile response from his follow colonists, Las Casas returned to Spain to campaign against the mistreatment of the native peoples in the New World. He established a colony at Cumaná in Venezuela where he endeavored to have the natives and Spaniards peacefully coexist with the colonists, paying the natives fair wages and teaching them farming techniques. The experiment ended in failure when during Las Casas's absence a group of the colonists initiated slave raids against neighboring Caribs that led to the Caribs attacking the colony and destroying it. Las Casas then moved to a Dominican monastery in Santo Domingo in 1523 and from there continued to write and lobby on behalf of the native peoples under Spanish dominion.

Las Casas paid a visit to newly conquered Guatemala in 1531 and in 1533 the head of the Guatemalan See, Francisco Marroquín, asked Las Casas to move to Guatemala.[55] Las Casas did not accept the offer at the time, but in 1537 an agreement was reached between the Dominican Order and Marroquín in which the Dominicans were given the right to carry out conversions in an area known as Tuzulutlan (the land of war), which was inhabited primarily by Kekchi Maya, and other Spanish colonists were to be barred from it for an initial period of five years. Pedro de Alvarado, the conqueror of Guatemala, opposed this agreement and went ahead and gave the area to two Spaniards in 1540.[56] In the meantime, Pope Paul III had issued two bulls in mid–1537 (*Sublimus Dei* and *Altituda Divini Consolii*) declaring that the native people of the Americas were humans and not to be robbed of their freedom or possessions along with a letter (*Pastorale Officium*) declaring that not anyone abiding by the bulls would be automatically excommunicated. These documents generated considerable controversy within the Catholic Church and in Spain and its colonies. For his part, Las Casas quickly translated them into Spanish and used them to further his campaign for native rights.[57] Las Casas had returned to Spain in order to continue his campaign and to recruit new missionaries. He sent Luis Cancer to Tuzulutlan (which came to be renamed Verapaz, "true peace") in 1541 and helped to draft the New Laws of the Indies, which were signed by the Spanish King Charles V in 1542. In addition, the king also "signed an edict endorsing Las Casas' ideas for peaceful conquest of the Verapaz and had dispatched letters guaranteeing the Indians of Tuzulutlan their land."[58]

Las Casas was offered the position of bishop of Cuzco in Peru, but he turned this down and instead accepted the post of bishop of Chiapa (in what is now southern Mexico and then including parts of what is now Guatemala) and was confirmed in this office in 1544. He remained in Spain until Tuzulutlan and the neighboring Lacandon were added to his bishopric by a papal bull and the granting of land in Tuzulutlan to the two Spaniards by Alvarado was annulled by royal decree. Local Spanish settlers greeted him with open hostility when his ship arrived in Santo Domingo from Spain. When he reached Cuidad Real de Chiapa (renamed San Cristóbal de Las Casas in 1848) to take up his post he was met with three months of violent demonstrations and threats to his life by the local Spaniards. Spanish colonists in Guatemala also protested and established their own settlement (Nueva Sevilla). The priests in Verapaz succeeded in converting many of the Kekchi and settling them in new communities (called *reducciones*). As these conflicts continued, Las Casas visited Verapaz and then returned to Spain in an effort to lobby on behalf of the Dominican efforts in Verapaz and the native peoples. Back in Spain he was forced to defend himself against charges of treason, which he did successfully. He resigned as bishop of Chiapa in 1551 to devote himself full time to writing and lobbying in Spain. The following year (1552) he published his most famous work, *A Short Account of the Destruction of the Indies*.[59] He died in Madrid in 1566.

Of the four main Catholic orders operating missions outside of Europe in the 1500s only the Jesuits were formed primarily for this purpose.[60] Ignatius of Loyola along with six other students at the University of Paris—four from Spain (including Francisco Xavier), one from France, and one from Portugal — met in 1534 to form the Company of Jesus. Their aim was to carry out hospital and missionary work in Jerusalem. They traveled to Rome in 1537, where Pope Paul III commended them and allowed them to be ordained as priests in Venice. Warfare made a trip to Jerusalem impossible and they devoted themselves to work in Italy. Ignatius became the first head of the order and once they were established the Jesuits focused on founding schools throughout Europe and beyond (Jesuit teachers were rigorously trained in both classical studies and theology) and converting non–Christians to Catholicism. Such activities were also linked to their goal to stop the spread of Protestantism. In regard to the first activity, the Jesuits had established a network of 74 colleges in Europe, Asia, and the Americas by the time of Ignatius' death in 1556.

Francisco Xavier (aka Francis Xavier, 1506–52) is among the most famous of the early Jesuits. His name is associated especially with the Catholic Church in Asia. As a founding member of the order he first worked in Europe. He left Europe from Lisbon in

1541 and remained for a time in Mozambique before continuing on to Goa in 1542. After working in various parts of south India and Sri Lanka, in 1545 he sailed to Malacca. The following year he sailed to Ambon and other Maluku islands, including Ternate and Morotai. He returned to Malacca in late 1547 and from there sailed back to Goa. He remained in Goa until 1549, when he sailed east again, returning to Malacca and then continuing on to Canton and finally to Japan, where he met the Japanese emperor and undertook missionary work. After establishing several congregations in Japan Xavier decided to return to Goa, making stops in China and Malacca on the way. Reaching Goa in early 1552, he soon headed back to Malacca and then sailed for China, but died off the coast of China before he was able to resume his work there. Unlike Las Casas, Xavier was not an especially tolerant individual. He promoted the introduction of the Inquisition in Goa, where it became notorious for its cruelty and use of torture. In Japan he stridently denounced idolatry, homosexuality, and a range of other beliefs and practices and urged those he converted to destroy temples and shrines.

Fellow Jesuit Alexander de Rhodes (1591–1660), who to some extent followed in Xavier's footsteps, was more tolerant of local customs and beliefs.[61] Wilson quotes Rhodes as commenting on efforts of some Jesuits to abolish local practices in East Asia, "though there are some practices which Christians cannot rightly indulge in, most of them are very innocent and we have judged that they may be retained without prejudice to true religion."[62] He is remembered especially for his role in creating the Romanized form of writing Vietnamese called *quoc ngu* in place of Chinese characters. Rhodes was born in Avignon, France, and joined the Society of Jesus (Jesuits) in Rome in 1612 in order to dedicate his life to missionary work. He left Rome for Lisbon in 1618 and from there, in April 1619, he sailed to the Portuguese colony of Goa with five other Jesuits on a small flotilla of three Portuguese ships. He spent his time in Goa preaching to Portuguese prisoners and galley slaves. He left Goa in April 1622 and after a brief stopover in Sri Lanka he arrived in Malacca (then also under Portuguese control) in July. He remained in Malacca for 9 months waiting for favorable winds for the onward journey to Macau, conducting baptisms while he waited. He arrived in Macau in May 1623 and was attached to a Jesuit college.

The Jesuits had established a mission in Dong Kinh (spelled Tonkin by Europeans) in 1615, which was ruled at the time by Trinh Tung (reigned 1570–1623). Following a struggle over the succession, Trinh Trang (reigned 1623–1654) assumed the throne. His reign was marked by conflict with the Nguyen lords who controlled much of what is now central Vietnam and who refused to recognize Trinh authority. Rhodes traveled to Dong Kinh from Macau towards the end of Trinh Tung's reign. While he was there he wrote a Vietnamese catechism and commenced work on a Portuguese-Latin-Vietnamese dictionary (*Dictionarium Annamiticum Lusitanum et Latinum*), which was published in Rome in 1651. This dictionary formed the basis of the *quoc ngu* writing system. He was also active in making converts and it was his success in this regard that led Trinh Trang to banish him in 1630. Rhodes returned to Macau for a time.

Figuring that it was safe to work in Nguyen-controlled territory, in 1640 Rhodes went to their capital at Phu Xuan (modern Hue). Nguyen Phuc Lan (reigned 1635–48) was the ruling Nguyen lord at this time and he maintained cordial relations with the Portuguese. Once again Rhodes set about making converts with relative success. During his time with the Nguyens he also made a trip to the Philippines. Eventually Nguyen Phuc Lan also reacted against the growing number of Catholic converts and arrested Rhodes, initially sentencing him to death but finally deciding to expel him. Rhodes went back to Macau one more time and then left for Malacca in early 1646.

By this time Malacca was under Dutch control and Rhodes received a hostile reception from the Dutch Protestants. Persisting, he then sailed to Java, where the Dutch imprisoned him for three months. After his release he went to Bantam (modern Banten) in western Java, where the English had established a trading post in 1603. Although they were also Protestants, the English there treated him well. Later in 1646 he sailed to Makassar (an important trading port on the island of Sulawesi in eastern Indonesia). He sailed to Makassar on a Portuguese ship and then returned to Bantam on an English ship.

Rhodes next sailed from Bantam to Surat in India on an English ship and from there on to the Persian port of Bandar Gombrun (modern Bandar Abbas) adjacent to the Strait of Hormuz, where he arrived in March 1648. From Bandar Gombrun he traveled overland in the company of two Calvanists (one French and one Flemish) to Isfahan. From there he traveled for a month with an Armenian caravan to Tabriz and then went to Erivan (in Armenia), which is located near Mt. Ararat where Noah's Ark is supposed to repose and where there was an important Carmelite monastery. Here he left behind a young Chinese companion whom he had baptized in Macau for fear of his being mistreated by the Turks and continued on alone to Rome, where he arrived in June 1649.

Back in Europe Rhodes unsuccessfully lobbied the pope and the Portuguese to support further Catholic missions in Vietnam. Pope Alexander III did agree, however, to allow Rhodes and two of his associates, François Pallu and Pierre Lambert de la Motte, to found the *Séminaire des Missions Étrangères* (Society of Foreign Missions) in Paris in 1659 (its name was changed later to *Missions Étrangères de Paris* or MEP). The Society of Foreign Missions of Paris was not a religious order, but a missionary organization composed of priests and lay persons. It was founded to engage in missionary work in areas outside of territories that were not under Spanish and Portuguese colonial rule. Rhodes himself went back to Isfahan where he died in 1660. The MEP later sent missionaries back to Vietnam. In the mid–1800s persecution of MEP missionaries by local authorities in Vietnam, China, and Korea provided a pretext for French military intervention in these countries and its subsequent conquest of Indochina. The MEP remains actively involved in missionary activity in Asia. A commemorative volume notes that in its 350 years of existence the society has sent over 4,200 missionary priests to Asia, commenting that they have sought to adapt to local customs and establish a local clergy, while keeping close contact with Rome.[63] The society's website mentions that in 2009 there were 260 priests working in Asia and that the society also sends 150 youth envoys to the region each year.[64]

As for the Jesuits, today the Society of Jesus is the largest order in the Catholic Church. In 2008 there were over 13,000 Jesuit priests in 112 countries. While focusing their activities on education, members of the order also engage in missionary work and a range of other activities including the promotion of social justice. The order's head-quarters (the General Curia) remains in Rome. The head of the order is referred to as the Superior General (SG). The current SG is Adolfo Nicolas Pachon (Spanish, born 1936–). After studying in Spain he went to Sophia University in Tokyo in 1960 to study theology. He then went to the Pontifical Gregorian University in Rome where he received a Masters degree in theology in 1971. He returned to Tokyo and then moved to the Philippines to serve as Director of the East Asian Pastoral Institute at the Ateneo de Manila University in Quezon City from 1978 to 1984. Fr. Pachon went back to Tokyo and in 1999 began working among poor immigrants in Tokyo. The year before, in 1998, he and other bishops in Asia had clashed with the Vatican when they requested greater local power in decision-making. Fr. Pachon became Moderator of the Jesuit Conference for Eastern Asia and Oceania (based in the Philippines) in 2004. He was elected the order's 30th Superior General in 2008 (the prior SG, Fr. Peter Hans Kolvenbach, was Dutch).

Just as the of spread of Catholicism to the Americas and elsewhere was closely associated with Spanish and Portuguese colonial expansion, the spread of the Church of England (Anglicans) around the world was linked to England's colonial presence. The Church of England considers itself to be both a Catholic and Reformed church, although its head is the ruling monarch of England rather than the Pope. Throughout its early history the Church of England was closely associated with the English state and its colonies. Although its roots go back to the initial establishment of Christianity in England, its origin as a distinct church is associated with its break with papal authority by King Henry VIII in 1534. Over the next few decades it evolved into a more distinct church from the Catholic Church.

The Church of England moved beyond the United Kingdom with the arrival of English explorers and settlers in North America. Robert Wolfall, chaplain to Martin Frobisher's expedition, held the first recorded Anglican religious service in North America in Baffin Island's Frobisher Bay in 1578. The English settlers in Newfoundland, sponsored by Humphrey Gilbert, held Anglican services in 1583 as did the English settlers who established the Roanoke Colony on Roanoke Island (in modern North Carolina) in 1584. The English settlers at Jamestown, Virginia, celebrated Anglican religious services in 1607 and the success of their colony led to the permanent establishment of the Church of England in North America.

The early activities of Anglicans in North America were twofold: serving the religious needs of English settlers and converting native peoples. While the church focused on the former activity, the latter was also important—although the two activities sometimes were in conflict especially when it related to the issue of slavery (see below). A native Croatan named Manteo,[65] who served as an interpreter for the settlers, was the first Native American to be converted to the Church of England in 1587. Manteo accompanied Walter Raleigh on his voyages and exploration and traveled with them back to England for a visit. The Society for the Propagation of the Gospel in Foreign Parts (aka SPG) was formed as the missionary arm of the Church of England in 1701 (under its charter the society was formed as an independent entity). It was established in response to a report prepared by Thomas Bray at the request of the Bishop of London, Henry Compton, on the state of the Church of England in the American Colonies. Bray found the Anglican Church in North America to be in a poor state and this prompted the founding of the SPG "to send priests and schoolteachers to America to help provide the Church's ministry to the colonists."[66] SPG missionaries arrived in North America in 1702 and in the West Indies the year after (1703).

It should be noted that the initial charter referred only to work among the English colonists. By 1710 the society had modified its charter to include work among African slaves in the West Indies and Native Americans in North America. Generally work among colonists on the one hand and slaves and Native Americans on the other hand were separate activities with the congregations kept apart. In the case of the West Indies, slaves were not allowed to join the church since plantation owners were afraid that this would undermine their authority. In fact, in 1710 the SPG inherited the Codrington Plantation on the island of Barbados with about 350 slaves and thereby became a slave owner.[67] The SPG hired managers to run the plantation on its behalf under the direction of a committee in England comprised of the Archbishop of Canterbury and a group of bishops. Not all Anglicans in England were happy with this state of affairs and in 1783 Beilby Porteus, then Bishop of Chester and later Bishop of London, called on the Church of England to end its involvement in the slave trade and to seek to improve conditions of the slaves in Barbados in a sermon delivered to a group of prominent members of the SPG. His plea was ignored, but Bishop Porteus went on to campaign against the evils of slavery and to become one of England's leading abolitionists. A second Anglican missionary society, the Church Missionary Society (CMS) was formed in 1799 by a group of clergy and laypeople (Bishop Porteus was a patron of the CMS) in part to send clergy to the West Indies to work among slaves and to lobby for the eradication of slavery. Such lobbying efforts led eventually to the British Parliament passing the Slavery Abolition Act in 1833 and in 1838 the Anglican Church freed its slaves in Barbados.

Bishop Porteus was also a founding member of the British and Foreign Bible Society (BFBS).[68] This society was formed in 1804 in response to concern on the part of a group of Anglicans about the lack of affordable Bibles in Welsh for Welsh-speaking Christians. BFBS Bible salesmen subsequently spread across Europe as far as Croatia and Albania and to India and elsewhere in the world to sell Bibles in local languages to Christians. Branches were formed in the United States (the Pennsylvania Bible Society in 1808 and the American Bible Society in 1816), Australia (1817), Colombia (1825), and New Zealand (1846). Delegates from Bible societies in 13 countries gathered in England in 1946 to form a separate non-denominational organization known as the United Bible Societies. Headquartered in London, the UBS in 2006 had 141 member societies in over 200 countries and is responsible for distributing the majority of the Bibles in the world.

The history of the Anglican Church in the Caribbean serves to highlight the changing nature of the Anglican Church as a whole in regards to its decentralization and the composition of church membership. Beyond the issue of slavery there was also the issue of organizational responsibility. From 1660 to 1813, for example, the church in Barbados was directly under the Bishop of London. In 1813 the Bishop of London declared that he was no longer solely responsible for appointments to local church posts in Barbados and that such appointments were to be made on the recommendation of the local governor. In 1824 two dioceses were created to cover the British West Indies: the Diocese of Barbados and the Diocese of Jamaica. This meant that the bishops in these two dioceses were also responsible for Anglican clergy on other islands and made occasional visits to these islands. Thus, the Bishop of Jamaica visited British Honduras (now Belize) in 1826 to consecrate St. John's Church. However, "Visits by the Bishop [to British Honduras] were very infrequent and the Anglican Church lost much ground to the Nonconformist missionaries and the Roman Catholics who had many converts among the Yucatecan migrants."[69] As the official church in British Honduras (as in other colonies) the Anglican Church in British Honduras received public funds and was influential in government affairs. As Dobson notes, "the Anglican clergy played an important role in the hierarchical colonial society" and "Few of these clergy were concerned with missionary work; they seem to have considered it their primary duty to minister to the more prosperous sections of the community in the town of Belize itself. Occasionally one of the clergy took some interest in the welfare of the slaves, but this usually led to criticism from the mahogany cutters who owned them."[70]

The Anglican Church in the Caribbean and elsewhere began to change dramatically in the 1800s. For one thing, in the Caribbean the abolition of slavery in the 1830s resulted in many ex-slaves becoming Anglicans. For instance, a survey of church membership in Barbados in 1871 indicated that 90 percent of the inhabitants of the island — the majority of whom were ex-slaves — were Anglicans. In other locales, however, the Anglican Church remained primarily the church of the English settler establishment while most other people joined different churches that were actively proselytizing (e.g., Wesleyans, Baptists, and Presbyterians).

The issue of the Anglican Church's relation to the colonial administration was also entangled with widespread controversy within the church in England and in the colonies between supporters of the so-called High Church and Low Church. Those favoring the High Church were closely identified with the colonial administration. Dobson comments that in British Honduras the Superintendents (who were the heads of the local colonial administration) tended "to regard themselves as the Supreme Heads of the [Anglican] Church and to make pronouncements on various aspects of Church governance."[71] This close identification waned to some extent during the latter part of the 1800s, but did not disappear entirely.

Financial support for the Anglican Church was one aspect of the link to the colonial administration. In British Honduras as the number of non–Anglican Christians increased, pressure was put on the colonial government to disestablish the Anglican Church and the Presbyterian Church. The government established a committee to look into this in 1866 and recommended that they be disestablished since it was unfair for the other poorer churches to pay to support these two wealthier ones. This took place over the next five years and as Dobson remarks, "This seems to have had a more beneficial effect on the Anglican Church than might have been anticipated, for the colony was now regarded as a suitable field for missionary work."[72]

The changing relationship of the Anglican Church to the colonial administration and in the nature of its local membership beyond the confines of the settler elite led to further decentralization in the international administrative structure of the church. In the British Caribbean this was marked by the creation of new dioceses within the Province of the West Indies. Thus, the Bahamas and the Turks and Caicos Islands separated from the Jamaican diocese to form a separate diocese in 1861, British Honduras formed a separate diocese in 1880, and Antigua and neighboring islands separated from the Diocese of Barbados in 1884 to form a separate diocese (it became the Diocese of the North East Caribbean and Aruba in 1987). While such structural changes allowed for greater local autonomy to a degree, bishops still often came from other areas within the Anglican Domain (the first bishop sent to British Honduras, Bishop Tozzer, came from a post in Zanzibar) and their link with England was affirmed by the practice of the bishops being consecrated at Lambeth Palace, the London Residence of the Archbishop of Canterbury.

Growing local autonomy within the Anglican Church also emerged within the Lambeth Conferences. These are conferences that are held approximately every 10 years in London. All of the Anglican bishops gather to debate issues of doctrine. The first Lambeth Conference was held in 1867. Resolution 8 of that year's conference deals with the question of unity and autonomy: "That, in order to the binding of the Churches of our colonial empire and the missionary Churches beyond them in the closest union with the Mother-Church, it is necessary that they receive and maintain without alteration the standards of faith and doctrine as now in use in that Church. That, nevertheless, each province should have the right to make such adaptations and additions to the services of the Church as its peculiar circumstances may require. Provided, that no change or addition be made inconsistent with the spirit and principles of the Book of Common Prayer, and that all such changes be liable to revision by any synod of the Anglican Communion in which the said province shall be represented."[73]

As the British Empire spread so too did the Anglican Church and its missionary arms, the SPG and CMS. Beyond North America, the Anglican Church was especially active in British-controlled territories in Africa and the South Pacific and remains an important religious institution in both of these parts of the world. We will focus on the acclivities of the church in Africa because of the importance of this region within the Anglican Church today in regard to the changing nature of its transnational relations in particular.

The history of the Anglican Church in Africa begins with the Rev. Thomas Thompson and Philip Quaque.[74] Quaque was born in Cape Coast (in modern Ghana) around 1741, the son of a local chief. The Rev. Thomas Thompson arrived in Cape Coast in 1752 as a chaplain for the small British garrison stationed there. He also established a school for African children and Quaque was among his students. Partially in response to his own health problems and recognizing the extent to which Europeans in general suffered illnesses in this part of Africa, Thompson promoted the training of Africans as missionaries. He approached the SPG with a plan to send some of the better African students to England for further education with the intention that they would then return to Africa as missionaries. The SPG approved the plan the following year and allocated funds for six boys. Three boys were sent to England in 1854, but two of them died there and only Philip

Quaque survived to become the first non–European to be ordained as a priest by the
Church of England. While in England, in 1765 he married an English woman. The next
year the couple left England for Cape Coast, where Quaque took over Thompson's position.

Although today Quaque is regarded as an indigenous pioneer in spreading Christianity in West Africa, he was not particularly successful as a missionary at the time, in
part because so much of his life had been spent away in England. He found himself something of a marginal man from the perspectives of both African and English society. For
one thing, he had forgotten the local language and had to work through an interpreter.
His English wife died a year after coming to Africa and he subsequently remarried, but
his family life was marked with conflict. British support for his missionary activities was
limited and he received little encouragement from the local English population. He had
been forced to support himself partially by bartering goods and when he died in 1816 the
SPG owed him 369 pounds.

Anglican missionary work in Africa did not begin in earnest until the 1840s with the
arrival of Anglican missionaries in Badagry (Nigeria) on the west coast of Africa in 1842
and Mombasa on the east coast of Africa in 1844. The roots of the Anglican Church lie
in the arrival of Henry Townsend (1815–86) and Samuel Ajayi Crowther at Badagry
among the Yoruba people. Later they moved to Abeokuta (in present Ogun State).

Samuel Ajayi Crowther (1809–91) was born in the Yoruba region, and in 1821 a
Muslem Fulani slave raider captured him and sold him to Portuguese slave traders.[75] He
was freed by a British naval ship and sent to Freetown in Sierra Leone, where he was
looked after by CMS missionary John Raban. Crowther was sent to school in England in
1826 and returned to Freetown the next year for further schooling and then taught school
there. He went back to England for training as a minister in 1842 and sailed back to Freetown with Townsend the following year. Crowther worked on translations of the Bible
and the Book of Common Prayer into Yoruba, Igbo, and Nupe. He returned to England
for a time, where he worked on his translations and on one occasion "engaged with Lord
Palmerston in placing before him the condition of things at Abeokuta, enlisting his sym-
pathy and help for the native Christians."[76]

Crowther became the first African Anglican bishop in 1864. Page provides the following description of the event: "We have now reached a point when we find Crowther
once more in England. He had come to plead his own cause on the platform of our English
May Meetings, and was the principal attraction at the Annual Meeting of the Church
Missionary Society at Exeter Hall. The excited interest of that immense gathering was in
a great part due to the fact that a negro, one of the very races from the distant African
regions, was to tell his own tale.... On St. Peter's Day, 1864, perhaps the most important
event of his life took place, when in Canterbury Cathedral Samuel Crowther was consecrated as the first Bishop of the Niger."[77] He was also awarded a Doctor of Divinity degree
by Oxford University in 1864.

Anglican missionary activities in other parts of Africa increased in the 1860s and
1870s as the British colonial presence spread into these regions. Charles Mackenzie went
to Natal from England to serve as archdeacon in 1855 and initially worked among the

English settlers. Then in 1860 he became head of the Universities' Mission to Central Africa (UMCA), which Anglicans at the universities of Oxford, Cambridge, Durham, and Dublin had established in 1857 in response to a call by Protestant missionary David Livingstone that the Anglicans establish bishoprics in Zanzibar and Nyasaland (modern Malawi). This was the first missionary organization to be established by High Church Anglicans. Mackenzie was made a bishop in 1861 and headed off to work in Nyasasland, where he died in early 1862 of Blackwater fever. Bishop Tozer became the next head of the UMCA and he moved its headquarters to Zanzibar in 1864, where it received a friendly reception from the island's inhabitants and soon set about expanding its activities on the island and the mainland (including its mission at Mpwapwa in what is now Tanzania). The UMCA merged with the SPG in 1965 and they became known as the United Society for the Propagation of the Gospel (USPG).[78] The CMS was also active in eastern Africa, establishing missions in Uganda in 1877 and the Sudan (at Omdurman) in 1899.

As the Anglican Church lost ground in the United Kingdom and the former settler colonies such as Canada and Australia in the post-colonial world of the latter part of the twentieth century, Anglican Churches in Africa and other former colonies assumed a more prominent role in church affairs. At present there are around 77 million Anglicans worldwide. Of this number only about 13.5 million live in the United Kingdom (17.5 percent), 3.8 million in Australia, 600,000 in Canada, under 600,000 in New Zealand, and 2.3 million in the United States. This compares with about 50 million Anglicans in Africa: 18 million in Nigeria, 8 million in Uganda, 5 million in Sudan, 2.5 million in Kenya, 2 million in Tanzania, 2 million in southern Africa, 1 million in other parts of West Africa, and 600,000 in Central Africa.

In a relatively democratic institution such as the modern Anglican Church the changing demographic characteristics of its membership has had a profound impact on the church as a whole and on transnational relations among church members. The Anglican churches in Africa, the South Pacific, and the West Indies come to play a more important role in the church not just numerically but also culturally. The changes taking place in the Anglican Church internationally can be seen in the Anglican Communion, which is the unifying body of the Anglican Church. Its membership includes the 38 Anglican provinces. Each province is considered to be independent with an elected primate serving as its head. Some provinces incorporate single states (such as the Ecclesiastical Province of Canada, which was founded in 1860 and includes 7 dioceses) or a region (such as the Province of Melanesia).

The headquarters of the Anglican Communion is in London and is closely associated with the Archbishop of Canterbury, but the authority of the Archbishop of Canterbury is much more limited than it was in the past. The Anglican Communion's website says that he "is more of the media spokesman for the church than its leader."[79] The Archbishop of Canterbury is considered to be one of the Anglican Communion's four "Instruments of Communion." The other three include the Lambeth Conference, the Primates' Meeting (the first of these was held in 1979 and they are held every two years), and the Anglican Consultative Council (created at the 1968 Lambeth Conference). Bishops attend the Lambeth Conference at the invitation of the Archbishop of Canterbury (there were 880 bishops in 2008), primates attend the Primates' Meeting (there were 38 of these in 2008), while bishops, clergy, and laity attend the Anglican Consultative Council (ACC). ACC membership includes representatives of the different provinces. The number of church members in the province determines the allocation of representatives. Thus, large provinces appoint one bishop, one priest, and one layperson; intermediate provinces appoint one bishop or priest and one layperson; and small provinces appoint one representative that is preferably a layperson. With the demographic shift in church membership, the majority of bishops, primates, and laypersons attending these Instruments of Communion now come from Africa, the Asia-Pacific region, and the West Indies.

In recent years Lambeth Conferences and Primates' Meetings have become forums for debate of liturgical and social issues that frequently have seen sharp differences between the Anglican clergy from developed Western countries and those from elsewhere. One of the most contentious issues in recent years has centered on homosexuality. The debate began in North America when the diocese of New Westminster in British Columbia authorized the blessing of same-sex unions in 2002 and the election of openly gay, noncelibate priest Gene Robinson as Bishop of New Hampshire in 2003. The issue divided the North American churches and was addressed in a report by Archbishop Robin Eames, known as the Windsor Report, published in 2004.[80] The primates at the 2005 Primates' Meeting debated the report and then requested that the Episcopal Church in the United States and Anglican Church of Canada voluntarily withdraw from the Anglican Consultative Committee until the issue could be debated further at the 2008 Lambeth Conference. The issue arose again at the 2007 Primates' Meeting in Dar es Salaam, Tanzania. Attendance at the Lambeth Conference is by invitation of the Archbishop of Canterbury and Gene Robinson was among those not invited. Also not invited was Martyn Minns, considered to be a missionary bishop to the United States by the Church of Nigeria (more on this below).

Prior to the Lambeth Conference the primates of Nigeria, Uganda, Kenya, and Rwanda announced that they would be boycotting the gathering because of their opposition to the Episcopal Church USA's support of homosexual clergy and same-sex unions. Other clergy also announced that they would not be attending, including Peter Jensen, the Archbishop of Sydney. As Anglican clergy in New Zealand and the United Kingdom blessed same-sex unions in June 2008, opponents of church support for such unions were meeting in Jerusalem at the Global Anglican Future Conference (GAFCON), which some saw as an alternative Lambeth Conference.[81] Archbishop Peter Akinola of the Church of Nigeria played a leading role in GAFCON. Others involved include the Church of the Province of West Africa, the Church of Uganda, the Anglican Church of Kenya, the Anglican Province of the South Cone, the Episcopal Church in Jerusalem and the Middle East, the Church of the Province of Myanmar, the Church of the Province of Southeast Asia, the Church of the Province of Rwanda, and Martyn Minns and others in North America who are associated with the newly formed Anglican Church in North America (see below).

In regard to the study of religious transnationalism, the Rev. Martyn Minns is a particularly interesting figure in this debate. The Rev. Minns became the rector of Truro Church in Fairfax, Virginia, in 1991. A champion of biblical fundamentalism, under his leadership the church became active in local outreach programs for the poor as well as foreign evangelical missionary work, especially in Africa. For his work in Africa he was made an honorary canon of All Saints Cathedral in Mpwapwa, Tanzania, in 2002. In December 2006, 92 percent of the congregation of the Rev. Minns' Truro Episcopal Church voted to withdraw from the Episcopal Church of the United States and join the Convocation of Anglicans of North America (CANA), which was a mission initiative of the Church of Nigeria.[82] Eleven other parishes in Virginia also switched to CANA. Later in the month Archbishop Peter Akinola consecrated the Rev. Minns as a Missionary Bishop of CANA. The Truro church now lists its denomination as Church of Nigeria. As evidence of its close ties to the Church of Nigeria the Truro Church launched a "Church and Islam Project" in response to the persecution of Anglicans in northern Nigeria by Muslim fundamentalists.

CANA joined with several other Anglican organizations in North America (including in Canada the Anglican Coalition of Canada, the Anglican Network in Canada, and Anglican Essentials Canada) to form the Anglican Church in North America (ACNA), which is headquartered in Ambridge, Pennsylvania. Essentially its members believe that the Episcopal Church in the United States and the Anglican Church in Canada have moved away from traditional Christian values. By August 2009 it claimed to have over 100,000 members in 682 parishes. It is not affiliated with the Anglican Communion, but rather with the Anglican churches in Nigeria and Uganda.

Recent decades have seen a dramatic increase in missionary activity around the world by Evangelical Christians. Evangelical churches in the United Kingdom formed the Evangelical Alliance in 1846. This movement assumed worldwide dimensions with the founding of the World Evangelical Alliance (WEA) in London in 1951. At present the WEA claims to be "a network of churches in 128 nations that have each formed an evangelical alliance and over 100 international organizations joining together to give a worldwide identity, voice and platform to more than 420 million evangelical Christians."[83] Its headquarters is located in Vancouver, British Columbia. It has an International Director, Executive Council, and a General Assembly, which meets every four years.

Evangelical missionary work is also associated with the International Congress on World Evangelization (ICOWE). The first of these congresses was held in Lausanne, Switzerland, in 1974 and resulted in the Lausanne Covenant and formation of the Lausanne Committee for World Evangelization (LCWE). The impetus for ICOWE came from the 1966 World Congress on Evangelism in Berlin. A committee headed by evangelist Billy Graham organized ICOWE. The congress in Lausanne brought together around 4,000 evangelical church leaders from 150 countries. The theme of the congress was "Let the earth hear His voice." The Lausanne Covenant, which was drafted by a committee headed by John Stott of England, provided a manifesto for the promotion of Christian evangelism worldwide. The original document was in English and it has since been translated into over 20 languages. The signatories of the covenant expressed shame at their failure to not have been more successful in spreading the Gospel of Jesus and committed themselves to working harder to spread their version of Christianity throughout the world. LCWE was critical of the bureaucratic nature of other such Christian bodies and chose to organize itself in a more decentralized fashion consisting of networks of local leaders connecting them to world leaders.

The Second International Congress on World Evangelization (aka Lausanne II or Lausanne '89) was held in Manila in 1989. It resulted in the Manila Manifesto, which renewed and expanded the commitment of its signatories to the Lausanne Covenant. Evangelist Luis Bush spoke at the Manila congress about the need to focus activities in what he called the "Resistant Belt" in the Middle East. Bush was born in Argentina, raised in Brazil, and attended university in the United States. After working for an accounting firm in Chicago, in 1973 he decided to devote his life to Christian ministry. In 1978 he went to El Salvador as a missionary. After the Manila congress he began promoting the 10/40 Window concept, urging fellow evangelists to focus on the regions of the world with the greatest human suffering and the least exposure to Christianity. He moved to Singapore to work with an evangelical organization known as Transform World Connections, which held its first international Transform World gathering in Indonesia in 2005 with the aim of creating a community of evangelical missionaries. The Third International Congress on World Evangelization was held in Cape Town October 2010.[84]

Muslem Missionaries

Islamic missionary activities are associated with the Arabic term *dawah,* meaning to call to Islam. As Poston points out, the term is used not only in reference to calling or converting non–Muslims, but also in reference to inviting Muslims to attain a higher degree of Islamicity.[85] Muhammad and his followers employed this to spread the religion. After his death in AD 632 most of the expansion of Islam over the next few centuries was a result of conquest. Along with conquest and commerce, Sufism played an important role in Islamic conversion in Africa, Asia, and the Balkans from the 1200s to the 1600s. Cook writes, "Sufis, more than any other single group in Islam, have been responsible for large-scale conversions to Islam."[86]

The "development of *da'wa* within the *Ummah* [Muslim community] in the last two centuries is closely connected to so-called Islamic revivalism, both religious and political" as championed by Muhammad Ibn Abd al-Wahhab (born Najd, Saudi Arabia; 1703–92).[87] Ibn Abd al-Wahhab's movement sought to purify Islam by returning to what he perceived to be Islam's original principles: "Abd al-Wahhab drew a line between those whom he considered true believers, *muslimun* (his own followers, naturally), and those whom he accused of *shirk*, associationism (worshiping anything but God alone)."[88] Moreover, he stressed the importance of inviting both Muslims and non–Muslims to embrace his version of Islam.

Ibn Abd al-Wahhab's daughter married the son of Muhammad ibn Saud of the House of Saud in 1744, which ruled over the Najd region of Saudi Arabia. Since then the House of Saud has been closely linked to Wahhabism, which is closely associated with Salafism (*salaf* meaning pious ancestor) and the two terms are sometimes used interchangeably. The rise of Wahhabism paralleled that of the House of Saud as it gained control over

Saudi Arabia and grew in importance internationally as a result of the exploitation of the country's oil riches following World War II. Saudi Arabia's oil wealth allowed the country to assume a position of leadership within Sunni Islam and therefore allowed it to promote Wahhabism (or Salafism) around the world from Indonesia to Western Europe.[89] While not all Salafis have direct relations with Saudi Arabia, the country nonetheless has played an important role in promoting this version of Islam globally.[90]

Saudi Arabia also promotes Wahhabism through a wide variety of relief, educational, and charitable organizations. The Muslim World League (MWL), founded in Mecca in 1962, is one of these. While some support for the MWL comes from other countries, most is provided by Saudi Arabia. The MWL seeks to promote the propagation of Islam worldwide by providing support for Islamic preachers, developing methods for the propagations of Islam, holding symposia and courses for Islamic scholars and preachers, supporting the construction of mosques, and providing relief assistance. The MWL oversees eight different bodies, including the International Islamic Relief Organization (aka International Islamic Relief Organization of Saudi Arabia, IIRO, and IIROSA), which is based in Saudi Arabia. The IIRO was formed by the MWL in 1979. The IIRO funds mostly relatively small projects and operates in over 80 countries. In addition to such activities as disaster relief and building mosques, the IIRO is often commonly viewed as serving as a front for terrorist activities by international bodies and Western governments.

Individuals associated with al-Qaeda and the Taliban have worked with the IIRO in the Philippines and Indonesia.[91] Undoubtedly the most prominent of these was Mohammad Jamal Khalifa, a brother-in-law of Osama bin Laden. Prior to moving to the Philippines, Khalifa had been a member of the Muslim Brotherhood in Lebanon and ran the MWL's office in Peshawar, Pakistan. Khalifa arrived in the Philippines in 1988 as Southeast Asian regional directors for the IIRO and head of various IIRO-funded bodies such as the Benevolence International Corporation. He then used the IIRO to channel funds to the local terrorist groups Abu Sayyaf and Moro Islamic Liberation Front (MILF), recruit local Muslims to fight in Afghanistan, and other such activities. Staff of the local IIRO offices in the Philippines included a number of individuals associated with Abu Sayyaf and the MILF. While the IIRO in the Philippines under his direction did carry out some charitable work, most of its funds went to terrorist groups. A story in *Newsweek International,* for example, mentions that one of these front organizations claimed to have built 30 orphanages, but in fact only built one.[92]

A CBS News story reported, "intelligence agencies say bin Laden sent him to the Philippines in 1988, where Khalifa helped set up an al Qaeda network that planned a spectacular series of attacks. They included the 1993 World Trade Center bombing, and a 1995 plot to assassinate the Pope in the Philippines and simultaneously hijack a dozen American airliners, crashing them into the Pacific, the Pentagon and the CIA. Intelligence experts say it was a blueprint for 9/11. 'There are a number of allegations that Khalifa was behind a number of charities that were linked to al Qaeda and that these charities funded the initial plan of 9/11,' said Rohan Gunaratna, author of 'Inside Al Qaeda.' But no government had enough evidence to put him behind bars. Khalifa was arrested in America, in Jordan, and after 9/11, in Saudi Arabia, and on each occasion was eventually released. Today he is a free man — just a businessman, he says — who used to run charities."[93] He later broke with Al-Qaeda and settled in Madagascar, where he was killed in 2007.

The Cham in Cambodia provide a useful case study of the activities of international Muslim missionary and charitable organizations at work.[94] The Cham in Cambodia suffered considerably at the hands of the Pol Pot regime between 1975 and 1979, with around 90,000 of the 250,000 Cham being killed by the regime. Moreover, 85 percent of the Cham mosques were destroyed by the Khmer Rouge and of the 113 imams who had been alive in 1975 only 21 were still living after the overthrow of the regime. Today they are a poor ethnic minority of around 400,000 in a largely Buddhist country that has received considerable attention from Islamic governments and religious organizations in the Middle East. The Cham in Cambodia have a history of close association with Malay Muslims and as a result their local variant of Islam developed more along the lines of the lines of Islam in Malaysia than the more localized and isolated version that predominates among Cham in Vietnam, but prior to 1975 it was still highly localized in nature.

The destruction of their traditional religious institutions and the trauma of life under the Pol Pot regime left the Cham especially susceptible to Middle Eastern Muslim influence. Starting in 1991 the Cambodian Cham began to receive aid not only from fellow Muslims in Malaysia but also from Muslim organizations in South Asia and the Middle East to build mosques and religious schools and for pilgrimages and study overseas. The version of Islam that these benefactors promoted were contemporary revivalist ones rather than the older more syncretic localized style. An interview by Graceffo highlights differences between the older and newer versions of Islam within Cambodian Cham society: "'There are two types of Muslims in Cambodia,' said Sary Abdulah, president of the Islamic National Movement for Democracy of Cambodia. The two groups include: Sunni, traditional Muslims, along the lines of Arab Muslims, who pray five times per day, and Fojihed Muslims, who follow an ancient Cham interpretation of the religion. 'They only pray once a week. They speak Cham, and keep the old Cham traditions.' Sary Abdulah went on to explain that the Fojihed maintained many of their pre–Muslim beliefs, particularly in the supernatural, and magical powers. 'They believe that they can pray, and achieve great internal power, called Chai. It is similar to what Kung Fu people call Chi.'"[95]

Cornerstone University provides an overview of some of the variants of Islam found among Cham Muslims at present: In Cambodia, there are a few Islamic groups such as Chang Veng, Imam San, Da'wa and Wahhaiyya. The Chang Veng group of villages tends to mix more Malay words with their vocabulary than those from the Imam San group of villages. This is because of their strong connections with, and support received from, Muslims in Malaysia. The Imam San group has fewer connections with outside Muslims because of their stance on animistic traditions that are unacceptable to fundamental Muslims. The Da'wa is a missionary movement from a variety of Islamic countries outside Cambodia. Visiting groups of Da'wa missionaries can be seen in Cham villages of Cambodia today. They travel from village to village spreading their beliefs and normally preach in village mosques where they also live during their stay. The Wahhabiyya is also a missionary movement similar to the Da'wa in that they also preach a more fundamentalist type of Islam.[96]

The missionary aid to the Cham from outside of Southeast Asia arrived at different times.[97] The first to arrive was Wahhabist from Saudi Arabia, the United Arab Emirates and Kuwait. Later in the 1990s Islamic organizations from Pakistan and India promoting a less politicized version known as *Tablighi Jamaat* arrived in Cambodia. These two groups succeeded in reviving Islam among the Cham (thus, by 2007 there were 280 Cham imams), but also created a division within the Cham community between followers of the two variants. This is reflected in architecture, with the newly built mosques resembling Gulf State style (called "Dubai" by the Cham) or South Asian rather than the pre–1975 Cham mosques that were similar to local Buddhist temples. In general the Cham have also increasingly adopted Middle Eastern styles of dress rather than the more traditional Malay style.

While such forms of assistance are generally viewed favorably by non–Muslims, there are concerns related to the nature of such foreign influence. Within Cambodia there is concern on the part of some Khmer (the national majority who are largely Buddhists) that the fundamentalist versions of Islam being promoted favors loyalty to Islam over loyalty to the state and that such fundamentalism may hamper efforts to develop the country economically. There is also concern that links with foreign fundamentalists may serve to promote support for terrorism both within Cambodia and in the region (i.e., for violent Muslim separatists in southern Thailand). While to date there is little evidence of Cambodian Cham expressing such support, there have been incidents that have heightened concern. Thus, in 2003 four Muslim teachers from Cambodia, southern Thailand, and Egypt at the *Om al-Qora* school (funded by a Kuwaiti-based charitable organization) in Phnom Penh were arrested as alleged members of the regional terrorist organization *Jemaah Islamiyah* and for using the school as a terrorist training center. In relation to these arrests, Abuza refers to southern Thai militants being "arrested in conjunction with a JI cell in Cambodia that was implicated in laundering money for al-Qaeda through the *Om Al Qura* Foundation."[98] Moreover, authorities discovered that the well-known Indonesian terrorist Riduan Isamuddin (aka Hambali and born Encep Nurjaman) had resided at the school for several months before his capture in Thailand in August 2003. At the time Hambali was widely considered to be the leading Muslim terrorist in Southeast Asia. While attending an Islamic school in Java he had become involved with *Jemaah Islamiyah* in his teems and traveled to Afghanistan in 1983, where he met Osama bin Laden and came to be closely associated with Al-Qaeda. He was associated with numerous bombings in Indonesia and with terrorist activities in other Southeast Asian countries as well.

One other group of Muslims needs to be mentioned in regard to Islamic missionary work, the *Ahmadiyya Muslim Jama'at*. The Ahmadiyya movement played an important role in spreading Islam to Western countries. Mirza Ghulam Ahmad (born Punjab; 1835–1908) founded the *Ahmadiyya Muslim Jama'at* (community) in 1889 and under his leadership it gained a substantial following within India. He claimed to be a promised messiah, preached the final triumph of Islam over all other religions, and sought to gain adherents through peaceful means. Sunni Muslims in particular do not consider followers of the Ahmadiyya movement to be Muslims and Saudi religious officials have banned its members from taking part in the *hajj*. Followers of the movement have been subjected to demonstrations and violent attacks in Indonesia in recent years and the Indonesian government passed a bill to curtail the movement's proselytizing.

The Ahmadis began actively to engage in missionary activities outside of India during the early 1900s. Thus, they established the Shahjehan mosque in Woking, England, in 1913 and became active among Afro-Americans in the 1920s. Poston likens the movement's missionary methods to those of Christianity.[99] Racius provides the following account of their activities: "To foster their missionary activities in a given area, Ahmadis are quick to build their own mosques, which they turn into their local base or headquarters. Ahmadis have succeeded in building these mosques in a number of European cities as well as in cities in other non–Muslim lands, often being the first to build a mosque in the vicinity. There are in excess of some 500 Ahmadi mosques around the world.... Ahmadi communities are also known to be engaged in hospital building and setting up institutions of education. Ahmadis have made translations of the whole Quran into over 50 languages and translations of selected verses in over 100 languages, among them minor languages of Africa, Asia, and smaller European languages like Swedish, Lithuanian, Latvian, Catalonian, and even Yiddish.... [T]he activities of their missionaries around the world have been and still continue to be controlled directly from the headquarters, first in India and, since the partition of India, in Rabwa, Pakistan, a town built by Ahmadis themselves. The movement has its Missionary Training College in Rabwa to train professional da'is (studies last as long as seven years). The Ahmadis publish widely on Islam, both polemical and theological, espousing their version of it. Most of this literature is translated into other languages, making Ahmadis' ideas accessible to quite a large public."[100]

The Ahmadis played a pioneering role in converting African-Americans in the 1920s. A small number of Muslims were among the slaves brought to the United States prior to the abolition of the slave trade, but the religion ceased to be practiced under slavery. Edward Wilmot Blyden (born Saint Thomas, U.S. Virgin Islands; 1832–1912), an influential writer, diplomat, and politician in Liberia and Sierra Leone, and widely regarded as the founder of Pan-Africanism, provided an intellectual basis for the spread of Islam among Afro-Americans in his book *Christianity, Islam and the Negro Race*.[101] In this work he portrayed Christianity as the religion of European colonizers and argued that Islam, as a major religion of sub–Saharan Africa, could play a more positive role in unifying African peoples. Using copies of the Qur'an that the Ahmadis had translated into English, Shaikh Al-Haj Daoud Ahmed Faisal (born Morocco), who had immigrated to the United States from Grenada, established the State Street Mosque and Islamic Mission to America in New York City in 1924. Other Islamic communities were established among Afro-Americans during he late 1920s and early 1930s, including the Lost-Found Nation of Islam in the Wilderness of North America (aka The Nation of Islam) founded by Wali D. Fard in Detroit in 1929 (Fard claimed to be the "Mahdi" or Savior) and a Sunni group known as the Addeynu Allah Universal Arab Association founded by "Professor" Ezeldeen (aka Brother Lomax Bey), but the Ahmadis remained the dominant presence among Afro-American Muslims for the next couple of decades. The Ahmadis established the American Fazl Mosque in Washington, D.C., in 1950 that served as the American headquarters of the movement in the United States until 1994. By the 1940s, however, the presence and influence of Ahmadi missionaries within the Afro-American community had declined.

8

DRESS

While wearing clothing made from woven cloth is a fairly recent human invention, humans have been decorating themselves for tens of thousands of years. Dress includes the wearing of clothing as well as other forms of decoration such as tattooing, hair styling, and wearing jewelry. Assessing similarities or differences in styles of dress (i.e., fashion) includes attention both to the overall style as well as small details. In regard to particular aspects of the style of dress this can include the manner in which items are worn, the shapes or tailoring of items of attire, how they are decorated, the colors that are used, and the contexts within which they are worn.

Technology, Fashion and Trade

Dress does not merely serve as a means of personal adornment or protection, but also serves important social functions as a marker of status and identity. It is its function as an indicator or national or ethnic identity that is one of the primary concerns in the present context. More particularly, we are interested in how this function as a marker of transnational identity serves to link people across borders. In this regard it is important to revisit the issue of state-level national identity versus ethno-national identity that was discussed in the first chapter. Thus, in terms of transnational identity styles of dress may serve to identify the wearer either with a state or ethnic group of origin or heritage. It is also necessary to examine the choices that people make in regard to wearing such dress in regard to the contexts within which they wear particular styles of dress and the factors that influence their choices. Thus, while some migrants may retain styles of dress associated with their original homeland as everyday wear and shun wearing the style of dress associated with their new home, others adopt the dress style of their new home and either cease to wear the dress style of their original homeland or they may choose to wear such dress only on special occasions.

Beyond such nationally specific notions of dress style, it is also important to consider how dress styles associated with a particular group, country, or region travel across borders and are adopted by people with no direct or ancestral link. How people dress is influenced by a variety of factors that include technology, trade, tradition, comparison, emulation, and differentiation. People often seek to emulate at least certain aspects of the dress style of others for a variety of reasons such as the belief that such dress is more modern and this can manifest itself in terms of the transnational spread of fashions and even to the transformation of a national fashion into more of a global one.

Another transnational aspect of dress concerns the commercial side of producing and trading in cloth and clothing. Even though most people for most of human history until quite modern times have produced at least some of their own clothing locally, cloth has been an important item of trade since ancient times. Two dimensions of the transnational cloth trade are how such trade serves to introduce new fashions across borders and how producers make cloth and clothing in accordance with the existing tastes of the importers. The first of these dimensions relates to the transnational diffusion of new fashions while the second concerns how transnational relations support existing fashions. In addition to the cloth, clothing, and fashions involved in such transnational interchanges there are also the people involved in these interchanges to be considered. In ancient times silk did not carry itself along the Silk Road, long-distance traders carried it on camels. Today, there are huge cloth and clothing industries scattered across the world and linked to consumers through a large commercial network employing thousands of people who move these goods across borders, including many people who live transnational lives as a result of such trade.

The Industrial Revolution

Local styles of dress evolved in the past not only within the context of the local environment, but also in relation to cultural traditions that were shaped by technical knowledge of cloth production and trade in cloth and clothing. Whereas the oldest types of cloth made from beaten bark or treated animal skins required only relatively simple technology and knowledge that could be acquired with relative ease, producing woven cloth is far more difficult. At its most basic it requires making thread and a loom and knowing how to weave on the loom. In the past the fact that some people knew how to do this and others did not gave rise to trade in cloth. Such trade was further stimulated by differences in levels of skills and available materials such as cotton, silk, and dyes.

The industrial revolution drastically changed not only the weaving and dyeing processes of cloth making but also the nature of the textile industry and trade in textiles. Combined with innovations in transportation and the dramatic increase in global trade from the 1800s onward the industrialization of cloth production promoted the development of a global trade in cloth and clothing on an unprecedented scale. This in turn resulted in the widespread demise of local weaving traditions and promoted the development of dress fashions that were increasingly global at the expense of national ones. This globalization of fashion, however, has not been complete and distinctive national fashions continue to play an important role in the world.

The industrial revolution in weaving began in England with the invention of the flying shuttle that was patented by John Kay in 1733. This invention allowed weavers to double their productivity, which in turn produced demand for more thread. Making thread by hand is an extremely time-consuming task. James Hargreaves invented a multi-spool spinning wheel known as the spinning jenny around 1764. This invention allowed a single worker to operate several spools producing thread at once. Next, Edmund Cartwright invented a power loom that he patented in 1785. Looms based on Cartwright's idea allowed for the development of a number of weaving factories around Manchester by the beginning of the 1800s. Further loom innovations, such as the Roberts Loom in 1830 and the semi-automatic Lancashire loom in 1841, resulted in a substantial growth in industrial textile production first in England and then elsewhere in the industrial world. Such looms were not only faster than previous looms but they also allowed a single worker with relatively little skill to operate between four and eight looms simultaneously — this is an especially important innovation since previously weaving had to be carried out by highly skilled people. The weaving process was further revolutionized in the 1940s with the introduction of the Sulzer loom and rapier looms that were even faster and more efficient than their predecessors. Contemporary looms employ air-jets and water-jets and computers to speed the weaving process and reduce labor even further.

The development of modern aniline dyes was an international effort involving scientists from a number of Western European countries. Prior to the industrial revolution cloth was colored using a variety of natural dyes. The production and use of these dyes, again, required both considerable skill and labor. In ancient times the purple dye produced by the Phoenicians of Tyre was of considerable importance in fashion and international trade in the ancient Mediterranean.[1] It is perhaps not surprising then that modern synthetic dyeing begins with this color with the discovery of mauvine or aniline purple by 18-year-old university student William Henry Perkin (1838–1907) who was attempting to synthesize the anti-malaria drug quinine. Perkin patented mauvine, making it the first synthetic organic dye, and began mass production of the dye in London.[2] Marketed under the name Tyrian purple or aniline purple, in 1859 the color was named mauve (French for the mallow flower). Queen Victoria made the color popular by wearing a silk dress colored with the dye at the Royal Exhibition in 1862.

The name aniline was used for Perkin's dye in relation to processes that had been developed by German chemist Friedrich Runge (1795–1867) — who is best known for his discovery of caffeine in coffee — involving the isolation of a blue colored substance from coal tar in 1834 and by C.J. Fritsche involving the treatment of indigo with caustic potash in 1841. Fritsche named the blue-colored oil that he produced aniline after the Sanskrit word *nila* for blue used in reference to the indigo plant, *Indigofera anil*. The work of French chemist Pierre Jacques Antoine Béchamp (1816–1908) combining aniline with arsenic acid to produce atoxyl in 1859 made the large-scale production of such synthetic dyes as Perkin's mauve possible.

Perkin's mauve went out of fashion by the end of the 1860s as additional colors became available using synthetic dyes. Indigo was probably the most important dye to be synthesized later in the 1800s. Indigo has a long history as an especially important blue dye. As Cardon notes, "Indigo was the dye used for both the blue Genoa-made fustian known in 16th-century England as 'Gene fustian' (which gave its name to 'blue jeans') and for the *bleu de Nîmes,* the more familiar 'denim.' Indigo had therefore already had a long and prestigious history weathering the fluctuations of fashion, when by crossing the ocean, it joined the legend of the pioneers of the Wild West, giving its colour to the cowboys' 'waist overalls,' the forerunners of today's jeans.... With the ability to withstand the rigours of weather and war, natural indigo was regarded as the 'colour of kings and the king of colour' until the end of the 19th century."[3]

German chemist Adolf von Baeyer (1835–1917) identified the chemical structure of the indigotin molecule that is the primary determinant of the blue color in indigo in 1883. It was not until 1897, however, that chemists working for Badische Anilin und Soda Fabrik (BASF) were able to produce synthetic indigo dye. The impact of this was profound: "This invention meant that for the first time, millions of people in all parts of the world could wear clothes of a beautiful and colourfast blue, the supply of which could barely have been met by the combined harvests of all the indigo plants of the world (one only has to think of Mao's China or the extraordinary worldwide popularity of blue jeans). And yet, at the same time, the synthesis of indigotin caused the demise of one of the last bastions of natural dyes, of crops that had brought fabulous riches to whole countries, and of an age-old tradition of technical expertise."[4]

Over the past two centuries industrial textile production has largely supplanted hand weaving and the use of natural dyes, although both processes survive in some isolated regions and elsewhere to meet the demands of particular markets as the work of skilled artists and artisans. It is important to recognize, however, that well into the 1900s most of the industrially produced cloth that was exported around the world was exported as cloth and then transformed into clothing domestically, often at the household level, rather than being transformed into tailored clothing prior to export. While the export of such cloth served to make woven cloth more readily available worldwide it did not dictate how cloth was used to make clothing or other objects.

Although not made into clothing, industrially produced cloth made for export has a long history of being produced to meet local market tastes—thus serving more as a substitute for hand-woven cloth than necessarily as something that leads inevitably to fundamental changes in dress or decoration. *Sarita* produced industrially in the Netherlands for the Toraja market on the Indonesian island of Sulawesi between 1880 and 1930 provide an example of this. *Sarita* are long, narrow pieces of cloth that the Toraja use during festivals. Prior to the 1880s the Toraja made these cloths themselves. They were made of hand-woven white cotton and decorated using wooden or bamboo stamps and natural indigo dye. The decorative patterns on the cloths include a variety of local motifs including fairly abstract representations as well as more realistic ones of people, water buffalo, and other animals. Using these indigenous textiles as models Van Vlissingen and Co., Ltd. of the Netherlands began producing *sarita* industrially at its cotton mills in the 1880s.[5] Workers at the Van Vlassingen factory employed wooden blocks with copies of the Toraja motifs cut out in felt attached to them that were dipped in a dye-resistant paste. After the industrially produced cotton cloth was stamped it was wound on a large rack and then dipped in a vat of synthetic indigo dye. These cloths were then exported to Sulawesi where the Toraja used them alongside locally produced *sarita* (which by then were also commonly decorated using synthetic indigo dye).

Fashion

The above point does not mean that industrial production does not influence how people dress, but such changes are part of broader cultural developments of which the availability of industrially produced cloth is only one element. An understanding of how styles of dress change requires a look at the concept of fashion. As Cannon points out, "Fashion develops in all contexts as the result of the assertion of self-identity and social comparison ... individuals use visual media to indicate to themselves and others whether they think they belong with another individual or group, or whether they consider themselves another's equal or superior. These expressions may involve an infinite range of comparisons depending on degrees of similarity or distinction, but the essential process of comparison remains the same in all contexts."[6] The self-identity expressed through fashion is linked to a desire to create a positive self-image and these in turn are shaped by individual choices that are made within a social and cultural context.

In the case of small-scale societies the social context is likely to be one of relative homogeneity with a cultural emphasis on conservatism and conformity in dress. This is not to say that variety does or did not exist and that changes do or did not occur in such societies, but these tend to be fairly circumscribed. There may be differences in dress according to status, such as between most people and those who perform special functions like that of a priest, and people may dress differently according to gender and age, but the repertoire of dress tends to represent a coherent whole, there are relatively few different ensembles available, and there is little variety within each of these ensembles. Such a situation was often equally true even of larger scale societies in the past.

The impediments to rapid or major changes in styles of dress in small-scale and many pre-industrial societies include technical and economic factors. If most people are relatively poor and rely mainly on their own productive capacity to produce clothing, change is not easy. Mothers teach their daughters how to make thread, weave, and dye cloth in much the same way as their mothers taught them. It is important to recognize that most people in such societies have few items of clothing because of the amount of domestic labor that is required to make the cloth needed by a family. Also, in societies where most people must carry out fairly demanding labor clothing tends to wear out faster than if people are sitting in shops or offices.

The hand-woven cloth used by the Hmong of the highlands of northern Vietnam provides an example of the technical limitations of non-industrial production.[7] In the past most Hmong women wore pleated skirts made of hand-woven hemp thread. Making the thread requires considerable work and the time from harvesting the hemp to completion of thread making is two to three months. A kilogram of thread is enough to produce 1 to 2.5 meters of cloth. The weaving season begins in the cold months of November and December and weaving must be completed prior to the start of the planting season. A woman is able to weave about four to five pieces of hemp cloth a year. This is enough to make one skirt and perhaps an additional shirt or blouse or a pair of trousers for her husband. Hmong women sometimes decorate the hemp cloth with batik patterns and also add strips of cloth to their clothing that are decorated using a variety of embroidery, crochet, and appliqué techniques. In addition to making clothing for the members of her immediate family a Hmong woman is also expected at some point to make sets of clothing for her parents and parents-in-law to wear when they are buried. Wearing their new clothing is an important part of Hmong New Year celebrations around February.

Greater access to industrially produced cloth since the 1980s has had an impact on Hmong dress in Vietnam, but not led to fundamental changes in the style of dress. Many Hmong women now use commercial cotton or synthetic fiber cloth rather than hand-woven hemp cloth for their skirts. The use of such cloth means that Hmong families now have more clothing than in the past and women spend less time making cloth, although the new fabrics are not as durable as the hand-made ones. The skirts are still decorated as in the past, although now strips of commercial cotton of synthetic fiber cloth with printed patterns made to resemble the Hmong batik ones are available from the PRC, where it is made for the Chinese Hmong market. In addition there is a wide variety of decorative items imported from PRC ranging from pompoms made of synthetic fiber to narrow strips of colorful patterned cloth that are often added to women's blouses. This represents an elaboration of tradition-based fashion rather than a new fashion.

Changes of fashion within non-industrial societies generally have been limited and slow. Cannon lists some of the circumstances that can lead to marked changes in fashion in non-industrial societies: personal charisma, uncontrolled influx of resources, rapid population growth or aggregation, rapid depopulation, and political power shift.[8] The role of social elites in setting fashion standards and in changing fashions was as evident in past societies as it is today and, although non-elites might not be able to wear the more sumptuous clothing of these elites they often would seek to wear clothing modeled on such clothing except when this was banned. Thus, whereas elite women in feudal societies might wear clothing made with silk and decorated with gold thread, common women might wear clothing modeled on the styles of the elite but made of cotton and with less elaborate decoration. That elites in such societies would be at the forefront of changing fashions is not surprising since it was such people who had the most surplus wealth that allowed them more access to trade goods and they were also likely to be the ones most exposed to outside ideas.

As an example of the role of elites and external fashions in non-industrial society let us look at changing fashion within Thailand. The early feudal rulers of the kingdoms of Ayutthaya and Lanna in what is now modern Thailand wore styles of clothing that was a blend of their heritage as Tai people along with influences from the neighboring Khmer and Burmese as well as from India. Prior to migrating to what is now Thailand, Tai men in northern Vietnam, including feudal nobles, had worn loincloths and gone bare-chested, a fashion that allowed them to expose their extensively tattooed bodies. Women wore tubeskirts with wide waistbands that could also serve as breast-covers and sometimes blouses.[9] Certain styles of female attire (including types of tubeskirt and in some instances blouses) and particular motifs used to decorate clothing (such as dragon motifs on the waistband) were reserved for women of the noble class.

The Tai people who migrated to the southwest and settled in what is now Laos and Thailand came into contact with Buddhism through the Mon people of what is now southern Burma (Myanmar) and central Thailand and with the culture of the Khmer who came to rule over a large part of Thailand. Indian fashion influenced the clothing styles of Mon and Khmer elites and through them the Tai elites as well. However, the styles of clothing worn by these elites, although influenced by Indian fashion, were distinctive and reflected a fashion of Indian and local fashions. Such fashion included a large rectangular piece of cloth that was usually woven with silk thread and wrapped around the waist. Whereas Tai commoners continued to wear loincloths in the case of men and tubeskirts in the case of women, Tai elites preferred to wear these large wrap-around hip-cloths that were associated with the dress of the Khmer who initially ruled the most powerful kingdom in the region. This fashion persisted among Tai elites even after they became dominant in what is today Thailand with the rise of the kingdom of Ayutthaya in the late 1300s, no doubt in part because of its association with the ancient traditions of India and Cambodia.

Not only did the feudal elite of Ayutthaya wear styles of clothing based on foreign traditions, but they also imported expensive textiles as an indication of their wealth and high status. Writing about Ayutthaya, Gittinger remarks, "Exotic textiles were a declaration of the separate status of the monarchy. As costume and as fittings, textiles proclaimed the wealth of the royal household in the luxurious quality and quantity. This display of imported cloth represented the center's strength and influence beyond the state. In all instances, however, textiles of the court were markers of status which delineated the 'sacredness' of center from the rest of the realm just as clearly as the palace walls."[10] As the power and wealth of the kingdom of Ayutthaya grew, the clothing of the king and his court became increasingly elaborate with relative status within the court being marked by differences in dress. Most of the cloth imported to Ayutthaya came from India and China. Europeans became involved in the cloth trade, but mainly as suppliers of cloth from elsewhere in Asia and they had virtually no influence on local fashion at this time.

Elite fashions and patterns of textile trade remained much the same after the fall of Ayutthaya and founding of the kingdom of Siam in the late 1700s, but by the mid–1800s the situation began to change as a result of the increased political and economic power of Western Europe. European fashion and industrially produced cloth began to make an appearance in the Siamese court during the reign of King Mongkut (aka Rama IV, reigned 1851–68) as the king sought to develop relationships with the dominant European powers (as highlighted in the musical/movie *The King and I*). Although older Asian fashions continued to be dominant in King Mongkut's court, European attire was introduced, leading to the creation of a mixed Siamese-European fashion.

The influence of Western fashions in the Siamese court increased markedly after King Mongkut's son Chulalongkorn (aka Rama V) assumed the throne. Following King Chulalongkorn's return from a visit to Singapore and Batavia in 1869 he decreed that tailored clothing in a European style be worn at court as part of a policy to promote the modernization of the country. The fashion was still a mixed one. Rama V wore a specially designed long-sleeved shirt that was modeled on European jackets (called a royal shirt) rather than a copy of a European jacket. In addition to the jacket, men at court wore either European-style trousers or the more traditional long skirt-cloth that was wrapped around the waist and drawn up between the knees. Women at court continued to wear long lengths of cloth and a shoulder-cloth in accordance with the older fashion, but they now also sometimes wore a European-style blouse. As for the cloth used to make the courtly attire, previously the Siamese elite had worn clothing made of cloth either made domestically or imported from India (where it was made in accordance with Siamese tastes). During Rama V's time, Indian cloth (such as silk with gold brocade) was still imported, but European industrially produced cloth was increasingly used.[11]

Elsewhere I have noted, "Reflecting the nature of social stratification within Siam, however, such Western influence [during the reign of King Chulalongkorn] was seen primarily among the dress of a small number of elites and better off urban dwellers, while the vast majority of Siamese continued to wear non–Western types of clothing."[12] European industrially produced cloth and synthetic dyes were increasingly available to even poorer people in Siam, but this did not carry over to adoption of European fashion. To the extent that fashions were changing away from the court in Bangkok the growing number of Chinese migrants had a greater influence, including the growing popularity of Chinese-style indigo-dyed cotton trousers and shirts, which people in Siam gradually came to view as their own national fashion, especially for rural people.

The spread of Western fashion increased markedly around the world during the early part of the twentieth century. This was related not simply to economic factors, but also to its association with modernity. The forces of modernization in relation to the adoption of Western styles of dress in Siam were given a boost with the overthrow of the monarchy in 1932. The military rulers of the country that they re-named Thailand in 1939 were avid proponents of modernization and this included the promotion of Western styles of dress. During the last decades of the 1800s the rise of European power in Asia had begun to influence fashion among local elites and the emerging middle classes of the region. Limited at first, by the 1920s this influence had become more pronounced among those who identified with modernity, including many anti-colonial nationalists. Such fashion spread beyond the colonial world of Asia to Japan, which the young military officers of Siam often looked upon as a role model. Western dress had been adopted to a limited extent in Japan during the Meiji Period (1868–1912), but in the 1920s it emerged as a major fashion trend among Japanese modernists whose sense of dress was strongly influenced by Hollywood movies such as those starring Charlie Chaplin. Among Japanese women, those adopting Western garb included the *atarashii onna* (new woman) of the 1910s and the *moga* (modern girl) of the 1920s. Upon assuming power in Siam in 1939 Phibun Songkhram issued a series of cultural mandates between 1939 and 1942 to promote national identity and modernization. The mandates included dress and men were to wear Western style trousers and shirts and women Western style skirts and blouses. To urban elites of the new Thailand, attire such as the traditional tubeskirt "came to be seen as suitable clothing for servants and poor people or for leisure wear around home" and were associated with backwardness.[13]

The adoption of generic Western fashion spread around the world to an even greater extent in the wake of World War II and in concert with the end of European colonialism and the rise of nationalism and of nationalist proponents of modernization. In Thailand and many other countries around the world, "government employees and institutions played an important role in spreading Western-style fashions and positive values associated with such clothing."[14] I cite a conversation with a Thai who grew up during this period outside of Bangkok: "he noted that when he was a boy in school he felt embarrassed to wear handmade clothing to school, even if it was made of silk. Such clothing was seen as inferior to the white shirts and dark pants made of commercial cloth. In addition, he recalls that his father and fellow teachers were the first men to wear T-shirts and khaki trousers in the community and he remembers female member of his family becoming excited whenever new imported cloth became available in local shops."[15]

Ready-Made Clothing and International Trade

In addition to the industrial production of cloth and the cultural context of fashion another important factor to consider in the global evolution of dress is the development of the industrial production of tailored clothing and the marketing of such clothing. A limited range of men's tailored clothing (mainly costs and jackets, which were referred to as outerware, and undergarments) was available in predetermined sizes prior to the latter part of the 1800s. Ready-made clothing became increasingly available for men in Western industrial countries during the latter part of the 1800s. In the case of the United States, the Civil War played a crucial role in promoting the mass production of ready-made clothing. When the war began uniforms were made either by members of a soldier's own family or in the homes of contract workers. As the war continued the demand for uniforms grew and manufacturers built factories to meet the demand. Soldiers were measured and uniforms were produced in a range of standard sizes. These measurements continued to be used to produce ready-made clothing for men after the war until the 1880s, when the Jno. J. Mitchell Company of New York devised and published a new system that became the standard in the industry.

By the 1890s men in the United States and many other Western industrial countries could easily purchase ready-to-wear trousers and shirts along with jackets and undergarments in stores. The development of women's ready-to-wear clothing was slower and did not emerge on a large scale until the first decade of the 1900s. Even then, most clothing for women continued to be custom made until the 1920s. The first item made available to women on this basis was a style of blouse called a shirtwaist. A standardized system of sizing for women was created following a study of women's body measurements by the Department of Agriculture in the United States. Increasing demand by women for ready-to-wear apparel was associated with the emergence of growing numbers of urban women who were working outside of the home.

The growing popularity of ready-to-wear clothing was linked to the spread of chain stores and mail order catalogs. Mail order catalogs initially catered mainly to markets within single states and sold goods for the most part manufactured in the same state. Aaron Montgomery Ward produced the first mail-order catalog in 1872 selling general merchandise mainly to farmers in the American Midwest from a rented room in Chicago. This first catalog was a single sheet listing 163 products. By the 1890s the Montgomery Ward catalog had grown into a 540-page book listing over 20,000 products. Ward's success led other to copy him in the United States and Canada, including Timothy Eaton (1884, 32 pages), Robert Simpson (1893, 82 pages), and Robert Sears (1896). Mail order shopping developed later in Europe, such as with the entry of Littlewoods into the mail order business in the United Kingdom in 1932. Sears was one of the few companies associated with these catalogs to eventually grow into a transnational company, opening its first store in Mexico City in 1947 and forming a joint-venture with Simpsons to form Simpsons-Sears in 1952 (as well as having stores in Guatemala City under the name Homeart S A).

For expatriates and locals desiring to wear such clothing who lived in other countries, such ready-to-wear merchandise continued to be imported by local merchants and the clothing pictured in mail-order catalogs by Sears and other such companies could only be copied rather than ordered. Throughout the colonial world during the 1800s and first decades of the 1900s there were numerous retail stores that imported ready-to-wear clothing from Europe and North America for expatriates and a few local elites, but most clothing continued to be custom-made domestically. There were also clothing manufacturers that specialized in exporting clothing to the colonies. A look through the "Advertiser" section in the *Colonial Office List for 1921* catering to colonial civil servants of the British Empire includes advertisements for a variety of such companies in London — e.g., "Miller, Rayner & Haysom Limited. Naval, Military & Colonial Outfitters, Established in 1818. Complete Equipment for Colonial Officers. Uniform and Mufti Clothing, Hosiery, Shirts, Boots, Helmets, Air-tight Cases, Trunks, Etc.... Agencies: Paris and Antwerp.... Estimates and Price Lists on Application."[16]

The transnational market for such ready-to-wear European colonial clothing as described in the above paragraph was relatively small and in the post-colonial world of the 1950s and beyond it virtually disappeared. However, the widespread popularity of ready-to-wear clothing within developed countries, where most people viewed such apparel as modern and fashionable, laid the groundwork for a post–World War II boom in the production of ready-to-wear clothing in developed countries. Most of this ready-to-wear clothing was produced within the countries where it was worn and international trade continued to focus on textiles rather than clothing (also referred to as apparel). Moreover, for the most part, people in developing countries continued to make their own clothing or to have it made by local tailors. The history of Indian clothing provides an example of this, as outlined in a speech by Shiri Kashiram Rana, the Minister of Textiles, at the CIAE International Fashion Awards: "If one were to look at the history of Indian exports they started with low value, low quality products and hence not much importance was given to strengthening production facilities. The concept of 'Ready to wear' is quite new in India. Even though ready made garments have been produced and sold in domestic market from as early as 1960's, these were restricted to certain product categories like kidswear and select products in men's wear like shirt, pajamas and kurtas. Easy availability of tailors and low tailoring charges made custom made products afford- able. In the late 70's and 80's, branded products were introduced in the domestic market. This was the time when apparel exports also started gaining momentum."[17]

The ready-to-wear industry and market began to become more global in the 1970s as clothing manufacturers in developed countries began to shift production to lower cost locations in developing countries. An entry in the *Encyclopaedia of Global Industries* on the apparel industry notes: "Apparel has long been made in locations around the world, and the global clothing market represents a substantial area of consumer spending, but in the last decades of the twentieth century there was a pronounced migration of its mass production from higher-wage industrial economies to lower cost labor markets in the developing world. Through the mid- to late 1990s and into the 2000s, apparel manufac- turers in industrial nations continued to seek countries with low-cost labor for produc- tion. Developing economies in Asia and South America received the bulk of these production contracts. Simultaneously, apparel companies in developed economies began reducing their domestic workforces as a direct result of sourcing labor from low-wage countries. Meanwhile, apparel firms that could not compete with low-cost manufacturers either merged with larger companies, diversified, or closed."[18]

During this period developed countries came to import an increasing amount of their clothing. The trend is evident if we compare the value of clothing imports in these countries for 1990 and 2007 (in millions of U.S. dollars): Australia $711 to $3,703, Canada $2,388 to $7,604, European Union (2000 and 2007) $83,181 to $162,806, Japan $8,765 to $23,999, Russia (2000 and 2007) $2,688 to $14,505, and the United States $26,977 to $84,853. In global terms, the value of clothing exports rose from U.S. $108,129 million in 1990 to U.S. $345,301 million in 2007. It is also important to note that the growth in international clothing trade was not due solely to developed countries importing clothing made in developing countries, but that there was also an increase in clothing imports of clothing by developing countries. Thus, Thailand, for example, exported $2,817 million worth of clothing in 1990 while importing only $29 million worth. By 2007 the value of its clothing exports had increased to $4,073 million, while the value of its imports had risen to $331 million. Such imports included both inexpensive items largely from the PRC aimed at the mass market as well as more expensive items from Western Europe and elsewhere for the middle class and elite markets.

The history of the trousers made from denim (a strong cotton twill textile) that are commonly called jeans provides a useful case study of the changing nature of the global clothing industry and how what began as essentially an occupational fashion in a few Western countries became a global one.[19] There are two aspects of such denim clothing in regard to transnationalism, one of a cultural nature and the other economic. The cul- tural side has to do with how such clothing has gradually lost its identification with specific states to become more broadly identified with Western fashion and then, increas- ingly, with a fairly generic modernization often in opposition to more traditional national dress. In a fashion sense, then, it has gradually lost its transnational character. In economic terms, the denim industry has grown from a local one that at most crossed a few state borders to an important global one that serves to link a variety of businesses transnationally to serve an international market.

In the 1500s denim was produced in France (Nîmes), Italy (Chieri), and India (Dongari Killa, Mumbai) to make durable work trousers and overalls. The denim trousers made in Chieri, Italy, in the 1500s were sold throughout northwestern Italy, including in the port city of Genoa. Among those wearing them were sailors in the Genoese navy and Genoese stevedores working both in Genoa and in neighboring parts of southern France. Having become popular as work-wear among Europeans, wearing denim trousers spread to the United States in the mid–1800s, where people wore them engaged in hard labor such as miners and cowboys in the American west. Their commercial development is closely linked to a Jewish businessman named Levi Strauss.

Born Löb Strauss in Bavaria in 1829 (died 1902), Levi Strauss migrated to New York City to join his two brothers who had established a wholesale dry goods business. The family sent Levi to San Francisco to open a branch of the business named Levi Strauss & Co. in 1853. Among the items sold by this company was blue denim fabric that local tailors made into trousers. The development of the modern blue jeans resulted from the work of a tailor in Reno, Nevada, named Jacob Davis, who used metal rivets to strengthen the trousers that he made from denim bought from Levi Strauss in 1870. The pair patented the use of copper rivets to make denim trousers in 1873 and Levi Strauss & Co. began having them manufactured by Amoskeag Manufacturing Co. in Manchester, New Hampshire.

There were other important producers of denim clothing as well, located either in the United States or western Canada. Lee Mercantile Company, founded by Henry David Lee in Salina, Kansas, in 1889, also emerged as a major manufacture of denim clothing in the late 1880s. The company began making denim trousers called dungarees and jackets and in 1913 introduced the Union-All work jumpsuit. Lee introduced the zipper fly to its trousers in the 1920s. Great Western Garment Co. of Edmonton, Alberta, which was founded in 1911, was one of the major manufacturers of denim clothing in Canada. It was acquired by Levi Strauss in the 1970s and closed down in 2004.

Denim clothing fashion and production underwent important changes in the 1960s and 1970s. The transformation of blue jeans from work-wear to everyday fashion has its origins in the 1955 Hollywood movie *Rebel Without a Cause* in which the young star James Dean wore blue jeans. Dean's style of dress was widely adopted by American teenagers in the late 1950s and by the 1970s jeans had become common informal attire for teenagers and adults in North America. This change in the market for blue jeans was reflected in the Lee company, which shifted the focus of its marketing and advertising from work-wear to mass-market fashion in the 1970s. The fashion market for jeans also spread beyond North America to Europe, Latin America, and elsewhere.

The spread of blue jeans fashion played a particularly important role in the communist world of the 1970s and 1980s, where the demand for blue jeans was widely viewed as the most important symbol of growing consumer demands that led to the transformation of the countries under communist rule and to the fall of their communist regimes. Writing on why the Soviet Union collapsed, Nick Wolf answers, "Blue Jeans! As with most questions there is always a very simple answer, blue jeans! There was a reason that every time a Russian athlete or other citizen representative left the country they were accompanied by a KGB escort. They weren't being protected, they were being coerced to return and not to defect. Each trip by each citizen brought home stories of the West. Mostly disbelieved, how could there be so much? And so much that was thrown away? Food rotting in stores, cloths hanging on racks as far as the eye could see. It was culture shock at its finest and one day a chink appeared in the armor of the state and the people were ready to grab their chance to get a part to the west, they wanted blue jeans and all that that embodied. Of course it helped that their glorious leader had a penchant for the taste of the beverage of choice, but the stage had been set by then to take advantage of an opportunity for the masses to get their blue jeans."[20]

Another article on blue jeans in the Soviet Union and contemporary Russia by Robert Bridge draws attention not just to the global spread of blue jeans fashion but also to changes in the production of jeans: "Last week, I decided to do something that I have never done before in the Russian capital: buy a pair of blue jeans, that quintessential western product that flaunts the liberal slogan of freedom and fun from every backside ... this is a far cry from the communist days when a pair of Wranglers allegedly fetched a fashionable Bolshevik's 200-ruble monthly stipend. In those days, as one Soviet scholar told me, the demand for denim (and other Western 'abominations') gave rise to the so-called *fartsovshchiki,* a back-alley market where Russians secretly purchased their coveted western apparel from 'speculators.' Another observer even went so far as to suggest that rebellious blue jeans, with a little help from Rock 'n' Reagan, of course, played no small role in toppling the Soviet Union. 'Blue jeans were the best counterargument against Soviet propaganda,' writes Sergei Boukhonine, on the website www.lewrockwell.com. 'In the pantheon of objects that brought down the Soviet communism, blue jeans have a very special place, second to none.' ... Okay, back to the brutal reality of ultra-expensive Moscow.... With the help of a long metal pole, Natasha plucked a pair of jeans down for me. I inquired about the legitimacy of the goods as I inspected the holographic sticker and the myriad labels claiming authenticity. Natasha explained that the Levis were hand-made by the industrious people of Turkey, and I could not find fault with the quality."[21]

As blue jeans fashion spread across the globe the production of denim and finished blue jeans increasingly moved from North America to other parts of the world. According to the *World Denim Report 2007*, at present "Over 50 percent of denim production is based in Asia with China, India, Turkey, Pakistan and Bangladesh leading in that order."[22] In India, for example, the Lalbhai Group's Arvind Mills are the country's largest producer of denim. The company headquarters is in Ahmedabad, Gujarat — a city with a long history of cotton textile production. Three brothers of the Lalbhai family — one of the city's leading families — established the mills in 1931. Since their founding the mills have produced a variety of cotton materials, but in 1987 they were modernized in large part to increase production of denim for export in response to the growing global demand for this fabric. By 1991 the mills were producing 100 million meters of denim per year and the company was the fourth largest producer of denim fabric in the world. The company also began to manufacture finished blue jeans through its subsidiary Arvind Fashions.

Arvind Fashions has its headquarters in Bangalore and its factories are located in nearby Chamarajanagar, Karnataka. With an agreement to produce jeans for Lee, Arvind Fashions introduced advanced technology into its factories in 1997 that allowed it to double its production of jeans. In 2006 Arvind Fashion announced plans to employ 60,000 workers to produce 5,000 Lee jeans per day.[23]

The shift of production of blue jeans to countries such as India is part of the general trend in ready-to-wear production mentioned above. Domestic and international trade agreements have played an important role in this trend. As the *Encyclopaedia of Global Industries* states, "World trade in apparel was highly regulated through the late twentieth century, but the movement away from trade barriers in the 1990s and early 2000s profoundly affected the industry, paving the way — in the view of many analysts—for China to become the world's dominant player. In 2002, according to the *Miami Herald,* 70 percent of all growth in apparel imports to the United States came from China and Vietnam. According to the American Textile Manufacturers Institute (ATMI), China's share of the U.S. import market, averaging about 9 percent in the 1990s when quotas were in effect, skyrocketed to 53 percent in 2003 after several categories of clothing were removed from quota requirements. This trend intensified after 2005, when remaining trade quotas expired. Indeed, in January 2005 alone, the value of Chinese apparel exports to the United States increased by more than 41 percent, and the value of its clothing exports to the European Union in the first four months of 2005 grew by 80 percent."[24]

Where is ready-to-wear clothing being made at present? If we take out the intra–EU share of ready-to-wear exports, this leaves U.S. $266,690 million worth of clothing exports in 2007. The remaining clothing exports are dominated by the PRC ($115,238 million, 43.2 percent of the total) and Hong Kong ($23,765 million, excluding exports to the PRC, 8.9 percent of the total), which combined accounts for 52.1 percent of the total. Other major exporters include (2007 figures): Turkey $14,001 million, Bangladesh $10,060 million, India $9,655 million, Vietnam $7,186 million, Indonesia $5,870 million, and Mexico $5,150 million.

The *Encyclopaedia of Global Industries* entry cited above reviews the pattern of outsourcing by companies in developed countries: "France depended on manufacturers in Spain and North Africa, while Germany outsourced to Eastern Europe and Turkey for lower-cost production. In addition to Mexico, the United States relied on countries across the globe, such as India and Singapore, for low-wage manufacturing. Finally, Japan contracted manufacturers in developing Asian countries." The entry also points to another transnational trend in the ready-to-wear business: "Besides internationalizing production, apparel firms in industrial countries sought to expand cross-border trade of their goods. This was necessary as the markets matured in many of the major apparel-producing countries, leaving them with few available channels of expansion. Consequently, apparel firms from the United States, France, Germany, Italy, Japan, and other maturing countries started to market their products in places such as South Korea, Russia, and Turkey, as well as South America."[25]

Despite the continued dominance of the international ready-to-wear industry by the PRC, in fact that industry has become increasingly diffuse over the years. The PRC's rise as a clothing exporter can be seen if we compare 1978 with 2000 production figures: from 670 million pieces of apparel in 1978 to 11.6 billion in 2000 with the value of clothing exports rising fifty times to $36.1 billion in 2000 (representing 14.5 percent of the value of the country's merchandise exports). The value of the PRC's clothing exports further increased to $74.2 billion in 2005 and to $115 billion in 2007 (representing 9.5 percent of the value of merchandise exports). The value of Hong Kong's clothing exports also increased substantially during this period to $15.4 billion in 1990 and $18.8 billion in 2007. In 2002 there were around 45,000 garment producers in the PRC, located primarily along the coast in Guangdong, Zhejiang, Jiangsu, Shandong, and Shanghai.

During the 1990s a growing number of developing countries were becoming involved in the global apparel trade, providing increased competition for the PRC and Hong Kong. In the case of the United States this diversification was linked in part to new trade agreements such as the 1984 Caribbean Basin Initiative that allowed countries in Central America and the Caribbean to export apparel to the United States duty free and the 2000 Trade and Development Act that allowed 48 sub–Saharan African countries to export a wide range of apparel items free of duties and quotas. The impact of these initiatives can be seen particularly in the case of Honduras, where clothing exports (primarily to the United States) increased in value from $64 million in 1990 to $2,275 million in 2000. The 1994 North American Free Trade Agreement was of even more significance in regard to the boost that it gave to apparel production in Mexico, which saw the value of its clothing exports (mainly to the United States) increased from $587 million in 1990 to $8,631 in 2000. Even without such trade agreements, other countries such as Sri Lanka and Bangladesh were able to increase their exports to countries such as the United States by offering lower costs of production than the PRC. Thus, the value of Bangladesh's clothing exports increased from $643 million in 990 to $5,067 in 2000 (and to $10,060 million in 2007) and Sri Lanka's from $638 million to $2,812 million in 1990 and 2000 respectively.

Since 2005 the international apparel trade has become increasingly free of duties and quotas. The PRC has been a prime beneficiary of this change, while other countries have found themselves less able to compete without protective agreements. Thus, while the value of the PRC's clothing exports, as noted above, have continued to increase since 2005, the value of Mexico's clothing exports decreased from $7,306 million in 2005 to $5,150 million in 2007 and Honduras's from $2,790 million to $2,693. Other countries have done better at weathering the changes in the international clothing trade. We will look at Mauritius as a case study, focusing on the role of local ethnic Chinese and their transnational links.

The history of Chinese migration to the Indian Ocean begins in the 1740s when a group of Chinese laborers were forcibly taken from Sumatra by French Admiral Charles Hector in the 1740s to work in Mauritius.[26] They refused to work and were sent back to Sumatra. The French then recruited several thousand voluntary migrants in Guangdong in the 1780s (mostly Cantonese-speakers) that were taken to Mauritius on British, French, and Danish ships to work in a variety of trades. This group settled on Mauritius and formed a small Chinatown. An additional 3,000 migrants arrived between 1840 and 1843 after the British assumed control of the island. Later migrants included a large number of Hakka-speakers from Mei County in Guangdong. Local Chinese who established businesses began bringing relatives to Mauritius. After becoming accustomed to the colonial environment these relatives were then sent to Réunion, South Africa, and other locales on the African mainland to establish satellite businesses. Chinese migrants also settled on the island of Madagascar. In this way transnational networks of ethnic Chinese were formed in the western Indian Ocean and nearby areas of Africa. At present there are around 40,000 ethnic Chinese in Mauritius.

When Mauritius gained independence in 1968 it was a fairly poor country with an economy that was heavily dependent on the production and export of sugar. Today it is one of the success stories of the developing world with a diversified economy and a per capita GDP in 2008 of around $12,100. Moreover, its economy is characterized by a relative equitable distribution of wealth and incomes and the country ranks relatively high on most other indices such as life expectancy. The country's textile and clothing industry has played an important role in this transformation. As noted by Joomun, "The setting up of the textile and clothing industry [in Mauritius] was successful in terms of income generation employment creation and capacity building for local entrepreneurs" and he highlights three aspects that contributed to this success: a conducive environment for investment, exogenous factors, and preferential trade arrangements.[27]

The government of Mauritius's interest in the clothing industry dates back to the late 1960s when a consultant's report recommended developing an export-oriented clothing industry as a means of diversifying the island's sugar-dependent economy. A first step in this direction was the creation of the country's first export processing zone in 1971. Many other countries have also tried such a strategy, but with less success than Mauritius. Jooman lists a series of exogenous factors that contributed to the development of the country's clothing industry and several of these involve transnational relations of Sino-Mauritians.[28] These exogenous factors begin with the 1982 international Multi-Fibre Agreement that served to constrain clothing exports from a number of countries with well-established exporting industries. Among these was Hong Kong and investors from Hong Kong came to Mauritius following implementation of the agreement and established firms there. Next, appreciation of the Taiwanese dollar made clothing exports from Taiwan more expensive and Taiwanese investors also came to Mauritius to establish businesses. During the 1990s political uncertainties in Hong Kong encouraged more investors to relocate in Mauritius.

The initial success of Mauritius's textile and clothing industry, which by 2000 contributed about 12 percent to its GDP and employed 81,438 people (71.1 percent of all employment in manufacturing), also owed a good deal to favorable exchange rates between the Mauritius rupee and the currencies of most of its trading partners and to preferential trade agreements, including the Lomé Convention in relation to the European Union and the 2000 African Growth and Opportunity Act in relation to the United States. The global liberalization of clothing trade in 2005 created concern for the country's clothing industry. Writing the following year Joomun noted, "the dismantling of the Multi-Fibre Agreement and the new challenges of an extremely competitive world market has left the [Mauritian clothing] industry in a weakened state. The positive conditions, which have contributed to the thriving of the industry have now almost all disappeared."[29] The government responded to the threat posed by the dismantling of the Multi-Fibre Agreement by establishing a Textile Emergency Support Team in 2003 to assist companies to become more competitive.

Mauritius's textile and clothing industry was already facing problems prior to 2005 in large part because of the country's overall economic success. Labor costs increased during the 1990s and it became more and more difficult to find local people willing to work in the textile and garment factories. Labor shortages were met by recruiting foreign workers with their number growing from 6,145 in 1995 to 13,792 in 2004 (about 20 percent of the workforce). Some companies also moved their operations to nearby Madagascar, where labor costs were less. Floreal Garments was the first to do so in 1990 and by 2000 it employed about 5,000 workers in Madagascar.[30] Political instability in Madagascar in 2002 forced Floreal and other companies from Mauritius to close their operations there and bring their equipment back to Mauritius (Floreal lost $14 million as a result). Some companies returned to Madagascar the following year, but investment was slow to return to previous levels. There were a total of 384 textile and clothing companies in Mauritius in 1997 (270 of these in the Export Processing Zone). Although some companies had moved to Madagascar, the number of companies in Mauritius grew to 420 in 2000 with the number of these in the Export Processing Zone growing to 286. After 2000, however, the number of companies began to decline with 265 operating in the Export Processing Zone in 2004. There was an accompanying drop in employment to 67,249 in 2004.

Writing in early 2008, Nassem Ackbarally asked "Is There life After 40 Years of Trade Preferences?"[31] pointing out that following "The European Union's decision to cut sugar prices by 36 percent and the end of the multi-fibre arrangement in January 2005" the textile and clothing and sugar industries in Mauritius were forced to lay off large numbers of workers: "Some 40,000 were lost during the past three years in the textile and clothing industry and more than 10,000 in the sugar sector." The same author answered the question in an article two days later with the title "Trade-Mauritius: Clothing Sector Not Hanging by a Thread Anymore."[32] He began by noting that revenue generated by the clothing and textile industry in Mauritius had grown from $1.25 billion in 2006 to $1.45 billion in 2007 and that "Plenty of jobs are now available in the textiles and clothing sector but there are not enough local takers. Hence the island is importing more foreign labour from India, China and Bangladesh who already number more than 33,000. Almost 7,000 arrived last year." As a new efficiency, he reported, "Some large enterprises have opened warehouses in Europe and South Africa where they stock their products. As soon as an order is received, the goods are shipped directly from there."

Of added relevance was the Tianli Development project at the Riche Terre business park that was inaugurated in early 2008: "The multi-billion Tianli Development project of Riche Terre has now been stepped up to reach Rs 20 billion. It has been qualified by the Prime Minister as the biggest integrated project ever to be developed in Mauritius. It is not only an industrial park but also an integrated project that takes into account the whole environment. The industrial projects will be particularly oriented to high-end value added industries and a school of Technology which will provide training and solutions to manpower problems. The zone is expected, in 5 years, to provide direct employ-ment to some 34,000 people while 8,000 will benefit from indirect jobs."[33] The company involved is Shandong Tianli Drying Equipment Inc. on Shandong in the PRC. The Shan-dong Academy of Sciences (SDAS) and Energy Research Institute attached to SDAS estab-lished the company in 1994. This represents the first large investment by a company from the PRC in Mauritius. The investment in the Riche Terre site is apparently around $600 million. Plans are for around 40 companies from the PRC to operate at the site, including clothing manufacturing, hardware assembly, and food processing. Thus, another East Asian company is setting up shop in Mauritius to produce clothing using local and South Asian labor for export to Europe and North America.

Dress and Religion

Beyond exhortations to dress modestly, the major religions of the world have had an important influence of the ways that people dress around the world. This in large part reflects the fact that notions of appropriate dress are grounded in attitudes towards the prevalent fashions of the times and locales of the founding religious figures as well as those of the later proponents of these religions. Thus, such religiously inspired attire reflects the fashion and cultural notions of particular places and peoples even though its proponents may view it in more universal terms.

In discussing the influence of religion on dress it is necessary to recognize that many religions make distinctions between the style of dress of religious specialists and the laity. Thus, from a transnational perspective, the influence of a particular religion on its fol-lowers around the world is likely to be most evident in the case of such specialists and their distinctive attire, which marks them as members of an international religious body. Religion may also influence local fashion on the part of laypeople, sometimes in the wholesale adoption of a religiously inspired fashion, but more often as an external influence on local fashion.

Christianity

Christianity's attitude towards dress draws on ancient fashions and cultural traditions in the eastern Mediterranean. There are relatively few passages in the Bible relating specifi-cally to dress. In the Old Testament there are passages in Deuteronomy dealing with dress: "A woman shall not wear anything that pertains to a man, nor shall a man put on woman's garment; for whoever does these things is an abomination to the Lord your God" (22:5), "You shall not wear a mingled stuff, wool and linen together" (22:11), and "You shall not make yourself tassels on the four corners of your cloak with which to cover yourself" (22:12). In response to the argument that some modern Christians make that the first of these passages indicates that women should not wear pants, other Christians point out that in light of the similarity of men's and women's clothing in Biblical times and the fact that pants were not worn by either sex at that time, that conclusion would be difficult to justify.[34] The second passage follows another passage which reads, "You shall not plow with an ox and an ass together" (22:10), indicating that the reference may have something to do with not mixing such things that God has created separately in what is perceived to be an unnatural way, but the meaning remains obscure.

Whatever appears in the Old Testament concerning dress, Christians generally believe that these are superseded by the New Testament and are not necessary to follow. There are a number of passages relating to appropriate dress in the New Testament. Thus, Timothy in his first letter to Paul says he would like for women to "adorn themselves modestly and sensibly in seemly apparel, not with braided hair or gold or pearls of costly attire" (1 Timothy 2:9). He follows this by saying that rather than wearing fancy dress they should do good deeds (2:9) and with statements that "a woman should learn in silence with all submissiveness," that she should "keep silent," and that she "will be saved through bearing children, if she continues in faith and love and holiness, with modesty" (2:11–15). Peter writes along similar lines. After telling wives to "be submissive to your husbands" he asks them not to adorn themselves "with braiding of hair, decoration of gold, and wearing of robes, but let it be the hidden person of the heart with the imperishable jewel of a gentle and quiet spirit" (1 Peter 3:1–4). Using clothing in a symbolic sense, Peter also urges males, young and old alike, to "Clothe yourselves, all of you, with humility toward one another, for 'God opposes the proud, but gives grace to the humble'" (1 Peter 6:5).

Paul discussed appropriate dress in regard to covering the face and head in his first letter to the Corinthians: "Any man who prays or prophecies with his head covered dishonors his head, but any woman who prays or prophecies with her head unveiled dishonors her head — it is the same as if her head were shaven. For if a woman will not veil herself, then she should cut off her hair but if it is disgraceful for a woman to be shorn or shaven, let her wear a veil. For a man ought not to cover his head, since he is the image and glory of God; but woman is the glory of man.... That is why a woman ought to have a veil on her head, because of the angels" (1 Corinthians 11:4–7, 10). Paul adds, "Does not nature itself teach you that for a man to wear long hair is degrading him, but if a woman has long hair, it is her pride? For her hair is given to her for a covering" (1 Corinthians 11:14–15). These lines need to be seen within their context. It was common in the eastern Mediterranean at the time for men to remove their head coverings when in the presence of a superior as a sign of respect and likewise when praying. Pagan men, however, covered their heads when praying to avoid distractions and Christian men were urged to remove their head coverings to avoid association with Paganism. As for veils, although Jewish women at the time normally did not wear veils, Greek and Roman women did in part to demonstrate their modesty and respect for their husband. The general public in Corinth would have viewed a woman removing her veil in public as an act of disrespect. Paganism also has a role here since Pagan priestesses sometimes removed their veils while praying and making prophesies and the early Christian wished to dissociate themselves with such practices.

In general the modern Christian attitude towards appropriate dress is that references to specific items of attire in the Bible (e.g., cloaks, tunics, turbans, and veils) are not relevant since particular dress fashions change, but that the principal of modesty, especially in regard to worship in public, should be adhered to. Paul's letter to the Corinthians stresses the desire of early Christians to fit in with local dress customs rather than trying to distinguish themselves, but at the same time it seeks to distance Christian dress from undesirable association with Paganism. Thus, while in general the notion of appropriate dress is relativistic there are limits. Ideas of what constitutes appropriate dress for Christians became especially important as European Christian missionaries encountered peoples with standards of dress that were very different from their own. Paul's discussion of appropriate dress was in the context of comparing appropriate dress for Christians and non–Christians from similar cultural backgrounds. European Christians from the 1500s onward commonly viewed their mission not only to convert people but also to uplift them in accordance with European morals, which included standards of dress.

While some European Christian missionaries simply wished to have non–European converts dress like Europeans since the missionaries considered European dress superior and more in keeping with Christian ideals, the process was usually more complex. Many European Christian missionaries expressed a sympathetic view of local dress traditions even though they might consider it inferior to their own. Thus, the English Methodist missionary Thomas Williams, who worked as a missionary in Fiji from 1840 until 1853, wrote the following about traditional Fijian dress: "In their dress, scanty as it is, the Fijians display great care and pride. In judging this matter, it is very difficult for a civilized stranger to form a right opinion, influenced, as he must be, by the conventionalities of costume to which he is accustomed. Hence the natives are frequently spoken of as naked; but they only seem so when compared with other nations. It must be borne in mind that the character of the climate and the quality of their skin both render dress as far as mere utility is concerned, unnecessary; the people, therefore, ought to receive full credit for modesty in the partial covering which they adopt, and about the use of which they are scrupulously particular."[35]

Even those Christian missionaries who were sympathetic to indigenous styles of dress usually advocated people wearing clothing that was more in the European fashion when attending church services and felt that modesty entailed covering a person's breasts. Thus, while such missionaries might consider it to be acceptable for people to continue wearing their traditional clothing at home or at work, they set different standards when worshipping. More often, however, missionaries advocated completely replacing the more offensive styles of dress with ones that adhered to prevailing European notions of decency. In the case of Hawaii, for example, Arthur notes in regard to the early contact period, "Commoners traditionally covered only the genitals, and women wore a short pa'u [bark-cloth skirt] with the bust exposed; missionaries took offense and would not allow naked-ness near the missions."[36] As the missions became more established and the number of converts grew the missionary wives established Christian women's organizations that, among other things, promoted European notions of modesty. Lucy Thurston, one of these early missionaries, comments that by 1829 missionaries had come to insist that local converts "uniformly have a full covering for their person, both at home and abroad."[37] Hawaiians also covered their bodies to different degrees, but as Arthur (1997) points out, "The missionaries and Hawaiians had different motives for covering the body. The main motive of the missionaries was to cover nakedness and uphold the western social conventions of modesty and propriety. According to the missionaries, the Hawaiians used clothing primarily to display status, 'rather than as a covering for their deformity.' While covering nakedness was essential to the missionaries, Hawaiians considered dress to be optional, depending on rank and the social occasion."[38]

In the case of Christian converts in Hawaii, as elsewhere, more was at work than people slavishly following the dictates of the missionaries. Contact between European Christian missionaries and non–Europeans commonly led to the development of distinct new forms of local attire that drew on European fashions in keeping with the processes of comparison, emulation, and differentiation mentioned earlier in the chapter. Converts and even many non-converts often viewed the missionaries as bringers of modern fashion, which they wished to emulate in order to present themselves as being modern. However, it was also common for local people to modify such fashions in accordance with local tastes—a practice that the European missionaries sometimes encouraged since it served to mark ethnic differences between themselves and the locals.

Prior to the arrival of Americans and Europeans, Hawaiian Islanders wore clothing made of bark-cloth. Bark-cloth wrap-around skirts of Hawaiian women were worn in such a way as to demarcate status. The skirts of women of the nobility (ali'i) covered their bodies from just beneath their breasts to their knees. Commoners wore them from their waists to their knees. Women of the noble class were the first to obtain imported commercial cloth and to design new styles of clothing based on American and European fashion.[39] Citing nineteenth century writings by Thurston and Kotzebue, Arthur argues, "The ali'i continued to use clothing, either indigenous or western, to symbolize their upper class position. Travelers noted that the Hawaiians from the upper classes eagerly acquired and wore western clothing and textiles."[40]

Kotzebue remarked that when Christian missionaries arrived in Hawaii the Hawaiian nobles "met the ship dressed in honour of us with the utmost neatness, in fine English clothes."[41] On formal occasions Hawaiian noble women at the time in fact commonly wore American/European style dresses made of imported cloth over slips made of bark-cloth. The cloth dresses that the nobles wore in 1820 were tailored in an older European fashion ("with a long, tight waist"), whereas the dresses of the missionary women were styled in the latest 1819 fashion ("with a high waist, narrow skirt and long, tight sleeves").[42] Thurston, who was one of these missionary wives, describes how the Hawaiian noble women, Queen Kalakua in particular, wished to have new dresses made mirroring this newer fashion. When asked by Queen Kalakua to make a dress for her to wear when accompanying the missionaries to meet King Liholiho using a bolt of white cambric cloth that she gave them, the missionaries produced a style of dress based on the ones that they wore, but modified to suit the large size of the queen and the warm, humid climate.[43] This dress was loose fitting with a full, straight skirt attached to a yoke above the bust and a high neck and tight sleeves. Queen Kalakua's new dress proved to be a hit with other Hawaiian noble women and served as the basis for what became known as the holok. A chemise referred to as a mu'umu'u was introduced at the same time as the holok. Arthur comments about them: "Both garments continue to be very important in Hawai'i. While the mu'umu'u is regarded by those from outside the islands as Hawaiian dress, the lesser-known holoku is more closely associated with Hawaiian ethnicity although it is virtually unknown outside of Hawai'i. Once worn by Hawaiian women as everyday wear, the holoku is now formal wear worn for ritual events related to Hawaiian ethnicity."[44]

The influence of European Christian missionaries on another group of Pacific islanders, Tongans, is particularly relevant in regards to transnationalism since Tongans, like many other Pacific Islanders, have taken their mission-inspired forms of dress with them as they have migrated to other countries. Prior to European contact Tongans wore clothing made of bark-cloth and pandanus mats. Tongan dress was an indication of status, with nobles wearing painted bark-cloth and pandanus mats and commoners wearing either plain bark-cloth, a pandanus mat, or a girdle made of leaves. When in the presence of nobles, however, commoners would wear two layers of clothing, usually a leaf girdle on top of bark-cloth. As in Hawaii, Tongan nobles were quick to adopt European cloth and clothing. Addo notes, "European garments were quickly embraced by high-ranking Tongans as signs of their distinction and of their new modern selves."[45] The Christian missionaries encouraged this since they viewed it as an important part of religious conversion. Commoners also sought to emulate the nobles and missionaries, but they were constrained "by lack of resources" and, thus, wishing still to be able to show respect "began to layer traditional textiles with garments introduced by the mission."[46] The fashion that gradually evolved comprised wearing a small pandanus mat wrapped around the waist over European-style clothing or clothing made of imported cloth but based more on pre–European traditions on formal occasions.

Since the late 1960s large numbers of Tongans have settled in New Zealand (especially in and around Auckland and Wellington) as well as in Australia and the United States. Most overseas Tongans continued to be members of Methodist, Catholic, Anglican, or Mormon churches and for them, "Clothing operates as an immediate visual indicator of cultural, and in some cases, religious devotion."[47] With the exception of Mormons, the dress of overseas Tongan Christians when attending church services still tends to reflect status differences and, even when wearing Western fashion there is a tendency to layer out of a sense of modesty. Moreover, even Mormons, who advocate not devoting too much attention to traditional Tongan styles of dress, will wear traditional hybrid clothing at funerals and during mourning periods out of respect for the deceased.[48] Thus, men who normally wear slacks to church will wear a tailored sarong (*tupenu*) and waist mat at funerals. In the case of Tongans living in Auckland, clothing styles at church are largely controlled by groups of prominent women. These and other women also gather to make bark-cloth and mats for traditional attire. As an alternative to actual bark-cloth some women wear cotton and viscose cloth with bark-cloth patterns that is produced by local Indo-Fijian migrants on commission as a substitute. Thus, while there are some changes from what is worn in Tonga, the Tongans in Auckland still retain many of the fashions and the sense of what is appropriate wear associated with Tonga in religious settings.

Islam

Attempts to instill dress codes among Muslims have generated considerable controversy in recent years. The Koran instructs Muslims to dress modestly. There are a few passages in the Koran dealing with dress. Surah 24:31 says: "And say to the believing women that they should lower their gaze and guard their modesty; that they should not display their beauty and ornaments except what (must ordinarily) appear thereof; that they should draw their veils [*khimar*] over their bosoms and not display their beauty except to their husbands, their fathers, their husbands' fathers, their sons, their husbands' sons, their brothers or their brothers' sons, or their sisters' sons, or their women, or the slaves whom their right hands possess, or male servants free of physical needs, or small children who have no sense of the shame of sex; and that they should not strike their feet in order to draw attention to their hidden ornaments. And O ye Believers! Turn ye all together towards Allah, that ye may attain Bliss." The verse Surah 33:59 has the following to say: "O Prophet! Tell thy wives and thy daughters and the women of the believers to draw their cloaks [*jilbab*] close round them (when they go abroad). That will be better, so that they may be recognised and not annoyed. Allah is ever Forgiving, Merciful."

Two other verses, Surah 33:32–33, discuss the dress of the wives of Muhammad and are also sometimes used as a directive for appropriate dress for all Muslim women: "O ye wives of the Prophet! Ye are not like any other women. If ye keep your duty (to Allah), then be not soft of speech, lest he in whose heart is a disease aspire (to you), but utter customary speech. And stay in your houses. Bedizen not yourselves with the bedizenment of the Time of Ignorance. Be regular in prayer, and pay the poor-due, and obey Allah and His messenger. Allah's wish is but to remove uncleanness far from you, O Folk of the Household, and cleanse you with a thorough cleansing."

The above verses have been widely used among Muslims as justification for having Muslim women wear various items of attire. While it is unknown precisely what a *jilbab* looked like at the time of the writing of the Koran, in general it refers to a type of garment that covers the head and is wrapped around a woman's body so as to cover virtually all of it. Most Muslims interpret *khimar* to refer to a headscarf (*hijab*). While it is debatable whether the Koran requires Muslim women to wear *jilbabs* or *khimars*[49] beliefs in the appropriateness of such attire have led to the spread of Middle Eastern styles of dress among Muslims around the world. Sometimes this has resulted in hybrid forms of dress that blend Middle Eastern Muslim fashion with local fashions. In other cases it has resulted in Middle Eastern Muslim fashion replacing local fashion entirely. Elsewhere, the two styles of dress co-exist with some members of a community wearing the imported style and others the local style or the same individuals wearing the imported style on some occasions and the local or another style on other occasions.

Let us use Muslims in Indonesia as a case study. Islam arrived in the northwestern part of Indonesia, in Aceh, in the 1200s and gradually spread to many other parts of the archipelago over the next few centuries. Muslim traders from the Middle East and South Asia introduced Middle Eastern fashion associated with Islam to Indonesia and local rulers usually were the first to convert and to adopt the new fashion. Dijk cites accounts of visitors to Indonesia from Ibn Battuta in the 1300s to Rijkloff van Goens in the 1600s commenting on how local Muslim rulers would wear Middle Eastern style attire on some occasions and local styles of dress on others.[50] Goens describes how the nobles of the kingdom of Mataram in Java in the mid–1600s would assemble and "with great diligence watch to see how the king's head is decked, with a Javanese cap or with a Turkish turban; if the King is wearing a turban, everybody abandons his ordinary cap and takes the other from his servant in order to be like the king."[51] In reference to such situations, Dijk refers to choices of attire as an "expression of the struggle for cultural hegemony which started after the arrival of Islam and the subsequent restoration of Javanese values within a Muslim setting."[52] He mentions as an example of this struggle the story of Raden Patah, who was the legendary founder of Demak, which was Java's first Muslim state. According to legend, "Raden Patah either fell ill or lost consciousness each time he tried to sit down on the throne while dressed as a *haji*. Only after he had put on his Javanese royal headdress and ear ornaments could he do so unscathed."[53]

The arrival of the Dutch in Indonesia in the 1600s created an additional fashion option for local Muslims and non–Muslims, although for the most part, at least initially, the Dutch tried to reserve European fashion for themselves and local Christian converts. Moreover, in areas under their control the Dutch preferred to have different groups wear their own particular style of clothing rather than the newer Muslim or Christian fashions (including ethnic Chinese). Dijk argues that this made it easier for the Dutch to keep track of people.[54] Such rules were not always enforceable and some local rulers wore Dutch fashion on occasion while others wore Middle Eastern Muslim fashion. One account from the 1600s illustrates a Makassarese man wearing a shirt and robe that covers his body from shoulder to knee in Middle Eastern fashion and mentions that while most Acehnese men and women simply wrapped a piece of cloth around their waists, wealthy Acehnese wore "a thin silk or cotton dress-coat ... after the fashion of the Moors [i.e., Middle Eastern Muslims]."[55]

In the case of the Muslim rulers such as the one from Mataram, Muslim fashion was often worn to emphasize the ruler's role as a religious leader. Gradually other Indonesians also adopted the fashion of wearing at least some items of attire associated with Islam when taking part in religious functions. Very few Muslim Indonesians during the Dutch colonial period adopted wearing distinctive Middle Eastern Muslim fashion on daily basis. Among those who did were the few who had taken part in the *hajj*. A few local Muslims who advocated more fundamentalist versions of Islam also wore such dress: "To bring society into conformity with the stricter prescription of Islam, they propagated a somewhat puritanical way of life, and spoke out against gambling, alcoholic drinks, the smoking of opium and tobacco, and the like."[56]

Wearing foreign-inspired fashions was sometimes associated with politics in colonial Indonesia. There are interesting examples of Javanese and Sumatrans adopting Middle Eastern Muslim fashion to indicate their opposition to Dutch colonialism. Kathirithamby-Wells mentions opponents of the Dutch in Banten, Java, discarding "Javanese dress in favour of Arab garb" in the 1670s.[57] Dijk cites examples of anti–Dutch rebels such as the Javanese Prince Dipanagara and the Pradi rebels of central Sumatra in the early 1800s wearing Middle Eastern Islamic attire to emphasize the holy nature of their rebellions.[58] The Pradi, for example, wore white Arab-style clothing and sought to impose strict rules of dress based on their interpretation of Islam.[59] The dress of such rebels led the Dutch often to associate Middle Eastern Muslim fashion in the context of Indonesia with rebelliousness and anti-colonialism.

By the early 1900s an increasing number of Indonesians were adopting European style clothing. Some nationalists saw wearing such clothing as "a sign of emancipation and of defiance towards the Dutch and the rules of dress they wanted to impose."[60] Other nationalists disagreed and advocated retaining local fashion as part of their cultural heritage. The Muslim community itself at this time was divided on the issue of dress. Delegates to the first Sarekat Islam Congress (an Islamic nationalist movement) in 1916 "dressed either in evening dress with a white tie or in a dinner jacket."[61] While some Muslims advocated wearing modern, European-style clothing others argued in favor of Middle Eastern style dress. There was debate over whether it was appropriate for Muslim boys in the Boy Scouts to wear shorts and whether women should wear head shawls. Dijk cites a 1917 article in *Islam Bererak* (Islamic Movement) taking "the side of a schoolgirl of seventeen who did not agree with the practice in Yogyakarta of wearing a veil to safeguard a woman's virtue, reasoning that Java is not Arabia, and following Islam does not necessarily mean complying with Arab rules," although the writer added the girl "should not think that the wearing of the head shawl was an imitation of Arab ways" since "In Arabia there is no woman who wears a head shawl of the type customary in Yogyakarta."[62] Such divergent attitudes highlighted religious differences among Indonesian Muslims: "Muslims from different camps avoided each other's religious gatherings, including the rites and ceremonies marking important stages of the life cycle, such as marriage and death."[63]

In post-colonial Indonesia Western-style dress has become dominant, but often with national touches such as batik shirts. For Indonesian men, Middle Eastern style dress has become a rarity with a white *haji* cap serving as one indictor of religiosity. In addition, men sometimes wear a sarong instead of trousers when going to the mosque. Women's attire, however, continues to be contentious. The growing influence of Middle Eastern Islamic ideas in Indonesia since the 1980s has resulted in the spread of Islamic fashions associated with Arabian Islam in particular, including wearing the *jilbab*. Dijk mentions various Indonesian authors writing on the subject of whether transvestites should wear the *jilbab*: "The comforting answer was that men do not have to wear a *jilbab*; only when a transvestite feels more female than male should s/he do so."[64] Whereas some Muslims influenced by Arabian Islam advocate austere dress for women, the general tendency within Indonesia has been to favor clothing that is viewed as relatively modest in terms of what is covered while still favoring colorful clothing.

Debate surrounding Islamic dress in Indonesia has increased in the 2000s since the fall of Suharto. As Warburton remarks, "Since the fall of Suharto, there's been a serious shift in Indonesian society concerning the jilbab (Islamic headscarf). In the past, most Indonesians considered Islamic dress a matter of private interpretation. But since reformasi local governments and Islamic institutions have begun to force women to cover, while at the national level the proposed anti-pornography laws place restrictions on women's dress and emphasise control of the female body as a tool for social reform. Supporters of these new regulations argue that this is a necessary step for addressing what they see as 'moral crises' of Indonesian society, claiming that jilbab-wearing women will create a more moral and stable community. This increasing public emphasis on female bodies means that women are losing their right to choose if or when they will wear the veil. What was a personal choice has become a political battleground."[65] The Indonesian parliament passed the anti-pornography law mentioned by Warburton in late October 2008 in the face of a variety of criticisms, including from Hindu Balinese who fear that the law will target non–Muslims and hurt the island's tourist industry.[66]

While supporters of the anti-pornography law sought to control women's dress at the national level, greater autonomy of Indonesia's provinces since the fall of Suharto has also allowed some provinces to pass their own laws regulating female dress. The province of Aceh was at the forefront of this following the introduction of *syariah* law in that province in 2001. Syariah police and unofficial Islamic groups have sought to enforce the province's dress code that includes the requirement for women to wear a veil in public. Other local governments in West Java, Banten, and South Sulawesi subsequently passed similar laws. The fear expressed by Balinese Hindus that non–Muslims would be forced to adhere to conservative Muslim dress codes has become a reality in some instances. Thus, in the city of Padang a law was introduced to require female civil servants and female students at state schools to wear veils regardless of their religion. A number of other local governments have passed laws requiring female civil servants and sometimes others to wear veils, headscarves, or other forms of modest attire.

The issue of appropriate attire for Muslim women surfaced in October 2009 when 18-year-old Qory Sandioriva won the Miss Indonesia title. Ms. Sandioriva was born in Jakarta, but entered the contest as an Acehnese because of her mother being Acehnese. She did not wear a veil in the contest and Muslim clerics in Aceh accused her of betraying her Acehnese roots. Ms. Sandioriva responded to the criticism saying that she believed that hair is beauty and that she is proud of beauty. One reporter commented at the time, "The controversy is likely to return next year when she goes on to compete in the Miss Universe contest where she will have to don a swimsuit as part of the pagent." [67] Not only swimming suits, but also tennis/badminton skirts, jogging shorts, and other forms of women's sports wear have often been criticized by conservative Muslims in Indonesia.

Similar developments have taken place in neighboring Malaysia, where in addition to pressure for Malay Muslim women to dress in a particular manner the dress of foreign female and male popular music performers has attracted criticism from local Malay Muslim conservatives in recent years. This is interesting both in regard to it being an attempt by local Muslim conservatives to impose their dress codes on non–Muslims (who in the case of Malaysia represent a considerable proportion of the population), but also in that it pits Arabian-inspired religiously-based views about dress against the Western secular fashion of youth oriented popular entertainers. One of the initial clashes came when the rap-rock group Linkin Park was scheduled to perform in Malaysia in 2003. The Malaysian Ministry of Culture, Arts and Tourism, which must give its permission for such foreign groups to perform in Malaysia, set conditions, stating that "Male artists must cover their bodies from the chest to knee level" and must not wear anything "obscene, linked to drugs or related to negative elements."[68]

Foreign female pop music performers have generated most of the controversy concerning dress in Malaysia with the youth wing of the country's Pan-Malaysian Islamic Party (PAS) taking the lead in this regard. After the Ministry of Culture, Arts and Tourism gave its permission, provided that her costumes not give offense, female singer Mariah Carey was to perform in Malaysia in February 2004. Carey had indicated her willingness to comply with this request. Nevertheless, PAS youth wing leader Ahmad Sabki Yusof wrote a letter to the ministry asking it to rescind its permission: "Everyone knows Mariah Carey presents herself in a sexy, unacceptable and almost vulgar manner. Allowing such concerts promotes and condones values that are totally contrary to our way of life and our culture. We don't want immoral values for our children, whether Muslim or not."[69]

The issue emerged again in 2006 in response to a performance by the group Pussycat Dolls that resulted in a tightening of conservative Muslim-inspired dress regulations. CBS News reported: "A local city council fined organizers for allowing the chart-topping singers to wear skimpy costumes and perform 'sexually suggestive' routines at a recent concert. Foreign artists will now have to follow strict guidelines in their on-stage acts, the government said Thursday. 'We have to have guidelines,' said Siti Zaleha, a senior official at the Culture and Arts ministry. 'We have enforcement officers that will check acts, and report to the relevant authorities for action.' Absolute Entertainment, the local organizer of the Pussycat Dolls concert, was fined $2,714 for flouting decency regulations.... Guidelines for foreign artists were initially drawn up last year, Siti said. The official guide includes: no jumping, shouting or throwing of objects onstage or at the audience; no hugging or kissing audience members or fellow artists; no unnecessary baring of skin, which a female artist needs to cover from the top of her chest to her knees; and clothes should not have obscene or drug-related images or messages. Local sponsors will have to sign a form accepting the guidelines, Siti said, and it will be their responsibility to inform performers of the rules."[70] This new dress code for performers led American pop singer Beyoncé to cancel a proposed performance in 2007 since she would have been required to cover herself from shoulders to knees and show no cleavage. She did, however, perform in Indonesia, "where rules governing stage performances are more relaxed."[71]

The youth wing of the PAS asserted itself again in 2008 in response to a proposed performance by pop star Avril Lavigne. A representative of the youth wing is quoted as saying Lavigne's show was "considered too sexy for us. We don't want our people, our teenagers, influenced by their performance. We want clean artists, artists that are good role models."[72] Under pressure from the youth wing, the ministry revoked permission for the performance. Later, however, the show was allowed to go ahead. A spokesman from the PAS youth wing responded threatening, "If the concert organisers do not heed this warning to cancel the concert, PAS youth will order all Muslim youth to turn up and protest the concert in order to prevent it from taking place."[73] Faced with similar protests from the PAS youth wing against "Western sexy performances," Beyoncé postponed a proposed performance in Malaysia in October 2009 following negotiations between her agents and the ministry over appropriate costumes.

The debate in Malaysia concerning the attire of Western pop music performers concerns a variety of issues surrounding tradition and modernity and a battle to influence the dress of Malaysian youth. How a person dresses is often seen as reflecting either traditional or modern values, usually in oppositional terms. Thus, while conservative Malay Muslims seek to have women dress according to dress traditions harking back 1500 years to the fashions of early medieval Arabia as a symbol of Muslim morality, performers such as the Pussycat Dolls see their attire as representing the cutting edge of modern popular fashion. Of course, what is considered to be traditional dress today at one time was also considered a cutting edge fashion — as, undoubtedly were the first women's veils introduced to the Arabian Peninsula from the eastern Mediterranean.

Dress and Ethnic Identity

There is a long tradition of styles of dress being associated with ethnic identity. This should be seen in a context whereby until recently most people in the world made their own clothing and to a greater extent dress styles reflected local technology and ideals about dress. The history of textile production and styles of dress is largely one of diffusion, followed by local adaptation. What concerns us here is where such local adaptations by particular groups come to be viewed as a manifestation of their identity. The use of dress as an identity marker has a number of aspects that are of relevance. Thus, part of the nation-building efforts of political leaders in states often involves the promotion of some form of national — i.e., state — dress. Examples include batik decorative clothing in Indonesia and the Vietnamese *ao dai*. The modern *ao dai* (long shirt) is a modified version of the *ao ngu than,* a five paneled gown worn by members of the Nguyen court in Hue following a decree by Nguyen Phuc Khoat in 1744 creating a fashion that was distinct from the clothing worn by the rival Trinh Lords in Hanoi. The *ao dai* was designed by a group of artists, including Nguyen Cat Tuong, affiliated with Hanoi University in the 1920s who were influenced by trends in Paris fashion. Initially it was worn mainly in southern Vietnam and it fell out of favor during the early years of communist rule. With the onset of economic and cultural revival in Vietnam in the early 1990s the government sought to promote the *ao dai* as a national dress for all Vietnamese.[74] In regard to transnationalism, ethnic Vietnamese women in countries around the world commonly wear the *ao dai* when wishing to highlight their ethnic identity. Moreover, *ao dai* fashions are constantly changing and there is considerable interest among overseas Vietnamese in keeping up with *ao dai* fashion trends in Vietnam.

Although promoted as the national dress of Vietnam, the *ao dai* is essentially a style of dress associated with the ethnic majority. This is a fairly common trend, whereby the political ascendancy of a particular ethnic group may also result in their style of ethnic dress being elevated to national dress at a state level. In the case of Vietnam, most of Vietnam's ethnic minorities do not wear *ao dai,* often have their own distinctive style of dress, and tend to view the *ao dai* as Kinh dress. Moreover, the government of Vietnam has not only been tolerant of these tendencies, but has promoted the wearing of distinctive ethnic dress among the country's minorities rather than pursuing a rigid policy of assimilation in regard to dress. This usually is not much of an issue in transnational terms since most overseas Vietnamese are from the Kinh ethnic majority of Vietnam or from the culturally similar Sino-Vietnamese ethnic group. It becomes of relevance in the case of refugees from the Central Highlands of Vietnam who have their own dress traditions. These people often identify themselves more with their particular ethnic group than with the Vietnamese state and tend not to mix with overseas Vietnamese of Kinh or Sino-Vietnamese backgrounds. As mentioned previously, there are also ethnic Thai from Vietnam living overseas. These people also tend to wear their distinctive ethnic dress rather than *ao dai* and to identify more closely with other Tai-speaking peoples such as Lao from Laos than with Kinh from Vietnam. In general, of course, overseas Vietnamese, whether Kinh or non–Kinh, do not wear *ao dai* on an everyday basis. With the rise of more generic ready-to-wear clothing globally it is increasingly common for ethnic styles of dress to be worn only on special occasions.

Hmong-speaking peoples who have settled around the world provide an interesting example of transnational ethnic dress in relation to a people who have often sought to retain a distinctive identity in a variety of states. The Hmong's homeland is in China. The expansion of Han political power in northern and central China starting around 2,300 years ago resulted in the gradual assimilation of some Hmong and was one of the factors leading to the southward migration of other Hmong. Today the Hmong people are found scattered across parts of southern China and Mainland Southeast Asia in Vietnam, Laos, Thailand, and Burma. In addition, largely as a result of the communist seizure of power in Laos in 1975 there are also Hmong living in many other parts of the world, especially in the United States, where they went initially as refugees.

The spread of the Hmong from their original homeland within China led to the emergence of numerous sub-groups of Hmong. Sub-groups in Vietnam, for example, include the White Hmong, a sub-group of White Hmong called Striped Hmong, Flowery Hmong, Blue Hmong, Black Hmong, and Red Hmong. In Laos, where there are fewer Hmong, White Hmong and Blue Hmong are the largest sub-groups. Many of the Hmong in Laos fought against the communists in the 1960s and 1970s and a large number of them subsequently fled across the Mekong River to Thailand after the communist victory in Laos in 1975, where they were placed in refugee camps. In these camps there was considerable mixing of White Hmong and Blue Hmong. Relatively few of these Hmong refugees were allowed to settle outside of the camps in Thailand. Most were forced to migrate to third countries with the Untied States taking by far the largest number. At present there are around 250,000 Hmong in the United States. Elsewhere there are around 15,000 in France, 2,000 in Australia, 2,000 in French Guyana, and small numbers in Canada, Argentina, and Germany.

The dress of each of the Hmong sub-groups is different and their names reflect dominant aspects of their dress, largely in relation to the color of clothing worn by women. Thus, White Hmong women wear wrap-around skirts that are predominantly white,

Flowery Hmong women wear wrap-around skirts featuring a variety of colors, Red Hmong women wear wrap-around skirts with more red than the skirts of others, and Black Hmong women wear wrap-around skirts with more black than the skirts of others. The relative isolation of most Hmong within the countries where they settled meant until recently that there was relatively little external influence on their styles of dress. The Na Hmong of northern Vietnam provide an example of a group of Hmong who settled near Tay and Nung and adopted the dress styles of these groups,[75] but there are few other examples of such acculturation. The influence of Han (Chinese) fashion on Hmong dress is most evident in regard to the adoption of trousers not only on the part of men but also by women. It is relatively common among many groups of Hmong in Southeast Asia in recent times for women to wear plain dark-colored trousers, often made of commercial cotton fabric, for everyday wear and to reserve their decorative wrap-around skirts for special occasions.

Life in the refugee camps of Thailand influenced Hmong dress and textile production in a number of ways. To begin with there was some blurring of dress differences as Blue Hmong and White Hmong mixed in these camps. The camps also saw the introduction of commercial production of textiles as a means of generating income starting in 1975. Previously, textiles were produced solely for use within the family or as gifts. Cohen argues that the textiles produced in these camps for sale "tend to lose their individuality, and come to resemble industrial products."[76] Efforts to promote economic development in the camps led in particular to the creation of an entirely new type of textile known as story blankets.[77]

Both commercialization of textile production and a blending of dress styles continued among the Hmong groups that were resettled outside of Southeast Asia. The production of story cloths as other textile forms featuring embroidered and appliqué patterning continued to be developed as a means of generating income especially by the Hmong who settled in the United States.[78] In addition, however, the Hmong in these countries had become ethnic minorities living in close proximity to others and subject to a much greater extent to acculturative pressures. This was especially true of young Hmong who attended ethnically mixed schools and generally developed a better command of the local language than older Hmong. Regardless of their age most Hmong quickly adapted local dress styles, while traditional Hmong dress was worn only on special occasions, such as at weddings or New Year celebrations. Lynch in a discussion of Hmong in the United States describes the clothing worn by young Hmong at New Year celebrations in St. Paul, Minnesota, in the 1980s: "it was generally designed by older women in the community. Older styles of Lao Hmong dress were transformed through the process of cultural authentification to reflect American as well as Hmong culture. Teenagers and the older women who sewed the garments drew inspiration from the range of cloth and trims available in American fabric stores to create ensembles that, while rooted in Hmong prototypes, were a creative blend of both Hmong and American influences."[79]

As for particular styles of dress that are associated with different groups of Hmong back in Southeast Asia, Lynch comments that at a 1988 New Year celebration she noticed that while the clothing that Hmong girls were wearing were designed to reflect the styles of the different groups, rather than girls wearing only the style associated with their particular group, they sometimes wore the styles of other groups. She found that "Teenage girls typically owned and wore a variety of sub-styles of dress" and when she asked the girls about this "Most teenagers simply told me it was the new style, the American way" and that "being a Hmong American rather than a Lao Hmong was often associated with the freedom to wear other sub-groups' styles."[80]

A new development in recent years among overseas Hmong is to import part or all of their costumes from Laos. Political reforms in Laos, making communication with Hmong in Laos and even visits back to Laos possible, has generated a trade with Hmong in Laos providing traditional clothing to overseas Hmong communities. Restrictions imposed by the United States on trade with Laos, however, created some obstacles for Hmong living in the United States. After the communist seizure of power in Laos in 1975 Laos became one of a handful of countries in the world that was denied Normal Trade Relations by the United States government. This meant that while goods from Laos could be imported into the United States they were assessed at much higher rates of duty than goods from countries with NTR status. Writing on the rate assessed for Laos, Gresser noted, "The average country receiving NTR tariff rates faced 2.4 percent tariffs on average.... By contrast, Laos faced a rate of over 45 percent. In actual dollar terms, Lao and Hmong businesses paid $1.8 million to the U.S. Customs Services in order to sell $3.9 million worth of goods."[81] Gresser also points out that while "Traditional clothing is a successful export for Hmong families in Thailand" it is "difficult, given the high tariffs, for Hmong families in Laos to export."[82] This situation ended after the United States extended normal trade relations to Laos in December 2004 and a Bilateral Trade Agreement came into force in February 2005. Since then there has been an increase in exports from Laos to the United States, including Hmong clothing.

9

THE ARTS

The arts are an important component of transnational relations. They may serve as reminders of links across borders, as symbols of ties to another place or society, and as a means of promoting a feeling of being part of a transnational community. In addition to such symbolic aspects of the arts, artists themselves may lead transnational lives as they move between locales where their art is appreciated or in demand.

Since antiquity, with the formation of states and empires, artists have migrated to centers of political and economic power. In the case of empires, such as those of ancient Rome and China, not only were artists attracted to the capital and other urban centers, but artists also toured throughout the empires. Thus, there was a flow of artistic forms and of the artists themselves within the empires. This was made possible by the political unity of the empire and the spread of a common language. The spread of artistic forms served to help bind the empire together. In modern times artists have moved around the globe both between different cultures and among peoples with similar cultures scattered around the world. Those artists moving across cultures often serve to blend or spread artistic traditions while those moving within scattered migrant communities help to maintain artistic traditions across borders.

The impetus for the creation of transnational arts can come from a variety of sources. For example, members of migrant communities who view the arts of their homeland or the homeland of their ancestors as a part of their heritage and as serving a role in creating their ethnic identity often seek to bring these arts with them. Such individuals may actively import art forms, sponsor visits by artists, or promote instruction in the arts from their homeland. Art forms may also travel across borders to those who do not necessarily have a link of birth or ancestry, but because they are associated with what is perceived to be a higher civilization or simply out of a desire for variety and because they represent something different. In modern times the export and import of arts also may have a commercial dimension as companies and entrepreneurs seek to profit from international trade in the arts.

Transnational art may have political dimensions as well, as in cases where countries seek to export their arts in an effort to promote their influence abroad. This may be part of a strategy of spreading their cultural values beyond state borders to promote trade or political influence. In this regard, the arts can become a tool of what Nye refers to as "soft power," which rests on "the ability to shape the preferences of others" in order to get them to do what you want without having to "use carrots or sticks to make you do it."[1] Such strategies may focus on other states with which the exporting country wishes to strengthen relations. They sometimes also focus more specifically on overseas migrant communities with which the state wishes to promote relations. In recent years the communist regime in the PRC has sought to employ the arts as part of its soft power strategy. Kurlantzick discusses the "tools of culture" that the PRC has come to employ as part of its strategy to enhance its influence around the world: "tools related to Chinese culture and arts and language and ethnicity."[2] Nyíri notes how the arts are part of an effort by the PRC to construct "a 'global Chinese' identity with shared values, raising cultural Chineseness and transnational modernity in importance above the immediate environment" of ethnic Chinese living outside of the PRC.[3]

Categorizing the Arts and Their Cultural Context

The arts are comprised of performing arts, plastic arts, and literature. Performing arts include story telling, music, dance, and theater. Plastic arts include drawing, iconography, painting, sculpture and carving, textile arts, pottery, and architecture. In the case of transnationalism, we are especially interested in artists who lead transnational lives and transnational contexts within which works of art appear, especially where they serve as an important part of ties that bind transnational communities together across borders.

Establishing what constitutes an art or work of art as distinct from, for example, a craft is not an easy matter. In general, artistic expression is associated "with the production or performance of something that is judged to have a special aesthetic quality to it either by members of a particular society or cross-culturally."[4] According to this definition, crafts have the potential to be works of art. Thus, while most ceramic bowls or woven pieces of cloth are not works of art, people may judge exceptional ones to be, based on special aesthetic qualities that set them apart from their utilitarian functions.

It is a common practice to distinguish between folk arts and fine arts or courtly arts. This is a distinction that reflects the emergence of hierarchy and specialization. Even in societies with relatively little hierarchy or specialization there is recognition of individual differences in talent, and some individuals are singled out for their abilities to produce items or performances of exceptional quality. Thus, works of art can be produced in such societies. What is generally lacking in these societies is the occupation of artist. The existence of external markets, however, can create opportunities for individuals of talent to become specialized artists who produce works of folk art. In the case of courtly/fine arts such specialization is the norm. The individuals producing these works of art commonly have received specialized training and devote themselves on a full-time basis to their art. The occupation of artist is especially important in relation to transnationalism in regard to such artists who themselves and whose works of art cross borders.

Whether folk art or fine art, the arts take place within a cultural context. This is certainly true in regard to views concerning what constitutes a fine art. Thus, in the Western world it is not common for textiles to come to mind in the realm of art and certainly in terms of fine arts. Since Western perceptions of art have tended to be dominant globally in the modern world this perception has spread beyond the West even to parts of the world such as Asia, where finely woven textiles have a long history of being more highly regarded than in the West.

Some idea of differing views of art can be seen in contrasting the fairly low regard for artisanal crafts in comparison with what are categorized as fine arts in the West with the relatively high status that the Japanese assign to artisanship. Fearing the loss of valued traditional arts after World War II the Japanese government initiated a program of recognizing and supporting important intangible cultural properties in 1954.[5] Grants were given to individuals and they were encouraged to train students. Pottery making was the first art form recognized under this program. Subsequent artists to be recognized under this system of awards have included weavers, *yuzen* (designers and dyers of kimono fabrics), bamboo plaiters, paper-makers, Bunraku puppeteers, sword-makers, other metal casters, Noh dramatic theater actors, Kabuki theater actors, potters, and traditional musicians. Over time the system came to focus more on the individual artists than the art form and awards were given to those designed National Living Treasures.

Western views about what constitutes art is of relevance to transnationalism both in terms of how this notion has spread to other countries in modern times as a result of the dominance of the West as well as in regard to how the arts of non–Western migrants to predominantly Western countries are judged by the population of these countries at large. Thus, whereas Western fine arts are promoted as fine art in a general sense in countries such as the United States and Canada, there has been a tendency to judge the arts of non–Western migrants to these countries or of their indigenous inhabitants by Western standards as if these standards were universal and to associate them with a particular ethnic group, thereby placing them in the lesser category of ethnic arts.

Despite claims of universality, artistic forms are deeply embedded in particular cultures in relation to perceptions of beauty and aesthetics, the language employed, preferences concerning the materials used, and their association with religious, political, and other beliefs.

Transnational Performing Arts

Our look at the performing arts will focus on forms of music, dance, and theater that developed in Western Europe and Asia first as local art forms, then as regional ones, and finally as transnational forms spanning the globe. To the ancient Greeks the arts of music, dance, and theater were associated with the Muses who, so they believed, lived on Mt. Helicon, near the birthplace of the poet Hesiod who composed the *Theogony,* the genealogy of the gods. Seven of the nine Muses are of relevance here: Euterpe the muse of lyric poetry, Thalia of comic drama and idyllic poetry, Melpomene of tragedy, Terpsichore of choral dance and song, Erato of love verse and mimicry, Polymnia of hymns, and Caliope of epic poetry.[6] The cult of the Muses had its origins in Thrace, which was the home of the singers and bards Orpheus, Musaeus, and Thamyris, who Durant refers to as "the half legendary founders of Greek music."[7] The cult of the Muses diffused from Thrace throughout the Hellenic world.

The spread of Greek colonies around the Mediterranean served to diffuse the Greek performing arts among Greek migrant communities, but it was the Roman Empire that served to ensure that these arts became a fundamental element of Western culture transcending their national association. The popularity of Greek arts in Rome and their spread throughout its empire helped to ensure that these arts became an integral part of Western civilization over the next two thousand years. In modern times they assumed a transnational importance by providing cultural links between different Western states and a context within which artists could move across borders. Greco-Roman performing arts went into decline following the fall of Rome, but underwent a renaissance with the onset of the Modern Era, when they became an important element of the emerging transnational culture of Western Europe. This renaissance began in Italy, where modern art forms such as ballet and opera were created that often had links to the Greco-Roman past and then spread to other parts of Europe largely via the feudal courts.

European Opera

The creation of modern European opera is closely linked to ancient Greek drama: "Toward the close of the sixteenth century a group of musical and literary enthusiasts, meeting in the home of Giovanni Bardi in Florence, proposed to revive the musical drama of the Greeks by freeing song from the heavy polyphony and drowned-out language of the madrigals, and restoring it to what they believed to be the monodic style of ancient tragedy." *Dafne,* the story of Apollo falling in love with the nymph Daphne, composed by Jacopo Peri in 1597 was the first opera to be produced as a result of this initiative. Next came *Euridice* in 1600, produced to celebrate the marriage of Henry IV and Maria de Medici in Florence, and *Orfeo* in 1607.

Opera spread from Italy to Germany. Heinrich Schutz was born in Saxony in 1585 and in 1609 he went to Venice to study music. He then returned to Saxony, where he became the director of music at the court of John George, the Elector of Saxony. Schutz wrote a German version of Peri's *Dafne* in 1627 to celebrate the marriage of the Elector of Saxony — making it the first German opera. He made another visit to Italy after this and worked for various royal courts before returning to Dresden in 1645. Italian influence on opera in Germany is also evident in the case of later operas composed by Christoph Willibald Gluck (1714–87) and Wolfgang Amadeus Mozart (1756–91).

Although Mozart is primarily associated with Austria and the German-speaking world, his life had a broader transnational side to it. He was born in Salzburg and then performed around Europe for a time as a child prodigy. He performed before the courts in Munich, Vienna, Prague, Mannheim, Paris, London, The Hague, Zurich, and Donaueschingen. He traveled to Italy with his father from late 1769 to early 1771. While in Milan in 1770 he wrote the opera *Mitridate, re di Ponto.* The success of this opera resulted in commissions for two additional operas, *Ascanio in Alba* and *Lucio Silla*. He traveled to Milan from Austria for the premieres of both operas. Mozart's father hoped that these operas would lead to his son finding employment in Italy. Instead he became a court musician for Prince Archbishop Hieronymus Colloredo of Salzburg.[9]

The pay was poor in Salzburg and there was no local support for the opera. These circumstances led Mozart to look for work elsewhere in Europe, including to Munich, where he was able to have his opera *La finta giardiniera* performed. His mother, who accompanied him, died during one of these trips in search of work in Paris in 1778. Unable to find employment, he returned to work in Salzburg in 1779. While there he wrote a new opera, *Idomeneo,* which was performed in Munich in 1781. Following this he again left Salzburg and moved to Vienna to work on a freelance basis. The following year he wrote another opera, *Die Entführung aus dem Serail* (The Abduction from the Seraglio). After its premiere in Vienna it was performed elsewhere in German-speaking Europe.

Mozart returned to opera in 1785, when he began work on *The Marriage of Figaro* in collaboration with Venetian librettist Lorenzo Da Ponte. *The Marriage of Figaro* premiered in Vienna in 1786 and was performed in Prague the following year. The two men then went to work on a new opera, *Don Giovanni*, which premiered in Prague 1787 and was performed in Vienna in 1788. In 1787 he also gained an appointment as chamber composer for Emperor Joseph II (the position had become vacant with the death of Gluck, to be discussed below). In part to augment his income, Mozart traveled to a variety of German-speaking cities in 1789 and 1790. Prior to his death the following year he composed additional operas, *The Magic Flute* and *La clemenza di Tito.*

Christoph Willibald Gluck (1714–87) was even more of a transnational artist than Mozart.[10] Gluck was born in Bavaria and went to Prague to attend university in 1731. He then moved to Milan to study music in 1737, where he wrote his first opera. In 1745 he was invited to be the house composer at London's King Theater. In 1747 and 1748 he wrote operas for Dresden and Vienna and joined Pietro Mingotti's opera company (which traveled throughout Western Europe from the 1730s through the 1750s) as musical director. Gluck went with Mingotti's company to Copenhagen at the invitation of Queen Louise to perform for the royal court. In 1750 he left Copenhagen to join a new troupe and return to Prague. He married and began commuting between Prague and Vienna as well as spending a short time in Naples to write another opera. He settled in Vienna in 1754. Among the operas that he composed after his court appointment was *Orfeo ed Euridice* in 1762, in which Orfeo seeks to rescue his wife Euridice from the Underworld. One of his former students, Marie Antoinette, married Louis XVI of France in 1770, and she invited him to write eight operas for the Paris Opera. A number of these were based on Classical Greek themes, including *Iphigénie en Aulide* in 1774 and *Iphigénie en Tauride* in 1779.

Opera was already well established in France by the 1770s, having been introduced during the reign of Louis XIV (reigned 1643–1715), in part through the influence of the king's regent, Cardinal Mazarin, who had been born in Italy. Francesco Sacrati's Italian opera *La finta pazza* was performed before the court in 1645. These and other Italian operas were not particularly popular since many at the court were hostile to Cardinal

Mazarin. Opera gained in popularity after Louis XIV assumed full royal powers in 1661. Giovanni di Lulli (Jean-Baptiste Lully) (1632–87) had been born in Florence and came to France in 1646. He gained employment as a dancer in Louis XIV's court in 1653 and came to the king's attention with the performance of the *Ballet de la Nuit* for which he composed the music. The king made him a court composer and he proceeded to produce a number of ballets (in which he performed) and musical comedies based on the work of Molière. By 1670 the king had lost his interest in ballet and Lulli no longer was able to perform. Lulli shifted his interest to opera. Pierre Perrin and Robert Cambert had opened the country's first *salle de l'opera* in 1671, with the patronage of Louis XIV. Lulli bought the rights to the opera from Perrin and came to monopolize opera in Paris until his death. He composed 14 operas starting with *Cadmus et Hermione* in 1673 and ending with *Achille et Polyxène* in 1687 (which was completed by Pascal Collasse). As with *Cadmus et Hermione,* which is a love story involving Cadmus, the founder and king of Thebes, and Hermione, daughter of Venus and Mars, many of these operas were based of Classical Greek stories. Lulli adopted Venetian opera to suit French tastes in a style known as *tragédie en musique.* In addition to these serious operas there was also a genre known as Comédie-Italienne, which was initially performed by Italian actors speaking Italian, but later performances were based on the work of French playwrights.

During the 1800s, although local styles of opera flourished around Europe, there continued to be considerable interaction across borders as artists toured and moved about the continent and opera houses staged performances of both national and foreign operas. One thing that remained constant was the popularity of Italian opera. Gioachino Antonio Rossini (1792–1868) was undoubtedly the most popular opera composer of the century. Born in Pesaro, Italy, he composed his first opera, a comedy named *La cambiale di matrimonio,* in Venice in 1810. An additional fifteen operas later he composed another comedy, *Il barbiere di Siviglia,* in Rome in 1816. He then composed more than a dozen dramatic operas. The popularity of his operas outside of Italy led to his being invited to London in 1823 by the manager of the King's Theatre. He was introduced to King George IV, paid a handsome stipend, and took up residence there for five months. He had stopped off in Paris on his way to London and was now invited to take up to post of musical director of the Théâtre-Italien, which he took up in 1824. Along with this he also became the chief composer to the king and inspector-general of singing in France. He composed six more operas in Paris, including *Ivanhoe* in 1826, *Le siège de Corinthe* in 1826, *Moïse et Pharaon* in 1827, and *Guillaume Tell* in 1829. He was now a fairly rich man and with the close of the opera season in 1829 he left Paris and moved to Bologna.

The Teatro San Carlo in Naples was widely considered to be the premiere opera house in Europe in the late eighteenth century and it attracted the leading opera performers from around Europe. One of these was the singer Isabella Colbran (1785–1845). She was born in Madrid and moved to Naples where she became the prima donna of the Teatro San Carlo. The theater's impresario, Domenico Barbaia, commissioned Rossini to compose a number of operas to feature the singing of Colbran. The first of these, written in 1815, was *Elisabetta, regina d'Inghilterra,* followed by *Otello, ossia il Moro di Venezia.* Colbran and Rossini were married in 1822. The two then traveled to Vienna and

Venice, where she starred in the opera *Semiramide* that Rossini had composed. The couple separated in 1837.

Angelica Catalani (1780–1849) was one of Europe's leading female opera singers in the early nineteenth century. She was born in Italy and began performing in Venice in 1795. Her popularity in Italy resulted in invitations to perform throughout Europe, starting with London in 1806. In addition to being a prima donna who performed around Europe, she also took up the post of manager of the Paris opera. During one of her tours in 1827 she was made a member of the Royal Swedish Academy of Arts. She retired from performing in 1828 and moved to Florence in 1830, where she established a singing school for girls. She continued to travel around Europe and died of cholera in Paris in 1849.

The transnational character of the European opera world changed significantly during the late nineteenth and early twentieth centuries as a result of improvements in transportation that facilitated long-distance travel of performing artists and with introduction of gramophone records. These technological innovations allowed for European performing arts such as opera to be performed and heard around the world, especially in those countries with large European settler populations. Emile Berliner who began marketing them in Europe through his Berliner Gramophone company in 1889, which later became Deutsche Gramophone, first produced gramophone records. He then founded the United States Gramophone Company in 1894 to market records in the United States. This company became the Victor Talking Machine Company in 1900, which was purchased by RCA in 1929. He established the Gramophone Company in the United Kingdom in 1897, which became the Gramophone & Typewriter Company and then became part of EMI in 1931.

The Italian tenor Enrico Caruso (1873–1921) was one of the early recording industry's most successful artists.[11] He was born in Naples and first performed at the Teatro Nuovo in Naples in 1895 and in 1900 he was given a contract to perform at La Scala opera house, which at the time was widely considered to be the best in Italy. Like other opera stars before him, Caruso then performed in other Europe cities, such as Monte Carlo, Warsaw, London, and St. Petersburg. In the case of London, the Royal Opera House arranged for him to appear in eight different Italian operas over a season. Unlike opera stars of a century earlier, however, he also traveled to Buenos Aires, where there was a large Italian settler population, to perform at the city's Teatro Colón (to be discussed below). After performing in Italy, Portugal, and South America, in 1903 he went to New York City where he had a contract with the Metropolitan Opera.

Prior to his performing debut in the English-speaking world, Caruso had made a series of recordings for the Gramophone & Typewriter Company of the United Kingdom in a hotel room in Milan. By the time he came to New York City the ten disk set that had come out of this recording session was a bestseller in the recording industry and had spread his popularity throughout the English-speaking world. Shortly after his first performance in New York City Caruso's agent, Pasquale Simonelli, negotiated a recording contract for him with Victor Talking Machine Company. He made his first record for the company in 1904 and between then and 1920 he made over 260 recordings for the company. These records were immensely successful and served not only to boost Caruso's career and to help make him a very wealthy man (as well as producing significant profits for the Victor company), but also allowed people throughout the United States and around the world to listen to him through these recordings rather than having to rely on live stage performances. Also important was the fact that those who bought his records as well as who came to hear him perform included not only aristocrats and wealthy elites, but also many members of the middle class of Europe, North America, and Latin America. Outside of Europe, his recordings were sold especially to Italian migrants, but many non–Italians were also introduced to opera through these recordings.

Between 1904 and 1920 Caruso performed at the Metropolitan Opera in New York City for eighteen seasons, while also continuing to tour extensively. These tours took him to cities throughout the United States, Canada, Latin America, and Western Europe. In Latin America he performed in Argentina, Uruguay, and Brazil in 1917, in Mexico City in 1919, and in Havana in 1920 (where he was paid U.S. $10,000 for a one-night perform-ance). Caruso bought a large country house near Florence in 1904, where he lived in between his time in New York City and tours. In New York City he lived mainly in the famous Knickerbocker Hotel, which was built by John Jacob Astor and opened in 1906. Caruso married New Yorker Dorothy Park Benjamin in 1918 and he died in Italy in 1921.

Performances of the Metropolitan Opera commenced with Charles Goudod's *Faust* with Swedish soprano Christina Nilsson in the starring role at the opera house in New York in 1883 and in Philadelphia in 1884. Germans performed most of the initial operas, but in the 1890s its finances improved and it began to evolve into one of the world's leading opera theaters that attracted artists from a number of different countries, includ-ing, as in the case of Caruso, from Italy. The Metropolitan Opera was also a pioneer in the production of live radio broadcasts of its operas. Two live performances were broadcast as far as Newark, New Jersey, in 1910. Then on Christmas Day in 1931, motivated in part by a desire to expand its audience in the face of financial difficulties following the onset of the Great Depression, it broadcast a performance of Englebert Humperdinck's opera *Hänsel und Gretel* over national network radio. Regular network radio broadcasts of its performances began in 1933.

While opera was popular among elites of European background, in many parts of the world outside of Europe, as noted above, it was also popular among members of the middle classes of European background. Increasing numbers of Italian and German settler migrants to countries like the United States, Argentina, and Brazil during the latter part of the nineteenth century resulted in the building of opera houses in cities where large numbers of European migrants settled. For example, there were over 500,000 Italians liv-ing in New York City in Caruso's time. By the end of the nineteenth century Argentina and Brazil were home not only to a large Italian and German migrant population, but also to several important opera houses and local opera companies. The opera companies employed local talent, imported artists from Europe, and also sponsored performances by visiting opera stars.

A 2008 article in *The Economist*, refers to the Teatro Colón in Buenos Aires as "Latin America's most famous opera house."[12] The city's growing European migrant population and economic prosperity in the 1850s was accompanied by increasing demand for European-style opera with 54 operas being performed by a variety of touring companies in 1854. The popularity of these operas led to the construction of the first Teatro Colón, which opened in Buenos Aires in 1857 with a performance of Verdi's *La Traviata* with Italian tenor Enrico Tamberlik (1820–89) appearing in the role of Alfredo. Construction of a new Teatro Colón commenced in 1889. Italian businessman Angelo Ferrari financed the project and the building was designed by two Italian-born architects, Francesco Tamburini (1846–91) and Vittorio Meano (1860–1904). Tamburini migrated to Argentina from Naples in 1881 and in 1883 he was appointed inspector general of National Architecture. Meano migrated to Argentina from Turin in 1884 and was employed by Tamburini. They designed the new theater in an Italian style and it was intended to have features that compared with the best of European opera houses. Construction of the new theater was beset with financial and other difficulties, including the death of Tamburini in 1891 followed by the death of Ferrari and murder of Meano in 1904. Completion of the building fell to a Belgian-born architect, Julio Dormal (1846–1924), who had studied architecture in Paris and migrated to Argentina in 1868. Dormal modified the original plans by adding French decorative features. The theater finally opened in 1908 with a performance of Verdi's *Aïda* and assumed a status in the opera world comparable to La Scala in Milan and the Metropolitan Opera in New York City. In the years following its opening the Teatro Colón saw performances by many of the world's leading composers, conductors, opera singers, and ballet dancers.

Other prominent theaters catering to performances of European-style opera, orchestral music, and ballet were built in Argentina in the nineteenth century. The second most important of these after the Teatro Colón is the Teatro Argentina de La Plata. Italian-born architect Leopoldo Ricchi designed it. Construction commenced in 1887 and it opened in 1890 with a performance of Verdi's *Otello*. Another was Teatro Opera in Buenos Aires, which opened in 1872 with a performance of Verdi's *Il Trovatore*.

Foreign, primarily European, opera singers who came to Buenos Aires to perform also often included other South American cities such as Montevideo, Rio de Janeiro, and São Paulo in their tours. These cities also boasted large opera theaters such as the Teatro D. Pedro II that was named after Brazil's ruling monarch and opened in 1871. In 1875 it was renamed Teatro Imperial D. Pedro II and after the end of the monarchy it was renamed Teatro Lyrico in 1890.

Brazil also possessed another, more remote opera theater, the Teatro Amazonas, in the city of Manaus located on the Amazon River. This theater was a manifestation of the wealth created by the rubber boom in the Amazon region that commenced in 1879 and lasted until 1912. The boom attracted large numbers of migrants to the region and boosted infrastructural construction there as well. The plan was proposed and approved by politicians representing the region in 1881–2 and the budget for construction came from state funds. Its supporters saw it as a means of promoting the city as a center of civilization—in this case, European civilization. An Italian-born architect, Celestial Sacardim, was commissioned to plan the theater and construction began in 1884. Many of the items used in construction and decoration of the theater were imported from Europe, including 32,000 tiles for its roof from Alsace, steel for the walls and wrought iron staircases from England, marble for the stairs and columns from Italy, furniture and other furnishing from Paris, and marble statues from Italy, Murano glass chandeliers from Venice, a curtain with a painting of the "Meeting of the Waters" by Crispim do Amaral was made in Paris. Even the wood used in construction, though it was Brazilian, was sent to Europe to be carved and polished. The theater was finally completed in late 1896 and opened on New Year's Eve 1897 with a performance of Ponchielli's *La Gioconda.*

The collapse of the rubber boom two years later, however, resulted in the opera house being closed. Lamb, who refers to it as a "folly" of the rubber boom that was "immortalised in Werner Herzog's film *Fitzcarraldo* about an Irishman who dreams of Caruso performing in the jungle," describes its subsequent history: "The rubber barons went back to Europe and for years the theatre sat rotting in the tropical heat. Sporadic attempts to renovate and reopen it spluttered out. The stage was used as a football pitch, the auditorium as storage for petrol. The last restoration was in 1990 but plans for a grand opening were thwarted when Brazil's then President, Fernando Collor, decided to freeze the nation's bank accounts."[13] Then in the mid–1990s the state's newly elected governor Amazonio Mendes sought to resurrect the theater with a high quality orchestra, choir, and ballet. The artists had to be imported: "Manaus has become the focus of a most unlikely musical migration. Some of Eastern Europe's best musicians have been tempted from such orchestras as the Kirov to Manaus with the lure of much higher wages. In fact, 39 of the 54-member Amazon Philharmonic orchestra are from Bulgaria, Belarus and Russia. Even the archivist hails from Belarus."[14] The government also opened a music school to encourage the development of local talent. The first Festival Amazonas de Opera was held in 2001. The 2008 festival featured a contemporary opera named *Ca Ira* by former leader of the rock group Pink Floyd Roger Waters about the French Revolution that had premiered in Rome in 2005.[15]

Chinese Opera

The other major form of opera is associated with China. Early forms of opera known as *canjun* opera developed as early as the Three Kingdoms Period (AD 220–280). Classic Chinese opera (*xiqu*) came into being during the reign of Emperor Xuanzong (reigned AD 712–56) of the Tang Dynasty (AD 618–907). Chang and Halliday make the point that "Unlike opera in the West, Chinese opera was popular entertainment ... different regions had developed their distinctive styles, performed in village markets as well as city theaters, danced in the northern mountains amidst winds and dust, and sung under moonlight and kerosene lamps on southern islets, listened to by fishermen on houseboats."[16]

Traditional Chinese opera within China virtually vanished after the communists led by Mao Tse Tung came to power, especially when he launched the so-called Great Proletarian Cultural Revolution in the 1960s that sought to destroy such traditional aspects of Chinese culture. Older forms of drama employing song and dance were replaced with new ones with highly propagandistic themes. Mao's wife Jiang Qing (1914–91) had run away from home at the age of 14 to join a traveling opera troupe,[17] though she later became a movie actress. Mao's love of opera and Jiang's operatic background did not spare this art form and Mao launched a movement to suppress traditional opera (along with many other traditional arts) in 1963, including a bonfire made of opera costumes and sets lit by members of the Red Guard at the outset of the Cultural Revolution in 1966.[18]

After the death of Mao in 1976 traditional art forms slowly revived, although still within a context of communist political influence.[19] The government sponsored a revival of traditional Peking Opera in the early 1990s, including a Peking Opera Festival in Tianjin in 1995. However, as Mackerras comments, this remains only a partial revival and it is premature to judge it success.[20]

Chinese opera began to be performed outside of China in the mid–nineteenth century as large numbers of Chinese migrated overseas. The style of opera performed outside of China by immigrant communities was primarily Cantonese opera since most of the migrants came from the coastal areas of southeastern China, where this style of opera was very popular.[21] Chinese opera troupes, especially those performing Cantonese operas, were to be found performing in overseas Chinese communities in Southeast Asia, North America, and in Australia in the nineteenth and early twentieth centuries. Just as European opera spread along with European migrants, "Those Chinese communities which left China in substantial numbers in the early stages of emigration often simply took their local theatre style with them, occasionally even acting as a source of attraction for actors to come from their original home."[22] Thus, as the spread of European opera gave rise to opera performers from Europe traveling around the world, Chinese opera performers also performed before Chinese migrant audiences. Mackerras cites the example of Cantonese opera star Ma Shuzeng (1900–64) who spent most of the period between 1920 and 1933 away from his native Guangdong performing in Vietnam, Singapore, and California.[23]

The California Gold Rush and resultant growth in San Francisco's wealth and population gave rise to both European and Chinese opera in the city. The first Italian opera was staged in San Francisco in 1851. Wealthy Chinese merchants in San Francisco also began to support Cantonese performing arts for the growing Chinese population of the city.[24] In 1852 a troupe of Chinese jugglers performed, followed a couple of months later by a performance of a selection of Chinese operas, including *The Eight Genii,* by the 123-member Tung Hook Tong troupe from China. The troupe also performed in New York in 1854. Before long other troupes were coming to the United States from China, performing Cantonese and Peking operas in San Francisco and New York (in its Chinatown and on Broadway). By the late 1850s there were two Chinese opera troupes resident in San Francisco. Initially they performed at the Adelphi and Union theaters, but in the 1860s members of the Chinese community built the 1,500-seat Hing Chuen Yuen/Royal Chinese Theater. Lei argues such operas catered to nostalgia and reinforced national consciousness among Chinese immigrants while also helping to forge a distinct Californian identity.[25] Chinese opera continues to be performed in San Francisco and other cities in the United States, catering both to the ethnic Chinese community and to the wider community. The 2008 performance of *The Bonesetter's Daughter* represents an attempt at fusion. Based on a novel by Amy Tan, the opera is by Stewart Wallace, with Amy Tan writing the libretto.

Tan Dun (born 1957) is the most prominent example of a contemporary transnational composer of Chinese operas. Born in China to professional parents who were banished to the countryside to work as farm laborers during the Cultural Revolution, he later joined the Beijing Opera and studied at the Central Conservatory. He received a fellowship to study at Columbia University in New York City in 1986 and subsequently moved back and forth between New York City, and the PRC (with some time spent in England as well), before settling in New York City in 2000. His first opera was *Ghost Opera* that premiered in 1994. Don Mager in his column *Making Time* refers to it as "Tan Dun's hybridizing of classical Chinese musical techniques with Western methods."[26] It was followed by the opera *Marco Polo* in 1995 and *Peony Pavillion* in 1998.

Tan Dun's opera *The Gate* is an example of a contemporary Chinese-style fusion opera. The opera premiered in 1999 in Japan with performances by a female Peking Opera singer, a Western opera soprano, and a Japanese puppeteer and music performed by the NHK Symphony, conducted by Charles Dutoit. The following year he won Academy and Grammy awards for his score to the movie *Crouching Tiger, Hidden Dragon.* His opera *Tea: A Mirror of Soul* premiered in 2002 at the Suntory Hall in Japan, performed by De Nederlandse Opera. He composed a concerto *The Map* in 2002, which was performed before a rural audience in Hunan in 2003, the first time that such Western music had been performed before such an audience in the PRC. His opera *The First Emperor* premiered with a performance by the Metropolitan Opera in New York City in 2006, featuring the opera singer Plácido Domingo. In 2008 he was commissioned by the International Olympic Committee to compose music for the Summer Olympic Games and Paraolympic Games in Beijing.

As noted above, Chinese opera performances have taken place in other overseas Chinese communities, but less often than in the United States. In recent years the promotion of Chinese arts overseas has been a significant part of the People's Republic of China's effort to increase its influence and stature around the world. This has included staging Chinese operas in many cities around the world. This has often taken place in cooperation with local Chinese cultural groups. The Vancouver Society for the Chinese Performing Arts, for example, has sponsored bringing Chinese performers to Vancouver (including Kunqu, Sichian, and Beijing opera).

There have been a few locales outside of the United States where ethnic Chinese communities have formed professional opera troupes. The Chinese Theatre Circle was established in Singapore in 1981.[27] It initiated a program of "Bringing Chinese Opera to the People" series in 1984 by performing in community centers around Singapore. Growing relations between Singapore and the People's Republic of China resulted in the Singapore group staging the opera *A Costly Impulse* in Beijing in 1993. In 1995 the group was given the status of a non-profit professional performing Chinese opera company. It performed its first full-length opera, *Madam White Snake,* in 2000, with dialogue and singing in English. This event was viewed as creating a unique Singapore brand of Chinese opera. This opera was staged in Mandarin in 2001 and in the same year the company presented "Chinese Opera in Malay." The Chinese Theatre Circle became the first Chinese opera company from outside the PRC to be invited to perform in the PRC in 2002. The company's playwright Leslie Wong wrote a Chinese opera *Tragedy of an Emperor* in English and this was staged in 2002. It was re-named *Intrigues in the Qing Imperial Court* and staged in Guangzhou in 2004 at the Guangzhou International Cantonese Opera Festival. The company undertook a world tour in 2000 and has performed to date in 23 countries. The Singapore International Cantonese Opera Festival was held in 2008.

Vietnamese Opera

The Vietnamese have a variant of Chinese opera known as *hat tuong* in northern dialect and *hat boi* in southern dialect. The Mongols unsuccessfully invaded Dai Viet (modern northern Vietnam) on several occasions in the 1200s. During one of these invasions Vietnamese troops captured a renowned Chinese actor named Ly Nguyen Cat. The Dai Viet court asked him to teach acting to the children of influential families and this laid the basis for the origin of *hat tuong.* Ly Nguyen Cat produced the first operatic drama in Vietnam, *The West Queen Offering Peaches.* The successful adaptation of this art form reflects the shared cultural heritage of the two countries since the region occupied by Dai Viet had been under Chinese rule for almost 1,000 years. *Hat tuong* represents a combination of indigenous Vietnamese singing, dancing, and music with Chinese drama.

By the time of the Le dynasty (1428–1788), theater had come to be held in ill repute. The emperor Le Thanh Tong (reigned 1460–97) banished dramatic art from the royal palace and public officials who married a theatrical person were to be publicly flogged and forced to divorce. Sons of theatrical people were barred from taking government examinations. Drama continued to be popular among the population at large, but remained out of royal favor until the late 1600s. *Hat tuong* performances for nobles began again by the mid–1700s and it gained in popularity under the Nguyen Lords, who ruled over central Vietnam and conquered southern Vietnam. Nguyen Hoang (1525–1613) brought the theatrical form with him to the south as he established himself as ruler of the south. The Binh Dinh area developed into an important center of *hat boi,* as it came to be known in the southern dialect. The Nguyen Lords initially used it as a form of entertainment for the troops and later as a means of upholding traditional moral principles. It was also popular among the troops associated with the Tay Son rebels (1771–1802) and some of its generals appear to have been *hat boi* artists. The nobles of the Nguyen Dynasty (1802–1945) favored *hat tuong/boi* and opera troupes were created under royal sponsorship. By the mid–nineteenth century there were numerous important playwrights, most of whom were also well-known Confucian scholars. Many of these plays were based on older works of Chinese fiction, but some were entirely local creations.

During the French period (1887–1954) *hat tuong/boi* went into decline. Its disadvantages in the modern context included the use of numerous words of Chinese origin and a style of delivery that made it hard for audiences to understand. Also the long scenes and overall style required long and exacting training. In its place a new form of drama known as *cai luong* emerged in southern Vietnam in the 1920s. It incorporated elements of Western spoken drama, but also drew on *hat boi*'s style of acting. *Cai luong* was much more accessible to modern audiences and grew in popularity while *hat boi* went into decline. *Hat boi* remained popular mainly among the rural poor rather than the wealthier urban-dwellers. The communists associated *hat tuong/boi* with feudalism and initially banned it when they came to power in northern Vietnam in 1954. Before long, however, it came to be viewed as having merit and state support was revived. By the 1960s there were several professional troupes and training schools for performers in the north. Under the southern Saigon government from the 1950s until 1975 troupes had existed in Saigon, Danang, and Qui Nhon, but in general the theater was not very popular. After the communists took over the south they also introduced state support for *hat boi* in that region.

From the perspective of transnationalism and in contrast to Chinese opera, while *hat tuong/boi* has been revived to some extent in recent years within Vietnam, it is not generally performed outside of Vietnam and appears to be of little interest to overseas Vietnamese. The government of Vietnam has sponsored occasional foreign performances of *hat tuong* by national performers, but such performances are directed more at non–Vietnamese international audiences than overseas Vietnamese. The arts tend not to be well supported in overseas Vietnamese communities and there have been relatively few *hat tuong/boi* performers among Vietnamese refugees or migrants. Most overseas Vietnamese are from the south and they commonly associate traditional art forms with the north and with communism. Unlike the Chinese migrant community that established itself in North America in the nineteenth century and was able and desired maintaining connections with China, Vietnamese came almost exclusively as refugees who until recently were unable to maintain contact with Vietnam. Ongoing opposition to the communist government in Vietnam by vocal members of the overseas Vietnamese community has made it difficult for the Vietnamese government to promote arts overseas. While such opposition has begun to moderate, support for the arts within the overseas ethnic Vietnamese community remains tepid and the government of Vietnam has no policy in place of using the arts to promote its interests internationally as does the government of the PRC.

Transnational Plastic Arts

Unlike performing artists who in the past personally had to appear before their audiences to create their arts, practitioners of the plastics arts such as painters could stay in one place and let their works of art do the traveling. This is not to say that painters, sculptors, and the like did not move around in the past, but prior to the nineteenth century such artists tended to travel far less than performing artists. When painters or sculptors did travel in the past it was often in the form of one-way or at least long term migration in search of improved opportunity or to an environment that they perceived to be better for their art — e.g., to political, economic, and cultural centers such as the capitals of empires. As travel became easier in the nineteenth century, painters and other artists began to travel more and, more importantly, to move back and forth between countries with more frequency. In particular, many aspiring painters from around the world spent time in Europe or the United States and recognition there as an artist often played an important role in boosting an artist's career back home. While spending a part of one's life in the perceived cultural capitals of Europe and the United States early in one's career, along with periodic trips back to these locales later in life, has been increasingly common among artists from around the world over the past couple of centuries, giving their work a transnational aspect, less common are artists who develop more thoroughly transnational lifestyles that entail establishing important roots in more than one country. Such artists, however, are beginning to become more common in recent years.

Transnational Painters in the Colonial Philippines

As a Spanish colony, painting developed in the Philippines influenced by European culture and Catholicism. Casal and Trota Jose, Jr., describe the origins of colonial painting in the Philippines: "The Chinese Christians were probably the first to master the art of painting in Manila.... Fr. Sedeño would gather these *sangleyes* in his house and teach them to paint religious images, which he then encouraged other churches to procure and display. These *sangleyes* were apt pupils, and in 1590 Bishop Salazar praised their skill.... Paintings from Europe and America were quite scarce and difficult to obtain, and the religious were, therefore, obliged to teach the basic artistic skills to satisfy the great demand for religious works of art. Prints of saints, many of Flemish origin, such as those from the presses of Christophe Plantin, were often the only models at hand. Since they were in black and white, the local artist could freely indulge in his own color preference."[28]

The Philippines remained a Spanish colony until the end of the 1800s and Spain continued to influence the arts in the Philippines during this century. Formal art classes in the Philippines began with the founding of the Academia de Dibujo (Academy of Drawing) in Manila in 1821.[29] Damian Domingo y Gabor (1790–1832) became its director. His father was Spanish, his mother from Tondo in Manila, and he was born in Manila. He was a painter who was known especially for painting portraits of middle class Filipinos and he helped to introduce non-religious subjects to Filipino painting.

The academy closed following Domingo's death because of a lack of money, but reopened in 1849 as the Academia de Dibujo y Pintura (Academy of Drawing and Painting) with a faculty that included three painters recruited from Spain to teach the latest European techniques. Other Spanish artists who taught there included Agustin Saez and Lorenzo Rocha. The status of the school was enhanced in 1893 when it became the Escuela Superior de Pintura, Escultura y Grabado (Superior School of Painting, Sculpture, and Engraving) under royal decree. Spanish artist Agustin Saez served as its director. Spanish artists such as Velazquez, Ribera, Zurbaran, and especially Murillo served as models for the students trained at the academy. The academy produced a number of acclaimed painters. Lorenzo Guerrero (1835–1904) was the first of these. Saez also taught Juan Luna y Novicio (1857–99), whom he dismissed from the academy but encouraged to go to Europe for further study. Several artists associated with the academy traveled and studied in Europe, mainly at Madrid's Academia de Bellas Artes de San Fernando and some won foreign awards for their work, which greatly added to their prestige back in the Philippines.

Juan Luna enrolled in the Academia de Bellas Artes de San Fernando in 1877. He left the school and went to Rome to work with one of his teachers from the academy, Don Alejo Vera. Luna's paintings were exhibited at the Exposición Nacional de Bellas Artes in Madrid in 1878 and again in the 1881 exposition, where his painting "The Death of Cleopatra" won a silver medal. His success in Spain resulted in Luna being awarded an annual stipend by the municipal government of Manila to produce paintings based on Philippine history, which he began in 1883. One of these paintings was sent to Madrid for the 1884 exposition and received a gold medal. He moved to Paris in 1885, where he opened a studio and continued to produce paintings for the Manila municipal government. The Spanish king commissioned him to produce a painting for the Spanish Senate. This painting, "The Battle of Lepanto," won an award at the 1887 exposition. He moved back to the Philippines in 1891.

Luna took a trip to Japan in 1896, returning in time for the onset of the war for independence from Spain. He was arrested on charges of being involved with anti–Spanish elements but was pardoned the following year. After his pardon he became a member of the revolutionary government's executive board. He was part of the delegations that went to Paris in 1898 to negotiate the independence of the Philippines and to Washington, D.C., to seek recognition of the new government. Shortly after returning to the Philippines in late 1899 he went to Hong Kong when his brother, who had been living in exile, died there. Luna himself died of a heart attack while in Hong Kong. He was buried there, but his remains were moved to the Philippines in 1920.

The Spanish connection in the arts remained strong in the Philippines after independence from Spain and even under American colonialism. Filipino painter Fernando Amorsolo y Cueto (1892–1972), one of the country's most important artists, provides an example of this. He was born in Manila and studied painting under Don Fabian de la Rosa (a cousin of his mother). After one of his paintings won an award in a competition held by the local international artists association he attended the Liceo de Manila's art school and then the School of Fine Arts at the University of the Philippines (where Rosa was teaching), from where he graduated in 1914. His work while a student won a number of local awards. After graduation he took up a job as a commercial artist and worked part-time teaching at the University of the Philippines. In 1917 the prominent businessman Enrique Zobel de Ayala gave Amorsolo a grant to go to Madrid and study at the Academia de San Fernando as well as to visit New York City. He returned to the Philippines after seven months abroad and set up his own studio. While he spent most of his life in the Philippines, and most of his paintings were exhibited and sold in Manila, there were several exhibitions of his work outside of the Philippines during his life, including one at the Exposición de Panama (including a portrait of President Woodrow Wilson) in Belgium in 1914, a solo show at New York's Grand Central Gallery in 1925, and a showing of two of his paintings at the Missionary Art Exhibit in Rome in 1950.

Transnationalism and Thai Plastic Arts

Thailand, known as Siam until 1938, provides an interesting case study of European influence on the arts of a non-colonized country. As in Europe, the monarchs of Siam were important patrons of the arts. Art in Thailand prior to the 1800s was largely religious in nature, focusing either on Buddhist themes or at least being set within Buddhist religious structures, and its plastic arts were influenced largely by other Asian artistic traditions (especially those of China and India) rather than Europe. European influence of Siam's arts developed in the mid–nineteenth century. Siam's King Mongkut played an important role in developing relations between his kingdom and Western countries and this included the appearance of European works of art in Siam, largely in the form of gifts to the king. Mongkut's son Chulalongkorn (reigned 1868–1910) in turn became a great patron of the arts when he assumed the throne. He took a particular interest in Western art and not only imported works of art and interacted with European artists when he toured Europe in 1897 and 1907,[30] but also commissioned European artists to produce works for the palace and encouraged local artists to study European arts.

In addition to commissioning artists in Europe to produce works for him, King Chulalongkorn hired artists to come to Bangkok to work. In 1904 he hired Cesare Ferro, who had been trained at the Accademia Albertina in Turin, as court painter.[31] Prince Naris (another of Mongkut's sons) was another important patron of European arts and artists in his role as head of the departments of public works and fine arts. Many works of art (murals, architecture, and statues) feature Siamese and Buddhist themes using European techniques and styles of representation. In 1907 the Public Works Department hired a group of eight Italian engineers, architects, painters (including Cesare), and sculptors to help construct and decorate the Ananta Samakhom Throne Hall. One of the painters at the court, Luang Soralaklikhit, studied technique with Ferro and then accompanied the king on his trip to Europe in 1907. After Luang's return he was appointed court painter. One of the artists working on the throne room, Carlo Rigoli, also gave art lessons in Bangkok. Not all of the European artists in Siam were from Europe. Edward Healey came from the Royal Academy in London

Poshyananda makes the point that under King Chulalongkorn the European artists coming to Siam were mainly painters, while under King Vajiravudh (reigned 1910–25) sculptors became more evident.[32] He associates this with the custom of sending young princes to Europe to study where they saw numerous monuments and sculptures on display in public places and their subsequent desire to promote this type of art back in Siam. Prince Vajirvudh studied in the United Kingdom at the Royal Military Academy Sandhurst between 1891 and 1894 and at Christ Church College, Oxford, from 1899 and 1901. As Chulalongkorn's health deteriorated, Vajiravudh was made regent in 1906 and during this time he commissioned the Chulalongkorn Equestrian Statue in 1908. Posyananda argues that European sculptors were brought to Siam in part because it was cheaper to bring them to Siam to work than to commission the works from artists in Europe and ship the works to Siam.[33] An added benefit was that these artists could then also train local artists. Corrado Feroci (1892–1962) was undoubtedly the most important European artist to move to Siam during King Vajiravud's reign. He graduated from the Academia di Bella Arti (Academy of Fine Arts) in Florence in 1914 and "soon gained a reputation as a sculptor of war memorials" while also teaching at the academy under the regime of fascist dictator Benito Mussolini.[34] Feroci came to Bangkok in 1923 as a result of a request by the Fine Arts Department to the Italian government for a sculptor to train local artists.

After the fall of the absolute monarchy in Siam in 1932 the royal court's role as a patron of the arts was greatly diminished. This role shifted to the Department of Fine Arts under the directorship of Luang Wichitwatakan (aka Luang Wichit) from 1933 to 1942, who was a fervent proponent of modernism and of using the arts as a tool of nation building. Luang Wichit had written a book on Italian dictator Benito Mussolini in 1932 and was influenced by Mussolini's use of art as propaganda. In 1933 Feroci was assigned the task of creating a new fine arts curriculum for the School of Fine Arts that had been established to train local artists to produce paintings and sculptures for government departments.

Feroci settled in Bangkok, but made return visits to Europe in 1930 and 1938. These visits served to keep him up to date with trends in fascist art in Europe, which inspired his own work back in Thailand such as the Democracy Monument, which was completed in 1940. The successful career that Feroci had developed in Thailand meant that when Italy surrendered to the Allies in 1944 he decided to take Thai citizenship (a decision that was also motivated by a desire to avoid possible arrest by the occupying Japanese) and to change his name to Silpa Bhirasi. He had divorced his first wife in Italy and later he remarried one of his Thai students. He played a key role in the founding of Silpakorn University in Bangkok, Thailand's fine arts university, and is widely viewed as the father of modern Thai art, whereas he is largely unknown in Italy. The approach to art that he promoted in Thailand has its parallel in the Novocentro movement in Italy that favored realism and naturalism in opposition to avant-garde Futurism. In both Italy and Thailand this meant creating art with strong roots in their respective cultural and artistic traditions.[35]

Under Bhirasi's tutelage, Thai artists participated in a number of international exhibitions in Europe, the United States, and Japan during the 1950s. Thailand also became a member of the International Association of Plastic Art (IAPA), based in Paris, in 1953. Established and aspiring Thai artists also went abroad to study. Sculptor Khien Yimsiri studied at the Academy of Fine Arts in Rome in 1953–4 before becoming an instructor at Silpakorn University. Sculptor Paitun Muangsomboon visited galleries and museums in Europe and North America under sponsorship of UNESCO's Creative Artists' Scheme in 1958–59.[36] Fua Haripitak, one of Thailand's most influential painters in the mid–twentieth century, went to study in India in 1941, where he was influenced by the work and thought of Rabindanath Tagore, and was interned in India for the duration of World War II, and returned to Bangkok only after the war in 1946. He then went to Rome to study at the Academy of Fine Arts in 1954–5 supported by a scholarship from the Italian government. He produced a large number of drawings and paintings in Italy and his style and technique was influenced by his trip to Europe. Another prominent painter of the period, Sawasdi Tantisuk, was awarded a four-year scholarship to study at the Academy of Fine Arts in Rome, where he "became attracted to the monochromatic paintings of Santomaso."[37]

Phillips writes about foreign influence on the education of Thai artists: "Thai artists began to study overseas in significant numbers over forty years ago [i.e., prior to 1950], and these numbers have increased exponentially in the intervening years. In fact, there are now so many artists who have studied overseas, and who have taught about both Euroamerican art and the personal impact their foreign experience has had on them, that it is essentially impossible to separate the indigenous and international components of Thai art education."[38] Such foreign influences reflect both foreign training of those who instruct artists within Thailand as well as trips abroad by the artists themselves. Phillips cites the example of painter Kamin Lertchaiprasert who at the time of his writing had "recently spent a year studying in New York, but even before leaving Bangkok, he had already studied under three instructors trained in Thailand and America, whose own roots reach back through two generations of instructors who had studied in Italy."[39] He lists various prominent Thai painters who had studied in Amsterdam, Salzburg, London, Kyoto, and various locales in the United States.

Mention should also be made of the prominent Thai sculptor Inson Wongsam. Inson was born in Pasang near Chiang Mai in 1934. Of his background, the Dhamma Park website notes, "His father was a Jeweller & Goldsmith who encouraged his son's talent from the earliest age. His grandfather was a Merchant who traded in Burma & the stories of his adventurous journeys inspired his grandson with a strong desire to travel abroad."[40] After graduating from Silpakorn University in 1961 he traveled overland on a Lambretta Scooter to Florence, Italy, to visit the birthplace of Corado Feroci. Inson exhibited woodcut prints made during his trip along the way in New Delhi, Lahore, Karachi, Tehran, Istanbul, and Athens. He lived on the island of Corfu for six months and produced more woodcuts, which he exhibited in Florence, Vienna, and Zurich. He then settled in Paris in 1963 to study at the École Nationale Supérieure des Arts Decoratifs. After a successful exhibit of his work at the Haut Pave gallery in Paris in 1966 he moved to New York City, where he lived and worked (focusing on sculpture and producing so-called happenings) for six years. He moved to Atlantic Highlands, New Jersey, where he lived for another two years. He returned to Thailand in 1974 and settled in the countryside near Pasang. Back in Pasang he worked mainly at producing sculptures from pieces of wood gathered from his surroundings. He exhibited his work at Silpakorn University in 1974 and at the USIS in Chiang Mai in 1975. Since returning to Thailand his exhibitions have been almost entirely held in Thailand (there was one in the PRC in 1985). He was named a National Artist of Thailand in the field of visual arts (sculpture) in 1999.

So far we have discussed European artists coming to Thailand and Thai artists going abroad to study and then returning home to Thailand. Phillips writes about five Thai artists who had come to reside outside of Thailand (four in the United States and one in the Netherlands), commenting that although they are few in number "they loom large in Thailand for having successfully pursued their talents in a foreign setting while maintaining their professional and personal connections with their colleagues and friends back home. When they visit Thailand, they are attended to and often celebrated, and when living abroad they are perceived as critical contacts for traveling artists, art students, and other members of the art community. Above all, they are considered the most reliable, up-to-date sources of knowledge on what is happening in the Euroamerican art world."[41]

Of these five, Phillips portrays Kamol Tassananchalee and Wattana Wattanapun as the most transnational, in that they have maintained very strong ties with Thailand while also developing strong roots in the United States.

Kamol Tassananchalee was born in Bangkok in 1944. After graduating from Srinakharinwirot University in Bangkok in 1969 he moved to Los Angeles in 1970. He received his MFA degree from the Otis Art Institute of Los Angeles in 1977 and during the 1970s exhibited his work on a number of occasions in California. Los Angeles by the 1970s had become the home to the largest overseas Thai community. Kamol settled in Los Angeles, where his parents and other members of his family joined him. His studio is located in Chatsworth, California. While the market for his work was in the United States, he not only maintained his identity himself as a Thai artist living in the United States, but as his career developed he sought to promote linkages between Thai artists in Thailand and the United States. He established the Thai Art Center in Los Angeles in 1979 and founded the Thai Art Council in the United States in association with the Pacific Asia Museum in Pasadena in 1982.[42] Through the latter organization he came to sponsor visits by artists from Thailand to Los Angeles and to promote an appreciation of Thai art in Los Angeles.

Back in Thailand, the National Gallery of Thailand exhibited his work in 1980, "Ten years of art in the U.S.A., 1970–1980." This was followed by an exhibition of his drawings at Silpakorn University in 1985 and another exhibition of his work, marking twenty years in the United States, by the National Gallery in 1990. His connection with Thailand was affirmed in 1997, when he was given the National Artist Award for a Visual Artist.

Kamol has continued to promote artistic links between Thailand and the United States in recent years. Thus, in 2002 he took part in an exhibition of Thai artists at the Thai consulate in Los Angeles. In 2005, in addition to an exhibition of his work at Silpakorn University to honor his 60th birthday, he also took part in a group exhibition featuring the works of seven Thai and three American artists at Chiang Mai University that was co-sponsored by the university and Kamol's Thai Art Council of the USA. Writing on the exhibit, Jittawong says, "The main objective of the exhibition is to exchange knowledge in art and culture and to build a stronger relationship between Thai and American artists."[43] In 2006–7 Kamol took part in a group exhibition entitled "Identity" at Bangkok's CP Seven Art Gallery as well as an exhibition entitled "Visions of Dharma: Thai Contemporary Art" featuring his work and that of Thai artist Thawan Duchanee (who live near Chiang Rai) at the Cantor Arts Center at Stanford University in California. The Center's description of the exhibition refers to them as "two of Thailand's most important living artists" and notes that both are recipients of the title National Artist of Thailand. In regard to Kamol the text notes that although he resides in Los Angeles, "He has become almost a cult figure in Thailand, where his work is very popular, yet few Americans collect his work."[44]

Wattana Wattanapun was born in 1941 in a small town to the west of Bangkok.[45] He graduated from Silpakorn University in 1968 and then went to the United States to study at the Rhode Island School of Design, from where he graduated in 1976. He spent the next ten years living in the United States, and worked primarily within an American art environment, making only a few visits back to Thailand. He took up a variety of teaching posts in the United States at Oberlin College (1974–5), the Rhode Island School of Design (1976), Haverford College (1979–81), and the Prat Fine Arts Center in Seattle (1982–8). His work was featured in 20 exhibitions in the United States during this period and his paintings were sold almost exclusively to Americans. He took part in only one exhibition in Thailand, a group exhibition in Bangkok in 1979 sponsored by the German Culture Institute in Bangkok. He also contributed to a joint German-Thai stage production in Bangkok in 1984 of *Prah Sang-Iphegenie* that blended Gluck's German opera with Thai theater. Although the artists involved liked it, Wattana remarked that the Thai audience hated the production, as did the German sponsor. They wanted something that was either Thai or German, but not a blend.

Wattana moved back to Thailand in 1986 and took up a teaching post at Chiang Mai University. His critical response to changes that he saw taking place in Thailand at the time was expressed in a series of works called *Sun, Sand, Silk, Sex*. The series was not popular in Thailand and he found himself being branded "as a Western brain-washed artist."[46] He staged two exhibits in Chiang Mai in 1988, one sponsored by the university and another by the USIS. The following year the British Council sponsored an exhibition of his work in Bangkok. Although there was a growing art market in Thailand, few Thais bought his work and most of his paintings were sold to Westerners. While living in Thailand he also continued to exhibit in the United States, where his work sold well and in 1990 he moved back to the United States and took up a teaching post at the Watkins Institute in Nashville. Three of his paintings were included in the 1991 *Essence of Contemporary Thai Art* exhibition that toured the United States from 1991 to 1993.[47]

He returned to Chiang Mai and to teaching at Chiang Mai University in 1993, this time for good. He took part in a group exhibition at the National Culture Center in Bangkok in 1993, but continued to find that his work was more appreciated in North America than in Thailand. The lukewarm response to his work in Thailand encouraged him to continue to visit the United States, where his work appeared in a number of exhibits, as well as semester-long visits to Simon Fraser University in Canada in 1996 and 1999 and an exhibition of his work at Centre A gallery of the Vancouver International Centre for Contemporary Asian Art in 2001. He also made frequent visits back to the United States and remains a member of the Nashville Artist Guild.

Wattana took part in group exhibitions at Chiang Mai University in 1995, 1996, and 1998 and gradually became more established as an artist in Thailand through his work at Chiang Mai University and exhibits that attracted a growing number of Thais. In particular he came to be viewed as part of the community of prominent artists living in northern Thailand and as an important proponent of northern Thai culture and arts. The growth of his artistic status within Thailand was manifest in a series of exhibits of his work — at the Surapon Gallery in Bangkok in 2002, solo exhibitions at galleries in Chiang Mai in 2005 and 2008, a group exhibition with two other northern artists entitled "Three Passages to Lanna" at the Thailand Cultural Center in Bangkok in 2006, and a solo exhibition "Weaving Paradise" at the Jim Thompson Art Center in Bangkok in 2008. He was also made a consultant to the Thai art magazine *Fine Art* that began publication in 2003, commissioned by the National Culture Commission of Thailand's ministry of Culture to write a biography of Inson Wongsam (that was published in 2003), and asked by the Office of the Ministry of Interior and Office of the National Culture Commission to head the Chiang Mai–San Kamphaeng Culture Road Project in 2004–5. Reflecting his transnational status as an artist, *Fine Art* magazine published an article in English and Thai featuring Wattana as its "Artist of the Month" with the title "An Artist in Two Cultures."[48]

Wattana has sought to express his experience as an artist in the different worlds of the United State and Thailand through the visual concepts of opaque and transparent. "He sees his experience in the United States as adding an opaque quality to his life and work — 'more complications, less certainty, more multiple layers, and more convolutions.' In contrast, 'my Thai Buddhist background and myself as a Thai perhaps are more transparent in nature.'"[49]

CHAPTER NOTES

Chapter 1

1. William Little, H.W. Fowler, and J. Coulson (revised and edited by C.T. Onions), *The Oxford Universal Dictionary on Historical Principles: Third Edition* (Oxford: Clarendon, 1955), 1311.

2. Ibid., 2005.

3. There is often confusion in regard to use of the terms Tai and Thai. Tai commonly refers to a large group of related languages and to the Tai-speaking ethnic or ethno-national groups associated with those languages (such as the Black Tai), whereas Thai is used in reference to a particular Tai-speaking ethnic group in Vietnam and to citizens of the country of Thailand.

4. Kinh refers to the ethnic majority in Vietnam. Non-Vietnamese sometimes refer to them as Viet.

5. See Yasmin Saikia, *Fragmented Memories: Struggling to be Tai-Ahom in India* (Durham, NC: Duke University Press, 2004).

6. See David Brown, *The State and Ethnic Politics in Southeast Asia* (New York: Routledge, 1994), 112–57; and Gerry Van Klinken, "Ethnicity in Indonesia," in *Ethnicity in Asia*, ed., C. Mackerras (London: RoutledgeCurzon, 2003), 64–87.

7. Michael C. Howard, "Dress and Ethnic Identity in Irian Jaya," *Sojourn* 15 (2000), 19–22.

8. *VietNamNet Bridge,* 28 February (2008), online at http://english.vietnamnet.vn/.

9. Ulf Hannerz, *Transnational Connections: Culture, People, Places* (New York: Routledge, 1996), 6.

10. Peter Dicken, *Global Shift: Reshaping the Global Economic Map in the 21st Century,* Fourth Edition (New York/London: Guilford, 2003), 1.

11. Thomas Faist, "Transnationalization in International Migration: Implications for the Study of Citizenship and Culture," *Ethnic and Racial Studies* 23 (2000), 189–222.

12. Katie Willis, Brenda S.A. Yeoh, and S.M. Abdul Khader Fakhri, "Introduction: Transnationalism as a Challenge to the Nation," in *State/Nation/Transnation: Perspectives on Transnationalism in the Asia-Pacific,* ed. K. Willis, B.S.A. Yeoh, and S.M.A.K. Fakhri (New York: Routledge, 2004), 1.

13. Arjun Appadura, "Disjuncture and Difference in the Global Cultural Economy," *Theory, Culture and Society* 7 (1990), 305.

14. Willis, Yeoh, and Fakhri, "Introduction," 3.

15. Anthony D. Smith, "Towards a Global Culture?," *Theory, Culture & Society* 7 (1990), 171.

16. See Gary Cartwright, "The World's First Hamburger," *Texas Monthly* August (2009); and Josh Ozersky, *Hamburger: A History* (New Haven, CT: Yale University Press, 2009).

17. See James L. Watson, ed., *Golden Arches East: McDonald's in East Asia* (Palo Alto, CA: Stanford University Press, 1997).

18. Internet World Stats, online at http://www.internetworldstats.com/stats.htm.

19. See John Holm, *Pidgins and Creoles, Volume II: Reference Survey* (New York: Cambridge University Press, 1989).

20. Hannerz, *Transnational Connections,* 66.

21. Ibid., 67.

22. Ibid., 68.

23. Ibid., 74.

24. Ibid.

25. Faist, "Transnationalization in International Migration," 191. Also see P. Jackson, P. Crang, and C. Dwyer, "Introduction: The Spaces of Transnationality," in *Transnational Spaces,* eds., P. Jackson, P. Crang, and C. Dwyer (New York: Routledge, 2004), 1–23.

26. Faist, "Transnationalization in International Migration," 195.

27. Ibid.

28. Ibid., 193.

29. A. Portes, L.E. Guarnizo, and P. Landolt, "The Study of Transnationalism: Pitfalls and Promises of an Emergent Research Field," *Ethnic and Racial Studies* 22 (1999), 219–237.

30. William Bernstein, *A Splendid Exchange: How Trade Shaped the World* (New York: Atlantic Monthly, 2008), 7.

31. Walt W. Rostow, *The World Economy: History and Prospect* (Austin: University of Texas Press, 1978).

32. World Trade Organization, *World Trade Report 2007* (Geneva: World Trade Organizaation, 2007).

33. Dicken, *Global Shift,* 10, 12.

34. Ibid.

35. Ibid., 89.

36. Bernstein, *Splendid Exchange*, 12.

37. Hannerz, *Transnational Connections*, 3.

38. Lionel Casson, *Travel in the Ancient World* (London: George Allen and Unwin, 1974), 65.

39. See William L. Schurz, *The Manila Galleon* (New York: E.P. Dutton, 1959).

40. Gerald S. Graham, "The Ascendancy of the Sailing Ship 1850–1885," *Economic History Review* 9 (1956), 79.

41. Charles K. Harley, "The Shift from Sailing Ships to Steamships, 1850–1890: A Study in Technological Change and its Diffusion," in *Essays on a Mature Economy*, ed. D.N. McClosky (Princeton, NJ: Princeton University Press, 1971), 215–225.

42. Norway-Heritage: Hands Across the Sea, online at http://www.norwayheritage.com/.

43. Bob Dickinson and Andy Vladimir, *Selling the Sea: An Inside Look at the Cruise Industry* (New York: John Wiley and Sons, 1997).

44. Martin Caidin, *Indiana Jones and the Sky Pirates* (New York: Bantam, 1993).

45. William T. Larkins, *The Ford Tri-Motor, 1926–1992* (Atglen, PA: Schiffler 1992).

46. Thijs Postma, *Fokker: Aircraft Builders to the World* (London: Jane's, 1979).

47. "Civil Aviation in Dutch East Indies," *Flight*, 4 March (1932), 196.

48. Jennifer M. Gradidge, *The Douglas DC-1/DC-2/DC-3: The First Seventy Years* (London: Air-Britain, 2006).

49. Bill Yenne, *Seaplanes and Flying Boats: A Timeless Collection from Aviation's Golden Age* (New York: BCL, 2003).

50. See Barnaby Conrad, *Pan Am: An Aviation Legend* (Emeryville, CA: Woodford, 1999); and Roger E. Bilstein, *Flight in America* (Baltimore, MD: Johns Hopkins University Press, 2001).

51. Bernstein, *Splendid Exchange*, 307.

52. Internet World Stats, online at http://www.internetworldstats.com/stats.htm.

Chapter 2

1. See Faist, "Transnationalization in International Migration."

2. Ibid.

3. Ibid.

4. Ibid.

5. See Walter Nugent, *Crossings: The Great Transatlantic Migrations, 1870–1914* (Bloomington: Indiana University Press, 1992).

6. See Herbert S. Klein, *The Atlantic Slave Trade* (New York: Cambridge University Press, 1999).

7. See Matthew Gibney and Randall Hansen, eds., *Immigration and Asylum: From 1900 to the Present* (Santa Barbara, CA: ABC-CLIO, 2005).

8. Michael C. Howard, *A World Between the Warps: Southeast Asia's Supplementary Warp Textiles* (Bangkok: White Lotus, 2008), 16–7.

9. John E. Fagg, *Latin America: A General History* (New York: Macmillan, 1963), 60.

10. Ibid., 60.

11. See Henry Charles Lea, *The Inquisition in the Spanish Dependencies* (New York: Macmilan, 1908).

12. Leon Poliakov, *Jewish Bankers and the Holy See* (London: Routledge and Kegan Paul, 1977), 173–4.

13. See Jonethan I. Israel, *Dutch Primacy in World Trade, 1585–1740*. Oxford: Clarendon, 1989), 161–8.

14. Horace Stern, "The First Jewish Settlers in America: Their Struggle for Religious Freedom," *Jewish Quarterly Review* 45 (1955), 289, 292–3. Also see Jonathan D. Sarna, "American Jewish History," *Modern Judaism* 10 (1990), 244–5.

15. See Taner Akçam, *A Shameful Act: The Armenian Genocide and the Question of Turkish Responsibility* (New York: Metropolitan, 2006); Donald Bloxham, *The Great Game of Genocide: Imperialism, Nationalism, and the Destruction of the Ottoman Armenians* (Oxford: Oxford University Press, 2005); and Vahakn N. Dadrian, *The History of the Armenian Genocide: Ethnic Conflict from the Balkans to Anatolia to the Caucasus* (Oxford: Berghahn, 1995).

16. Arnold Toynbee, "A Summary of Armenian History up to and Including the Year 1915," in *The Treatment of Armenians in the Ottoman Empire 1915–16: Documents Presented to Viscount Grey of Fallodon, Secretary of State for Foreign Affairs by Viscount Bryce* (New York and London: G.P. Putnam's Sons, for His Majesty's Stationary Office, London, 1916), 637–53.

17. David Wolff, *To the Harbin Station: The Liberal Alternative in Russian Manchuria, 1898–1914* (Stanford, CA: Stanford University Press, 1999).

18. Seraphim Rose and Abbot Herman, *Blessed John the Wonderworker* (Platina, CA: St. Herman of Alaska Brotherhood, 1987).

19. See Gary Nash, *The Tarasov Saga: From Russia through China to Australia* (Castlecrag, NSW: Rosenberg, 2002); and Alexander P. Saranin, *Child of the Kulaks* (St. Lucia: University of Queensland Press, 1998).

20. See Solomon M. Bard, *Light and Shade: Sketches from an Uncommon Life* (Hong Kong: Hong Kong University Press, 2009).

21. See Alfred W. McCoy, *The Politics of Heroin in Southeast Asia* (New York: Harper and Row, 1972), 126–35.

22. Amara Pongsapich and Noppawan Chonwattana, "The Refugee Situation in Thailand," in *Indochinese Refugees: Asylum and Resettlement*, eds., S. Chantavanich and E. B. Reynolds (Bangkok: Institute of Asian Studies, Chulalongkorn University, 1988), 14.

23. Human Rights Watch, *No Sanctuary* (2006), available in PDF format online at http://www.hrw.org/en/reports/2006/06/13/no-sanctuary-0.

24. S. Castles, "Contract Labour Migration" in *The Cambridge Survey of World Migration*, ed., R. Cohen (Cambridge: Cambridge University Press, 1995), 510–22.

25. See David Northrup, *Indentured Labor in the Age of Imperialism, 1834–1922* (New York Cambridge University Press, 1995).

26. See Hugh Tinker, *Indians Overseas 1830–1920* (London: Oxford University Press, 1974).

27. Kingsley Davis, *The Population of India and Pakistan* (Princeton, NJ: Princeton University Press, 1951), 99.

28. John Wesley Coulter, *Fiji: Little India of the Pacific* (Chicago: University of Chicago Press, 1942), 96.

29. Deryck Scarr, *Fiji: A Short History* (Sydney: George Allen and Unwin, 1984), 144.

30. Coulter, *Fiji*, 106.

31. Ibid., 84.

32. Robert Norton, *Race and Politics in Fiji* (St. Lucia: University of Queensland Press, 1977), 104.

33. See Michael C. Howard, *Fiji: Race and Politics in an Island State* (Vancouver: University of British Columbia Press, 1991).

34. See Carmen Voigt-Graf, "Transnationalism and the Indo-Fijian Diaspora: The Relationship of Indo-Fijians to India and Its People," *Journal of Intercultural Studies* 29 (2008), 81–109, and Kyung-Hak Kim, "Transnational Indo-Fijians in Australia," *Man in India* 87 (2007), 303–321.

35. Northrup, *Indentured Labor in the Age of Imperialism*, 54.

36. See Sheila Marriner and F.E. Hyde, *The Senior John Samuel Swire 1825–98: Management in Far Easter Shipping Trades* (Liverpool: Liverpool University Press, 1967); and F.E. Hyde and J. Harriss, *Blue Funnel: A History of Alfred Holt and Co. of Liverpool from 1865 to 1914* (Liverpool: Liverpool University Press, 1957).

37. See John Haskell Kemble, "The Big Four at Sea: The History of the Occidental and Oriental Steamship Company," *The Huntington Library Quarterly* 3 (1940), 339–357; and Robert J. Chandler and Stephen J. Potash, *Gold, Silk, Pioneers & Mail: The Story of the Pacific Mail Steamship Company* (El Cerrito, CA: Glencannon and Friends of the San Francisco Maritime Museum Library, 2007).

38. Arnold J. Meagher, *The Coolie Trade: The Traffic in Chinese Laborers to Latin America* (San Francisco: Chinese Materials Center, 1975, and Bloomington, IN: Xlibris, 2008), 148.

39. Joao de Piña-Cabral, *Between China and Europe: Person, Culture and Emotion in Macao* (New York: Berg, 2002), 24.

40. Northrup, *Indentured Labor in the Age of Imperialism*, 54–5.

41. Erika Lee, "Defying Exclusion: Chinese Immigrants and Their Strategies During the Exclusion Era," in *Chinese American Transnationalism*, ed., S. Chang (Philadelphia: Temple University Press, 2006), 8.

42. Ibid., 8.

43. Barbara Watson Andaya and Leonard Y. Andaya, *A History of Malaya* (London: Macmillan Education, 1982), 137.

44. See M.R. Frost, *Transcultural Diaspora: The Straits Chinese in Singapore, 1819–1918*, Working Paper Series No. 10 (Singapore: Asia Research Institute, 2003).

45. Andaya and Andaya, *A History of Malaya*, 176.

46. See Lucy M. Cohen, *Chinese in the Post-Civil War South: A People without a History* (Baton Rouge: Louisiana State University Press, 1984).

47. Andrew Gyory, *Closing the Gate: Race, Politics, and the Chinese Exclusion Act* (Chapel Hill: University of North Carolina Press, 1998).

48. See Erika Lee, *At America's Gates: Chinese Immigrants during the Exclusion Era, 1882–1943* (Chapel Hill: University of North Carolina Press, 2007).

49. Ralph S. Kuykendall, *Hawaiian Kingdom 1874–1893, the Kalakaua Dynasty* (Honolulu: University of Hawaii Press, 1967), 147.

50. See W. Willmott, "Chinese Contract Labour in the Pacific Islands during the Nineteenth Century," *Journal of Pacific Islands Studies* 27 (2004), 165.

51. Victor Purcell, *Malaya: Outline of a Colony* (London: Thomas Nelson and Sons, 1946), 45.

52. Ibid., 28.

53. Lee, Defying Exclusion," 8–9.

54. See Sucheng Chan, *Chinese American Transnationalism: The Flow of People, Resources, and Ideas between China and America during the Exclusion Era* (Philadelphia, PA: Temple University Press, 2005).

55. See Liu, "Chinese Herbalists in the United States."

56. Mary F. Somers Heidhues, *Bangka Tin and Mentok Pepper: Chinese Settlement on an Indonesian Island* (Singapore: Institute of Southeast Asian Studies, 1992), 188.

57. Ibid., 199.

58. See "Philippines Approves New Migrant Worker Act," *Migration New* 1, 3 (1995).

59. William H. Mercer, A.E. Collins, and A.J. Harding, *The Colonial Office List for 1924* (London: Waterlow and Sons, 1924), 725.

60. *The Cyclopedia of Fiji* (Sydney, NSW: Cyclopedia Company of Fiji, 1907), 307–12.

61. See David A. Price, *Love and Hate in Jamestown: John Smith, Pocahontas, and the Start of a New Nation* (New York: Knopf, 2003).

62. See Geoffrey Serle, *The Golden Age: A History of the Colony of Victoria, 1851–1861* (Melbourne: Melbourne University Press, 1963).

63. See Katherine Cronin, *Colonial Casualties: Chinese in Early Victoria* (Melbourne: Melbourne University Press, 1982).

64. James Foreman-Peck, *A History of the World Economy: International Economic Relations since 1850* (Brighton: Wheatsheaf, Harvester, 1983), 50.

65. See Ion L. Idriess, *Forty Fathoms Deep: Pearl Divers and Seas Rovers in Australian Seas* (Sydney: Angus and Robertson, 1945); and Hugh Edwards, *Port of Pearls* (Adelaide: Rigby, 1983).

66. See Philip Jones and Anna Kenny, *Australia's Muslim Cameleers: Pioneers of the Inland 1860s– 1930s* (Kent Town, South Australia: Wakefield, 2007).

67. P. Taylor, *The Distant Magnet: European Migration to the United States* (London: Eyre and Spottiswoode, 1971).

68. Foreman-Peck, *A History of the World Economy*, 149–50.

69. See J.G. Williamson, *Late Nineteenth Century American Development* (New York: Cambridge Uni-

versity Press, 1974); and J.D. Gould, "European Intercontinental Emigration," *Journal of European Economic History* 8 (1979), 593–679.

70. See M.J. Piore, *Birds of Passage: Migrant Labour and Industrial Societies* (New York: Cambridge University Press, 1979).

71. See Michael LeMay and Elliott R. Barkin, eds., *U.S. Immigration and Naturalization Laws and Issues: A Documentary History* (Westport, CT: Greenwood, 1999); and Aristide Zolberg, *A Nation by Design: Immigration Policy in the Fashioning of America* (Cambridge, MA: Harvard University Press, 2006).

72. See Harry Reicher, *The Post-Holocaust World and President Harry S. Truman: The Harrison Report and Immigration Law and Policy* (Online at http://www.schnader.com/files/Uploads/Documents/post-holocaust.pdf, 2002).

73. See David M. Reimers, "Post–World War II Immigration to the United States: America's Latest Newcomers," *The Annals of the American Academy of Political and Social Sciences* 454 (1981), 1–12.

74. Peter S. Costellos, "Obama Victory took Root in Kennedy-inspired Immigration Act," *The Boston Globe,* 11 November 2008.

75. United States Census Bureau, *The Asian Population: 2000* (Washington, D.C.: United States Census Bureau, 2002).

76. United Nations press release (POP 844), 28 October 2002.

77. United Nations, *International Migration Report for 2002.*

78. Using data obtained online from http://www.migrationinformation.org/datahub/.

79. Rainer Muenz, *Europe: Population and Migration in 2005.* Migration Information Source, June (2006), online at http://www.migrationinformation.org/Feature/display.cfm?ID=402

80. R. Skeldon, "The Emergence of Trans-Pacific Migration," in *The Cambridge Survey of World Migration,* ed., R. Cohen (Cambridge: Cambridge University Press, 1995), 510–22.

81. Ibid.

Chapter 3

1. Clark W. Sorenson "P'yongyang North Korea," in *Encyclopedia of Urban Cultures,* Volume 3, eds., Melvin Ember and Carol R. Ember (Danbury, CT: Grolier, 2002), 489.

2. See J.H. Hann, "Origin and Development of the Political System in the Shanghai International Settlement," *Journal of the Hong Kong Branch of the Royal Asiatic Society* 22 (1982), 31–64.

3. Ibid., 36.

4. See Jean-Paul Crespelle, *La Vie quotidienne a Montmarte au temps de Picasso, 1900–1910* (Paris: Hachette Literature, 1978).

5. Charles Allen, ed., *Tales from the South China Seas: Images of the British in South-East Asia in the Twentieth Century* (London: Futura, 1983), 86.

6. See George Dutton, *The Tây Son Uprising: Society and Rebellion in Eighteenth-Century Vietnam*

(Honolulu: University of Hawai'i Press, 2006), 199–205.

7. Naval Intelligence Division, *Indo-China* (Cambridge: Cambridge University Press, 1943), 233.

8. Ibid., 472.

9. See Yong Chen, *Chinese San Francisco, 1850–1943: A Trans-Pacific Community* (Palo Alto, CA: Stanford University Press, 2000); and Thomas W. Chin, *Bridging the Pacific: San Francisco Chinatown and its People* (San Francisco: Chinese Historical Society of America, 1989).

10. Will Durant, *Caesar and Christ: A History of Roman Civilization and of Christianity from their beginnings to A.D. 325* (New York: Simon and Schuster, 1944), 457. Also see John M. Fritz and George, eds., *New Light on Hampi: Recent Research at Vijayanagar* (Mumbai: MARG, 2001).

11. See V.A. Smith, *The Oxford History of India* (New York: Oxford University Press, 1981), 304–13.

12. Nicolo de Conti, *The Travels of Nicolo Conti in the East in the Early Part of the Fifteenth Century* (London: Hakluyt Society, 1857); W.H. Moreland and Atul Chandra Chatterjee, *A Short History of India* (New York : David McKay, 1962), 177; K.A. Nilakanta Sastri, *A History of South India from Prehistoric Times to the Fall of Vijayanagar* (New Delhi: Oxford University Press, 2002), 304–6; and Robert Sewell, *A Forgotten Empire, Vijayanagara* (Delhi: Asian Education Services, 1982), 246–7.

13. Suryanath U. Kamath, *A Concise History of Karnataka: From Pre-Historic Times to the Present* (Bangalore: Jupiter, 2001), 181.

14. Monica L. Smith, "The Archaeology of South Asian Cities," *Journal of Archaeological Research* 14 (2006), 129.

15. Halil Inalcik, "The Policy of Mehmed II Toward the Greek Population of Istanbul and the Byzantine Buildings of the City," *Dumbarton Oaks Papers* 23 (1969), 236.

16. See Janet L. Abu-Lughod, *Cairo: 1001 Years of the City Victorious* (Princeton, NJ: Princeton University Press, 1971).

17. See V. Minorsky and S.S. Blair, "Tabriz," in *Encyclopedia of Islam,* Volume X, eds., P.J. Bearman, et al. (Leiden: Brill, 2009).

18. William B. Fisher, ed., *The Cambridge History of Iran: The Land of Iran* (New York: Cambridge University Press, 1968), 14.

19. See Jan de Vries, *European Urbanization, 1500–1800* (New York: Routledge, 1984).

20. See Jocelyn Hunt, *Spain, 1474–1598* (New York: Routledge, 2001); and Patrick O'Flanagan, *Port Cities of Atlantic Iberia, c. 1500–1900* (Farnha, Surrey, UK: Ashgate, 2008).

21. O'Flanagan, *Port Cities of Atlantic Iberia.*

22. Michael E. Smith, "City Size in Late Post-Classic Mesoamerica," *Journal of Urban History* 31 (2005), 403–34.

23. Anthony Reid, "Economic and Social Change, c. 1400–1800," in *The Cambridge History of Southeast Asia, Volume One: From Early Times to c. 1800,* ed., N. Tarling (New York: Cambridge University Press, 1992), 473.

24. Ibid., 474.

25. David K. Wyatt, *Thailand: A Short History* (New Haven, CT: Yale University Press, 1982), 65.

26. Ibid., 67.

27. Ibid., 105.

28. Ibid., 108.

29. Ibid., 109.

30. Ibid., 110.

31. George V. Smith, *The Dutch in Seventeenth-Century Thailand* (DeKalb, IL: Center for Southeast Asian Studies, Northern Illinois University, 1977), 35.

32. See Humayun Ansari, *The Infidel Within: The History of Muslims in Britain, 1800 to the Present* (London: C. Hurst, 2004); Michael H. Fisher, "Excluding and Including 'Natives of India': Early-Nineteenth-Century British-Indian Race Relations in Britain," *Comparative Studies of South Asia, Africa and the Middle East* 27 (2007), 303–314; and Michael H. Fisher, Shompa Lahiri, and Shinder Thandi, *A South Asian History of Britain: Four Centuries of Peoples from the Indian Subcontinent* (London: Greenwood, 2007).

33. "Curry House Founder in Honoured," BBC News, 29 September (2005).

34. Fisher "Excluding and Including," 304–5.

35. See John May, "The Chinese in Britain, 1869–1914," in *Immigrants and Minorities in British Society*, ed., Colin Holmes (London: George Allen and Unwin, 1978), 111–24; Kwee Choo Ng, *The Chinese in London* (London: Oxford University Press, 1968); Gregor Benton and E.T. Gomez, *The Chinese in Britain, 1800–Present: Economy, Transnationalism, and Identity* (London: Palgrave, 2007); John Seed, "Limehouse Blues: Looking for Chinatown in the London Docks, 1900–1940," *History Workshop Journal* 62 (2006), 58–85; and David Parker, "Chinese People in Britain: Histories, Futures and Identities," in *The Chinese in Europe*, eds., Gregor Benton and F.N. Pieke (Basingstoke: Macmillan, 1998).

36. John Mark Carroll, *A Concise History of Hong Kong* (London: Rowman and Littlefield, 2007), 100.

37. See Jeffrey Auerbach, *The Great Exhibition of 1851: A Nation on Display* (New Haven, CT: Yale University Press, 1999); Charles H. Gibbs-Smith, *The Great Exhibition of 1851* (London: HMSO, 1981); and Michael Leapan, *The World for a Shilling: How the Great Exhibition of 1851 Shaped a Nation* (London: Headline, 2001).

38. Susan Abeyasekere, *Jakarta: A History* (Singapore: Oxford University Press, 1987), 19.

39. Norman Lewis, *Golden Earth: Travels in Burma* (New York: Charles Scribner's Sons, 1952), 15.

40. R. Talbot Kelly, *Burma: The Land and the People* (London: L. Beling Tetens/Boston: J.B. Millet, 1910), 6–7.

41. Mercer, Collins, and Harding, *The Colonial Office List for 1924*, 397.

42. Carl Trocki, *Singapore: Wealth, Power and the Culture of Control* (New York: Routledge, 2005), 31.

43. Saskia Sassen, *The Global City: New York, London, Tokyo* (Princeton, NJ: Princeton University Press, 1991).

44. A.T. Kearny and the Chicago Council on Global Affairs, "The 2008 Global Cities Index," *Foreign Policy*, November/December (2008), online at http://www.foreignpolicy.com/articles/2008/10/15/the_2008_global_cities_index.

45. Ibid.

46. "The Principal Agglomerations of the World," online at http://www.citypopulation.de/world/Agglomerations.

47. Brenda S.A. Yeoh, "Singapore: Hungry for Foreign Workers at All Skill Levels," *Migration Information Source*, January (2007), online at http://www.migrationinformation.org/Profiles/display.cfm?ID=570.

48. Mark Jacobson, "The Singapore Solution," *National Geographic* 217, 1 (2010), 140.

49. Online at http://www.studiesinaustralia.com.

50. See Wena Poon, ed., *Lions in Winter* (Singapore: MPH Group, 2007).

51. See, for example, www.expat-blog.com/nationalities/singaporean/in/north-america/canada/.

52. Museum Victoria, "Singapore," *Origins: Immigrant Communities in Victoria*, online at http://museumvictoria.com.au/origins/gallery.aspx?pid=53&img=352.

53. See Kevin Teo, "Of Migration and the Singaporean Diaspora," *The Kent Ridge Common*, 14 April (2009).

Chapter 4

1. John Kenneth Galbraith, *The Age of Uncertainty* (Boston: Houghton Mifflin, 1977), 68.

2. Ibid., 68.

3. Ibid., 68.

4. Tomoko Makabe, *Picture Brides: Japanese Women in Canada* (Toronto: Multicultural Historical Society of Canada, 1995). Also see Evelyn Nakano Glenn, *Issei, Nisei, War Bride: Three Generations of Japanese American Women in Domestic Service* (Philadelphia: Temple University Press 1986); and Jenifer Gee, "Housewives, Men's Villages, and Sexual Respectability: Gender and the Interrogation of Asian Women at the Angel Island Immigration Station," in *Asian/Pacific Islander Women: A Historical Anthology*, eds., S. Hune and G.N. Nomura (New York: NYU Press, 2003), 90–4, concerning Japanese picture brides going to the United States.

5. Makabe, *Picture Brides*, 6.

6. Ibid., 7.

7. Ibid., 8.

8. Ibid., 46–7.

9. Ibid., 11.

10. Lili M. Kim, "Redefining the Boundaries of Traditional Gender Roles: Korean Picture Brides, Pioneer Korean Korean Immigrant Women, and Their Benevolent Nationalism in Hawai'i," in *Asian/Pacific Islander Women: A Historical Anthology*, eds., S. Hune and G.M. Nomura (New York: NYU Press, 2003), 107. Also see Eun Sak Yang, "Korean Women of America: From Subordination to Partnership, 1903–1930," *Amerasia* 11, 2 (1984), 1–28; and Alice Chai, "Korean Women in Hawaii, 1903–1945, The Role of Methodism in Their Liberation and Their Participa-

tion in the Korean Independence Movement," in *Women in New Worlds,* eds., H.F. Thomas and R.S. Keller (Nashville, TN: Abingdon, 1981), 328–344.

11. Kim, "Redefining the Boundaries of Traditional Gender Roles," 107.

12. Helen Papanikolas, *An Amulet of Greek Earth: Generations of Immigrant Folk Culture* (Athens: Ohio University Press, 2002), 122.

13. Ibid., 126.

14. Isabel Kaprielian-Churchill, "Armenian Refugee Women: The Picture Bride, 1920–1930," *Journal of American Ethnic History* 3, 3 (1993), 3.

15. Chitra Divakaruni, "Uncertain Objects of Desire," *The Atlantic Online,* March (2000). Also in the paper version in *The Atlantic,* 285, 3 (2000), 22–27.

16. Neena Bhandari, "Indian Brides Spearhead Oz Migration," *Overseas Indian,* October (2008), published online by the Ministry of Overseas Indian Affairs at http://www.overseasindian.in.

17. Ibid.

18. Ibid.

19. Ellen Oxfeld, "Cross-Border Hypergamy? Marriage Exchanges in a Transnational Hakka Community," in *Cross-Border Marriages: Gender and Mobility in Transnational Asia,* ed., N. Constable (Philadelphia: University of Pennsylvania Press, 2005), 17–33.

20. Ibid., 32.

21. Ibid., 22–3.

22. Ibid., 24.

23. Ibid., 25.

24. Ibid., 26.

25. Ibid., 29.

26. Nicole Constable, "Introduction: Cross-Border Marriages, Gendered Mobility, and Global Hypergamy," in *Cross-Border Marriages: Gender and Mobility in Transnational Asia,* ed., N. Constable (Philadelphia: University of Pennsylvania Press, 2005), 1–16.

27. Ibid., 10.

28. Ibid., 10–1.

29. Nobue Suzuki, "Tripartite Desires: Filipina-Japanese Marriages and Fantasies of Transnational Traversal," in *Cross-Border Marriages: Gender and Mobility in Transnational Asia,* ed., N. Constable (Philadelphia: University of Pennsylvania Press, 2005), 124–44.

30. Hung Cam Thai, "Clashing Dreams in the Vietnamese Diaspora: Highly Educated Overseas Brides and Low-wage U.S. Husbands," in *Cross-Border Marriages: Gender and Mobility in Transnational Asia,* ed., N. Constable (Philadelphia: University of Pennsylvania Press, 2005), 145–165; and Hung Cam Thai, *For Better of for Worse: Vietnamese International Marriages in the New Global Economy* (Piscataway, NJ: Rutgers University Press, 2008).

31. See Carol Fallows, *Love and War: Stories of War Brides from the Great War to Vietnam* (Milson Point, NSW: Bantam, 2002).

32. David M. Reimers, "The Korean-American Immigrant Experience." Conference paper, The Legacy of Korea: a 50th Anniversary Conference, Truman Presidential Museum and Library and the University of Missouri–Kansas City (2001), available online at http://www.trumanlibrary.org/korea/reimers.htm#reimers.

33. Elfrieda Shukert and Barbara Scibetta, *War Brides of World War II* (Novato, CA: Presidio, 1988), 209.

34. Ibid., 216.

35. Reimers, "The Korean-American Immigrant Experience."

36. Brendan O'Malley, "Japanese War Brides Light Up Citizenship Ceremony," *Couriermail,* 20 January (2009), online at http://www.couriermail.com.au/. Also see Keiko Tamura, *Michi's Memories: The Story of a Japanese War Bride* (Canberra: Research School of Pacific Studies, Australian National University, 2001).

37. Constable, "Introduction."

38. Ibid., 4.

39. Suzuki, "Tripartite Desires."

40. Constable, "Introduction," 7.

41. Ibid., 7.

42. Yaan-Ju Lee, Dong-Hoon Seol, and Sung-Nam Cho, "International Marriages in South Korea: The Significance of Nationality and Ethnicity," *Journal of Population Research* 23, 3 (2006), 165–182.

43. Hyun Mee Kim, "Current Situation and Challenges in South Korea, Taiwan and Japan — Integration for Whom?: Married Migrant Women Policies in South Korea and Patriarchal Imagination," paper presented at "International Marriage from the Women's Human Rights Perspective" symposium, Seoul, 3 August (2007). Synopsis provided in Koonae Park, "Korea-Japan Symposiums on 'International Marriage' and 'Female Migrant Workers,'" online at http://www.hurights.or.jp/asia-pacific/050/08.html.

44. "South Korea's Birthrate World's Lowest," *The Korea Times,* 22 May 2009.

45. Lee, Seol, and Cho, "International Marriages in South Korea."

46. Kim, "Current Situation and Challenges in South Korea, Taiwan and Japan."

47. Lee, Seol, and Cho, "International Marriages in South Korea."

48. Kim, "Current Situation and Challenges in South Korea, Taiwan and Japan."

49. Norimitsu Onishi, "Marriage Brokers in Vietnam Cater to S. Korean Bachelors," *International Herald Tribune,* 21 February 2007.

50. Ibid.

51. Hsiao-Chuan Hsia, "The Development of Immigrant Movement in Taiwan — the Case of Alliance of Human Rights Legislation for Immigrants and Migrants," paper presented at "Multicultural Families and the Local Community — Examining Co-existence in Japan, Korea and Taiwan" symposium (2007). Synopsis provided in Park, Koonae, and Nobuki Fujimoto, "Symposium on Multi-cultural Families and the Local Community," online at http://www.hurights.or.jp/asia-pacific/055/05.html.

52. "Taiwan Curbs Foreign Bride Firms," BBC News, 8 January 2009.

53. Ibid.

54. Hsia, "The Development of Immigrant Movement in Taiwan."

55. Hsia, "The Development of Immigrant Movement in Taiwan."

56. "Vietnam State to Run Bride Agency," BBC News, 08 January 2009.

57. Ibid.

58. Nicole Constable, *Romance on a Global Stage: Pen Pals, Virtual Ethnography, and "Mail-Order" Marriages* (Berkeley: University of California Press, 2003), 217.

59. Ibid.

60. See Lynn Visson, *Wedded Strangers: The Challenges of Russian-American Marriages* (New York: Hippocrene, 2001).

61. Craig Harris, "Marriage Brokers Scrutinized: Critics Fear Exploitation of Foreign Women: Local Dating Service Defends Romance Tours," *The Arizona Republic,* 15 October (2005).

62. Ibid.

63. See Visson (2001).

64. Harris, "Marriage Brokers Scrutinized."

65. Constable, *Romance on a Global Stage.*

66. Harris, "Marriage Brokers Scrutinized."

67. Ibid.

68. James A. Tyner, "Global Cities and Circuits of Global Labor: The Case of Manila," in *Filipinos in Global Migrations,* ed., F.V. Aguilar, Jr. (Quezon City: Philippine Migration Research Network and Philippine Social Science Council, 2002), 65.

69. Haiming Liu, *The Transnational History of a Chinese Family: Immigrant Letters, Family Business, and Reverse Migration* (Piscataway, NJ: Rutgers University Press, 2005).

70. Constable, *Romance on a Global Stage,* 183.

71. Ibid., 185.

72. Ibid., 184.

73. Graeme J. Hugo, *Population Mobility and Wealth Transfers in Indonesia and Other Third World Societies* (Honolulu: East-West Center Population Institute, 1983), 2.

74. Ibid., 25.

75. Suzuki, "Tripartite Desires," 127.

76. Ibid. Also see Rhacel Salazar Parreñas, *Servants of Globalization: Women, Migration, and Domestic Work* (Stanford, CA: Stanford University Press, 2001).

77. Skeldon, "The Emergence of Trans-Pacific Migration."

78. See United Nations, *Working Towards the Elimination of Crimes Against Women Committed in the Name of Honour: Report to the Secretary-General* (New York: United Nations General Assembly, Report A/57/169, 2002).

Chapter 5

1. See Jan de Vries and Ad Van Der Woude, *The First Modern Economy: Success, Failure, and Perseverance of the Dutch Economy, 1500–1815* (New York: Cambridge University Press, 1997).

2. Ibid., 436–7.

3. Division of Commerce of the Department of Agriculture, Industry and Commerce, Java (Buitenzorg), *Handbook of the Netherlands East-Indies* (Batavia: G. Kolff, 1924), 225.

4. See Stephen Howarth, Joost Jonker, Keetie Sluyterman, and Jan Luitan van Zanden, *The History of Royal Dutch Shell* (New York: Oxford University Press, 2007).

5. Royal Dutch Shell, online at http://www.shell.com/home/content/aboutshell/who_we_are/our_history/.

6. See http:/www.energyintel.com/.

7. Fluor Corporation, *Insight: 2009 Annual Report:* Form 10-K, pg. 2.

8. Online at http://money.cnn.com/magazines/fortune/global500/2010/.

9. Timothy W. Mair, "China's Military May Get U.S. Base" *Insights of the News,* 17 May 1999. Also see Softwar, "The Panama Canal in Transition: Threats to U.S. Security and China's Growing Role in Latin America (2000), online at http://www.softwar.net/panama/.

10. Peter S. Goodman, "China Invests Heavily In Sudan's Oil Industry: Beijing Supplies Arms Used on Villagers," *Washington Post,* 23 December (2004), A01. Also see Shaofeng Chen, "Motivations Behind China's Foreign Oil Quest: A Perspective from the Chinese Government and the Oil Companies," *Journal of Chinese Political Science* 13, 1 (2008), 79–104.

11. CNPC homepage at http://www.cnpc.com.cn/en/.

12. Debra Highley, *The Talara Basin Province of Northwestern Peru: Cretaceous-Tertiary Total Production System,* U.S. Geological Survey Bulletin 2206-A (Washington, D.C.: U.S. Department of the Interior, U.S. Geological Survey, 2004), 8.

13. See Eurasia Group, *China's Overseas Investments in Oil and Gas Production* (New York: Eurasia Group, 2006), 21; and Goodman, "China Invests Heavily in Sudan's Oil Industry."

14. Goodman, "China Invests Heavily In Sudan's Oil Industry."

15. Ibid.

16. Ibid.

17. Parker (2009).

18. Dilip K. Das, "Globalisaton and an Emerging Middle Class," *Economic Affairs* 29, 3 (2009), 89–92.

19. Quoted in John Parker, "Burgeoning Bourgeoisie," *The Economist,* 12 February 2009.

20. Ibid.

21. See "China's Mr. Golf Looks to Tee Up Business," BBC News, 15 July 2010.

22. "Golf Today Course Guide: Courses in China," *Golf Today,* online at http://www.golftoday.co.uk/clubhouse/coursedir/world/china/mainindex.html.

23. Parker, "Burgeoning Bourgeoisie."

24. Ibid.

25. Bibek Dibroy, "Who Are the Middle Class in India?," *The Indian Express,* 24 March 2009, online at http://www.indianexpress.com/.

26. Ibid.

27. See Hsin-Huang Michael Hsiao, ed., *East Asian Middle Classes in Comparative Perspective* (Taipei: Institute of Ethnology, Academia Sinica,

1999); and Hsin-Huang Michael Hsiao, *The Changing Faces of the Middle Classes in Asia-Pacific* (Taipei: Center for Asia-Pacific Studies, 2006).

28. Nguyen Thanh Tuan, "About the Current Middle Class in Vietnam," *Tap chi Cong san* (Communist Review), 8 March 2007.

29. Grant McCool, "Middle Class in Vietnam Likes to Buy Things, Too," *International Herald Tribune,* 9 October 2006.

30. Damien Cave, "This Ho Chi Minh Trail End at the 18th Hole," *The New York Times,* 9 March 2008.

31. McCool, "Middle Class in Vietnam."

32. "Vietnam Automobile Industry Forecast (2007–2010)," http://www.prlog.org/10031685-vietnam-automobile-industry-forecast-2007-2010.html.

33. Business Monitor International, *Vietnam Automotives Report* (2007).

34. "Vietnam July Car Sales Drop 13 pct yr/yr — Industry," Reuters, 9 August 2010, online at http://www.reuters.com/article/idUSSGE67902A20100810.

35. McCool, "Middle Class in Vietnam."

36. See a summary of Vidamco's history online at http://www.vidamco.com.vn/history.php.

37. The company vision online at http://www.vidamco.com.vn/Vision.php.

38. The company's board of directors online at http://www.vidamco.com.vn/board.php.

39. TNS Global refers (www.tnsglobal.com) to itself as "the world's largest Custom Market Research specialists. We provide quality marketing information delivered by Global Industry Sector expert consultants, innovative Market Research Expertise across the product life-cycle, in 75 countries.... We have the strongest Market Research custom network in Asia Pacific" and its branch in Vietnam is "The only full service market research group in Vietnam."

40. McCool, "Middle Class in Vietnam."

41. Ibid.

42. Carrefour homepage at http://www.carrefour.com/.

43. See "Retailers Jump in for Carrefour SE Asia Assets," Reuters, 1 September 2010, online at http://www.reuters.com/article/idUSTRE6800ZQ20100901?dbk; "Retailers Race to Bid on Carrefour's Asian Assets," *New York Times,* 1 September 2010, online at http://dealbook.blogs.nytimes.com/2010/09/01; and "Carrefour Said to Seek Buyers for Three Southeast Asia Units," Bloomberg, 5 July 2010, online at http://www.bloomberg.com/news/print/2010-07-05/.

44. Online at http://www.absoluteastronomy.com/topics/E-Land.

45. Aeon Group, *Aeon 2010: Fully Global, Truly Local* (Chiba: Aeon, 2010); also see Aeon's homepage online at http://www.aeon.info/en/.

46. Ibid., 4.

47. Ibid., 14.

48. *Business Standard,* 14 May 2008.

49. Metro Cash & Carry India homepage at http://www.metro.co.in/.

50. Metro Cash & Carry Pakistan homepage at http://www.metro.pk/servlet/PB/menu/-1_l2/index.html.

51. Jean-Joseph Cadilhon and Andrew P. Fearne. "Lessons in Collaboration: A Case study from Vietnam: A Grocery Wholesaler Proves that Effective Supply Chain Partnerships can be Built on Basic Information-sharing and Coordination Practices," *Supply Chain Management Review,* May (2005).

52. "Metro Supermarkets Close after Five-year Decline," *The Jakarta Post,* 31 March 2009.

53. Laura Liebeck, "Kmart Czechs into Europe — K Mart Corp.'s Czechoslovakian Acquisitions," *Discount Store News,* 15 June (1992).

54. See C. Louise Sellaro, Therese Maskulka, and David J. Burns, "(R)evolution of Retailing in the Former Czechoslovakia: The Case of Kmart," *International Journal of Commerce and Management* 7, 1 (1997), 74–87.

55. Susie Measure and David McNeil, "Tesco Builds Presence in Japan with Acquisition of Debt-laden Fre'c Chain," *The Independent,* 28 April 2004.

56. "Retailers Jump in for Carrefour SE Asia Assets," Reuters, 1 September 2010, online at http://www.reuters.com/article/idUSTRE6800ZQ20100901?dbk.

57. Big C press release at http://bigc.com.vn/, 28 November 2007.

58. Kwok-bun Chan and Leo Douw, "Introduction: Differences, Conflict and Innovations: The Emergence of a Transnational Management Culture in China," In *Conflict and innovation: Joint Ventures in China,* eds., L. Douw and C. Kwok-bun (Leiden: Brill, 2006), 3.

59. Geert Hofstede, *Culture's Consequences: International Differences in Work-Related Values* (Beverley Hills, CA: Sage, 1980).

60. James R. Lincoln, Harold R. Kerbo, and Elke Wittenhagen, "Japanese Companies in Germany: A Case Study in Cross-Cultural Management," *Industrial Relations: A Journal of Economy and Society* 34, 3 (2008), 417–40.

61. Chan and Douw, "Introduction," 6.

62. Ibid., 4.

63. See May M.L. Wong, "Shadow Management in Japanese Companies in Hong Kong," *Asia Pacific Journal of Human Resources* 34, 1 (1996), 95–110.

64. Chan and Douw, "Introduction," 9–10.

65. Ibid., 10.

66. Ibid., 10–11.

67. Ibid., 11.

68. Lincoln, Kerbo, and Wittenhagen, "Japanese Companies in Germany."

69. Irmtraud Munder and Renate Krieg, "Sino-German Joint Ventures: Shared Values and Cultural Divides," in *Conflict and Innovation: Joint Ventures in China,* eds., L. Douw and C. Kwok-bun (Leiden: Brill, 2006), 116–38.

70. Pankaj Ghemawat, *Redefining Global Strategy: Crossing Borders in a World Where Differences Still Matter* (Cambridge, MA: Harvard Business School Press, 2007).

71. Christopher A. Barlett and Sumantra Ghohal, "Japan's Achilles Heel — Its Corporate Global Strategies are Hindered by a History of Highly Centralized Operational Control." *Los Angeles Times,* 12 November 1989; and see Christopher A. Barlett Barlett and Sumantra Ghohal, *Managing Across Borders: The Transnational Solution* (Cambridge, MA: Harvard Business School Press, 2002).

72. Bartlett and Ghohal," Japan's Achilles Hill."
73. Ibid. For a study of Japanese companies in Hong Kong in this regard see Wong, "Shadow Management."
74. Yoshida (2001).
75. "The True Story of Carlos Ghosn," CNN.com/World Business, 16 June 2008, online at http://edition.cnn.com/2008/BUSINESS/06/11/ghosn.profile/index.html#cnnSTCText.
76. See "Carlos Ghosn," online at http://www.notablebiographies.com/supp/Supplement-Fl-Ka/Ghosn-Carlos.html.
77. See David Magee, *Turnaround: How Carlos Ghosn Rescued Nissan* (New York: Collins, 2003); and Ghosn, *Shift: Inside Nissan's Historic Revival* (New York: Doubleday, 2005).
78. Reiji Yoshida, "International Rationale: Language among New Survival Skills: Foreign Managers bring Change to Corporate Life," *The Japan Times Online,* 24 May (2001).
79. James Brooke, "Shake-up at Sony: Japan's Reaction; Western Chief? Most Japanese are Unfazed," *The New York Times,* 8 March 2005.
80. Ibid.
81. Ibid.
82. Ibid.
83. Ibid.
84. Ibid.
85. Hiroshi Suzuki and Masaki Kondo, "Sony's CEO Stronger Ousts Chubachi in Overhaul of Management," Bloomberg, 27 February 2009, online at http://www.bloomberg.com/.
86. Yoshida, "International Rationale."
87. Suzuki and Kondo, "Sony's CEO Stronger Ousts Chubachi."
88. "Aeon Appoints First Foreign Exec," *Japan Times Online,* 25 January 2009, online at http://search.japantimes.co.jp/cgi-bin/nb20090125a3.html.
90. "Kurt Salmon Associate Appoints Jerry Black as CEO," *Positions & Promotions,* online at http://www.poandpo.com/who-is-promoted/kurt-salmon-associates-appoints-jerry-black-as-ceo/.
91. Kurt Salmon homepage online at http://www.kurtsalmon.com/.
92. "Kurt Salmon Associate Appoints Jerry Black as CEO."
93. Kurt Salmon Associates, "Japan," online at http://www.kurtsalmon.com/team_group.php?id=14.
94. Yoshida, "International Rationale."
95. Ibid.
96. Ibid.
97. Susan Lund, Charles Roxburgh, and Bruno Roy, "Sovereign Investors Still Strong in Asia," *Far Eastern Economic Review* 172, 7 (2009), 53.
98. Lund, Roxburgh, and Roy, "Sovereign Investors Still Strong in Asia," 55.

Chapter 6

1. Henk van de Bunt and Dina Siegel, "Introduction," in *Global Organized Crime: Trends and Developments,* eds., H. van de Bunt and D. Siegel (Dordrecht: Kluwer Academic, 2003) 3.
2. Bunt and Siegel, "Introduction," 4–5.
3. Mark Shaw and Gail Wannenburg, "Organized Crime in Africa," in *Handbook of Transnational Crime and Justice,* ed., P. Reichel (Thousand Oaks, CA: Sage, 2005), 373.
4. Ibid.
5. United Nations Office on Drugs and Crime, *Transnational Organized Crime in the West African Region* (New York: United Nations, 2005), 1.
6. Donald R. Liddick, Jr., *The Global Underworld: Transnational Crime and the United States* (Westport, CT: Praeger, 2004), 35.
7. Online at http://www.fas.org/irp/congress1996_hr.
8. Gail Wannenburg, "Organised Crime in West Africa," *African Security Review,* 14, 4 (2005), online at http://www.iss.co.za.
9. "That's All They Needed: Illicit Drugs Flow in From All Over and Then Flow Out to Europe," *The Economist,* 06 December 2007.
10. United Nations Office on Drugs and Crime, *Transnational Organized Crime,* 21.
11. *The Times of India,* 11 June 2006.
12. "Nigerians Top in Drug Trafficking," *Times of India,* 7 December 2009.
13. Online at http://www.libraryindex.com/pages/2361/Drug-Trafficking-HEROIN.html.
14. Online at http://wwwlibraryindex.com/pages/2361/Drug-Trafficking-HEROIN.html.
15. National Drug Intelligence Center, "Methamphetamine Drug Threat Assessment," online at http://www.usdoj/gov/ndic/pubs11/13853/product.htm.
16. Online at http://www.danwei.org, 24 June 2009.
17. "Women and the Hard Drug Trade," *Daily Sun,* 12 December 2008.
18. Shaw and Wannenburg, "Organized Crime in Africa," 373; Mark Shaw, "West African Criminal Networks in South and Southern Africa," *African Affairs,* 101, 404 (2002), 291–316
19. United Nations Office on Drugs and Crime, *Transnational Organized Crime,* 2.
20. Jeffrey Robinson, *The Merger: The Conglomeration of International Organized Crime* (Woodstock, NY: Overlook, 2000), 281.
21. United Nations Office on Drugs and Crime, *Transnational Organized Crime,* 4.
22. Ibid., 5.
23. Ibid.
24. Ibid., 15.
25. Ibid.
26. Ibid., 16.
27. Ibid., 17.
28. Jørgen Carling, *Migration, Human Smuggling and Trafficking from Nigeria to Europe* (Geneva: International Organization for Migration, 2006), 25.
29. Carling, *Migration, Human Smuggling and Trafficking,* 26.
30. Ibid., 24–5.
31. Ibid., 26.
32. Ibid., 27.
33. Ibid.

34. See R. van Dijk, "'Voodoo' on the Doorstep: Young Nigerian Prostitutes and Magic Policing in the Netherlands," *Africa*, 71, 4 (2001). 558–586.

35. United Nations Office on Drugs and Crime, *Transnational Organized Crime*, 17.

36. Ibid.

37. Robinson, *The Merger*, 284; and see Toyyin Falola, "Lebanese Traders in Southwestern Nigeria, 1900–1960," *African Affairs*, 89 (1990), 523–53.

38. McCoy, *The Politics of Heroin in Southeast Asia*, 76.

39. Ibid., 76–7.

40. Ibid., 89.

41. Ibid., 91–2.

42. Ibid., 121.

43. Ibid., 153, 160, 253.

44. Ibid., 252.

45. Ibid., 430, fn. 34.

46. Ibid., 253.

47. See Eugène Saccoman, *Bandits à Marseille* (Paris: Julliard, 1968); Robin Moore, *The French Connection: A True Account of Cops, Narcotics, and international Conspiracy* (Guilford, CT: Lyons, 2003).

48. McCoy, *The Politics of Heroin in Southeast Asia*, 173.

49. Ibid., 181.

50. Ibid.

51. Ibid., 247.

52. Ibid., 239–40.

53. *New York Times*, 06 June 1971, 2.

54. McCoy, *The Politics of Heroin in Southeast Asia*, 248.

55. Robinson, *The Merger*, 221.

56. See Bertil Lintner, *Burma in Revolt: Opium and Insurgency Since 1948* (Boulder, CO: Westview, 1994); Bertil Lintner and Michael Black, *Merchants of Madness: The Methamphetamine Explosion in the Golden Triangle* (Chiang Mai: Silkworm, 2009); and Ronald Renard, *The Burmese Connection: Illegal Drugs and the Making of the Golden Triangle* (Boulder: Lynne Rienner, 1996).

57. See *The Times*, May 11, 2007.

58. See Ko-Lin Chin, *The Golden Triangle: Inside Asia's Drug Trade* (Ithaca, NY: Cornell University Press, 2009); and Lintner and Black, *Merchants of Madness*.

59. Lintner and Black, *Merchants of Madness*, 92.

60. "Eight High-Ranking Leaders of Southeast Asia's Largest Narcotics Trafficking Organization Indicted by a Federal Grand Jury in Brooklyn, New York," U.S. Drug Enforcement Administration, News from DEA, Domestic Field Divisions, New York City News Releases, 24 January 2005 (online at www.justice.gov/dea/pubs/states/.../nyc012405.html).

61. See Linter and Black, *Merchants of Madness*, 67–72, 153–4.

62. Ibid., 67.

63. Ibid., 113–7.

64. See Sirivanh Khontaphane, Sathanbandith Insisisangmay, and Vanthana Nolintha, *Impact of Border Trade in Local Livelihoods: Lao-Chinese Border Trade in Luang Namtha and Oudomxay Provinces*, Technical Background Paper for the Third National Human Development Report (Vientiane: International Trade and Human Development/UNDP, 2006).

65. Lintner and Black, *Merchants of Madness*, 115.

66. See Anthony Bruno, "The Yakuza: Origins and Traditions," Time Warner Crime Library, 2007, available online at: http://www.crimelibrary.com; Peter E. Hill, *The Japanese Mafia: Yakuza, Law, and the State* (New York: Oxford University Press, 2003); David E. Kaplan and Alec Dubro, *Yakuza: The Explosive Account of Japan's Criminal Underworld* (Berkeley: University of California Press, 2003); and Christopher Seymour, *Yakuza Diary* (New York: Atlantic Monthly, 1996).

67. Liddick, *The Global Underworld*, 28.

68. Bertil Linter, *Blood Brothers: Crime, Business, and Politics in Asia* (Chiang Mai: Silkworm, 2002), 4.

69. Jake Adelstein, "This Mob Is Big in Japan," *The Washington Post*, 11 May 2008, B02; and Bruno, "The Yakuza."

70. Adelstein, "This Mob Is Big in japan."

71. Kaplan and Dubro, *Yakuza*, 7–8.

72. Ibid.

73. Ibid.

74. Ibid., 9–10.

75. Ibid., 224.

76. Ibid.

77. Sonia Ryang, *Koreans in Japan: Critical Voices from the Margin* (New York: Routledge, 2000).

78. See Kaplan and Dubro, *Yakuza*, 228–31.

79. Ibid., 232.

80. Antonio Nicaso and Lee Lamothe, *Global Mafia: The New World Order of Organized Crime* (Toronto: Macmillan Canada, 1995), 93–4.

81. Richard H. Ward and Daniel J. Mabrey, "Organized Crime in Asia," in *Handbook of Transnational Crime and Justice*, ed., P. Reichel (Thousand Oaks, CA: Sage, 2005), 393.

82. Linter, *Blood Brothers*, 5.

83. Kaplan and Dubro, *Yakuza*, 280.

84. Ibid., 282.

85. Ibid.

86. Ibid.

87. Testimony before the Senate's Permanent Subcommittee of Investigations during a hearing on Asian organized crime in the United States, 03 October 1991.

88. Briane M. Grey, "The Poisoning of Paradise: Crystal Methamphetamine in Hawaii." Testimony before the House Government Reform Committee's Subcommittee on Criminal Justice, Drug Policy and Human Resources, 2 August 2004.

89. Kaplan and Dubro, *Yakuza*, 289–90.

90. See Kingsley Bolton and Chris Hutton, eds., *Triad Societies: Western Accounts of the History, Sociology and Linguistics of Chinese Secret Societies* (London: Taylor and Francis, 2000); Martin Booth, *The Triads: The Chinese Criminal Fraternity* (London: Grafton, 1990); Martin Booth, *The Dragon Syndicates: The Global Phenomenon of the Triads* (New York: Basic, 2001); Fenton S. Bresler, *The Trail of the Triads: An Investigation into International Crime* (London: Weidenfeld and Nicolson, 1980); James Main, "The Truth About Triads," *Policing* 7, 2 (1991), 144–163; W.P. Mor-

gan, *Triad Societies in Hong Kong* (Hong Kong: Government Press, 1960); and Frank Robertson, *Triangle of Death: The Inside Story of the Triads, the Chinese Mafia* (London: Routledge and Kegan Paul, 1978).

91. See Dian H. Murray, *The Origins of the Tiandihui: The Chinese Triads in Legend and History* (Sanford, CA: Stanford University Press, 1994).

92. Leonard P. Adams II, "China: The Historical Setting of Asia's Profitable Plague," in *The Politics of Heroin in South East Asia,* A.W. McCoy, et al (Singapore: Harper and Row, 1972), 371–3.

93. Lintner, *Blood Brothers,* 28.

94. Ibid., 32, 38–40.

95. Adams, China," 371.

96. McCoy, *The Politics of Heroin in Southeast Asia,* 225.

97. Ko-Lin Chin, *Chinese Subculture and Criminality: Non-Traditional Crime Groups in America* (Westport, CT: Greenwood, 1990).

98. McCoy, *The Politics of Heroin in Southeast Asia,* 228.

99. Ibid., 229.

100. Ibid., 233.

101. Permanent Subcommittee on Investigations of the Committee on Governmental Affairs, United States Senate, *The New International Criminal and Asian Organized Crime: Report, December 1992* (Washington, D.C.: United States Government Printing Office, 1993).

102. Lintner, *Blood Brothers,* 80.

103. Ibid., 79–8.

104. See "Macau Moves Against Gangs," BBC News, 4 May 1998; and "'Broken Tooth' Sent to Jail," BBC News, 23 November 1999.

105. Lintner, *Blood Brothers,* 9–10.

106. Ibid., 8.

107. Permanent Subcommittee on Investigations of the Committee on Governmental Affairs, *The New International Criminal.*

108. Antonio Nicaso, "The Dragon's Fire: Part 18 — The Chinese Triads are Digging their Claws into Canadian Businesses," *Tandem,* 24 June (2001), online at http://www.tandemnews.com/.

109. Permanent Subcommittee on Investigations of the Committee on Governmental Affairs, *The New International Criminal.*

110. Parliamentary Joint Committee on the National Crime Authority, Australian Parliament, *Asian Organized Crime,* Discussion Paper (1995), available online at http://www.fas.org/irp/world/australia/docs/ncaaoc2.

111. Angela Veng Mei Leong, "The 'Bate-ficha' Business and Triads in Macao Casinos," *QUT Law & Justice Journal,* 5 (2002), online at http://www.austlii.edu.au/Au/journals/QUTLJJ/2002/5.

112. Loeng, "The 'Bate-ficha' Business and Triads."

113. A. Pinho, "Gambling in Macau," in *Macau: City of Commerce and Culture,* ed., R.D. Cremer (Hong Kong: API, 1991), 249.

114. Loeng, "The 'Bate-ficha' Business and Triads."

115. Ibid.

116. Parliamentary Joint Committee on the National Crime Authority, *Asian Organized Crime.*

117. On their involvement in American Chinatowns see Chin, *Chinese Subculture and Criminality:* Ko-Lin Chin, *The Golden Triangle: Inside Asia's Drug Trade* (Ithaca, NY: Cornell University Press, 2000); and Jeoffrey Scott Mcillwain, "From Tong War to Organized Crime: Revising the Historical Perception of Violence in Chinatown," *Justice Quarterly* 14, 1 (1997), 25–52.

118. See W.L. Blythe, *The Impact of Chinese Secret Societies in Malaya: A Historical Study* (London: Oxford University Press, 1969).

119. Andaya and Andaya, *A History of Malaya,* 141.

120. Ibid.

121. Ibid., 142.

122. Leon Combe, *The Hung: Chinese Secret Societies in 1950's Malaya and Singapore* (Glasgow: Talisman, 2009).

123. McCoy, *The Politics of Heroin in Southeast Asia,* 234.

124. On postwar activities of the Triads in this area see Lau-Fong Mak, *Chinese Secret Societies in Ipoh Town, 1945–1969* (Singapore: Working Paper, Department of Sociology, University of Singapore, 1975); Lau-Fong Mak, *The Sociology of Secret Societies: A Study of Chinese Secret Societies in Singapore and Peninsular Malaysia* (Kuala Lumpur: Oxford University Press, 1981); and Combe, *The Hung.*

125. Nicaso, "The Dragon's Fire."

126. Liddick, *The Global Underworld,* 29.

127. Ward and Mabrey, "Organized Crime in Asia," 389.

128. Ibid.

129. Ibid.

130. Parliamentary Joint Committee on the National Crime Authority, *Asian Organized Crime.*

131. 22 June (1988), reproduced on page 66 of the National Crime Authority's *Annual Report 1987–88.*

132. Parliamentary Joint Committee on the National Crime Authority, *Asian Organized Crime.*

133. 22 June (1988), reproduced on page 66 of the National Crime Authority's *Annual Report 1987–88.*

134. Parliamentary Joint Committee on the National Crime Authority, *Asian Organized Crime.*

135. Ibid.

136. Nicaso, "The Dragon's Fire."

137. Nicaso and Lamothe, *Global Mafia,* 114.

138. Nicaso, "The Dragon's Fire."

139. Terry Gould, *Paper Fan: The Hunt for Triad Gangster Steven Wong* (Toronto: Random House Canada, 2004).

Chapter 7

1. Will Durant, *The Age of Faith: A History of Medieval Civilization — Christian, Islamic, and Judaic — from Constantine to Dante: A.D. 325–1300* (New York: Simon and Schuster, 1950), 215.

2. Ibid., 216.

3. Robert R. Bianchi, *Guests of God: Pilgrimage*

and Politics in the Islamic World (New York: Oxford University Press, 2004), 3.

4. See http://www.hajinformation.com/main/l.htm.

5. Bianchi, *Guests of God,* 5.

6. Ibid., 4.

7. Ibid.

8. Howard M. Federspeil, *Sultans, Shamans, and Saints: Islam and Muslims in Southeast Asia* (Honolulu: University of Hawaii Press, 2007), 67.

9. See Christiaan Snouck Hurgronje, "Notes sur le mouvement du pelerinage de la Macque aux indes néederlandaises," *Revue du Monde Musulman* 10, October (1911), 397–413; Christiaan Snouck Hurgronje, "Le pelerinage a la Mekke," in *Selected Works of C. Snouck Hurgronje,* eds., G.H. Bousquet and J. Schacht (Leiden: E.J. Brill, 1957), 173–207; and Harry J. Benda, "Christiaan Snouck Hurgronje and the Foundations of Dutch Islamic Policy in Indonesia," *Journal of Modern History* 30 (1958), 338–347.

10. Federspeil, *Sultans, Shamans, and Saints,* 100.

11. Ibid., 108.

12. Bianchi, *Guests of God,* 195.

13. Ibid., 195–6.

14. "Garuda Gears Up to Take Pilgrims to Saudi Arabia," *Jakarta Globe,* 20 August 2009.

15. David Clingingsmith, Asim Ijaz Khwaja, and Michael Kremer, *Estimating the Impact of the Hajj: Religion and Tolerance in Islam's Global Gathering,* Weatherhead Center Working Paper No. 2008-0128 (Cambridge, MA: Harvard University, 2008).

16. Ibid., 2.

17. "43 Percent Surge in Christian Pilgrims," *Jerusalem Post,* 03 April 2009.

18. Ibid.

19. "60,000 Christian Pilgrims to Visit Holy Land this Christmas," *Christian Telegraph,* 01 March 2008.

20. http://www.holyland-pilgrimage.org/.

21. http://www.catholicpilgrimages.com/.

22. Such as James McCormick, *The Holy Land: The First Ecumenical Pilgrim's Guide* (Bloomington IN: IUniverse, 2000); Charles Dyer and Gregory Hetteberg, *The New Christian's Traveler's Guide to the Holy Land* (Chicago, IL: Moody, 2006); and Hela Crown-Yamir, *How to Walk in the Footsteps of Jesus and the Prophets: A Scripture Reference Guide for Biblical Sites in Israel and Jordan* (Jerusalem: Gefen, 2000).

23. Vida Bajc, "Christian Pilgrimage to Jerusalem and Normalization of Crises: Of Tradition, Modernity, and Security," paper presented at the annual meeting of the American Sociological Association, Montreal, Canada (2006).

24. http://www.custodia.fr.

25. "Christian Pilgrim Leaves for Jerusalem," *sify.com,* 25 November 2008, online at http://www.sify.com/.

26. Peter Abelson, "Schopenhauer and Buddhism," *Philosophy East and West* 43, 2 (1993), 255–278; and James Heisig, *Philosophers of Nothingness* (Honolulu: University of Hawaii Press, 2001).

27. See Brooks Wright, *Interpreter of Buddhism to the West: Sir Edwin Arnold* (New York: Bookman, 1957).

28. Edwin Arnold, *The Light of Asia* (Cambridge, UK: Windhorse, 2004, reprint, originally published in 1879).

29. See Daniel H. Caldwell, ed., *The Esoteric World of Madame Blavatsky: Insights Into the Life of a Modern Sphinx* (Wheaton, IL: Quest, 2000); and Gertrude Marvin Williams, *Priestess of the Occult, Madame Blavatsky* (New York: Alfred. A. Knopf, 1946).

30. See "Blavatsky and Buddhism," online at http://www.blavatsky.net/.

31. See Stephen Prothero, *The White Buddhist: The Asian Odyssey of Henry Steel Olcott* (Bloomington: Indiana University Press, 1996).

32. See Ananda Gurunge, ed., *Return to Righteousness: A Collection of Speeches, Essays, and Letters of the Anagarika Dharmapala* (Colombo: Ministry of Education and Cultural Affairs, 1965); David L. McMahan, *The Making of Buddhist Modernism* (New York: Oxford University Press, 2008), 91–7, 110–3; Gananath Obeyesekere, "Personal Identity and Cultural Crisis: the Case of Anagarika Dharmapala of Sri Lanka," in *The Biographical Process,* eds., F.E. Reynolds and D. Capps (The Hague: Mouton, 1976), 221–52; and D.C. Ahir, *Buddhism in Modern India* (Delhi: Sri Satguru, 1991).

33. See John McRae, "Oriental Verities on the American Frontier: The 1893 World's Parliament of Religions and the Thought of Mason Abe," *Buddhist-Christian Studies* 11 (1991), 7–36.

34. See its website at http://www.parliamentofreligions.org/. Also see "Melbourne Hosts Multi-faith Fest," BBC News, 3 December 2009.

35. Seonaigh MacPherson, Anne-Sophie Benz, and Dawa Bhuti Ghoso, "Global Nomads: The Emergence of the Tibetan Diaspora," *Migration Information Source,* September (2008).

36. MacPherson, Benz, and Ghoso, "Global Nomads."

37. http://www.tibet.com/.

38. MacPherson, Benz, and Ghoso, "Global Nomads."

39. http://www.gomang.org/.

40. "Tibetans in Switzerland," *Tibet Sun,* 27 June 1964, onlime at http://www.tibetsun.com/archive/1964/06/27/tibetans-in-switzerland/.

41. http://www.tcccgc.org/.

42. ABC News, 11 August 2007.

43. See, for example, "Dalai Lama Sees Taiwan visit as 'Moral Responsibility,'" CBC News, 31 August 2009; and "Dalai Lama Meets Protests, Tears in Taiwan," Time.com, 01 September 2009.

44. See Jessica Mai Sims, *Empowering Individuals and Creating Community — Thai Perspectives of Life in Britain* (Runnymede Trust, 2008), online at www.runnymedetrust.org/.../EmpoweringIndividualsCreatingCommunity-2008.pdf.

45. See Sandra Cate, *Making Merit, Making Art: A Thai Temple in Wimbledon* (Honolulu: University of Hawai'i Press, 2003).

46. http://www.buddhapadipa.org/.

47. See Stanley Jeyaraja Tambiah, *The Buddhist*

Saints of the Forest and the Cult of Amulets (New York: Cambridge University Press, 1984), 136–8.

48. J.L. Taylor, *Forest Monks and the Nation-State: An Anthropological and Historical Study in Northeastern Thailand* (Singapore: Institute of Southeast Asian Studies, 1993), 124.

49. See Robert W. Funk, Ron W. Hoover, and The Jesus Seminar, *The Five Gospels: The Search for the Authentic Words of Jesus* (Sonoma, CA: Polebridge, and New York: Macmillan, 1993).

50. See J.S. Cummins, ed., *Christianity and Missions, 1450–1800* (Aldershot, UK: Ashgate, 1997). On Christian missionaries in the Americas in particular see Charles H. Lippy, Robert Choquette, and Stafford Poole, *Christianity Comes to the Americas: 1492–1776* (New York: Paragon House, 1992).

51. From the English translation of the *Inter Caetera* online at http://www.catholic-forum.com/saints/pope1214a.htm/.

52. Fagg, *Latin America*, 101.

53. Ibid., 102.

54. See Bartolomé de Las Casas, *Short Account of the Destruction of the Indies* (London: Penguin, 1999); David Brading, "Prophet and Apostle: Bartolomé de las Casas and the Spiritual Conquest of America," in *Christianity and Missions, 1450–1800*, ed., J.S. Cummins (Aldershot, UK: Ashgate, 1997), 117–138; Juan Friede and Benjamin Keen, eds., *Bartolomé de las Casas in History: Toward an Understanding of the Man and His Work* (DeKalb, IL: Northern Illinois University Press, 1971); Lewis Hanke, *Bartolomé de Las Casas: Bookman, Scholar and Propagandist* (Philadelphia: University of Pennsylvania Press, 1952); and Francis Augustus MacNutt, *Batholomew de las Casas: His Life, His Apostolate and His Writings* (Cleveland, OH: Arthur H. Clark, 1909).

55. Arden R. King, *Coban and the Verapaz: History and Cultural Process in Northern Guatemala* (New Orleans: Middle American Research Institute, Tulane University, 1974), 17.

56. Ibid., 19.

57. Armando Lampe, *Christianity in the Caribbean: Essays on Church History* (Kingston: University of West Indies Press, 2001), 17.

58. King, *Coban and the Verapaz*, 20.

59. Las Casas, *Short Account of the Destruction of the Indies*.

60. See Andrew Steinmetz, *History of the Jesuits* (London: R. Bentley, 1848).

61. See Alexandre de Rhodes, *Rhodes of Vietnam: The Travels and Missions of Fathers Alexander de Rhodes in China and Other Kingdoms of the Orient* (Westminster, MD: Newman, 1966); and Arnold T. Wilson, "History of the Missions of the Fathers of the Society of Jesus in China and Other Kingdoms of the East," *Bulletin of the School of Oriental Studies, University of London*, 4, 1 (1926), 47–57.

62. Wilson, "History of the Missions," 49.

63. Missions Étrangères de Paris, *Missions étrangères de Paris: 350 ans au service du Christ* (Paris: Editeurs Malesherbes, 2008), 4.

64. http://www.mepasie.org/.

65. See Alden T. Vaughan, "Sir Walter Raleigh's Indian Interpreters, 1584–1618," *The William and Mary Quarterly* 59, 2 (2002), 341–76.

66. See Thomas Bray, *A Memorial Representing the Present State of Religion, on the Continent of North-America* (London: John Brudenell, 1701).

67. J. Harry Bennett, Jr., *Bondsmen and Bishops—Slavery and Apprenticeship on the Codrington Plantations of Barbados, 1710–1838* (Berkeley: University of California Press, 1958).

68. See William Canton, *A History of the British and Foreign Bible Society* (London: J. Murray, 1904–10).

69. Narda Dobson, *A History of Belize* (London: Longman Caribbean, 1973), 160.

70. Ibid., 317–8.

71. Ibid., 318.

72. Ibid., 319.

73. http://www.lambethconference.org/resolutions/1867/1867-8.cfm.

74. *Papers of Philip Quaque,* Collection 151, Billy Graham Center, Wheaton University, online at http://www.wheaton.edu/bgc/archives/GUIDES/151.htm. Also see J Kofi Agbeti, *West African Church History: Christian Missions and Church Foundations*. Leiden: Brill, 1986).

75. See Jesse Page, *Samuel Crowther: The Slave Boy Who Became Bishop of the Niger* (London: S.W. Partridge, 1892).

76. Ibid., Ch. VI.

77. Ibid., Ch. X.

78. See http://www.uspg.org.uk/.

79. http://www.anglicancommunion.org/.

80. Online at http://www.anglicancommunion.org/windsor2004/.

81. See http://www.gafcon.com/.

82. See http://www.canaconvocation.org/.

83. http://www.worldevangelicals.org/.

84. See the Lausanne Movement homepage at http://www.lausanne.org/.

85. Larry Poston, *Islamic Da'wah in the West: Muslim Missionary Activity and the Dynamics of Conversion to Islam* (New York: Oxford University Press, 1992), 6.

86. David Cook, *Martyrdom in Islam* (New York: Cambridge University Press, 2007), 74.

87. Egdunas Racius, *The Multiple Nature of the Islamic Da'wa,* Academic Dissertation (Helsinki: University of Helsinki, 2004), 155.

88. Ibid., 103.

89. See Roel Meijer, ed., *Global Salafism: Islam's New Religious Movement* (London: C. Hurst, 2009).

90. On Salafism in Indonesia, where Salafi Da'wa emerged in the 1980s, see Noorhadi Hasan, "The Salfi Movement in Indonesia: Transnational Dynamics and Local Development," *Comparative Studies of South Asia, Africa and the Middle East* 27, 1 (2007), 83–94.

91. See Zachary Abuza, *Funding Terrorism in Southeast Asia: The Financial Network of Al Qaeda and Jemaah Islamiyah* (National Bureau of Asian Research, *NBR Analysis* 14, 5, 2003).

92. "Taking from the Poor," *Newsweek International,* 22 October 2001, online at http://www.newsweek.com/2001/10/22/taking-from-the-poor.html.

93. "A Blueprint for 9/11," CBS News, 17 January 2003.

94. See Agnes de Feo, *Les Musulmans du Cambodge et du Vietnam* (Bangkok: Institute de Recherché sur l'Asie du Sud-Est Contemporaine, 2009).

95. Antonio Graceffo, "Cham Muslims: A Look at Cambodia's Muslim Minority" (2005), online at http://www.talesofasia.com/rs-50-cham.htm.

96. Cornerstone University, "Cham of Cambodia," online at http://intercultural-mandate.wiki spaces.com/Meghan+Jones+People+Group

97. Feo, *Les Musulmans du Cambodge.*

98. Zachary Abuza, "The Islamist Insurgency in Thailand," *Current Trends in Islamist Ideology* 4 (2006).

99. Poston, *Islamic Da'wah in the West*, 112.

100. Racius, *The Multiple Nature of the Islamic Da'wa*, 159.

101. Edward Wilmot Blyden, *Christianity, Islam and the Negro Race* (London: W.B. Whittingham, 1887).

Chapter 8

1. See Dominique Cardon, *Natural Dyes: Sources, Tradition, Technology and Science* (London: Archetype, 2007), 553–606.

2. See K. Hubner, "History — 150 Years of Mauvine," *Chemie in unserer Zeit* 40, 4 (2006), 274–275; and Anthony S. Travis, "Perkin's Mauve: Ancestor of the Organic Chemical Industry," *Technology and Culture* 31, 1 (1990), 51–82.

3. Cardon, *Natural Dyes*, 335.

4. Ibid., 336.

5. See Hetty Nooy-Palm, "The Sacred Cloths of the Toraja: Unanswered Questions," in *To Speak With Cloth: Studies in Indonesian Textiles*, ed., M. Gittinger (Los Angeles: Museum of Cultural History, University of California, Los Angeles, 1989), 170–2.

6. Aubrey Cannon, "The Cultural and Historical Contexts of Fashion," in *Consuming Fashion: Adorning the Transnational Body*, eds., A. Brydon and S. Niessen (New York: Berg, 1998), 24.

7. Michael C. Howard and Kim Be Howard, *Textiles of the Peoples of Northern Vietnam: Mon-Khmer, Hmong-Mien, and Tibeto-Burman* (Bangkok: White Lotus, 2002), 29–46.

8. Cannon, "The Cultural and Historical Contexts of Fashion," 26.

9. See Michael C. Howard and Kim Be Howard, *Textiles of the Daic Peoples of Vietnam* (Bangkok: White Lotus, 2002), 10–11.

10. Mattiebelle Gittinger, "Textiles in the Service of the Kings," in *Textiles and the Tai Experience in Southeast Asia*, eds., M. Gittinger and L. Lefferts (Washington, D.C.: Textile Museum, 1992) 143.

11. John Guy, *Woven Cargoes: Indian Textiles in the East* (London: Thames and Hudson, 1998), 150.

12. Michael C. Howard, "Identity and Traditional and Tradition-based T'ai Textiles in Contemporary Thai Society," in *Traditional T'ai Arts in Contemporary Perspective*, eds., M.C. Howard, W. Wattanapun, and A. Gordon (Bangkok: White Lotus, 1998), 22.

13. Ibid.

14. Ibid., 22–23.

15. Ibid., 23.

16. "Colonial Office List Advertiser," in *The Coloinal Office List for 1921*, eds., William H. Mercer, A.E. Collins, and A.J. Harding (London: Waterlow and Sons, 1921).

17. Address delivered on 24 November 2000, online at http://texmin.nic.in.

18. *Encyclopaedia of Global Industries*, 4th Edition (Detroit: Gale, 2007).

19. See Rachel Louise Snyder, *Fugitive Denim: A Moving Story of People and Pants in the Borderless World of Global Trade* (New York: W.W. Norton, 2009); and James Sullivan, *Jeans: A Cultural History of an American Icon* (London: Gotham, 2006).

20. Nick Wolf, "Why the Soviet Union Collapsed," online at http://www.helium.com/items/223412-why-the-soviet-union-collapsed.

21. Robert Bridge, "Russia's Blue Jean Blues," *Moscow News*, 31 January 2008, online at http://mn weekly.rian.ru.

22. *World Denim Report 2007*, online at http://www.fibre2fashion.com/. See L. Y Li and K.W. Yeung, *The China and Hong Kong Denim Industry*, Woodhead Texile Series No. 30 (Cambridge: Woodhead, 2003) on the PRC.

23. K. Giriprakesh, "Building a Rural Workforce," *Business Line*, 14 September 2006, online at http://www.thehindubusnessline.com.

24. *Encyclopaedia of Global Industries.*

25. Ibid.

26. Lynn Pan, *Sons of the Yellow Emperor: A History of the Chinese Diaspora* (Tokyo: Kodansha Globe, 1994), 28–9. Also see Ly-Tio Fane, *La diaspora chinoise dans l'Ocean Indien occidental* (Mauritius: Editions de l'Ocean Indien, 1985).

27. Gilles Joomun, "The Textile and Clothing Industry in Mauritius," in *The Future of the Textile and Clothing Industry in Sub-Saharan Africa*, eds., H. Jauch and R. Traub-Merz (Bonn: Friedrich-Ebert Stiftung, 2006), 193.

28. Ibid., 194. Also see Deborah Brautigam, "Local Entrepreneurship in Southeast Asia and Sub-Saharan Africa: Networks and Linkages to the Global Economy," in *Asia and Africa in the Global Economy*, eds., Ernest Aryeetey, Julius Court, and Beatrice Weder (Tokyo: United Nations University Press, 2003), 106–28.

29. Jooman, "The Textile and Clothing Industry in Mauritius," 194.

30. Ibid., 204.

31. Inter Press Service News Agency, 12 March 2008, online at http://ipsnews.net/.

32. Inter Press Service News Agency, 14 March 2008, online at http://ipsnews.net/.

33. *Indian Ocean News*, 05 February 2008.

34. "What Does the Bible Say About Proper Dress?," online at http://www.twopaths.com/faq_dress.htm.

35. Thomas Williams, *Fiji and the Fijians, Volume*

I: The Islands and their Inhabitants (London: Alexander Heylin, 1858), 156.

36. Linda B. Arthur, "Cultural Authentication Refined: The Case of the Hawaiian Holoku," *Clothing and Textiles Research Journal* 15, 3 (1997), 129–39.

37. Lucy G. Thurston, *Life and Times of Mrs. Lucy G. Thurston, Wife of Rev. Asa Thurston, Pioneer Missionary to the Sandwich Islands, Gathered from Letters and Journals Extending Over a Period of More than Fifty Years, Selected and Arranged by Herself* (Ann Arbor, MI: S.C. Andrews, 1882), 98.

38. Arthur, "Cultural Authentication Refined." Her quotation is from the Missionary Herald, *Extracts from the Joint Letters of the Hilo Mission* (Hilo, HI: Lyman House Memorial Museum, 1832), 222.

39. See Gail Stewart, *Ancient Hawaiian Dress and the Influence of European Dress on It, 1778–1820,* unpublished master's thesis, University of Hawai'i (1977); and Otto von Kotzebue, *Kotzebue's Voyage of Discovery 1815–1818* (London: Longman, Thirst, Rees, Orme and Brown, 1821).

40. Thurston, *Life and Times of Mrs. Lucy G. Thurston;* Kotzebue, *Kotzebue's Voyage of Discovery;* and Arthur, "Cultural Authentication Refined."

41. Kotzebue, *Kotzebue's Voyage of Discovery,* 252.

42. Arthur, "Cultural Authentication Refined."

43. Thurston, *Life and Times of Mrs. Lucy G. Thurston,* 32.

44. Arthur, "Cultural Authentication Refined."

45. Ping-Ann Addo, "God's Kingdom in Auckland: Tongan Christian Dress and the Expression of Duty," in *Clothing the Pacific,* C. Colchester (Oxford: Berg, 2003), 142.

46. Ibid.

47. Ibid., 154.

48. Ibid.

49. See Leila Ahmed, *Women and Gender in Islam: Historical Roots of a Modern Debate* (New Haven, CT: Yale University Press, 1992); and Fadwa El Guindi, *Veil: Modesty, Privacy, and Resistance* (Oxford: Berg, 1999).

50. Kees van Dijk, "Sarong, Jubbahs, and Trousers: Appearance as a Means of Distinction and Discrimination," in *Outward Appearances,* ed., H. Schulte Nordholt (Leiden: KITLV, 1997), 44.

51. Rijkloff van Goens, "Reijsbeschrijving van den weg uit Samarangh nae de konincklijke hoofdplaets Mataram," *Bijdragen tot de Taal-en Volkenkunde* 4 (1856), 323.

52. Dijk, "Sarong, Jubbahs, and Trousers," 44.

53. Ibid.

54. Ibid., 45.

55. Johanes Nieuhoff, *Voyages and Travels into Brasil and the East-Indies* (London: Linton and John Osborn, 1744), 76; cited by Dijk, "Sarong, Jubbahs, and Trousers," 49.

56. Dijk, "Sarong, Jubbahs, and Trousers," 55.

57. J. Kathirithamby-Wells, "Ahmed Shan Ibn Iskander and the Late 17th Century 'Holy War' in Indonesia," *Journal of the Malaysian Branch of the Royal Asiatic Society* 43 (1970), 50.

58. Dijk, "Sarong, Jubbahs, and Trousers," 55.

59. See Charles Dobbin, *Islamic Revivalism in a Changing Peasant Economy: Central Sumatra, 1784–1847* (London: Curzon, 1983), 132.

60. Ibid., 62.

61. Ibid., 63.

62. Ibid., 65.

63. Ibid., 63.

64. Ibid., 75.

65. Eve Warburton, "No Longer a Choice: Veiling has Become a Highly Politicised Practice in Indonesia," *Inside Indonesia* 89, January–March (2007), online at http://www.insideindonesia.org/.

66. See "Indonesia Passes Anti-porn Bill," BBC News, 30 October 2008.

67. Vaswami, Karishma. "Aceh Outrage over Miss Indonesia," BBC News, 12 October 2009.

68. Charles Oliver, "Rap-rock Band Linkin Park will Play in Malaysia.... On a Few Conditions," *Reason,* 1 January 2004.

69. "Mariah Upsets Malaysian Muslims," BBC News, 16 January 2004.

70. "Pussycat Dolls Too Frisky for Malaysia," CBS News, 10 August 2006.

71. "Beyonce Postpones Malaysia Show," BBC News, 20 October 2009.

72. 19 August (2008), online at http://newsvine.com/.

73. 28 August (2008), online at http://nme.com/.

74. See Ann Marie Leshkowich, "The *Ao Dai* Goes Global: How International Influences and Female Entrepreneurs have Shaped Vietnam's 'National Costume.'" in *Re-orienting Fashion: The Globalization of Asian Dress,* eds., S.A. Niessen, A.M. Leshkowich, and C. Jones (Oxford: Berg, 2003), 79–116.

75. Howard and Howard, *Textiles of the Peoples of Northern Vietnam,* 29–30.

76. Erik Cohen, "The Commercialization of Ethnic Crafts," *Journal of Design History* 2, 2–3 (1989), 164.

77. See Theresa Reilly, *Richly Woven Traditions: Costumes of the Miao of Southwest China and Beyond* (New York: China House Gallery, 1987), 28.

78. See Nancy D. Donnelly, *Changing Lives of Refugee Hmong Women* (Seattle: University of Washington Press, 1994).

79. Annette Lynch, "Hmong American New Year's Dress: The Display of Ethnicity," in *Dress and Ethnicity,* ed., J.B. Eicher (Oxford: Berg, 1995), 260–1.

80. Ibid., 262.

81. Edward Gresser, "NTR and Trade Normalization: and U.S.–Lao Trade," Progressive Policy Institute, 22 May (2002), online at http://www.ppionline.org/.

82. Ibid.

Chapter 9

1. Joseph S. Nye, Jr., *Soft Power: The Means of Success in World Politics* (New York: Public Affairs, 2004), 5–6.

2. Joshua Kurlantzick, *Charm Offensive: How China's Soft Power is Changing the World* (New Haven, CT: Yale University Press, 2007), 61.

3. Pál Nyíri, "Expatriating is Patriotic? The Discourse on 'New Migrants' in the People's Republic

of China and Identity Construction among Recent Migrants from the PRC," in *State/Nation/Transnation,* eds., B.S.A. Yeoh and K. Willis (New York: Routledge, 2004), 129.

4. Michael C. Howard, "Introduction," in *Traditional T'ai Arts in Contemporary Perspective,* eds., M.C. Howard, W. Wattanapun, and A. Gordon (Bangkok: White Lotus, 1998), 1.

5. See Sheikla Hamanaka and Ayano Ohmi, *In Search of the Spirit: The Living National Treasures of Japan* (New York: HarperCollins, 1999).

6. Will Durant, *The Life of Greece* (New York: Simon and Schuster, 1939), 186.

7. Ibid., 69.

8. Durant, *The Age of Reason Begins* (New York: Simon and Schuster, 1961), 255.

9. Ruth Halliwell, *The Mozart Family: Four Lives in a Social Context* (Oxford: Oxford University Press, 1998), 172, 183–5.

10. See Bruce Allen Brown, *Gluck and the French Theatre in Vienna* (Oxford: Clarendon, 1991); and Patricia Howard, *Gluck and the Birth of Modern Opera* (London: Barrie and Rockliff, 1963).

11. See Michael Scott, *The Great Caruso* (London: Hamish Hamilton, 1988).

12. "Argentina's Teatro Colón," *The Economist,* 9 July 2008.

13. Christina Lamb, "A Night at the Opera — and 14 Days on the Amazon to Get There," *Daily Telegraph,* 17 June 2001, online at http://www.telegraph.co.uk/.

14. Ibid.

15. See "Começam os ensaios de ópera de Roger Waters no mítico Teatro Amazonas," *O Globo,* 18 March 2008, online at http://oglobo.globo.com/.

16. Jung Chang and Jon Halliday, *The Unknown Story of Mao* (New York: Anchor, 2006), 477.

17. Ibid., 195.

18. Ibid., 476–7, 495–6, 507–8.

19. See Colin Mackerras, "Identity, Modernity and Power in the Performing Arts among the Chinese Diaspora," in *Diaspora and Interculturalism in Asian Performing Arts,* ed., H. Um (New York: Routledge-Curzon, 2005), 19.

20. Ibid., 20.

21. Ibid., 22.

22. Ibid.

23. Colin Mackerras, *The Chinese Theatre in Modern Times: From 1840 to the Present Day* (London: Thames and Hudson, 1975), 151–2.

24. See Daphne P. Lei, *Operatic China: Staging Chinese Identity Across the Pacific* (New York: Pal-

grave Macmillan, 2006); and Nancy Yunwa Rao, "Racial Essence and Historical Invisibility: Chinese Opera in New York, 1930," *Cambridge Opera Journal* 12, 2 (2000), 135–62.

25. Lei, *Operatic China.*

26. Online at http://www.eclectica.org/v1n10/making_time.html.

27. Tong Soon Lee, "Chinese Theatre, Confucianism and Nationalism: Amateur Chinese Opera Tradition in Singapore," *Asian Theatre Journal* 24, 2 (2007), 397–421.

28. Gabriel Casal and Regalado Troata Jose, Jr., "Colonial Artistic Expressions in the Philippines (1566–1898)," in *The People and Art of the Philippines,* Gabriel Casal, et al. (Los Angeles: Museum of Cultural History, University of California, Los Angeles, 1981) 103.

29. Ibid., 93, 106.

30. Apinan Poshyananda, *Modern Art in Thailand* (Singapore: Oxford University Press, 1992), 12.

31. Ibid., 16.

32. Ibid., 21.

33. Ibid.

34. Ibid., 34.

35. Ibid., 55.

36. Ibid., 65.

37. Ibid., 76.

38. Herbert P. Phillips, *The Integrative Art of Modern Thailand* (Berkeley: Lowie Museum of Anthropology, University of California at Berkeley), 51.

39. Ibid., 52.

40. Dhamma Park Foundation homepage at http://dhammapark.com/default.aspx.

41. Phillips, *The Integrative Art of Modern Thailand,* 54.

42. See Thai Art Council and Thai Art Center homepage at http://www.thaiartcouncilusa.org/.

43. Preeyanoot Jittawong, "Thai–U.S. Modern Art Show," *Chiang Mai Mail,* 13–19 August (2005), online at http://www.chiangmai-mail.com/.

44. "Works from Two of Thailand's Most Important Living Artists," Cantor Arts Center at Stanford University News Room, online at http://museum.stanford.edu/news_room/Thai1.html.

45. See Wattana Wattanapun homepage at http://www.wwattanapun-art.com/.

46. Michael C. Howard, "An Artist of Two Worlds," *Asian Art News* 4, 2 (1994), 65.

47. Philips, *The Integrative Art of Modern Thailand,* is the catalog.

48. *Fine Art* 4, 28 (2007), 26–37.

49. Howard, "An Artist of Two Worlds," 66.

REFERENCES

Abelson, Peter. "Schopenhauer and Buddhism." *Philosophy East and West* 43, 2 (1993), 255–278.

Abeyasekere, Susan. *Jakarta: A History.* Singapore: Oxford University Press, 1987.

Abu-Lughod, Janet L. *Cairo: 1001 Years of the City Victorious.* Princeton, NJ: Princeton University Press, 1971.

Abuza, Zachary. *Funding Terrorism in Southeast Asia: The Financial Network of Al Qaeda and Jemaah Islamiyah.* National Bureau of Asian Research, *NBR Analysis* 14, 5 (2003).

_____. "The Islamist Insurgency in Thailand." *Current Trends in Islamist Ideology* 4 (2006).

Adams, Leonard P. II. "China: The Historical Setting of Asia's Profitable Plague." In A.W. McCoy, *The Politics of Heroin in South East Asia:* 355–375. Singapore: Harper and Row, 1972.

Addo, Ping-Ann. "God's Kingdom in Auckland: Tongan Christian Dress and the Expression of Duty." In C. Colchester (ed.), *Clothing the Pacific:* 141–163. Oxford: Berg, 2003.

Adelstein, Jake. "This Mob is Big in Japan." *The Washington Post,* 11 May 2008, B02.

Agbeti, J. Kofi. *West African Church History: Christian Missions and Church Foundations.* Leiden: Brill, 1906.

Ahir, D.C. *Buddhism in Modern India.* Delhi: Sri Satguru, 1991.

Ahmed, Leila. *Women and Gender in Islam: Historical Roots of a Modern Debate.* New Haven, CT: Yale University Press, 1992.

Akçam, Taner. *A Shameful Act: The Armenian Genocide and the Question of Turkish Responsibility.* New York: Metropolitan, 2006.

Allen, Charles (ed.). *Tales from the South China Seas: Images of the British in South-East Asia in the Twentieth Century.* London: Futura, 1983.

Andaya, Barbara Watson, and Leonard Y. Andaya. *A History of Malaya.* London: Macmillan Education, 1982.

Ansari, Humayun. *The Infidel Within: The History of Muslims in Britain, 1800 to the Present.* London: C. Hurst, 2004.

Appadura, Arjun. "Disjuncture and Difference in the Global Cultural Economy." *Theory, Culture and Society* 7 (1990), 295–310.

Arnold, Edwin. *The Light of Asia.* Cambridge, UK: Windhorse, 2004 (reprint, originally published in 1879).

Arthur, Linda B. "Cultural Authentication Refined: The Case of the Hawaiian Holoku." *Clothing and Textiles Research Journal* 15, 3 (1997), 129–139.

Auerbach, Jeffrey A. *The Great Exhibition of 1851: A Nation on Display.* New Haven, CT: Yale University Press, 1999.

Bajc, Vida. "Christian Pilgrimage to Jerusalem and Normalization of Crises: Of Tradition, Modernity, and Security." Paper presented at the annual meeting of the American Sociological Association, Montreal, Canada, 2006.

Bard, Solomon M. *Light and Shade: Sketches from an Uncommon Life.* Hong Kong: Hong Kong University Press, 2009.

Bartlett, Christopher A., and Sumantra Ghohal. "Japan's Achilles Heel — Its Corporate Global Strategies are Hindered by a History of Highly Centralized Operational Control." *Los Angeles Times,* 12 November (1989).

_____. *Managing Across Borders: The Transnational Solution.* Cambridge, MA: Harvard Business School Press, 2002.

Benda, Harry J. "Christiaan Snouck Hurgronje and the Foundations of Dutch Islamic Policy in Indonesia." *Journal of Modern History* 30 (1958), 338–347.

Bennett, J. Harry, Jr. *Bondsmen and Bishop: Slavery and Apprenticeship on the Codrington Plantations of Barbados, 1710–1838.* Berkeley: University of California Press, 1958.

Benton, Gregor, and E.T. Gomez. *The Chinese in Britain, 1800–Present: Economy, Transnationalism, and Identity.* London: Palgrave, 2007.

Bernstein, William J. *A Splendid Exchange: How Trade Shaped the World.* New York: Atlantic Monthly, 2008.

Bhandari, Neena. "Indian Brides Spearhead Oz Migration." *Overseas Indian,* October 2008, published online by the Ministry of Overseas Indian Affairs at www.overseasindian.in.

Bianchi, Robert R. *Guests of God: Pilgrimage and Politics in the Islamic World.* New York: Oxford University Press, 2004.

Bilstein, Roger E. *Flight in America.* Baltimore, MD: Johns Hopkins University Press, 2001.

Bloxham, Donald. *The Great Game of Genocide: Imperialism, Nationalism, and the Destruction of the Ottoman Armenians,* Oxford: Oxford University Press, 2005.

Blyden, Edward Wilmot. *Christianity, Islam and the Negro Race.* London: W.B. Whittingham, 1887.

Blythe, W.L. *The Impact of Chinese Secret Societies in Malaya: A Historical Study.* London: Oxford University Press, 1969.

Bolton, Kingsley, and Chris Hutton (eds.). *Triad Societies: Western Accounts of the History, Sociology and Linguistics of Chinese Secret Societies.* London: Taylor and Francis, 2000.

Booth, Martin. *The Dragon Syndicates: The Global Phenomenon of the Triads.* New York: Basic, 2001.
_____. *The Triads: The Chinese Criminal Fraternity.* London: Grafton, 1990.

Brading, David. "Prophet and Apostle: Bartolomé de las Casas and the Spiritual Conquest of America." In J.S. Cummins (ed.), *Christianity and Missions, 1450–1800:* 117–138. Aldershot, UK: Ashgate, 1997.

Brautigam, Deborah. "Local Entrepreneurship in Southeast Asia and Sub-Saharan Africa: Networks and Linkages to the Global Economy." In Ernest Aryeetey, Julius Court, and Beatrice Weder (eds.), *Asia and Africa in the Global Economy:* 106–128. Tokyo: United Nations University Press, 2003.

Bray, Thomas. *A Memorial Representing the Present State of Religion, on the Continent of North-America.* London: John Brudenell, 1701 (available online at anglicanhistory.org/england/tbray/memorial 1701.html).

Bresler, Fenton S. *The Trail of the Triads: An Investigation into International Crime.* London: Weidenfeld and Nicolson, 1980.

Brooke, James. "Shake-up at Sony: Japan's Reaction; Western Chief? Most Japanese are Unfazed." *The New York Times,* 8 March 2005.

Brown, Bruce Alan. *Gluck and the French Theatre in Vienna.* Oxford: Clarendon, 1991.

Brown, David. *The State and Ethnic Politics in Southeast Asia.* New York: Routledge, 1994.

Bruno, Anthony. "The Yakuza: Origins and Traditions." Time Warner Crime Library 2007 (available online at: www.crimelibrary.com).

Bunt, Henk van de, and Dina Siegel. "Introduction." In H. van de Bunt and D. Siegel (eds.), *Global Organized Crime: Trends and Developments:* 3–5. Dordrecht: Kluwer Academic, 2003.

Cadilhon, Jean-Joseph, and Andrew P. Fearne. "Lessons in Collaboration: A Case Study from Vietnam: A Grocery Wholesaler Proves that Effective Supply Chain Partnerships can be Built on Basic Information-Sharing and Coordination Practices." *Supply Chain Management Review,* May 2005.

Caidin, Martin. *Indiana Jones and the Sky Pirates.* New York: Bantam, 1993.

Caldwell, Daniel H. (ed). *The Esoteric World of Madame Blavatsky: Insights Into the Life of a Modern Sphinx.* Wheaton, IL: Quest, 2000.

Cannon, Aubrey. "The Cultural and Historical Contexts of Fashion." In A. Brydon and S. Niessen (eds.), *Consuming Fashion: Adorning the Transnational Body:* 23–38. New York: Berg, 1998.

Canton, William. *A History of the British and Foreign Bible Society.* 5 volumes. London: J. Murray, 1904–1910 (reprinted by Bibliolife in 2008).

Cardon, Dominque. *Natural Dyes: Sources, Tradition, Technology and Science.* London: Archetype, 2007.

Carling, Jørgen. *Migration, Human Smuggling and Trafficking from Nigeria to Europe.* Geneva: International Organization for Migration, 2006.

Carroll, John Mark. *A Concise History of Hong Kong.* London: Rowman and Littlefield, 2007.

Cartwright, Gary. "The World's First Hamburger." *Texas Monthly,* August 2009.

Casal, Gabriel, and Regalado Troata Jose, Jr., "Colonial Artistic Expressions in the Philippines (1566–1898)." In Gabriel Casal, et al., *The People and Art of the Philippines:* 85–121. Los Angeles: Museum of Cultural History, University of California, Los Angeles, 1981.

Casson, Lionel. *Travel in the Ancient World.* London: George Allen and Unwin, 1974.

Castles, S. "Contract Labour Migration." In R. Cohen (ed.), *The Cambridge Survey of World Migration:* 510–522. Cambridge: Cambridge University Press, 1995.

Cate, Sandra. *Making Merit, Making Art: A Thai Temple in Wimbledon.* Honolulu: University of Hawai'i Press, 2003.

Cave, Damien. "This Ho Chi Minh Trail End at the 18th Hole." *The New York Times,* 9 March 2008.

Chai, Alice. "Korean Women in Hawaii, 1903–1945, The Role of Methodism in Their Liberation and Their Participation in the Korean Independence Movement." In H.F. Thomas and R.S. Keller (eds.), *Women in New Worlds:* 328–344. Nashville, TN: Abingdon, 1981.

Chan, Kwok-bun, and Leo Douw. "Introduction: Differences, Conflict and Innovations: The Emergence of a Transnational Management Culture in China." In L. Douw and C. Kwok-bun (eds.), *Conflict and Innovation: Joint Ventures in China:* 1–22. Leiden: Brill, 2006.

Chan, Sucheng. *Chinese American Transnationalism: The Flow of People, Resources, and Ideas between China and America during the Exclusion Era.* Philadelphia, PA: Temple University Press, 2005.

Chandler, Robert J., and Stephen J. Potash. *Gold, Silk, Pioneers and Mail: The Story of the Pacific Mail Steamship Company.* El Cerrito, CA: Glencannon and Friends of the San Francisco Maritime Museum Library, 2007.

Chang, Jung, and Jon Halliday. *The Unknown Story of Mao.* New York: Anchor, 2006.

Chen, Shaofeng. "Motivations Behind China's Foreign Oil Quest: A Perspective from the Chinese Government and the Oil Companies." *Journal of Chinese Political Science* 13, 1 (2008), 79–104.

Chen, Yong. *Chinese San Francisco, 1850–1943: A Trans-Pacific Community.* Palo Alto, CA: Stanford University Press, 2000.

Chin, Ko-Lin. *Chinatown Gangs: Extortion, Enterprise, and Ethnicity.* New York: Oxford University Press, 2000.

_____. *Chinese Subculture and Criminality: Non-Traditional Crime Groups in America.* Westport, CT: Greenwood, 1990.

_____. *The Golden Triangle: Inside Asia's Drug Trade.* Ithaca, NY: Cornell University Press, 2009.

Chin, Thomas W. *Bridging the Pacific: San Francisco Chinatown and its People.* San Francisco: Chinese Historical Society of America, 1989.

"Civil Aviation in Dutch East Indies." *Flight,* 4 March 1932, 196.

Clingingsmith, David, Asim Ijaz Khwaja, and Michael Kremer. *Estimating the Impact of the Hajj: Religion and Tolerance in Islam's Global Gathering.* Weatherhead Center Working Paper No. 2008-0128. Cambridge, MA: Harvard University, 2008.

Cohen, Erik. "The Commercialization of Ethnic Crafts." *Journal of Design History* 2, 2–3 (1989), 161–168.

Cohen, Lucy M. *Chinese in the Post-Civil War South: A People without a History.* Baton Rouge: Louisiana State University Press, 1984.

Combe, Leon F. *The Hung: Chinese Secret Societies in 1950s Malaya and Singapore.* Glasgow: Talisman, 2009.

Conrad, Barnaby. *Pan Am: An Aviation Legend.* Emeryville, CA: Woodford, 1999.

Constable, Nicole. "Introduction: Cross-border Marriages, Gendered Mobility, and Global Hypergamy." In N. Constable (ed.), *Cross-Border Marriages: Gender and Mobility in Transnational Asia:* 1–16. Philadelphia: University of Pennsylvania Press, 2005.

_____. *Romance on a Global Stage: Pen Pals, Virtual Ethnography, and "Mail-Order" Marriages.* Berkeley: University of California Press, 2003.

Conti, Nicolo de (tr. J.W. Jones). *The Travels of Nicolo Conti in the East in the Early Part of the Fifteenth Century.* London: Hakluyt Society, 1857.

Cook, David. *Martyrdom in Islam.* New York: Cambridge University Press, 2007.

Costellos, Peter S. "Obama Victory Took Root in Kennedy-Inspired Immigration Act." *The Boston Globe,* 11 November 2008.

Coulter, John Wesley. *Fiji: Little India of the Pacific.* Chicago: University of Chicago Press, 1942.

Crespelle, Jean-Paul. *La Vie quotidienne a Montmarte au temps de Picasso, 1900–1910.* Paris: Hachette literature, 1978.

Cronin, Katherine. *Colonial Casualties: Chinese in Early Victoria.* Melbourne: Melbourne University Press, 1982.

Crown-Yamir, Hela. *How to Walk in the Footsteps of Jesus and the Prophets: A Scripture Reference Guide for Biblical Sites in Israel and Jordan.* Jerusalem: Gefen, 2000.

Cummins, J.S. (ed.). *Christianity and Missions, 1450–1800.* Aldershot, UK: Ashgate, 1997.

Dadrian, Vahakn N. *The History of the Armenian Genocide: Ethnic Conflict from the Balkans to Anatolia to the Caucasus.* Oxford: Berghahn, 1995.

Das, Dilip K. "Globalisaton and an Emerging Middle Class." *Economic Affairs* 29, 3 (2009), 89–92.

Davis, Kingsley. *The Population of India and Pakistan.* Princeton, NJ: Princeton University Press, 1951.

Dibroy, Bibek. "Who Are the Middle Class in India?" *Indian Express,* 24 March 2009, online at www.indianexpress.com.

Dicken, Peter. *Global Shift: Reshaping the Global Economic Map in the 21st Century.* Fourth Edition. New York/London: Guilford, 2003.

Dickenson, Bob, and Andy Vladimir. *Selling the Sea: An Inside Look at the Cruise Industry.* New York: John Wiley and Sons, 1997.

Dijk, Kees van. "Sarong, Jubbahs, and Trousers: Appearance as a Means of Distinction and Discrimination." In H. Schulte Nordholt (ed.), *Outward Appearances:* 39–83. Leiden: KITLV 1997.

Dijk, R. van. "'Voodoo' on the Doorstep: Young Nigerian Prostitutes and Magic Policing in the Netherlands." *Africa* 71, 4 (2001), 558–586.

Divakaruni, Chitra. "Uncertain Objects of Desire." *The Atlantic Online,* March 2000, also in the paper version in *The Atlantic* 285, 3 (2000), 22–27.

Division of Commerce of the Department of Agriculture, Industry and Commerce, Java (Buitenzorg). *Handbook of the Netherlands East-Indies.* Batavia: G. Kolff, 1924.

Dixon, Peter. *Global Shift: Reshaping the Global Economic Map in the 21st Century.* Fourth Edition. New York: Guilford, 2003.

Dobbin, Charles. *Islamic Revivalism in a Changing Peasant Economy: Central Sumatra, 1784–1847.* London: Curzon, 1983.

Dobson, Narda. *A History of Belize.* London: Longman Caribbean, 1973.

Donnelly, Nancy D. *Changing Lives of Refugee Hmong Women.* Seattle: University of Washington Press, 1994.

Durant, Will. *The Age of Faith: A History of Medieval Civilization — Christian, Islamic, and Judaic — from Constantine to Dante: A.D. 325–1300.* New York: Simon and Schuster, 1950.

_____. *The Age of Reason Begins.* New York: Simon and Schuster, 1961.

_____. *Caesar and Christ: A History of Roman Civilization and of Christianity from Their Beginnings to A.D. 325.* New York: Simon and Schuster, 1944.

_____. *The Life of Greece.* New York: Simon and Schuster, 1939.

Dutton, George. *The Tây Son Uprising: Society and Rebellion in Eighteenth-Century Vietnam.* Honolulu: University of Hawai'i Press, 2006.

Dyer, Charles, and Gregory Hatteberg. *The New Christian's Traveler's Guide to the Holy Land.* Chicago, IL: Moody, 2006.

Edwards, Hugh. *Port of Pearls.* Adelaide: Rigby, 1983.

El Guindi, Fadwa. *Veil: Modesty, Privacy, and Resistance.* Oxford: Berg, 1999.

Encyclopaedia of Global Industries, 4th Edition. Detroit: Gale, 2007.

Eurasia Group. *China's Overseas Investments in Oil and Gas Production.* New York: Eurasia Group, 2006.

Fagg, John E. *Latin America: A General History.* New York: Macmillan, 1963.

Faist, Thomas. "Transnationalization in International Migration: Implications for the Study of Citizenship and Culture," *Ethnic and Racial Studies* 23, 2 (2000), 189–222.

Fallows, Carol. *Love & War: Stories of War Brides from the Great War to Vietnam.* Milson Point, NSW: Bantam, 2002.

Falola, Toyyin. "Lebanese Traders in Southwestern Nigeria, 1900–1960." *African Affairs* 89 (1990), 523–553.

Fane, Ly-Tio. *La diaspora chinoise dans l'Ocean Indien occidental.* Mauritius: Editions de l'Ocean Indien, 1985.

Federspeil, Howard M. *Sultans, Shamans, and Saints: Islam and Muslims in Southeast Asia.* Honolulu: University of Hawaii Press, 2007.

Feo, Agnes de. *Les Musulmans du Cambodge et du Vietnam.* Bangkok: Institute de Recherché sur l'Asie du Sud-Est Contemporaine, 2009.

Fisher, Michael H. "Excluding and Including 'Natives of India': Early-Nineteenth-Century British-Indian Race Relations in Britain." *Comparative Studies of South Asia, Africa and the Middle East* 27, 2 (2007), 303–314.

_____, Shompa Lahiri and Shinder Thandi. *A South Asian History of Britain: Four Centuries of Peoples from the Indian Subcontinent.* London: Greenwood, 2007.

Fisher, William B. (ed.). *The Cambridge History of Iran: The Land of Iran.* New York: Cambridge University Press, 1968.

Foreman-Peck, James. *A History of the World Economy: International Economic Relations since 1850.* Brighton: Wheatsheaf, Harvester, 1983.

Friede, Juan, and Benjamin Keen (eds.). *Bartolomé de las Casas in History: Toward an Understanding of the Man and His Work.* DeKalb: Northern Illinois University Press, 1971.

Fritz, John M., and George Mitchell (eds.). *New Light on Hampi: Recent Research at Vijayanagar.* Mumbai: MARG, 2001.

Frost, M.R. *Transcultural Diaspora: The Straits Chinese in Singapore, 1819–1918.* Working Paper Series No. 10. Singapore: Asia Research Institute, 2003.

Funk, Robert W., Ron W. Hoover, and The Jesus Seminar. *The Five Gospels: The Search for the Authentic Words of Jesus.* Sonoma, CA: Polebridge, and New York: Macmillan, 1993 (reprinted in 1996 by HarperOne).

Galbraith, John Kenneth. *The Age of Uncertainty.* Boston: Houghton Mifflin, 1977.

Gee, Jenifer. "Housewives, Men's Villages, and Sexual Respectability: Gender and the Interrogation of Asian Women at the Angel Island Immigration Station." In S. Hune and G.N. Nomura (eds.), *Asian/Pacific Islander Women: A Historical Anthology:* 90–105. New York: NYU Press, 2003.

Ghemawat, Pankaj. *Redefining Global Strategy: Crossing Borders in a World Where Differences Still Matter.* Cambridge, MA: Harvard Business School Press, 2007.

Ghosn, Carlos, *Shift: Inside Nissan's Historic Revival.* New York: Doubleday, 2005.

Gibbs-Smith, Charles H. *The Great Exhibition of 1851.* London: HMSO, 1981.

Gibney, Matthew, and Randall Hansen (eds.). *Immigration and Asylum: From 1900 to the Present.* 3 Volumes. Santa Barbara, CA: ABC-CLIO, 2005.

Giprakesh, K. "Building a Rural Workforce." *Business Line,* 14 September 2006, online at www.the hindubusnessline.com.

Gittinger, Mattiebelle. "Textiles in the Service of the Kings." In M. Gittinger and L. Lefferts (eds.), *Textiles and the Tai Experience in Southeast Asia:* 143–176. Washington, D.C.: Textile Museum, 1992.

Glenn, Evelyn Nakano. *Issei, Nisei, War Bride: Three Generations of Japanese American Women in Domestic Service.* Philadelphia: Temple University Press 1986.

Goens, Rijkloff van. "Reijsbeschrijving van den weg uit Samarangh nae de konincklijke hoofdplaets Mataram." *Bijdragen tot de Taal-en Volkenkunde* 4 (1856), 307–350.

Goodman, Peter S. "China Invests Heavily In Sudan's Oil Industry: Beijing Supplies Arms Used on Villagers." *Washington Post,* 23 December 2004, A01.

Gould, J.D. "European Intercontinental Emigration." *Journal of European Economic History* 8 (1979), 593–679.

Gould, Terry. *Paper Fan: The Hunt for Triad Gangster Steven Wong.* Toronto: Random House Canada, 2004.

Graceffo, Antonio. "Cham Muslims: A Look at Cambodia's Muslim Minority." Online at www.talesofasia.com (2005).

Gradidge, Jennifer M. *The Douglas DC-1/DC-2/DC-3: The First Seventy Years.* London: Air-Britain, 2006.

Graham, Gerald S. "The Ascendancy of the Sailing Ship 1850–1885." *Economic History Review* 9, 1 (1956), 74–88.

Gresser, Edward. "NTR and Trade Normalization: and U.S.–Lao Trade." *Progressive Policy Institute,* 22 May 2002, online at www.ppionline.org.

Grey, Briane M. "The Poisoning of Paradise: Crystal Methamphetamine in Hawaii." Testimony before the House Government Reform Committee's Subcommittee on Criminal Justice, Drug Policy and Human Resources, 2 August 2004, available online at www.usgodoj.gov/dea/pubs.

Gurunge, Ananda (ed.). *Return to Righteousness: A Collection of Speeches, Essays, and Letters of the Anagarika Dharmapala.* Colombo: Ministry of Education and Cultural Affairs, 1965.

Guy, John. *Woven Cargoes: Indian Textiles in the East.* London: Thames and Hudson, 1998.

Gyory, Andrew. *Closing the Gate: Race, Politics, and the Chinese Exclusion Act.* Chapel Hill: University of North Carolina Press, 1998.

Halliwell, Ruth. *The Mozart Family: Four Lives in a Social Context.* Oxford: Oxford University Press, 1998.

Hamanaka, Sheila, and Ayano Ohmi. *In Search of the Spirit: The Living National Treasures of Japan.* New York: HarperCollins, 1999.

Hanke, Lewis. *Bartolomé de Las Casas: Bookman, Scholar and Propagandist.* Philadelphia: University of Pennsylvania Press, 1952.

Hann, J.H. "Origin and Development of the Political System in the Shanghai International Settlement." *Journal of the Hong Kong Branch of the Royal Asiatic Society* 22 (1982), 31–64.

Hannerz, U. *Transnational Connections: Culture, People, Places.* New York: Routledge, 1996.

Harley, Charles K. "The Shift from Sailing Ships to Steamships, 1850–1890: A Study in Technological Change and its Diffusion." In D.N. McClosky (ed.), *Essays on a Mature Economy:* 215–225. Princeton, NJ: Princeton University Press, 1971.

Harris, Craig. "Marriage Brokers Scrutinized: Critics Fear Exploitation of Foreign Women: Local Dating Service Defends Romance Tours." *The Arizona Republic,* 15 October 2005.

Hasan, Noorhadi. "The Salfi Movement in Indonesia: Transnational Dynamics and Local Development." *Comparative Studies of South Asia, Africa and the Middle East* 27, 1 (2007), 83–94.

Heidhues, Mary F. Somers. *Bangka Tin and Mentok Pepper: Chinese Settlement on an Indonesian Island.* Singapore: Institute of Southeast Asian Studies, 1992.

Heisig, James. *Philosophers of Nothingness.* Honolulu: University of Hawaii Press, 2001.

Highley, Debra. *The Talara Basin Province of Northwestern Peru: Cretaceous-Tertiary Total Production System.* U.S. Geological Survey Bulletin 2206-A. Washington, D.C.: U.S. Department of the Interior, U.S. Geological Survey, 2004.

Hill, Peter B.E. *The Japanese Mafia: Yakuza, Law, and the State.* New York: Oxford University Press, 2003.

Hofstede, Geert. *Culture's Consequences: International Differences in Work-Related Values.* Beverley Hills, CA: Sage, 1980.

Holm, John. *Pidgins and Creoles, Volume II: Reference Survey.* New York: Cambridge University Press, 1989.

Howard, Michael C. "An Artist of Two Worlds." *Asian Art News* 4, 2 (1994), 64–66.

_____. "Dress and Ethnic Identity in Irian Jaya." *Sojourn* 15, 1 (2000), 1–29.

_____. *Fiji: Race and Politics in an Island State.* Vancouver: University of British Columbia Press, 1991.

_____. "Identity and Traditional and Tradition-Based T'ai Textiles in Contemporary Thai Society." In M.C. Howard, W. Wattanapun, and A. Gordon (eds.), *Traditional T'ai Arts in Contemporary Perspective:* 13–45. Bangkok: White Lotus, 1998.

_____. "Introduction." In M.C. Howard, W. Wattanapun, and A. Gordon (eds.), *Traditional T'ai Arts in Contemporary Perspective:* 1–11. Bangkok: White Lotus, 1998.

_____. *A World Between the Warps: Southeast Asia's Supplementary Warp Textiles.* Bangkok: White Lotus, 2008.

_____, and Kim Be Howard. *Textiles of the Daic Peoples of Vietnam.* Bangkok: White Lotus, 2002.

_____, and _____. *Textiles of the Peoples of Northern Vietnam: Mon-Khmer, Hmong-Mien, and Tibeto-Burman.* Bangkok: White Lotus, 2002.

Howard, Patricia. *Gluck and the Birth of Modern Opera.* London: Barrie and Rockliff, 1963.

Howarth, Stephen, Joost Jonker, Keetie Sluyterman, and Jan Luitan van Zanden. *The History of Royal Dutch Shell.* 4 volumes. New York: Oxford University Press, 2007.

Hsia, Hsiao-Chuan. "The Development of Immigrant Movement in Taiwan: The Case of Alliance of Human Rights Legislation for Immigrants and Migrants," paper presented at "Multicultural Families and the Local Community — Examining Co-Existence in Japan, Korea and Taiwan" symposium (2007). Synopsis provided in Koonae Park and Nobuki Fujimoto, "Symposium on Multi-Cultural Families and the Local Community," online at http://www.hurights.or.jp/asia-pacific/055/05.html.

Hsiao, Hsin-Huang Michael (ed.). *The Changing Faces of the Middle Classes in Asia-Pacific.* Taipei: Center for Asia-Pacific Studies, 2006.

_____. *East Asian Middle Classes in Comparative Perspective.* Taipei: Institute of Ethnology, Academia Sinica, 1999.

Hubner, K. "History — 150 Years of Mauvine." *Chemie in unserer Zeit* 40, 4 (2006). 274–275.

Hugo, Graeme J. *Population Mobility and Wealth Transfers in Indonesia and Other Third World Societies.* Honolulu: East-West Center Population Institute, 1983.

Human Rights Watch. *No Sanctuary.* Online at www.hrw.org (2006).

Hunt, Jocelyn. *Spain, 1474–1598.* New York: Routledge, 2001.

Hurgronje, Christiaan Snouck. "Notes sur le mouvement du pelerinage de la Macque aux indes néederlandaises." *Revue du Monde Musulman* 10, October (1911), 397–413.

_____. "Le pelerinage a la Mekke." In G.H. Bousquet and J. Schacht (eds.), *Selected Works of C. Snouck Hurgronje:* 173–207. Leiden: E.J. Brill, 1957.

Hyde, F.E., and J. Harriss. *Blue Funnel: A History of Alfred Holt and Co. of Liverpool from 1865 to 1914.* Liverpool: Liverpool University Press, 1957.

Idriess, Ion L. *Forty Fathoms Deep: Pearl Divers and Seas Rovers in Australian Seas.* Sydney: Angus and Robertson, 1945.

Inalcik, Halil. "The Policy of Mehmed II Toward the Greek Population of Istanbul and the Byzantine Buildings of the City." *Dumbarton Oaks Papers* 23 (1969), 229–249.

Israel, Jonathan I. *Dutch Primacy in World Trade, 1585–1740.* Oxford: Clarendon, 1989.

Jackson, P., P. Crang, and C. Dwyer. "Introduction: The Spaces of Transnationality." In P. Jackson, P. Crang, and C. Dwyer (eds.), *Transnational Spaces:* 1–23. New York: Routledge, 2004.

Jacobson, Mark. "The Singapore Solution." *National Geographic* 217, 1 (2010), 132–149.

Jittawong, Preeyanoot. "Thai–U.S. Modern Art Show." *Chiang Mai Mail,* 13–19 August 2005, online at www.chiangmai-mail.com.

Jones, Philip, and Anna Kenny. *Australia's Muslim Cameleers: Pioneers of the Inland 1860s–1930s.* Kent Town, South Australia: Wakefield, 2007.

Joomun, Gilles. "The Textile and Clothing Industry in Mauritius." In H. Jauch and R. Traub-Merz (eds.), *The Future of the Textile and Clothing Industry in Sub-Saharan Africa:* 193–211. Bonn: Friedrich-Ebert Stiftung, 2006.

Kamath, Suryanath U. *A Concise History of Karnataka: From Pre-Historic Times to the Present.* Bangalore: Jupiter, 2001.

Kaplan, David E., and Alec Dubro. *Yakuza: The Explosive Account of Japan's Criminal Underworld.* Berkeley: University of California Press, 2003.

Kaprielian-Churchill, Isabel. "Armenian Refugee Women: The Picture Bride, 1920–1930." *Journal of American Ethnic History* 3, 3 (1993), 27.

Kathirithamby-Wells, J. "Ahmed Shan Ibn Iskander and the Late 17th Century 'Holy War' in Indonesia." *Journal of the Malaysian Branch of the Royal Asiatic Society* 43 (1970), 48–64.

Kearney, A.T., and the Chicago Council on Global Affairs. "The 2008 Global Cities Index." *Foreign Policy,* November/December 2008, online at www.foreignpolicy.com.

Kelly, R. Talbot. *Burma: The Land and the People.* London: L. Beling Tetens/Boston: J.B. Millet, 1910.

Kemble, John Haskell. "The Big Four at Sea: The History of the Occidental and Oriental Steamship Company." *The Huntington Library Quarterly* 3, 3 (1940), 339–357.

Khonthaphane, Sirivanh, Sathanbandith Insisisangmay, and Vanthana Nolintha. *Impact of Border Trade in Local Livelihoods: Lao-Chinese Border Trade in Luang Namtha & Oudomxay Provinces.* Technical Background Paper for the Third National Human Development Report. Vientiane: International Trade and Human Development/ UNDP, 2006.

Kim, Hyun Mee. "Current Situation and Challenges in South Korea, Taiwan and Japan — Integration for Whom?: Married Migrant Women Policies in South Korea and Patriarchal Imagination," paper presented at International Marriage from the Women's Human Rights Perspective symposium, Seoul, 3 August 2007. Synopsis provided in Koonae Park, "Korea-Japan Symposiums on 'International Marriage' and 'Female Migrant Workers,'" online at http://www.hurights.or.jp/asia-pacific/050/08.html.

Kim, Kyung-Hak. "Transnational Indo-Fijians in Australia." *Man in India* 87, 3–4 (2007), 303–321.

Kim, Lili M. "Redefining the Boundaries of Traditional Gender Roles: Korean Picture Brides, Pioneer Korean Korean Immigrant Women, and Their Benevolent Nationalism in Hawai'i." In S. Hune and G.M. Nomura (eds.), *Asian/Pacific Islander Women: A Historical Anthology:* 106–122. New York: NYU Press, 2003.

King, Arden R. *Coban and the Verapaz: History and Cultural Process in Northern Guatemala.* New Orleans: Middle American Research Institute, Tulane University, 1974.

Klein, Herbert S. *The Atlantic Slave Trade.* New York: Cambridge University Press, 1999.

Klinken, Gerry Van. "Ethnicity in Indonesia." In C. Mackerras (ed.), *Ethnicity in Asia:* 64–87. London: RoutledgeCurzon, 2003.

Kotzebue, Otto von. *Kotzebue's Voyage of Discovery 1815–1818.* London: Longman, Thirst, Rees, Orme and Brown, 1821.

Kurlantzick, Joshua. *Charm Offensive: How China's Soft Power is Changing the World.* New Haven, CT: Yale University Press, 2007.

Kuykendall, Ralph S. *Hawaiian Kingdom 1874–1893, the Kalakaua Dynasty.* Honolulu: University of Hawaii Press, 1967.

Lamb, Christina, "A Night at the Opera — and 14 Days on the Amazon to Get There." Online at Telegraph.co.uk, 17 June 2001.

Lampe, Armando. *Christianity in the Caribbean: Essays on Church History.* Kingston: University of West Indies Press, 2001.

Larkins, William T. *The Ford Tri-Motor, 1926–1992.* Atglen, PA: Schiffler, 1992.

Las Casas, Bartolomé de (trans. Nigel Griffin). *Short Account of the Destruction of the Indies,* London: Penguin, 1999.

Lea, Henry Charles. *The Inquisition in the Spanish Dependencies.* New York: Macmilan, 1908.

Leapman, Michael. *The World for a Shilling: How the Great Exhibition of 1851 Shaped a Nation.* London: Headline, 2001.

Lee, Erika. *At America's Gates: Chinese Immigrants during the Exclusion Era, 1882–1943.* Chapel Hill: University of North Carolina Press, 2007.

_____. "Defying Exclusion: Chinese Immigrants and Their Strategies During the Exclusion Era." In S. Chang (ed.), *Chinese American Transnationalism:* 1–21. Philadelphia: Temple University Press, 2006.

Lee, Tong Soon. "Chinese Theatre, Confucianism and Nationalism: Amateur Chinese Opera Tradition in Singapore." *Asian Theatre Journal* 24, 2 (2007), 397–421.

Lee, Yaan-Ju, Dong-Hoon Seol, and Sung-Nam Cho. "International Marriages in South Korea: The Significance of Nationality and Ethnicity." *Journal of Population Research* 23, 3 (2006), 165–182.

Lei, Daphne P. *Operatic China: Staging Chinese Identity Across the Pacific.* New York: Palgrave Macmillan, 2006.

LeMay, Michael, and Elliott R. Barkan (eds.). *U.S. Immigration and Naturalization Laws and Issues: A Documentary History.* Westport, CT: Greenwood, 1999.

Leong, Angela Veng Mei. "The 'Bate-ficha' Business and Triads in Macao Casinos." *QUT Law & Justice Journal* 5 (2002), online at http://www.austlii.edu.au/Au/journals/QUTLJJ/2002/5.

Leshkowich, Ann Marie. "The *Ao Dai* Goes Global: How International Influences and Female Entrepreneurs have Shaped Vietnam's 'National Costume.'" In S.A. Niessen, A.M. Leshkowich, and C. Jones (eds.), *Re-Orienting Fashion: The Globalization of Asian Dress:* 79–116. Oxford: Berg, 2003.

Lewis, Norman. *Golden Earth: Travels in Burma.* New York: Charles Scribner's Sons, 1952.

Liddick Jr., Donald R. *The Global Underworld: Transnational Crime and the United States.* Westport, CT: Praeger, 2004.

Liddle, Alan. "Jollibee Doing Brisk Business in U.S., Plans Expansion." *BNET,* 13 July 1998.

Liebeck, Laura. "Kmart Czechs into Europe — K Mart Corp.'s Czechoslovakian Acquisitions." *Discount Store News,* 15 June 1992.

Lincoln, James R., Harold R. Kerbo, and Elke Wittenhagen, "Japanese Companies in Germany: A Case Study in Cross-Cultural Management." *Industrial Relations: A Journal of Economy and Society* 34, 3 (2008), 417–440.

Lintner, Bertil. *Blood Brothers: Crime, Business, and Politics in Asia.* Chiang Mai: Silkworm, 2002.

_____. *Burma in Revolt: Opium and Insurgency Since 1948.* Boulder, CO: Westview, 1994.

_____, and Michael Black. *Merchants of Madness: The Methamphetamine Explosion in the Golden Triangle.* Chiang Mai: Silkworm, 2009.

Lippy, Charles H., Robert Choquette, and Stafford Poole. *Christianity Comes to the Americas: 1492–1776.* New York: Paragon House, 1992.

Little, William, H.W. Fowler, and J. Coulson (revised and edited by C.T. Onions). *The Oxford Universal Dictionary on Historical Principles.* Third Edition. Oxford: Clarendon, 1955.

Liu, Haiming. "Chinese Herbalists in the United States." In S. Chang (ed.), *Chinese American Transnationalism:* 136–155. Philadelphia: Temple University Press, 2006.

_____. *The Transnational History of a Chinese Family: Immigrant Letters, Family Business, and Reverse Migration.* Piscataway, NJ: Rutgers University Press, 2005.

Lund, Susan, Charles Roxburgh, and Bruno Roy. "Sovereign Investors Still Strong in Asia." *Far Eastern Economic Review* 172, 7 (2009), 51–55.

Lynch, Annette. "Hmong American New Year's Dress: The Display of Ethnicity." In J.B. Eicher (ed.), *Dress and Ethnicity:* 255–267. Oxford: Berg, 1995.

Mackerras, Colin. *The Chinese Theatre in Modern Times: From 1840 to the Present Day.* London: Thames and Hudson, 1975.

_____. "Identity, Modernity and Power in the Performing Arts Among the Chinese Diaspora." In H. Um (ed.), *Diaspora and Interculturalism in Asian Performing Arts:* 17–29. New York: RoutledgeCurzon, 2005.

MacNutt, Francis Augustus. *Batholomew de las Casas: His Life, His Apostolate and His Writings.* Cleveland, OH: Arthur H. Clark, 1909.

MacPherson, Seonaigh, Anne-Sophie Benz, and Dawa Bhuti Ghoso. "Global Nomads: The Emergence of the Tibetan Diaspora." *Migration Information Source,* September 2008.

Magee, David. *Turnaround: How Carlos Ghosn Rescued Nissan.* New York: Collins, 2003.

Main, James. "The Truth About Triads." *Policing* 7, 2 (1991), 144–163.

Mair, Timothy W. "China's Military May Get U.S. Base." *Insights of the News,* 17 May1999.

Mak, Lau-Fong. *Chinese Secret Societies in Ipoh Town, 1945–1969.* Singapore: Working Paper, Department of Sociology, University of Singapore (distributed by Chapman Enterprises), 1975.

_____. *The Sociology of Secret Societies: A Study of Chinese Secret Societies in Singapore and Peninsular Malaysia.* Kuala Lumpur: Oxford University Press, 1981.

Makabe, Tomoko (trans. K. Chisato Merken). *Picture Brides: Japanese Women in Canada.* Toronto: Multicultural Historical Society of Canada, 1995.

Marriner, Sheila, and F.E. Hyde. *The Senior John Samuel Swire 1825–98: Management in Far Easter Shipping Trades.* Liverpool: Liverpool University Press, 1967.

May, John. "The Chinese in Britain, 1869–1914." In Colin Holmes (ed.), *Immigrants and Minorities in British Society:* 111–124. London: George Allen and Unwin, 1978.

McCool, Grant. "Middle Class in Vietnam Likes to Buy Things, Too." *International Herald Tribune,* 9 October 2006.

McCormick, James. *The Holy Land: The First Ecumenical Pilgrim's Guide.* Bloomington IN: IUniverse, 2000.

McCoy, Alfred W. *The Politics of Heroin in Southeast Asia.* New York: Harper and Row, 1972.

Mcillwain, Jeffrey Scott. "From Tong War to Organized Crime: Revising the Historical Perception of Violence in Chinatown." *Justice Quarterly* 14, 1 (1997), 25–52.

McMahan, David L. *The Making of Buddhist Modernism.* New York: Oxford University Press, 2008.

McRae, John R. "Oriental Verities on the American Frontier: The 1893 World's Parliament of Religions and the Thought of Mason Abe." *Buddhist-Christian Studies* 11 (1991), 7–36.

Meagher, Arnold J. *The Coolie Trade: The Traffic in Chinese Laborers to Latin America.* San Francisco: Chinese Materials Center, 1975, and Bloomington, IN: Xlibris, 2008.

Measure, Susie, and David McNeil. "Tesco Builds Presence in Japan with Acquisition of Debt-laden Fre'c Chain." *The Independent,* 28 April 2004.

Meijer, Roel (ed.). *Global Salafism: Islam's New Religious Movement.* London: C. Hurst, 2009.

Mercer, William H., A.E. Collins, and A.J. Harding. *The Colonial Office List for 1921.* London: Waterlow and Sons, 1921.

_____. *The Colonial Office List for 1924.* London: Waterlow and Sons, 1924,

Migration News. "Philippines Approves New Migrant Worker Act." *Migration News* 1, 3 (1995).

Minorsky, V., and S.S. Blair. "Tabriz." In P.J. Bearman, et al. (eds.), *Encyclopedia of Islam, Volume X.* Leiden: Brill, 2009.

Missionary Herald. *Extracts from the Joint Letters of the Hilo Mission.* Hilo, HI: Lyman House Memorial Museum, 1832.

Missions Etrangeres de Paris. *Missions étrangères de Paris. 350 ans au service du Christ.* Paris: Editeurs Malesherbes, 2008.

Moore, Robin. *The French Connection: A True Account of Cops, Narcotics, and international Conspiracy.* Guilford, CT: Lyons, 2003.

Moreland, W.H., and Atul Chandra Chatterjee. *A Short History of India.* New York : David McKay, 1962.

Morgan, W.P. *Triad Societies in Hong Kong.* Hong Kong: Government Press, 1960.

Muenz, Rainer. *Europe: Population and Migration in 2005.* Migration Information (2006), online at migrationinformation.org.

Munder, Irmtraud, and Renate Krieg. "Sino-German Joint Ventures: Shared Values and Cultural Divides." In L. Douw and C. Kwok-bun (eds.), *Conflict and Innovation: Joint Ventures in China:* 116–138. Leiden: Brill, 2006.

Murray, Dian H. *The Origins of the Tiandihui: The Chinese Triads in Legend and History.* Sanford, CA: Stanford University Press, 1994.

Nash, Gary. *The Tarasov Saga: From Russia through*

*China to Austra*lia. Castlecrag, NSW: Rosenberg, 2002.

Naval Intelligence Division. *Indo-China*. Cambridge: Cambridge University Press, 1943.

Ng, Kwee Choo. *The Chinese in London*. London: Oxford University Press, 1968.

Nguyen Thanh Tuan. "About the Current Middle Class in Vietnam." *Tap chi Cong san* (Communist Review), 8 March 2007.

Nicaso, Antonio. "The Dragon's Fire: Part 18 — The Chinese Triads are Digging Their Claws into Canadian Businesses." *Tandem*, 24 June 2001, online at www.tandemnews.com.

_____, and Lee Lamothe. *Global Mafia: The New World Order of Organized Crime*. Toronto: Macmillan Canada, 1995.

Nieuhoff, Johanes. *Voyages and Travels into Brasil and the East-Indies*. London: Linton and John Osborn, 1744.

Nooy-Palm, Hetty. "The Sacred Cloths of the Toraja: Unanswered Questions." In M. Gittinger (ed.), *To Speak With Cloth: Studies in Indonesian Textiles*: 163–180. Los Angeles: Museum of Cultural History, University of California, Los Angeles, 1989.

Northrup, David. *Indentured Labor in the Age of Imperialism, 1834–1922*. New York Cambridge University Press, 1995.

Norton, Robert. *Race and Politics in Fiji*. St. Lucia: University of Queensland Press, 1977.

Nugent, Walter. *Crossings: The Great Transatlantic Migrations, 1870–1914*. Bloomington: Indiana University Press, 1992.

Nye Jr., Joseph S. *Soft Power: The Means of Success in World Politics*. New York: Public Affairs, 2004.

Nyíri, Pál. "Expatriating is Patriotic? The Discourse on 'New Migrants' in the People's Republic of China and Identity Construction among Recent Migrants from the PRC." In B.S.A. Yeoh and K. Willis (eds.), *State/Nation/Transnation*: 120–143. New York: Routledge, 2004.

Obeyesekere, Gananath. "Personal Identity and Cultural Crisis: the Case of Anagarika Dharmapala of Sri Lanka." In F.E. Reynolds and D. Capps (eds.), *The Biographical Process*: 221–252. The Hague: Mouton, 1976.

O'Flanagan, Patrick. *Port Cities of Atlantic Iberia, C. 1500–1900*. Farnha, Surrey, UK: Ashgate, 2008.

O'Malley, Brendan. "Japanese War Brides Light Up Citizenship Ceremony." *Couriermail*, 20 January 2009, online at http://www.couriermail.com.au/.

Onishi, Norimitsu. "Marriage Brokers in Vietnam Cater to S. Korean Bachelors." *International Herald Tribune*, 21 February 2007.

Oxfeld, Ellen. "Cross-border Hypergamy? Marriage Exchanges in a Transnational Hakka Community." In N. Constable (ed.), *Cross-Border Marriages: Gender and Mobility in Transnational Asia*: 17–33. Philadelphia: University of Pennsylvania Press, 2005.

Ozersky, Josh. *Hamburger: A History*. New Haven, CT: Yale University Press, 2009.

Page, Jesse. *Samuel Crowther: The Slave Boy Who Became Bishop of the Niger*. London: S.W. Partridge, 1892.

Pan, Lynn. *Sons of the Yellow Emperor: A History of*

the Chinese Diaspora. Tokyo: Kodansha Globe, 1994.

Papanikolas, Helen. *An Amulet of Greek Earth: Generations of Immigrant Folk Culture*. Athens: Ohio University Press, 2002.

Parker, David. "Chinese People in Britain: Histories, Futures and Identities." In Gregor Benton and F.N. Pieke (eds.), *The Chinese in Europe*. Basingstoke: Macmillan, 1998.

Parker, John. "Burgeoning Bourgeoisie." *The Economist*, 12 February 2009.

Parliamentary Joint Committee on the National Crime Authority, Australian Parliament. *Asian Organized Crime*, Discussion Paper (1995), available online at www.fas.org/irp/world/australia/docs/ncaaoc2.

Parreñas, Rhacel Salazar. *Servants of Globalization: Women, Migration, and Domestic Work*. Stanford, CA: Stanford University Press, 2001.

Permanent Subcommittee on Investigations of the Committee on Governmental Affairs, United States Senate. *The New International Criminal and Asian Organized Crime: Report, December 1992*. Washington, D.C.: United States Government Printing Office, 1993.

Phillips, Herbert P. *The Integrative Art of Modern Thailand*. Berkeley: Lowie Museum of Anthropology, University of California at Berkeley, 1991.

Pina-Cabral, Joao de. *Between China and Europe: Person, Culture and Emotion in Macao*. New York: Berg, 2002.

Pinho, A. "Gambling in Macau." In R.D. Cremer (ed.), *Macau: City of Commerce and Culture*. Hong Kong: API, 1991.

Piore, M.J. *Birds of Passage: Migrant Labour and Industrial Societies*. New York: Cambridge University Press, 1979.

Poliakov, Leon (M. Kochan, trans.). *Jewish Bankers and the Holy See*. London: Routledge and Kegan Paul, 1977.

Pongsapich, Amara, and Noppawan Chongwattana. "The Refugee Situation in Thailand." In S. Chantavanich and E.B. Reynolds (eds.), *Indochinese Refugees: Asylum and Resettlement*: 12–47. Bangkok: Institute of Asian Studies, Chulalongkorn University, 1988.

Poon, Wena (ed.). *Lions in Winter*. Singapore: MPH Group, 2007.

Portes, A, L. E. Guarnizo, and P. Landholt. "The Study of Transnationalism: Pitfalls and Promises of an Emergent Research Field." *Ethnic and Racial Studies* 22, 2 (1999), 219–237.

Poshyananda, Apinan. *Modern Art in Thailand*. Singapore: Oxford University Press, 1992.

Postma, Thijs. *Fokker: Aircraft Builders to the World*. London: Jane's, 1979.

Poston, Larry. *Islamic Da'wah in the West: Muslim Missionary Activity and the Dynamics of Conversion to Islam*. New York: Oxford University Press, 1992.

Price, David A., *Love and Hate in Jamestown: John Smith, Pocahontas, and the Start of a New Nation*. New York: Knopf, 2003.

Prothero, Stephen. *The White Buddhist: The Asian Odyssey of Henry Steel Olcott*. Bloomington: Indiana University Press, 1996.

Purcell, Victor. *Malaya: Outline of a Colony*. London: Thomas Nelson and Sons, 1946.

Racius, Egdunas. *The Multiple Nature of the Islamic Da'wa*. Academic Dissertation. Helsinki: University of Helsinki, 2004.

Rao, Nancy Yunwa. "Racial Essence and Historical Invisibility: Chinese Opera in New York, 1930." *Cambridge Opera Journal* 12, 2 (2000), 135–162.

Reicher, Harry. *The Post-Holocaust World and President Harry S. Truman: The Harrison Report and Immigration Law and Policy*. Available online at www.schnader.com (2002).

Reid, Anthony. "Economic and Social Change, c. 1400–1800." In N. Tarling (ed.), *The Cambridge History of Southeast Asia, Volume One: From Early Times to c. 1800*: 460–507. New York: Cambridge University Press, 1992.

Reilly, Theresa. *Richly Woven Traditions: Costumes of the Miao of Southwest China and Beyond*. New York: China House Gallery, 1987.

Reimers, David M. "The Korean-American Immigrant Experience." Conference paper, The Legacy of Korea: a 50th Anniversary Conference, Truman Presidential Museum & Library and the University of Missouri–Kansas City (2001), available online at www.trumanlibrary.org/korea/.

_____. "Post-World War II Immigration to the United States: America's Latest Newcomers." *The Annals of the American Academy of Political and Social Sciences* 454, 1 (1981), 1–12.

Renard, Ronald D. *The Burmese Connection: Illegal Drugs and the Making of the Golden Triangle*. Boulder, CO: Lynne Rienner, 1996.

Rhodes, Alexandre de (trans. S. Hertz). *Rhodes of Vietnam: The Travels and Missions of Fathers Alexander de Rhodes in China and Other Kingdoms of the Orient*. Westminster, MD: Newman, 1966.

Robertson, Frank. *Triangle of Death: The Inside Story of the Triads, the Chinese Mafia*. London: Routledge and Kegan Paul, 1978.

Robinson, Jeffrey. *The Merger: The Conglomeration of International Organized Crime*. Woodstock, NY: Overlook, 2000.

Rose, Seraphim, and Abbot Herman. *Blessed John the Wonderworker: A Preliminary Account of the Life and Miracles of Archbishop John Maximovitch*. Third Edition. Platina, CA: St. Herman of Alaska Brotherhood, 1987.

Rostow, Walt W. *The World Economy: History and Prospect*. Austin: University of Texas Press, 1978.

Ryang, Sonia. *Koreans in Japan: Critical Voices from the Margin*. New York: Routledge, 2000.

Saccomano, Eugène. *Bandits à Marseille*. Paris: Julliard, 1968.

Saikia, Yasmin. *Fragmented Memories: Struggling to be Tai-Ahom in India*. Durham, NC: Duke University Press, 2004.

Saranin, Alexander P. *Child of the Kulaks*. St. Lucia: University of Queensland Press, 1998.

Sarna, Jonathan D. "American Jewish History." *Modern Judaism* 10, 3 (1990), 244–245.

Sassen, Saskia. *The Global City: New York, London, Tokyo*. Princeton, NJ: Princeton University Press, 1991.

Sastri, K.A. Nilakanta. *A History of South India from Prehistoric Times to the Fall of Vijayanagar*. New Delhi: Oxford University Press, 2002.

Scarr, Deryck. *Fiji: A Short History*. Sydney: George Allen and Unwin, 1984.

Schurz, William L. *The Manila Galleon*. New York: E.P. Dutton, 1959.

Scott, Michael. *The Great Caruso*. London: Hamish Hamilton, 1988.

Seed, John. "Limehouse Blues: Looking for Chinatown in the London Docks, 1900–1940." *History Workshop Journal* 62, Autumn (2006), 58–85.

Sellaro, C. Louise, Therese Maskulka, and David J. Burns. "(R)evolution of Retailing in the Former Czechoslovakia: The Case of Kmart." *International Journal of Commerce and Management* 7, 1 (1997), 74–87.

Serle Geoffrey. *The Golden Age: A History of the Colony of Victoria, 1851–1861*. Melbourne: Melbourne University Press, 1963.

Sewell, Robert. *A Forgotten Empire (Vijayanagara)*. Delhi: Asian Education Services, 1982.

Seymour, Christopher. *Yakuza Diary*. New York: Atlantic Monthly, 1996.

Shaw, Mark. "West African Criminal Networks in South and Southern Africa." *African Affairs* 101, 404 (2002), 291–316.

_____, and Gail Wannenburg. "Organized Crime in Africa." In P. Reichel (ed.), *Handbook of Transnational Crime and Justice*: 367–385. Thousand Oaks, CA: Sage, 2005.

Shukert, Elfrieda, and Barbara Scibetta. *War Brides of World War II*. Novato, CA: Presidio, 1988.

Sims, Jessica Mai. *Empowering Individuals and Creating Community — Thai Perspectives of Life in Britain*. Runnymede Trust online at www.runnymedetrust.org (2008).

Skeldon, R. "The Emergence of Trans-Pacific Migration." In R. Cohen (ed.), *The Cambridge Survey of World Migration*: 510–522. Cambridge: Cambridge University Press, 1995.

Smith, Anthony D. "Towards a Global Culture?" *Theory, Culture & Society* 7, 2 (1990), 171–191

Smith, George V. *The Dutch in Seventeenth-Century Thailand*. DeKalb, IL: Center for Southeast Asian Studies, Northern Illinois University, 1977.

Smith, Michael E. "City Size in Late Post-Classic Mesoamerica." *Journal of Urban History* 31, 4 (2005), 403–434.

Smith, Monica L. "The Archaeology of South Asian Cities." *Journal of Archaeological Research* 14 (2006), 97–142.

Smith, V.A. *The Oxford History of India*. New York: Oxford University Press, 1981.

Snyder, Rachel Louise. *Fugitive Denim: A Moving Story of People and Pants in the Borderless World of Global Trade*. New York: W.W. Norton, 2009.

Softwar. "The Panama Canal in Transition: Threats to U.S. Security and China's Growing Role in Latin America. Online at www.softwar.net/panama (2000).

Sorensen, Clark W. "P'yongyang North Korea." In Melvin Ember and Carol R. Ember (eds.), *Encyclopedia of Urban Cultures, Volume 3*: 488–496. Danbury, CT: Grolier, 2002.

Steinmetz, Andrew. *History of the Jesuits: From the*

Foundation of Their Society to Its Suppression by Pope Clement XIV; Their Missions Throughout the World; Their Educational System and Literature; wit Their Revival and Present State. London: R. Bentley, 1848 (vol. 2 reprinted by BiblioLife in 2008).

Stern, Horace. "The First Jewish Settlers in America: Their Struggle for Religious Freedom." *Jewish Quarterly Review* 45, 4 (1955), 289, 292–293.

Stewart, Gail. *Ancient Hawaiian Dress and the Influence of European Dress on It, 1778–1820.* Unpublished master's thesis, University of Hawai'i, 1977.

Sullivan. James. *Jeans: A Cultural History of an American Icon.* London: Gotham, 2006.

Suzuki, Hiroshi, and Masaki Kondo. "Sony's CEO Stronger Ousts Chubachi in Overhaul of Management." *Bloomberg,* 27 February 2009, online at www.bloomberg.com.

Suzuki, Nobue. "Tripartite Desires: Filipina-Japanese Marriages and Fantasies of Transnational Traversal." In N. Constable (ed.), *Cross-Border Marriages: Gender and Mobility in Transnational Asia:* 124–144. Philadelphia: University of Pennsylvania Press, 2005.

Tambiah, Stanley Jeyaraja. *The Buddhist Saints of the Forest and the Cult of Amulets.* New York: Cambridge University Press, 1984.

Tamura, Keiko. *Michi's Memories: The Story of a Japanese War Bride.* Canberra: Research School of Pacific Studies, Australian National University, 2001.

Taylor, J.L. *Forest Monks and the Nation-State: An Anthropological and Historical Study in Northeastern Thailand.* Singapore: Institute of Southeast Asian Studies, 1993.

Taylor, P. *The Distant Magnet: European Migration to the United States.* London: Eyre and Spottiswoode, 1971.

Teo, Kevin. "Of Migration and the Singaporean Diaspora." *The Kent Ridge Common,* 14 April 2009.

Thai, Hung Cam. "Clashing Dreams in the Vietnamese Diaspora: Highly Educated Overseas Brides and Low-Wage U.S. Husbands." In N. Constable (ed.), *Cross-Border Marriages: Gender and Mobility in Transnational Asia:* 145–165. Philadelphia: University of Pennsylvania Press, 2005.

_____. *For Better of for Worse: Vietnamese International Marriages in the New Global Economy.* Piscataway, NJ: Rutgers University Press, 2008.

Thurston, Lucy G. *Life and Times of Mrs. Lucy G. Thurston, Wife of Rev. Asa Thurston, Pioneer Missionary to the Sandwich Islands, Gathered from Letters and Journals Extending Over a Period of More than Fifty Years, Selected and Arranged by Herself.* Ann Arbor, MI: S.C. Andrews, 1882.

Tinker, Hugh. *Indians Overseas 1830–1920.* London: Oxford University Press, 1974.

Toynbee, Arnold. "A Summary of Armenian History up to and Including the Year 1915." In Viscount Bryce, *The Treatment of Armenians in the Ottoman Empire 1915–16: Documents Presented to Viscount Grey of Fallodon, Secretary of State for Foreign Affairs by Viscount Bryce:* 637–653. New York and London: G.P. Putnam's Sons, for His Majesty's Stationary Office, London, 1916.

Travis, Anthony S. "Perkin's Mauve: Ancestor of the Organic Chemical Industry." *Technology and Culture* 31, 1 (1990), 51–82.

Trocki, Carl A. *Singapore: Wealth, Power and the Culture of Control.* New York: Routledge, 2005.

Tyner, James A. "Global Cities and Circuits of Global Labor: The Case of Manila." In F.V. Aguilar, Jr. (ed.), *Filipinos in Global Migrations:* 60–86. Quezon City: Philippine Migration Research Network and Philippine Social Science Council, 2002.

United Nations. *Working Towards the Elimination of Crimes Against Women Committed in the Name of Honour: Report to the Secretary-General.* New York: United Nations General Assembly, Report A/57/169, 2002.

United Nations Office on Drugs and Crime. *Transnational Organized Crime in the West African Region.* New York: United Nations, 2005.

United States Census Bureau. *The Asian Population: 2000.* Washington, D.C.: United States Census Bureau, 2002.

Vaughan, Alden T. "Sir Walter Raleigh's Indian Interpreters, 1584–1618." *The William and Mary Quarterly* 59, 2 (2002), 341–376.

Visson, Lynn. *Wedded Strangers: The Challenges of Russian-American Marriages.* New York: Hippocrene, 2001.

Voigt-Graf, Carmen. "Transnationalism and the Indo-Fijian Diaspora: The Relationship of Indo-Fijians to India and Its People." *Journal of Intercultural Studies* 29, 1 (2008), 81–109.

Vries, Jan de. *European Urbanization, 1500–1800.* New York: Routledge, 1984.

_____, and Ad Van Der Woude. *The First Modern Economy: Success, Failure, and Perseverance of the Dutch Economy, 1500–1815.* New York: Cambridge University Press, 1997.

Wannenburg, Gail. "Organised Crime in West Africa." *African Security Review* 14, 4 (2005), online at www.iss.co.za.

Warburton, Eve. "No Longer a Choice: Veiling Has Become a Highly Politicised Practice in Indonesia." *Inside Indonesia* 89, January–March 2007, online at www.insideindonesia.org.

Ward, Richard H., and Daniel J. Mabrey. "Organized Crime in Asia." In P. Reichel (ed.), *Handbook of Transnational Crime and Justice:* 387–401. Thousand Oaks, CA: Sage, 2005.

Watson, James L. (ed.). *Golden Arches East: McDonald's in East Asia.* Palo Alto, CA: Stanford University Press, 1997.

Williams, Gertrude Marvin. *Priestess of the Occult, Madame Blavatsky.* New York: Alfred. A. Knopf, 1946.

Williams, Thomas. *Fiji and the Fijians, Volume I: The Islands and their Inhabitants.* London: Alexander Heylin, 1858 (reprinted by the Fiji Museum, Suva, 1972).

Williamson, J.G. *Late Nineteenth Century American Development.* New York: Cambridge University Press, 1974.

Willis, Katie, Brenda S.A. Yeoh, and S.M. Abdul Khader Fakhri. "Introduction: Transnationalism as a Challenge to the Nation." In B.S.A. Yeoh and K. Willis (eds.), *State/Nation/Transnation: Perspec-*

tives on Transnationalism in the Asia-Pacific: 1–15. New York: Routledge, 2004.

Willmott, W. "Chinese Contract Labour in the Pacific Islands During the Nineteenth Century." *Journal of Pacific Islands Studies* 27, 2 (2004), 161–176.

Wilson, Arnold T. "History of the Missions of the Fathers of the Society of Jesus in China and Other Kingdoms of the East." *Bulletin of the School of Oriental Studies, University of London* 4, 1 (1926), 47–57.

Wolff, David. *To the Harbin Station: The Liberal Alternative in Russian Manchuria, 1898–1914.* Stanford, CA: Stanford University Press, 1999.

Wong, May M.L. "Shadow Management in Japanese Companies in Hong Kong." *Asia Pacific Journal of Human Resources* 34, 1 (1996), 95–110.

World Trade Organization. *World Trade Report 2007.* Geneva: World Trade Organization, 2007.

Wright, Brooks. *Interpreter of Buddhism to the West: Sir Edwin Arnold.* New York: Bookman Associates, 1957.

Wyatt, David K. *Thailand: A Short History.* New Haven CT: Yale University Press, 1982.

Y Li, L. Yao, and K. W. Yeung. *The China and Hong Kong Denim Industry.* Woodhead Texile Series No. 30. Cambridge: Woodhead, 2003.

Yang, Eun Sik. "Korean Women of America: From Subordination to Partnership, 1903–1930." *Amerasia* 11, 2 (1984), 1–28.

Yene, Bill. *Seaplanes and Flying Boats: A Timeless Collection from Aviation's Golden Age.* New York: BCL, 2003.

Yeoh, Brenda S.A. "Singapore: Hungry for Foreign Workers at All Skill Levels." *Migration Information Source,* January (2007), online at http://www.migrationinformation.org/Profiles/display.cfm?ID=570.

Yoshida, Reiji. "International Rationale: Language among New Survival Skills: Foreign Managers Bring Change to Corporate Life." *The Japan Times Online,* 24 May 2001.

Zolberg, Aristide. *A Nation by Design: Immigration Policy in the Fashioning of America.* Cambridge, MA: Harvard University Press, 2006.

INDEX